# The Archaeology of Rock-Art

Pictures, painted and carved in caves and on open rock surfaces, are amongst our loveliest relics from prehistory. This pioneering set of sparkling essays goes beyond guesses as to what the pictures mean, instead exploring how we can reliably learn from rock-art as a material record of distant times: in short, rock-art as archaeology.

Sometimes contact-period records offer some direct insight about indigenous meaning, so we can learn in that informed way. More often, we have no direct record, and instead have to use formal methods to learn from the evidence of the pictures themselves.

The book's nineteen chapters range wide in space and time, from the Palaeolithic of Europe to nineteenth-century Australia. Using varied approaches within the consistent framework of informed and of formal methods, they make key advances in using the striking and reticent evidence of rock-art to archaeological benefit.

**Christopher Chippindale** is a Senior Assistant Curator at the Cambridge University Museum of Archaeology and Anthropology. He edited the journal *Antiquity* from 1987 to 1997.

**Paul S. C. Taçon** is Senior Research Scientist in the Division of Anthropology at the Australian Museum in Sydney. He is Head of the Museum's People and Place Research Centre.

**Edited by Christopher Chippindale and Paul S. C. Taçon**

# The Archaeology of
# Rock-Art

**CAMBRIDGE**
UNIVERSITY PRESS

PUBLISHED BY THE PRESS SYNDICATE OF THE UNIVERSITY OF
CAMBRIDGE
The Pitt Building, Trumpington Street, Cambridge,
United Kingdom

CAMBRIDGE UNIVERSITY PRESS
The Edinburgh Building, Cambridge CB2 2RU, UK
    http://www.cup.cam.ac.uk
40 West 20th Street, New York, NY 10011–4211, USA
    http://www.cup.org
10 Stamford Road, Oakleigh, Melbourne 3166, Australia
Ruiz de Alarcón 13, 28014 Madrid, Spain

First published 1998
Reprinted with corrections 2000

Printed in the United Kingdom at the University Press,
Cambridge

Typeset in Columbus 10/12.5pt [VN]

*A catalogue record for this book is available from the
British Library*

*Library of Congress Cataloguing in Publication data applied for*

ISBN 0 521 57256 8 hardback
ISBN 0 521 57619 9 paperback

For Andrée and for George;
for Joan and for David
– our great teachers and friends

# Contents

Contents

# Figures

# Tables

# Contributors

Carolyn E. Boyd
*Department of Anthropology, Texas A and M University,*
*College Station, Texas, USA*

Richard Bradley
*Department of Archaeology, University of Reading, England*

Christopher Chippindale
*Museum of Archaeology and Anthropology, University of*
*Cambridge, England and Australian National University,*
*Canberra and Darwin, Australia*

John Clegg
*School of Archaeology, Classics and Ancient History,*
*University of Sydney, Australia*

Jean Clottes
*International Committee on Rock Art, CAR-ICOMOS,*
*Foix, France*

Thomas A. Dowson
*Department of Archaeology, University of Southampton,*
*England*

Henri-Paul Francfort
*CNRS Paris, France*

Ralph Hartley
*NPS Midwest Center, Lincoln, USA*

Pieter Jolly
*Department of Archaeology, University of Cape Town,*
*South Africa*

Michael A. Klassen
*Vancouver, Canada*

Jo McDonald
*Sydney, NSW, Australia*

Sven Ouzman
*Rock Art Department, National Museum, Bloemfontein,*
*South Africa*

Benjamin Smith
*Rock Art Research Unit, University of the Witwatersrand,*
*Johannesburg, South Africa*

Kalle Sognnes
*Stjørdal Museum, Stjørdal, Norway*

Anne Solomon
*Department of Archaeology, University of Cape Town,*
*South Africa*

Paul S. C. Taçon
*Anthropology Division, The Australian Museum, Sydney,*
*Australia*

Anne M. Wolley Vawser
*NPS Midwest Center, Lincoln, USA*

Eva M. Walderhaug
*Institute of Archaeology, University of Bergen, Norway*

David S. Whitley
*Institute of Archaeology, University of California at Los*
*Angeles, USA*

Meredith Wilson
*Department of Archaeology and Anthropology, Australian*
*National University, Canberra, Australia*

# Note on dates

Dates given as BC, AD, BP ('Before Present') are in
calendar years, however they have been arrived at.
Dates given as 'b.p.' are uncalibrated radiocarbon
determinations, and are measures of 'radiocarbon
years' that do not equate exactly with calendar years.

# Acknowledgements

# The speared bighorn sheep

The editors thank the contributors for the speedy, good-humoured and efficient way in which they have worked with us. We thank also Margaret Deith, Alison Gascoigne, Jessica Kuper, David Lewis-Williams, John Parkington, Benjamin Smith and Jim Specht for their assistance in several ways.

The image decorating chapter headings is from a rock-engraving of a bighorn sheep from the Coso Range, eastern California; it was traced from a photograph by Christopher Chippindale.

Paul S. C. Taçon and Christopher Chippindale

# 1. An archaeology of rock-art through informed methods and formal methods

As the millennium draws to a close, the world is undergoing unparalleled change, affecting virtually every living creature on Earth. Human beings, the primary agents of change, also are intensely affected by it. In particular, over the past few hundred years indigenous peoples of every continent have undergone radical transformations to their ways of life. But with the dawning of the computer and space age so too have individuals from the more dominant cultures. One global response to this intense social, environmental and technological change has been a creative explosion, not only in technology but also in the arts, as contemporary artists draw on cultures the world over for inspiration. The result is an unrivalled fusion of form, aesthetics and subject-matter. Alongside this wondrous burst of creativity, and the embracing of all that is new, has been an increased interest in the past, the remote, the exotic, the 'other'. The western disciplines of archaeology and anthropology were born to chart, to describe and to tabulate the 'old' and 'new' peoples encountered through this exploration and conquering of 'other' lands; museums were established to assemble, curate and display the material culture and products of the peoples that populated those lands.

## Rock-art

Nevertheless, there have been many periods of intense change in human history (see, for instance, Allen and O'Connell 1995) and many 'creative explosions' (Pfeiffer 1982). The post-glacial transformation of most of the globe – beginning 10,000 years ago – from the lands of mobile gatherer-hunters into the territories of farmers and kings is another in a series (but see Sherratt 1997). Evidence of those earlier revolutions may be scant in most places, and for some aspects – like the prehistory of song and music – we have scarcely no evidence. One record is enduring. The accumulations of ancient rock-paintings and engravings are testament to visual art as a medium of mediating, recording, recounting and a new means of more fully experiencing those profound human events and changes which have shaped our histories. Through what we now collectively refer to as 'rock-art', we see how different peoples, at various times of the past, represented or interpreted change *for themselves*. What is remarkable is not so much the particular images of certain regions but rather the widespread and truly global nature of this phenomenon. For at least 40,000 years (Chase and Dibble 1987; Davidson and Noble 1989; Lindly and Clark 1990; Mellars 1989, 1991; Taçon 1994), and perhaps for much longer (Bednarik 1994; Lorblanchet 1993; Fullagar *et al.* 1996; Taçon *et al.* 1997), human beings have increasingly marked landscapes in symbolic ways. A characteristically human trait, this is one of the ways we socialise landscapes. The result is a great and a scattered array of visually striking imagery as time and chance have let it survive to us at sites or within regions over vast periods of time.

## The archaeology of rock-art

In this volume we explore some of that imagery. This exploration is not a complete one – there is too much to explore, too many ways to explore it. We do not here explore the inspiration these ancient images give to contemporary artists (Fig. 1.2), or the aesthetics of

**Fig. 1.1.** Roger Yilarama, *Mardayin Dreaming: Water Dreamings of My Father's Country (Mardayin Djang)*, ochres and clay on stringy-bark tree bark, 1993.

Where most rock-art traditions – like all those of prehistoric Europe – have perished, a few continue, largely in other media.

In central Australia, the now-celebrated 'dot' paintings of the desert country, generally in acrylic on canvas, derive their iconography from the ancient traditions seen in the region's rock-engravings. The painting of central desert designs and images in synthetic materials on to portable surfaces is not at all ancient; it began at Papunya, about 200 km west of Alice Springs, in 1971 (Caruana 1993: 107).

On the central north coast of Australia, the long tradition of painting seen on the rocks and crags of Arnhem Land is lively today in portable paintings made on the bark of eucalyptus trees (Brody 1985) and, increasingly, on art paper (Dyer 1994), of

the ancient pictures – if those can be discerned from them (see Scarre 1994).

The sole subject of this book – which could have been much larger – is the *archaeology* of rock-art, where archaeology is the systematic study of past human lives as they can be discerned through a knowledge of their material traces. The special merit, and the special attraction, of rock-art as the subject of archaeological enquiry is its directness. These are images from ancient worlds as ancient human minds envisioned them; these are neither stray fragments of ancient garbage nor chance stumps of perished buildings. They are all direct material expressions of human concepts, of human thought. The directness carries a matching special obstacle. While one hopes speedily to deduce from the grubby old stones and bones reasonably secure facts about these ancient objects, the rock-art is a more immediate record, both easier to see and harder to make sense of. So interpretations of its nature and meaning have been famously eccentric: some still are.

A scholarly interest in rock-art is not new. It is often said that Europeans began their fascination with rock-art in 1879, after a young girl and her father investigated a large cave at Altamira, Spain, and were awed by the sight of majestic bulls on the ceiling above them (Grant 1967: 3), but serious study is now recognised to have begun at least by the 1860s (Bahn and Vertut 1988: 19). The study of rock-art in Central Asia, remarks Henri-Paul Francfort in Chapter 17, *Central Asian petroglyphs: between Indo-Iranian and shamanistic interpretations,*

which this is a fine recent example. The ochre and clay pigments are those used on the rocks; the subject and manners of depiction are equally in the same tradition. It is not just an illustration for its own sake, but derives from knowledge of the country, as related by the varied 'inside' and 'outside' stories the images stand for.

We mention these details to illustrate how pertinent modern traditions of depiction and iconography can hint at the real nature of the many traditions of rock-art we approach only by formal means.

Reproduced by permission of the artist and of Cambridge University Museum of Archaeology and Anthropology.

Photograph by Gwil Owen.

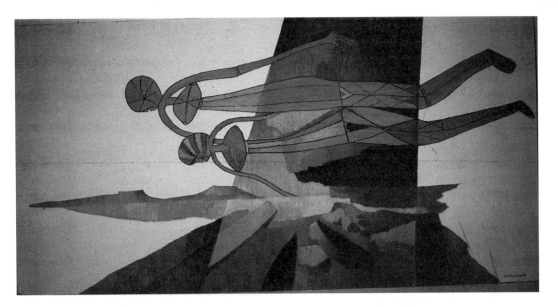

**Fig. 1.2.** George Chaloupka, *Spirits in the Land*, oil on canvas, 1972.

This book is about the archaeology of rock-art, so other aspects to the images are not developed. Here is a picture inspired by rock-art to stand for what is missing.

George Chaloupka, the senior researcher on Australian rock-art, is himself an artist. He painted this image at a time when Arnhem Land was being presented as a desert, which deserved development if that was financially advantageous, and otherwise had no merit. In its subject and its manner of depiction, Chaloupka was inspired by the rock-art images, especially those which had been painted not many years before by Najolbombi, last of the famous rock-painters, in western Arnhem Land. This is one of about twenty paintings that were exhibited in Canberra and largely sold there. The last of those left over from the exhibition, it survived the destruction of Chaloupka's home in Darwin by Cyclone Tracy in 1977. The whereabouts of those sold in 1972 is not known.

We mention these details to illustrate – again, and in another context – how particular can be the reasons for which images are created, and how capricious can be their survival and our access to knowledge of them.

Reproduced by permission of the artist.

began in the seventeenth century and has never ceased. The ancient little figures pecked into the ice-smoothed rocks of Valcamonica, in Alpine north Italy, were known to its country people, who had a dialect word for them. And in Arnhem Land, north Australia, Aboriginal people know the old art of the Mimi – the other kind of human being who were in their stone country long long before them and who still live there as frail-bodied spirits, sheltered within the cracks in the ancient rocks (Brandl 1973; Chaloupka 1993; Lewis 1988; Taçon 1989; Taçon and Brockwell 1995; Taçon and Chippindale 1994).

Much of the apparatus with which archaeologists approach rock-art (Whitley in press) is the usual kit of the archaeologist's trade: the drawing, photo-graphic, recording and survey gear is standard. So are some of the methods, increasingly science-based, and their technical languages – direct AMS dating, strati-graphic sequence, co-variation, taphonomy. And so are many frames of ideas. Rock-art is seen as structured by distinct, distinctive and distinguishable style, so amenable to stylistic studies (e.g. Francis in press, *contra* Lorblanchet and Bahn 1993). And the images of rock-art lend themselves to contemporary research interest in ancient meanings and their social expression (e.g. Tilley 1991). But rock-art research remains distanced from other special interests within archae-ology; and the special circumstances of survival and study mean the methods developed for studying art in other contexts may not transfer across either. Some

**Fig. 1.3.** Eric Gill, *Crocodile*, carved into exterior brick wall, Mond Laboratory, Free School Lane, Cambridge, 1930–1.

Rock-engravings are rare in the artificial landscapes of the world's contemporary cities. This is in a built surface of brick, fittingly a synthetic rock, as it is in a humanly created city-scape.

The celebrated engraver and illustrator carved the image, about 1.8 metres high, to a subject chosen by the Russian physicist Peter Kapitsa. It is Russian in its symbolism: the crocodile as the 'great unknown' in created things. (There are crocodiles of two types, freshwater and saltwater, in Roger Yilarama's bark-painting, Fig. 1.1: in his Australian country, the two beasts are vital creatures, important in the land and in the stories – not alien curiosities in the zoological garden!) Gill's own comment on his image of the crocodile – refined by visits to London Zoo to see and draw the real creatures – was, 'What should we know of reptiles who only reptiles know?' (MacCarthy 1989: 273).

The Mond Building now houses the Cambridge University collection of air photographs, a unit within the University much concerned with archaeology. Staff there think of their crocodile as a fierce beast that stands guardian at the door to their precious archive.

We mention these details to illustrate – yet again, and in yet another context – how the meanings of images are varied and shifting.

Photograph by Christopher Chippindale.

methods and many frames of ideas translate uncertainly into the different language of pictures on the rocks. Researchers use an eclectic mix of approaches, some of them new (if any approach in twentieth-century research can wholly be called new), some of them borrowed (and adapted in or after the borrowing to the circumstance of studying rock-art).

In Valcamonica – as in other parts of the world – the tradition of marking the rocks tellingly stops as its sheltered communities were overwhelmed by an outside world of commanding people whose culture was a literate one of reading and writing (Anati 1976: 153–6): for those communities, the swallowing power of the growing Roman Empire. In a great many regions, it was the first fleets of the European expansion and their landing passengers who closed down the world in which the rock-art had been made; the regions are not numerous where we have good ethnohistorical accounts of the rock-painters and very few where the painting traditions are still strong (for one, western Arnhem Land, see e.g. Chaloupka 1993; West 1995). The worlds of texts and the world of written words are different in fundamental ways, as Sven Ouzman, *Towards a mindscape of landscape: rock-art as expression of world-understanding*, shows in Chapter 3. Even the rock-arts of our culture in our own day – among which one should include the inscriptions monumentally engraved into and the graffiti sprayed on to the artificial rock surfaces of buildings in our urban landscapes – often offer words alongside or instead of pictures (Figs. 1.3, 1.4).

Inasmuch as rock-art is rather an archaeological subject apart, so will the methods of its study be set rather apart. Many of them will have novelty. Since no settled or standard approach has emerged – Whitley (in press) will be the first general handbook on the archaeological study of rock-art to be published – this is the time to explore the diversity of fruitful approaches, and to recognise their unities. Rock-art has been a subject-matter of archaeology for centuries, at least in Scandinavia – yet the title of this book, *The archaeology of rock-art*, seems not to have

**Fig. 1.4.** Artist unknown, graffiti piece, spray-paint on brick bridge abutment, Cambridge (Long Road railway bridge, old Bedford line archway), c. 1995.

Images officially set on walls in the contemporary urban environment are primarily directional signs, in words alone, or in words treated with graphic care, sometimes in pictures alone: 'This is the way out', 'This is the way to the aeroplane.' Distinctive 'rock'-paintings on artificial hard-rock surfaces of our own culture include the spray-painted graffiti, said to have originated in New York in the 1970s (Castleman 1982; Cooper and Chalfant 1984), then seen in cities across the world (Stahl 1990).

Individual graffiti artists declare their identity with small 'tags' contrived from their initials or nicknames. Often they make a 'piece', a large and ambitious composition; the word 'piece' derives from 'masterpiece' and echoes the original meaning of that word, as denoting the grand project with which an apprentice craftsman proves his skill and is thereby made a master.

Imagery in 'pieces' has many forms. Often central, as in this piece, is an elaborated polychrome geometrical form, again a kind of lettering – nicknames, initials, or favoured word – treated with such graphic force that the letters are barely or not recognised. We find it striking, and telling of late twentieth-century values, that spray-graffiti artists – the famous marginals who make a special iconography in our society – nevertheless make their graphics on the model of those words which define the power of the controlling literates against them.

We mention these details to illustrate – yet again, and in yet another context – how varied can be the ways in which images derive from a society, and relate to its values.

Artist unknown, therefore reproduced without permission of the artist. Photograph by Christopher Chippindale.

been used before. Rock-art is old, but this kind of study seems perhaps young.

The diversity is represented by the eighteen remarkable essays that make up this book, by researchers whose academic standing runs from senior professors to graduate students, and whose immediate subject-matter spans the world. The unity is given by a deep structure both to the book and to individual papers. Since doubt surrounds just what best to *do* in studying rock-art, the group emphasises considered and rigorous *methods*. Since methods do not exist in the abstract, they show themselves in application by effective case-studies that begin with the *essentials*:

● what the stuff is;
● what date it is;
● how it is studied with informed methods;
● how it is studied with formal methods;
● how it is studied by analogy.

The group has not attempted a specific definition of 'rock-art'. We hold it to refer to human-made marks on natural, non-portable rocky surfaces; the more common being those which are either applied *upon* the rock and called *pictographs* – including paintings, drawings, daubings, stencils, prints, beeswax motifs – or which are cut *into* the rock and called *petroglyphs* – engravings, incisings, peckings, gougings, symbolic grindings, etchings, and so forth. 'Rock' will do as a term for the surface that bears them, although sometimes the rock is a geological surface as soft as mud (Bednarik 1986; Faulkner 1986). 'Art' is a less happy term, because art has a rather specific meaning in recent western societies, not suited to those many societies where the crafty making of images and pictures was a business centrally integrated with other concerns. In the absence of a better term – 'rock image', 'rock picture', 'rock marking', 'rock trace', 'rock glyph', and so on are also unhappy – we stay with rock-art. (In consequence we have to tolerate the confusion by which the term 'rock-art' also refers to the iconography of rock-and-roll music!) We hyphenate 'rock-art', against common modern habit, in a slight attempt to make this term into a portmanteau.

## Dating

Chronology has always been important to rock-art studies, and remains generally difficult.

Carbon is present usually in minute traces only, and it is generally supposed rather than known that the 'carbon event' which will be measured by radiocarbon is actually to be equated reliably with the 'art event', the subject of study for which we would like a date. Accordingly carbon dating of rock-art is a new field of endeavour, made possible only by the AMS radiocarbon method with its scanty sample size, and still at an experimental stage (Nelson 1993). The disputes of 1995–6 over the age of the Foz Côa petroglyphs engravings, for which dates are argued that run from the later Palaeolithic (Zilhão 1995) to the eighteenth century or later of our own era (Bednarik 1995), shows how large the uncertainties can be.

Dating is here addressed by Jean Clottes, *The 'Three Cs': fresh avenues towards European Palaeolithic art*, Chapter 7. The material available from the European Palaeolithic, often charcoal safely preserved in deep and still caves, is far more satisfactory for trustworthy carbon-dating than are the materials of such exposed surface imagery as Jo McDonald studies in *Shelter rock-art in the Sydney Basin – a space–time continuum: exploring different influences on change*, Chapter 18. Our own Chapter 6, Christopher Chippindale and Paul S. C. Taçon *The many ways of dating Arnhem Land rock-art, north Australia*, takes dating as its central theme, for a region with exceptional and fortunate opportunities for varied dating methods.

## Informed methods

By *informed methods* we mean those that depend on some source of insight passed on directly or indirectly from those who made and used the rock-art – through ethnography, through ethnohistory, through the historical record, or through modern understanding known with good cause to perpetuate ancient knowledge; then, one can hope to explore the pictures from the inside, as it were. In Arnhem Land, for instance, the recent rock-painting tradition continues in fine paintings on bark and paper, full of layered and intricate meaning (Fig. 1.1); so the image of a croco-dile in Thompson Nganjmirra's painting *Crocodile Dreaming* (1992) relates not to a mere beast, but to 'the first Crocodile Ancestor, who was a man before he turned into a crocodile with large jaws and gnawed through the Liverpool Ranges to see what lay beyond' (Dyer 1994: 54). The 'hybrid' creature in another of the same artist's paintings, with snake body and crocodile head, we know to represent the Rainbow Serpent, one of the creator-beings who in the found-ing days passed through the country, making its water-holes and creeks, filling it with creatures, and peopling it with its several clans, each in its proper place in the land. And we know there is not just one Rainbow Serpent, for in the Dreamtime Yingarna, the Mother Rainbow Serpent, grew two eggs in her body and gave birth to a son, Ngalyod, and a daughter, Ngalkunburriyaymi (Taylor 1990: 330). By their common traits we – both Aboriginal Arnhem Landers and western researchers who have been give that knowledge – can recognise late Rainbow Serpents in the rock-art, and then trace this distinctive subject back in the long dated sequence. In this way, we come to see how the Rainbow Serpent starts as a motif in Arnhem Land rock-art when the rising sea-level of the post-glacial brings the ocean across settled land; and an element in its founding ethnography is a creature of the sea – a pipefish rather than a land snake (Taçon, Wilson and Chippindale 1996).

Importantly, because iconographic meanings seem to be variable and historically idiosyncratic – rather than standardised and accessible by some generalis-ing rules in an anthropology of art – that ethno-graphic insight into an informed knowledge is essen-tial to that kind of understanding. Without it, one might *suppose* this snaky creature, because of its non-natural combination of limbs and traits, might not be of the everyday, mundane world – but one would not *know* just what it stood for, with just what meaning and just what power. The crocodile as a picture, because natural in its traits, one could think is wholly a subject from the natural world; nothing in the image itself tells the ignorant outsider that it is not only a

beast but Crocodile Ancestor, a man before he turned into a crocodile. The cross-hatching that fills the creatures' bodies one might suppose mere decorative infill, whilst in truth it is *rarrk,* a design that carries strong meaning and is particular to the individual artist's clan. Equally, in the Coso Range of California one would not have immediate cause to suppose, from the pictures of bighorn sheep and of rattlesnakes, that these images of everyday creatures in the Mojave drylands stood for different and deep meanings – as the old ethnohistoric records show (see Whitley's *Finding rain in the desert: landscape, gender and far western North American rock-art,* Chapter 2).

There are practically no rock-art traditions that continue into the present, and precious few of which there is a good ethnographic or ethnohistoric record available. Even the rich records of San knowledge, on which an understanding of South African rock-paint-ings has been built (e.g. Lewis-Williams 1981 and subsequent work), come from Bushmen who were not themselves painters and whose country was far re-moved from that region of the Drakensberg where a compelling account of the rock-art has now been made through treating their knowledge as informed about that art's meaning. For some regions, the relev-ance of potentially informed sources is uncertain: are the rock-engravings of the later prehistoric Alps to be comprehended through seeing in them Indo-Euro-pean structures of religious knowledge as these have later been discerned (Masson 1995)? Or are those understandings no kind of true knowledge when it comes to the ancient Alpine panels (de Lumley *et al.* 1995)?

## Formal methods

For much prehistoric art, beginning with the Palaeo-lithic art of the deep European caves, we have no basis for informed knowledge. There we must work with *formal methods,* those that depend on no inside knowledge, but which work when one comes to the stuff 'cold', as a prehistorian does. The information available is then restricted to that which is immanent in the images themselves, or which we can discern from their relations to each other and to the landscape, or by relation to whatever archaeological context is available. This includes inference by location in landscape (Richard Bradley, *Daggers drawn: depictions of Bronze Age weapons in Atlantic Europe*, Chapter 8; Sven Ouzman, *Towards a mindscape of landscape: rock-art as expression of world-understanding*, Chapter 3), the figuring out of what a picture shows by the geometry of its shape (Benjamin Smith, *The tale of the chameleon and the platypus: limited and likely choices in making pictures*, Chapter 12), inference from a mathematical measure of information content and from site location (Ralph Hartley and Anne M. Wolly Vawser, *Spatial behaviour and learning in the prehistoric environment of the Colorado River drainage (south-eastern Utah), western North America*, Chapter 11), and the relationship of similar but widely separated forms through the use of multivariate analyses (Meredith Wilson, *Pacific rock-art and cultural genesis: a multivariate exploration*, Chapter 10) or by other techniques.

Even where there is informed knowledge, the formal methods can be useful, just as one can study the geometry of pictures from any cultural context as an interest separate from their meaning, or as one can usefully find kinds of modern understanding in aspects of paintings in the western tradition which in their own time were not a concern (see, e.g., Carrier 1991).

## Analogy

Finally, *analogy* relates to, but does not duplicate, the formal methods: when we cannot observe $x$ but we can $y$, which is sufficiently like it, we can hope to infer things about $x$ based on observations of $y$. Aspects are necessarily particular to the distinctive nature of rock-art as a class of archaeological materials, but the issues of method that arise are the difficult and well-known ones that concern archaeological reasoning by analogy in general.

## The studies in this book, and the book's structure

Some of this book's authors can say little or nothing by informed methods: when enigmatic images come from a remote prehistory, we can have no inside knowledge of them; study must proceed by formal methods and/or analogy. Most authors touch upon more than one aspect, and do so with more than one method; a diversity of approaches to studying rock-art is evident. Four chapters primarily approach their subject-matters from informed perspectives: David Whitley, *Finding rain in the desert: landscape, gender and far western North American rock-art*, Sven Ouzman, *Towards a mindscape of landscape: rock-art as expression of world-understanding*, Michael A. Klassen, *Icon and narrative in transition: contact-period rock-art at Writing-On-Stone, southern Alberta, Canada*, Chapter 4, and Thomas A. Dowson, *Rain in Bushman belief, politics and history: the rock-art of rain-making in the south-eastern mountains, southern Africa*, Chapter 5. One concentrates on different strands of dating evidence: Christopher Chippindale and Paul S. C. Taçon, *The many ways of dating Arnhem Land rock-art, north Australia*. Two rely on dating and formal methods: Jean Clottes, *The 'Three Cs': fresh avenues towards European Palaeolithic art* and Richard Bradley, *Daggers drawn: depictions of Bronze Age weapons in Atlantic Europe*. Three focus on the formal: Kalle Sognnes, *Symbols in a changing world: rock-art and the transition from hunting to farming in mid Norway*, Chapter 9, Meredith Wilson, *Pacific rock-art and cultural genesis: a multivariate exploration* and Benjamin Smith, *The tale of the chameleon and the platypus: limited and likely choices in making pictures*. Five use a combination of formal methods and analogy: Carolyn E. Boyd, *Pictographic evidence of peyotism in the Lower Pecos, Texas Archaic*, Chapter 13, Pieter Jolly, *Modelling change in the contact art of the south-eastern San, southern Africa*, Chapter 14, Anne Solomon, *Ethnography and method in southern African rock-art research*, Chapter 15, Eva M. Walderhaug, *Changing art in a changing society: the hunters' rock-art of western Norway*, Chapter 16, and Henri-Paul Francfort, *Central Asian petroglyphs: between Indo-Iranian and shamanistic interpretations*. Then Jo McDonald's *Shelter rock-art in the Sydney Basin (Australia) – a space–time continuum: exploring different influences on diachronic change* weaves dating, formal methods and analogy. We close with a Chapter 19 that combines aspects of dating, formal methods and analogy with flashes of insight, inspiration and exasperation: John Clegg, *Making sense of obscure pictures from our own history: exotic images from Callan Park, Australia.* His chapter humbles us too, in showing how mysterious figures can be that are from our own culture, and nearly from our own time.

These case-studies explore a wide range of petroglyphs and pictographs from seven key regions of the world: Australia (three-and-a-half chapters), southern Africa (three-and-a-half), North America (three), Scandinavia (two), western Europe (two), continental Asia (one) and the Pacific Islands (one). The chapters are not ordered by geographical location but rather by the primary methods researchers employed, moving from informed towards formal, and then to analogy. Interestingly, five of the chapters – Whitley, Ouzman, Klassen, Boyd, Francfort – focus on aspects of shamanism for interpretation.

## Celebrating rock-art, learning from rock-art

Rock-art represents a great and shared legacy: a visual, illustrated history of human endeavour, aggression, co-operation, experience and accomplishment. As Australian Aboriginal colleagues of ours in Kakadu National Park and Arnhem Land are fond of pointing out to us, these sites are history; these are history books that tell of pasts more varied and more diverse than what declares itself in the written record. They give insight into the present – a theme not developed in this book – as well as into the past. Ultimately, the lessons of the past do help to shape our futures: this is one of the reasons human ancestors the world over recorded their experiences on such durable media as stone and rock. They explored, fought over, farmed and marked places with aspects of their cultural, group or individual identities. In so doing, they made statements to themselves and to others about the nature of *place.* They also made statements about themselves, defining landscapes for future use. We continue this process on a daily basis: in our cities, our parks, our gardens, our homes. We map, mark and immortalise places. We journey; we remember. Already our species has sent contrived objects out of the solar system, and left traces upon the rocks of the moon. The legacy of the first artists will continue in unimagined new ways. But through books such as this one the accomplishments of some of the earliest creators, our original artists, poets and story-tellers, will not be forgotten! Read, reflect, relax and rejoice. Embark with us on a journey through time and space that explores the visually creative essence of early humanity.

Paul S. C. Taçon and Christopher Chippindale
*Sydney and Cambridge*
*1997*

## REFERENCES

Allen, J. and J. F. O'Connell (eds.). 1995. *Transitions: Pleistocene to Holocene in Australia and Papua New Guinea.* Antiquity 69: Special Number 265.

Anati, E. 1976. *Evolution and style in Camunian rock art.* Capo di Ponte (BS), Edizioni del Centro.

Bahn, P. G. and J. Vertut. 1988. *Images of the Ice Age.* Leicester, Windward.

Bednarik, R. 1986. Parietal finger markings in Europe and Australia, *Rock Art Research* 3: 30–61, 159–70.

1994. The Pleistocene art of Asia, *Journal of World Prehistory* 8(4): 351–75.

1995. The Côa petroglyphs: an obituary to the stylistic dating of Palaeolithic rock art, *Antiquity* 69: 877–83.

Brandl, E. 1973. *Australian Aboriginal paintings in western and central Arnhem Land: temporal sequences and elements of style in Cadell River and Deaf Adder Creek art.* Canberra, Australian Institute of Aboriginal Studies.

Brody, A. 1985. *Kunwinjku Bim: western Arnhem Land paintings from the collection of the Aboriginal Arts Board.* Melbourne, National Gallery of Victoria.

Carrier, D. 1991. *Principles of art history writing.* University Park (PA), Pennsylvania State University Press.

Caruana, W. 1993. *Aboriginal art.* London, Thames and Hudson.

Castleman, C. 1982. *Getting up: subway graffiti in New York.* Cambridge (MA), MIT Press.

Chaloupka, G. 1993. *Journey in Time.* Sydney, Reed Books.

Chase, P. and H. Dibble. 1987. Middle Palaeolithic symbolism: a review of current evidence and interpretations, *Journal of Anthropological Archaeology* 6: 263–96.

Cooper, M. and H. Chalfant. 1984. *Subway art*. London, Thames and Hudson.

Davidson, I. and W. Noble. 1989. The archaeology of perception: traces of depiction and language, *Current Anthropology* 30(2): 125–55.

Dyer, C. A. (ed.). 1994. *Kunwinjku art from Injalak 1991–1992: the John W. Kluge Commission*. North Adelaide (SA), Museum Art International.

Faulkner, C. H. (ed.). 1986. *The prehistoric Native American art of Mud Glyph Cave*. Knoxville (TN), University of Tennessee Press.

Francis, J. In press. Classification and taxonomy, in D. Whitle (ed.), *Handbook of rock art research*. Walnut Creek (CA), AltaMira.

Fullagar, R. L. K., D. M. Price and L. M. Head. 1996. Early human occupation of northern Australia: archaeology and thermoluminescence dating of Jinmium rock-shelter, Northern Territory, *Antiquity* 70: 751–73.

Grant, C. 1967. *Rock art of the American Indian*. New York, Promontory Press.

Lewis, D. 1988. *The rock paintings of Arnhem Land: social, ecological, and material culture change in the post-glacial period*. Oxford, British Archaeological Reports, International Series 415.

Lewis-Williams, J. D. 1981. *Believing and seeing: symbolic meanings in southern San rock painitnings*. London, Academic Press.

Lindly, J. M. and G. A. Clark. 1990. Symbolism and modern human origins, *Current Anthropology* 31(3): 233–61.

Lorblanchet, M. 1993. Response to Bednarik, Mathpal and Odak, *International Newsletter on Rock Art* 6: 14–16.

Lorblanchet, M. and P. Bahn (eds.). 1993. *Rock art studies: the post-stylistic era, or, Where do we go from here?* Oxford, Oxbow Books.

de Lumley, H. *et al.* 1995. *Le Grandiose et la sacré: gravures rupestres protohistoriques et historiques de la région du Mont Bégo*. Paris, Editions Edisud.

MacCarthy, F. 1989. *The life of Eric Gill*. London, Faber.

Masson, E. 1992. Découverte et signification des gravures de l'Age du bronze ancien du Mont Bégo (Alpes-Maritimes) dans leur ensemble, *Comptes Rendus de l'Académie des Sciences Paris*, Series II, 314: 313–17.

Mellars, P. 1989. Major issues in the emergence of modern humans, *Current Anthropology* 30(3): 349–85.

1991. Cognitive changes and the emergence of modern humans, *Cambridge Archaeological Journal* 1(1): 63–76.

Nelson, D. E. 1993. Second thoughts on a rock-art date, *Antiquity* 67(257): 893–5.

Pfeiffer, J. E. 1982. *The creative explosion: an inquiry into the origins of art and religion*. Ithaca, Cornell University Press.

Scarre, C. (ed.). 1994. Is there a place for aesthetics in archaeology?, *Cambridge Archaeological Journal* 4(2): 249–69.

Sherratt, A. 1997. Climatic cycles and behavioural revolutions: the emergence of modern humans and the beginning of farming, *Antiquity* 71: 271–87.

Stahl, J. 1990. *Graffiti: zwischen Alltag und Aesthetik*. Munich, Scaneg.

Taçon, P. S. C. 1989. From Rainbow Snakes to 'X-ray' fish: the nature of the recent rock painting tradition of western Arnhem Land, Australia. Unpublished Ph.D. thesis, Australian National University, Canberra.

1994. Socialising landscapes: the long-term implications of signs, symbols and marks on the land, *Archaeology in Oceania* 29(3): 117–29.

Taçon, P. S. C. and S. Brockwell. 1995. Arnhem Land prehistory in landscape, stone and paint, *Antiquity* 69(265): 676–95.

Taçon, P. S. C. and C. Chippindale. 1994. Australia's ancient warriors: changing depictions of fighting in the rock art of Arnhem Land, N.T., *Cambridge Archaeological Journal* 4(2): 211–48.

Taçon, P. S. C., R. Fullagar, S. Ouzman and K. Mulvaney. 1997. Cupule engravings from Jinmium-Granilpi (northern Australia) and beyond: exploration of a widespread and enigmatic class of rock markings, *Antiquity* 71: 942–65.

Taçon, P. S. C., M. Wilson and C. Chippindale. 1996b. Birth of the Rainbow Serpent in Arnhem Land rock art and oral history, *Archaeology in Oceania* 31:103–24.

Taylor, L. 1990. The Rainbow Serpent as visual metaphor in western Arnhem Land, *Oceania* 60: 329–44.

Tilley, C. 1991. *Material culture and text: the art of ambiguity*. London, Routledge.

West, M. 1995. *Rainbow Sugarbag and Moon: two artists of the stone country: Bardayal Nadjamerrek and Mick Kubarkku*. Darwin (NT), Museum and Art Gallery of the Northern Territory.

Whitley, D. (ed.). In press. *Handbook of rock art research*. Walnut Creek (CA): AltaMira.

Zilhão, J. 1995. The age of the Côa valley (Portugal) rock-art: validation of archaeological dating to the Palaeolithic and refutation of 'scientific' dating to historic or proto-historic times, *Antiquity* 69: 883–901.

David S. Whitley

# 2. Finding rain in the desert: landscape, gender and far western North American rock-art

It will soon be a century since Ishi, a Yahi man from California, came into a white settlers' camp and into anthropological fame as the 'last wild Indian' of the far American west. Does this place the rock-art of the region now into, effectively, a prehistoric context, accessible only through formal methods? Or is there sufficient understanding, recorded in abundant ethnographies and quietly continuing in some present-day knowledge, to grasp what its striking iconography meant? Distinctive formal traits, consistent with grounded insight, can be observed within some frame of dating.

## Art on the natural landscape

Like much of our professional jargon, the term 'rock-art' is one inherited from our archaeological forebears yet, as with most such standard terms, it is not without its definitional problems. Whether or not it is actually 'art' (in the European sense of this term), for example, is problematic. But regardless of one's position on that unresolved issue, the definitional basis of 'rock-art' is worth considering for an additional reason: what we know as 'rock-art' qualifies as such not so much because of its association with rocks (sculptures and mobile art too are made from stone), nor simply due to its placement on parietal surfaces (murals, on built walls, would also qualify). Instead, the defining characteristic of 'rock-art' is its placement on geological substrates, which is to say the natural landscape. Long before Robert Smithson and Michael Heizer (not coincidentally the son of early rock-art researcher Robert Heizer) initiated the modern 'earthworks' art movement, rock-art too was landscape art.

I raise this simple point to emphasise that, with only occasional exceptions (provided by archaeologists such as Ralph Hartley (1992) and Richard Bradley (1991)), we have largely ignored this defining contextual attribute of rock-art in our analyses of it. Moreover, this neglect of context has occurred even while our symbolic analyses of the art have become increasingly more detailed, and they have therefore run counter to a basic principle of symbolic analysis: the importance of context in symbolic meanings. Using the ethnohistorical record, I consider in this chapter specifically the landscape symbolism of far western North America, and how an understanding of the symbolism of the landscape informs and amplifies our symbolic interpretation of the rock-art contained thereon. After some background material, I look in particular at the symbolism of the rock-art site as a sacred place in the landscape; how rock-art sites related to the gender symbolism of the landscape; and, finally, why male ritual specialists then went to the outskirts of Death Valley, the most xeric region in the Great Basin, to make rain.

## Far western North American rock-art

Far western North America (California, the Great Basin and the Columbia Plateau) is a region that, into the last century, was occupied by hunter-gatherer groups, the results of which are twofold: as with many such regions, it contains a rich record of rock-art; and, because occupation by traditional groups is recent, this rock-art record is matched by substantial ethnohistorical documentation. As regards the nature of the art, a recent synthesis has identified five rock-art traditions, each containing various geographical, stylistic and socio-functional variants, within the far west (Whitley 1998a). The two of primary interest in the current discussion account for the large majority of Californian rock-art, my primary focus in this chapter: the *Californian Tradition,* generally restricted to the mesic or western half of California; and the *Great Basin Tradition,* found in the more xeric desert regions in the Mojave Desert of eastern California, and the Great Basin generally (Fig. 2.1).

Californian Tradition rock-art is primarily painted, typically monochrome, and usually displayed in small rock-shelters consisting of one or a few panels, each of which has less than roughly a dozen motifs. Red, black and white are the most common colours employed, although occasional yellows, oranges and even blues sometimes appear (Fig. 2.2). Simple 'geometric' patterns of various sorts are by far the most common category of Californian Tradition motifs, with circles, disc-forms, 'rakes' and 'ladders', 'tick-marks', diamonds, diamond-chains and zigzags common. Although diamond-chains and zigzags were ethnographically identified as rattlesnake (*Crotalus* sp.) drawings (because they mimic the scale pattern on the back of the Western Diamondback, or the track of the Sidewinder, respectively), other readily identifiable 'iconic' motifs are relatively rare. When present, they most commonly portray stick-figure humans, hand prints, lizards and lizard-like motifs.

There is, of course, regional, ethnic, social and functional (and presumably temporal) variation within this tradition, reflecting the ethnographically expected range of variability found in the arts of any given traditional culture (including what is typically glossed as 'stylistic' variability by rock-art researchers; see Whitley 1982). Of particular note in this regard is the South-Central Painted Variant of the Californian Tradition, found extending from the Santa Barbara Channel region, near Los Angeles, north-eastwards into the southern Sierra Nevada. This variant contains the renowned Chumash and Tulare sites (see Grant 1965; Wellmann 1979), where certain spectacular polychrome panels are located. These, like other Californian Tradition sites, are frequently associated with living sites which, almost invariably, date within the last 1500 years.

**Fig. 2.1.** Far western North America, showing the location of the Coso Range within the southern Great Basin. Great Basin Tradition sites are found within the Great Basin and the desert region along the Colorado River of eastern California; Californian Tradition sites typically occur to the west, extending into the coastal zone.

**Fig. 2.2.** Californian Tradition rock-painting panel: the ceiling of Pleito Cave, an elaborate South-Central Painted Variant site. The site, in the mountains north of Los Angeles, is painted with red, yellow, black, white and blue-green pigments. It is believed to be historical in age.

Scale: width of circular 'cartouche' about 30 cm.

The Great Basin Tradition differs from the rock-art to the west on a number of counts. First, it is heavily dominated by rock-engravings, rather than paintings. Second, the locations, sizes and archaeological contexts of the Great Basin Tradition sites vary in important ways from the Californian sites. Massive concentrations of engravings, comprising hundreds and sometimes tens of thousands of motifs, are found in this region. These are typically located on open basalt cliffs and boulders, often with no clear associations with other archaeological features or sites. The Coso Range, in eastern California, is the best known example (see Whitley 1994a). Some estimates place the total number of motifs present in the Cosos in the 100,000 range. Other major concentrations of Great Basin Tradition engravings include Black Mountain, eastern California; Harney Basin, south-eastern Oregon; and the Dinwoody/ Big Horn Basin, western Wyoming. Third, the motif assemblages themselves differ from Californian Tradition sites. Although there is, in fact, considerable regional variation within the Great Basin Tradition, and geometric designs similar to those in the Californian Tradition are still very common at all sites, iconic motifs are significant components of these site assemblages: bighorn sheep (*Ovis canadensis*), humans (including elaborate 'patterned body' figures), skin bags and weapons, and other animals – felines, canids, snakes and lizards – all commonly appear in Great Basin art (Fig. 2.3). In the Cosos, for example, one quantitative study indicates that iconic motifs contribute 74 per cent of the assemblage, with fully 51 per cent of the assemblage total comprising bighorn engravings alone. Although the Cosos represent an extreme case, it is still apparent that the iconography of the Great Basin Tradition varies significantly from the Californian sites (Whitley 1998a).

## Chronology of Californian and Great Basin Traditions rock-art

Considerable research has been conducted on the age of the Great Basin Tradition engravings (e.g., Whitley

**Fig. 2.3.** A Great Basin Tradition panel: an engraving from 'the Wadi' (site CA-SBR-5383), Fort Irwin, central Mojave Desert, California. The bighorn sheep is the most common zoomorphic motif at Great Basin sites. This example is notable because it is portrayed with plantigrade feet rather than hoofs, signalling that it is a shaman transformed into his spirit helper *alter ego*, the bighorn.
Scale in cm.

and Dorn 1987, 1988, 1993; Whitley 1998a; Whitley *et al.* 1996), with much less on the Californian Tradition; a variety of lines of evidence suggest the general chronological parameters for both traditions of rock-art. Independent weathering rind organics (WRO) AMS radiocarbon assays, varnish microlamination (VML) studies, cation-ratio (CR) dating, and ancillary geomorphological data all confirm that Great Basin Tradition engravings were made as early as 16,500 b.p. (Whitley *et al.* 1996), a chronological conclusion supported by the depictions of extinct Pleistocene megafauna in western North American rock-art (Agenbroad 1994). The direct chronometric evidence, further, indicates continued rock-art production through the entirety of the Holocene, into the last 500 years. This evidence also suggests that the basic motif assemblage repertoire of bighorn sheep and simple and complex geometric patterns was employed for the duration of this lengthy time-period; notably, the palaeontological evidence demonstrates that bighorn sheep have been present throughout the far west for at least the last 25,000 years. Late Holocene art production is also evidenced in the subject-matter: the engravings include depictions of atlatls or throwing boards, and bows and arrows. The latter weaponry replaced the atlatl and dart at approximately AD 500. Finally, depictions of horses and riders indicate continued engraving into the last century, which is confirmed by ethnographic commentary. Although the chronometric and other evidence then indicates a very lengthy period of rock-art manufacture within the Great Basin Tradition, a systematic study of the relative degree of revarnishing in Coso Range motifs concluded that the majority of them display little or no visible evidence of revarnishing. While revarnishing provides only the grossest sense of motif ages, this still suggests that the majority of the rock-engravings were probably made during the last 2000 years (Whitley 1994a).

Chronological evidence for the Californian Tradition is much more limited. The fundamental instability of mesic California's sandstone and grano-diorite bedrocks suggests little likelihood of the Californian Tradition panels being preserved much beyond 2000 years. These environmental factors alone favour the inference that extant Californian Tradition sites are necessarily relatively recent in age. This inference is supported by analyses of historical photos of painted panels, which reveal visible and significant deterioration at a number of sites in as little as a few decades. While it is impossible from this evidence to determine how ancient the Californian Tradition might be, the majority of the extant examples of it probably date to the last thousand or so years. Clear evidence that it continued to be made into the period of Euro-American contact is present in occasional depictions of horses, riders and ships and – again – by ethnographic commentary.

**Symbolism and meaning in the art**

Recent research on Californian and Great Basin Tradition rock-art has employed ethnohistorical sources to elucidate the symbolism of this art (see Whitley 1992, 1994a, 1994b, 1994c, 1998a, 1998b, in press a, in press b). This is most profitably summarised by, first, outlining the common cultural patterns in ethnographic rock-art production that are found throughout the far west, and, second, by looking at some regional variations on this underlying pattern, as well as the variation between these two rock-art traditions.

A basic ethnographic pattern underlies far western North American rock-art production, which appears to have been common to most or all hunter-gatherer groups in North America (for example, Vastokas and Vastokas 1973; Snow 1977; Whitley 1988, 1992, 1998a; Rajnovich 1989, 1994; Conway and Conway 1990; York *et al.* 1993; Callahan in press; Hann, Keyser and Minthorn in press). Furthermore, based on analogical studies, this same pattern also appears to pertain to earlier Archaic hunting groups, about which we have no direct ethnographic information (see Zintgraff and Turpin 1991; Schaafsma 1994; Turpin 1994; Boyd in press; Hyland in press). This ethnographic pattern involved the production of rock-art by shamans to depict the altered state of consciousness (ASC) experiences of their vision quests and rituals. The art then commonly depicts ASC mental imagery which – due to the neuropsychological universals of the *Homo sapiens sapiens* central and peripheral nervous systems – comprises a series of cross-cultural regularities in motif forms. It has been argued that the principles by which these forms were perceived and therefore depicted are also cross-culturally regular (see Lewis-Williams and Dowson 1988).

Because the ASC of shamanic visions has somatic effects, the art displays more than simply the mental imagery of trances. It also encodes a set of themes whose origin lies in the natural models provided by the physiological effects of ASC. These effects are likewise constrained by human neuropsychology and thereby again result in a limited, but cross-culturally shared, range of physical responses, which are triggered by various neurotransmitters activated by an ASC. These somatic hallucinations include feelings of death, of weightlessness or flight, of drowning or swimming, of aggression and fighting, of bodily transmogrification, and of sexual arousal and release. Because the ASC experience is, in essence, an ineffable event, these cross-cultural somatic responses served as commonly employed metaphors for the shaman's visionary experience. The cross-cultural regularities observable in many shamanic rituals and symbols, first synthesised by Eliade (1964), then are not solely attributable to historical relationships or to some universally shared psychic principles; instead they are largely based on the natural models provided by neuropsychological universals (Whitley 1994b). It is then understandable that motif forms *and* subject-matter *and* the principles by which both were depicted are equivalent at a structural level for most if not all North American hunter-gatherer rock-art. And it is also then understandable why the subject-matter of the art is precisely duplicated in recorded verbal descriptions of shamans' trances (Whitley 1994b, 1998a, 1998b).

The underlying North American pattern of rock-art production to depict ASC experiences has suggested a monolithic interpretation of the function and meaning of this art to some archaeologists, who object on principle to any interpretation of human behaviour without apparent internal variability. The shamanic interpretation of this art is advantaged by being ethnographically rather than inductively based; the question is then whether we choose to believe informed indigenous commentaries or Euro-American scientists' speculations. Yet two points are still important to emphasise. The first is that Native American hunter-gatherer cultures were themselves thoroughly and undeniably shamanistic in belief, world-view and ritual practice. Acknowledgement that their rock-art had any connection to religious beliefs, practices or symbolism, therefore, necessarily implies symbolism founded on this underlying and unifying shamanistic religious system. Second, and in keeping with this first comment, while the shaman entered into ASC, believed to represent an entry into the supernatural, in order to acquire and manipulate supernatural power, there was no single function or purpose universal to all such shamanic acts. Although a shaman's initial vision quest was usually undertaken to obtain potency, typically manifest in a number of animal spirit helpers and various ritual talismans, subsequent ASCs were sought for very different purposes – curing, sorcery, weather control, clairvoyance, controlling game animals, finding lost objects, and so on. Furthermore, what was depicted when the shaman entered an ASC to perform these various functions also varied considerably, even at the categorical level: although primarily portraying spirit helpers and the shaman himself transformed into a power being, the art also depicts a miscellany of supernatural beings – the guardians of the supernatural, ghosts, individuals bewitched by a shaman, the mythic origin of the world, and supernatural ceremonies and rituals – which the shaman then duplicated in the mundane world. Consequently, even though the art was widely made to depict visionary experiences, the function or purpose of this art varied considerably, a fact simply reflective of the varied functions and kinds of shamans present in North American indigenous groups.

2    In addition to this shamanic origin, rock-art was also made by puberty initiates in shamanistic group ceremonies in certain parts of the far west. Of particular note is the Southwest Painted Variant of the California Tradition, found in the region between Los Angeles and the Mexican border. Sites of this variant are invariably red monochrome paintings, dominated by zigzags, diamond-chains and hand prints (Fig. 2.4). These sites were made into the 1890s by young girls at the completion of their puberty initiations. A primary purpose of this puberty initiation was the girls' acquisition of a single spirit helper (in contrast to shamans, who maintained many such spirit tutelaries). In an inversion of gender symbols, phallic rattlesnake was considered the ideal spirit helper for these young girls; hence this girls' art is dominated by schematicised rattlesnake paintings. In contrast, within the Mojave Desert portion of the Great Basin Tradition, no such puberty rock-art site production is indicated in the ethnographic record. The production of puberty ritual rock-art is documented for boys, during their nasal septum-piercing ceremony, among a restricted group of Yuman-speakers along the

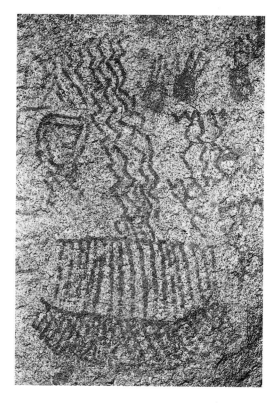

**Fig. 2.4.** A red painted panel from a Southwest Painted Variant site, CA-RIV-16 or 'Puberty Rock', which is part of the larger Californian tradition. This site, located inland from Los Angeles, is known ethnographically to have been painted by girls during a group puberty initiation, sometime during the last century. The zigzags and diamond-chain net patterns are said to represent rattlesnake, the preferred spirit helper for females.

Scale: hand prints at top right are about 13 cm long.

Colorado River, to the south (Whitley 1998a). Again, the intention here was the acquisition, and depiction, of supernatural power.

## Symbolism of the rock-art site

Given the above similarities and differences in the origin and symbolism of Californian and Great Basin rock-art, it is possible to turn to the specific questions at hand. I begin with the symbolism of the rock-art site (as opposed to motif), as a ritual location placed in the landscape. This logically leads to the larger symbolism of the landscape, specifically its gender symbolism, and finally to the way that this landscape symbolism articulated with beliefs about creating rain.

The first point that is apparent in the far western North American ethnohistorical record is that rock-art sites – their physical location in the landscape, geomorphological attributes (rock outcrop, cliff face, rock-shelter walls and ceilings) and the rock-panel faces themselves – were, in fact, important symbols in their own right; instead of serving as neutral back-drops for rock-art motifs, they were in a real sense as symbolically important as the iconography. Indeed, while this iconography could be duplicated by the shaman in other contexts (such as on ceremonial clothing, shields), it was the contextual association between site/panel and motif which gave material potency to the iconographic image; and it was this association which provided the particular meaning among the many meanings that, otherwise, might inhere in a given drawing or engraving. The rock-art site served as the instrumental symbol, in Turner's (1967) terms, of the ritual practices involved in rock-art production.

The symbolism of the site involved the belief that sites were portals into the sacred realm (Whitley 1988, 1992): the site was thought an entrance into the supernatural while the painted or engraved panel was believed a permeable barrier, with rocks and cracks in the panel face opening to allow the shaman to move between the natural and supernatural realms. Making reference to the related belief that shamans kept their ritual paraphernalia *inside* the supernatural (that is, within their rock-art sites), Gayton (1948: 207) noted that in the southern Sierra Nevada a shaman danced in front of a rock-art site and talked

to the rock, which would open up so he could get his things. Each doctor [shaman] had his own place; his things would be in a basket set in a hole in the rock which he had created by means of his power. The opening thereto was not palpable to others: 'you could go over that rock a thousand times and not find the place'.

Likewise, Gayton (1948: 113) noted elsewhere that 'cracks indicated the door, which opened at the owner's command'.

Detailed verbal descriptions of shamans' ASC experiences then often recount the opening of the rock face or an entry through a crack, into the supernatural beyond, as the first event of a shaman's trance (Blackburn 1975: 234; Zigmond 1980: 175–6). Similarly, widespread belief maintained that spirits too entered and exited the natural world through cracks in rocks, further reflecting the belief that rocks were numinous (Dixon 1908: 23; DuBois 1908: 231; Chalfant 1933: 52–3; Turney-High 1937: 13, 33, 1941: 95; Park 1938: 27–8; Steward 1938: 131, 187–8, 1941: 258, 1943: 283; Voegelin 1938: 69; Patencio 1943: 54; Kelly 1977: 127; Hill-Tout 1978a: 152, 1978b: 73; Olofson 1979: 16; True and Waugh 1986: 270–2; Bean *et al.* 1991: 9; Curtin n.d.; Teit n.d.).

The symbolic importance of the rock-art site was then manifest in a number of ways. The first pertains to the naming of rock-art sites. Californian Tradition rock-art sites were referred to generically by terms (in different dialects/languages) such as *choishishiu, pusin tinliw, taakwitc puki* and *kutsitcqove.* Although there are minor translational differences between some of these, they may all be glossed as a toponymic meaning '[shaman's] spirit helper' place, emphasising that the sites were locations within which supernatural beings resided. Similarly, Great Basin Tradition sites were called *pohaghani,* 'house of [supernatural] power' (Whitley 1994b: 3–4). In both regions, then, generic names for rock-art sites were explicit acknowledgements of their connection to the supernatural. The few known site-specific names further emphasise this fact: *pahdin, mawyucan* and *aatogwinaa* (Whitley 1998a). The first term translates literally as place 'to go under', meaning 'to drown'; the second as 'whirlwind' place and the third as place 'to be lifted up' – meaning in both the last two cases 'to fly'. Each is an allusion to the shaman's somatic metaphors for his ASC: the sites are the places where he drowned or where he flew. Each of these referents would be understood precisely as the place where the shaman entered the supernatural realm: they were his portals into the sacred.

A second manifestation of the symbolic importance

**Fig. 2.5.** Engraving from McCoy Spring, in the Colorado Desert west of the Colorado River. This Great Basin Tradition engraving shows a rattlesnake shaman transforming back into his human form as he emerges from a crack in the rock face – his portal into the supernatural realm.

Scale in cm.

of the rock-art site/panel is displayed in the iconography: the placement of paintings or engravings is, in many cases, not random but instead intended to articulate with features on the panel face. Small declivities in the rock panel are commonly used for paintings, while it is not uncommon for paintings and engravings to begin or terminate in a crack on a panel. A good example is provided by an engraving from the Great Basin Tradition site of McCoy Spring, in the Colorado Desert of eastern California (Fig. 2.5). On this panel a zigzag 'emerges' out of a crack and, as it proceeds up the panel face vertically, straightens into a stick-figure human. Inasmuch as zigzags were universally identified in this portion of the far west as rattlesnakes, rattlesnake shamans were among the most common of the shamanic specialists, and all shamans were believed capable of transmogrifying into and out of the form of their animal spirit helpers, this motif may be understood as a rattlesnake shaman, emerging from the supernatural and transforming out of his power form back into his natural self, from a crack in the rock face – the portal to the sacred.

Another manifestation of the important symbolic function of rock-art sites, apart from their iconography, involved the folk (i.e., non-shamanic) use of the sites for general curing activities, during which no rock-art was made. This was a particularly common use of Great Basin Tradition sites (Steward 1943: 283; Heizer and Baumhoff 1962: 48; Grosscup 1974: 23; Fowler 1992: 178), which were called in English 'Doctors' Rocks'. In these secondary uses of sites a supplicant would approach the panel, pray and leave offerings, usually of small things such as twigs, lithic flakes and pennies, which were often stuck in cracks in the rocks. Californian Tradition sites were also used in similar ways (see Crampton 1957: 65; McQueen 1995; Whitley 1998a). In both cases, these sites functioned in folk curing rituals for precisely the same reason that shamans drew or pecked their art on the rocks: because they were locations where humans could access the supernatural realm, and the powers therein.

### Gender and rock-art sites

At one level rock-art sites served as symbolic portals into the supernatural. Yet as is always true with symbolic systems, the sites had different meanings, and different levels of meaning, beyond this fundamental symbolic attribute. One constellation of such meanings pertains to the gender symbolism associated with these sites which, as we shall see, was ultimately a determinant of rock-art site location.

Throughout California and the Great Basin, shamans' rock-art sites were feminine-gendered places, even though they were primarily (if not exclusively) used by male shamans. This conceptual organisation itself reflected a widespread far western North Ameri-

can inversion in gender symbolism, and was manifest in a number of ways. As regards the inversion in gender symbolism, first, I have noted above the very strong association between female puberty initiates and rattlesnake which, for obvious reasons, was a masculine-gendered symbol. Mythic rattlesnake, accordingly, was male (Goss 1972: 125). But the rattlesnake–female inversion involved more than puberty initiates: rattlesnake iconography, for example, was widely used as a gender sign on such mundane artefacts as female infants' cradleboards, as well as on all forms of (female-made and owned) basketry. Likewise, the vaginas of mythic females were believed to be guarded by rattlesnake 'skirts'. That feminine places were used by males, then, was not a contradiction in terms, but instead reflective of the general symbolic logic of far western North America.

The feminine gender symbolism of rock-art sites, second, is then demonstrated in a few different ways. Rock-art sites, most importantly, were described by a series of generic terms which were, themselves, feminine-gendered. I noted one of these above, *choishishiu*, which translates literally as 'bitch'; that is, female dog. This reflects the common Native Californian use of the term 'dog' to signify 'spirit helper' (thus the gloss 'spirit helper place' for *choishishiu*); what is important about this particular generic term is that 'bitch' was substituted for the much more common referent for spirit helper, *pu'us*, literally meaning 'male dog' (as seen in the variant *pusin tinliw*, literally 'male dog cave', noted earlier). Moreover, the use of this generic feminine-gendered term is neither idiosyncractic nor the result of rock-art sites which may have been made by female shamans. One of the best-documented uses of *choishishiu* as a generic rock-art term was recorded for the site Bell Bluff by two separate ethnographers, working with different informants (Gayton 1948: 58–9; Latta 1977: 185). Yet this site can be attributed to a historical male shaman, Jim Hangton (Whitley 1992: 93). But more to the point, the generic terms *pachki* and *taiwan* were also used for rock-art sites and, like *choishishiu*, each of these has strong feminine referents: *pachki* is the colour red, the feminine colour (from menstrual blood), associated with the direction west and the Land of the Dead; *taiwan* is the basketry gambling tray, made by women and used by them in the women's walnut dice game. In each of these three cases, then, generic rock-art site terms were feminised.

The logic of sites as feminine-gendered places used by male shamans is further reflected in their sexual symbolism, which was tied to one of the natural models and somatic metaphors of the shaman's ASC: sexual intercourse. The sites were, in essence, symbolic vaginas. The Numic shaman, for example, was said to use his ritual staff to open the crack in the rock, the earth's vagina, and thereby restore life and fecundity to the world (Laird 1976: 216); that is, to enter the supernatural in order to maintain cosmic balance. From this belief the logic of the generic term *taiwan*, 'basket', for 'rock-art site', is apparent: baskets too were symbolic wombs (Kroeber 1907a: 266–72; Laird 1976: 214, 1984: 59), with mythic beings then invariably born out of them (see Kroeber 1907b: 225–7; Gayton and Newman 1940: 23–6; Zigmond 1980: 69; Myers 1987). Furthermore, the shaman's altered state was metaphorically expressed as coitus: nocturnal emissions, for example, were considered supernatural sexual encounters with spirits (Lowie 1909: 224–5; Gayton 1948: 111; Devereux 1949: 111; Zigmond 1972: 133, 1977: 62, 70, 72), while shamans' visionary experiences were sometimes described as sexual encounters with a supernatural being (Gifford 1932: 50; Rogers and Gayton 1944: 207; Laird 1975: 54).

The natural model for sexual intercourse provided, in some cases, by the shamans' ASC involves an enlargement of the pupils, which occurs during an ASC and as a result of sexual arousal (La Barre 1980: 63; Boyd in press). It is also due to the fact that certain of the hallucinogens taken to achieve altered states, such as jimsonweed (*Datura wrightii*), are aphrodisiacs (Stone 1932: 55), and may result in priapism. Notably, jimsonweed itself was feminine-gendered, as a personified spirit among some groups

(Blackburn 1975: 36), and was prepared in a ritual mortar and pestle, with the pestle often consisting of an immensely exaggerated penis-effigy. At least one kind of epileptic seizure which was known to occur in Native Californian populations resulted in priapism and ultimately sexual release, and was equated with a supernatural experience (Devereux 1961: 76). And in keeping with this perceived association between sexuality and altered states, and therefore with shamans, shamans were believed to maintain unusual virility; so much so, in fact, that they were thought sexually predatory, and young girls were cautioned to keep away from them (Gayton 1930: 382, 392–3, 397, 1948: 36, 195, 209, 259; Toffelmeier and Luomala 1936: 223; Stewart 1973: 317; Latta 1977: 693; Boscana 1978: 48; Laird 1984: 266). Indeed, one account indicates that the shaman even received a 'sexual name' during his first ASC, with the connection between male (hetero)sexuality and shamanism so strong that homosexuals could not be shamans (Toffelmeier and Luomala 1936: 197, 214). But perhaps most importantly, it is clear that ritual coitus occurred during certain ceremonies or ceremonial periods, which is to say during the sacred times equated with group entry into the supernatural (Harrington 1934: 40; Ray 1963: 81; Blackburn 1975: 82; Harrington in Boscana 1978: 167; Hudson 1979: 119–20), while brazen allusions to intercourse occurred in other rituals (Steward 1938: 187). Male shamans used feminine-gendered rock-art sites, because on one level their entry into the supernatural was conceived as a kind of ritual intercourse.

Following this gender and sexual symbolism, rock-art sites in portions of the far west were thought to be 'guarded' by rattlesnakes, just as were the vaginas of mythic women. A supernatural rattlesnake was believed to reside immediately inside the rock-art site (that is, at the entrance to the supernatural), which a shaman had to cross to enter the sacred (Zigmond 1977: 76, 93, 1980: 175–9; Harrington n.d.: 355, 523). This snake spirit served as one of the ritual retributors responsible for the enforcement of supernatural taboos and proscriptions (Kroeber 1907b: 216–18; Gayton and Newman 1940: 17–19, 35, 99–100). Rattlesnake motifs, following this symbolic logic, are particularly common at far western rock-art sites, signalling the fact that the sites are guarded by serpent spirits.

Of course, the conceptualisation of a rock-art site as a symbolic vagina is apparent in the physical analogy between caves and rock-shelters, and wombs. But it appears in rock-art sites and motifs in additional ways. The most dramatic is at Painted Rock, a South-Central Painted Variant site; this large rock outcrop has been almost universally identified as resembling a massive vagina on the landscape (Fig. 2.6). At the apex of the U-shaped outcrop is a painted panel displaying a series of human figures standing in a *tomol*, or Chumash plank canoe (Fig. 2.7). 'Getting into the canoe' was a Chumash metaphor for sexual intercourse (Blackburn 1975: 208) and, from the natural model outlined above, for the

**Fig. 2.7.** The red and black panel at the apex of the U-shaped interior of Carrizo Painted Rock, now vandalised and eroded. It portrays a *tomol*, or plank canoe, which contains six standing figures: five small dancers (three to the left and two to the right) arrayed around a large central figure, now only evident by the extant feet, legs and lower torso (historical photographs, taken before the vandalism, provide a clearer illustration of these motifs). 'Getting into a canoe' was a metaphor for sexual intercourse, which was itself a metaphor for a shaman's entry into the supernatural. The combination of this men-in-canoe image with the vulva-shaped outcrop alludes to this metaphoric association, along with the fact that rock-art sites were considered feminine-gender places on the landscape.

Scale: length of *tomol*, about 50 cm.

**Fig. 2.6.** Painted Rock, on the Carrizo Plain in inland south-central California. This large U-shaped sandstone outcrop, in the centre of the photograph, contains one of the largest and most elaborate concentrations of South-Central Painted Variant rock-art, unfortunately now badly vandalised. The site has been likened to a natural vulva by numerous authors and commentators.

shaman's ASC. Like much far western rock-art, then, this painted motif is a graphic metaphor for entry into the supernatural.

The second overt manifestation of rock-art sexual symbolism is found in so-called 'vulva-form' motifs. Male sexual potency was so much associated with supernatural power that among some groups, the word for 'intelligence' or 'having sense' – both of which were also strongly associated with shamans as ritual specialists and men of knowledge – translates literally as 'having semen' (Laird 1976: 84, 1984: 181). Female sexuality (and by extension the feminine-gender connotations of rock-art sites), in contrast, was not viewed so favourably: boys were instructed never to look at vaginas; the clitoris was equated with a knife; mythic women were believed to have had toothed vaginas; female sexual promiscuity was considered deadly; menstrual blood was thought so inimical to supernatural potency that women, during menstruation, were prohibited from participating in rituals, and effectively excluded from becoming shamans; and the twitching of the vulva, that is, female orgasm, was considered the most deadly kind of sorcery that could be rendered unto a man (Kroeber 1907b: 323; Harris 1940: 62; Whiting 1950: 62; Laird 1984: 113, 214, 257; Myers 1987).[1]

The results of these beliefs were twofold. First, even though sacred and often adjacent to mundane activity areas, rock-art sites were themselves inherently dangerous and feared. Californian Tradition sites, for example, were avoided and never casually loitered about or touched (Gayton 1930: 391, 1948: 33, 34, 110, 113, 168; Latta 1977: 600; Zigmond 1977: 71; Whitley 1996), even when they were located within living sites, because of, at one level, their dangerous symbolism and associations. Second, inasmuch as male shamans were primarily responsible for making far western rock-art sites (with the exception of the puberty art, noted above), and since female sexuality generally and the vagina specifically were associated with bewitching, it then follows that the vulva-form engravings that are found at certain sites most likely represent examples of shamans' activities as sorcerers: in this case, harnessing the malevolent powers of the supernatural to steal another's soul, or otherwise cause them harm. Just as the phallic rattlesnake was a symbol strongly associated with women, so too was the vagina symbol employed by men. And while male sexuality was equated with intelligence and controlled supernatural potency, female sexuality was unbridled, danger-

ous, and generally malevolent, just as was the rock-art site – except of course to the shaman, who could control the power contained in it.

## Landscape, gender and rock-art site locations

This discussion has highlighted the importance of the rock-art site, a physical location in the landscape, as a symbol in its own right, and has provided a few comments on how this site symbolism is sometimes reflected iconographically. It is now possible to turn to the question of landscape symbolism at a regional scale, and how the rock-art site fits into this topographical symbolism.

My first concern is rock-art site distribution, which plays to the issue of sites as symbolic portals into the supernatural. As should be clear, this site symbolism implies that the distribution of sites was some function of the perceived distribution of supernatural power in the landscape. Such power spots were universally believed to be rock outcrops, caves and rock-shelters, springs and other permanent water sources and – especially – high mountain peaks (Bean 1976: 408, 415; Miller 1985: 58–9; Fowler 1992: 179–80). For example, springs were believed inhabited by supernatural spirits (Kroeber 1925: 514; Park 1938: 16; Patencio 1943: 92; Blackburn 1975: 38, 289; Zigmond 1977: 74; Fowler 1992: 180), and shamans were thought able to enter or exit the supernatural through them (Kroeber 1925: 514; Cline 1938: 141; Patencio 1943: 93; Zigmond 1977: 177–9). Hence, frequent swimming at these locations was an important part of a shaman's training, sites are often adjacent to springs, and aquatic iconography is a common attribute of the art, reflecting the drowning/swimming metaphor for the shaman's ASC (see Whitley 1994b: 19–21). Mountain peaks were considered particularly potent; so much so that the highest peak in any group's region was generally believed both the point where the world was created (e.g. Kroeber 1957: 231; Goss 1972: 128; Laird 1976: 119–22; Hudson and Underhay 1978; Miller 1983: 72; Fowler 1992: 39, 171), and a place inhabited by powerful spirits

---

[1] These conceptualisations point to the fundamentally androcentric nature of many far western North American hunter-gatherer groups (Collier 1988; Whitley 1994a), a circumstance further reflected in a generalised Evil:Good, Female:Male opposition seen among some far western groups (Goss 1972: 125).

(Gifford 1933: 308; Patencio 1943: 44–5; Shipek 1985: 68; Bean *et al.* 1991: 32).

Within the region encompassed by the Californian Tradition, rock outcrops and rock-shelters tend to be ubiquitous (with the exception of the alluvial Central Valley, which has no rocks and therefore no rock-art); there is little physical constraint, then, on potential site locations. Though there are occasional exceptions, generally speaking rock-art sites are associated with important inland (as opposed to coastal) villages or living sites in this region (Latta 1977: 600; Whitley 1987), which themselves are necessarily near water sources. Shamans' rock-art sites were apparently owned by individual medicine men (Gayton 1948: 113; Whitley 1994c: 85); the placement of the rock-art in or near villages, and the resulting implications of the distribution of these supernatural portals as roughly correlating with the distribution of villages, can be taken as a function of the well-integrated social function of shamans in Native Californian society (e.g., see Gayton 1930). As is clear, on at least one level the distribution of power followed the distribution of human settlement, and thus political power, within Native California.

Within the Great Basin, in contrast, the distribution of rock-art sites is not so closely tied to village locations. Certainly, all major villages in this desertic region were necessarily located near water sources, and rock-art sites are relatively commonly associated with living sites, and thus water. Yet there are major concentrations of rock-art, such as the Coso Range, which show no obvious association with other aspects of settlement pattern; these probably constitute the majority of Great Basin Tradition rock-art. In other words, the distribution of power within the Great Basin was only partly reflective of human settlement and social organisation.

In both regions, one attribute of site distributions stands out. This is the apparent paradox by which mountain peaks were universally cited as especially potent sacred places, yet do not commonly have rock-art. This occurs even though, within the Great Basin at least, there was no constraint *vis-à-vis* associations with villages that necessarily would have restricted such placement. For example, the 3667 m high Charleston Peak, in the Spring Range west of Las Vegas, Nevada, was recognised by the Southern Paiute and Chemehuevi as the place where the earth was created, the home of the creator spirit Ocean Old Woman, and a locale of great power (Goss 1972: 128; Laird 1976: 122; Miller 1983: 72). While imbued with significant power, and therefore used for certain rituals, it lacks rock-art, although a number of such sites are present below about 1230 m, in the foothills of the Spring Range. Similarly, the 1735 m high Newberry Peak, near the Colorado River in southernmost Nevada, was recognised as the home of the creator deity Mastamho, the place of origin for Yuman-speakers, and the locale from which these Colorado River shamans received their supernatural power (Kroeber 1925: 770, 1957: 207; Devereux 1957: 1036; Stewart 1970: 15, 1973: 315). Yet the rock-art associated with this Yuman vision quest location is found in Grapevine Canyon, below about 860 m elevation, at the foot of the mountain. Even within the confines of the dense concentration of rock-engravings in the Coso Range, the art is similarly found in a series of canyons and upland valleys below approximately 1800 m, and is nowhere present on Maturango Peak, at 2695 m the highest peak in the region. Finally, Mount Piños at 2717 m, north of Los Angeles, was the centre of the world and origin point for the Chumash (Hudson and Underhay 1978: 40–1). As in the above and other far western examples, the rock-art sites associated with this sacred mountain are not located on it, but instead are at lower elevations within the surrounding Los Padres Mountains, below approximately 1550 m. Rock-art site location, then, was clearly not simply a function of the perceived distribution of power on the landscape.

This was because the symbolism of the landscape – like that of the sites themselves – was gendered. It was based on a widespread directional opposition, which equated males with up/high/mountain, and females with down/low/valley.[2] Thus, far western cosmology maintained that the world was created through the union of a masculine principle, the sky, and a feminine principle, represented by the earth (Bourke 1889: 178; DuBois 1901: 181; Harrington 1934: 10; Devereux 1961: 155–6; Blackburn 1975; Hudson and Underhay 1978; Applegate 1979: 74; Miller 1983: 77), resulting in the belief that high places were masculine locales, low spots feminine. Indeed, this directional symbolism was sufficiently strong that, among some groups, it even affected the sexual division of labour: Miller (1983: 74) notes that in Numic house-building, men were responsible for erecting the upright pole supports, while women made the floor mats and the wall-coverings and, during the pine-nut harvest, men climbed the trees to knock down the nut-laden cones, while women gathered them on the ground.

The masculine landscape symbolism of mountains was partly reflected among some groups in word terminations for certain place-names. These correspond to 'peak' in English, but translate literally as 'penis' or 'penis-erected' (see Loud 1929: 162; Laird 1976: 123, 131), contrasting nicely with the feminine-gendered terms for rock-art sites noted previously. When the masculine symbolism of mountain peaks is then matched against the feminine symbolism of rock-art sites, the symbolic logic of rock-art site distribution becomes apparent. Even though the distribution of the sites reflected the distribution of supernatural power on the landscape, rock-art sites as feminine places only logically fit within the feminine-gendered portions of the supernatural landscape: rock outcrops and caves, and water sources, found at relatively lower elevations. It is not surprising that certain of the landscape features at which rock-art sites are commonly found were sometimes themselves linked linguistically to women and vulvas (e.g. Loud 1929: 160; Laird 1976: 131, 304).

## Finding rain in the desert

The discussion has, so far, emphasised three points: the symbolic function of rock-art sites as portals to the supernatural; the related gender and sexual symbolism of the sites and how this articulated with the larger gender symbolism of the landscape; and the important role of symbolic inversion in site symbolism and iconographic associations. These principles may be used to understand a larger problem in far western North American rock-art: the existence of very large concentrations of rock-art in the landscape within the Great Basin. My focus here is the engravings of the Coso Range, in which bighorn sheep motifs predominate.

The first point important to understanding the symbolic logic of this large concentration of engravings in the landscape concerns the iconography, *per se.* The bighorn sheep was a specialised spirit helper for the rain-shaman (for reasons discussed in Whitley 1998b, in press a); in a variation on the somatic death metaphor for trance, and because the shaman and his helper were conceptually indistinguishable, 'to kill a bighorn' was a verbal and graphic metaphor for a rain-shaman's ASC (his auto-sacrifice), within which he was thought to control weather; the Cosos were then widely renowned as the locale from which rain-making power could be obtained; and shamans are documented as having travelled for hundreds of miles to come to the Cosos, to obtain this specialised power (Whitley 1992, 1994a, 1998b, in press b). The bighorn sheep engravings are depictions of the spirit helper of the rain-shaman; drawings of 'hunters and sheep' have nothing to do with 'hunting magic' but instead are graphic metaphors for creating rain; and even many of the elaborate 'patterned-body anthropomorph' figures from this region display a characteristic quail topknot feather head-dress – the specialised ritual headgear of the rain-maker (Fig. 2.8). In the light of the iconography, the question then may be rephrased: Why is there an immense

---

[2] Note that, although far western North America was gendered in terms of the 'cosmic' Male : Female opposition, this duality did not hold for all of Native America. Among the Maricopa, a Southwestern group in Arizona, for example, the landscape was apparently conceptualised in terms of three genders: male, female and transvestite (Drucker 1941: 163; Kroeber 1957: 229).

**Fig. 2.8.** 'Patterned-body anthropomorphs' from Little Petroglyph Canyon, Coso Range, eastern California, which depict shamans transformed into supernatural power forms. The central motif in this frequently illustrated panel of engravings is wearing a quail topknot feather head-dress, the special ritual headgear of the rain-shaman, reflecting the fact that the Cosos served as a nexus for rain-making power. He is also portrayed with a concentric circle face. The spiral and concentric circle were conventionalisations for the whirlwind, which concentrated supernatural power, just as the shaman did through his rituals.
Scale in cm.

west, with the Cosos as the effective terminus in that search. Yet the high Sierra Nevadas, immediately to the west of the Cosos, create an orographic rain shadow over the Cosos and other nearby areas, resulting in one of the driest landscapes in North America, with precipitation only 7.5–16 cm annually (Troxell and Hoffman 1954: 15). Even though rain came from the south-west, very little of it fell within these regions. Reflecting this fact, *coso* translates literally as 'fire'.

This last circumstance plays to the second level of symbolic logic which supported the development of the Cosos as a concentration of rain-shamanism engravings – symbolic inversion. Another aspect to the role of inversion in the symbolism of far western rock-art is the supernatural world conceptualised as precisely the opposite of the natural. In the far west this was most commonly expressed in beliefs about the Land of the Dead, a specific aspect of the larger supernatural realm. As one Mohave informant stated concerning this widespread perception:

In [the Land of the Dead] everything is reversed. That's the reason they cremate the body face down, because 'down' is 'up' in [the Land of the Dead]. Everything is backwards there. 'Yes' means 'no', and 'no' means 'yes'. 'East' is 'West'. Words are backwards. Day and night is [*sic*] reversed. Everything tastes good there. There's a long line of everlasting watermelons, and a torch with everlasting fire. (Stewart 1977: 18)

As is implied in this comment, rituals in general operated on the principle of inversion, to correlate with the reversal of things in the sacred. One means of entering a trance was by eating sand – the opposite of water, the purifying element – because 'It is said that as the prophet [clairvoyant shaman] eats the sand it turns to water in him and he just swallows that' (Kroeber 1957: 227). Rituals were held at night, to correspond to daytime in the supernatural. But more to the immediate point: the Coso region, in the most xeric region of the Great Basin, was particularly apposite as a location from whence rain-making power could be obtained. To enter the supernatural

concentration of rain-shamanism rock-art within the Coso Range, an arid landscape only one valley west of Death Valley, the driest spot in the Great Basin?

Two levels of logic appear to have supported the symbolism of the Cosos as the location on the landscape associated with rain. The first is physiographic: as the Cosos are the south-westernmost corner of the Great Basin, rain coming off the Pacific Ocean most commonly approaches the Basin from this direction. To find rain in the Great Basin, one travelled south-from a rock-art site in the 'Mountains of Fire' was to access the inverse in the sacred; and the inverse of fire and dryness was, of course, water. Shamans came to the unusually arid Cosos to find the most verdant aspect of the supernatural and, from this experience, to make rain in the natural world.

That the supernatural was the inverse of the natural, moreover, further amplifies an understanding of the gender symbolism of sites (above). For it is also clear that, while one level of meaning in the gender and sexual symbolism of male rock-art sites pertained to the shaman's ASC as a kind of ritual intercourse, at another the hyper-virile shaman still desired a masculine supernatural power – most easily obtained by entering the supernatural from the inverse in the natural, feminine-gendered rock-art sites, rather than masculine mountain peaks. And it is then understandable why male shamans' rock-art sites were given feminine generic names, while girls' puberty initiation rock-art sites were known instead as the '[male] shaman's house'. Just as the male shaman entered the supernatural at feminine places to obtain masculine kinds of power, or at dry places to acquire rain-making power, so too then did young girls enter the sacred at masculine locations on the landscape, to obtain the feminine powers needed for childbirth, which was the emphasis of their puberty initiation.

## Rock-art, landscape symbolism and the supernatural

To close this sketch of far western North American rock-art and landscape symbolism, a few general points need be made. The first concerns rock-art sites as symbolic portals to the supernatural. As such, they clearly fit a widespread pattern in the conceptualisation of Native American sacred places which, regardless of physical form, Walker (1991, n.d.) has identified as entrances to the sacred. Rock-art sites are not unique in having been conceptualised in such terms, and fit well within the larger landscape symbolism of Native America as a whole. However, Walker (n.d.) has also contended that there is little to support the common anthropological notion, stemming from Durkheim (1947: 40), that north-western Native American groups maintained a conceptual organisation of the universe into sacred versus profane places. Walker's contention is well supported by the rock-art data from California and the Great Basin: although the sites were sacred, this did not preclude mundane activities from occurring at and around them, as the ethnohistorical record demonstrates in many ways. The sacred inhered everywhere, even though its presence was more strongly felt (or, in essence, rested closer to the mundane) at some spots because, as Walker (n.d.) notes: 'the sacred is an embedded, intrinsic attribute lying behind the external, empirical aspect of all things, but not a domain set aside or forbidden'.

There is an important archaeological implication of this last fact. Although there is no denying that we have much to gain in our understanding of rock-art rituals through the archaeological excavation of rock-art sites, as Loendorf (1994) has shown, the belief that simple locational associations between rock-art panels and adjacent artefactual assemblages in all cases will reveal 'functional' information about the art (e.g., Singer and Gibson 1978) is clearly naive. For such an interpretation assumes precisely the kind of segregation of sacred versus profane space which is nowhere suggested by the western North American ethnohistorical record.

My final point then concerns the symbolic inversions that are reflected in both the iconography and landscape symbolism of the rock-art sites. Blackburn (1975: 81) has noted that such inversions are common in many circumstances in which the sacred is distinguished from the profane, and thus the use of inversions in the above described cases should not be seen as idiosyncratic so much as, perhaps, circumstances to be expected. Their implication for the rock-art researcher, furthermore, is straightforward: things are not always as they at first seem to be. Certainly, any simple equation of masculine or feminine designs (whatever these may be) with exclusively masculine or feminine activities or rites, such as the commonly inferred (but nowhere ethnographically supported) interpretation of vulva-forms as resulting from female fertility rituals (e.g. Davis 1961), can only be considered anthropologically naive. Instead, as should now be clear, rock-art, and the landscape that it sits within, was part of a symbolic system that was at once layered with nuanced meaning, yet was also ultimately logical and coherent in its conceptualisation. The point of rock-art interpretation, then, is not to despair at the seeming ambiguity that is present in any symbolic system (e.g. Tilley 1991), but instead to find the cognitive keys that give coherency and meaning to the whole.

## REFERENCES

Agenbroad, L. 1994. Paleo-Indian rock-art on the Colorado Plateau: 11,000 years of petroglyphs. Paper presented at the 1994 International Rock Art Congress, Flagstaff, Arizona.

Applegate, R. B. 1979. The black, the red, and the white: duality and unity in the Luiseño Cosmos, *Journal of California and Great Basin Anthropology* 1: 71–88.

Bean, L. J. 1976. Power and its application in Native California, in L. J. Bean and T. C. Blackburn (eds.), *Native Californians: a theoretical retrospective*, pp. 407–20. Socorro (NM), Ballena Press.

Bean, L. J., S. B. Vane and J. Young. 1991. *The Cahuilla landscape: the Santa Rosa and San Jacinto mountains.* Menlo Park (CA), Ballena Press Anthropological Papers 75.

Blackburn, T. C. 1975. *December's child: a book of Chumash oral narratives.* Berkeley (CA), University of California Press.

Boscana, G. 1978. *Chinigchinich: an historical account of the Indians of the Mission of San Juan Capistrano called the Acagchemem Tribe*, trans. by A. Robinson, annotated by J. P. Harrington. Banning (CA), Malki Museum.

Bourke, J. G. 1889. Notes on the cosmogony and theogony of the Mojave Indians of the Rio Colorado, Arizona, *Journal of American Folk Lore* 2(4): 169–89.

Boyd, C. E. In press. Datura, peyote, and their animal counterparts identified in the pictographs of the Lower Pecos, Texas Archaic, in D. S. Whitley (ed.), *Ethnography and western North American rock art.* Albuquerque (NM), University of New Mexico Press.

Bradley, R. 1991. Rock art and the perception of landscapes, *Cambridge Archaeological Journal* 1: 77–101.

Callahan, K. In press. Shamanism, dream symbolism and altered states of consciousness in Minnesota rock-art: ethnohistorical accounts regarding Pipestone, Jeffers and Nett Lake, in D. S. Whitley (ed.), *Ethnography and western North American rock art.* Albuquerque (NM), University of New Mexico Press.

Chalfant, W. A. 1933. *The story of Inyo.* Revised edition. Bishop (CA), privately printed.

Cline, W. 1938. Religion and world view, in L. Spier (ed.), *The Sinkaietk or Southern Okanagan of Washington,* pp. 133–82. Menasha (WI), General Series in Anthropology 6, Contributions from the Laboratory of Anthropology 2.

Collier, J. F. 1988. *Marriage and inequality in classless societies.* Stanford (CA), Stanford University Press.

Conway, T. and J. Conway. 1990. *Spirits on stone: the Agawa pictographs.* San Luis Obispo, CA, Heritage Discoveries.

Crampton, C. G. (ed.). 1957. *The Mariposa Indian War, 1850–1851: diaries of Robert Eccleston: the California gold rush, Yosemite, and the High Sierra.* Salt Lake City (UT), University of Utah Press.

Curtin, J. N.d. Unpublished ethnographic fieldnotes, Modoc and Klamath. Washington (DC), National Anthropological Archives, Smithsonian Institution.

Davis, E. L. 1961. The Mono Crater petroglyphs, California, *American Antiquity* 27: 236–9.

Devereux, G. 1949. Magic substances and narcotics of the Mohave Indians, *British Journal of Medical Psychology* 22: 110–16.

1957. Dream learning and individual ritual differences in Mohave shamanism, *American Anthropologist* 59: 1036–45.

1961. *Mohave ethnopsychiatry: the psychic disturbances of an Indian tribe*, Bureau of American Ethnology, Bulletin 175. Washington (DC), Smithsonian Institution.

Dixon, R. 1908. Some shamans of northern California, *Journal of American Folk Lore* 17: 23–7.

Drucker, P. 1941. *Culture element distributions: XVII, Yuman-Piman.* Berkeley (CA), University of California Anthropological Records 6(3).

DuBois, C. G. 1901. The mythology of the Diegueños, *Journal of American Folk Lore* 14: 181–5.

1908. Ceremonies and traditions of the Diegueño Indians, *Journal of American Folk Lore* 21: 228–36.

Durkheim, E. 1947. *The elementary forms of religious life.*

Glencoe (IL), Free Press.

Eliade, M. 1964. *Shamanism: archaic techniques of ecstasy*. Princeton (NJ), Princeton University Press.

Fowler, C. S. 1992. *In the shadow of Fox Peak: an ethnography of the Cattail-Eater Northern Paiute people of Stillwater Marsh*. Fallon (NV), Stillwater National Wildlife Refuge. Cultural Resource Series No. 5.

Gayton, A. H. 1930. Yokuts-Mono chiefs and shamans, *University of California Publications in American Archaeology and Ethnology* 24: 361–420.

1948. Yokuts and Western Mono ethnography, *University of California Anthropological Records* 10: 1–290.

Gayton, A. H. and S. S. Newman. 1940. Yokuts and Western Mono myths, *University of California Anthropological Records* 5: 1–110.

Gifford, E. W. 1932. The Northfork Mono, *University of California Publications in American Archaeology and Ethnology* 31(2): 15–65.

1933. The Cocopa, *University of California Publications in American Archaeology and Ethnology* 31(5): 257–334.

Goss, J. A. 1972. A basin–plateau Shoshonean ecological model, in D. D. Fowler (ed.), *Great Basin cultural ecology: a symposium*, pp. 123–8. Reno (NV), Desert Research Institute. Publications in the Social Sciences 8.

Grant, C. 1965. *The rock paintings of the Chumash*. Berkeley (CA), University of California Press.

Grosscup, G. 1974. Northern Paiute archaeology, in *Paiute Indians* IV, pp. 9–52. New York, Garland Publications.

Hann, D., J. Keyser and P. Minthorn. In press. Columbia Plateau rock-art: a window to the spirit world, in D. S. Whitley (ed.), *Ethnography and western North American rock-art*. Albuquerque (NM), University of New Mexico Press.

Harrington, J. P. (ed.). 1934. *A new original version of Boscana's Historical account of the San Juan Capistrano Indians of Southern California*. Washington (DC), Smithsonian Miscellaneous Collections 92(4).

N.d. Unpublished ethnographic fieldnotes, Yokuts. Washington (DC), National Anthropological Archives, Smithsonian Institution.

Harris, J. S. 1940. The White Knife Shoshoni of Nevada, in R. Linton (ed.), *Acculturation in seven American Indian tribes*, pp. 39–116. New York, Appleton-Century.

Hartley, R. J. 1992. *Rock art on the northern Colorado Plateau*. Aldershot, Avebury.

Heizer, R. F. and M. Baumhoff. 1962. *Prehistoric rock-art of Nevada and eastern California*. Berkeley (CA), University of California Press.

Hill-Tout, C. 1978a. *The Salish People 1: The Thompson and Okanagan*. Vancouver (BC), Talonbooks.

1978b. *The Salish People 2: The Squamish and Lillooet*. Vancouver (BC), Talonbooks.

Hudson, D. T. (ed.). 1979. *Breath of the sun: life in early California as told by a Chumash Indian, Fernando Librado to John P. Harrington*. Banning (CA), Malki Museum.

Hudson, D. T. and E. Underhay. 1978. *Crystals in the sky: an intellectual odyssey involving Chumash astronomy, cosmology and rock-art*. Socorro (NM), Ballena Press.

Hyland, J. In press. Talking with the dead: the peninsular ceremonial complex and the great mural tradition of Baja California, in D. S. Whitley (ed.), *Ethnography and western North American rock-art*. Albuquerque, (NM), University of New Mexico Press.

Kelly, W. H. 1977. *Cocopa ethnography*. Tucson (AZ), University of Arizona Anthropological Papers 29.

Kroeber, A. L. 1907a. The religion of the Indians of California, *University of California Publications in American Archaeology and Ethnology* 4(6): 319–56.

1907b. Indian myths of south-central California, *University of California Publications in American Archaeology and Ethnology* 4(4): 169–250.

1925. *Handbook of the Indians of California*. Washington (DC), Smithsonian Institution, Bureau of American Ethnology. Bulletin 78.

1957. Mohave clairvoyance: ethnographic interpretations 1–6, *University of California Publications in American Archaeology and Ethnology* 47(2): 226–33.

La Barre, W. 1980. *Culture in context*. Durham (NC), Duke University Press.

Laird, C. 1975. *Encounter with an angry god: recollections of my life with John Peabody Harrington*. Banning (CA), Malki Museum.

1976. *The Chemehuevis*. Banning (CA), Malki Museum.

1984. *Mirror and pattern: George Laird's world of Chemehuevi mythology*. Banning (CA), Malki Museum.

Latta, F. 1977. *Handbook of the Yokuts Indians*. 2nd edition. Santa Cruz (CA), Bear State Books.

Lewis-Williams, J. D. and T. A. Dowson. 1988. The signs of all times: entoptic phenomena in Upper Palaeolithic art, *Current Anthropology* 29: 201–45.

Loendorf, L. L. 1994. Traditional archaeological methods and their applications at rock-art sites, in D. S. Whitley and L. L. Loendorf (eds.), *New light on old art: recent advances in hunter-gatherer rock-art research*, pp. 95–104.

Los Angeles (CA), Institute of Archaeology, University of California. Monograph 36.

Loud, L. L. 1929. Notes on the Northern Paiute, *University of California Publications in American Archaeology and Ethnology* 25: 125–64.

Lowie, R. H. 1909. The Northern Shoshone, *Anthropological Papers, American Museum of Natural History* 2(2): 165–306.

McQueen, C. M. 1995. A Kawaiisu healing cave. Paper presented at the 1995 meeting of the Society for California Archaeology, Eureka (CA).

Miller, J. 1983. Basin religion and theology: a comparative study of power (Puha), *Journal of California and Great Basin Anthropology* 5: 66–86.

1985. Shamans and power in western North America: the Numic, Salish, and Keres, in Great Basin Foundation (ed.), *Woman, poet and scientist: essays in New World anthropology, honoring Dr Emma Lou Davis*, pp. 56–66. Los Altos (CA), Ballena Press.

Myers, L. D. 1987. *Levels of context: a symbolic analysis of Numic origin myths.* Ph.D dissertation, Rutgers University. Ann Arbor (MI), University Microfilms.

Olofson, H. 1979. Northern Paiute shamanism revisited, *Anthropos* 74: 11–24.

Park, W. Z. 1938. *Shamanism in western North America: a study in cultural relationships.* Evanston (IL), Northwestern University Studies in the Social Sciences 2.

Patencio, F. 1943. *Stories and legends of the Palm Springs Indians.* Palm Springs (CA), Palm Springs Desert Museum.

Rajnovich, G. 1989. Vision in a quest for medicine: an interpretation of the pictographs of the Canadian Shield, *Midcontinental Journal of Archaeology* 14(2): 179–225.

1994. *Reading rock art: interpreting the Indian rock paintings of the Canadian Shield.* Toronto (Ont.), Natural Heritage/Natural History.

Ray, V. 1963. *Primitive pragmatists: the Modoc Indians of northern California.* Seattle, University of Washington Press.

Rogers, B. T. and A. H. Gayton. 1944. Twenty-seven Chukchansi Yokuts myths, *Journal of American Folklore* 57: 190–207.

Schaafsma, P. 1994. Trance and transformation in the canyons: shamanism and early rock-art on the Colorado Plateau, in S. Turpin (ed.), *Shamanism and rock art in North America*, pp. 45–72. San Antonio (TX), Rock Art Foundation. Special Publication 1.

Shipek, F. C. 1985. Kuuchamaa: the Kumeyaay sacred mountain, *Journal of California and Great Basin Anthropology* 7: 67–74.

Singer, C. A. and R. O. Gibson. 1978. Ven-195: treasure house of prehistoric cave art, in C. W. Clewlow, Jr (ed.), *Four rock-art studies*, pp. 45–64. Socorro (NM), Ballena Press.

Snow, D. 1977. Rock-art and the power of shamans, *Natural History* 86(2): 42–9.

Steward, J. H. 1938. *Basin–Plateau Aboriginal sociopolitical groups.* Washington (DC), Smithsonian Institution, Bureau of American Ethnology. Bulletin 120.

1941. Culture element distributions: XIII, Nevada Shoshoni, *University of California Anthropological Records* 4(2): 209–359.

1943. Culture element distributions: XXIII, Northern and Gosiute Shoshoni, *University of California Anthropological Records* 8(3): 263–392.

Stewart, K. M. 1970. Mojave Indian shamanism, *Masterkey* 44(1): 15–24.

1973. Witchcraft among the Mohave Indians, *Ethnology* 12: 315–24.

1977. Mojave Indian ghosts and the Land of the Dead, *Masterkey* 51(1): 14–21.

Stone, E. 1932. *Medicine among the American Indians.* New York, Paul B. Hoeber.

Teit, N.d. Notes on rock paintings in general (1918). Manuscript; Glenbow Alberta Institute archives.

Tilley, C. 1991. *Material culture and text: the art of ambiguity.* London, Routledge.

Toffelmeier, G. and K. Luomala. 1936. Dreams and dream interpretation of the Diegueño Indians of southern California, *Psychoanalytic Quarterly* 5: 195–225.

Troxell, H. C. and W. Hoffman. 1954. Hydrology of the Mojave Desert, in R. H. Jahns (ed.), Geology of southern California, *California Division of Mines Bulletin* 170: 13–17.

True, D. L. and G. Waugh. 1986. To-Vah: a Luiseño power cave, *Journal of California and Great Basin Anthropology* 8: 269–73.

Turner, V. 1967. *The forest of symbols: aspects of Ndembu ritual.* Ithaca (NY), Cornell University Press.

Turney-High, H. H. 1937. *The Flathead Indians of Montana.* Washington (DC), American Anthropological Association. Memoir 48.

1941. *Ethnography of the Kutenai.* Washington (DC), American Anthropological Association. Memoir 56.

Turpin, S. 1994. On a wing and a prayer: flight metaphors

in Pecos River art, in S. Turpin (ed.), *Shamanism and rock art in North America*, pp. 73–102. San Antonio (TX), Rock Art Foundation. Special Publication 1.

Vastokas, J. M and R. K. Vastokas. 1973. *Sacred art of the Algonkians: a study of the Peterborough petroglyphs*. Peterborough (Ont.), Mansard Press.

Voegelin, E. W. 1938. Tubatulabal ethnography, *University of California Anthropological Records* 2: 1–90.

Walker, D., Jr. 1991. Protection of American Indian sacred geography, in C. Vecsey (ed.), *Handbook of American Indian religious freedom*, pp. 100–15. New York, Crossroad Publishing Company.

N.d. Sacred geography in northwestern North America. Manuscript to appear in Ted Stern Festschrift.

Wellmann, K. F. 1979. *A survey of North American Indian rock art*. Graz (Austria), Akademische Druck-u. Verlagsanstalt.

Whiting, B. B. 1950. *Paiute sorcery*. New York, Viking Fund. Publications in Anthropology 15.

Whitley, D. S. 1982. The study of North American rock art. Ph.D dissertation, University of California, Los Angeles. Ann Arbor (MI), University Microfilms.

1987. Socioreligious context and rock art in east-central California, *Journal of Anthropological Archaeology* 6: 159–88.

1988. Bears and baskets: shamanism in California rock art, in T. Dowson (ed.), *The state of the art: advances in world rock-art research*, pp. 34–42. Johannesburg, University of the Witwatersrand, Archaeology Department.

1992. Shamanism and rock-art in far western North America, *Cambridge Archaeological Journal* 2: 89–113.

1994a. By the hunter, for the gatherer: art, social relations and subsistence change in the prehistoric Great Basin, *World Archaeology* 25(3): 356–77.

1994b. Shamanism, natural modelling and the rock art of far western North America, in S. Turpin (ed.), *Shamanism and rock art in North America*, pp. 1–43. San Antonio (TX), Rock Art Foundation. Special Publication 1.

1994c Ethnography and rock art in far western North America: some archaeological implications, in D. S. Whitley and L. L. Loendorf (eds.), *New light on old art: recent advances in hunter-gatherer rock-art research*, pp. 81–94. Los Angeles (CA), Institute of Archaeology, University of California. Monograph 36.

1996. *A guide to rock-art sites: southern California and southern Nevada*. Missoula (MT), Mountain Press.

1998a. *Les chamanes de Californie: art rupestre Amenindien de California*. Paris, Editions du Seuil.

1998b. Meaning and metaphor in the Coso petroglyphs: understanding Great Basin rock-art, in E. Younkin (ed.), *Coso rock art: a new perspective*, pp. 109–74. Ridgecrest (CA), Maturango Museum.

In press a. The Numic vision quest: ritual and rock art in the Great Basin, in D. S. Whitley (ed.), *Ethnography and western North American rock art*. Albuquerque (NM), University of New Mexico Press.

In press b. Ethnohistory and south-central California rock art, in K. Hedges (ed.), *Proceedings of the 1994 International Rock-art Congress*. Flagstaff, American Rock Art Research Association.

Whitley, D. S. and R. I. Dorn. 1987. Rock-art chronology in eastern California, *World Archaeology* 19: 150–64.

1988. Cation-ratio dating of petroglyphs using PIXE, *Nuclear Instruments and Methods in Physics Research* B35: 410–14.

1993. New perspectives on the Clovis versus pre-Clovis controversy, *American Antiquity* 58: 626–47.

Whitley, D. S., R. I. Dorn, J. Francis, L. L. Loendorf, T. Holcomb, R. Tanner and J. Bozovich. 1996. Recent advances in petroglyph dating and their implications for the pre-Clovis occupation of North America, *Proceedings of the Society for California Archaeology* 9: 92–103.

York, A., R. Daly and C. Arnett. 1993. *They write their dreams on the rock forever: rock writings in the Stein River valley of British Columbia*. Vancouver (BC), Talonbooks.

Zigmond, M. 1972. Some mythological and supernatural aspects of Kawaiisu ethnography and ethnobiology, in D. D. Fowler (ed.), *Great Basin cultural ecology: a symposium*, pp. 129–34. Reno (NV), Desert Research Institute. Publications in the Social Sciences 8.

1977. The supernatural world of the Kawaiisu, in T. C. Blackburn (ed.), *Flowers of the wind: papers on ritual, myth and symbolism in California and the Southwest*, pp. 59–95. Socorro (NM), Ballena Press.

1980. *Kawaiisu mythology: an oral tradition of south-central California*. Socorro (NM), Ballena Press.

Zintgraff, J. and S. Turpin. 1991. *Pecos River rock art: a photographic essay*. San Antonio (TX), McPherson Publishing Company.

**Sven Ouzman**

# 3. Towards a mindscape of landscape: rock-art as expression of world-understanding

Rock-art imagery represents one of the most theoretically informed classes of material culture relating to archaeologically observed forager communities. Unlike most other items of material culture, the visual primacy of rock-art imagery is able simultaneously to present a wealth of associations for the viewer. In order to establish which of these associations are relevant and meaningful, reliable relations of relevance linking contemporary and forager thought need to be constructed. These relations of relevance should, ideally, be composed of multiple strands of evidence. In this manner we may move from material, observable manifestations towards an exploration of certain non-material elements of the forager mindscape. Rock-art interpretations suffer from a visual and language bias which – though essential to research – does tend to close off less easily described research directions. I suggest three strands of archaeological evidence that may go some way towards a consideration of non-visual and non-verbal meanings of certain rock-arts. The three strands are: forager cognitive systems, shamanism and forager landscape perceptions.

## Rock-art, visual imagery and signification

In archaeological discourse, phrases such as 'the evidence shows', 'from the data it is clear' and, indeed, 'rock-art' indicate that our construction and perception of data is overwhelmingly visual in nature. Though we have numerous other ways of articulating with external realities (Derrida 1982; Claasen 1993), we largely restrict ourselves to what we can see. Sight, as a very powerful form of sensory perception, is justifiably central to archaeological discourse (see, for example, Skotnes 1994). Reliance on a single trope does, however, run the risk of closing off research into other less easily definable ways of acquiring knowledge.

The visual primacy of rock-art imagery has attracted researchers from all walks of life to the engravings, paintings and sculptures of forager[1] communities. It is largely because of the detailed iconography of rock-art that researchers have been able actively to interpret, rather than passively to describe, what they perceive. Rock-art interpretations do not always agree and are often in competition with each other, but it is precisely this dynamic and creative context that has made rock-art a theoretically informed class of material culture which is arguably the best positioned to approach the ways in which archaeologically observed foragers thought and lived. Yet this is also where our dilemma lies.

Foragers work with a system of signification which is in many ways maximally different from our own. For this reason, the very language we use is unable to capture the hints, metaphors, nuances, resonances and textures of forager existence. We assume, for example, that forager ethnographies contain information our non-forager sensibilities are able to assimilate, despite the radical transformation aurally perceived information undergoes when represented in an ethnographic trope (Wylie 1985; Clifford and Marcus 1986; Aunger 1995). Many non-western societies construct their world according to senses other than sight, using smell, emotional shades and even temperature to classify certain topographical locations (Claasen 1993; see also Car-

---

[1] I use 'forager' as a generic term. This does, however, run the risk of masking enormous variability in forager social organisation, belief and material culture signatures which are the product of specific social, historical and intellectual conditions. I make no comment on non-forager rock-arts.

michael *et al.* 1994). We use visual and linguistic metaphors that are, at times, inappropriate. Unfortunately, both the visual and our language are essential and unavoidable to archaeological thought and discourse. We cannot step wholly outside the bounds of our intellectual tradition.[2] We would seem at an impasse; logically unable to transcend our intellectual tradition, we are without a means of independent verification by which we could know whether we are simulating an emic understanding of forager material culture or not.

Fortunately, recent archaeological research may provide a practicable way of approaching certain non-visual and non-verbal aspects of rock-art imagery and, at the same time, establish necessary and sufficient relations of relevance between contemporary thought and the forager mind. These relations of relevance may be thought of as strands of evidence that can be twisted together to form a 'cable' of archaeological inference, the combined 'weight' of which allows an argument to hold together for a time, even though the individual strands cannot (Bernstein 1983; Wylie 1989; see also Lewis-Williams 1991). I consider three such strands of evidence, namely forager cognitive systems, shamanism and forager landscape perception. I specifically exclude dating as a strand of evidence, as it is, at best, an archaeological technique which can provide us with a relative chronological reference frame. Though the absolute or even relative dating of rock-art imagery will be immensely helpful, it does seem as if rock-art images were produced in intellectual milieux that were largely independent of age because they rely on the articulation of social variables that can occur and recur at any and many times.

## Forager cognitive systems

Most rock-arts appear to have been the product of people who engaged in hunting, gathering, fishing and scavenging subsistence activities. Archaeological and anthropological evidence suggests that these people lived in groups of between fifteen and forty people (for example, Conkey 1985; Bahn and Vertut 1988; Barnard 1992; Sales 1992) who aggregated in larger social groups at certain times for purposes of marriage-brokering (Lee 1979), forming alliances (Weissner 1984), information exchange (Moore 1983), feasting (Hayden 1990), religious and ritual activities (David *et al.* 1994; Katz 1982). Forager technology varied from the relatively simple to the complex. Other items of material culture, such as rock-art imagery, appear to be highly complex and speak of an altogether different, non-technological order of things. The visual magnificence and intricacy of, for example, Australian Aboriginal, French Upper Palaeolithic, Native American and San rock-arts was difficult for nineteenth-century researchers to reconcile with stereotypes of foragers' apparently simple ways of life (for example, Bahn and Vertut 1988; Whitley and Loendorf 1994). This contradiction led to racist and condescending stereotypes of foragers. In particular, the notion of the 'noble savage' as somehow naturally and inevitably connected to a higher reality – and thus a passive conduit through which elements of that higher reality found visual expression – was a favoured interpretation. In some instances, however, such as in 1879 when Don Marcelino Sanz de Sautuola offered his daughter's discovery of the rock-paintings at Altamira as authentic forager rock-art, the discrepancy between 'primitive' foragers and 'great' art was too great for the reigning social order to accept; this is why forager authorship of that rock-art was rejected for a further twenty-three years (Bahn and Vertut 1988: 25).

Today the sheer weight of evidence makes such rejection untenable, and the forager authorship of most rock-arts is uncontested. There is also general consensus that rock-art imagery is not 'ordinary' but is somehow 'extra-ordinary' though we do not fully understand the forces that drove these foraging communities to engrave, paint and sculpt. For example, the Magdalenian phase engravings and paintings of

---

[2] The intellectual tradition referred to is principally post-Enlightenment thinking, in particular the philosophies of Descartes, Kant and Wittgenstein, though there is reference to an earlier Classical tradition.

the French Upper Palaeolithic, made some 12,000 to 17,000 years ago, tend to be found deep within dark and potentially dangerous caves (Clottes 1990, 1995). Sites such as Le Tuc d'Audoubert, Les Trois Frères and the Salon Noir in Niaux strongly suggest conscious placing of images and thus manipulation of space. The literal and conceptual journey of the Magdalenian artists into the depths of the earth must have been driven by something both immensely powerful and fundamental to forager existence.

It is at this juncture that it is useful to consider forager cognition or world-understanding more closely. Foragers, it is understood, did not have a written tradition but an oral one. This is so, yet forager oral discourse does not neatly correspond with our understanding of language (see Derrida 1982). The present 'San' or 'Bushman'[3] communities of southern Africa, whose ancestors produced rock-art, have a language that is unparalleled in its complexity. The use of tone, register and between one and five 'click' sounds enables them not only very precisely to denote words, objects, concepts and so forth, but also very precisely to express tones, textures, presentiments and ambiguous meaning fields. In this way, the San approach what Wittgenstein called the 'unspeakable' or the transcendent, something our language is largely incapable of.

Similarly, foragers' construction of internal and external reality, what we would call 'the self' and 'the world', is unique. We largely subscribe to a Cartesian unity of self quite separate from the world – which we perceive as external to the self. Certain categories of forager, particularly ritual specialists such as shamans, were able, apparently unproblematically, to undergo multiple ego divisions on their hallucinatory journeys to the spirit realms. Certain of these shamans have been documented as 'hearing voices', a condition we would call schizophrenia or madness,

**Fig. 3.1.** Rock-painting of a hand print, Western Cape Province, South Africa.
Scale bar is 3 cm.

but which foragers took to be a manifestation of another reality. Jaynes (1976) has written of the breakdown of the bicameral mind, an event which happened sometime in antiquity and which severed the mental or cognitive link we had with the minds of foragers.

The relevance of this strand of evidence to rock-art is that it indicates that the engraved, painted and sculpted imagery is not a form of language, nor is it a text, though it does communicate. This view is contrary to the 'material culture as text' school of thought. Tilley (1991) has analysed the Nämforsen rock-engravings in Scandinavia as if they constituted a text, even a document. Archaeological material culture, rock-art imagery in particular, cannot be neatly bounded and interpreted using a linguistic model for two reasons. First, a rock-art panel is not reducible to the linearity of text; instead individual motifs are visually apprehended in an unstable, often

---

[3] While neither 'San' nor 'Bushman' is a satisfactory term for South Africa's first people, the issue of nomenclature appears insoluble as San communities have no generic name for themselves. I reject any negative connotations 'San' or 'Bushman' may have.

random manner and their meanings are thus constantly shifting. One cannot then say rock-art images constitute subjects, objects and the like (see Lenssen-Erz 1989; Lewis-Williams 1990). Sentences and texts progressively limit the potential meanings of an image, compromising its polysemy. Secondly, rock-art images are not like signifiers and have no necessary and sufficient relation of relevance with a signified. Images are often things in themselves and not something standing for something else. Rock-art imagery works in a synergistic fashion in which ethnographic analogy, the viewer's experiences and a certain amount of creativity simultaneously combine in a synthesis so complex language cannot hope to capture it.

One possible example of a non-visual meaning encoded by rock-art may be evident in depictions of hand prints and hand stencils (Fig. 3.1). Hand prints/stencils are an astoundingly enduring and widespread image class and are among the most frequent motifs on every continent. They occur in Africa, the Americas, Asia, Australia and Europe. Their meaning, however, remains recondite. If we were to consider these images, not as something to be seen, but as the expression of a desire to touch or have contact with the rock surface, entirely new research possibilities are opened. Just as the San believed the rock surface to be more than a neutral canvas (Lewis-Williams and Dowson 1990), so many foragers may have believed that the rock surface, and even rock-art sites, such as caves, were entrances to another reality. They may have, literally, wanted to get 'in touch' with this reality (see Whitley, this volume, above). Hand prints, with their often enigmatic 'mutilations', though highly visible, may be referring to an altogether different sensory perception.

Rock-art images were thus consciously selected for and juxtaposed, superimposed, placed in unusual physical settings and articulated within specific social and historical circumstances so that the synthesis the images represent is considerably more than the sum of its parts.

I now move from the conceptual space of forager cognitive systems to the otherworldly space of forager shamanism.

## Shamanism

One consequence of forager cognition is that it tends to be associated with a shamanistic form of belief. In her study of forager communities, Halifax (1991; see also Winkelman 1986, 1992) found most to be shamanistic in one form or another. Briefly, as its defining characteristic shamanism has institutionalised altered states of consciousness in which the religious specialist, or shaman, experiences visual and somatic hallucinations which are said to constitute the central truths of forager religion (Dobkin de Rios 1986; Eliade 1989; Lewis 1989). Theoretical and methodological caution is essential in studying forager shamanism. Shamanism is not a monolithic category, but a polyvalent and pervasive phenomenon that has ingress to all facets of forager life (Halifax 1991). Shamanism is enormously variable as regards content and expression; so, where possible, specific social groups should be analysed. Yet despite this variability, there is also a remarkable correspondence in shamanistic belief and practice between forager groups that are spatially and temporally separate. These correspondences are most adequately explained as the product of a shared, human universal – the central nervous system (Lewis-Williams and Dowson 1988). For the past 100,000 years we have all shared the same central nervous system which – if stimulated by vigorous dancing, percussive sound or the ingestion of psychoactive substances – will, at some level, produce near-identical hallucinatory visions and experiences (Furst 1976; Harner 1973; Jacobs 1984; Winkelman 1992). These visions and experiences are then embedded in a specific cultural matrix and given culturally specific meaning. Shamans are a category of person well suited to handle these hallucinatory experiences; they are visually and symbolically 'literate'. They translate their otherworldly experiences into an idiom their group can understand. This idiom is both verbal, as the shaman orally relates her/his experiences, and visual, as imagery including rock-art is produced (Lommel 1967). Images are particularly appropriate vehicles for the shaman's aims as they are able powerfully and simultaneously to presence a flood of associations, not all of which are readily understandable without the exegesis of the shaman.

A shamanistic origin for rock-art imagery is enjoying increasing support from researchers in Africa (Lewis-Williams 1981; Yates and Manhire 1991), Australia (Sales 1992), Europe (Bradley 1989; Lewis-Williams 1991; Goodman et al. 1995; see also Clottes 1996: 284, 287) and North America (Boyd and Dering 1996; Turpin 1994; Whitley and Loendorf 1994; see also Le Moine et al. 1995). Not all forager rock-art is shamanistic, but the many correspondences between much rock-art iconography and shamanic experience are too great to ignore. Furthermore, many rock-art traditions, such as those in southern Africa and France, persisted with remarkable continuity of expression for thousands of years. Rather than interpreting this as an indication of stasis or degeneration, it is more rewarding to see the continuity as the product of a deeply held, universal forager tenet such as shamanism. What we perceive as rock-art images are, in fact, the distillate of the mental efforts of generations of shamans adding layer upon layer of meaning in a fascinating and complex synthesis.

I now move from the inner space of forager shamanism to the outer space of the landscape.

## Forager landscape perception

Just as language, the self and shamanism are problematic categories, so is the forager construction of space. Cross-culturally, it appears as if most societies have a stratified concept of the universe with upper, middle and lower realms, which may be further subdivided (Eliade 1989; Lewis 1989). The middle realm is usually the space of ordinary reality, while the upper and lower realms constitute spaces of extra-ordinary reality. In the increasingly secular context of western society, the Judaeo-Christian construction of heaven and hell has today lost much of its force and is now principally a didactic device. But for foragers, these realms were real and carried great force. Many San communities believed, for example, that the upper and lower realms constituted real, definable territories with specific, though supernatural, beings and resources that ran roughly parallel to the world of normal experience and were everywhere immanent (for example, Deacon 1988; see also Taçon 1990; Ingold 1993; Carmichael et al. 1994). I argue that southern African rock-art sites represented physical and conceptual places at which these worlds connected and interpenetrated. It is useful to make a distinction between 'spaces' and 'places'. 'Spaces' are fairly undifferentiated areas which nevertheless provide the general character, texture and context of a 'place', a specific, defined topographical location at which human activity is focused (Tilley 1994). I discuss two San rock-art sites in this light.

### Site 1: the spirit world emergent

The first site is located in the well-watered and mountainous Eastern Cape Province of South Africa (Fig. 3.2). The site is an unusually large cave overhang over which runs a waterfall (Fig. 3.3). In the northwestern portion of the cave, a 0.5 m to 1.5 m deep archaeological deposit contains lithics and material culture signatures characteristic of Later Stone Age[4] foragers. Two panels of rock-paintings are located 20 m apart. On the one panel the images depicted are densely painted with complex super- and juxtapositionings, indicating multiple authorship, probably over an extended period. The painted images include ochre and white felines, seventy shaded polychrome eland, a red and black buck-headed serpent, and forty human figures in a variety of postures generally considered to be diagnostic of San shamanistic practice (see Lewis-Williams 1981). However, it is the second painted panel that provides the real insight into San perceptions of landscape.

---

[4] The Later Stone Age in southern Africa refers to forager history from approximately 25,000 years ago until the time of living memory.

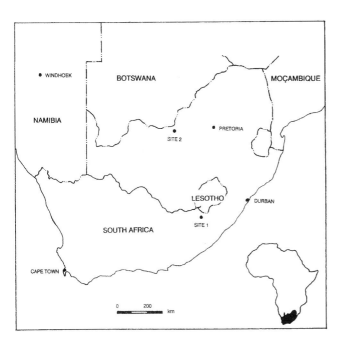

**Fig. 3.2.** Locations of Sites 1 and 2, in South Africa.

**Fig. 3.3.** View of Site 1, Eastern Cape Province, South Africa.

**Fig. 3.4.** View of two rain-animals apparently emerging from a water-pool at the base of the dark stain in the rock. The second rain-animal has been painted as though emerging from a step in the rock face.
  Site 1, Eastern Cape Province, South Africa.

In an extraordinary painted panel 10 m long, there is a vision of an event of singular importance to San communities – the rain-making ritual. San communities conceived of the rain in zoomorphic terms as a composite hallucinatory animal that inhabited deep water-pools (Bleek 1933a). This rain-animal had to be found, captured and bound by the rain-shamans who would then slaughter the rain-animal so that its milk and blood could mix to form rain (Bleek 1933a, 1933b). This entire ritual was, in fact, a complex interdigitation of the real and the non-real, the observable and the hallucinatory. The rain-making ritual existed largely in the minds of shamans, and in order to make visible what was ordinarily invisible to all but the shamans, the rain-making ritual found expression in painted idiom.

At this site a particularly good insight into a San world-understanding is presented by the painting of an elaborate rain-making ritual (Fig. 3.4). It comprises four huge (each 1.5 m to 2 m in length) rain-animals which are depicted in procession, apparently pursuing over fifty human figures; some of them are running, others bend forward and bleed from the nose, while still others hold containers of what is probably *buchu* or powerful, even narcotic, plant substances (for example, Dobkin de Rios 1986) in front of the on-coming rain-animals. This rain-making panel, unparalleled in size in southern Africa, is most probably the work of a particularly gifted San shaman-artist or artists. This assertion is strengthened by the shaman-artist's use of the non-visual.

The second-from-hindmost rain-animal has been depicted as emerging from a step in the rock face (Fig. 3.4). This convention is a persistent feature of southern African rock-art indicative of a San belief that the rock face constituted an interface between this world and the spirit world (Lewis-Williams and Dowson 1990). Steps, cracks and the like were construed as pathways which connected the two worlds. These pathways could only be followed by shamans and inhabitants of the spirit world. The use of this natural rock feature – together with the iconography and related San rain-making and shamanistic beliefs – indicates that rock-paintings are not so much images put *on* to the rock surface as experiences of the spirit world brought out *from behind* the rock face. The

**Fig. 3.5.** View of the main hill site.
Site 2, North-West Province, South Africa.

paintings, not only depictions representing something else, exist as entities sufficient in themselves.

In addition, the symbolically literate shamans used a further non-visual element in the multi-nuanced composition. All four painted rain-animals appear to be proceeding from the plunge pool of the waterfall that falls over the cave overhang. It seems no accident that these rain-animals – which were believed to inhabit deep pools of water – were painted in such a way as to indicate that they were being led both out of their home and, thus, out of the spirit world. The water-pool is not a visual entity as such but a topographical feature that, had any other image been painted, would not have formed part of the meaning field of this composition. Using the water-pool, the shaman-artist(s) were able to free the painted rain-animals from the rock support. These painted rain-animals are thus ambiguous constructions, simultaneously residing behind the rock face, on the rock face, in the water-pool and in the space between water-pool and rock face.

This meaning field, though it has a visual element, is equally a product of topographical features, San rain-making beliefs and multiple, subtle links between them. Site 1 is a place where multiple worlds interconnect, where the spirit world is emergent.

*Site 2: reconsidering 'site'*
The second site useful in understanding San constructions of landscape is a rock-engraving locale in the arid, almost featureless terrain of the North-West Province of South Africa (Fig. 3.2). The 'site' is, in fact, a cluster of six engraving locales. Locales 1–5, on low ground or gently rising prominences, have between one and twenty-seven images. Locale 6 is an 8.5 m high hill bounded by twenty-seven standing stones (Fig. 3.5). Over 559 identifiable images cluster very precisely on the slopes and summit of the

hill. The number, range and complexity of the images at locale 6 strongly suggests that it was a major San ritual centre which provided the space around it with a conceptual focus and resonance (Ouzman 1996). The pre-eminence of this locale finds accord with research in the same general area which indicates that certain low hills were especially favoured ritual centres by San foragers (Deacon 1988, 1994). In fact, so powerful is this resonance, that contemporary Tswana-speaking communities in the area use locale 6 for a variety of religious rituals, some of which bear a striking resemblance to ethnographically observed San rituals (Ouzman 1995). Though speculative, 'topophilia' (Tuan 1974), or the feeling of attachment and belonging to a place, is a pervasive cross-cultural phenomenon – not easily reducible to language but exerting a profound effect on people, even across the millennia. Site 2 has such an effect on people: the challenge is to articulate this feeling into a scientifically arguable and defensible form.

Site 2 is also important for another reason. We tend to define archaeological sites by visual inspection of the presence or absence of archaeological material culture. As a result, sites are most typically represented as dots on a map (for example, Fig. 3.2), serving to focus our perception on a specific place. Yet, in this case, all six engraving locales are within 1.5 km of each other, and locale 6 is visible from the other five locales. Though there is unengraved space between the locales, I offer that all six locales were considered a single 'place' by San foragers. Each engraving locale is also different, and this difference may indicate different aspects of San ritual practice. Locale 6 appears to be a suitable place at which large groups of people could converge for corporate activities – communal healing, dancing, and so forth. The dense engraving distribution both mimics and informs the similarly dense and thick texture of these large-scale gatherings. Locales 1–5 suggest a more private, contemplative use, possibly even by an individual who wanted to focus on specific aspects of San belief without the distraction of a large gathering. Vision-questing is an obvious activity suited to this context.

**Fig. 3.6.** Non-representational hammer marks. Site 2, North-West Province, South Africa. Scale bar is 3 cm.

Traces of foragers' use of these engraved locales may be encoded by a number of engraved rocks, principally locale 6, on which there are diffuse and concentrated clouds of hammer marks (Fig. 3.6). The most adequate explanation for these visually confusing marks is that they were not created as things to be seen; instead they are the residue of certain San rituals at which the production of percussive sound such as hammering or drumming was required. Cross-culturally, the use of percussion is especially marked at rituals at which an altered state of consciousness is induced (Needham 1967; Dobkin de Rios and Katz 1975; Tuzin 1984; Hedges 1993; Waller 1993), as percussion affects one's sense of association with the body. In fact, at certain rock-art sites in France, such as in the Ariège, researchers have supposed the practice of beating of stalactites in order to set up a resonance within the cave (Scarre 1989; see also Dams 1985).

Just as music may have helped people journey to different realities, the actual journey between rock-art locales may have been considered just as important as the locales (Smith 1994). The journey, in this context, could have assumed the form of a pilgrimage, the undertaking of which was intended to transform a person from one state, such as impurity, to another such as catharsis. Shamanistic and foraging societies have the metaphor of a journey deeply ingrained into their consciousness. It would be profitable to see how the physical approaches or paths to rock-art sites, as well as the sites, manipulate space, human movement and hence perceptions of rock-art at a site (Tilley 1994). The Australian Aborigines' belief in 'song lines' (Lewis 1976) that criss-cross the landscape is a useful heuristic device in bringing about the realisation that forager landscapes consisted of places that constituted nodal points on the interstices of a landscape resonant with meaning.

## Rock-art and the forager landscape

Ritual, sound and journey represent non-visual and non-verbal ways in which rock-art imagery may have been embedded in the forager social firmament. Forager constructions of landscape perception often show remarkable parallels which often find expression in rock-art imagery. Rock-art sites were places at which ordinary reality was suspended and re-ordered, and the forager universe a scape of both the land and the mind. I have discussed three strands of archaeological evidence – forager cognitive systems, shamanism and forager landscape perception – that go some way towards addressing the current visual and verbal bias in our discourse. Insights arrived at from visual and from non-visual approaches – logically difficult to define precisely – do appear to represent a dynamic, creative process that may provide ways of thinking, if not specific details. Possibly we need to step slightly outside of current intellectual tradition and subtly realign our understanding of 'foragers' and 'rock-art' to include information which is novel and which exists somewhat uneasily beside received and accepted knowledge. In short, we may have to learn to live with some ambiguity in our interpretations of rock-art imagery. It is somewhere in that creative tension between the known and unknown that our most profound insights will emerge (Derrida 1982) and we will appreciate even more what remarkable realities rock-art represents.

## REFERENCES

Aunger, R. 1995. Ethnography: storytelling or science?, *Current Anthropology* 36: 97–130.

Bahn, P. G. and J. Vertut. 1988. *Images of the Ice Age.* Leicester, Windward.

Barnard, A. 1992. *Hunters and herders of southern Africa: a comparative ethnography of the Khoisan peoples.* Cambridge, Cambridge University Press.

Bernstein, R. J. 1983. *Beyond objectivism and relativism: science, hermeneutics, and praxis.* Oxford, Blackwell.

Bleek, D. F. 1933a. Beliefs and customs of the /Xam Bushmen. Part V: The rain, *Bantu Studies* 7: 297–312.

1933b. Beliefs and customs of the /Xam Bushmen. Part VI: Rain-making, *Bantu Studies* 7: 375–92.

Boyd, C. E. and J. P. Dering. 1996. Medicinal and hallucinogenic plants identified in the sediments and pictographs of the Lower Pecos, Texas Archaic, *Antiquity* 70: 256–75.

Bradley, R. 1989. Deaths and entrances: a contextual analysis of megalithic art, *Current Anthropology* 30: 68–75.

Carmichael, D. L., J. Hubert, B. Reeves and A. Schanche. 1994. *Sacred sites, sacred places.* London, Routledge.

Claasen, C. 1993. *Worlds of sense: exploring the senses in history and across cultures.* London, Routledge.

Clifford, J. and G. Marcus. (eds.). 1986. *Writing culture: the poetics and politics of ethnography.* Berkeley (CA), University of California Press.

Clottes, J. 1990. The parietal art of the late Magdalenian, *Antiquity* 64: 527–48.

1995. *Les Cavernes de Niaux: art préhistorique en Ariège.* Paris, Editions du Seuil.

1996. Thematic changes in Upper Palaeolithic art: a view from the Grotte Chauvet, *Antiquity* 70: 276–88.

Conkey, M. W. 1985. Ritual, communication, social elaboration and variable trajectories of Palaeolithic archaeology, in T. D. Price and J. A. Brown (eds.), *Prehistoric hunter-gatherers: the emergence of social and cultural complexity*, pp. 299–323. London, Academic Press.

Dams, L. 1985. Palaeolithic lithophones: descriptions and comparisons, *Oxford Journal of Archaeology* 4: 31–46.

David, B., I. McNiven, V. Attenbrow, J. Flood and J. Collins. 1994. Of Lightning Brothers and White Cockatoos: dating the antiquity of signifying systems in the Northern Territory, Australia, *Antiquity* 68: 241–51.

Deacon, J. 1988. The power of a place in understanding southern San rock engravings, *World Archaeology* 20: 129–40.

1994. Rock engravings and the folklore of Bleek and Lloyd's /Xam San informants, in T. A. Dowson and J. D. Lewis-Williams (eds.), *Contested images: diversity in southern African rock art research*, pp. 237–56. Johannesburg, Witwatersrand University Press.

Derrida, J. 1982. *Margins of philosophy*. Brighton, Harvester Press.

Dobkin de Rios, M. 1986. Enigma of drug-induced altered states of consciousness among the !Kung Bushmen of the Kalahari Desert, *Journal of Ethnopharmacology* 15: 297–304.

Dobkin de Rios, M. and R. Katz. 1975. Some relationships between music and hallucinogenic ritual: the 'jungle gym' in consciousness, *Ethos* 3: 64–76.

Eliade, M. 1989. *Shamanism: archaic techniques of ecstasy*. Guernsey, Arkana.

Furst, P. T. 1976. *Hallucinogens and culture*. Novato (CA), Chandler and Sharp.

Goodman, J., P. E. Lovejoy and A. Sherratt (eds.) 1995. *Consuming habits: drugs in history and anthropology*. London, Routledge.

Halifax, J. 1991. *Shamanic voices: a survery of visionary narratives*. New York, Arkana.

Harner, M. J. 1973. *Hallucinogens and shamanism*. New York, Oxford University Press.

Hayden, B. 1990. Nimrods, piscators, pluckers and planters: the emergence of food production, *Journal of Anthropological Archaeology* 9: 31–69.

Hedges, K. 1993. Places to see and places to hear: rock art and features of the sacred landscape, in J. Steinbring, A. Watchman, P. Faulstich and P. Taçon (eds.), *Time and space: dating and spatial considerations in rock art research*, pp. 121–7. Melbourne, Australian Rock Art Research Association. Occasional AURA Publication No. 8.

Ingold, T. 1993. The temporality of the landscape, *World Archaeology* 25: 152–72.

Jacobs, B. L. (ed.). 1984. *Hallucinogens: neurochemical, behavioural, and clinical perspectives*. New York, Ravan.

Jaynes, J. 1976. *The origin of consciousness in the breakdown of the bicameral mind*. London, Chatto and Windus.

Katz, R. 1982. *Boiling energy: community healing among the Kalahari !Kung*. Cambridge (MA), Harvard University Press.

Le Moine, G., J. Helmer and D. Hanna. 1995. Altered states: human–animal transformational images in Dorset art, in K. Ryan and P. J. Crabtree (eds.), *The symbolic role of animals in archaeology*, pp. 38–49. Philadelphia, University of Pennsylvania Museum of Archaeology and Anthropology. MASCA Research Papers in Science and Archaeology.

Lee, R. B. 1979. *The !Kung San: men, women, and work in a foraging society*. Cambridge, Cambridge University Press.

Lenssen-Erz, T. 1989. Catalogue, in H. Pager, *The rock paintings of the Upper Brandberg* Part 1: *Amis Gorge*, pp. 343–502. Cologne, Heinrich Barth Institute.

Lewis, D. 1976. Observation on route finding and spatial orientation among the Aboriginal peoples of the Western Desert region of central Australia, *Oceania* 46: 249–82.

Lewis, I. M. 1989. *Ecstatic religion: a study of shamanism and spirit possession*. Second edition. London, Routledge.

Lewis-Williams, J. D. 1981. *Believing and seeing: symbolic meanings in southern San rock paintings*. London, Academic Press.

1990. Documentation, analysis and interpretation: dilemmas in rock art research, *South African Archaeological Bulletin* 45: 126–36.

1991. Wrestling with analogy: a methodological dilemma in Upper Palaeolithic rock art research, *Proceedings of the Prehistoric Society* 57: 149–62.

Lewis-Williams, J. D. and T. A. Dowson. 1988. The signs of all times: entoptic phenomena and Upper Palaeolithic art, *Current Anthropology* 29: 201–45.

1990. Through the veil: San rock paintings and the rock face, *South African Archaeological Bulletin* 45: 5–16.

Lommel, A. 1967. *Shamanism: the beginning of art*. New York, McGraw-Hill.

Moore, J. A. 1983. The trouble with know-it-alls: information as a social and ecological resource, in J. A. Moore and A. S. Keene (eds.), *Anthropological hammers and theories*, pp. 173–91. New York, Academic Press.

Needham, R. 1967. Percussion and transition, *Man* 2: 606–14.

Ouzman, S. 1995. Spiritual and political uses of a rock engraving site and its imagery by San and Tswana-speakers, *South African Archaeological Bulletin* 50: 55–67.

1996. Thaba Sione: place of rhinoceroses and rock art, *African Studies* 55: 31–59.

Sales, K. 1992. Ascent to the sky: a shamanic initiatory engraving from the Burrup Peninsula, Northwestern Australia, *Archaeology in Oceania* 27: 22–35.

Scarre, C. 1989. Painting by resonance, *Nature* 338: 382.

Skotnes, P. 1994. The visual as a site of meaning: San parietal painting and the experience of modern art, in T. A. Dowson and J. D. Lewis-Williams (eds.), *Contested images: diversity in southern African rock art research*, pp. 315–29. Johannesburg, Witwatersrand University Press.

Smith, A. B. 1994. Metaphors of space: rock art and territoriality in southern Africa, in T. A. Dowson and J. D. Lewis-Williams (eds.), *Contested images: diversity in southern African rock art research*, pp. 373–84. Johannesburg, Witwatersrand University Press.

Taçon, P. 1990. The power of place: cross-cultural responses to natural and cultural landscapes of stone and earth, in J. M. Vastokas (ed.), *Perspectives of Canadian landscape: Native traditions*, pp. 11–43. York University (Ont.), Robarts Centre for Canadian Studies.

Tilley, C. 1991. *Material culture and text: the art of ambiguity*. London, Routledge.

1994. *A phenomenology of landscape: places, paths and monuments*. Oxford, Berg.

Tuan, Y.-F. 1974. *Topophilia: a study of environmental perception, attitudes and values*. Englewood Cliffs (NJ), Prentice-Hall.

Turpin, S. (ed.). 1994. *Shamanism and rock art in North America*. San Antonio (TX), Rock Art Foundation.

Tuzin, D. 1984. Miraculous voices: the auditory experience of numinous objects, *Current Anthropology* 25: 579–96.

Waller, S. J. 1993. Sound and rock art, *Nature* 363: 501.

Weissner, P. 1984. Reconsidering the behavioural basis for style: a case study among the Kalahari San, *Journal of Anthropological Archaeology* 3: 190–234.

Whitley, D. S. and L. L. Loendorf (eds.). 1994. *New light on old art: recent advances in hunter-gatherer rock art research*. Los Angeles (CA), University of California Los Angeles, Institute of Archaeology. Monograph 36.

Winkelman, M. 1986. Trance states: a theoretical model and cross-cultural analysis, *Ethos* 14: 174–203.

1992. *Shamans, priests and witchdoctors: a cross-cultural study of magico-religious practitioners*. Tempe (AZ), Arizona State University. Anthropological papers 44.

Wylie, A. 1985. The reaction against analogy, *Advances in Archaeological Method and Theory* 8: 63–111.

1989. Archaeological cables and tacking: the implications of practice for Bernstein's '*Options beyond objectivism and relativism*', *Philosophy of the Social Sciences* 19: 1–18.

Yates, R. and T. Manhire. 1991. Shamanism and rock paintings: aspects of the use of rock art in the southwestern Cape, South Africa, *South African Archaeological Bulletin* 46: 3–11.

Michael A. Klassen

# 4. Icon and narrative in transition: contact-period rock-art at Writing-On-Stone, southern Alberta, Canada

The pictures at Writing-On-Stone, greatest petroglyph site on the Great Plains of North America, include vivid depictions of cultures in contact and conflict. Horses and guns arm warriors who, before, fought with bow and arrow and were protected by great shields. Sometimes, the imagery provides the dating means securely to place individual motifs and groups at a certain point in the transformations of contact. And – as often – the insights of informed methods combine with the observation of key points in the figures, as formally observed, to tease out the varied visions of different artistic traditions. Analogies in other imagery – painted on tipis or buffalo robes and inscribed in ledger-books – assist.

## Writing-On-Stone and its rock-art

This chapter focuses on the rock-art of Writing-On-Stone, located in the Milk River valley of southern Alberta, Canada (Fig. 4.1). Situated in a region of rolling prairie, Writing-On-Stone is placed near the northern limits of the Great Plains and some 150 km east of the Rocky Mountains. A prominent group of isolated peaks, the Sweetgrass Hills, is located approximately 10 km south of the locality; they rise more than 1200 m above the surrounding plains. The Milk River valley and tributary coulees in the Writing-On-Stone area are deeply incised into the surrounding grassland, forming extensive areas of exposed sandstone outcrops ('hoodoos') and creating vertical sandstone cliffs above the river (Figs. 4.2 and 4.3).

Almost without exception, Blackfoot oral traditions concerning Writing-On-Stone involve the sacred nature of the site, and informants have been nearly unanimous in ascribing a spiritual origin to the rock-art (Dempsey 1973); the earliest recorded explanations describe the images as 'written by spirits' (Doty 1966; Maclean 1896: 118). The spirits created the 'writings' in order to communicate with the living. For those with the 'power' to decipher them, the images could warn them of their fate or foretell the future (Dempsey 1973: 26–7). The use of Writing-On-Stone as a sacred site persists to the present day, and members of Blackfoot communities continue to visit for religious purposes. Despite the secularisation and desecration of the site through government control and tourism, the fundamental role of the Milk River valley as a sacred place remains intact.

With more than 280 separate panels at 93 sites, the Writing-On-Stone area encompasses the largest collection of rock-art on the Great Plains. Most panels are found on cliff faces near the river, with sites concentrated in two areas (Fig. 4.4). The vast majority of the images are incised and scratched petroglyphs, although some twenty panels with monochrome painted images and a few panels with pecked or abraded images are also known. According to recent classification attempts, as many as five different Plains rock-art traditions are represented at Writing-On-Stone, some of which may have originated before 1000 years BP (Keyser and Klassen, in prep.). Of concern here is the rock-art generally referred to as the Plains Ceremonial and Plains Biographic Traditions (Keyser 1977, 1984, 1990; Keyser and Klassen, in prep.; Klassen 1994).

The Plains Ceremonial Tradition developed during the late pre-contact period, AD 250–1725, and continued well into the post-contact era. The Plains Biographic Tradition arose near the end of the

Fig. 4.1. Location of Writing-On-Stone on the Northwestern Plains.

Fig. 4.2. View of Writing-On-Stone area. Hoodoo outcrops in foreground, Sweetgrass Hills in background.

Fig. 4.3. Sandstone cliffs lining the Milk River valley at Writing-On-Stone Provincial Park.

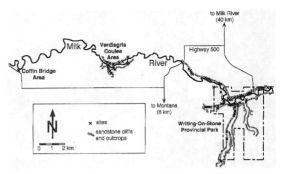

Fig. 4.4. Location of rock-art sites in Writing-On-Stone area.

pre-contact era, but flourished during the early post-contact period, AD 1725–1850. On the North-western Plains, the contact transition began with the arrival of the first horses, approximately AD 1725, and ended with the onset of permanent European settlement around AD 1850. Both traditions have been dated primarily by the presence (or absence) of subject-matter of known age – body shields and the bow and arrow for pre-contact panels, guns and horses for post-contact images. The late pre-contact ages of a few Ceremonial Tradition sites have also been corroborated by other dating methods (Loendorf 1990; Francis, Loendorf and Dorn 1993).

The anthropological study of Ceremonial and Biographic rock-art at Writing-On-Stone can be approached from the perspective of both informed and formal methods. Both traditions are well represented by sites dating from the 'historic' period. As such, a number of ethnographic, historical and traditional knowledge sources make direct reference to the rock-art. More important, the rock-art is closely related to the well-documented Plains tradition of painting representational images on material culture, including bison robes, clothing, shields and tipis. The extensive ethnographic record for painting on material culture provides a direct analogical model for interpreting the rock-art. Long-term cultural and formal continuities are also apparent in the rock-art, allowing these sources of external evidence to be applied to pre-contact images.

From the perspective of formal methods, subject-matter and composition are the most useful attributes. Both traditions consist almost exclusively of representational subject-matter, dominated by anthropomorphs, zoomorphs and depictions of material culture. Although many motifs are shared by the traditions, their frequency and associations differ, while certain motifs are exclusive to one tradition. The traditions are primarily differentiated on the basis of their distinct compositional qualities. Whereas Ceremonial rock-art consists of static images occurring singly or in small juxtaposed groups, Biographic rock-art consists of active images involved in interactive scenes depicting recognisable events.

The presence of an extensive pictorial record at Writing-On-Stone, spanning the contact transition, provides us with an unequalled opportunity for assessing variation and change in the visual traditions of Plains cultures. The Ceremonial and Biographic Traditions can be seen to represent two modes of pictorial expression – iconic and narrative – which reflect differing conceptions of the world. Moreover, shifts in the relative importance of the two traditions illustrate the significant material and social transformations resulting from indirect and direct contact with European culture.

### Icon and narrative

Until recently, the Ceremonial and Biographic Traditions were considered unrelated, each having distinct ethnic origins, temporal spans and cultural functions (Keyser 1977, 1979, 1984, 1990). In this view, Ceremonial rock-art was believed to be primarily pre-contact in age, affiliated with Shoshonean people, and related to vision quests. Biographic rock-art, on the other hand, was thought to be primarily post-contact in age, affiliated with Algonkian groups, and related to graded war honours. Ethnic and temporal discontinuity was invoked because it was felt that the formal variation between the two traditions and the increase in Biographic rock-art after contact could best be explained in terms of a cultural displacement of the Shoshone during the contact transition.

Elsewhere, I have argued that archaeological and ethnohistorical evidence of a cultural displacement on the Northwestern Plains during the contact transition is lacking (Klassen 1995: 72–105; see also Greiser 1995; Schlesier 1995; Vickers 1995). I have also tried to demonstrate that long-term formal continuities in both Ceremonial and Biographic rock-art exist, and that the traditions coexisted throughout the contact transition (Klassen 1995: 106–40). Given the evidence for cultural continuities on the Northwestern Plains, ethnic displacement is inadequate for explaining the presence of two traditions at Writing-On-Stone and a diachronic shift in their relative importance.

An alternative, and more promising, explanation is offered by the contention that two fundamentally different modes of expression are present within the pictorial traditions of Native groups (Vastokas 1985, 1990; see also Maurer 1992: 27). These modes of expression closely correspond to the Ceremonial and Biographic categories first proposed by Keyser (1977), but they are more appropriately termed 'iconic' and 'narrative' imagery (see Vastokas 1985: 429–30, 1990: 65–6). Iconic and narrative modes of expression are not restricted to a specific time, place, or culture. Each mode exhibits distinct formal and iconographic characteristics, and in turn, these differences underlie the bulk of variation in the rock-art at Writing-On-Stone. The form of each mode 'is not mere stylistic difference, but serves instead a different function and communicates a different meaning' (Vastokas 1990: 65). In other words, the form of imagery at Writing-On-Stone is more closely tied to function and meaning than to ethnicity.

In formal terms, iconic images can be defined as static, frontal, symmetrical, non-interactive motifs, found alone or in small juxtaposed groups. Such images are 'presented' to the viewer in such a way that their 'symmetry and frontality serve to arrest or to demand the beholder's attention' (Vastokas 1990: 65). Indications of narrative or 'time-sequence' relationships are not apparent (Maurer 1992: 23), and they do not represent a specific time, place, or event, but rather evoke the eternal present of the spirit world. Iconic images can be recognised as presentations of sacred subject-matter and themes, such as the objects and beings associated with visions and medicine powers. Furthermore, the thematic and formal repetition of iconic motifs reflects the ritualised nature of sacred activities.

In the ethnographic context of the Northwestern Plains, the iconic mode is well represented by the 'medicine' paintings found on shields and tipis. The form and function of these images closely correspond to those characteristics noted for iconic depictions. Medicine imagery generally consists of isolated anthropomorphic and zoomorphic figures, ceremonial objects and astronomical phenomena; the typical pictorial conventions and compositional associations which suggest a 'historical' or linear narrative are not employed (Fig. 4.5). Medicine images, primarily depicting the spirits and beings encountered in dreams, represent the spiritual or 'medicine' powers obtained through visions, as well as the ceremonial paraphernalia and ritual performances associated with these spirit visions (Benedict 1922; Brasser 1978; Ewers 1939, 1976, 1982; Grinnell 1901; Hall 1926a, 1926b; McClintock 1936; Nagy 1994; Raczka 1992; Szabo 1994).

The narrative mode of expression, on the other hand, describes the world in a very different formal and meaningful manner (Maurer 1992: 36). Narrative imagery employs both profile and frontal representations, various perspectives, and more complex compositions and combinations of motifs. Individual figures may be animated and asymmetrical; they are depicted interacting with other motifs to create 'time-sequenced' narratives or stories (Maurer 1992: 26). Certain pictorial conventions are used to suggest movement through space and the passage of time: 'In contrast to the hypnotic visual grip of iconic images, the eye of the beholder travels across and around the narrative imagery, led by pictorial cues such as repetitions in the sequence of like motifs, by explicit and

**Fig. 4.5.** Hide-painting with primarily iconic imagery. Canadian Museum of Civilization, V-B-536, Blackfoot, c. 1880, elk hide.

implicit directional lines, by animal tracks, and the like' (Vastokas 1990: 66). Space–time references, such as landscape features, may be included in the composition, while 'frames' may even be employed to separate pictorial from actual space (Vastokas 1990: 66). Narrative imagery is used to relate a specific event, generally biographical or historical in origin, but also occasionally mythological in nature. Whether mythological or historical, narratives may have both literal and metaphorical meanings (Taçon and Chippindale 1994: 217).

The narrative mode clearly corresponds to the ethnographically documented Plains Tradition of 'war record' imagery found on painted bison robes and shirts. War records consist of multiple images, often found in complex compositional arrangements. They rely on various pictorial conventions to represent the passage of time and location in space, including the use of animation and perspective (Fig. 4.6). This imagery was used primarily to chronicle the war honours and heroic deeds of an individual, although other 'historical' events may also be depic-

**Fig. 4.6.** Hide-painting with primarily narrative imagery. Royal Ontario Museum, 975.73.6, Blackfoot, pre-1898, deer hide.

while significant events undergo a process of 'mythicisation', transforming them into an event with a celestial origin (Eliade 1959: 39). In the historical conception of the world, time entails a linear progression of unique events, each with intrinsic value. Individual events are not seen as repetitions of cosmic precedents, but are given their own singular 'historical' significance. Historical events derive from the experiential or 'real' world, and they are linked to specific times, places and individuals.

'Cosmology' and 'history', however, are not necessarily mutually exclusive concepts. Although one perspective may tend to predominate in a specific culture, 'the two modes of knowledge about the world – historical (experiential, empirical) and mythic (cosmic, archetypal) – are present within the cultural systems of every group' (Vastokas 1990: 55). Each mode of thought fulfils its separate cultural function, but these modes often intersect and collaborate through the 'vehicles of art and ritual' (Vastokas 1990: 55). Just as both world-views may coexist to varying degrees within a single culture, so too can the pictorial modes which reflect those conceptions.

At Writing-On-Stone, iconic (or cosmic) and narrative (or historical) imagery can be identified in both pre-contact and post-contact contexts. Iconic imagery demonstrates considerable continuity throughout the contact transition (despite some diachronic shifts in form and subject-matter), indicating an underlying long-term cosmic view. However, during the contact transition an increasing predominance of narrative compositions in the rock-art becomes evident. The shift towards increasing narrativity in the post-contact era may reflect an increased emphasis on a 'historical' conception of the world. In the following sections, iconic continuity and heightened narrativity over the contact transition are explored from the perspective of formal evidence, iconography and ethnographic analogy.

### Continuity in iconic depiction

Five common iconic motifs at Writing-On-Stone clearly demonstrate overall continuity in formal char-

ted (Barbeau 1960: 224–5; Boyle 1904; Doty 1966; Dunn 1968: 144–8; Ewers 1983; Grinnell 1892: 249; Hall 1926a; Harper 1970; Horse Capture 1993: 82–4; Maclean 1896; Nagy 1994; Rodee 1965; Schultz 1962: 264; Schuster 1987; Vatter 1927; Walton et al. 1985: 224–8; Willoughby 1905). War shirts and robes were worn publicly to display the 'coups' obtained by individuals while on hunting expeditions, horse raids or warfare (Brownstone 1993; Ewers 1939: 17; see also Hassrick 1988: 126 and Thomas and Ronnefeldt 1976: 137).

Iconic and narrative modes of expression essentially reflect the difference between 'cosmic' and 'historic' conceptions of the world, as distinguished by Mircea Eliade (1959). In a cosmic world-view, physical objects and human acts derive their meaning and value from 'sacred' or celestial powers (Eliade 1959: 3–4). Space reflects a cosmic order, while time is apprehended as cyclical or as eternally present. Every act is a repetition of a 'celestial archetype' or mythical precedent (Eliade 1959: 27–8), acteristics and iconographical significance over the contact transition. The *Shield Figure* motif depicts a frontal, standing human figure with a large circular shield covering the torso. In all cases, legs and heads extend from behind the shield, while arms are also frequently portrayed. A design is depicted on many of the shields. Most authors agree that the Shield Figure motif depicts a pedestrian warrior carrying a large 'body shield', and that the majority of these figures date from the late pre-contact era (Klassen 1995: 59–64). Body shields, in use on the Plains before the introduction of the horse, were quickly abandoned during the equestrian period in favour of much smaller shields which were more practical on horseback.

The *Bow/Spear* motif includes depictions of bows, spears and bow-spears. The bow and arrow were introduced on to the Plains approximately 1750 years BP, and continued to be used until the end of the nineteenth century, while the spear or lance was used throughout the same time period. The bow-spear is a ceremonial object consisting of a large bow with a spear head and feather flights attached to opposite ends. The bow-spear appears to have been a common object during pre-contact times, but was also used during the post-contact era. The *Gun, Horse* and *Mounted Horse* motifs date from the post-contact period. The gun appears to have preceded the horse on to the Northwestern Plains by perhaps a decade, arriving around AD 1715. All five motifs are executed as incised carvings, or paintings using an ochre-based red pigment.

Almost without exception, Shield Figures are depicted in static poses and either individually or in small juxtaposed groups. For example, the three painted Shield Figures in Fig. 4.7 are found in a triangular grouping in isolation from other motifs. A crescent shape, undoubtedly a bow, 'floats' beside one Shield Figure while another bow is attached by a thin line to a second figure with a definite pattern on the shield. Similar painted Shield Figures on other panels (Fig. 4.8) are depicted as single or small groups of juxtaposed motifs. Despite their greater detail, the three incised Shield Figures in Fig. 4.9

bear a remarkable compositional likeness to those in Fig. 4.7, and their resemblance to the painted versions is reinforced by the presence of a faint smear of ochre across one incised shield. Two bow-spears and a spear appear to 'float' beside these figures, lending n iconic air to these objects, which are clearly not depicted in an animated fashion. One of the Shield Figures wears an elaborate head-dress, an object with ceremonial values used to denote the medicine powers of its owner.

Other incised Shield Figures share iconic characteristics with the preceding examples. Although badly weathered, an incised design is still visible on one of the Shield Figures in Fig. 4.10, while the entire lower portion of the shield also bears the faint traces of red ochre. In Fig. 4.11, two Shield Figures are associated with several human figures and other motifs in a juxtaposed group. Ochre has been used to enhance the incisions of the lower of the two Shield Figures (as well as one of the human figures), and ochre smears are also found across much of the panel, including across the lower shield. The large, isolated, carefully incised Shield Figure in Fig. 4.12 exhibits fine detailing, such as 'feathering' on the margins of the shield and above the head, and a distinct crescent and circle design on the shield. Found high above the ground on a small but prominent face and completely isolated from other motifs, the 'presentational' qualities of this figure serve to make it stand out clearly from the surrounding rock surface.

All of the Shield Figures described above clearly fit the formal definition for iconic images, and evidence of activity or narrativity (interaction between figures or a sequence of events over time and space) is not apparent. Their consideration as iconic images is supported by ethnographic evidence and iconographic analysis. Within documented post-contact Plains cultures, shields were more than simply a form of practical defence in battle: they also functioned symbolically. Shields were considered to be invested with supernatural powers, which protected their owners from harm during battle. These 'medicine' powers were transferred to shields by painting their

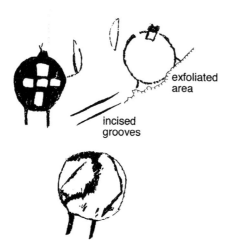

**Fig. 4.7.** Juxtaposed group of iconic Shield Figures (DgOv-2:1).

**Fig. 4.8.** Painted iconic Shield Figures (not to scale).

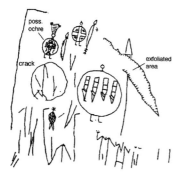

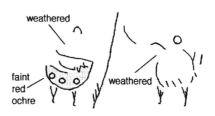

**Fig. 4.10.** Incised Shield Figures, one with ochre pigment (DgOw-2:17C).

**Fig. 4.9.** Incised, juxtaposed iconic Shield Figures with bow-spears and detailed shield designs (detail from DgOv-2:26F).

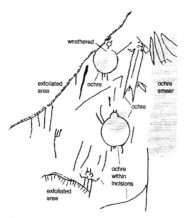

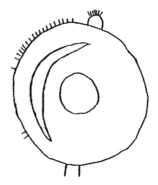

**Fig. 4.12.** Incised, isolated Shield Figure motif with shield design (DgOv-2:11A).

**Fig. 4.11.** Incised Shield Figures with ochre infilling and smears (detail from DgOv-2:16A).

surfaces with images of personal guardian spirits seen during a vision quest, and the powers of the shields were then ritually 'blessed' or sanctioned by 'medicine men' (Ewers 1955: 203). By way of analogy, we may suggest that decorated body shields had a similar function in a pre-contact context.

Given the spiritual connotations of medicine shields in Plains culture, we may propose that most iconic representations of shields are related to the personal medicine powers obtained through visions. Many of the rock-art images exhibit distinct shield designs, undoubtedly mirroring medicine designs painted on real shields. This interpretation is substantiated by the red ochre used in conjunction with several of the petroglyphs. The use of ochre reflects its properties as a sacred substance as much as it does its practicality as a pigment (see McClintock 1968: 32, 215). By extension, the sanctity of painted Shield Figures may have been enhanced by the symbolic properties of the very pigment itself. Furthermore, a human is almost always depicted as an extension of the shield, suggesting that the maker of the image conceived of the shield and its bearer as one and the same, a common entity manifesting the powers of the spirit world.

Overall, the iconography of Shield Figures reflects a timeless, 'cosmic' conception of the world. The images represent the powers of the eternal spirit world invested in shields and the transfer of these powers to humans. In both their material and representational forms, shields are a physical manifestation of personal medicine powers obtained through ritual dreaming. Through this motif, warriors depicted their medicine power as a rock-art icon.

The iconic depiction of the Shield Figure clearly persisted briefly into the post-contact period. For example, a gun is depicted beside a Shield Figure in Fig. 4.13, indicating this scene may date to shortly after the introduction of guns and before the arrival of the horse. Shown with an obvious shield decoration and in typically iconic fashion, the presentational quality of this Shield Figure is heightened by its upraised arms and open hands, in the position of

giving and receiving medicine power (Rajnovich 1994: 75). The persistence of this motif into the post-contact era underscores the continuity in the underlying cultural system at Writing-On-Stone.

Continuity in iconic imagery is also demonstrated by the gun in Fig. 4.13. In the same manner as bow-spears (Fig. 4.9), the gun floats beside the Shield Figure, as if it has an iconographic significance equal to that of the shield itself. The gun is not held as property, or brandished to demonstrate the authority it gives to its owner. In short, it is not depicted as if it were simply acquired or used in a secular fashion. Rather, the gun is displayed as a separate entity, indicating its intrinsic sacred value as an object invested with medicine power. The representation of this 'historical' trade object, introduced by Europeans during the contact transition, has seemingly acquired the same iconographic significance as that of bow-spears, perhaps because the bow-spear and the gun were charged with the same spiritual, as well as destructive, power. This is much like the case described by Miller and Hamell (1986; Hamell 1987) for the proto-contact Woodland region, where trade goods were quickly incorporated into ceremonial contexts alongside traditional sacred items of similar appearance or qualities.

Continuity in iconic significance is further exemplified by the depiction of guns at other sites, including one where at least six separate guns are painted on four different faces. In particular, a distinct red painting of a single, isolated flintlock stands out clearly from the surrounding rock (Fig. 4.14). There is no pictorial narrativity in this type of image, nor does the image function as part of a sequence of events – a story does not directly unfold from this single representation. This does not mean that a story may not lie *behind* the image: indeed, each depiction of a gun may be related to an event at a specific time and place (and the accompanying oral narrative of that event).

Evidence suggests that the pictorial depiction of guns, either singly or in groups, on hide-paintings and other surfaces represents a 'tally' of objects acquired

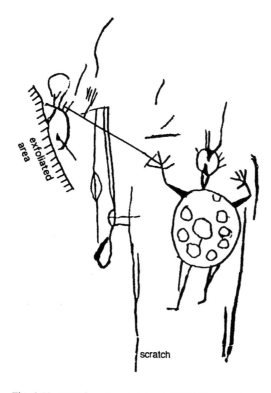

**Fig. 4.13.** Incised, post-contact, iconic Shield Figure and associated gun (detail from DgOv-29:10).

**Fig. 4.14.** Painted, isolated gun (iconic Gun motif) at DgOv-78:2 (detail).

through raids and battles, where each object symbolises a war honour or 'coup' (Brownstone 1993: 18; Ewers 1983: 52; Keyser and Brady 1993: 15; Maclean 1896: 120). Ethnographic accounts indicate that the capture of weapons was an important way of counting coup, particularly among the Blackfoot (Grinnell 1892: 248). For instance, one informant told Wissler (1912: 40) that the capture of a gun ranked ahead of killing an enemy, as the former placed the warrior in a state of greater danger. On one level, each coup represents a physical act of bravery or daring, but on a deeper level, it symbolises the medicine power giving an individual courage and protecting him from harm. Not only did coups serve to heighten an individual's status and respect, but through these deeds the medicine powers of an individual were confirmed and strengthened.

As such, images of isolated guns often represent more than a mere record of coups. They have a deeper intrinsic meaning arising from the spiritual connotations of each coup: the bravery of the individual, the strength of the medicine power which protected and inspired the warrior, and the respect, status and ceremonial rights that were conferred for capturing this trophy of war. In the terms of Erwin Panofsky (1955), the pre-iconographical identification is of a gun, while the iconographic significance records a specific coup event. But on a much deeper level, the *iconological* meaning of the gun/coup image relates to its overall cultural and spiritual significance. The image in Fig. 4.14 is an icon of everything that capturing a gun represents, a metaphorical reference to spiritual power and status.

In Fig. 4.15, a large, deeply incised flintlock displays classic iconic characteristics. Near by, a single deeply incised horse image clearly shares many of the same formal and compositional characteristics as the gun. At Writing-On-Stone, horses are frequently represented as iconic images. Many examples of the Horse motif exhibit a variety of minor 'stylistic' differences, while sharing important formal characteristics. Most horse images have been conventionalised to such a degree that they have been

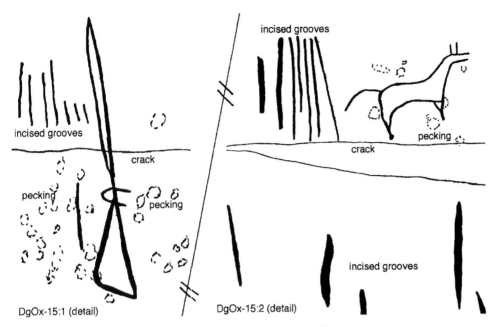

**Fig. 4.15.** Incised, iconic gun and horse on separate panels at DgOx-15 (detail).

reduced to a few simple but elegant strokes (Fig. 4.16). To this basic form, details such as ears, manes, tails, hoofs and body markings are often added. The smooth, flowing shape of this motif emphasises the grace and speed of horses, and the profile depiction also suggests movement and direction. Many depictions of the Horse motif exhibit the same presentational qualities as other iconic images. They are isolated motifs without reference to visual narrativity.

Like guns, images of isolated horses may record animals acquired during raids, therefore representing a war honour. The capture of horses was certainly an important way of counting coup, although among the Blackfoot it generally ranked well below the capture of guns (Ewers 1955: 311; Wissler 1912: 40). On hide-paintings, groups of horses often represent the number captured during specific raids, but these representations are generally depicted in association with other motifs, such as a human figure representing the successful raider, or in conjunction with a narrative scene representing the actual event. In other cases, a large group of horses is depicted to

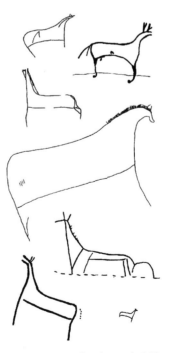

**Fig. 4.16.** Incised and scratched Horse motifs from various panels (not to scale).

51

indicate the total number captured during the lifetime of an illustrious warrior.

While groups of horses in rock-art may have acted as a biographical tally, this does not seem to be an adequate explanation for single, isolated horse images. These motifs are not associated with any narrative scenes, and their typically iconic depiction suggests a deeper significance. Indeed, the belief that the horse possessed supernatural powers was widespread among Plains cultures, and the power of certain horses was considered to be greater than others (Ewers 1955: 290–1). Horses also appeared in visions, through which they transferred their power to the visionary, giving rise to Horse Medicine cults in most Plains groups.

Among the Blackfoot, horse medicine was considered one of the strongest of all medicines, and gave wide-ranging powers to the owners of horse-medicine bundles (Ewers 1955: 317). The sudden appearance of horses on the Plains may have initially seemed a unique and unprecedented event, but perhaps because of their 'miraculous' appearance these animals were quickly incorporated into the cosmic conception of the world. The origin of horses was 'mythologised', and the historical event was incorporated into Plains cosmology, with the horse becoming a sacred icon, a metaphor of power (Penney 1992: 70). The Blackfoot, for instance, widely credited the origin of horses to both the sky and the underwater spirits, from which horses obtained their supernatural powers (Ewers 1955: 297).

As a component of the cosmic order of things, it is not surprising that the horse was frequently represented in the iconic mode of depiction (Maurer 1992: 35). Accordingly, many images of horses may symbolise their sacred value and potent medicine, perhaps created as part of a prayer for power (Penney 1992: 70). The horses illustrated in Fig. 4.17 seem to support this interpretation. Although somewhat different in 'style' from the horses considered so far, these images are rendered in complete isolation from other motifs and clearly are not part of a pictorial narrative composition. The images are deeply in-cised, and the smooth, flowing lines are executed with precision and control. Most significantly, red ochre has been used to enhance the incisions of at least one of the horses. All of these characteristics suggest that the maker of these images intended to convey the sanctity of the subject-matter.

Numerous horses at Writing-On-Stone are also depicted with riders (Fig. 4.18). Like the unmounted Horse motif, many examples of the Mounted Horse motif are found as isolated images, without clear compositional associations. Again, the horses and their riders are depicted in a variety of 'styles', but some basic characteristics remain constant. The general form is essentially identical to that of the horses described earlier, with a human figure added as a rider. While the horses are shown in profile, riders are usually depicted frontally, a continuation of the traditional iconic manner of depicting human figures. Some difficulty was encountered in combining a frontal human with a profile horse, and in most cases both legs of the rider are simply drawn across the body of the horse. This technical problem seems to have been of little concern, as the depictions were never intended to convey a sense of realism and perspective in the first place. Indeed, the riders are frequently depicted without arms, and legs are sometimes omitted as well.

Elaborations are occasionally added to the Mounted Horse motif, including riders wearing headdresses or holding reins, weapons, or quirts (leather whips). Other mounted horses, such as those in Fig. 4.19, are depicted with objects identified as War Bridle bundles (Keyser 1991: 265). These bundles, consisting of feathers hanging from a thin stick, are associated with the Horse Medicine cult. They were attached to the halter of a horse to give it power and protection during hunting and raiding (Ewers 1955: 277–8). The addition of the War Bridle emphasises the medicine powers of the horse.

In some cases, iconic Mounted Horse motifs are found in juxtaposed compositions (Fig. 4.20). Despite the basic similarities of the horses in Fig. 4.20, the images illustrate the variation in form possible

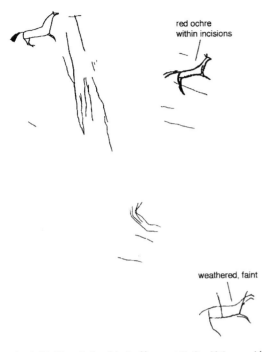

Fig. 4.17. Three isolated, incised horses at DgOv-42:1, one with ochre within incisions.

red ochre
within incisions

weathered, faint

for this motif. The motifs are scattered almost randomly across the panel, with all oriented at different angles. Although an ambiguous figure is found directly in front of the horse and rider on the far left, none of the motifs on this panel are clearly interacting. Overall, the motifs on this panel exhibit iconic characteristics.

Mounted Horse motifs do not intrinsically display a greater degree of narrativity than that noted for the unmounted Horse motif. Except for the addition of riders and their associated elaborations, the overall presentation of these motifs is essentially identical to that of unmounted horses. Given this similarity of expression, it seems plausible that the Mounted Horse had an iconic significance similar to that of the Horse motif. Rather than simply a coup tally or a depiction of an event, this motif may represent the supernatural powers invested in the horse. In this case, however, the horse medicine is shown in conjunction with the human recipients of these powers.

In iconological terms, the Mounted Horse motif appears to be a direct replacement for the Shield Figure motif of the pre-contact era. Although

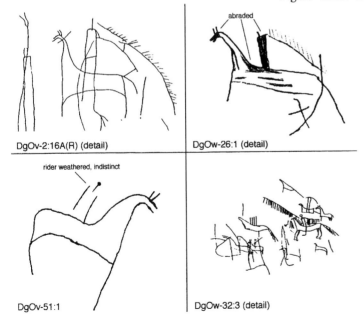

DgOv-2:16A(R) (detail)

abraded

DgOw-26:1 (detail)

rider weathered, indistinct

DgOv-51:1

DgOw-32:3 (detail)

Fig. 4.18. Incised and scratched, isolated Mounted Horse motifs on various panels (not to scale).

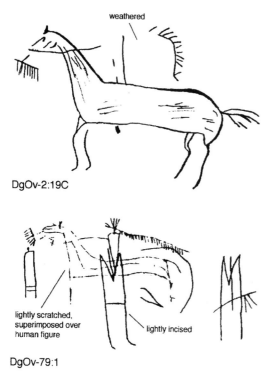

DgOv-2:19C

DgOv-79:1

**Fig. 4.19.** Incised Mounted Horse motifs with 'War Bridle' bundle (not to scale).

medicine shields continued to be used in the post-contact period, their importance was quickly over-shadowed by the practical and spiritual powers of the horse. Whereas before contact the medicine shield conferred supernatural powers upon the bearer of the shield, after contact it was the horse that transferred its powers to the rider. No longer did the shield and its power alone protect a warrior, and increasingly the medicine powers of the horse filled this role. Just as the horse eventually replaced the body shield as an object which provided a warrior with power and protection, so was the Shield Figure replaced by the Mounted Horse motif. And just as the shield and human figure were conceptualised as one single entity, so too were the horse and rider one and the same. The importance of the Mounted Horse motif as a symbol of sacred power, rather than of a secular entity, is accentuated by the iconic form and context of the images. Once again, we have an example of how iconographic significance has been transferred from one motif to another, and of iconic continuity amidst significant cultural change.

### The rise of narrativity in the post-contact era

Narrative rock-art at Writing-On-Stone includes similar subject-matter as iconic imagery, including representations of shield figures, weapons and both mounted and unmounted horses. In the narrative

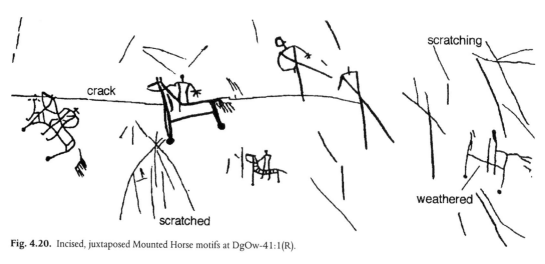

**Fig. 4.20.** Incised, juxtaposed Mounted Horse motifs at DgOw-41:1(R).

imagery, the subject-matter is depicted in a completely different compositional context: the motifs appear as part of integrated scenes which portray specific events. Although many types of activities and events are represented by narrative scenes, this section will focus on depictions of combat, horse raids and battles.

While the narrative mode of expression flourished at Writing-On-Stone in the post-contact period, it originated before the contact transition, as indicated by the narrative use of the Shield Figure motif. For example, two Shield Figures in Fig. 4.21 clearly exhibit a rudimentary degree of narrativity. A feathered spear, originating from the larger figure on the left, is directed at the head of the smaller figure, which holds a raised weapon or club in defence. In this case, the two figures are not placed in static juxtaposition, but are clearly in direct association with each other. Indeed, the asymmetrical composition provides a 'time sequence' to the narrative, leading our eyes from the larger figure on the left to the smaller figure on the right. The specific event depicted may represent an actual combat between two individuals (Keyser 1979: 45); it may *directly* represent the physical act of counting a coup.

Even in this narrative scene, the iconic features of shield images continue to be apparent, as both Shield Figures have simple shield markings. The combination of icon and narrative is even more evident in Fig. 4.22, where two detailed, precisely executed Shield Figures holding weapons are depicted in apparent combat. Both figures closely resemble the iconic Shield Figures described previously, particularly in the depiction of elaborate shield decorations, but these figures are also portrayed using simple narrative conventions. The figures face one another, with weapons brandished, serving to create movement between the two figures, and the impression of a sequence of events. The 'cosmic' significance of the shields, in terms of medicine power, are integrated with the 'historical' narrative unfolding on the panel. Personal medicine powers and counting coup are closely related and mutually reinforcing cultural con-

cepts. As such, a narrative of a conflict which also depicts iconic Shield motifs provides strong evidence of the spiritual connotations associated with counting coup.

Other iconic Shield Figures may also exhibit a rudimentary degree of narrativity, but this association is not always clear. In particular, the distinctions between iconic and narrative modes of expression are blurred by the Shield Figures in Fig. 4.23. In

**Fig. 4.21.** Narrative combat scene with interacting, incised Shield Figures (detail from DgOv-2:12A).

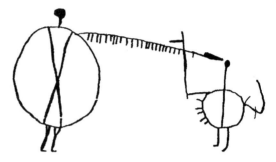

**Fig. 4.22.** Combat scene with incised Shield Figures (DgOw-29:2D). Note iconic shield designs.

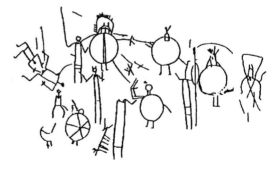

**Fig. 4.23.** Incised Shield Figures at DgOv-2:17A(R) in a complex, integrated narrative scene.

the central portion of this panel, five Shield-bearers are associated with at least six human figures, creating a complex composition. Almost all the figures are frontal and essentially static, with the exception of two figures at the extreme left. One of the Shield Figures exhibits a detailed and elaborate head-dress and two vertical marks on the shield itself. Taken individually, the majority of the motifs exhibit iconic characteristics, but taken as a whole they give the impression of a narrative scene. Two of the Shield Figures in direct opposition seem to be pointing weapons at each other. A third Shield Figure at bottom centre appears to be brandishing an object above a human figure, while other human figures also are arranged as if interacting. Each of these small groupings of interacting figures may represent a separate act within a larger event. The compositional arrangement gives an overall impression of interaction, movement and a sequence of events. Regardless of the specific event depicted, this panel illustrates the integration of motifs exhibiting iconic characteristics into a relatively complex narrative scene.

The preceding examples clearly represent narrative scenes occurring in pre-contact rock-art. The use of the Shield Figure in visual narratives also persisted into the early post-contact period. One of the more significant panels at Writing-On-Stone contains three separate scenes in which a number of 'classic' Shield Figures are shown in obvious interaction with human figures mounted on horses (Fig. 4.24). On the lower left, a warrior mounted on a horse attacks a pedestrian human, who appears to fall backward. The rider appears to be carrying a large shield, while the body of the horse is amorphous in shape and rendered with a cross-hatched design, interpreted by some as representing 'horse armour' (Keyser 1977). On the upper right, another mounted warrior attacks a standing Shield Figure. Although sketchy and indistinct, the horse also appears to be depicted with horse armour, while an indistinct circular shape or shield surrounds the body of the rider. However, the figure being attacked in this group is a classic Shield Figure. Carved with precision and detail, it has the

unusual distinction of revealing an elaborated human body through a 'transparent' shield. Finally, at the lower right, a third mounted warrior, carrying a large decorated shield, attacks yet another Shield Figure. The horse is considerably different in form from the flowing, conventionalised horses described earlier. The pedestrian Shield Figure is also detailed and precise in execution, and the body of the shield-bearer can be seen through the outline of the shield. This Shield Figure is brandishing a large club or axe above the rider, while a large spear is being thrust by the rider towards the shield. The orientation of the Shield Figure at a slight diagonal makes this figure appear to be falling backwards.

All three groupings in Fig. 4.24 show evidence of narrativity. In each case, two figures are clearly interacting as part of an event. The use of bent legs and raised arms, the positioning and the orientation of the figures, and the dynamic profile opposition of the 'actors' all convey a sense of directionality, movement and action. Each group seems to represent a specific event which occurred at a specific place and time: combat between pedestrian and mounted warriors, a form of conflict first encountered during the earliest years of the contact period. The co-occurrence of pedestrian Shield Figures and horses suggests a very early post-contact date for this panel, before body shields were abandoned. The possible presence of horse armour, which was apparently used for a brief period of time after the introduction of horses to the Plains (Ewers 1955), also suggests an early date. Others have pointed to the human figures 'awkwardly mounted on crudely-drawn' horses – as if the image makers were unfamiliar with the subject-matter – as evidence of their early post-contact age (Keyser 1979: 43). Regardless of the competence of their representation, the horses are certainly different in 'style' from most other depictions of horses and riders at Writing-On-Stone, particularly those known to date from late in the post-contact era. Although it may be impossible to confirm, it seems reasonable to suggest that this panel depicts one of the very earliest conflicts between pedestrian and

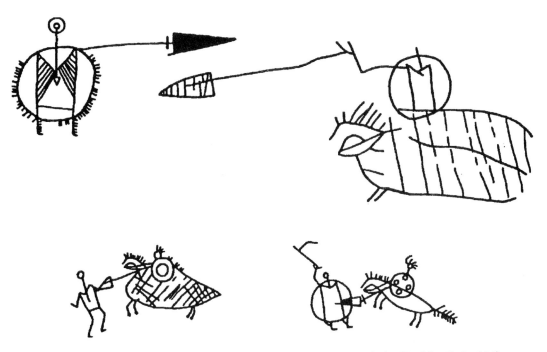

**Fig. 4.24.** Early post-contact narrative combat scenes, including incised Shield Figures and riders (detail from DgOw-32:1).

equestrian Plains groups, an undoubtedly significant historical event. In fact, the events depicted in Fig. 4.24 may represent some of the initial experiences leading to the shift in emphasis from a 'cosmic' to a 'historical' conception of the world, and from an iconic to a narrative mode of expression.

The greater prevalence of narrative compositions in post-contact rock-art at Writing-On-Stone is certainly evident, perhaps reflecting the growing need to recognise unusual personal experiences as historical events. For example, panels on which the Mounted Horse motif is closely associated with unmounted horses may represent a pictorial narrative of horse raiding (Fig. 4.25). The composition of these scenes – a rider 'chasing' one or more horses, with the figures all facing the same way – provides a sense of movement and uniform direction, giving these scenes a narrative character, of action taking place over time and space. What appears to be a brand or symbol on the flank of one of the mounted horses in Fig. 4.25, perhaps identifying the owner of

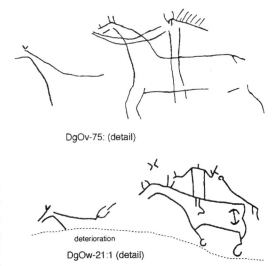

DgOv-75: (detail)

deterioration

DgOw-21:1 (detail)

**Fig. 4.25.** Possible horse raid scenes (not to scale).

57

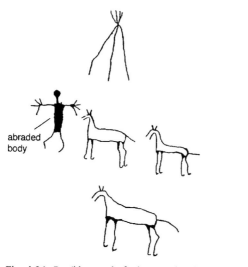

Fig. 4.26. Possible record of a horse raid with incised, juxtaposed horses, human and tipi (DgOv-2:26D).

the horse, adds to the historical specificity of the event and the individuality of the representation.

When depicted in association with pedestrian or mounted humans, groups of horses seem to represent tallies of horses captured in a raid. The three horses juxtaposed with a human figure and a tipi in Fig. 4.26 make a group similar in form and composition to images commonly found on Plains hide-paintings and other painted material culture. The ethnographic documentation for hide-paintings reveals that these scenes depict the number of horses captured on a specific raid by the individual represented. Although this type of imagery is not a pictorial narrative in the formal sense – the individual figures are not interacting, nor do they represent the passage of time (although space is suggested) – it does act as a 'biographical' record of a specific event. The formal characteristics of other rock-art scenes, such as the two rows of horses in Fig. 4.27, suggest they are

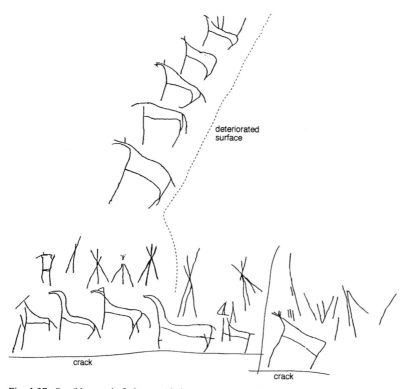

Fig. 4.27. Possible record of a horse raid, showing two rows of horses, associated human and tipis (DgOv-2:26G).

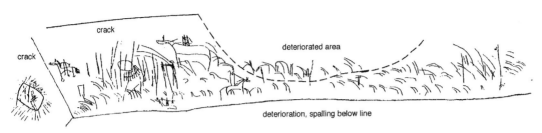

crack

crack

deteriorated area

deterioration, spalling below line

**Fig. 4.28.** Large, complex scene of a horse raid, with horse 'ideograms' and mounted riders (DgOv-60:2).

more profane than sacred in nature: the horses are scratched, lacking details or elaborations; and little care appears to have been taken to control the precision and form of the lines, suggesting a hasty execution. These characteristics suggest the visual documentation of a secular event.

'Horse raid' imagery is developed to its furthest extent on the panel shown in Fig. 4.28. Along with several Mounted Horse motifs, as many as eighty horses are represented as nothing more than a pair of curving and roughly parallel lines, a pictorial convention undoubtedly derived from the characteristic head and neck shape of the Horse motif. Through this schematisation the horse form has become simplified to its bare essentials, and the images have become essentially ideographic in nature. They no longer resemble the natural form of the entity they are meant to represent, and it is only by reference to the less schematised horses on this panel (and elsewhere) that they can be recognised for what they are. This 'ideogram' is a simple and effective shorthand for quickly depicting large numbers of horses. This certainly suggests the intention of this panel was to tally the number of horses owned or captured by one or more individuals. As these images also lack the formal characteristics associated with iconic images, this deliberate record seems to refer more directly to experiential reality than to cosmic themes. The several Mounted Horse motifs among the horse ideograms – which ethnographic accounts indicate represent the individuals involved in capturing the horses – also suggest that this panel represents a specific event accomplished by specific individuals.

Indeed, the placement of these mounted horse images leaves the impression that they are actively taking part in the capture of these horses. More than just a tally, this panel depicts a narrative representation of a horse raid, a recognition of the historical significance of this event.

Although it may represent a specific event rooted in experiential reality, the image in Fig. 4.28 is not necessarily entirely profane or historical in nature. It may exhibit an incipient narrativity, but this panel nevertheless manifests elements of iconic expression, particularly evident in the Mounted Horse motif on the far upper left of the panel. Slightly separated from the other motifs on the panel, this image is depicted with greater technical control and in greater detail, and exhibits the presentational features of an iconic motif. Juxtaposed against the busy composition, this carefully executed and disengaged motif displays the potency of the medicine arising from the combination of the horse and rider which made the capture of so many horses possible. In this image, it seems that both icon and narrative are combined, sacred and profane are integrated, and cosmic and historical conceptions of the world coexist.

Simple narrative scenes involving the Mounted Horse motif engaged in personal combat are also relatively common (Fig. 4.29). In each case, the scene involves a single mounted warrior directly confronting a pedestrian human figure, with both combatants wielding weapons and in obvious conflict. The images are carefully incised and quite detailed, and the combatants are depicted with weapons pointed at

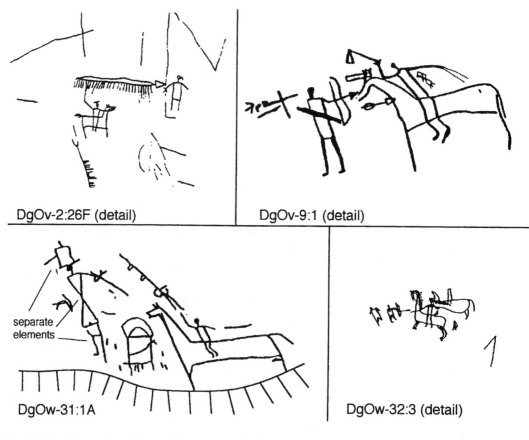

DgOv-2:26F (detail)

DgOv-9:1 (detail)

separate
elements

DgOw-31:1A

DgOw-32:3 (detail)

**Fig. 4.29.** Incised narrative combat scenes between mounted and pedestrian human figures on various panels (not to scale).

each other. These post-contact combat scenes appear to be directly equivalent to those involving pedestrian Shield Figures, but the degree of narrative action in these depictions is more developed, with a greater use of pictorial narrative conventions. Several pictorial devices serve to create a greater sense of place, movement and animation: the imaginary ground lines on which the horses are depicted are at an angle slightly oblique to the horizontal; the riders on at least two of the horses are leaning strongly forward with raised arms brandishing weapons; three of the pedestrian figures are shown leaning slightly backwards; and the bent legs on one horse make it seem as if it is rearing up. These combat scenes apparently represent specific events in which

warriors counted coup on their enemies, while the degree of narrativity evident indicates the emphasis is placed on the physical event itself.

The use of narrative devices in Fig. 4.29 does not necessarily indicate that a complete distinction between sacred and profane acts was intended, or that the meaning of the imagery was entirely divorced from sacred powers. The feathered spear in one of the scenes is greatly exaggerated in proportion to the actors, suggesting that the emphasis was placed on the power of this weapon, or the fact that the weapon itself was used to count coup. Furthermore, a close examination of one of the mounted horses reveals that a small object is depicted behind the back of the rider. Similar objects depicted on a

Blackfoot hide-painting may represent a war medicine bundle (Fig. 4.6), made from the skin of a weasel or otter, worn in battle as a form of spiritual protection (Brownstone 1993: 19). The formal likeness to the hide-painting, and the similar narrative context, suggest that the object in Fig. 4.29 also depicts a medicine bundle. The narrative scene on this panel may represent not only a specific coup, but also the warrior's medicine powers which made this coup possible. The role of medicine power in this narrative depiction is reinforced by the presence of what appears to be red ochre within the incisions and smeared across the scene. Again, the distinctions between profane and sacred activities are blurred, and the historical event and cosmic power are conflated.

A different form of visual narrative seems to be represented in Fig. 4.30, where a hatchet, a spear and at least two guns are clearly associated with a simple human figure. From our knowledge of hide-paintings, this composition clearly represents several coups being counted on an enemy. However, the narrative emphasis in this scene is focused on the *action* relating to the specific coup event, and not on the *actor*. The author of this narrative, the individual counting coup, is outside the picture, and is only implicated by representations of 'floating' weapons. Unlike previous iconic depictions of isolated weapons, these are clearly involved in an event. They are not a static tally of objects, but instead act as 'verbs' to carry the action of the narrative forward through use of a pictorial convention akin to true pictography. The weapons have become 'pictograms' representing the action of the subject upon the object. This is most evident in the gun on the upper right, where a series of dots lead from the muzzle to the head of the victim, not only indicating how the victim was killed or coup was counted, but also serving as a pictorial convention to depict the event in time and space, moving the sequence of events from right to left, from (implied) subject to object.

The presence of this greater degree of narrativity,

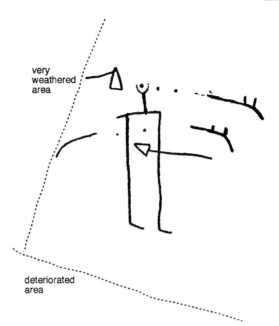

**Fig. 4.30.** Incised 'pictographic' narrative depicting the act of counting coup on an enemy (DgOw-38).

developed to the level of incipient pictography, distinguishes post-contact rock-art from its pre-contact manifestations. Several large post-contact compositions employing pictorial narrative conventions exhibit a degree of complexity and narrativity unlike anything known from the pre-contact era. The panel in Fig. 4.31 depicts a large number of lightly incised images – including a mounted horse, three pedestrian human figures and several free-floating spears and guns – clearly involved in a single conflict or battle. The presence of only one horse and a limited number of guns suggests a relatively early post-contact age. The mounted horse bears a remarkable formal resemblance to those depicted in Fig. 4.24, but the degree of complexity and narrativity of the composition in this case is much greater. While several human figures are depicted in some detail, most of the actors in this scene are represented only by the weapons they used in the battle.

An extensive amount of interaction is depicted in Fig. 4.31, with at least three pairs of depicted or

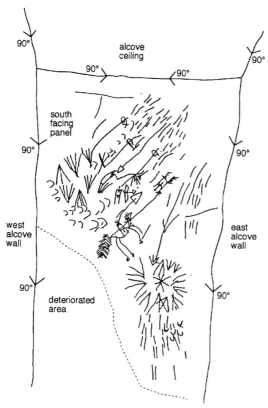

90°
alcove
ceiling
90°
90°
90°
south
facing
panel
90°
90°
west
alcove
wall
east
alcove
wall
90°
deteriorated
area
90°

**Fig. 4.31.** Complex, incised narrative battle scene showing the use of multiple perspective and pictographic conventions (DgOv-43:1A).

implied combatants in direct conflict. The narrativity is also heightened by a number of formal characteristics and pictorial conventions not noted in the previous examples. First of all, the actors and objects are rendered in multiple perspective, including various combinations of frontal, profile and 'bird's-eye' views, all of which help to create the illusion of activity occurring in a three-dimensional space. In particular, an attempt at reproducing perspective is evident in the depiction of a pedestrian human in conflict with the mounted figure. Secondly, the interactions between the human combatants are depicted alongside objects not directly involved with the action, specifically two groups of tipis, which indicates a physical setting. Altogether, this panel exhibits

many of the characteristics associated with pictorial narratives, having the overall effect of causing the viewer to glance from action to action, producing a sense of movement and a sequence of events which recreate the chaotic activity of a battle, while also placing it in the context of recreated space. The pictorial conventions and formal characteristics employed probably stem from an attempt to represent a specific event, involving multiple actors and occurring in a physical setting, from multiple points of view – in other words, the reproduction of a sequence of events based on experiential reality. The overall narrative action of this panel is made even more apparent by the use of additional pictorial conventions, namely the use of a series of dashes and 'C' shapes to depict sequential movement and direction – a convention more clearly illustrated in the following example.

In Fig. 4.32, the narrative scene involves the use of similar pictorial conventions. Some of these have been termed by Keyser (1987) a 'lexicon' of pictorial conventions characteristic of 'picture-writing' or pictography, including those used to convey the passage of time and space (what Keyser (1987: 62) refers to as 'tense') and the consequences of specific actions and events. The panel consists primarily of four horses and riders in conflict with five pedestrian humans, while a horizontal row of three or four standing human figures is depicted near a group of tipis. Two of the riders carry guns, while the uppermost rider holds a feathered spear and a shield. Three of the pedestrian figures carry guns, one wields a sword, and the last holds a bow. Among the 'pictographic' conventions, a series of C-shaped marks, leading from the tipis to a nearby horse, represent tracks which show the direction of movement by the rider, while the series of dashes on the right of the panel probably represent the tracks of the pedestrian figures and their movement from what may be another camp on the far right. The series of dots connecting guns to specific human figures represents the path of bullets, as well as who was killed or injured by whom. The spear wielded by the upper-

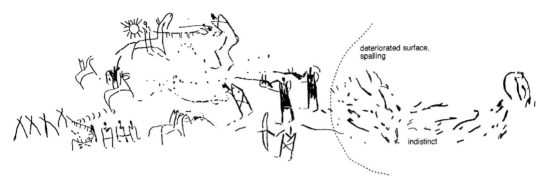

**Fig. 4.32.** Painted narrative battle scene, with pictographic conventions (DgOv-57).

most rider also points directly at a pedestrian human, and may represent a significant coup against an enemy. The probable victim appears to be doubled over, perhaps indicating this individual was killed or wounded.

As in the previous scene, the pictorial conventions used to depict action in Fig. 4.32 represent a sequence of specific events occurring over time and space, creating a fairly complex narrative of a battle involving a number of actors. A single perspective and a suggestion of visual depth are created by the orientation of all figures in relation to an implied ground line, providing an overall organising element to the composition. This, in combination with the narrative characteristics already noted by Keyser (1987), creates the impression of an actual spatial environment. Furthermore, the images on this panel are engraved on a small, smooth face surrounded by large areas of deteriorated surface, which serves to 'frame' and contain the action, thereby helping to distinguish pictorial space from 'real' space. All of these characteristics emphasise the narrative intentions of this panel – the depiction of real events in real time and space – and heighten its underlying 'historicality', its concern with individualised, unique and unprecedented events.

The intensified narrativity found in post-contact imagery culminates in Fig. 4.33. This panel exhibits the largest number of images and the most complex composition of any narrative panel found at Writing-

On-Stone, and perhaps anywhere on the Great Plains. Many of the same pictorial conventions noted for the two previous panels are also employed here. On the far left, a large camp circle of profile tipis, depicted from several angles, surrounds two circles, a rectangle and a single tipi enclosing human figures. The depiction of interior space inside a tipi is unique at Writing-On-Stone. A series of hoof tracks leads away from the tipis, suggesting the movement of an individual from the camp. To the right of the camp circle, a row of 'warriors' defending the camp are represented by guns. That these guns stand for armed humans is clear from the fact that the uppermost two are held by human figures. Bullets issue from all the guns, producing a sense of movement towards the middle of the panel.

In the centre of the panel, two individual human figures, one firing a gun and another wielding a hatchet, are shown in direct conflict. The figure on the left leans towards the second figure, slightly bent at the waist. The row of bullets passes through the body of the leaning figure, perhaps indicating that this human was wounded or killed by the bullets. The central position of these figures on the panel, their direct involvement with each other, and the greater detail with which they are depicted, all suggest that their conflict was intended as the central event on this entire panel. To the right of these combatants a number of armed human figures hold guns. Bullets also emerge from these weapons, again

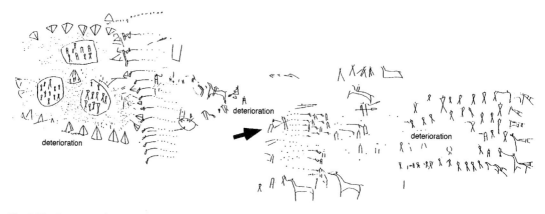

**Fig. 4.33.** Large, complex, incised battle scene (DgOv-81:1). Central conflict indicated by arrow.

directing our attention towards the centre of the panel. Finally, on the far right, a large group of generally unarmed human figures is depicted, several leading horses. They do not appear to be directly involved in the battle, but their positions suggest movement towards the central area.

This panel is clearly a narrative composition in which a number of pictorial conventions are used to indicate time and space. The use of the gun to represent a warrior is also conventionalised and could be considered a pictogram. Many of the conventions also serve to move the action in a certain direction, and present sequences of events leading towards the centre, where the decisive, central conflict appears to be taking place. The vast extent and complexity of this panel, the inclusion of references to a setting (such as the camp circle), the incorporation of motifs not directly involved in the 'action', the conventions used to create direction and movement, and the detailed specifics of the conflict all suggest that this panel represents a specific event. The lack of characteristically iconic images gives a sense of 'actuality' to this scene, and the considerable detail implies that it functions as a historical record of a real battle.

All three of the preceding examples reveal narrativity and historicity. There seems to be little doubt that the compositions were intended to represent events occurring in real time and space. Furthermore,

the degree of complexity found on these panels indicates a heightened awareness of, and concern with, unique and specific historical events. Unlike the iconic images of the pre-contact era, there are few references to cosmic themes on these panels. Nevertheless, the historical and cosmic views of the world are not mutually exclusive in Plains culture, and historical awareness was framed within an overarching cosmic conception of the world. In this conceptual view, even the most unique and unprecedented of events may eventually become 'mythologised' over time, as Eliade (1959: 38) suggests.

This mythologisation of profane events, transforming them into the sacred, is clearly illustrated by an oral tradition told by Bird Rattler (Dempsey 1973: 34–42). Bird Rattler describes a major battle in which a large band of Piikáni were attacked by a combined party of Atsina, Cree and Crow warriors. Known as the 'Retreat up the Hill' battle, and believed to have taken place in 1866, this conflict occurred along the Milk River near Writing-On-Stone (Dempsey 1973: 34; Ewers 1955: 195). For our purposes, the most significant aspect of this story is the role of the representations at Writing-On-Stone. According to Bird Rattler, certain petroglyphs appeared overnight warning the Piikáni of the impending attack, and this message from the spirit world allowed them to prepare for the battle.

The battle fought that day was a disastrous defeat

for the attacking party, with over 300 participants killed, and one of the most decisive Blackfoot victories. Dempsey (1973: 42) speculates that the large battle scene represented in Fig. 4.33 may, in fact, be the same panel alluded to in Bird Rattler's account of the battle. As he puts it, 'it is possible that the pictographs were placed there *after* the event, and over the years, in telling and re-telling the tale, they became a part of the story itself . . . By the time Bird Rattler told his story in 1924, the whole supernatural aura of the pictographs and their predictive powers had blended into the factual tale.' Whether this, or any other, rock-art panel actually depicts the battle of 1866 is uncertain, of course. What is significant is the possibility that battle scenes originally recorded an actual historical event, and that the depictions of these events, and the circumstances surrounding them, soon became mythologised. The historical and secular were thereby transformed into the cosmic and sacred.

## Narrativity and history

Iconic and narrative modes of pictorial expression clearly coexist at Writing-On-Stone in both pre- and post-contact contexts. If we accept the contention that the iconic and narrative modes of expression roughly correspond to cosmic and historical conceptions of time and space – as borne out by iconographical analysis and ethnographic analogy – then a continuity in the relationship of rock-art to cultural perceptions existed throughout the contact transition. At the same time, however, a shift in pictorial expression occurred during the contact transition, leading to a much greater development of the narrative mode during the post-contact period. Although the roots of narrativity are certainly present during the pre-contact, the degree of narrativity in the post-contact far exceeds anything seen from the earlier period. The pictorial conventions associated with pre-contact expressions of narrativity are relatively rudimentary, and no pre-contact period panels approach the narrative complexity exhibited by several post-contact panels.

Any explanation for the shift in narrative emphasis, and the concomitant variation in form and function, must take into account the overall cultural continuity at Writing-On-Stone. A plausible explanation for the increase in narrativity comes from the significant internal cultural changes originating from the effects of indirect and direct contact with European culture. Widespread and far-reaching cultural impacts arising from contact are well documented for the Northwestern Plains and adjacent regions, with the introduction of new diseases, the fur trade, and the arrival of guns and horses among the factors having the most significant material and social implications during the early contact era (Blick 1988; Lewis 1942; Ramenofsky 1987; Rogers 1993; Secoy 1953).

Of these, the single factor with perhaps the greatest impact on Plains groups was the introduction of the horse (Ewers 1955; Mishkin 1940; Penney 1992). Others have already noted that increased narrativity in post-contact rock-art at Writing-On-Stone may be linked to cultural change arising from the introduction of the horse (see Keyser 1979), but the specific cultural mechanism linking this change to a shift in pictorial expression has not been explored. The contention here is that cultural change arising from the arrival of the horse led to a shift in the relative importance of cosmic and historical conceptions of the world, with a subsequent increased emphasis on the importance of narrativity in Plains visual traditions (Klassen 1995).

Ewers (1955: 299–302) has carefully documented the significant effect the horse had on many aspects of Blackfoot culture, including its tangible influence on hunting, transportation and travel, warfare, trade, recreation, social organisation, religion and 'cultural innovation', as well as intangible effects on the 'psychology' of the Blackfoot. Many traits of the ensuing Blackfoot 'Horse Complex' were held in common by groups across the Plains (Ewers 1955: 323; see Mishkin 1940). The following description, largely summarised from Ewers (1955: 299–320) and Lewis (1942: 34–59), refers specifically to the effect of horses on Blackfoot culture, but in broad terms the Blackfoot experience can also be extended to other Plains groups.

Despite some initial misapprehension (see Glover 1962: 242), horses were quickly recognised by Plains Native groups for their enormous practical and utilitarian value. They permitted more efficient buffalo hunting, particularly in times of scarcity, by small groups and individuals, eliminating the necessity for the communal buffalo hunt. The bands could follow the herds more easily, and the complex social organisation of the communal hunt was no longer required. Horses also made transportation and camp movements much easier, as they carried heavier loads, travelled further and faster, and required less work to feed than the dogs previously used for this purpose. With the greater ease of travel also came increased inter-cultural contact and conflict. Greater access to horses also provided 'military' advantages, thereby altering the regional 'balance of powers' (Secoy 1953: 36–7, 58). The use of the horse in warfare led to an increasing emphasis on offensive mobility, and, consequently, smaller raiding parties became more common and more effective (Secoy 1953: 62). While this change in tactics brought combatants into closer contact during conflicts, increasing the potential for casualties, it also offered improved opportunities for capturing weapons and counting coup, thus increasing the emphasis placed on the system of graded war honours, scaled according to the degree of danger (Keyser 1979).

Horses undoubtedly improved the 'standard of living' among Plains groups. The more horses owned by members of a family, the greater the economic advantages they enjoyed. The substantial benefits accruing from their possession led to horse ownership becoming viewed as a form of wealth. Horses also became a major medium of exchange, used to purchase almost every type of material culture, with the best hunting and war horses most highly valued. They were also important as part of dowries, payments for membership in age-graded societies, and for the reciprocity and redistribution of wealth. Furthermore, ceremonial bundles and medicine powers could be purchased with horses, leading to the equation of wealth and religious stature. The buying and selling of horses became involved in many aspects of ritual and ceremonial life.

The ownership of horses became a major index of status, where wealth and social position depended upon the size of the herd owned by families or, more commonly, by individual men. Those men rich in horses enjoyed certain privileges, including the possession of elaborate clothes and trade objects, the ability to purchase many wives, membership in societies, influence in political and religious matters, and the ownership of sacred bundles and medicine powers. At the same time, status was solidified by the generous redistribution of horses as gifts to elders and the poor, and also by the fairness displayed in trades involving these animals. The ownership of the best hunting and war horses also permitted the greater accumulation of war honours through raiding, while wealth and status also contributed to opportunities to lead or participate in raids.

Overall, the accumulation of property and its relationship to status led to the increasing social stratification of Plains culture, and the disparities between the rich and poor grew in extent. According to Ewers (1955: 314–15), the poor were now worse off than they were in the time before horses, as they were now denied many privileges which only came through wealth in horses. In the past, the need for co-operative hunting, the limited opportunities for accumulating property, and the lack of social stratification based on wealth all tended to encourage egalitarianism. When social status was recognised in the pre-contact era, it was generally on the basis of an individual's medicine powers or outstanding war honours.

Yet, status and wealth were not entirely unattainable for the poor in the equestrian period, as horses — and honour — could be obtained through courage and ambition on horse raids. Because of their practical and social value, the supply of horses never met demand during the pre-treaty period (Ewers 1955:

312). In an attempt to fill this vacuum, the horse raid developed as the major source of inter-cultural conflict on the Plains (Ewers 1955: 312; Lewis 1942: 57; Secoy 1953: 62). The motive for the horse raid was primarily economic in nature, stemming from the desire to obtain the horses necessary for hunting, transportation and overall economic security. According to Ewers (1955: 311), 'Need, not greed or glory, was the major stimulus impelling most young men to engage in the hazardous . . . enterprise of the horse raid.' The war honours obtained by capturing horses provided a secondary motive, as this feat was a low-grade coup (Ewers 1955: 311). Nevertheless, the importance of horse raids in the system of graded war honours should not be underestimated. The feats of bravery displayed during particularly risky horse raids often counted as coups much greater in significance than those arising from capturing the horses themselves. Furthermore, the ownership of herds far larger than that needed for subsistence alone was an important factor in determining status and influence, thus providing an additional motivation for obtaining horses through raiding.

The importance of the horse, in both practical and social terms, led to the continual need for raiding. Small raiding parties were most effective, and organising and leading raids was an individual's prerogative. For young men, participating in or leading a horse raid was an important route to establishing economic and social security and improving status. As its frequency and intensity increased, horse raiding brought about significant social consequences. The role of the war chief and the authority of the elders over young warriors declined, and the rise of small-scale raiding parties led by interim war leaders fostered a tendency towards individualism in warfare (Secoy 1953: 62). The emphasis on individualism in warfare, coupled with the rising importance of social stratification, may have also placed a heightened emphasis on the system of graded war honours. A subsequent decline in the influence of religious leaders and elders took place, and the status derived from medicine powers was diminished in relative

importance. The status system shifted away from spiritual values and cosmic themes, and now emphasised personal valour, manifested through counting coup and material wealth. Overall, the influence of the horse on patterns of hunting, warfare and status led to a significant 'decentralisation in political organisation and a fluorescence of individualism', wherein group interests gave way to individual interests (Lewis 1942: 59). This emphasis on the personal and the individual reflects an increasing preoccupation with the unique and unprecedented – or in other words, with historicality itself.

In terms of pictorial representations, historicality and narrativity go hand in hand. As Hayden White (1980: 17) has speculated, 'the growth and development of historical consciousness . . . is attended by concomitant growth and development of a narrative capability'. An increasing emphasis on narrativity may reflect a greater preoccupation with a 'historical' conception of time and space. The idea that the degree of narrativity may be linked to 'historical consciousness' can be further explored in reference to the rock-art. In iconic representations, the imagery largely represented timeless, cosmic themes, ranging from supernatural visions to the medicine powers invested in objects and people. The images were not directly related to experiential reality, but were depictions of 'cosmic archetypes'. Yet, the very first appearance of the horse on the Plains would be difficult to place immediately within the existing cosmological order. The horses in Fig. 4.24 are perhaps some of the earliest depictions of this animal at Writing-On-Stone. Here we have the depiction of an entirely new category of event without an archetypal antecedent.

An individual's first encounter with horses would have been a unique, astonishing and totally unprecedented experience, which would not immediately fit within the explanatory cultural framework available. The uniqueness of this event, and its lack of cosmic or mythical precedence, may have on a certain level encouraged the recognition of its 'historicality'. The pictorial representation of a conflict between pedestrian warriors and mounted riders would only be possible after direct (or indirect) experience with such an event, and this experience would be utterly new and unreferenced. The earliest experience with the horse would have encouraged a historical conception of space and time, wherein unprecedented events were acknowledged. It would be difficult to accommodate the significance of this encounter using iconic pictorial conventions, and to record the unprecedented character of the event required the adoption of a narrative mode of expression.

While the horse and its sudden appearance would soon become mythologised and incorporated into the cosmological order, the cultural reverberations from the introduction of this animal seem correlated with a heightened awareness of history and the recognition of dynamic change. The rise of individualism, the importance of personal valour, and the significance placed on particular deeds, leading to the need for the promotion of personal accomplishments through pictorial records of specific events, are a reflection of an increasing historical conception of the world, a recognition of specific, unprecedented events which are not referred back to a cosmic antecedent but arise out of new experiences and individual experiential reality. The glorification of individual acts, self-promotion through story-telling, and pictorial 'war records' all require narrative structures. In the end, this need to record the historical and the specific led to an increasing narrativity in the pictorial conventions at Writing-On-Stone, culminating in complex battle scenes and incipient pictography.

Yet the growing historical conceptions associated with post-contact Plains culture, and the pictorial narrativity derived from them, were not entirely divorced from cosmic themes. Horses, wealth, status and war honours are all wrapped up in conceptions of medicine powers derived from the spirit world. The strength of an individual's medicine is increased with each coup, while wealth in horses also gives the ability to purchase medicine bundles and transfer sacred powers. While the acquisition of war honours

and success in horse raids are both products of an individual's skill and bravery, these qualities are derived from the powers of a guardian spirit. All in all, narrative renderings of 'historic' deeds are intimately associated with the 'cosmic' powers which made those deeds possible: 'Because the warrior depended on spiritual power and protection, any account of military exploits was by extension also a celebration of the validity and efficacy of those powers' (Maurer 1992: 39).

Cosmic and historical conceptions of the world structured and controlled pictorial expression within Plains cultures, leading to the presence of both iconic and narrative imagery in rock-art. While at any one point in time the traditions of a culture may emphasise one mode over another, iconic and narrative expressions are not mutually exclusive, and any image may share elements of both modes. Thus, while a shift towards increased historicality and narrativity in the rock-art of Writing-On-Stone occurred during the equestrian period, underlying continuities allied even the most narrative of scenes to an overarching cosmic conception of the world.

### Rock-art in a sacred landscape

The presence of two modes of expression in Plains cultures explains the coexistence of what appears to be two distinct rock-art traditions at Writing-On-Stone. Formal differences between iconic and narrative modes of expression provide a plausible explanation for most variation in subject-matter and composition in the rock-art. Indeed, the close relationship between iconic and narrative images at Writing-On-Stone suggests that the Ceremonial and Biographic Traditions are simply different manifestations of a single tradition of pictorial expression.

The concept of iconic and narrative imagery also provides a means of explaining variation over time which does not rely on temporal discontinuities in ethnicity. The relationship between historicity and narrativity provides a mechanism for explaining the shift in relative importance of the narrative mode of expression in the post-contact rock-art of Writing-

On-Stone. Variation over time is seen as a result of internal cultural change, as opposed to external cultural displacements or migrations. This does not necessarily imply that only a single ethnic group was responsible for all of the rock-art at Writing-On-Stone. Indeed, variation *within* the iconic and narrative traditions may reflect the differences between ethnic 'styles'. Rather, the presence of dual modes of expression was probably a pan-Plains tradition shared among multiple ethnic groups.

While the rise in narrativity during the post-contact period represents a significant shift in cultural perceptions, the continuity in iconic imagery suggests an underlying stability in cosmic connotations for the rock-art. Both the continuity in iconic depictions and the long-term use of Writing-On-Stone as a rock-art locality can be best explained from the perspective of sacred landscape. Within traditional Plains cultures, the entire landscape is charged with medicine powers, but this spiritual energy is also concentrated in certain sacred areas, generally unusual or outstanding landscape features (Paper 1990: 44; Taçon 1990: 13; see also Vastokas and Vastokas 1973: 47–8). Among the Blackfoot, impressive natural features such as unusually shaped 'medicine rocks', large glacial erratics, and isolated mountain peaks are all considered invested with medicine power (Dormaar and Reeves 1993: 162–6; Grinnell 1892: 262–3; Klassen 1995: 193–7; Reeves 1992; Vest 1990: 154–63), and, according to oral traditions, many of these sacred features had their genesis in supernatural circumstances. The connection between people and a sacred landscape must be reaffirmed through rituals and ceremonies, including the production of rock-art; through these activities individuals can 'tap into' the power of sacred places (Taçon 1990: 29).

Unusual landscape features certainly occur in great abundance at Writing-On-Stone. The Milk River valley, cut deep into the surrounding prairies, forms a wide, cliff-lined passage which frames an impressive view to the east (Fig. 4.3). The valley also intersects several narrow, winding canyons which lead to the near-by Sweetgrass Hills. The high cliffs offer spectacular views of the valley and the surrounding landscape, while numerous caves, overhangs, alcoves and ledges provide an abundance of suitable vision-quest locations. Above the cliffs, extensive areas have eroded into a fantastic array of strange sandstone hoodoos which share the physical characteristics and spiritual connotations of medicine rocks. The effects of light and sound among the hoodoos, cliffs and canyons create striking phenomenological experiences. All these features, both physical and phenomenological, lend an otherworldly air to Writing-On-Stone.

Most important, the landscape at Writing-On-Stone is dominated by the nearby presence of the Sweetgrass Hills (Fig. 4.2), one of the most powerful locations within the sacred geography of the Blackfoot (Dormaar and Reeves 1993; Grinnell 1892: 262; Reeves 1992; Schwab 1994). The Sweetgrass Hills have always been an important vision-quest location for the Blackfoot, and an enormous area of the surrounding Plains, including many other landscape features considered sacred by the Blackfoot, are visible from the summits of these hills. The Sweetgrass Hills undoubtedly influenced the ritual use of Writing-On-Stone, intensifying the medicine powers found within the valley itself.

It seems clear that the numinous landscape of Writing-On-Stone played an important role in the use of the site as a ceremonial area, a vision-quest locality, and a place to record human experience visually (both visionary and historical). It comes as no surprise, then, that more rock-art is found at Writing-On-Stone than anywhere else on the Great Plains. The rock-art is found here primarily because of a sacred landscape supercharged with spiritual forces – it graphically represents the dynamic relationship between a people, a sacred landscape and the spirit world. In the end, it is the enduring role of Writing-On-Stone as a sacred place which gives the rock-art such a high degree of underlying continuity in form, function and spiritual meaning.

## Acknowledgements

This chapter is derived from my Master of Arts thesis, which Joan Vastokas supervised, and Paul Taçon and Ted Brasser examined. Jim Keyser provided many helpful comments on the ideas presented in it. Numerous individuals assisted with the fieldwork for this research, and all deserve thanks. Fieldwork was supported by the Alberta Historical Resources Foundation, the Provincial Museum of Alberta, Alberta Parks Service, and Trent University. Figures are reproduced from original tracings by J. D. Keyser and M. A. Klassen.

## REFERENCES

Barbeau, M. 1960. *Indian days on the western prairies.* Ottawa, National Museum of Canada. Bulletin 163, Anthropological Series 43.

Benedict, R. F. 1922. The vision in Plains culture, *American Anthropologist* 24: 1–23.

Blick, J. P. 1988. Genocidal warfare in tribal societies as a result of European-induced culture conflict, *Man* (NS) 23: 654–70.

Boyle, 1904. Picture-writing, *Annual Archaeological Report 1904.* Appendix to the report of the Minster of Education, Ontario, pp. 54–7. Toronto, Warwick Bros. and Rulter.

Brasser, Ted J. 1978. Tipi paintings, Blackfoot style, in D. W. Zimmerly (ed.), *Contextual studies of material culture,* pp. 7–18. Ottawa, National Museum of Canada. Canadian Ethnology Service, Paper 43.

Brownstone, A. 1993. *War paint: Blackfoot and Sarcee painted buffalo robes in the Royal Ontario Museum.* Toronto, Royal Ontario Museum.

Dempsey, H. A. 1973. A history of Writing-On-Stone. Unpublished manuscript on file with Alberta Recreation and Parks and the Provincial Museum of Alberta.

Dormaar, J. F. and B. O. K. Reeves. 1993. Vision quest sites in southern Alberta and northern Montana, in B. O. K. Reeves and M. A. Kennedy (eds.), *Kunaitupii: coming together on Native sacred sites,* pp. 162–78. Calgary, Archaeological Society of Alberta.

Doty, J. 1966. A visit to the Blackfoot camps, *Alberta Historical Review* (summer): 17–26.

Dunn, D. 1968. *American Indian painting of the Southwest and Plains area.* Albuquerque (NM), University of New Mexico.

Eliade, M. 1959. *Cosmos and history: the myth of the eternal return.* Princeton (NJ), Princeton University Press.

Ewers, J. C. 1939. *Plains Indian painting: a description of an Aboriginal American art.* Palo Alto (CA), Stanford University Press.

1955. *The horse in Blackfoot culture.* Washington (DC), Bureau of American Ethnology. Bulletin 159.

1976. *Blackfeet Indian tipis: design and legend.* Bozeman (MT), Museum of the Rockies.

1982. The awesome bear in Plains Indian art, *American Indian Art Magazine* 7(3): 36–45.

1983. A century and a half of Blackfeet picture-writing, *American Indian Art Magazine* 8(3): 52–61.

Francis, J. E., L. L. Loendorf and R. I. Dorn. 1993. AMS radiocarbon and cation-ratio dating of rock art in the Bighorn Basin of Wyoming and Montana, *American Antiquity* 58(4): 711–37.

Glover, R. (ed.). 1962. *David Thompson's narrative 1784–1812.* Toronto, Champlain Society. Publication 40.

Greiser, S. T. 1995. Late prehistoric cultures on the Montana plains, in K. H. Schlesier (ed.), *Plains Indians, AD 500–1500: the archaeological past of historic groups,* pp. 34–55. Norman (OK), University of Oklahoma Press.

Grinnell, G. B. 1892. *Blackfoot lodge tales: the story of a prairie people.* New York (NY), Charles Scribner and Sons.

1901. The lodges of the Blackfoot, *American Anthropologist* 3: 650–68.

Hall, H. U. 1926a. A buffalo robe biography, *University of Pennsylvania Museum Journal* 17(1): 5–37.

1926b. Some shields of the Plains and Southwest, *University of Pennsylvania Museum Journal* 17(1): 37–61.

Hamell, G. R. 1987. Strawberries, floating islands, and rabbit captains: mythical realities and European contact in the northeast during the sixteenth and seventeenth centuries, *Journal of Canadian Studies* 21(4): 72–94.

Harper, J. R. 1970. *Paul Kane 1810–1871: catalogue for an exhibition organized for the Amon Carter Museum of Western Art, Fort Worth, Texas and the National Gallery of Canada, Ottawa, 1971–72.* Ottawa, National Gallery of Canada.

Hassrick, R. B. 1988. *The George Catlin book of American Indians.* New York (NY), Promontory Press.

Horse Capture, G. 1993. Des musées aux Indiens: la mémoire recomposée, in Anne Vitart (ed.), *Parures d'histoire: peaux de bisons peintes des Indiens d'Amérique du Nord*, pp. 61–91. Paris, Musée de l'Homme.

Keyser, J. D. 1977. Writing-On-Stone: rock art on the Northwestern Plains, *Canadian Journal of Archaeology* 1: 15–80.

1979. The Plains Indian war complex and the rock art of Writing-On-Stone, Alberta, Canada, *Journal of Field Archaeology* 6(1): 41–8.

1984. The North Cave Hills, in *Rock art of western South Dakota*, pp. 1–51. Sioux Falls (SD), South Dakota Archaeological Society. Special Publication No. 9.

1987. A lexicon for historic Plains Indian rock art: increasing interpretive potential, *Plains Anthropologist* 32(115): 43–71.

1990. Rock art of North American Northwestern Plains: an overview, *Bollettino del Centro Camuno di Studi Preistorici* 25–6: 99–122.

1991. A thing to tie on the halter: an addition to the Plains rock art lexicon, *Plains Anthropologist* 36: 261–7.

Keyser, J. D. and T. J. Brady. 1993. A war shirt from the Schoch Collection: documenting individual artistic expression, *Plains Anthropologist* 38: 5–20.

Keyser, J. D. and M. A. Klassen. In prep. *Indian rock art of the Northwestern Plains*. Seattle (WA), University of Washington Press.

Klassen, M. A. 1994. Spirit images and medicine rocks: results of the 1992–1993 Alberta rock art survey. Paper presented at the 1994 Canadian Archaeological Association meeting, Edmonton, Alberta, 1994.

1995. Icons of power, narratives of glory: ethnic continuity and cultural change in the contact period rock art of Writing-On-Stone. Unpublished MA thesis, Trent University, Peterborough, Ontario.

Lewis, O. 1942. *The effects of white contact upon Blackfoot culture, with special reference to the role of the fur trade*. Washington (DC), American Ethnological Society. Monograph 6.

Loendorf, L. L. 1990. A dated rock art panel of shield-bearing warriors in south central Montana, *Plains Anthropologist* 35(127): 45–54.

McClintock, W. 1936. Painted tipis and picture-writing of the Blackfoot Indians, *Masterkey* 10: 120–33, 168–79.

1968. *The Old North Trail: life, legends and religion of the Blackfeet Indians*. Lincoln (NE), University of Nebraska

Press.

Maclean, J. 1896. Picture-writing of the Blackfeet, *Transactions of the Canadian Institute* 5 (Part 1, No. 9): 114–20.

Maurer, E. M. 1992. Visions of the people, in E. M. Maurer (ed.), *Visions of the people: a pictorial history of the Plains Indian life*, pp. 15–45. Minneapolis (MN), Minneapolis Institute of the Arts.

Miller, C. L. and G. R. Hamell. 1986. A new perspective on Indian–White contact: cultural symbols and colonial trade, *Journal of American History* 73: 311–28.

Mishkin, B. 1940. *Rank and warfare among the Plains Indians*. Seattle (WA), University of Washington Press. American Ethnological Society Monograph 3.

Nagy, I. J. 1994. A typology of Cheyenne shield designs, *Plains Anthropologist* 39(147): 5–36.

Panofsky, E. 1955. Iconography and iconology: an introduction to the study of Renaissance art, in *Meaning in the visual arts: papers in and on art history*, pp. 26–54. Chicago (IL), University of Chicago Press.

Paper, J. 1990. Landscape and sacred space in Native North American religion, in J. Vastokas (ed.), *Perspectives of Canadian landscape: Native traditions*, pp. 44–54. North York (Ont.), York University, Robarts Centre for Canadian Studies.

Penney, D. W. 1992. The horse as symbol: equine representations in Plains pictographic art, in E. M. Maurer (ed.), *Visions of the people: a pictorial history of the Plains Indian life*, pp. 69–79. Minneapolis (MN), Minneapolis Institute of the Arts.

Raczka, P. M. 1992. Sacred robes of the Blackfoot and other Northern Plains tribes, *American Indian Art Magazine* (summer): 67–73.

Rajnovich, G. 1994. *Reading rock art: interpreting the Indian rock paintings of the Canadian Shield*. Toronto, Natural Heritage/Natural History.

Ramenofsky, A. R. 1987. *Vectors of death: the archaeology of European contact*. Albuquerque (NM), University of New Mexico Press.

Reeves, B. O. K. 1992. Vanished visions? Traditional Native American sacred sites in the twenty-first century. Paper presented at the 25th Chacmool Conference, University of Calgary.

Rodee, H. D. 1965. The stylistic development of Plains Indian painting and its relationship to ledger drawings, *Plains Anthropologist* 10: 218–32.

Rogers, J. D. 1993. The social and material implications of culture contact on the Northern Plains, in J. D.

Rogers and S. M. Wilson (eds.), *Ethnohistory and archaeology: approaches to postcontact change in the Americas*, pp. 73–88. New York, Plenum Press.

Schlesier, K. H. 1995. Commentary: a history of ethnic groups in the Great Plains, AD 500–1500, in K. H. Schlesier (ed.), *Plains Indians, AD 500–1500: the archaeological past of historic groups*, pp. 308–81. Norman (OK), University of Oklahoma Press.

Schultz, J. W. 1962. *Blackfeet and buffalo: memories of life among the Indians*. Norman (OK), University of Oklahoma Press.

Schuster, H. H. 1987. Tribal identification of Wyoming rock art: some problematic considerations, *Archaeology in Montana* 28(2): 25–43.

Schwab, D. 1994. The Sweetgrass Hills: cultural landmarks on the Northwestern Plains, *Archaeology in Montana* 35(2): 59–88.

Secoy, F. R. 1953. *Changing military patterns on the Great Plains (seventeenth century through early nineteenth century)*. Seattle (WA), University of Washington Press.

Szabo, J. M. 1994. Shields and lodges, warriors and chiefs: Kiowa drawings as historical records, *Ethnohistory* 41: 1–24.

Taçon, P. S. C. 1990. The power of place: cross-cultural responses to natural and cultural landscapes of stone and earth, in J. Vastokas (ed.), *Perspectives of Canadian landscape: Native traditions*, pp. 11–43. North York (Ont.), York University, Robarts Centre for Canadian Studies.

Taçon, P. S. C. and C. Chippindale. 1994. Australia's ancient warriors: changing depictions of fighting in the rock art of Arnhem Land, NT, *Cambridge Archaeological Journal* 4(2): 211–48.

Thomas, D. and K. Ronnefeldt. 1976. *People of the First Man: life among the Plains Indians in their final days of glory*. New York, E. P. Dutton.

Vastokas, J. M. 1985. Interpreting birch bark scrolls, in *Proceedings of the Fifteenth Algonquian Studies Conference*, pp. 425–44. Ottawa, Carleton University.

1990. Landscape as experience and symbol in Native Canadian culture, in J. Vastokas (ed.), *Perspectives of Canadian landscape: Native traditions*, pp. 55–82. North York (Ont.), York University, Robarts Centre for Canadian Studies.

Vastokas, J. M. and R. K. Vastokas. 1973. *Sacred art of the Algonkians: a study of the Peterborough petroglyphs*. Peterborough, Mansard Press.

Vatter, E. 1927. Historienmalerei und Heraldische Bilderschrift der Nordamerikanischen Präriestämme: Beiträge zu einer Ethnographischen und Stilistischen Analyse, *IPEK: Annual Review of Prehistoric and Ethnographic Art* 4: 46–81.

Vest, J. H. C. 1990. The Badger-Two Medicine Wildlands: sacred geography of the Blackfeet, *Western Wildlands* 15(3): 30–3, 36.

Vickers, J. R. 1995. Cultures of the Northwestern Plains: from the Boreal Forest edge to Milk River, in K. H. Schlesier (ed.), *Plains Indians, AD 500–1500: the archaeological past of historic groups*, pp. 3–33. Norman (OK), University of Oklahoma Press.

Walton, A. T., J. C. Ewers and R. B. Hassrick. 1985. *After the buffalo were gone: the Louis Warren Hill, Sr, Collection of Indian Art*. St Paul (MN), Northwest Area Foundation.

White, H. 1980. The value of narrativity in the representation of reality, *Critical Inquiry* 2(1): 5–27.

Willoughby, C. C. 1905. A few ethnological specimens collected by Lewis and Clark, *American Anthropologist* 7: 633–41.

Wissler, C. 1912. Ceremonial bundles of the Blackfoot Indians, *Anthropological Papers of the American Museum of Natural History* 7, Part 2.

Thomas A. Dowson

# 5. Rain in Bushman belief, politics and history: the rock-art of rain-making in the south-eastern mountains, southern Africa

The last quarter-century of studying southern African rock-art has been a famous success – although the art is still uncertainly dated. Formal methods have identified patterns in the art, of what was represented and what was overlooked. Informed methods, drawing on ethnohistorical records of Bushman knowledge, have found insight behind those patterns in a frame of visionary knowledge. This chapter – very much in that research spirit – extends beyond Bushman knowledge to a more widely informed perspective on the creatures associated with rain and with rain-making, and draws equally on formal traits of the rain-animals to place them within a socio-political context.

## Southern African rock-art: approaches and expectations

The study of southern African rock-art has been largely dominated by the rock-paintings of the mountainous landscape in and around Lesotho. The paintings in this area, the south-eastern mountains (Fig. 5.1), are very detailed and numerous, and more often make up large complex panels. It is not unusual to find five layers of paintings, and depictions with minute, pinhead-sized details. These complex panels are found in open rock-shelters of Triassic sandstones. Large sandstone boulders with slight overhangs have also been used, repeatedly or on single occasions. The subject-matter, incredibly rich and diverse, has been discussed in numerous papers and books. In this chapter I discuss paintings that relate specifically to beliefs about rain-making.

One difficult issue in researching the rock-art of the south-eastern mountains is its dating. There are no reliable dates; the subject-matter suggests that much of the art has been produced in the last thousand or so years. Many researchers believe that the

Fig. 5.1. The south-eastern mountains, showing places mentioned in the text. Numbers refer to illustrations to this essay.

lack of a 'firm chronological framework' hinders our ability to use rock-art in a meaningful way. But as Yates (1993: 70) suggests, 'Archaeological data is not limited, only the minds that interpret it.' Further, 'the way forward for rock-art analysis is *not* to address issues of chronology but to theorise the art – a theorisation which must extend way beyond the stale discussions of terminology – and study its appearance and meaning in local and regional terms' (Yates 1993: 35). This is what I have attempted for the south-eastern mountains (Dowson 1994). Studies like these go unnoticed by the chronocentrics because they effectively challenge their chronocentrism.

But how do we 'theorise the art'? Simply put, by employing a variety of informed and formal methods. Over the last decade or so rock-art studies have been developing rather rigorous methodologies to deal with a variety of limitations. That these studies are ignored or misconstrued by more mainstream archaeologists is a reflection of the inflexibility of archaeology that continues to hamper our understanding of the past.

In this chapter I utilise the wealth of ethnographic and historical records that we have for the various communities of the south-eastern mountains to further our understanding of the complex interactions between the various political/ethnic communities. But this 'informed method' is made more meaningful by examining the paintings of rain-making with formal methods, that is, examining distinctive features in the paintings of which we have no direct ethnographic record. Taken together, these 'informed' and 'formal' approaches show the way in which beliefs and images are transformed into resources for political power.

I begin by extending current discussions of Bushman people's rain-making rituals and art to a broader context across the southern African subcontinent, showing how these beliefs were implicated in rock-paintings of rain-making in the south-eastern mountains. I then discuss the social and political issues associated with these paintings. As I have outlined elsewhere (Dowson 1994, 1995), these images are documents in their own right which through informed and formal methods can be used to construct a history for the south-eastern mountains that goes beyond existing, rather simplistic constructions.

## Antiquity of rain-making in southern Africa

In the first place, it is important to note that rituals and beliefs about the control of rain are present in all indigenous groups in southern Africa; they are not exclusively Bushman. One striking aspect is the often detailed similarities of the beliefs held by different groups (see Schmidt 1979 for a review). Because these groups have not always lived in close proximity, an interesting question concerns which group had which beliefs first.

Examining ancient material remains is a somewhat limited response to this question, for ancient material remains can be interpreted only in terms of more recent ethnographies. It is highly unlikely we shall thereby detect subtle but important conceptual shifts taking place through time.

Archaeological studies have, nevertheless, suggested a high antiquity for southern African beliefs about rain-making. In a survey of the Lephalala drainage basin (Northern Province, South Africa), Aukema located a number of rock-shelters, often extremely small, containing clay pots and grindstones and unsuitable for habitation. The shelters are usually without other cultural deposit and are not defensively sited (Aukema 1989: 70). The material he found in the shelters, then, could not have been brought there by hunter-gatherers who were living there; nor could the sites have been used as living places by farmers.

Instead, Aukema links the remains of clay pots and grindstones to rain-making rituals of Bantu-speaking communities who lived in settlements some way off. In many Bantu-speaking communities rain-medicine is prepared and placed in a pot, which is then deposited in a secluded place – a cleft in a rock or a rock-shelter (Krige and Krige 1947: 273–4; Berglund 1976: 60; Jackson 1982: 46). Because some of the pottery recovered in these small, secluded shelters belongs to the Early Iron Age Eiland Tradition (tenth–twelfth centuries AD), Aukema (1989) argues that his finds extend at least some aspects of ethnographically observed rain-making practices back at least a thousand years from the present.

Important as these Early Iron Age remains are, they do not shed light on the complexity of the attendant beliefs; again, they can be explained only by much more recent ethnography. Further, the antiquity of the evidence found in the Lephalala drainage basin does not tell of the flow of beliefs about the control of rain between different communities. Indeed, trying to untangle the complex beliefs and to ascribe them to particular cultural groups may be an impossible task.

Nevertheless, the great time-depth suggested by this Early Iron Age material provides explanatory background to Schmidt's (1979: 202, 211) perceptive observation that the study of Bushmen's rain-making rituals and beliefs must necessarily involve looking at their neighbours' beliefs about rain as well. In trying to come to a better understanding of rock-paintings that relate to beliefs about rain, I therefore also consider the beliefs of farming communities.

## Rain-making and rain-creatures

A central aspect of the many beliefs about rain involves a creature of some kind – specifically identified or not. Following Orpen (1874), Stow (Stow 1905; Stow and Bleek 1930) and Bleek (1933a, 1933b), a number of researchers have identified rain-creatures in the rock-art, creatures that are like hippopotamuses, eland or cattle, or strange combinations derived from one or more of these animals. Because of the close association of snakes and water throughout Africa, Vinnicombe (1976: 233; see also Woodhouse 1992) has cautiously suggested that grotesque-looking serpents, relatively common in the art, were connected with Bushman rain-making rituals. Lewis-Williams (1981a: 103–16) instead followed an early trend in rock-art research (see Stow 1905; Stow and Bleek 1930; also Willcox 1963: 34, 1984: 55, who distinctly rules out snakes) in identifying as rain-creatures only those paintings that have close affinities with bovid, pachyderms or weird, hallucinatory transformations of these animals. He interprets painted snakes as depictions of transformed shamans (Lewis-Williams 1981a: 89; Lewis-Williams and Dowson 1989: 130–1) rather than rain-creatures.

That certain snakes were associated with rain-making was suggested as long ago as 1874 in a statement given by Qing to Orpen, the significance of which has not been explored. One painting about which Orpen obtained comments from Qing is of a hippopotamus-like rain-creature; it is being led by a 'rope' held by four human figures (Vinnicombe

1976: fig. 239). Today this is generally accepted as depicting a typical rain-making scene (Vinnicombe 1976: 336–9; Schmidt 1979; Lewis-Williams 1980, 1981a: 34, 103–15, 1990: 51–4). But Qing is reported to have said, 'That the animal which the men are catching is a snake(!)' (Orpen 1874: 10). The exclamation mark is Orpen's; he was surprised by the remark.

Schmidt (1979), demonstrating a close association between the oft-referred-to 'rain-bull' and snakes, believes that these widespread beliefs about snakes and their association with rain are reflected in the rock-paintings. More recently, Thackeray (1988) has argued that southern Nguni concepts about the 'river people', *abantubomlambo*, and one of the snake familiars, *ichanti*, may be relevant to understanding some rock-paintings.

Alongside these valuable pointers, there is further ethnography on rain-creatures that has not been discussed fully. Schapera (1971) notes that, for the Tswana, the fat of a large and powerful snake is one of the most potent medicines used in rain-making; this snake, *kgwanyape*, is said to live in a pool on top of a hill. Murray (1980: 123) believes this is the same snake that Basuto call *khanyapa*, which is sometimes identified as a python. This snake is also associated with deep pools; for example, a large snake is said to inhabit the pool at the Maletsunyane Waterfall, Semonkong, in Lesotho (Murray 1980: 123).

Also in an area occupied by Basuto, Stow met a number of Bushmen to whom he showed copies he had made of Bushman paintings. Kou'ke, an elderly woman, at once recognised a copy of a horned serpent, saying that in the days of their forefathers these enormous and powerful serpents had lived in the rivers; they measured, so she said, up to 30 feet (about 10 m) (Stow 1905: 131–2).

Perhaps the most detailed and vivid accounts of these aquatic snakes are in the southern Nguni ethnography; they highlight a key feature of *ichanti* directly relevant to our understanding of rock-paintings of serpents. According to Soga (1931: 193), *ichanti* can assume the appearance of almost anything from a snake to a goat, and transform itself from an iron chain to a feather to a honeycomb. The apparently random transformations of *ichanti* were clearly important to the Xhosa people whom Soga interviewed; they likened the rapidly changing patterns they observed in a kaleidoscope to *ichanti*. Perhaps because of these rapid transformations, *ichanti* has the power to mesmerise people. Significantly, Soga (1931: 195) associates this 'water-sprite', as he calls *ichanti*, with hallucinations of 'excessive nervous temperaments'. This linking of snakes and transformation to hallucination is significant.

These legendary, protean snakes are linked by the various cultural groups in differing ways to rain and rain-making. In some Bushman myths that Qing recounted there are references to personified snakes and their abilities. For instance, during a dispute between Cagn's (/Kaggen in Bleek's orthography) family and the snakes over his daughter, it was said the snakes 'would fill the country with water' (Orpen 1874: 5). It appears from this that the snakes had command of the rain.

The southern Nguni's mythical 'river people', whom some groups see as snakes (Hammond-Tooke 1975), have both a malevolent and benevolent nature. One benevolent trait is a close association with rain (Hammond-Tooke 1975: 21), evident in an account of a Pondo rain-making procedure:

The chief sends a black beast without a spot. It is killed at the kraal of the Yalo rain-maker, and the skin is prepared. A human being is killed, and in his skull is put the fat of the beast killed. The rain-maker goes to live in a hut by himself. He covers himself with the hide of the ox killed, and smears the hide with the fat from the human skull. Then a snake comes by night, and licks the fat off the hide. The grass is not burned round one side of that *umzi*, so that the snake may come and not be seen. It should not be seen by anyone except the rain-maker. No one goes on that side of the *umzi*. The name of the snake is Intlanthu. After that it rains. (Hunter 1979: 80–1)

This procedure is strikingly similar to the accounts Berglund (1976: 53–63) recorded for northern Nguni Zulu rain-makers. During a drought, men approaching a rain-maker must bring a fat black sheep or goat without any white or brown colouring. The animal is killed and skinned. The rain-maker takes the skin and his medicines (in horns) to a black rock in a stream. He lies on the rock with the medicines next to him and the skin covering his body. During the night, when all is still and quiet, a python emerges from a deep pool in the river and licks the fat off the skin. The snake then lies on the medicines 'for a long time until the horns are as cool as [the snake] is cool. Then it returns into the water from where it came' (Berglund 1976: 55–6). At dawn the rain-maker gets up, takes the medicine and 'makes rain just there next to the river' (Berglund 1976: 56).

The northern Nguni rain-makers whom Berglund met also burned the grass around their homestead, except for a part immediately to the east 'because that is the road for the great snake when it comes to my home to do its work' (Berglund 1976: 56). The medicines were kept in cool places, under rocks or in caves. The python is associated with coolness. When a female rain-maker hid her medicines in a cave where pythons were found, the 'snake of the sky' would come and keep the medicines cool (Berglund 1976: 60). It is essential to keep the medicines cool so that they may 'do their work'. The Nguni snake, like the /Xam rain-creature, is associated with the sky and with water-holes/rivers.

The evidence so far briefly discussed, together with that cited by Schmidt (1979), demonstrates the existence of subcontinental beliefs concerning large water-snakes and rain. These beliefs – not the same everywhere – have a virtual, rather than a fixed, reality. The stock of knowledge about snakes and rain was employed by knowledgeable agents in different communities during specific social practices. The rapidly transforming visual hallucinations experienced by Bushman shaman-artists during trance would have been much like the 'kaleidoscopic' transformations of *ichanti* to which Soga (1931: 195) refers. In this way, all beliefs – including those about rain-making and, for the Bushmen, about painting –

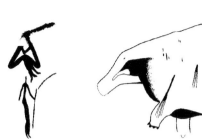

**Fig. 5.2.** Rock-painting showing a 'bleeding' rain-creature associated with trancing human figures. Colours: red and white; scale in cm.

were recursively implicated in daily social practice. These were the beliefs drawn upon during the production of paintings that concerned rain and rain-making. I now consider the differences between paintings of rain-creatures, a point not hitherto much noted. By analysing the differences between paintings I prepare the way for an account of the role of individual rain-makers in the history of the south-eastern mountains.

## Paintings of rain-creatures

There is a fundamental difference in the painted scenes in which rain-creatures appear: in some, human figures are an integral part, while in others they are absent. Qing told Orpen that rain-creatures were caught 'under water' by 'people spoilt by the [*moqoma*] dance'. Ethnographic research has shown how this remark is couched in Bushman idioms; it means that shamans entered trance (went 'under water' and were 'spoilt') at a trance dance and – in the spirit, or hallucinatory, world – captured the rain in the form of a creature of some kind (Lewis-Williams 1980, 1981a: 103–16). Qing went on to identify the people who captured the rain-creature as those whose 'noses bleed'; as the Bleek and Lloyd ethnography shows, shamans often experienced a nasal haemorrhage when they entered trance (Bleek 1935: 12, 19, 34). Human figures apparently bleeding at the nose are, in fact, frequently depicted in the

art and have often been noted (for example, Vinnicombe 1976: figs. 225, 231, 237, 240, 241; Lewis-Williams 1981a: figs. 19, 20, 21, 23, 24, 30, 31, 32, 33).

Despite Qing's identification of rain-creatures by nasal haemorrhage, the people capturing the rain-creature in the painting of which he was speaking are not bleeding from the nose, nor are people in the other paintings Orpen copied (see Orpen 1874). It seems likely that Qing must have shown Orpen other paintings depicting trance blood and that he was speaking of a category of people – shamans – identifiable in the art even if they were not always depicted with a nasal haemorrhage.

Although the human figures in Fig. 5.2 are not bleeding from the nose, several features – the arms-back posture (Lewis-Williams 1981a: 88), a hand raised to the nose (Lewis-Williams 1983: 542–3), kneeling in a shamanistic posture (Lewis-Williams 1981a: 75–102), having one leg raised (Katz 1982: 46, 62) – show they are indeed shamans.

A feature of the rain-creature itself may be similarly explained by beliefs about rain-making. Like two other known rock-paintings (see, for example, Vinnicombe 1976: fig. 245), the rain-creature in Fig. 5.2 appears to be bleeding from a number of wounds. One of W. H. I. Bleek's (Bleek 1933a: 310) informants, //Kabbo, spoke of a shaman of the rain who said, 'I will really ride the rain up the mountain

77

**Fig. 5.3.** A graphic metaphor of a rain-creature being 'led' from a 'water-hole' to the 'sky'. Colours: red (solid), ochre (stipple) and white; scale in cm.

on top of which I always cut the rain. It is high, so that the rain's blood flows down, for the Flat Bushmen live on the plains.'

The wounds depicted in these paintings, none of which actually has a spear or arrow in it, may depict 'cutting the rain'. Rain's blood was analogous to precipitation, and the blood streaming from the rain-creature's wounds should be seen in this light.

In summary, the painting in Fig. 5.2 has features that proclaim its association with trance performance, even though none of the human figures bleeds from the nose. The rain-creature itself displays a feature (bleeding from wounds) consistent with beliefs about rain-making. Both the people and the rain-creature are in the spiritual dimension of trance experience rather than the 'real' world.

A more remarkable painting (Fig. 5.3) omits human figures altogether, yet implies the trance experiences. The rain-creature here, like the previous example, bears some resemblance to a hippopotamus, but it does not bleed from any wounds. It is walking along a red line that is painted in three sections, a kind of line frequently – but not always – fringed with white dots. These lines, with or without dots, often seem to depict a path or track along which people and animals walk (see Lewis-Williams 1981b: figs. 1, 3); they also connect paintings by passing in and out of human figures and animals. In some instances the line wanders apparently (though I am sure not) aimlessly through densely painted panels.

The diversity of depictions of the line shows that many different painters were idiosyncratically ma-

nipulating their beliefs; it also makes full and unequivocal interpretation of each instance difficult. Nevertheless, some suggestions can be made about the painting illustrated in Fig. 5.3. The line may be a shaman, transformed by synaesthesia and participation, controlling the movements of a rain-creature (see Lewis-Williams 1986). The 'conceptual' direction in which the rain-creature is being controlled is established by a shoal of fish and a flock of birds; it is moving from the fish towards the birds. Both the fish and the birds express Bushman shamanistic metaphors. As we have seen, 'under water' is a metaphor of trance experience, frequently represented in Bushman rock-art by the depiction of fish, eels, turtles and, in one instance, by crabs (Dowson 1988). 'Flight' is equally a worldwide metaphor of trance experience with roots in somatic hallucinations of dissociation, rising up and floating. In one sense, the birds are complementary to the shoal of fish (both suggest trance experience), but they also point to two areas of Bushman cosmology: the realm above the earth and the realm below.

Now we can show that this painting reflects the same beliefs as Fig. 5.2, subtly varied. Shamans captured the rain-creature in a water-hole, the realm below, and then sometimes led it to the top of a mountain, the realm above, where they cut and killed it (Bleek 1933a: 310). The journey started under water and ended high up. In Fig. 5.3 the red line starts near the fish, enters the rock face, emerges again to run at the animal's feet, re-enters the rock and emerges once more near the birds. I see the painting as depicting a shaman who has been transformed into a controlling line of potency by his altered state of consciousness and who is leading a rain-creature from the water-hole to the top of a mountain or up into the sky. The shaman-artist achieved this alternative mode of depicting the essence of Fig. 5.2 by moving further away from 'reality' and deeper into the somatic and visual experiences of southern African shamanism.

This discussion of two specific rain-making scenes establishes how beliefs about rain-making are manipulated to produce such strikingly different paintings, which are about 25 km away from one another. In the following section I show how subcontinental beliefs about rain-serpents are manipulated in paintings associated with rain-making.

## Paintings of rain-snakes

Depictions of snakes are found throughout the south-eastern mountains. Many have hairs along their backs, tusks, ears and antelope heads. I have not yet noticed patterns in their distribution in the south-eastern mountains. Instead of specific features being confined to specific areas, there appears to be marked variation across the entire region – a diversity that may result from the ways in which individual shaman-artists drew on widely held beliefs. At the same time, because of these beliefs, some features of these paintings are repeated. One is the way in which the depictions of rain-serpents relate to natural features of the rock surface. I explain two examples.

First, an artist has painted a convoluted snake (Fig. 5.4) so that it fits neatly into one of many natural circular concavities in the roof of a rock-shelter. More commonly, serpents are depicted entering or emerging from steps or cracks in the rock face (see also Vinnicombe 1976: 228–37; Lewis-Williams 1981a: 89). In one of the most spectacular examples a snake, about 25 cm wide, emerges from a crack in the rock face. After nearly 4 metres it 'disappears' for about 40 cm behind a boss of rock; then its head emerges on the other side (this portion of the serpent is reproduced here, Fig. 5.5). One is always struck by

**Fig. 5.4.** A rain-snake that has been painted in such a way that it fills a natural, circular concavity in a rock-shelter's roof.
   Colours: white, light red (stipple) and red (solid); scale in cm.

**Fig. 5.5.** A large, fantastic serpent that emerges from a crack in the rock face, and disappears behind, and reappears from, a block of rock (indicated by the bold dot/dash line). It has an antelope head and is bleeding from the nose.
   Colours: white, light red (stipple) and red (solid); scale in cm.

the enormous size of such serpents, particularly in relation to associated human figures (Vinnicombe 1976: 230).

Passing through the rock face is linked to some beliefs I have cited. The accounts collected by Berglund show that snakes, particularly pythons, are associated with rain and are believed to be 'cool'. Rain-medicines are sometimes stored in caves as they are considered cool places (Berglund 1976: 60; see also Aukema 1989: 71). Cool snakes are thus linked with cool places that include caves, an association made more significant when the artists painted these snakes emerging from the walls of the cool shelters. The use of the hollow in the example depicted in Fig. 5.4, then, was probably drawing on subcontinental beliefs about snakes living in cool places. To ensure belief in the control of the rain, some artists, probably rain-makers themselves, manipulated the beliefs about snakes and their associations with coolness in their paintings. Even if the artists were not themselves rain-makers, they used features of the rock faces to convey the power of the rain-makers. These ideas made the placing of paintings of snakes, as rain-creatures, in rock-shelters highly appropriate for Bantu-speakers and for Bushmen.

Passing through the rock face and an association with pools are features of painted rain-snakes that relate directly to trance experience. The /Xam Bushmen spoke of trancing shamans going into a 'water-pit' where the water was 'alive' to capture a rain-creature (Bleek 1935: 32: see also Lewis-Williams 1981a: 103–16). Similarly, an old !Kung shaman, K'xau, told Biesele (1975, 1980) how he reached the spirit world. First, the giraffe, his power animal, 'took' him. Then Kauha (God) led him to a 'wide body of water' which they entered. His teacher, an experienced shaman, told him he would enter the earth (the realm below); he 'would travel through the earth and then emerge at another place' (Biesele 1980: 56). 'When people sing [medicine songs], I dance. I enter the earth. I go in at a place where people drink water. I travel in a long way, very far' (Biesele 1980: 61). /Kaggen, the southern Bushman

trickster-deity, who was probably himself a shaman, also dived into water-holes during trance episodes (Orpen 1874: 7; Bleek 1924: 17; Lewis-Williams 1996). In one myth he descended not into a pool but directly into the ground and came up again 'until he was close to an eagle whose honey he desired' (Orpen 1874: 8).

All these beliefs are versions of a subcontinental belief that the entrance to the spirit world was through holes in the ground, caves and pools of water. Travelling to the spirit world was metaphorically related to travelling under water, which is cool.

When painting rain-creatures, all artists drew on the same set of beliefs about rain-making. This is why serpents and other animals are treated similarly in the paintings. But the flexibility of these beliefs and the ways in which they are manipulated lead to considerable variations in the different panels. The painted variants discussed, which by no means exhaust this diversity, do show how complex this kind of painting is. At the same time, they show it is impossible to compile finite lists of criteria for the identification of certain subjects in Bushman rock-art (Willcox 1984: 55–6).

The following section examines the origins of the painted diversity I have described and the ways in which Bushman rain-makers related to diversity in highly personal ways. As I argue in the final section, it is the relationship between diversity and individual people that allows for the development of the art's political role.

### Idiosyncrasy as a resource

I begin by explaining the origins of conceptual and painted diversity and how Bushmen regard it, for it was the fundamental possibility of diversity that facilitated the harnessing of the art in political manoeuvres. Essentially, diversity derives from an infinitely varied combination of 'real' elements and hallucinatory elements. Bushman shamans speak of seeing supernatural potency, sickness, spirit animals and so forth during a trance dance. These things, entoptic and iconic hallucinations not to be seen by ordinary people, in a shaman's vision are superimposed on and become part of a 'real' dance. Depictions of trance dances that incorporate these elements present a shaman's privileged perspective, seeing a whole dimension invisible to other people. This combination of perception and hallucination, relating to a key feature of Bushman religion, explains an intriguing feature of paintings of rain-creatures.

In the Kalahari today Bushman religion is similarly culturally determined but, at the same time, idiosyncratic (Marshall 1960, 1962, 1969; Biesele 1975, 1978a, 1986; Katz 1982). All shamans' revelations of the spirit world are taken as valid, even if they appear to us to be contradictory (Biesele 1975, 1986). Some revelations, as they become generally accepted, are eventually experienced by other shamans; others remain idiosyncratic. Idiosyncratic beliefs are often associated with special and valuable revelations, believed to come from God; they are seen as particular favours rather than as aberrations (Biesele 1986).

Similarly, although there are clear likenesses between depictions, no two rain-creatures are identical; each 'scene' is a unique combination of features. On the one hand, the art's general uniformity derives from culturally determined expectations of what a shaman may see in trance and, of course, the 'real' world on to which hallucinations are often projected. By contrast, the idiosyncratic elements derive, at least in part, from the essentially uncontrollable functioning of the human nervous system in certain altered states. Inevitably, unique and unexpected mental images are generated from time to time. Some shamans ignore these because they do not match their expectations; others seize upon the more tractable ones as special revelations of the nature of the spirit world (Dowson 1988, 1989; Dowson and Holliday 1989). Why one shaman will ignore novel visions and another develop them depends on their respective social positions and on their desire, or lack of desire, to enhance their prestige.

That is why each painting of a rain-creature has

subtle variations that, looked at together, can provide an understanding of the complexity and nuances of the spiritual experience of rain-making. It is necessary to go from site to site examining the characteristics of a particular subject if we wish to understand culturally determined uniformity as well as idiosyncratic insights.

Inter-site comparison of this kind shows that depictions of rain-creatures are – compared with some other classes of depiction – highly idiosyncratic. This level of idiosyncrasy probably resulted, in part – but, as I shall show, only in part – from the simple fact that there are no rain-creatures in reality, as there are, say, eland or elephant. The existence of real animals clearly places stringent restrictions on the amount of variation a painter may introduce before his depiction ceases to be recognisable.

One facet of Bushman rain-making beliefs led directly to the high level of idiosyncrasy in the art and, at the same time, seems to have provided a foundation for the importance of rain-making in changing political and social circumstances. This facet, which also opens up the way to the notion of 'possession' and to the translation of potency into power, is evident in /Han‡kasso's remarks on a rain-shaman named //Kunn: 'I have seen him; I have seen the rain which he caused to fall . . . His rain came streaming from out of the west there, it went to the north, because he was from that part' (Bleek 1933b: 387). /Han‡kasso's statement associates //Kunn with a particular rain, not just rain in general: it was a rain that 'belonged' to //Kunn, one that he 'possessed'. And //Kunn's rain was associated with a 'place', the north, the area from which he himself came. This association of rain and water (for the /Xam the word was the same, *!khwa*) recalls //Kabbo's remark, 'My place is the Bitterpits' (see Deacon 1986). There is strong evidence that //Kabbo was a shaman (see Lewis-Williams 1996). The Bitterpits, a water-hole, may have been his personal entrance to the spirit world.

The same notion of shamans being associated with a particular rain rather than with an undifferentiated, generalised concept underlies a complex association between – on the one hand – kinds, not just directions, of wind and – on the other – specific people. This association also extended to animals. Dia!kwain told Lloyd, 'The springbok appeared to be moving away and the wind really blew following them . . . It was really father's wind, and you can feel yourself how it is blowing' (Bleek 1932: 329).

The special wind associated with Dia!kwain's father was caused by a 'mythical' interaction between himself and an animal he had killed: 'You know that when father used to shoot game, his wind blew like that' (Bleek 1932: 329). A /Xam informant also spoke of 'our brother whose wind blows hard from the north' (Bleek 1932: 336) and of 'another man whose wind is pleasant' (Bleek 1932: 338). The intimate relationship between a man and 'his' wind was succinctly summed up by /Han‡kasso: 'The wind is one with the man' (Bleek 1932: 338). A comment by Dia!kwain takes this idea further in explicitly linking a wind with rain: 'I felt the wind [his father's wind], when the rain water had fallen on the ground' (Bleek 1932: 338).

This kind of conceptual association may well be widespread; similar beliefs exist among the !Kung, who call this association between the weather and people n!ow (Marshall 1957; see also Biesele 1978b; Vinnicombe 1972). A person's n!ow is said to be good if it brings rain, bad if it brings cold. The !Kung say that when the blood of certain animals falls on the ground it can effect a change in the weather (Marshall 1957: 238–9; Marshall Thomas 1959: 161–2). If the blood of a giraffe is allowed to flow on to the ground instead of being saved and consumed, it will cause clouds, the forms and colours of which will be like giraffes. There seems a close association between /Xam rain-making rituals involving the cutting of a rain-creature and these !Kung beliefs about n!ow (Vinnicombe 1972: 200–10).

The southern Bushmen thus associated particular kinds of wind and rain with individual people in a particularity that seems, in turn, to have been expressed in the way a shaman conceived of, or hal-lucinated, *his* rain-creature. If each shaman had an idiosyncratic notion of what 'his' rain-creature looked like, this explains both the diversity and the underlying uniformity of depictions of those 'creatures'. The important point for the role of rock-art in historical processes is that it seems highly probable that a shaman-artist could point to a specific depiction and say, 'That is my *!khwa-ka xoro* [rain-creature].' Other people could look at an imposing, potency-filled painting of a rain-creature and say, perhaps with awe and respect, 'That is so-and-so's rain-creature.'

This close relationship between a shaman and his (or her, but for the reasons outlined elsewhere (Dowson 1994, 1995), I believe predominantly 'his') rain is very strongly suggested in two groups of unusual paintings.

The first group comprises five rain-creatures (Fig. 5.6), four close together, one relatively far away (Fig. 5.6e). The five examples are strikingly similar: all are bulky, unidentifiable quadrupeds, with a long trunk-like appendage. The rain-creatures illustrated in Figs. 5.6a and 5.6b are associated with fish. Those in Figs. 5.6a, 5.6b, 5.6c and 5.6d also have small white hairs on their bodies and 'trunks'. The similarities and close proximity of these rain-animals suggest they – except perhaps the far-off example (Fig. 5.6e) – were all painted by the same rain-shaman, moving from shelter to shelter.

The second set of similar rain-making 'scenes' includes human figures. In the first (Fig. 5.7a), one of two 'walking' figures has a small unidentifiable quadruped on its head that closely resembles a rain-creature. Lee and Woodhouse (1970: fig. 151) have published a close-up photograph of another, near-by example. In a third example (Fig. 5.7b), the human figure with the animal on its head is playing a musical bow. Proximity and similarity again suggest that these three examples were done by the same artist.

There is no ethnographic evidence that Bushmen had this sort of headgear. Rather, the amorphous, quadrupedal form of this animal, so much like that of

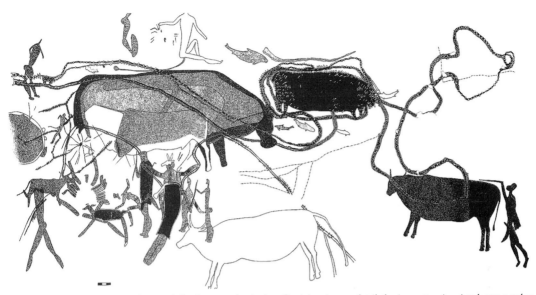

**Fig. 5.6a.** Part of a large, complex panel that has several episodes of activity. A more detailed rain-creature is painted over a rather simple rain-creature.

Colours white, ochre (solid), red (light stipple) and black (dense stipple); scale in cm.

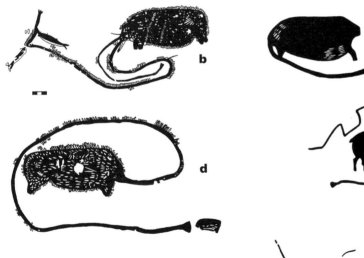

**Figs. 5.6b, c, d, e.** Rain-creatures that are remarkably similar to each other and the most recent rain-creature reproduced in Fig. 5.6a (b, after Pager 1975: 213; c, after Rosenthal and Goodwin 1953: fig. 9; d, after Pager 1975: 213; e, after Vinnicombe 1976: fig. 241).

Colours: red and white; scale, in each case, in cm, but un-recorded for 5.6c.

**Fig. 5.7a.** Two human figures, one of whom has an unidentifiable quadruped on its head that is interpreted as a rain-creature. Colours: white, light red (stipple) and red (solid); scale in cm.

**Fig. 5.7b.** A human figure with an unidentifiable quadruped on its head (a rain-creature) plays a musical bow, while two other members of the group clap.

Colours white, red (stipple) and black (solid); scale in cm.

many rain-animals, suggests that it is a rain-creature, painted idiosyncratically on the top of the shaman's head, the place from which his spirit leaves on out-of-body travel (Lewis-Williams 1981a: 86–100). Significantly, these three paintings are all in the region where, I argue, particularly powerful, male shamans existed and began to establish their individuality and power (Dowson 1994).

Depictions of rain-creatures, then, are not merely generalised representations of rain-making. Even though they have elements in common, they each preserve the unique religious experience of a particular shaman. When looked at together, the subtle variations in each painting provide an understanding of the complexity and nuances of the spiritual experience of rain-making. In the next section I show how this complexity, together with the association of a shaman with a particular rain-creature, was knowingly manipulated in attempts to control political change in the south-eastern mountains.

### Rain-creatures as a political resource

Two illuminating /Xam accounts show that shamans could use their control of rain not only for everyone's benefit but also against others in the group (LIV4. 2556–9; LV3. 4083–5 respectively).

The medicine men told them that the rain would be angry and not fall for the rain is willing to fall but anger does not let the rain fall, for the rain likes to fall, but not by anger will they make it fall. When the rain fell, they did wrong actions which were not good. They behaved badly when it was with them, they make it go away for they did not take good care of their fellows, medicine men.

And the rain's sorcerers returned, and they spoke, they told the people about it, that now they had made rain to fall for the people, and the people could now do that which they were accustomed to do; if the rain falls, they do not take care of one another; for, they are accustomed to do evil things; while they do not seek, feeding themselves; and they fight when they have made fat, when the rain has fallen for them. When they flourish, they become fat, and they do not remember that they had now asked the sorcerers for rain. For, those things they are those which the sorcerers do not always therefore make the rain to fall for them, on account of them.

The stories tell of shamans using beliefs as a political resource to exercise their power and to control the behaviour of other people. They told the people that if they were not treated in a proper manner the rain would be angry and not fall. People believed that the shamans had control of the rain, and hence the growth of plant foods for themselves and the animals.

Having painted a rain-creature by idiosyncratically manipulating beliefs about rain and shamans' control over it, a shaman-artist's image remained for consumption. As accounts such as Silayi's suggest (Stanford 1910), the consumers would not have been exclusively Bushmen, but probably included Bantu-speaking and Khoenkhoen people. Because the painter was drawing on widely held beliefs, these other people would have understood the 'meaning' of the painting and been susceptible to its impact. The artist could, through his painting, negotiate his status and power in communities other than his own. Indeed, some paintings of rain-creatures may well have been made principally for a Bantu-speaking audience.

The painted rain-creature was thus not simply a daily reminder of beliefs about the shaman and his specific rain (as in Lewis-Williams 1982); the image was actively implicated in social and political practices. The depiction became, recursively, a resource in that it was used to bring about certain actions that reproduced ritual dominance. Paintings of rain-creatures were made by shamans to negotiate a higher status than others, both shamans and non-shamans. To understand how individual rock-painters manipulated imagery to make their rain-animals different from others and so establish their personal status, we turn to some paintings in much the same region as we find paintings of high-status, male shamans. These paintings emphasise size, ferocity and elaboration.

First, there are some exceptionally large rain-animals. At one site, two rain-animals measure 635 × 1905 mm and 740 × 1600 mm respectively; in other regions, rain-animals are much smaller than

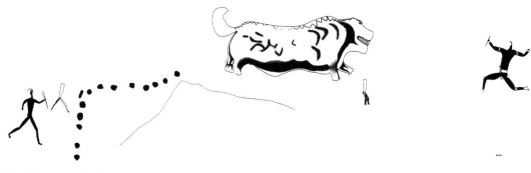

**Fig. 5.8.** A particularly large and somewhat menacing-looking rain-creature.
Colours: red and white; scale in cm.

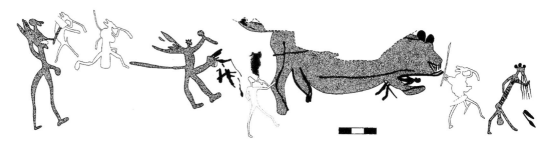

**Fig. 5.9.** A badly preserved rain-creature. The animal has teeth that are clearly visible, and it appears to be trampling a human being.
Colours: white, red (solid) and grey-black (stipple); scale in cm.

this. I argue that, in making these paintings, shaman-artists manipulated the size to draw attention to their own power and control of rain.

Secondly, some examples are not only large but particularly threatening in appearance (Fig. 5.8). Bushmen spoke to Stow not only about large dangerous aquatic snakes; they also mentioned other animals inhabiting the rivers in the days of their forefathers: 'great monstrous brutes, exceeding the elephant or hippopotamus in bulk' (Stow 1905: 131). Remarking on one of Stow's copies (Stow and Bleek 1930: plate 34) of a large unidentifiable animal, Kou'ke, a Bushwoman from the eastern Orange Free State, called it 'the master of the water' (Stow 1905: 132) – an animal, she said, far larger and more formidable than the hippopotamus. Stow (1905: 132) paraphrased her account:

The Bushmen captured it by making a very strong enclosure with reeds and poles, so strongly interwoven and bound together that it could not break through . . . When they succeeded in getting one of these brutes within the toils, as soon as the monster found he was entrapped his fury appeared to know no bounds; he made desperate attempts to free himself, and lashed the water about, in the impotence of his rage, until he raised such clouds of spray around him that the rainbow appeared upon them, as if crowning him. Hence his name [the Master of the Water], and this circumstance the Bushman artists attempted to depict in their paintings. But even after thus imprisoning him, it frequently happened that three or four Bushmen would be sacrificed to his uncontrollable fierceness before he was finally conquered and killed. He generally seized them by the middle of the back, crushed them with a single crunch of his teeth, and then pounded them to a shapeless mass beneath his feet. These and others she declared were animals that once lived in the land in the days of her father's fathers, but they had long since disappeared.

Numerous accounts in the Bleek and Lloyd ethnography also testify to the dangerous nature of rain-creatures (Bleek 1933a, 1933b). In one account Dia!kwain recounts how *buchu*, an aromatic herbal substance, was used to pacify angry rain-creatures (Bleek 1933b: 382). Moreover, the paintings themselves often depict the rain-creatures as dangerous and particularly ferocious. One example from the Zastron District (Fig. 5.9; see also Dowson *et al.* 1994) shows a rain-creature with large teeth apparently trampling a human figure in the manner described by Kou'ke. A number of other rain-creatures are depicted with large teeth (Fig. 5.8). Given the general nature of animal behaviour, depicting the teeth in this manner probably points to a threatening display of potential danger. By drawing attention to the dangers of their work, rain-shamans were able to restrict access to rain-making as a resource and hence maintain and enhance their own position in society.

Finally, in one instance (Fig. 5.6a), a very visible rain-animal is painted on top of an older, much more faded rain-animal. The newer is more elaborate; it has lines with hairs and dots on them protruding from its body; and it is surrounded by fish. The later shaman-artist was thus drawing attention away from the earlier, simpler rain-animal towards his own striking and elaborate rain-animal, again by manipulating iconographic content and colour. By painting patently different rain-creatures, a shaman-artist could entrench notions about 'his' rain and his ability to control it. His status and power were founded on these activities.

The four very similar, though not especially elaborate, paintings (Figs. 5.6a, b, c and d) suggest another aspect of a shaman's political power. As I have argued, these paintings were probably made by one rain-shaman who moved from shelter to shelter in a restricted area. His placing of recognisably similar paintings in different sites may have made a territorial statement. When people journeyed to him to ask him to make rain for them, they had to leave their own territories and enter his. In so doing, they acknowledged his control of land as well as his control of rain. The demarcation of tracts of land by painted imagery, as distinct from single rock-shelters, is a point that needs attention. The placing of distinctive images may well have been one of the shaman's responses to the encroachment of other communities on a Bushman community's land.

There are many other paintings of rain-creatures to which I have not referred. Although they support my position here, each example adds a nuance of its own, a nuance that relates to a particular producer's position in a particular community. The control of rain and the manipulation of imagery was every bit as real for the many different communities that produced and consumed these rock-paintings. This is very much a part of southern Africa's history – certainly no less important than the political events that continue to shape the subcontinent's future.

## REFERENCES

Aukema, J. 1989. Rain-making: a thousand-year-old ritual, *South African Archaeological Bulletin* 44: 70–2.

Berglund, A. 1976. *Zulu thought-patterns and symbolism.* Uppsala, Swedish Institute of Missionary Research.

Biesele, M. 1975. Folklore and ritual of !Kung hunter-gatherers. Doctoral thesis, Harvard University, Cambridge (MA).

1978a. Religion and folklore, in P. V. Tobias (ed.), *The Bushmen*, pp. 162–72. Cape Town, Human and Rousseau.

1978b. Sapience and scarce resources: communication systems of the !Kung and other foragers, *Social Science Information* 17: 921–47.

1980. 'Old K'xau', in J. Halifax (ed.), *Shamanic voices: a survey of visionary narratives*, pp. 54–62. Harmondsworth, Penguin.

1986. 'Anyone with sense would know': tradition and creativity in !Kung narrative and song, in R. Vossen and K. Keuthmann (eds.), *Contemporary studies on Khoisan* 1, pp. 83–106. Hamburg, Helmut Buske Verlag.

Bleek, D. F. 1924. *The Mantis and his friends.* Cape Town, Maskew Miller.

1932. Customs and beliefs of the /Xam Bushmen. Part IV: Omens, wind-making, clouds, *Bantu Studies* 6: 324–42.

1933a. Beliefs and customs of the /Xam Bushmen. Part V: The rain, *Bantu Studies* 7: 297–312.

1933b. Beliefs and customs of the /Xam Bushmen. Part VI: Rain-making, *Bantu Studies* 7: 375–92.

1935. Beliefs and customs of the /Xam Bushmen. Part VII: Sorcerors, *Bantu Studies* 9: 1–47.

Deacon, J. 1986. 'My place is the Bitterpits': the home territory of Bleek and Lloyd's /Xam San informants, *African Studies* 45: 135–55.

Dowson, T. A. 1988. Revelations of religious reality: the individual in San rock art, *World Archaeology* 20: 116–28.

1989. Dots and dashes: cracking the entoptic code in Bushman rock paintings, *South African Archaeological Society, Goodwin Series* 6: 84–94.

1994. Reading art writing history: rock art and social change in southern Africa, *World Archaeology* 25(3): 332–45.

1995. Hunter-gatherers, traders and slaves: the 'Mfecane' impact on Bushmen, their ritual and their art, in C. Hamilton (ed.), *The Mfecane aftermath: reconstructive debates in southern African history*, pp. 51–70. Johannesburg and Pietermaritzburg, Witwatersrand University Press and University of Natal Press.

Dowson, T. A. and A. L. Holliday. 1989. Zigzags and eland: an interpretation of an idiosyncratic combination, *South African Archaeological Bulletin* 44: 46–8.

Dowson, T. A., S. Ouzman, G. Blundell and A. L. Holliday. 1994. A Stow site revisited: Zastron District, Orange Free State, in T. A. Dowson and J. D. Lewis-Williams (eds.), *Contested images: diversity in southern African rock art research*, pp. 177–88. Johannesburg, Witwatersrand University Press.

Hammond-Tooke, W. D. 1975. The symbolic structure of Cape Nguni cosmology, in M. G. Whisson and M. West (eds.), *Religion and social change in southern Africa*, pp. 15–33. Cape Town, David Philip.

Hunter, M. 1979. *Reaction to conquest*. Cape Town, David Philip.

Jackson, A. O. 1982. *The Ndebele of Langa*. Pretoria, Government Printer. Ethnological Publication 54.

Katz, R. 1982. *Boiling energy: community-healing among the Kalahari !Kung*. Cambridge (MA), Harvard University Press.

Krige, E. J. and J. D. Krige. 1947. *The realm of the Rain Queen*. London, Oxford University Press.

Lee, D. N. and H. C. Woodhouse. 1970. *Art on the rocks of southern Africa*. Cape Town, Purnell.

Lewis-Williams, J. D. 1980. Ethnography and iconography: aspects of southern San thought and art, *Man* 15: 467–82.

1981a. *Believing and seeing: symbolic meanings in southern San rock paintings*. London, Academic Press.

1981b. The thin red line: southern San notions and rock paintings of supernatural potency, *South African Archaeological Bulletin* 36: 5–13.

1982. The economic and social context of southern San rock art, *Current Anthropology* 23: 429–49.

1983. Reply to C. K. Cooke and A. R. Willcox, *Current Anthropology* 24: 540–5.

1986. Cognitive and optical illusions in San rock art research, *Current Anthropology* 27: 171–8.

1990. *Discovering southern African rock art*. Cape Town, David Philip.

1996. 'A visit to the Lion's House': the structure, metaphors and sociopolitical significance of a nineteenth-century Bushman myth, in J. Deacon and T. A. Dowson (eds.), *Voices from the past: /Xam Bushmen and the Bleek and Lloyd collection*. Johannesburg, Witwatersrand University Press.

Lewis-Williams, J. D. and T. A. Dowson. 1989. *Images of power: understanding Bushman rock art*. Johannesburg, Southern Books.

Marshall, L. 1957. N!ow, *Africa* 27: 232–40.

1960. !Kung Bushman bands, *Africa* 30(4): 325–55.

1962. !Kung Bushman religious beliefs, *Africa* 32: 221–51.

1969. The medicine dance of the !Kung Bushmen, *Africa* 39: 347–81.

Marshall Thomas, E. 1959. *The harmless people*. Harmondsworth, Penguin.

Murray, C. 1980. Ritual practice and belief, in W. F. Lye and C. Murray (eds.), *Transformations on the Highveld: the Tswana and southern Sotho*, pp. 122–33. Cape Town, David Philip.

Orpen, J. M. 1874. A glimpse into the mythology of the Maluti Bushmen, *Cape Monthly Magazine* (NS) 9: 1–13.

Pager, H. 1975. *Stone Age myth and magic*. Graz, Akademische Druk-u. Verlagsanstalt.

Rosenthal, E. and A. J. H. Goodwin. 1953. *Cave artists of South Africa*. Cape Town, Balkema.

Schapera, I. 1971. *Rainmaking rites of Tswana tribes*. Leiden, Afrika-Studiecentrum.

Schmidt, S. 1979. The rain bull of the South African Bushmen, *African Studies* 38: 201–24.

Soga, J. H. 1931. *The Ama-Xhosa life and customs*. London, Lovedale.

Stanford, W. E. 1910. Statement of Silayi, with reference to his life among the Bushmen, *Transactions of the Royal Society of South Africa* 1: 435–40.

Stow, G. W. 1905. *The native races of South Africa*. London, Swan Sonnenschein.

Stow, G. W. and D. F. Bleek. 1930. *Rock paintings in South Africa*. London, Methuen.

Thackeray, J. F. 1988. Southern African rock art and Xhosa beliefs associated with *abantubomlambo*, *Pictogram* 1(2): 2–3.

Vinnicombe, P. 1972. Myth, motive and selection in southern African rock art, *Africa* 42: 192–204.

1976. *People of the eland: rock paintings of the Drakensberg Bushmen as a reflection of their life and thought*. Pietermaritzburg, Natal University Press.

Willcox, A. R. 1963. *The rock art of South Africa*. London, Nelson.

1984. Meanings and motives in San rock art: the views of W. D. Hammond-Tooke and J. D. Lewis-Williams considered, *South African Archaeological Bulletin* 39: 53–7.

Woodhouse, H. C. 1992. *The rain and its creatures, as the Bushmen painted them*. Rivonia, William Waterman Publications.

Yates, T. 1993. Frameworks for an archaeology of the body, in C. Tilley (ed.), *Interpretative archaeology*, pp. 31–72. Oxford, Berg.

Christopher Chippindale and Paul S. C. Taçon

# 6. The many ways of dating Arnhem Land rock-art, north Australia

Fortunate circumstances – and good work by the first generation of field researchers – have provided an unusually strong framework for dating the long and varied repertoire of rock-art in Arnhem Land, north Australia: it is now one of the very few regional rock-art sequences with a clear relative and absolute chronology. It now becomes possible to explore – rather than to suppose – whether conventional guiding assumptions are true, whether a distinctive 'style' is in fact a good marker of date. And a clear chronology guides the varied approaches from informed knowledge and from formal methods which together build an integrated knowledge of a complex and highly informative rock-art region.

## Arnhem Land and its rock-art

Arnhem Land (Berndt and Berndt 1954) is a large region on the central north coast of Australia, a block of land some 400 km east–west by 250 km north–south. It is bounded on the north by the Arafura Sea separating Australia from New Guinea, and on the east by the Gulf of Carpentaria. To the west is the modern city of Darwin, and the rest of the 'Top End' of the present-day Northern Territory. To the south, Arnhem Land runs into the semi-desert country as it approaches arid central Australia. The climate is tropical, with an annual nine months of dry season, and a flooding three months of monsoon wet.

Parts of Arnhem Land, especially the region of the three Alligator Rivers in western Arnhem Land, now partly in Kakadu National Park, have large exposures, with crags and cliffs, of ancient Precambrian sandstone. This 'western Arnhem Land' or 'Alligator Rivers' region (Fig. 6.1) is celebrated for the quantity, range and artistic quality of its rock-art (Brandl 1973; Chaloupka 1993). Several hundred sites are

known with many thousands of figures – so many not even a reliable estimate of the tally exists; since not all the area has been covered by intensive survey (for example Chaloupka et al. 1985; Chaloupka 1992), much probably remains to be rediscovered, and very few sites have been recorded in detail (see Chippindale and Taçon 1993). The bulk of the art is painted. There are also some engravings (Sullivan 1988), figures etched into the rock by the application of some corrosive fluid (Chaloupka 1993: 235–6), and figures made in the rare medium of moulded beeswax applied to rock-surfaces and making low-relief figures (Brandl 1968).

Western Arnhem Land, specifically the drainages of the Alligator rivers, has also benefited from palaeoecological and archaeological research of an intensity rare in Australia. There is a well-studied framework of ecological change, in relation to changing sea-levels and river regimes (Woodroffe et al. 1986); the consequent changes in flora and fauna can be sketched from that, and in turn the subsistence opportunities seen for hunter-gatherers who depend on varied resources and their seasonal availability. The archaeological deposits give well-dated sequences that relate to the palaeoecological record (for example, Schrire 1982); the Arnhem Land soils, acid sands that are soaked each wet season, are hostile to the continuing survival of any materials other than stone. The long-term archaeological record, accordingly, is overwhelmingly a story of lithics which is not easy to interpret in human terms.

It is not unfair to say that in Arnhem Land, the archaeology tends to offer 'chronology without information'; once below the upper levels where the

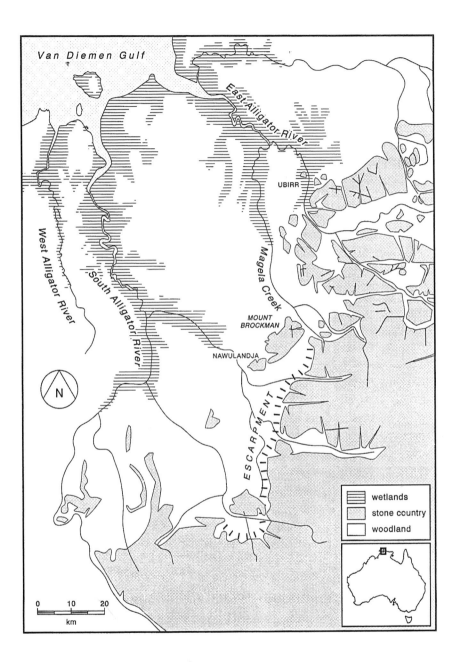

**Fig. 6.1.** The Alligator Rivers region, heart of the rock-art zone of western Arnhem Land. Its north-west limit is Van Diemen Gulf, the bay within the Arafura Sea into which flow the three Alligator Rivers. Along their courses are the present-day areas of wetlands. To the south and east is the 'stone country', often edged by a sheer escarpment. Within the area of woodland between low wetlands and high stone country are scattered rocky islands and outliers.

Rock-art may be found anywhere offering suitable protected surfaces on the rock. There are concentrations where outliers, such as Nawulandja, Mount Brockman and Ubirr, are close to the resources of the wetlands.

shells in middens shield materials from the acid soil, there are commonly only the lithics. Below a certain depth, even the charcoal and finely divided carbon perishes, so the basal dates for the sequences are by luminescent techniques applied to the sand matrix (for example Roberts *et al.* 1994). The rock-art, with its intricate record of humans and their activities, shows their kit of hunting and gathering gear and of ceremony. Nearly all the objects are in organic materials that perish in the archaeological record; at one time, it promised the complement – 'information without chronology'.

How a developed chronology for the rock-art has been established is the subject of this chapter: partly by working with features of the rock-art itself, partly by 'bridging' across to the palaeoecological and archaeological records, we now have information *and* chronology in the rock-art.

## Approaches to Arnhem Land art
### Dating
Unusually, painting on the rocks has continued in Arnhem Land up to the present. There are many rock-paintings from this century. The iconography, pigments, and design rules of the later rock-art continue in the celebrated bark-paintings of the region and – within the last few years – in paintings on fine art-paper. Traditional knowledge of the paintings is perpetuated along with the images themselves. By drawing on a variety of evidence, as detailed in this chapter, we are able to document a long sequence in which both the subjects and the manners of depiction change. Links between the pictures and the dated palaeoecological–archaeological sequence for western Arnhem Land permit this relative sequence to be tied, for its later portions, to an absolute chronology. And there are some radiocarbon dates directly from or pertinent to the art itself.

### Informed methods
The rare good fortune of Arnhem Land painting's having continued into present times allows opportunity of direct insight into the images. For a very few

pictures, one can today ask the artist directly what they depict, and why they were painted! A continuing knowledge and memory of hunter-gatherer ways, and of the stories of the country, enables many images to be understood, sometimes by reference to knowledge of the ancient Dreaming-time when the world was made and ordered, sometimes by everyday considerations: one type of fish, a mullet, is painted with its head snapped back – because you do well to break its neck when you catch one, lest it cheekily flaps and flips its way from the bank back into the water. Distinctive figures with distinctive attributes can be traced back from their appearance in the modern stories far through the art sequence.

### Formal methods
While a great many elements in the recent rock-art are known in modern times or ethnographically, elements in the older art are different. The *didjeridu*, the musical instrument of everyday life and of ceremony today, seems absent from the ancient art, and so is the modern spear-thrower; the boomerang, nowadays used only as clap-sticks in music-making, is seen in old art as a hunting and a fighting weapon. The intricate conventions of the X-ray manner of depiction, commonplace in recent art, are known from contemporary bark- and paper-painting. The older paintings use different conventions, as well as depicting other subjects; more formal methods are called for there.

### Analogy
With exceptional, even unique opportunities for insight from contemporary knowledge, with a good dating sequence, and with older paintings full of intricate well-drawn detail, Arnhem Land researchers have also worked in a framework of analogy (e.g. Lewis 1988: 68–70).

## 'Chains' and 'cables' in the dating of Arnhem Land art
Alison Wylie (1989) has usefully distinguished two habits of archaeological reasoning.

Commonly, we work by *chains* of logic: from observation $x$ of the evidence we develop proposition $y$, and from that there follows deduction $z$. Each is a link in a chain of reasoned deduction. Neither archaeological observation nor archaeological deduction is usually secure with any real certainty: a lengthening chain of reasoning accumulates the weaknesses in its numerous links. Many a link is qualified with a 'probably' or 'in all likelihood', and many an unqualified statement – 'this is a midden', 'these are the attributes of a state-level society' – in reality carries large uncertainty. Suppose a link from $x$ to $y$, so qualified or not, has a real certainty of 0.7; that is, it is true in 70 per cent of cases and un- or uncertainly true in 30 per cent. Suppose the next link, $y$ to $z$, has the same 0.7 certainty. Then the overall certainty, from $x$ to $y$ to $z$, is 0.7 times $0.7 = 0.49 - 49$ per cent, and less than 50 per cent. In just two steps of chained reasoning, we have reached an outcome which is more likely to be wrong than right! These rules, which apply to all reasoning by a sequence of deduction, are particularly telling for archaeology, where there is so often a weak coupling between what we are able to observe – 'what are the features of these chipped-stone pieces?' – and what we hope to study – 'did people move seasonally about the landscape, or was it divided into the territories of distinct groups?'

Against chains of reasoning, Wylie commends another approach, of 'cabling'. As a strong cable is made by combining together many threads, each one individually weak, so can a variety of forms of evidence, and individually weak deductions drawn from them, be tied and be pulled together, collectively to build a reasonably secure knowledge. This is the established habit of Arnhem Land rock-art research.

Certainly, cabling is the right spirit in which to approach the dating of Arnhem Land art. Relevant to date are many distinct sources of information, or aspects to sources of information, and distinct ways of working with them. Some apply to very few figures; for only a handful is there known to be a direct memory of their making. Some apply to fig-

ures of an infrequent class, such as those that depend on certain characteristic subjects. Some that apply to many figures are weak, such as those that depend on the relative weathering of different colours of pigment. Yet, taken together, these methods, each fallible by itself, build a chronology for Arnhem Land art which is unusually detailed and unusually secure by the standards of rock-art dating; they permit detailed studies of change over time, of a kind rarely possible with the materials of rock-art. Arnhem Land researchers now have grounds for sufficient confidence in rock-art chronology that we see anomalies and contradictions as fruitful opportunities to advance knowledge by exploring how the anomaly comes about, rather than challenges that upset the dating framework.

## Approaches to the dating of Arnhem Land rock-art

Dating has been a central issue since considered study of Arnhem Land rock-art began (Spencer and Gillen 1928: 823–4; McCarthy 1958, 1960: 297–414). Brandl (1973: 171–8), working with the distinctions amongst the paintings made by Aboriginal people in their country, recognised an earlier period of 'Mimi' art (divided into early and late), and a transitional period leading into the X-ray conventions that are seen both on the painted rocks and on bark-paintings, on which he developed a chronology. Lewis (1988) drew on changing technology as depicted in the pictures for a finer chronology. Chaloupka (1977, 1984, 1985) made further divisions into distinct successive styles of depiction, as well as changing subject-matter, and linked changes in the art to environmental shifts, tying the relative sequence in with the absolute dates. More recently, Harris matrices have been used to analyse sequences in detail (Chippindale and Taçon 1993), and the first radiocarbon dates directly applicable to beeswax art have become available (Nelson *et al.* 1995).

Most potential sources of information for dating Arnhem Land art were noticed a generation ago by Brandl (1973: 171–8). Although there has been some disputation between researchers (see, for example, Lewis 1988: 6–13; Haskovec 1992a), behind the differences there is a good consistency in the patterns discerned by different researchers emphasising each a certain aspect.

## Aboriginal knowledge of the antiquity of Arnhem Land paintings

Even the casual tourist is made aware of the lively present-day meaning of Arnhem Land rock-art (for example, by Breeden and Wright 1989: 27ff). Contemporary Aboriginal knowledge includes a history for Arnhem Land paintings imputing the old ones to the Mimi people (Carroll 1977). Arnhem Landers know the story of their rock-painting in these terms. Before us in the land were the Mimi people, and it was the Mimi people who taught us how to paint. You can see paintings on high ceilings that no human can reach; the Mimi must have pulled the roof down to reach the surface or flown up so they could paint up there. The Mimi have gone as people now, but they are still there as spirits, thin as they can slide into cracks in the rocks. Clever people sometimes see them.

Arnhem Landers, naturally enough, have no fixed definition of what constitutes the Mimi art, as Brandl (1973: 165, 167, 172–8) notes. They may recognise it by a faded red colour, by strange habits of depiction, by obsolete weapons and implements, by ceremonial dress unknown today – that is, by features which set it apart from the imagery of present-day knowledge.

In our archaeological view of the paintings we see a matching distinction, recognising a noticeable step in a long sequence between the archaic paintings – ones Arnhem Landers identify with the Mimi – and the more recent ones with conventions that Arnhem Landers recognise as their own. But this is not an abrupt or total break: there are continuities as well. (How different is different, how much the same is the same, when one is judging change through a long-term sequence?)

Recent art on bark and on paper from Gunbalanya

(Oenpelli), a painting centre in the heart of the western Arnhem Land rock-art region, often depicts the Mimi (see, for example, paintings by Garry Djorlom, Djawida Nadjongorle, Peter Nabarlambarl, in Dyer 1994: plates 30, 36, 38). In the contemporary way of painting them, Mimi are indeed narrow and thin like spirits that can slip into the cracks; but other present-day conventions of painting Mimi, in the treatment of the head and in the kind of spear-throwers they carry, come from the later traditions of the rock-art.

## Dating by reference to historical knowledge

Since rock-art in Arnhem Land continues into recent times, and since its conventions are perpetuated in contemporary paintings on bark and on paper, there is memory and historical knowledge of paintings and painting conventions.

*Memory and historical records of artists and their styles*
For now, the practice of rock painting has largely come to an end in western Arnhem Land. A number of pictures have been painted in the last twenty or so years, although often – it has been noted – in circumstances where non-Aboriginal people were present (or even at their prompting), and in that sense not painted in the traditional way. Still, it remains a remarkable fact that here one can go to rock-art with the painter, and hear directly and on the spot when and how a picture was made (Taçon 1992a; Taçon and Garde 1995).

Beyond these few are the paintings, still not numerous, by artists now passed away, but of which there is some record, particularly due to the work of Chaloupka, and thereby of known date. A beeswax composition of water-buffalo and buffalo-hunter with rifle and skinning knife in lower Deaf Adder Creek (Chaloupka 1984: fig. 25) is known to have been made by Najombolmi in the early 1950s (George Chaloupka, pers. comm.); at Nawulandja (Nourlangie) is a group of paintings, now the most celebrated in the region, by the same master artist, painted in 1964 (Chaloupka 1982: 22–5).

The Najombolmi paintings at Nawulandja have some distinctive conventions, within the elaborate X-ray manner of recent polychrome paintings that one can see elsewhere. The bark-painters have their own individual styles, of course, and with practice one can recognise the work of the individual artist. Bardayal Nadjamerrek paints his human figures always with a very large first toe (for example, West 1995: plates 7–8), and the *rarrk* (fine-line cross-hatching) of a painting follows an individual artist's habit. (One of us remembers feeling his eyes had begun to understand Arnhem Land painting, when he recognised an individual artist's *rarrk* on a piece glimpsed in a souvenir shop window and knew immediately who had painted it.) Since a distinct style is evident in the rock-paintings known to be by Najombolmi, one can hope to recognise his own personal style in other figures, and this has been done (Haskovec and Sullivan 1989). But Chaloupka (1993: 238; pers. comm.) and Lewis (pers. comm.) fear the style identified in that study with Najombolmi is not of a single individual but common also to his companions Djimongurr and Djorlom and/or others. Whatever the case, one can have confidence that figures with these distinctive traits are broadly of the period when this artist was active, since the others were his contemporaries.

*Subjects depicted, and pigments used, of known historical date*

European people and European things have been known in Arnhem Land since settlements were planted on the Coburg Peninsula about 160 years ago. Depictions of European people and things (Fig. 6.2) (Chaloupka 1993: 193–205) are datable to that period onwards.

Guns are seen in some paintings (Fig. 6.2), and some are painted so exactly they can be identified as the Martini-Henry rifle, British military-surplus and the favourite buffalo-hunting weapon for much of this century (Chaloupka 1993: plate 226). At Cannon Hill, there are stencils of European steel axes, and detailed paintings of aircraft (the Qantas airline's

'Kangaroo Route', 1940s: Chaloupka 1993: plate 230) and of ships, one with the name of a lugger that traded into Oenpelli Mission. At a remote shelter on the plateau is a picture of the whole wharf at Darwin with its buildings and boats, well painted with much detail although some hundreds of kilometres away (Chaloupka 1993). The Europeans themselves are painted, with their hats and pipes, and without hands (in their trouser pockets!); and a human figure near the East Alligator River crossing (Fig. 6.2) is painted with a gun and long pigtails down his back in the Chinese manner; he is surely one of the Chinese labourers brought in the late nineteenth century to Darwin, who worked the mines at Pine Creek to the south.

Domestic animals brought to the Coburg settlements quickly wandered away into the bush. When Leichardt came through western Arnhem Land on his famous walk across Australia in 1845, western Arnhem Landers' knowledge of white men and of their animals was his first notice that he was close to the goal of the Port Essington settlement. So paintings of cattle, horses and water-buffalo (Chaloupka 1993: plates 223–5) will post-date the Port Essington settlement of 1838–49 or the earlier failed plantation at Raffles Bay (1827–9), whose pigs, ponies, buffaloes and red cattle wandered the woods (Spillett 1972: 81, 91). Near the west bank of the East Alligator River is painted a line of horses, with riders and bells around their necks, who must be Europeans on their horses; Chaloupka (1979) identifies these as pictures of the McKinlay Expedition which lost itself in that region in 1865; and many buffalo-shooters, miners and others went on horseback through the country (e.g. Warburton 1944).

No natural blue pigments are used in Aboriginal art but the artificial pigment of laundry blue was adopted for some rock-paintings (Chaloupka 1993: plates 74, 75) when it became available at some point in the nineteenth century.

For some centuries before the European settlement (Macknight 1976; Clarke 1994), Macassan fishermen camped on Arnhem Land shores to cure

**Fig. 6.2.** Later Arnhem Land rock-art: much-overpainted panel from the Lower East Alligator River region, western Arnhem Land. Photograph and line drawing to identify images within the mass of paint.

The polychrome paint, and X-ray technique in the manner of depiction, are characteristic of the Estuarine. The large fishes are typical of the Freshwater period. The human figure, centre lower, with tobacco-pipe, rifle and Chinese hair-style, places that image into the Contact era.

**Fig. 6.3.** Later Arnhem Land rock-art: detail of panel from catchment of the South Alligator River.

In this much-overpainted panel of distinctive paintings, clear superpositions can be plotted. Many figures are from the recent period, with a range of features distinctive of a late date. These range from the comparative freshness of the white pigment, which even in sheltered surfaces is not enduring when applied over large areas of rock, to many distinctive features in the manner with which subjects are depicted. Underneath, in faded and blurred dark red, fragments of ancient paintings can sometimes be discerned, again distinctive in pigment, subject and manner of depiction.

the *trepang* they had caught. Images of their boats and huts (Chaloupka 1993: plates 214, 215) are dated without exactness in that way.

Images of these historically dated subjects are not frequent in the art, but they are useful beyond their own interest. One can be certain the European-sourced materials, conventions and manners of depiction applying here were active within the last

century and a half. The 'McKinlay paintings' of the ridden horses are in red and somewhat faded; they are a useful proof that red paintings can be recent, and that they can blur and fade in a matter of about a century.

*Distinctive subjects in relation to contact-era and recent Arnhem Land hunter-gatherer life-ways*

The European and Macassan subjects aside, there are many subjects and activities depicted which are clearly those known for Arnhem Land hunter-gatherers at the time of contact. It is reasonably supposed that many of these subjects were in use for many centuries before. Some can be specifically associated with landscape features of limited age, such as the freshwater swamps where magpie geese now flock and make a major food-source. Paintings of the distinctive fans made from the goose wings will be of that Freshwater era, and the distinctive spear-thrower of Arnhem Land today (Lewis 1988: 53–5) will indicate that a painting may be 'new'.

Palaeoecological evidence (below) shows the freshwater swamps are some hundreds of years old (rather than decades or thousands). Images specifically linked to the freshwater swamps and life-ways will fall within that age-range.

*Distinctive manners of depiction in relation to contact-era and recent Arnhem Land painting*

Modern Aboriginal knowledge and continuity in painting – nowadays on bark and on paper more often than on rock – identifies the many and distinctive conventions in picture-making of recent times. Again, these show a rock-painting may be new without ruling out that it is old. Among these are the distinctive and elaborate X-ray conventions where the interior features of an animal subject are shown within the body. It can be hazarded that the 'simple X-ray' variant of the convention, in which an un-elaborated empty space stands for the body cavity, or a single simple line stands for the gut, is a precursor of the elaborate convention – hence its other name, 'early X-ray' (Brandl 1973). Stratigraphic study of

**Fig. 6.4.** Earlier Arnhem Land rock-art: Dynamic Figure group.

These Dynamic Figures are characteristic in the 'mulberry' colour of pigment which sets 'in' rather than 'on' the rock surface (and reproduces in monochrome as a mid-grey), in the fine technique of 'brush-painting', in the Dynamic manner of depiction, and in aspects of the subject-matter (notice the boomerangs held by the human figure below and by the animal-headed being above).

These figures, in Upper Deaf Adder Creek, were unusually (and valuably for study of chronology) amended by the addition in a thicker line and different, darker-coloured pigment of the simple spear-thrower – an object and art-subject not present until a later period.

sequences in the paintings confirms that antiquity; and a radiocarbon date for a beeswax figure using the convention (below) now places a calendar age on it.

## Dating by reference to lack of historical knowledge

The several aspects to dating noted so far depend on historical knowledge of aspects of the pictures. It follows that aspects *not* known historically are likely not to be recent and have the potential to be old.

*Distinctive subjects not known in contact-era and recent Arnhem Land hunter-gatherer life-ways*
Equally, distinctive subjects seen in the paintings that

are not seen in contact-era paintings, and are not used in Arnhem Land life-ways today, will be old.

A frequent subject is boomerangs, sometimes stencilled, sometimes painted, and in use as hunting or fighting weapons (Fig. 6.4). Yet Arnhem Landers today use boomerangs only as clap-sticks in music-making. As well as the spear-throwers of the common modern type, there is a simpler form, painted as a simple hooked stick (Fig. 6.4): this will be archaic – if it can be separated from the variant spear-throwers known in modern times and called by Cundy (1989: 104) the 'North Australian cylindrical spear-thrower'.

An obvious group among these instructive subjects is the several animals that are extinct in the region. Chief among these is the thylacine (Tasmanian tiger: *Thylacinus*), commonly seen in older art styles painted with striped flanks and a distinctive tail (Brandl 1972; Lewis 1988). The thylacine is supposed to have been extinguished in mainland Australia consequent on its being out-competed by dingoes; the coming of the dingo into Australia is uncertainly dated about 3500 b.p. (Corbett 1995: 14–17). Identified with less certainty are pictures of the long-nosed echidna, because it closely resembles the common, and commonly painted, echidna; it is known today only in New Guinea, and its date of extinction – if it were in Arnhem Land – is unknown. The local disappearance of other sometimes-depicted creatures such as numbats is unknown. A bone of Tasmanian devil (*Sarcophilus harrisii*) dated after 3100 b.p. from the Paribari shelter (Schrire 1982: 53) is a reminder that extinctions may not be very ancient events. A clear and archaic painting of two strange creatures in Upper Deaf Adder Creek is identified without certainty as depicting *Palorchestes*, a species of the Australian Pleistocene megafauna (Murray and Chaloupka 1984), again with unknown date of regional extinction.

Many subjects may be of recent or of ancient date – dilly-bags, for example – and are therefore not evidence diagnostically.

*Distinctive manners of depiction not known in contact-era and recent Arnhem Land painting*
The same goes for conventions of picture-making and the manners in which things are depicted. Conventions that are not seen in paintings identifiable as of recent date by other characteristics will be archaic.

## Stratigraphic sequences on the painted surfaces

By their several common features, Arnhem Land researchers can establish paintings that together make a distinctive group (called by Chaloupka 'styles') – 'Dynamic Figures', 'Northern Running Figures', and so on. Often – as befits a refined art tradition of classical characteristics – particular traits are so distinctive one comes to recognise them with confidence even from a worn scrap on a ruined surface; the S-curve in the body of a Northern Running Figure, or the bobbles, trailers and tassels of Yam Figures are unmistakable. The energy of the Dynamic Figures, well named by Chaloupka, is such that even a static coiled snake, painted in that manner, appears dynamic to the eye.

The first means of establishing the sequence of these styles is provided by those many surfaces in which paintings lie one over the other, often so densely the rock surface itself is hidden and little patches of covered-over paintings are spied under and between those that lie on top (e.g. Yuwengayay: Walsh 1988: plate 314). We have some, but not complete, confidence that one can often discern on careful examination which line lies over which; therefore the order in which the paintings were placed can be deduced. It is harder to be sure when the more transparent yellow pigment is involved, when one line is thick and sharp and the other broad and indistinct, when the lines are old or faded, or when the paint of two lines is of similar hue. We are encouraged by the cautious confidence of workers in Baja California, where figures are in faded red ochre on sandstone as the older Arnhem Land figures are, when they attempt similar observations (Stanley Price, pers. comm.). It is valuable when multiple observations can be made at a single panel, and when a pattern of sequence is repeated at several panels, so an erroneous judgement as to any one superposition is not fatal.

From his observations at two sites on Mount Gilruth, Chaloupka (1977) was able to discern a stratigraphic sequence of styles (observations there since contested by Haskovec 1992a). A detailed study of a panel at Mount Brockman (137 figures) and another at Kungurrul (172 figures), which have many paintings with distinctive traits in some reasonably secure visible superposition, has confirmed essentials of the Gilruth sequence (Chippindale and Taçon 1993). The Kungurrul site, in particular, is valuable in including more styles, and therefore providing a fuller stratigraphy which may now have superseded those seen at Mount Gilruth.

One odd class of figures is the marks of 'thrown objects' seen generally on high ceilings in irregular lines and splotches of colour, and thought to have been made by throwing objects such as pieces of bush twine soaked in ochre. These, in high places all on their own, are not in useful superimposition in relation to other figures; they do not yet find a place in the sequence as observed stratigraphically.

Rarely, a more certain kind of sequence is provided by a rock-fall which covers or hides a painted surface; it may at the same time create a new surface which can be painted. Then the figures on the 'lost' surface must be older than those on the 'made' surface, while both may be coeval with pictures on the unaffected surfaces adjacent.

## Bridging to dated palaeoecological and archaeological evidence

The palaeoecology and archaeology of Arnhem Land provide well-dated sequences relevant to the art sequence in the same region. We have no direct links between them. The ecological changes have transformed the Arnhem Land environment without, so far as is known, making surfaces newly available for painting. Although many of the Arnhem Land archaeological sites are in shelters with paintings, the archaeological deposits do not include or cover painted surfaces – as if the water in the acid sands carries the paint off the wall once it is buried. Instead, one is obliged and able to 'bridge' across from aspects of the art to aspects of the palaeoecology and archaeology of Arnhem Land that share common features, together to make a history of Arnhem Land in landscape, stone and paint. Taçon and Brockwell (1995), a detailed study in this approach for the period 15,000–7000 BP, could be extended to a fuller time-span.

### Bridging across to the palaeoecological record

The region's environmental history divides into three distinct periods. The first began with initial human settlement; it ended when the post-glacial rising sea flooded across the broad and flat Arafura Plain to the north, converting it into the shallow Arafura Sea, and reaching about the position of the present shoreline about 6000 BP (Chappell and Grindrod 1983: 67–9, 87–8); this is the *Pre-Estuarine* period. There followed an era when the lowland ecology was dominated by the marine presence, and it is likely there were intensely saline flats, as nowadays persist in some lower reaches of the East Alligator River (Woodroffe *et al.* 1986, 1987; Woodroffe 1988); this is the *Estuarine* period. During the Estuarine, sand-bars and mangrove thickets grew up in the river systems, to the point that they blocked tidal access by sea-water. The salt water was gradually washed out by the wet-season flow of stormwater, and the upper portions of the estuarine systems were converted into freshwater swamps, an enormously rich and productive resource: this is the *Freshwater* period. This transformation is evident in the archaeological sequences from the sites near rivers; after a period without shell (*Pre-Estuarine*), marine shells appear at a date corresponding to the arrival of the sea (*Estuarine*), and give way to freshwater species at the time of freshwater conversion (*Freshwater*) (e.g. Schrire 1982 in respect of sites near the lower East Alligator River; Allen and Barton 1989: 101–2).

Images in the rock-art reflect the same changes. The dominant animals, and likely animal-food resources, in the old styles are the several varieties of macropod; there are fish, but it is noticeable that among these it is the eel-tailed catfish and other freshwater species which are frequent. In the later paintings, fish dominate over macropods; and the dominant fish are the species of the big swamps and of the freshwater rivers – commonly fork-tail catfish, barramundi and saratoga (Taçon 1988). The change in rock-art subjects, following the ecological sequence, is most evident in the northern sites that are close to the modern wetlands, such as Cannon Hill and Ubirr. It is less apparent or not visible at all in the upland sites on the southern plateau, a region above the escarpment not directly affected by the transformation of the low landscape downstream.

Accordingly, Chaloupka's scheme divides the art into four phases:

- *Pre-estuarine* to about 6000 BP;
- *Estuarine* about 6000–1200 BP;
- *Freshwater* about 1200–100 BP; and a recent
- *Contact* period from the mid–late nineteenth century up to the present.

The Contact period is distinguished by depictions of European people, subjects and introduced creatures and by other markers of a modern date (but ecologically part of the Freshwater).

*Bridging across to the archaeological record*
Just as one can bridge from the art to the environmental sequence, so one can bridge from the art to the archaeological sequence. Difficult soil conditions mean that the archaeology at most sites consists only of stone artefacts until the last several hundred years (e.g. Ngarradj Warde Djobkeng: Allen and Barton 1989). And stone artefacts are not frequent in the art – a plain reminder of how small a proportion of an elaborate material culture survives in the defining archaeological record. The recognisable stone artefact commonly seen in the paintings is the ground stone axe (e.g. Taçon and Brockwell 1995: figs. 8, 9), hafted with a withy passed round the stone head and bound together into a handle with gum/resin and bush-twine just as it always has been in Arnhem Land in recent times, and as it is so depicted in contemporary bark- and paper-paintings (e.g. paintings by Ralph Nganjmirra, Danny Djorlom and Garry Djorlom in Dyer 1994: plates 16, 27, 30). But the stone axe has a long history in Arnhem Land; its occurrences in sites near the East Alligator was many years ago shown to extend back to some 20,000 years (White 1967), and there are rotted fragments of igneous rock likely to be used for axe-making in old strata at Nauwalabila (Jones and Johnson 1985). So bridging across from axes in the pictures to axes in the archaeology – which can be reliably done for the hafted axe as a distinctive

subject – gives only slight indication of date (Lewis 1988: 46).

Recently recognised from a single painted example in the art is another stone artefact, the hafted chisel, introduced about 4000 BP, and therefore providing a sharper marker of date (Taçon and Brockwell 1995: 680). Depictions of various stone points can also set limits on the ages of particular paintings and their styles (Taçon 1991).

*Art materials within archaeological deposits*
Many art sites have no archaeological component because they are well above the ground surface, or because the rock at their base is washed clean by wet-season storms. A certain number of Arnhem Land sites have both an art and an archaeological component. Where paintings extend down towards the modern ground surface, they appear to vanish as they reach the earth; the soil conditions do not permit the pigments to persist on the rock, once buried. Nor are engravings of the region in a direct stratigraphic relation to archaeological deposits. So we have no direct stratigraphical links between art and archaeology.

A repeated feature of deep Arnhem Land archaeological sites is the occurrence of good-quality ochre, consistently from the earliest levels and – at Nauwalabila – shaped with distinct facets from a level dating to about 12,000 BP (Taçon and Brockwell 1995: 687). Does ochre mean that painting, and therefore the rock-art, goes back in Arnhem Land to the very beginning, with two sites now dated by luminescence as having sequences that begin some 50,000 to 60,000 years ago? Is Arnhem Land art therefore 'the world's longest continuing art tradition' (Chaloupka 1993)? As well as rock-art, ochre has many uses in modern Aboriginal ceremony, and is in repeated association with burial from the later Palaeolithic elsewhere in the world.

In Arnhem Land, there is no certainty either that ochre was used for painting from the beginning; or that painting with ochre was on rock surfaces (rather than on perishable subjects); or that the first paintings on rock surfaces are amongst the ones that survive. It is equally clear that a demonstrated potential for rock-art from that first settlement is shown by the presence of ochre.

At sites towards the Victoria River art province, beyond the south-west limits of Arnhem Land, excavated sequences show ochre appearing abruptly and in large quantities in strata dating from around 1400 years ago onwards (David *et al.* 1994). The ochre is there reasonably linked with the large ochre figures painted on the walls of the same shelters, without its being directly demonstrated that the ochre in the ground is the self-same stuff as the material on the walls. In Arnhem Land itself, no excavated site has provided or hinted at such a direct link, because nowhere is there a grand mass of ochre in the strata that can confidently be linked to a matching mass of ochre on the rock surface above; analysis of the sequences does show 'pulses' in ochre presence in the deposits, and these might correlate with new styles (Taçon and Brockwell 1995).

**Principles of continuity**

In resolving the sequence of different distinctive 'styles' – whether defined by subject, by manner of depiction, or by both aspects in combination – one can fairly expect that a particular feature will have been depicted over some continuous time-span rather than coming into the pictures, disappearing, and then recurring; therefore those styles with common features should fall adjacent to each other in the chronological sequence.

A subject illustrating this is the boomerang, depicted in the distinct painting styles of Dynamic Figure, Post-Dynamic Figure, Simple Figure, and Northern Running Figure. All of these, it is likely, will form a coherent group occupying a distinct block of time, rather than the boomerang's having entered, left and re-entered the repertoire of subjects (see Jones and Johnson 1985: 218, for a smiliar argument in respect of axes). *A priori*, one could expect also that the stencils of boomerangs will be of broadly the same era as the painted group.

In distinctive aspects to manners of depiction, the same expectation of continuity will apply as it does to what is depicted. In the depiction of how boomerangs are held in the hand, for example, one sees two distinct conventions. In the one, found in paintings of the Dynamic manner, the boomerangs – usual two or three – are drawn held together and crossing at the hand; they are commonly of much the same length. In the other, found in figures of the Post-Dynamic and Simple manners, the two or three boomerangs are drawn concentric, as if nested one inside the other and with the inner ones shorter. It is reasonable to expect these last two manners to be adjacent (or contemporary) within the sequence.

A puzzle in current knowledge of the Arnhem Land sequence is an apparent contradiction concerning archaic pictures of large animals, commonly macropods; these are the distinctive and defining element of Chaloupka's Large Naturalistic style, which he sets early in the sequence. Our field observations of superposition – since Lewis's (1988), Haskovec's (1992a) and Chippindale and Taçon's (1993) noticing the anomaly – lead us to conclude that closely similar subjects and manners of depiction exist in both that early phase and in the later Yam Figure/Simple Figure phase; between these, in our current understanding, is the Dynamic Figure style, where a different and distinctive manner of depicting animals is evident. Here, it appears, the continuity principle does not hold.

**Direct dating by radiocarbon**

Chemical analysis of paint from recent figures found its organic component to be nil (Clarke and North 1991). Painters of early modern times, it is remembered, used to use the juice of an orchid root as a binder, but one does not know whether it is preserved in the paint – apparently not, if those studies are relied on (and there is no reason to question them).

Direct dating has been attempted on organics from painted surfaces in Australia and elsewhere (Rosenfeld and Smith 1997). Sometimes plausible dates have been obtained (e.g. Tratebas 1993), sometimes dates are erratic for the same figures (e.g. McDonald *et al.* 1990); usually, it is not proven that the organic carbon being dated in fact relates to the painting of an image (e.g. Nelson 1993).

It remains to be demonstrated, therefore, whether Arnhem Land paintings *can* be dated directly by the radiocarbon method. Indeed, with a well-dated sequence established by other methods, it may be that Arnhem Land will have a special value as a region to check novel radiocarbon studies by reference to paintings of known age.

A small component in the Arnhem Land repertoire, especially in the region of the lower East Alligator River, is figures made by moulding wax from the nests of the native *Trigona* bee. The soft wax is kneaded into pellets or strips or sheets and applied to the rock in varied designs and images. Analytical study proves what one would suppose, that beeswax is a good material for carbon dating, made by the bees in a matter of not many months, collected and used for art soon after. Chemically, it is complex and stable, and a pilot programme of carbon dating has shown that one beeswax figure is some 4000 years old (Nelson *et al.* 1995). The majority, however, are at most a few hundred years old; radiocarbon dates for these, with their large error factors and unhelpful calibration curves, give a reliable but inexact date.

Where dated beeswax figures are stratified over or under paint, a date for the beeswax figures gives a minimum or a maximum age for the painted figure.

For the most part, the repertoire of beeswax forms is special to the medium rather than shared with paint; the lines and arrays of dots that are the most common motif are very rare in paint. Where characteristics are shared, the beeswax date is pertinent: the 4000-year-old beeswax figure is of a turtle drawn in the simple X-ray convention common in paint. It gives a certain date for when that creature was presnet and when that convention was in use.

## Weathering

Inspection of single figures and of larger surfaces shows that weathering of the art surfaces is very variable, both between surfaces and within any one surface. Often one can see how paint is worn away, where, for instance, water runs down otherwise protected surfaces. Sometimes one can see no such cause, and one remembers that water-runs will change their course as a shelter erodes.

In an approximate way, then, one can expect a weak rule that crisp and distinct images will be newer than worn and indistinct paint. Along with that pattern goes the different behaviour of the three common colours – red, yellow and white – in the art.

The red ochre, haematite, appears enduring; it is well said that, closely examined, the colour of ancient paintings is not *on* the rock but *in* the rock. Even paintings annually exposed to washes of water survive crisply when 'in' the rock; some surfaces that support early painting in red – like the celebrated emu-hunter panel at Mount Brockman (Chippindale and Taçon 1993) – are not well protected from sun and rain. A distinctive feature of some of the most archaic red paintings is the turning of the pigment to a bluer or pinker hue, aptly called 'mulberry' by Walsh (1994), who finds the same tone in archaic red-ochre paintings of north Western Australia.

The yellow ochre, limonite, is more often seen washing down a rock surface. Over the long term of many hundreds of years it is not chemically stable, turning slowly to haematite. A few of the Dynamic Figures, certain to be ancient, are in yellow while most are in red; most of these few yellow Dynamics are not in the clear 'chrome yellow' of recent figures, but are a more butterscotch tone, as if turning from yellow towards red.

The white, generally a kaolin-type clay (Clarke and North 1991: 84), makes a thicker pigment, which one can see sits very much out on the rock rather than passing into the surface; it does not seem to endure. A telling illustration is a solid picture of a wallaby painted by Bill Miyarki at Koongarra in 1972 (illustrated in Edwards 1979: 130) on an unprotected surface and over ancient red paint. Not a trace of the white pipe-clay from 1972 is seen on the surface today, but the ancient red figure it was painted over remains.

In general, it can be said that red is enduring, yellow transient, and white fugitive as pigments on the surfaces. In Northern Running Figures (Haskovec 1992b), otherwise complete pictures are missing portions of the whole subject: for instance, a figure with well-drawn arms will have no hands. In these cases, it seems the red only has endured, and it is conjectured that the white or yellow component of the full bi- or polychrome composition is lost.

The *appliqué* figures made of beeswax (above) show a distinctive weathering sequence: at first dark and shiny, they crack, fissure, become paler, as they are reduced to a white brittle skin which then disappears. Exposure to ultraviolet light, which weakens the chemical bonding of the wax, is the likely cause; when a single figure spreads over surfaces with differing exposure to light, its state of preservation varies accordingly.

The rare engravings in western Arnhem Land (Chaloupka 1993: 234–7) are mostly found heavily patinated, sometimes with a red mineral skin, sometimes with an uncoloured or dark skin. They are regarded as ancient.

### Direct dating of skins and other natural features in stratigraphic relation to art

Commonly, Arnhem Land paintings are on patination or mineral skins covering the exposed rock surface; sometimes skins cover paintings (Hughes and Watchman 1983; Watchman 1985, 1990). Preliminary radiocarbon studies of deposited salts in stratigraphic relation to rock-art gave determinations of up to 8000 years for a multi-layered crust on a surface with paintings (Watchman 1987). The chemistry and carbon-dating of rock skins and crusts, a difficult and a developing field, has yet decisively to contribute to dating in Arnhem Land.

Many painted shelters are frequented by mud-wasps, whose nests become robustly fixed on to the surface. There are nests over paint, and nests under paint. Luminescent study of the mineral component

as a means of dating mud-wasp nests, and thereby dating art in a stratigraphic relationship to it, has been reported from the Kimberley region of Western Australia (Roberts *et al.* 1997); it has potential for Arnhem Land.

### Diversity in dating Arnhem Land rock-art

*Multiple sources of evidence, 'cabling', and consistency in dating Arnhem Land rock-art*

We have reported on these approaches to dating Arnhem Land rock-art:

- Aboriginal knowledge of the antiquity of Arnhem Land paintings.
- Dating by reference to historical knowledge:
    Memory and historical record of artists and their styles;
    Subjects depicted, and pigments used, of known historical date;
    Distinctive subjects in relation to contact-era and recent Arnhem Land hunter-gatherer lifeways;
    Distinctive manners of depiction in relation to contact-era and recent Arnhem Land painting.
- Dating by reference to lack of historical knowledge:
    Distinctive subjects not known in contact-era and recent Arnhem Land hunter-gatherer lifeways;
    Distinctive manners of depiction not known in contact-era and recent Arnhem Land painting.
- Stratigraphic sequences on the painted surfaces.
- Bridging to dated palaeoecological and archaeological evidence:
    Bridging across to the palaeoecological record;
    Bridging across to the archaeological record;
    Art materials within archaeological deposits.
- Principles of continuity.
- Direct dating of images by radiocarbon (and implications therefrom by superposition, by subject depicted, and by manner of depiction).
- Weathering.
- Direct dating of skins and other natural features in stratigraphic relation to art.

Some of the subdivisions of these categories may run into each other: memory and the historical record of artists and their styles run into the distinctive manners of depiction in relation to contact-era and recent Arnhem Land painting; the distinctive subjects of known historical date shade into those of contact-era and recent hunter-gatherer life-ways; and these in turn, run into the sources of the palaeoecological. We think it convenient to keep them a little distinct, as each category of evidence makes a different contribution.

Other lines of reasoning can be brought to bear. Chaloupka (1993: 89) places the paint imprints of thrown objects (Chaloupka 1993: plate 79), grass-prints (thought to be made by striking paint-loaded grass stems against the surface) (Chaloupka 1984: fig. 4), and hand prints (Chaloupka 1993: plate 80) early in the sequence, in the expectation that prints – as direct images taken by imprinting from the object itself – may be earlier than the more developed artistry of painting images.

It was acknowledged above that the sources for dating vary in their applicability and in their strength. Their independence compensates here, when it is consistently found that the several lines of evidence are coherent with each other.

Chronology for the animated images of the Dynamic Figures, for example, depends on the following lines of evidence:

- Aboriginal knowledge they are Mimi paintings.
- Distinctive subjects not known in contact-era and recent Arnhem Land hunter-gatherer life-ways.
- Distinctive manners of depiction not known in contact-era and recent Arnhem Land painting.
- Stratigraphic sequences on the painted surfaces.
- Bridging across to the archaeological record.
- Principles of continuity.
- Weathering.

Chronology for the beeswax figures depends on the following:

- Aboriginal knowledge of the figures.
- Memory and historical record of artists and their styles.

- Subjects depicted of known historical date.
- Distinctive manners of depiction in relation to contact-era and recent Arnhem Land painting.
- Stratigraphic sequences of beeswax figures in relation to other beeswax figures, and in relation to paint.
- Principles of continuity.
- Direct dating of images by radiocarbon.
- Weathering.

In short, the dating of Arnhem Land rock-art illustrates Wylie's 'cabling', and the way in which varied lines of independent evidence – seven for one of these groups, eight for the other – can be brought together into a single coherent and strong strand (Table 6.1).

It is repeatedly found that the deductions made from each line of evidence are consistent with each other. It follows that when they are *not* consistent, one can have confidence that a real anomaly exists, rather than there being gross fault in the dating evidence. One example of this has been noted above, the discrepancy in the archaic large depictions of animal subjects, which leads us to think that there were two distinct periods when these subjects were portrayed: they will occur *both* as older Large Naturalistic and as younger Yam/Simple figures. By using clues as to which of the collected group may be late and which early, it may be possible to recognise distinctive features of subject or of manner of depiction peculiar to each, and thereby to divide the group reliably into its two components.

Stratigraphic study has shown another anomaly: Yam Figures are stratified over Simple Figures (regarded as earlier) – but Simple Figures are also stratified over Yam Figures. (Both successions are clearly seen on a key panel on Upper Twin Falls Creek: our unpublished field observations.) Accordingly, there is an overlap between 'Simple' and 'Yam', corresponding to a length of time when both manners of depiction were in use. This is consistent with other evidence: the repertoire of spears and early spear-throwers found with figures of each class appears to be the same. In considering the two classes, we are encouraged to explore a relationship between them other than a chronological sequence: we find that Simple Figures depict activities that appear to belong to the human domain (e.g. scenes of humans fighting), while Yam Figures depict activities in a spiritual domain (e.g. images of Rainbow Serpents).

Again, this seems to us to be a strength, rather than a weakness of the research approach to Arnhem Land art as it has developed. Unstated in much of the Arnhem Land literature is the fair starting premiss that, at any one period, a coherent range of subjects would be depicted with a coherent manner of depiction – the entities combined in the idea of a 'style' – and the expectations that the styles will form a chronological series. This is the common starting-point for rock-art studies everywhere. Nevertheless, recent Arnhem Land rock-art demonstrates a more complex pattern, for there are several coexisting 'styles' as well as the intricate X-ray depictions in polychrome colours for which modern Arnhem Land art is celebrated. With the 'Energetic' stick figures and many other elements these, taken together, make up Taçon's 'Complete Figure Complex' (1992b: 204–5). Unpublished preliminary results from the programme of radiocarbon dating for beeswax figures show the same finding: the variability evident in that repertoire of forms is not a simple function of changing time. If dating were precarious, or depended on a single line of evidence, this would be disconcerting. With a robust framework for dating and multiple lines of evidence, one can instead proceed with the working premiss that variability is primarily a function of time, and the expectation of a sequence of distinctive styles. When that premiss is contradicted, as it is for the large archaic animal images, for the Yam/Simple Figures, and for the beeswax figures, then one can use that anomaly to move from the simplifying premiss towards knowledge of a more complex reality.

*Arnhem Land chronology in summary, and its context*
Table 6.1, adapted from Taçon and Chippindale (1994: table 1), sets out our then understanding of the major elements in Arnhem Land rock-art chronology.

Our view of it has moved on a little since 1994, and other workers in the fast-moving field each have their own slightly different schemes (e.g. Lewis 1988; Chaloupka 1993; Haskovec 1992a). The fundamentals of the main features are largely held in common.

Arnhem Land is unusual among rock-art regions in Australia in our detailed grasp of its chronology. A consistency beyond the immediate region is provided by neighbouring regions of the Northern Territory. In the Katherine region to the south, at Dead Man Pocket near the west coast of the Northern Territory, in the Victoria River District, and at Keep River on the border with Western Australia a similar fundamental sequence is found (Lewis 1984): an archaic class of figures in red (sometimes mulberry) pigment, and a recent strand of polychrome figures well known to Aboriginal people of the regions today. On a larger scale, the same broad pattern seems to apply to the Kimberley region of Western Australia and to northern Queensland, united with the 'Top End' of the Northern Territory in a grand province (Morwood and Hobbs 1995b) of similarity across the north of the continent. Morwood and Hobbs (1995a), a study of first importance from north Queensland, bridges across between the archaeological and the art records to develop an integrated picture, following the model of Arnhem Land studies.

*Dating rock-art: a brief comparison of Arnhem Land and southern Africa*
The fair chronology that now exists for Arnhem Land enables varied study of change over time: Chaloupka (1993) is a good broad survey of changing subjects depicted and of changing manners of depiction. There are a few, and could be many, specialist studies to explore specific themes: as well as regional variants, in aspects specific to a period (e.g. Taçon 1989 on recent rock-art), in changing technology (e.g. Lewis 1988 on spear-throwers), in changing social relations (e.g. Taçon and Chippindale 1994 on fighting), in the changing sense of images (e.g. Taçon, Wilson and Chippindale 1996 on Rainbow Serpents).

What these have in common is a capacity to study

Table 6.1. *Chronology of western Arnhem Land art*

| Age | Nature | | Years before present |
|---|---|---|---|
| New | Rare rock-paintings + bark- and paper-paintings | | present-day |
| | 'Complete Figure Complex' rock-paintings + some rock-engravings + beeswax figures | | about 4000–3000 up to the 1960s AD |
| | 'Simple Figures' + 'Yam Figures' + large human figures + some large fauna + 'Early X-ray' rock-paintings | | about 6000 |
| Intermediate | 'Northern Running Figures' rock-paintings | 'Simple Figures with Boomerangs' + some large fauna rock-paintings | unknown |
| | ? | 'Post-Dynamic Figures' rock-paintings | unknown |
| | 'Dynamic Figures' rock-paintings + '3MF' stencils | | ?10,000 years |
| | ?break | | |
| | 'Large Naturalistic' fauna rock-paintings | | unknown |
| Old | ?break | | |
| | Panaramitee-like rock-engravings pigment in shelter deposits | | unknown ≥ 30,000–50,000 |

Revised from that published in 1994. We anticipate work in progress will lead to further revision. We think the relative chronology is sound, but the absolute dates for early 'intermediate' and before are uncertain.

Prints and stencils for which there is slight evidence of date are excluded, except for the distinctive 3MF hand stencil (made with the '3 Middle Fingers' pressed together), which is associated with Dynamic Figures.

Strong continuities are identified, alongside distinct changes, from the Dynamic Figures through to the present.

Adapted from Taçon and Chippindale (1994: table 1).

change and variation over time, that defining purpose of archaeology which is – unhappily – often elusive in rock-art research. Instead of a whole repertoire of images being treated as a single group without regard to change over time (because there is slight evidence for chronology), or some grasp of chronology being the goal of study, it becomes possible to *track* change. Importantly in Arnhem Land, this means one can deduce – on a basis of fairly secure dating – an understanding of archaic aspects not accessible by the informed knowledge of present-day and recent times. Only in that way is it possible to work well and fairly with that varied range of information offered by formal and by informed methods. And it means one can look beyond the changes visible in the imagery to other transformations – in landscape and in settlement – to which changing imagery may relate.

One can contrast that with the present state of research in southern Africa (Dowson and Lewis-Williams 1994), where ethnohistorical sources provide informed information, formal methods are available, but an effective chronology remains lacking, despite varied studies (e.g. in that collection

Deacon 1994; Hall 1994; Loubser and Laurens 1994; Morris and Beaumont 1994; Walker 1994; Whitley and Annegarn 1994; Yates *et al.* 1994; see Thackeray 1983 for an earlier survey). A late date for some panels is proved by contact-era figures with European subjects (Campbell 1987), and a late date has long been thought likely for those many panels which seem similar in style and state of preservation (Lewis-Williams 1981: 24). The possibility of a very early date is given by the charcoal, ochre and white images from the Apollo XI Cave, Namibia, dated to over 26,000 years (Wendt 1976). The ethnohistorical records – though they are accounts from San people who did not themselves paint – have clear relevance to recent paintings. But without a developed chronology in between, interpretation is 'flat', lacking time-depth, or the means well to study how picture-making has changed over time. One believes, or does not believe, that recent San knowledge informs all the paintings, rather than having the means to develop a secure knowledge.

## Acknowledgements

We work in Arnhem Land with the consent of its Aboriginal people, whom we thank for that permission and for their welcome into their country, as expressed through the Gagudju, Gunbalanya and Jawoyn Associations. We thank in particular those individuals concerned with granting that permission, and those who went with us as companions in the field. We are grateful to the Australian Nature and Conservation Agency (ANCA/ANPWS) and the Northern Land Council for permits. We thank colleagues, friends, acquaintances and strangers for assistance in and after the field, and for energetic comments on a draft of this chapter.

## REFERENCES

Allen, H. and G. Barton. 1989. *Ngarradj Warde Djobkeng: White Cockatoo Dreaming and the prehistory of Kakadu.* Sydney (NSW), Oceania Publications. Oceania Monograph 37.

Berndt, R. M. and C. H. Berndt. 1954. *Arnhem Land: its history and people.* Melbourne (Vic.), F. W. Cheshire.

Brandl, E. J. 1968. Aboriginal rock designs in beeswax and description of cave painting sites in western Arnhem Land, *Archaeology and Physical Anthropology in Oceania* 3(1): 19–29.

1972. Thylacine designs in Arnhem Land rock paintings, *Archaeology and Physical Anthropology in Oceania* 7(1): 24–30.

1973. *Australian Aboriginal paintings in western and central Arnhem Land: temporal sequences and elements of style in Cadell River and Deaf Adder Creek art.* Canberra (ACT), Australian Institute of Aboriginal Studies. Australian Aboriginal Studies 52, Prehistory and Material Culture series 9.

Breeden, S. and B. Wright. 1989. *Kakadu: looking after the country – the Gagudju way.* East Roseville (NSW), Simon and Schuster.

Campbell, C. 1987. Art in crisis: contact period rock art in the south-eastern mountains of southern Africa. Master's dissertation, University of Witwatersrand.

Carroll, P. J. 1977. Mimi from western Arnhem Land, in P. Ucko (ed.), *Form in indigenous art: schematisation in the art of Aboriginal Australia and prehistoric Europe*, pp. 119–30. Canberra (ACT), Australian Institute of Aboriginal Studies.

Chaloupka, G. 1977. Aspects of the chronology and schematisation of the prehistoric sites on the Arnhem Land plateau, in P. Ucko (ed.), *Form in indigenous art: schematisation in the art of Aboriginal Australia and prehistoric Europe*, pp. 243–59. Canberra (ACT), Australian Institute of Aboriginal Studies.

1979. Pack-bells on the rock face: Aboriginal paintings of European contact in north-western Arnhem Land, *Aboriginal History* 3(2): 92–5.

1982. *Burrunguy, Nourlangie Rock.* Darwin (NT), Northart.

1984. *From palaeoart to casual paintings.* Darwin (NT), Northern Territory Museum of Arts and Sciences. Monograph 1.

1985. Chronological sequence of Arnhem Land plateau rock art, in Rhys Jones (ed.), *Archaeological research in Kakadu National Park*, pp. 269–80. Canberra (ACT), Australia National Parks and Wildlife Service. Special Publication 13.

1989. *Groote Eylandt archipelago rock art survey 1988.* Report to the Heritage Branch, Conservation Commission of the Northern Territory. Darwin (NT), Northern Territory Museum.

1992. *Rock art survey: Arnhem Land Plateau – central region.* Report to the Heritage Branch, Conservation Commission of the Northern Territory. Darwin (NT), Northern Territory Museum.

1993. *Journey in time: the world's longest continuing art tradition.* Chatswood (NSW), Reed.

Chaloupka, G., N. Kapirigi, B. Nayidji and G. Namingum. 1985. A cultural survey of Balawurru, Deaf Adder Creek, Amarrkananga, Cannon Hill and the Northern Corridor. Darwin: Museum and Art Galleries Board of the Northern Territory: report to Australian National Parks and Wildlife Service. Unpublished report. Darwin (NT), Northern Territory Museum of Arts and Sciences.

Chappell, J. and A. Grindrod. 1983. 7 + 2 KA 'spike', in J. Chappell and A. Grindrod (eds.), *CLIMANZ*, pp. 87–8. Canberra (ACT), Department of Biogeography and Geomorphology, Research School of Pacific Studies, Australian National University.

Chippindale, C. and P. S. C. Taçon. 1993. Two old painted panels from Kakadu: variation and sequence in Arnhem Land rock art, in J. Steinbring *et al.* (eds.), *Time and space: dating and spatial considerations in rock art research*, pp. 32–56. Melbourne, Australian Rock Art Research Association. Occasional AURA Publication 8.

Clarke, A. 1994. *Winds of change: an archaeology of contact in the Groote Eylandt archipelago, Northern Territory.* Ph.D thesis, Australian National University, Canberra.

Clarke, J. and N. North. 1991. Pigment composition of post-estuarine rock art in Kakadu National Park, in C. Pearson and B. K. Swartz, Jr (eds.), *Rock art and posterity: conserving, managing and recording rock art*, pp. 80–7. Melbourne, Australian Rock Art Research Association. Occasional AURA Publication 4.

Corbett, L. 1995. *The dingo in Australia and Asia.* Sydney, University of New South Wales Press.

Cundy, B. J. 1989. *Formal variation in Australian spear and spearthrower technology.* Oxford, British Archaeological Reports. International Series 546.

David, B., I. McNiven, V. Attenbrow and J. Flood. 1994. Of Lightning Brothers and White Cockatoos: dating the antiquity of signifying systems in the Northern Territory, Australia, *Antiquity* 68: 241–51.

Deacon, J. 1994. Rock engravings and the folklore of Bleek and Lloyd's /Xam San informants, in Thomas A. Dowson and David Lewis-Williams (eds.), *Contested images: diversity in southern African rock art research*, pp. 237–56. Johannesburg, Witwatersrand University Press.

Dowson, T. A. and D. Lewis-Williams (eds.). 1994. *Contested images: diversity in southern African rock art research.* Johannesburg, Witwatersrand University Press.

Dyer, C. A. (ed.). 1994. *Kunwinjku art from Injalak 1991–1992: the John W. Kluge Commission.* North Adelaide (SA), Museum Art International.

Edwards, R. 1979. *Australian Aboriginal art: the art of the Alligator Rivers region, Northern Territory.* Canberra (ACT), Australian Institute of Aboriginal Studies.

Hall, S. 1994. Images of interaction: rock art and sequence in the Eastern Cape, in T. A. Dowson and D. Lewis-Williams (eds.), *Contested images: diversity in southern African rock art research*, pp. 61–82. Johannesburg, Witwatersrand University Press.

Haskovec, I. P. 1992a. Mt Gilruth revisited, *Archaeology in Oceania* 27: 61–74.

1992b. Northern Running Figures of Kakadu National Park: a study of a regional style, in J. McDonald and I. P. Haskovec (eds.), *State of the art: regional rock art studies in Australia and Melanesia*, pp. 148–58. Melbourne, Australian Rock Art Research Association. Occasional AURA Publication 6.

Haskovec, I. and H. Sullivan. 1989. Najombolmi: reflections and rejections of an Aboriginal artist, in H. Morphy (ed.), *Animals into art*, pp. 57–74. London, Unwin Hyman.

Hughes, P. J. and A. Watchman. 1983. The deterioration, conservation and management of rock art sites in the Kakadu National Park, in D. Gillespie (ed.), *The rock art sites of Kakadu National Park*, pp. 37–82. Canberra (ACT), Australia National Parks and Wildlife Service. Special Publication 10.

Jones, R. and I. Johnson. 1985. Deaf Adder Gorge: Lindner Site, Nauwalabila I, in R. Jones (ed.), *Archaeological research in Kakadu National Park*, pp. 165–227. Canberra (ACT), Australia National Parks and Wildlife Service. Special Publication 13.

Lewis, D. J. 1984. Mimi on Bradshaw, *Australian Aboriginal Studies* 2: 58–61.

1988. *The rock paintings of Arnhem Land, Australia: social, ecological and material culture change in the Post-Glacial period.* Oxford, British Archaeological Reports. International Series S415.

Lewis-Williams, J. D. 1981. *Believing and seeing: symbolic meaning in southern San rock paintings.* London, Academic Press.

Loubser, J. and G. Laurens. 1994. Depictions of domestic ungulates and shields: hunter/gatherers and agro-pastoralists in the Caledon River, in T. A. Dowson and D. Lewis-Williams (eds.), *Contested images: diversity in southern African rock art research*, pp. 83–118. Johannesburg, Witwatersrand University Press.

McCarthy, F. D. 1958. *Australian Aboriginal rock art.* Sydney, Australian Museum.

1960. The cave paintings of Groote Eylandt and Chasm Island, in C. P. Mountford (ed.), *Records of the American–Australian scientific expedition to Arnhem Land 2: Anthropology and nutrition*, pp. 297–414. Melbourne (Vic.), Melbourne University Press.

McDonald, J., K. Officer, T. Jull, D. Donahue, J. Head and B. Ford. 1990. Investigating C14 AMS: dating prehistoric rock-art in the Sydney Sandstone Basin, Australia, *Rock Art Research* 7: 83–92.

Macknight, C. C. 1976. *The voyage to Marege: Macassan trepangers in northern Australia.* Melbourne (Vic.), Melbourne University Press.

Morris, D. and P. Beaumont. 1994. Portable rock engravings at Springbokoog and the archaeological contexts of rock art of the Upper Karoo, in T. A. Dowson and D. Lewis-Williams (eds.), *Contested images: diversity in southern African rock art research*, pp. 11–28. Johannesburg, Witwatersrand University Press.

Morwood, M. J. and D. R. Hobbs. (eds.). 1995a. *Quinkan prehistory: the archaeology of Aboriginal art in SE Cape York Peninsula, Australia.* Brisbane, Anthropology Museum, University of Queensland. Tempus 3.

1995b. Themes in the prehistory of tropical Australia, in Jim Allen and James F. O'Connell (eds.), *Transitions: Pleistocene to Holocene in Australia and Papua New Guinea*, pp. 747–68. *Antiquity* 69 (Special number 265).

Murray, P. and G. Chaloupka. 1984. The Dreamtime animals: extinct megafauna in Arnhem Land rock art, *Archaeology in Oceania* 19: 105–16.

Nelson, D. E. 1993. Second thoughts on a rock-art date, *Antiquity* 67: 893–5.

Nelson, D. E., G. Chaloupka, C. Chippindale, M. S. Alderson and J. Southon. 1995. Radiocarbon dates for beeswax figures in the prehistoric rock art of northern Australia, *Archaeometry* 37(1): 151–6.

Roberts, R. G. 1996. Preliminary investigations using optically-stimulated luminescence to date fossil mud-wasp nests associated with rock pictures in the Kimberley. Unpublished paper presented at the First Workshop on Australian Rock Picture Dating, Lucas Heights (Sydney), February.

Roberts, R. G., R. Jones, N. A. Spooner, M. J. Head, A. S. Murray and M. A. Smith. 1994. The human colonisation of Australia: optical dates of 53,000 and 60,000 years bracket human arrival at Deaf Adder Gorge, Northern Territory, *Quaternary Geochronology, Quaternary Science Reviews* 13: 575–83.

Roberts, R., G. Walsh, A. Murray, J. Olley, R. Jones, M. Morwood, C. Tuniz, E. Lawson, M. Macphail, D. Bowdery and I. Naumann. 1997. Luminescence dating of rock art and past environments using mud-wasp nests in northern Australia, *Nature* 387: 696–9.

Rosenfeld, A. and C. Smith. 1997. Recent developments in radiocarbon and stylistic methods of dating rock art, *Antiquity* 71: 405–11.

Schrire, C. 1982. *The Alligator Rivers: prehistory and ecology in western Arnhem Land.* Canberra (ACT), Department of Prehistory, Research School of Pacific Studies, Australian National University. Terra Australis 7.

Spencer, W. Baldwin and F. J. Gillen. 1928. *Wanderings in wild Australia.* London, Macmillan.

Spillett, P. G. 1972. *Forsaken settlement: an illustrated history of the settlement of Victoria, Port Essington, North Australia 1838–1849.* Dee Why West (NSW), Lansdowne.

Sullivan, H. 1988. Rock engravings in Kakadu National Park. Unpublished paper, First AURA Congress, Darwin, August.

Taçon, P. S. C. 1988. Identifying fish species in the recent rock paintings of western Arnhem Land, *Rock Art Research* 5(1): 3–15.

1989. *From Rainbow Snakes to 'X-ray' fish: the nature of the recent rock painting tradition in western Arnhem Land, Australia.* Unpublished Ph.D. thesis, Australian National University, Canberra.

1991. The power of stone: symbolic aspects of stone use and tool development in western Arnhem Land, Australia, *Antiquity* 65: 192–207.

1992a. The last rock painters of Kakadu, *Australian Natural History* 23(11): 866–73.

1992b. Somewhere over the rainbow: an ethnographic and archaeological analysis of recent rock paintings of western Arnhem Land, Australia, in J. McDonald and I. P. Haskovec (eds.), *State of the art: regional rock art studies in Australia and Melanesia*, pp. 202–15. Melbourne, Australian Rock Art Research Association. Occasional AURA Publication 6.

Taçon, P. S. C. and S. Brockwell. 1995. Arnhem Land prehistory in landscape, stone and paint, in J. Allen and J. F. O'Connell (eds.), *Transitions: Pleistocene to Holocene in Australia and Papua New Guinea*, pp.

676–95. *Antiquity 69* (Special number 265).

Taçon, P. S. C. and C. Chippindale. 1994. Australia's ancient warriors: changing depictions of fighting in the rock art of Arnhem Land, N.T., *Cambridge Archaeological Journal* 4(2): 211–48.

Taçon, P. S. C. and M. Garde. 1995. *Kun-wardde bim*, rock art from western and central Arnhem Land, in M. West, *Rainbow Sugarbag and Moon: two artists of the stone country: Bardayal Nadjamerrek and Mick Kubarkku*, pp. 30–6. Darwin (NT), Museum and Art Gallery of the Northern Territory.

Taçon, P. S. C., M. Wilson and C. Chippindale. 1996. Birth of the Rainbow Serpent in Arnhem Land rock-art and oral history, *Archaeology in Oceania* 31:103–24.

Thackeray, A. I. 1983. Dating the rock art of southern Africa, in *New approaches to southern African rock art*, pp. 21–6. Cape Town, South African Archaeological Society. Goodwin Series 4.

Tratebas, A. 1993. Stylistic chronology versus absolute dates for early hunting style rock art on the North American Plains, in M. Lorblanchet and P. Bahn (eds.), *Rock art studies: the post-stylistic era, or where do we go from here?*, pp. 163–78. Oxford, Oxbow.

Walker, N. 1994. Painting and ceremonial activity in the Later Stone Age of the Matopos, Zimbabwe, in T. A. Dowson and D. Lewis-Williams (eds.), *Contested images: diversity in southern African rock art research*, pp. 119–30. Johannesburg, Witwatersrand University Press.

Walsh, G. L. 1988. *Australia's greatest rock art*. Bathurst (NSW), E.J. Brill – Robert Brown.

1994. *Bradshaws: ancient rock paintings of north-west Australia*. Carouge-Geneva, Edition Limitée.

Warburton, C. 1944. *Buffaloes*. Sydney, Consolidated Press.

Watchman, A. 1979. Summary and interpretation of petrological, geochemical and mineralogical studies, in P. J. Hughes, A. Watchman and D. Gillespie, The deterioration, conservation and management of rock art sites in the Kakadu National Park, NT. Report to Australian National Parks and Wildlife Service.

1985. Mineralogical analysis of silica skins covering rock art, in Rhys Jones (ed.), *Archaeological research in Kakadu National Park*, pp. 281–9. Canberra (ACT), Australia National Parks and Wildlife Service. Special Publication 13.

1987. Preliminary determinations of the age and composition of mineral salts on rock art surfaces in the Kakadu National Park, in W. Ambrose and J. Mummery (eds.), *Archaeometry: further Australasian studies*, pp. 36–42. Canberra (ACT), Australian National University, Department of Prehistory, Research School of Pacific Studies.

1990. A summary of occurrences of oxalate-rich crusts in Australia, *Rock Art Research* 7(1): 44–50.

Wendt, W. E. 1976. 'Art mobilier' from the Apollo 11 Cave, South West Africa: Africa's oldest dated works of art, *South African Archaeological Bulletin* 31: 5–11.

West, M. 1995. *Rainbow Sugarbag and Moon: two artists of the stone country: Bardayal Nadjamerrek and Mick Kubarkku*. Darwin (NT), Museum and Art Gallery of the Northern Territory.

White, C. 1967. Early stone axes in Arnhem Land, *Antiquity* 41: 147–52.

Whitley, D. S. and H. J. Annegarn. 1994. Cation-ratio dating of rock engravings from Klipfontein, northern Cape, in T. A. Dowson and D. Lewis-Williams (eds.), *Contested images: diversity in southern African rock art research*, 189–97. Johannesburg, Witwatersrand University Press.

Woodroffe, C. D. 1988. Changing mangrove and wetland habitats over the last 8000 years, northern Australia and southeast Asia, in Deborah Wade-Marshall and Peter Loveday (eds.), *Northern Australia: progress and prospects 2: Floodplains research*, pp. 1–33. Darwin (NT), North Australia Research Unit, Australian National University.

Woodroffe, C. D., J. Chappell, B. G. Thom and E. Wallensky. 1986. *Geomorphological dynamics and evolution of the South Alligator tidal river and plains, Northern Territory*. Canberra (ACT), Australian National University, North Australian Research Unit. Monograph 3.

Woodroffe, C. D., B. G. Thom, J. Chappell, E. Wallensky, J. Grindrod and J. Head. 1987. Relative sea level in the South Alligator River region, north Australia, during the Holocene, *Search* 18: 92–4.

Wylie, A. 1989. Archaeological cables and tacking: the implications of practice for Bernstein's 'Options beyond objectivism and relativism', *Philosophy of the Social Sciences* 19: 1–18.

Yates, R., A. Manhire and J. Parkington. 1994. Rock painting and history on the south-western Cape, in T. A. Dowson and D. Lewis-Williams (eds.), *Contested images: diversity in southern African rock art research*, pp. 29–60. Johannesburg, Witwatersrand University Press.

**Jean Clottes**

# 7. The 'Three Cs': fresh avenues towards European Palaeolithic art

Three great new discoveries within a few years – Cosquer, Chauvet, Côa – have overturned known understandings of European Palaeolithic art. New dating, by small-scale radiocarbon methods, provides a different view of the art's distribution in time. Far remote in time, and largely set in deep caves, European Palaeolithic art remains a domain of formal methods, and we are uncertain where it may find useful analogy. The first lesson from the 'Three Cs' is that new field observations can – rightly – upset comfortable frames of ideas!

## Dating Palaeolithic art

Until the late 1980s, it was not possible to date parietal art directly. One had to use the time-honoured archaeological methods that had been evolved by the Abbé Breuil and his successors. They can be summed up as:

- establishing as many and as firm fixed points as possible;
- by analogy, comparing the undated art with what was felt to have been securely dated.

Despite the advent of radiocarbon and other direct dating methods, this process is still very often used, even though it depends upon various unproved assumptions.

For lack of better means, Breuil (e.g. 1952) relied heavily upon superimpositions of figures, his idea being that the regular recurrence of stylistic conventions or of particular techniques either on top of or below others on the cave walls should enable him to establish a succession of styles and periods. Occasionally, this may prove correct in particular cases (Cosquer), yet this method is flawed because of two unknown variables: the duration of stylistic conven-

tions and the limited number of examples of super-impositions available.

When the entrance to a cave has been blocked by archaeological deposits, or when painted or engraved panels have been partially or totally covered by habitation layers, or again when painted blocks have fallen from the walls and have been found within well-dated layers, the art has often been considered to be securely dated. However, the unstated assumption is that a negligible amount of time elapsed between the moment when the art was made and the moment when it was sealed up, which may or may not be true.

Analogy then comes into play – even more fraught with dangers. Can we safely assume that the representation of an animal which looks very much like others from supposedly well-dated contexts belongs to the same period as they do? The same can be said for comparisons between portable and wall art (Ucko and Rosenfeld 1967). All sorts of phenomena may intervene. Convergence is one of them. For example, a painted deer from Cosquer was felt by Delluc and Delluc (1991b) to look like the deer in Lascaux, which may or may not be the case. They might have drawn the conclusion that the two were contemporary. In fact, they chose to interpret the resemblance as suspicious and indicated that the Cosquer deer could have been a fake: like the Lascaux deer, its antlers were on the top of its skull, it had been drawn with a tear bag, and its ears were behind its antlers. Now, all those features being anatomical characteristics that all deer possess, it is obvious that anybody drawing a deer accurately

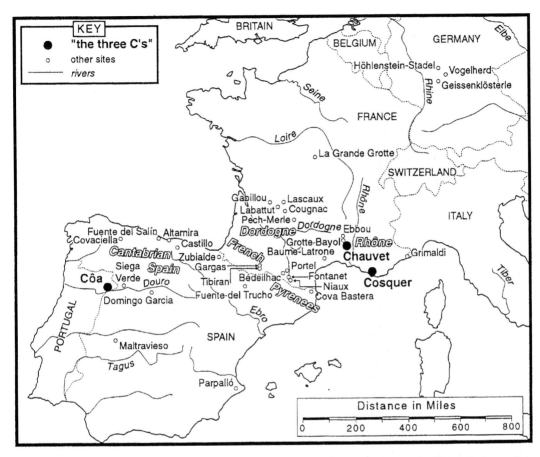

**Fig. 7.1.** Location of the 'Three Cs' (Cosquer, Chauvet, Côa), major regions of western European Palaeolithic parietal art, and sites mentioned in the text.

would reproduce them. Their presence just shows that deer had been carefully observed and faithfully painted at Cosquer, as at Lascaux. This case is enlightening as to the mental processes that may play a part in visual assessment of the art. First, a resemblance is perceived. Then, a conclusion is drawn which is wholly subjective and based upon unargued presuppositions.

Direct radiocarbon dating and systematic research on paint analysis became possible because technical advances allowed the lifting of minute samples. For Palaeolithic cave art, they began in the early 1990s (Lorblanchet *et al.* 1990; Valladas *et al.* 1992; Clottes,

Menu and Walter 1990; and Clottes 1993b). In arid countries, experimental methods were tried to date petroglyphs (e.g. Dorn 1992; Watchman and Lessard 1992; and Bednarik 1993). They were applied for the first time in Europe to the Côa valley engravings in 1995 (see below).

### The 'Three Cs': Cosquer, Chauvet, Côa
Coincidentally, several major discoveries of rock-art sites were made: Cosquer in mid 1991, Chauvet and the Côa valley petroglyphs at the end of 1994 (Fig. 7.1). For diverse reasons, their direct dating has proved extremely important. It played a major part in

settling a controversy about the authenticity of the art at Cosquer. At Chauvet, it was felt to be as much of a breakthrough as the discovery itself. Finally, it raised tremendous problems and arguments about the age of Foz Côa and about the validity of our knowledge of Palaeolithic art.

## La Grotte Cosquer

The discovery of the Cosquer Cave was hailed as an epoch-making event. The romantic circumstances of the exploration of that dangerous cave, and the tragedy that followed when three divers died exploring it on their own, undoubtedly played a major part in the public response to its announcement.

Right from the start, it was obvious that it was both an important and an original art find. It was located in Provence near Marseilles, an area where no Palaeolithic art had ever been discovered. The nearest sites were the Grimaldi ones to the east, on the Italian border (200 km away from Marseilles), and the Ardèche caves to the west – 180 km away. This highlighted a taphonomic problem, supposedly well known but rarely referred to whenever the location of Palaeolithic art is considered, which is the disappearance of uncounted caves under the sea all along the Mediterranean shores since Pleistocene times. Several large caves (Le Figuier, La Triperie) are next to Cosquer. A number of those caves could have been – and probably were – painted or engraved. In Cosquer, more than two-thirds of the galleries and chambers have been submerged and had the surface of their walls destroyed, so that the remaining art is most likely only a minor part of what there used to be, which prevents a structuralist study of the cave (Clottes and Courtin 1994).

Despite the destruction due to the sea, Cosquer ranks among the few caves where more than 100 animal figures have been found. After the latest dives (end of 1994) and the work Jean Courtin and Jacques Collina-Girard did then, their total is now 141, with, in addition, a single human figure overlaid by a spear-like sign, and the isolated representation of a realistic human penis with testicles. Horses are most common (48 = 34 per cent), followed by caprids (ibex and 4 chamois: 27 = 19 per cent), bovids (bison and 4 aurochs: 18 = 12.5 per cent), sea animals (9 seals and 4 auks: 13 = 11 per cent), cervids (2 *Megaloceros*, 11 deer including 2 does: 13 = 9 per cent), 1 feline; and 18 unidentified animals (12.5 per cent) (Clottes, Courtin and Collina-Girard 1996). Geometric signs are very numerous. Many linear ones (48), looking like spears, are on top of 28 different figures. Other signs are rectangles, with sometimes an infilling, zigzags, etc.

Hand stencils now total 55, the highest number in Europe except for Gargas. They are all located in the east side of the chamber, with one in the south. None is in the west. Right at the brink of the 25 m (80 ft) deep shaft (Fig. 7.2) they are all black. On other panels, they may be black or red. One positive red hand has been found. A number of hand stencils have been scratched or painted over (dots, bars). Only adult hands have been found. Many have incomplete fingers reminiscent of the Gargas stencils.

Even though Cosquer is far from having been exhaustively studied, it has significantly added to our knowledge of cave art. The presence of 13 sea animals, as well as the unusually numerous caprids, testifies to the influence the local biotope played in the painters' myths. At the time of its painting the Cosquer Cave was located a few miles from the shore in an environment of limestone hills favourable to ibex and chamois. It is no coincidence, then, that the artists chose to represent that local fauna. This has not always been the case. In the deep Vicdessos valley, where the Magdalenians of La Vache mostly hunted ibex, the cave art of Niaux shows an overwhelming majority of bison and horses (Clottes 1995a).

Hand stencils with incomplete fingers had until very recently been found in only a few caves (Gargas, Tibiran, Fuente del Trucho, Maltravieso). Now we know that the phenomenon was far more widely represented than had been thought (also see La Grande Grotte at Arcy-sur-Cure: Baffier and Girard 1992, 1995). The direct dating of two hands in

**Fig. 7.2.** Black hand stencils near the 25 m (80 ft) deep shaft in the Cosquer Cave.

Photograph Ministère de la Culture, Direction du Patrimoine, A. Chêné, Centre Camille Jullian, CNRS.

human groups living at such distances from one another should independently develop the same crippling diseases and should react in the same way by immortalising them on the walls of the caves by means of the same techniques?

Right from the beginning, by studying the superimposition of figures (Breuil's method), we could determine that there had been two main phases in the art, the earlier one including the hand stencils and the finger tracings, and a later phase to which most of the animal paintings and engravings appear to belong (Beltrán *et al.* 1992; Clottes, Beltrán *et al.* 1992a). This was confirmed by direct radiocarbon dating, when five dates obtained from three different animals ranged between 18,000 and 19,200 b.p. (Clottes *et al.* 1992). Since then, another animal was dated to 19,340 ± 200 b.p. (GifA-95135) (Clottes, Courtin and Valladas 1996), which perfectly fitted with our earlier results. However, we also got a surprising date for a bison (Bi2, Fig. 7.3) situated next to a second one (Bi1) (Fig. 7.4) which had previously been sampled and double-dated (18,010 ± 190 (GifA-91419) and 18,530 ± 180 b.p. (GifA-92492)). Instead of falling within the expected range, the result was 27,350 ± 430 b.p. (GifA-95195) (Clottes, Courtin and Valladas 1996). The dating of the humic fraction was 23,080 ± 640 b.p. (GifA-95308), which showed that some pollution had been eliminated by the acid–base–acid treatment. The date tallies with those already obtained for Cosquer's Phase 1. This cannot be a coincidence. Therefore, taking into account the similarity between the two bison (heads in three-quarters perspective, male sex organs explicitly indicated, which is not often the case; see Clottes, Garner and Maury 1994), only two possibilities can be contemplated. Either one bison was actually drawn more than 8000 years before the other, which would mean that the late-comers still used the same conventions as their predecessors or copied them, or more probably the two bison were contemporary. If this were true, the artist would have picked up some charcoal lying around in the cave to make his/her

Cosquer (27,110 ± 350 b.p.,[1] GifA-92491; and 24,840 ± 340 b.p., GifA-95358) has given dates which are the earliest ever obtained for hand stencils. In addition, the obvious comparison with Gargas has been strengthened by a date there of 26,860 ± 460 b.p. (GifA-92369), from a bone stuck in a crack in the wall next to some hand stencils with incomplete fingers (Clottes, Valladas *et al.* 1992). It is now established that at roughly the same time hand stencils were being made in sites hundreds of miles apart, a fact which should deal a death blow to the theory of pathological mutilations (Sahly 1966; Barrière and Suères 1993). How likely would it be that

[1] Most radiocarbon determinations for the figures in question are far beyond the limit of agreed calibration curves; all radiocarbon dates in this chapter are therefore uncalibrated.

**Fig. 7.3.** Cosquer Cave. This bison gave a date of more than 27,000 b.p. It could have been roughly sketched with charcoal from the ground.
Photograph Ministère de la Culture, Direction du Patrimoine, A. Chêné, Centre Camille Jullian, CNRS.

**Fig. 7.4.** Cosquer Cave. Next to the bison in Fig. 7.3 and very similar to it. This more detailed bison gave two dates, between 18,000 and 18,500 b.p.
Photograph Ministère de la Culture, Direction du Patrimoine, A. Chêné, Centre Camille Jullian, CNRS.

drawing, a possibility theoretically formulated before (Bednarik 1994a) but not substantiated.

Cosquer is the only rock-art site where so many radiocarbon datings have been made (seven from the charcoal scattered on the floor, nine directly from the works of art). These multiple analyses have already paid off by revealing a more complex picture than one might have imagined.

They also put a final and welcome stop to a long-drawn, bitter controversy about the authenticity of the art, when Vialou, followed by Delluc and Delluc, aired his doubts about it, mostly in the media (but see Bourdial 1992; Delluc and Delluc 1991b; for all details about the polemics see Clottes and Courtin 1994: 23–6). This has lately been used as an argument against the validity of stylistic evaluation and dating (Bednarik 1995a: 100), purported to be valueless since specialists could err so grossly. In fact, this unfortunate development reflects far less upon the method than upon the imprudence of a very few individuals – not 'many' as Bednarik (1995a: 91) erroneously said – who felt they could express an adverse opinion about the art without having seen anything but a few photographs published in the press, and without even asking to be shown the rest of the evidence that had been collected (Clottes, Beltrán *et al.* 1992b).

## La Grotte Chauvet

No such problems arose with the discovery of Chauvet, perhaps because Cosquer had provided a salutary warning about the dangers of rash pronouncements. Chauvet was immediately hailed as a new Lascaux, because of the hundreds of animal figures it seemed to contain, as well as because of their aesthetic quality and their originality, with so many rhinos and lions and even with a few animals that had never before been represented in Palaeolithic cave art, such as a long-eared owl, a panther and a possible hyena.

Close examination showed how a variety of sophisticated and at times unusual techniques had been used to make representations of animals (Clottes 1995b). On the main two black panels, the surface of the wall was scraped white prior to the drawing of the figures (Fig. 7.5). This was done not just once to get rid of previous figures but repeatedly, and the way some animals just fitted within the scraped areas (see Chauvet *et al.* 1995: fig. 82) indicated that the preparation of the rock surfaces had been carried out deliberately, with particular images in mind. In some places, the blank area was then painted over by spreading a faint layer of paint, as a kind of background to the animals to be painted on top (see Chauvet *et al.* 1995: fig. 88). In addition to these intricate preparations, the artists tried to give relief – and succeeded in doing so – to some animals by scraping the wall along their outlines, which stand out against the white band thus created (see Chauvet *et al.* 1995: fig. 81).

Another uncommon feature of the art is the expression of spatial perspective by different means. A lion with its head stretched out has been made to look as though it were standing behind several horses (Fig. 7.6). This was done by avoiding any overlapping between the line of its back and hindquarters and the horses that had been painted before. Then, with that effect achieved, the artist had not bothered to do more; the convex line of the lion's belly was superimposed upon the two neighbouring horses (see Chauvet *et al.* 1995: fig. 55). On the main

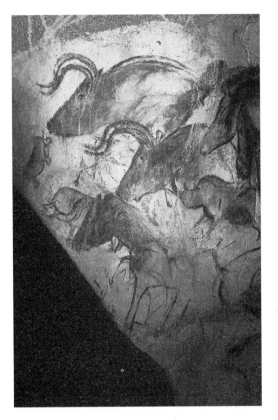

**Fig. 7.5.** Chauvet Cave. Aurochs, horses and rhinos were painted on a wall that had previously been scraped white.
Photograph J. Clottes.

panel in the last chamber, a number of rhinos were drawn as if they were standing in a row (see Chauvet *et al.* 1995: fig. 86). Their parallel horns are in true perspective, that is, the one in the foreground is larger than those in the background (Fig. 7.7). This the artist could not do for the lines of their backs, which, however, give the impression of several animals side by side, as was intended. In several other cases, involving both engravings and black paintings, the same technique has been applied to the rendering of perspective by multiplying the contours (see Chauvet *et al.* 1995: figs. 30, 64, 66, 79). A different way of showing an animal in spatial perspective has involved a clever use of a natural relief next to the panel of the lions and rhinos, where two

117

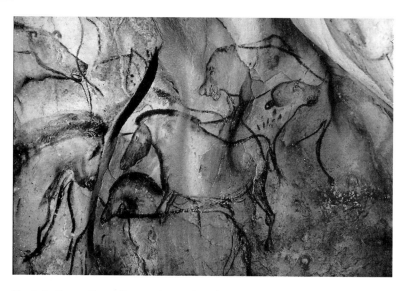

**Fig. 7.6.** Chauvet Cave. A lion stretching to the right has been put into spatial perspective in relation to three horses. Photograph J. Clottes.

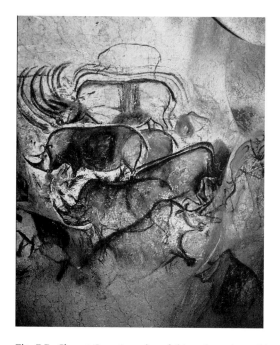

**Fig. 7.7.** Chauvet Cave. A number of rhinos shown in spatial perspective. Some of the outlines of rhinos in the middle of the panel have been scraped to make them stand out.
Photograph J. Clottes.

planes of the wall converge and make a 90° angle. There, a bison has been represented with its head facing us on the flat wall, while its body seems to be receding behind it on the other plane, exactly as the animal would look if it were right in front of us (Chauvet *et al.* 1995: fig. 88).

One of the main problems for the Chauvet art, as for so many other caves with numerous figures, is perceiving some semblance of unity amongst the diverse range of figures. We must assess whether the art belongs to a single period or whether much later works have been added to earlier ones, as was the case with Cosquer. For decades there had been no way of checking the validity of the answers proposed. They heavily depended upon the theoretical beliefs of their proponents. For the Abbé Breuil, the art had slowly accumulated over time during a great number of magic rituals. Each image had to be judged according to its stylistic characteristics, which made for great variety. Leroi-Gourhan (1965) took an opposite stance. For him the art was definitely structured, which implied an overall unity. Despite the advent of AMS dating and the widespread distrust in France of grand theories (GRAPP 1993: 405), one must still try to tackle the problem, at least in a preliminary stage, through direct observation and comparisons.

So far, the art in the Chauvet Cave seems coherent, because of the techniques used and the themes represented. Furthermore, certain details have been repeated over and over again.

In the first part of the cave – in the chambers and passages nearest the Palaeolithic entrance – the numerous animals and signs are mostly red, with very scarce engravings and only a couple of black figures. Then one comes to a middle area with hardly anything but engravings except for two black animals. The remotest parts of the cave include a great many black paintings. Engravings are not rare there, but red figures are exceptional. Red hand stencils and hand prints, as well as extensive panels of red dots and other geometric signs are only to be found in the 'red area', while reindeer, *Megaloceros*, bison, aurochs and horses are only black, in addition to a few engraved horses. Consequently, there does seem to exist a kind of structure to the art, with particular locations and themes having been favoured for particular techniques. This could be interpreted in two ways. If one supports unity, one might say that each location was chosen for a special function or was used by people of different status. On the other hand, one might also argue that the earlier art was done next to the cave entrance and that it was only later that people went to the deeper galleries – or the other way round. In that case, different techniques and a few themes could have a different chronological value.

In fact, distinct similarities can also be found which blur the differences between red and black figures. Even if red animals are rare amongst the black ones and vice versa, they do occur occasionally: a black horse with red stencils; a red rhino on the black Panel of Horses, and so forth. To a black rhino was added paint for the horns and something interpreted as 'breath'. Three lions were drawn in perspective with parallel lines, one red between two black ones. Finally, on the main panel in the last chamber, black paintings were superimposed on older red figures and signs. This shows that occasionally red and black were used before or after each other, and at times jointly. It is not surprising, then, to notice that stump drawing,[2] so prevalent with the black animals, is also present – albeit more discreetly – with a few red ones (see the bears in Chauvet *et al.* 1995: figs. 20, 21).

A tell-tale tiny detail can be observed on most rhino images, whether they be red, black or engraved. It is the distinctive way their ears were drawn, like two small wings, one on each side of the outline of the head and back (Fig. 7.8). This way of representing the ears is so peculiar that its constant reiteration can be neither coincidental nor caused by imitation of much earlier figures. Either all those rhinos were the work of one person or they were done by people who imitated one another. On the Panel of Horses, where the wall was scraped to prepare it for the black paintings, some earlier engravings were totally or partly erased. The surviving part of an engraved rhino at the top shows the distinctive wing-like ears, as do the several black rhinos on the panel.

Until Chauvet, rhinos had been among the rarest animals represented in Palaeolithic parietal art: irrespective of period, less than a score had been known for the whole of Europe (Barrière 1993: 158). The 53 rhinos thus far seen in Chauvet may be black (39), red (8) or engraved (6). The same observation holds for other fairly rare species, such as lions, bears and mammoths. There is a commonality of concepts, whatever the technique used.

The scale seems to be tipped in favour of an overall unity within the Chauvet body of art, whether it was created within a short period or over millennia, which we have no way of knowing at this early stage of research.

Despite current fashionable criticism of dating by

---

[2] Stump drawing is a way of rendering the shading and relief inside the body – here of animals – by spreading the paint either with the hand or with a piece of hide.

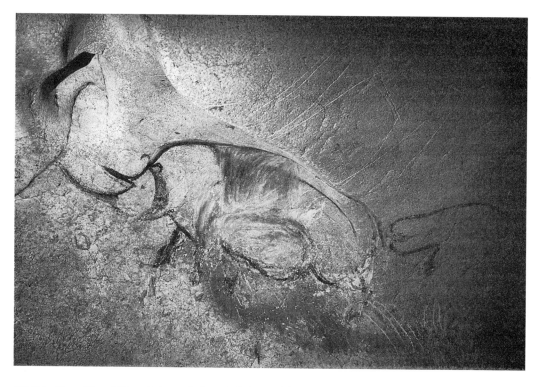

**Fig. 7.8.** Chauvet Cave. Rhino with its ears in the typical Chauvet fashion, like small arches on either side of the line of the head. Photograph J. Clottes.

stylistic analogy (Bednarik 1995b; Lorblanchet and Bahn 1993), this method is and will remain a necessary 'evil' until technical progress makes it possible to obtain a great number of direct dates for most cave art sites, if this ever happens. Meanwhile, one cannot sit back and wait for better times, which is why stylistic conventions are still so widely used by all specialists even when they criticise them (Clottes 1993c).

When Chauvet was discovered, it soon became apparent that various characteristics of the animals pointed to a pre-Lascaux date: all the bison had their horns in frontal ('twisted') perspective, which is a good marker of ancient art – as Breuil had argued – not for an isolated figure but only when it has been used systematically; the bellies of the mammoths were in the form of an arch, a convention so far found in Gravettian and Solutrean contexts (Combier

1995); one bison had the stiff, hoofless legs in the form of a Y prevalent at Cosquer; the horns of the aurochs had been drawn like an inverted S, as at Ebbou; the panels of big red dots had parallels in Pech-Merle; hand stencils were present and so far those that have been assigned a date (Cosquer, Gargas, Labattut, Fuente del Salín) are significantly older than 20,000 b.p. On the other hand, a few figures were reminiscent of Lascaux, such as a running aurochs (Chauvet *et al.* 1995: fig. 62), horses with very thick manes (Chauvet *et al.* 1995: figs. 70, 73), and animals with round hoofs (Chauvet *et al.* 1995: figs. 69, 76). Consequently, the art was provisionally attributed to a time-span – with the supposed date for Lascaux (17,000 b.p.) as a limit – mostly centred on the Solutrean (up to 22,000 b.p.), *or to an earlier period* (my emphasis) (Clottes 1995b: 114).

When four direct dates for three different animals

became available in the late spring of 1995, they created quite a stir, as they ranged from 30,340 to 32,410 b.p. (Clottes *et al.* 1995) – the earliest ever obtained for Palaeolithic paintings. Initial doubts and fears of contamination were soon allayed after checking with Hélène Valladas of the Gif-sur-Yvette Laboratory, who pointed out that those dates were corroborated by an analysis of a torch mark left on top of calcite covering some earlier paintings, very close to the ones (two rhinos) that had given the very early dates. The torch mark was dated to $26,120 \pm 400$ b.p. (GifA-95127). As there was a distinct stratigraphy, dates upwards of 30,000 for the original paintings were quite coherent. Charcoal from similar torch marks in a different chamber gave dates of $26,980 \pm 410$ b.p. (GifA-95129) and $26,980 \pm 420$ b.p. (GifA-95130), another corroboration. In addition, those results brought to mind the discovery of a number of sophisticated ivory statuettes in Aurignacian layers in the south-west of Germany at Vogelherd, Geissenklösterle and Höhlenstein-Stadel. Their elaboration had long been a challenge to theories of the very crude beginnings of art in the Aurignacian (Clottes 1993a). Chauvet was to parietal art what those statuettes were to portable art.

However, the Chauvet dates have already been challenged on stylistic grounds, either obliquely (Combier 1995) or more directly (Zuechner 1996). While admitting that the art is clearly pre-Magdalenian, Combier (1995) has stressed some themes (*Megaloceros*) and several peculiar features which are to be found in Gravettian and Solutrean art, particularly in the Ardèche Solutrean; he wonders whether Chauvet is homogeneous (see also Clottes 1995b: 110). Zuechner, going further than Combier, flatly refuses the Aurignacian dates because they do not fit with existing methods of dating by stylistic themes. He argues that some animals look Solutrean or even Magdalenian (but see Combier 1995) and cannot belong to earlier cultures (Zuechner 1996).

This raises three interesting questions. One is the duration of artistic conventions: we are far from knowing exactly when a convention first came into existence, how long it lasted and whether it could be found in unrelated contexts by chance through phenomena of convergence. Another is the dating of particular sites. Lascaux is generally considered as firmly dated to 17,000 b.p., although no painting there has yet been directly analysed. It is true that at Chauvet the horns of the aurochs are identical to those in Ebbou, which certainly poses a problem. But Ebbou has never been securely dated by its own evidence, only by comparison with other caves. Finally, one must never forget that one is dealing with a period of more than 20,000 years, with less than 300 parietal sites for the whole of Europe, from the tip of the Iberian Peninsula to the Urals. This scanty scattering of sites cannot provide an accurate picture of Palaeolithic rock-art (Bahn 1995), or else one would have to accept that over that huge area one site was painted or engraved every seventy years or so, which is most unlikely. We are dealing with an immensely long chain with very few remaining links. Therefore, not only are surprises and original or unique works possible but also they should be frequent. All discoveries cannot be expected to fit snugly into the comforting pigeon-holes that we have set up!

The discrepancy between the early guesses about the art of Chauvet and the results of direct radiocarbon dating has been quoted as still more evidence of the inanity and imprudence of stylistic evaluations (Bednarik 1995a; Lorblanchet 1995). Both authors conveniently forgot that, if at first the Chauvet paintings were cautiously assigned a tentative age between 17,000 and 22,000 b.p. ('or earlier', see above), an important proviso had also been made; taking into account the uniqueness of the cave, the possibility of surprises had been mentioned explicitey (Clottes 1995b: 114). It would have been much stranger and contrary to the initial stylistic analysis of the paintings if they had yielded Magdalenian dates!

Leroi-Gourhan's (1965) theories are no longer tenable after Chauvet. His Style I, equated with the Aurignacian, can now apply to only a few Dordogne sites. The new Ardèche cave is placed totally outside it by its originality and sophistication. Lions and rhinos are given great importance on the main panels where they are centrally situated. This is also contrary to Leroi-Gourhan's ideas about the organisation and structure of Palaeolithic parietal art, which would have placed lions, for example, either in the entrance or at the bottom of the cave in a secondary position. Furthermore, his belief is now challenged (Clottes 1996) that Palaeolithic cave art represented one single symbolic view of the world from the Aurignacian to the Magdalenian, with a continuity of the same themes and only minor variations (Leroi-Gourhan 1965: 137, 147).

The dominance in Chauvet of fearsome animals posed a problem; rhinos, lions, mammoths and bears constitute 61 per cent of the identifiable animals in the cave. Was this a freakish local phenomenon or are those themes found elsewhere in Aurignacian or other sites and thus testify to a major change in concepts at an unspecified date after the Aurignacian?

The well-dated Aurignacian sites of the Dordogne include about three times more 'dangerous' animals than those of the Gravettian in the same area (Delluc and Delluc 1991a). Those animals are also dominant for the Aurignacian German statuettes, with 7 mammoths, 4 felines, 1 rhino or bear, 2 bison, 1 horse, 1 human and 1 therianthrope with a lion head (Riek 1934; Hahn 1986). In Gargas, the Gravettian cave with most figures, only mammoths are still there – and they represent only 4 per cent of the bestiary (Barrière 1976: 380). Other caves, belonging to early periods of parietal art but still undated (Grande Grotte at Arcy-sur-Cure, Grotte Bayol and Baume-Latrone in the Gard), show that the enormous number of dangerous animals at Chauvet is not a unique phenomenon, isolated in time and space. Drastic thematic changes occurred at the end of the Aurignacian or during the Gravettian in south-west France, though perhaps not everywhere at the same time. In central and eastern Europe, the same dangerous animals went on being carved on the statuettes throughout the Pavlov (63 per cent) and Kostienki-Avdeevo periods (60 per cent) (Kozlowski 1992),

while in the same regions they become far fewer in the Magdalenian (9 per cent; Hahn 1990).

## The Côa valley petroglyphs

When the discovery of the Côa valley engravings was announced, in November 1994, it immediately became a world event because the art was under imminent threat of being flooded by the building of a huge dam (for details, see Bahn 1995; Chippindale 1995; Clottes 1995c; Bednarik 1995a, 1995b; Zilhão 1995a, 1995b; Oliveira Jorge 1995). The controversy between conflicting interests raged for months in the media and became a political issue. Eventually, the new government appointed after the October 1995 general election wisely decided not only to freeze the dam project until the art and its archaeological context had been studied in depth but to cancel the dam altogether. It was probably the first time in world history that such a major project was stopped because of rock-art study and preservation.

The engravings are scattered along the banks of a deep valley in a number of clusters over at least 17 km. After the initial work done by a team led by Antonio Martinho Baptista and Mario Varela Gomes (1995), thousands of mainly finely etched engravings had been found. Many figures are also pecked. They include aurochs and horses (the majority of figures), with deer and ibex, and one anthropomorph, as well as numerous geometric signs (Varela, pers. comm.). Few species seem to have been represented, but further research may reveal more.

From the first, the Côa rock-art has been declared a major discovery on two counts. It was attributed to the Upper Palaeolithic and, more specifically, to the Solutrean and early Magdalenian cultures because of the artistic conventions used. As such, it is one of the largest bodies of Ice Age rock-art ever found in Europe. In addition, it is an open-air site, which added to its interest, since most Palaeolithic art had so far been known from caves.

When I was asked by the Portuguese Institute for Architecture and Archaeology (IPPAR) of the Secretariat of State for Culture and by UNESCO to visit the site on 15–16 December 1994, which I did with Mario Varela Gomes, we were the first specialists in Palaeolithic art to see it. In my report (19 December 1994), I expressed the opinion that, in addition to Iron Age and Chalcolithic figures, most of the art was indeed Palaeolithic, as had been surmised by Nelson Rebanda who had found it, and that probably it was in great part Solutrean and early Magdalenian. We saw fine engravings representing deer with striations inside the bodies – what Spanish specialists call *estriado* – which were identical to those found on well-dated portable art in Spain (Castillo), where they are considered characteristic of the cultures mentioned. At Foz Côa, at least one of those deer was superimposed on a pecked animal, thus providing a minimum probable date. As to the pecked animals, they all had simple naturalistic bodies in profile, with short, barely sketched, hoofless legs, one per pair. Their horns were in frontal perspective (Fig. 7.9), one of them being often linked to the backline while the other was connected to the line of the head, with a central blank between the two. Those characteristics remind one of the Solutrean animals in Cosquer or Parpalló. In the first semester of 1995, many other European cave-art specialists saw the site and all concurred with that provisional estimate.

In my report, I had also suggested seeing whether the varnish covering the petroglyphs could be dated. In February 1995, EDP – the state-owned electricity company that was building the dam – asked me for the names and addresses of specialists in petroglyph direct dating. After checking that this was done with the approval of and in conjunction with IPPAR, I gave the names of Ron Dorn (University of Arizona) and Alan Watchman (Canada). Each suggested another person: Dorn asked for Fred Phillips (USA) and Watchman for Robert Bednarik (Australia). All were invited by EDP. Each came to Portugal separately and carried out sampling without any communication with the others, in a blind test.

When some of the initial results were leaked to the press, and thus became widely known, they caused

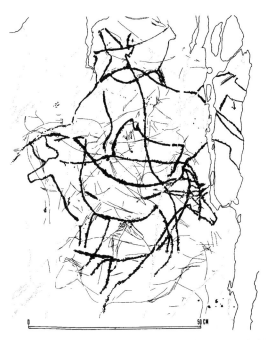

**Fig. 7.9.** Foz Côa. Pecked and engraved animals at Canada do Inferno.
From Martinho Baptista and Varela Gomes 1995 (part of fig. 3).

uproar. Instead of the Palaeolithic dates expected, Dorn, Watchman and Bednarik, while using different methods and not agreeing on exact dates, were reported as having obtained results that ranged from less than 200 to a few thousand years. This posed – and still does pose – a huge problem. Either the methods applied were at fault and the results unacceptable, which has implications for dates obtained by these methods elsewhere; or else the results could be trusted. If the latter were true, it would mean either that in the Holocene an independent reinvention of an art very close to that of the Ice Age took place in that area, or that a local Palaeolithic art tradition survived over ten or fifteen millennia in parallel to the well-known development of art in the Iberian Peninsula. Both hypotheses seemed most unlikely, the former even more than the latter. It was nevertheless necessary to confirm the dates by time-honoured methods, such as a geological study of the valley, an assessment of the ageing of the rock surfaces, or excavations close to the engraved panels (Clottes, Lorblanchet and Beltrán 1995).

Before any such results could be available, passions flared on both sides and culminated in emotional debates during sessions of the NEWS-95 rock-art conference at Turin, in September 1995 (see Bednarik 1995a, 1995b; and Watchman 1995 for a defence of the very late age of the art, and Zilhão 1995a, 1995b for a refutation of their arguments). However, within a few months, some new discoveries significantly changed the picture. At Salto do Bol, about 3 km upstream of the Penascosa engravings in the Côa valley, Zilhão found a habitation site with thousands of artefacts under 1 metre of colluvial sand. The assemblage is attributed to the late Gravettian (Zilhão 1995a). This means that – contrary to Bednarik's suppositions – the valley was not of such recent making and, in addition, that Upper Palaeolithic habitation sites were indeed present in the area. Although this is not direct proof, it strengthens the argument for a Palaeolithic date for some of the art.

The fact that the Foz Côa rock-art is in the open air, rather than being deep in caves, has also been presented as having major significance, after the discoveries of other major open-air Palaeolithic petroglyphs at Siega Verde, in Spain, just across the border from Portugal and the Côa valley (Balbín Behrmann et al. 1995), as well as at Domingo Garcia, also on the Spanish meseta (Ripoll Lopez and Muncio Gonzalez 1994). In the past few years, Bednarik (1994b) had argued that cave art was a kind of epiphenomenon, the importance of which had been vastly heightened if not exaggerated by its exceptional preservation. After the Spanish open-air sites, and more still after Foz Côa became known, some felt that cave art would soon be considered an exceptional activity, limited in time and space, as compared to art in the open (Balbín Berhmann et al. 1995: 105) or that, instead of being the rule as now, cave art sites used in fact to be exceptions (Zilhão 1995a: 111). Bahn (1995: 231) even went so far as to assert that cave art was 'unrepresentative and

uncharacteristic of the period, owing its apparent predominance in the archaeological record to a taphonomic fluke'.

These sweeping statements must be qualified on several accounts. First of all, the recent discoveries should not be construed as drastically upsetting our conceptions of Palaeolithic art. The likelihood of an extensive body of art having existed either in the open, or on media other than cave walls, had been hypothesised long before the recent discoveries were made (Breuil 1952: 24) and an engraved horse at Domingo Garcia had long been recognised as Palaeolithic (Balbín, Moure and Ripoll 1982). Côa, Siega Verde and the others confirm this supposition.

Secondly, the relative importance of open-air art versus cave art: it is indeed possible that the one may have been overwhelmingly more important than the other, and we may expect a number of other discoveries in the near future, now that attention has been forcefully drawn to open-air art sites. However, any statement as to their predominance rests upon two unproven assumptions. The first one is that both forms of art were similarly widespread, which we had no way of knowing up to now. Is the absence of art in the open in areas where cave art is well represented, such as the Dordogne and Quercy, the central and western Pyrenees, the south-east of France, southern Italy and Sicily, due to severe exposure or could it be that open-air rock-art was quite scarce or absent there for any number of reasons? Let us make a comparison. It is more than likely that wood was used during the Upper Palaeolithic. If, by some fluke, a hoard of Magdalenian engraved wooden artefacts was discovered in some Alpine lake or bog, should we then conclude that engravings on bones and antlers are unrepresentative and uncharacteristic of the period?

It is not only open-air sites that have disappeared over the millennia but also caves. Contrary to popular opinion, caves have a life of their own. Admittedly, paintings are obviously more likely to survive in deep caves, while they have no chance fully in the open. However, even in deep caves, they may be – and uncounted numbers were – destroyed by draughts (see the Passage in Lascaux), by water (Niaux), by spalling of the wall surface (Cosquer); both paintings and engravings may be calcited over or destroyed by all kinds of vandalism (entrance to Gabillou, Cova Bastera, Grande Grotte at Arcy-sur-Cure). Hundreds of caves have been flooded by the sea: less than one-third of Cosquer survived because part of a large chamber happened to remain above sea-level. In all limestone areas, where the caves are located, an abundance of scree and other slope deposits has blocked cave entrances. Innumerable caves are concealed under them, and the few painted ones that are known, such as Chauvet, Fontanet or Pech-Merle, owe their discovery to the existence of a passage other than the one used by Palaeolithic people. This means that it is certain that we know but a fraction of the caves which were painted and/or engraved. Precisely how small or large that fraction is we have no way of finding out. One must conclude that a comparison between two unknown variables cannot be anything but a futile exercise.

There should be more rewarding lines of research, such as the possibility that each form of art had different meanings and roles. The problem was raised a long time ago concerning deep caves and shelters (Laming-Emperaire 1962), that is, the difference between the art of the depths and the art of the light (Clottes 1997). From a psychological point of view, going into the subterranean world was a major undertaking, which is why – apart from the European Palaeolithic – if real cave art can occasionally be found elsewhere (Australia, USA (Tennessee, Kentucky), Santo-Domingo, for example), it still remains an exceptional occurrence. That change of worlds between outer light and inner darkness, which plays such a great part in many origin myths, for instance in the American South-west, may also be regarded as a metaphor or a substitute for shamanistic experiences (Lewis-Williams 1994). Even if animals such as horses, aurochs, deer and ibex are represented both outside and inside the caves, it is highly likely that each form of art played a different part in the lives of those people and was endowed with special signifi-

cance. For instance, one was very public while the other was much less accessible. Some of the directions future research might take could be assessing the archaeological context of the art outside, its relation to settlements and to the landscape. For example, the extensive sites of Côa and Siega Verde are both along rivers, and many engraved rock panels seem to face the stream: were those open-air sites chosen in relation to the water and why? It is also necessary to date this art precisely and to know what activities took place in its vicinity, as well as to compare the themes and techniques used with what the artists did in the caves, in order to determine whether major differences can be ascertained and what they could mean.

**Learning from the 'Three Cs'**

The 'Three Cs' (Cosquer, Chauvet, Côa) are a useful reminder that further major discoveries are still possible, which in a few years may change our outlook on major issues. With Cosquer, Provence is no longer a blank on maps, the nagging problem of hand stencils with incomplete fingers is probably solved, and the influence of the local environment upon the themes chosen has been strongly substantiated. With Côa, open-air Palaeolithic art is now in the limelight, and fruitful comparisons with cave art will become possible in the near future. Chauvet's early dates for very sophisticated images play havoc with current theories about the origins and development of Palaeolithic art. It can no longer be considered as starting in the Aurignacian with crude and awkward representations in the shelters of the Dordogne, and slowly improving in the course of the following millennia. As Ucko (1987) surmised, there must have been many heydays and many beginnings. This means that cave art – the tangible manifestation of complex cultural beliefs during the Upper Palaeolithic – has been more diverse than was thought. Instead of a linear evolution from awkward figures to elaborate ones, one must admit the simple and now obvious idea that panels with admirable works of art were painted long before or at the same time as others which appear to us cruder in different areas. Were the masterpieces of Chauvet preceded by thousands of years of trials and errors on other media such as bark, wood, sand or hide – as the Abbé Breuil long ago supposed? Perhaps not, since there is no reason why the development of artistic capacities and creativity in humankind should mimic that of a child. Chauvet has also made us realise that the contents of the art did change considerably over time.

All of this highlights our overall ignorance about the details of the evolution of Palaeolithic art, despite a century of research, discoveries and progress. From the beginnings of parietal art in the Aurignacian (or before?) to the end of the Magdalenian, there stretches a very long chain with many missing links. One must remain aware of this fact and be ready to accept conceptual changes when other discoveries *will* come to light. Does it mean, then, that our knowledge of Palaeolithic art is so shaky that specialists are nearly invariably wrong in their pronouncements?

Bednarik (1995a) has stressed a few unexpected results in the direct dating of several sites, concluding that stylistic datings 'appear to be totally random and irrelevant, offering no redeeming feature at all' (Bednarik 1995a: 100) and even that 'the Palaeolithic art specialists of the world have collectively demonstrated that they are not capable of determining whether a particular art corpus belongs to that *inferred* entity, Franco-Cantabrian Palaeolithic rock art' (1995a: 101). The same author states that specialists 'cannot produce consistently valid predictions', that is, 'predictions that are found to agree consistently with scientific dating estimates' (1995a: 100). He publishes a diagram supposed to demonstrate that there is no correlation between stylistic guesses and direct datings (Bednarik 1995a: 100, fig. 12).

That diagram and Bednarik's conclusions are flawed for two main reasons: he picked just four examples of dated art out of the nine available, and whenever there was a controversy (Cosquer, Zubialde) he chose to quote the opinion of the people who had initially misinterpreted the art and not the assessment of those who had been right from the first.

In fact, we now know of 32 direct AMS analyses for 26 figures in 9 different caves. They are: Niaux (3 determinations), Portel (2), Altamira (2), Castillo (2), Covaciella (2), Cosquer (9), Chauvet (5), Cougnac (6) and Pech-Merle (1). In addition, three sites have yielded very late Holocene dates which specialists do not accept because they most likely result from contamination in extensively frequented caves (Gargas, Bédeilhac) or from the use of methods that are still experimental (the Côa petroglyphs).

For the nine caves mentioned above, the results fit with the expectations for Niaux, Altamira, Castillo, Portel, Covaciella, Cosquer, Pech-Merle (seven out of nine). There are only minor differences, with dates later by 500 or 1000 years than had been assumed (Niaux, Portel), or earlier by 2 to 3 millennia for Cosquer Phase 1, while still remaining within the postulated culture (Magdalenian, Gravettian). For Cosquer Phase 2, the dates fitted perfectly well. For Pech-Merle, a recently published date ($24,640 \pm 390$ b.p., GifA-95357) for a spotted horse (Lorblanchet 1995) next to a row of stencilled bent thumbs seen sideways was a welcome confirmation: a Gravettian date had been contemplated after stylistic comparison with Gargas, where an identical row of thumbs had long been known in a Gravettian art context (itself also confirmed by the dating of a bone stuck in a crack next to some hand stencils) (Clottes, Valladas *et al.* 1992).

It is true that our knowledge about early art has dramatically increased and that we have had some unexpected results (about Chauvet see above; about Cougnac, see Lorblanchet 1994; Clottes 1994), but the landmarks for Magdalenian art seem now to be solidly fixed. All in all, when the evidence – *all* the evidence – about direct dating of the art is reviewed with a dispassionate eye, stylistic analyses do not fare that badly. New attempts at dating and new discoveries may add further pieces to the puzzle of

Palaeolithic art but they do not detract from the results of methodical stylistic studies in a detrimental way.

## REFERENCES

Baffier, D. and M. Girard. 1992. La Grande Grotte d'Arcy-sur-Cure (Yonne), nouveau sanctuaire paléolithique: résultats préliminaires, *Revue Archéologique de l'Est* 43(2): 195–205.

 1995. La Grande Grotte d'Arcy-sur-Cure (Yonne): second sanctuaire paléolithique bourguignon, *L'Anthropologie* 100(2): 208–16.

Bahn, P. G. 1995. Cave art without the caves, *Antiquity* 69(263): 231–7.

Bahn P. G. and J. Vertut. 1988. *Images of the Ice Age.* Leicester, Windward.

Balbín Berhmann, R. de, J.-J. Alcolea Gonzalez and M. Santonja Gomez. 1995. Siega Verde: un art rupestre à l'air libre dans la vallée du Douro, *L'art préhistorique*, Dossiers d'Archéologie 209: 98–105.

Balbín Berhmann, R. de, J.-A. Moure Romanillo and E. Ripoll Perello. 1982. Grabados esquematicos de la comarca de Santa Maria de Nieva (Segovia), *Coloquio Internacional sobre el Arte Rupestre Esquematico de la Peninsula Ibérica*, pp. 8–9. Salamanca, Resumen de Comunicacions.

Barrière, C. 1976. *L'art pariétal de la Grotte de Gargas.* Oxford, British Archaeological Reports. Supplementary Series 14(1).

 1993. Les Rhinocérotidés, in GRAPP, *L'art pariétal paléolithique: techniques et méthodes d'étude*, pp. 157–9. Paris, Ed. du Comité des Travaux Historiques et Scientifiques.

Barrière, C. and M. Suères. 1993. Les mains de Gargas, in *La Main dans la préhistoire*, Dossiers d'Archéologie 178: 46–54.

Bednarik, R. G. 1993. Geoarchaeological dating of petroglyphs at Lake Onega, Russia, *Geoarchaeology* 8(6): 443–63.

 1994a. About rock art dating, *INORA* 7: 16–18.

 1994b. A taphonomy of palaeoart, *Antiquity* 68: 68–74.

 1995a. The age of the Côa Valley petroglyphs in Portugal, *Rock Art Research* 12(2): 86–103.

 1995b. The Côa petroglyphs: an obituary to the stylistic dating of Palaeolithic rock art, *Antiquity* 69(266): 877–83.

Beltrán, A., J. Clottes, J. Courtin and H. Cosquer. 1992. Une grotte ornée paléolithique sur le littoral méditerranéen: la Grotte Cosquer à Marseille. *Comptes-Rendus de l'Académie des Sciences* series II 315: 239–46.

Bourdial, I. 1992. Une grotte bien ténébreuse, *Science et Vie* 894: 74–9, 164.

Breuil, H. 1952. *Quatre cents siècles d'art pariétal.* Montignac, Centre d'Etudes et de Documentation Préhistoriques.

Chauvet, J.-M., E. Brunel-Deschamps and C. Hillaire. 1995. *La Grotte Chauvet à Vallon-Pont-d'Arc.* Paris, Le Seuil. Postface by J. Clottes.

Chippindale, C. 1995. Editorial, *Antiquity* 69(266): 863–70.

Clottes, J. 1993a. La naissance du sens artistique, *Revue des Sciences Morales et Politiques* 173–84.

 1993b. Paint analyses from several Magdalenian caves in the Ariège region of France, *Journal of Archaeological Science* 20: 223–35.

 1993c. Post-stylistic? In P. G. Bahn and M. Lorblanchet (eds.), *Rock art studies: the post-stylistic era, or Where do we go from here?*, pp. 19–25. Oxford, Oxbow.

 1994. Dates directes pour les peintures paléolithiques, *Bulletin de la Société Préhistorique Ariège-Pyrénées* 49: 51–70.

 1995a. *Les Cavernes de Niaux: art magdalénien en Ariège.* Paris, Le Seuil.

 1995b. Postface: la Grotte Chauvet aujourd'hui, in J.-M. Chauvet, E. Brunel-Deschamps and C. Hillaire, *La Grotte Chauvet à Vallon-Pont-d'Arc*, pp. 81–120. Paris, Le Seuil.

 1995c. Paleolithic petroglyphs at Foz Côa, Portugal. *INORA* 10: 2.

 1996. Thematic changes in the art of the Upper Palaeolithic, *Antiquity* 70: 276–88.

 1997. Art of the light and art of the depths. In press.

Clottes, J., A. Beltrán, J. Courtin and H. Cosquer. 1992a. The Cosquer Cave on Cape Morgiou, Marseille, *Antiquity* 66: 583–98.

 1992b. Réponse à D. Vialou, *Bulletin de la Société Préhistorique Française* 89(8): 229–30.

Clottes, J., J.-M. Chauvet, E. Brunel-Deschamps, C. Hillaire, J.-P. Daugas, M. Arnold, H. Cachier, J. Evin, Ph. Fortin, C. Oberlin, N. Tisnerat and H. Valladas. 1995. Les peintures paléolithiques de la Grotte Chauvet-Pont-d'Arc, à Vallon-Pont-d'Arc (Ardèche, France): datations directes et indirectes par la méthode du radiocarbone, *Comptes-Rendus de l'Académie des Sciences* series IIa 320: 1133–40.

Clottes, J. and J. Courtin. 1994. *La Grotte Cosquer: peintures et gravures de la caverne engloutie.* Paris, Le Seuil.

Clottes, J., J. Courtin and J. Collina-Girard. 1996. More research on the Cosquer Cave, *INORA* 15: 1–2.

Clottes, J., J. Courtin and H. Valladas. 1996. New direct dates for the Cosquer Cave, *INORA* 15: 2–4.

Clottes, J., J. Courtin, H. Valladas, M. Cachier, N. Mercier and M. Arnold. 1992. La Grotte Cosquer datée, *Bulletin de la Société Préhistorique Française* 89(8): 230–4.

Clottes, J., M. Garner and G. Maury. 1994. Bisons magdaléniens des cavernes ariégeoises, *Bulletin de la Société Préhistorique Ariège-Pyrénées* 49: 15–49.

Clottes, J., M. Lorblanchet and A. Beltrán. 1995. Are the Foz Côa engravings actually Holocene?, *INORA* 12: 19–21.

Clottes, J., M. Menu and Ph. Walter. 1990. La préparation des peintures magdaléniennes des cavernes ariégeoises, *Bulletin de la Société Préhistorique Française* 87(6): 170–92.

Clottes, J., H. Valladas, M. Cachier and M. Arnold. 1992. Des dates pour Niaux et Gargas, *Bulletin de la Société Préhistorique Française* 89(9): 270–4.

Combier, J. 1995. Les grottes ornées de l'Ardèche, *L'Art préhistorique*, Dossiers d'Archéologie 209: 66–85.

Delluc, B. and G. Delluc. 1991a. *L'Art pariétal archaïque en Aquitaine.* Paris, Editions du CNRS, 28th suppl. to *Gallia Préhistoire.*

1991b. A propos de la découverte de la grotte de Sormiou à Cassis, dite Grotte Cosquer, *Bulletin de la Société Historique et Archéologique du Périgord* 108(4): 516–17.

Dorn, R. 1992. A review of rock varnish dating of rock engravings, *INORA* 2: 10–14.

GRAPP. 1993. *L'Art pariétal paléolithique. Techniques et méthodes d'étude.* Paris, Ed. Comité des Travaux Historiques et Scientifiques.

Hahn, J. 1986. *Kraft und Aggression: die Botschaft der Eiszeitkunst im Aurignacien Süddeutschlands?* Tübingen, Institut für Urgeschichte der Universität Tübingen, Verlag Archaeologica Venatoria.

1990. Fonction et signification des statuettes du Paléolithique supérieur européen, in J. Clottes (ed.), *L'Art des objets au Paléolithique* 2: *Les Voies de la recherche*, pp. 173–83. Paris, Ministère de la Culture.

Kozlowski, J.-K. 1992. *L'Art de la préhistoire en Europe orientale.* Paris, CNRS.

Laming-Emperaire, A. 1962. *La Signification de l'art rupestre paléolithique.* Paris, Picard.

Leroi-Gourhan, A. 1965. *Préhistoire de l'art occidental.* Paris, Mazenod.

Lewis-Williams, J. D. 1994. Rock art and ritual: southern Africa and beyond, *Complutum* 5: 277–89.

Lorblanchet, M. 1994. La datation de l'art pariétal paléolithique, *Bulletin de la Société des Etudes Littéraires, Scientifiques et Historiques du Lot* 115(3): 161–82.

1995. La datation de l'art pariétal paléolithique: état de la question (juin 1995), *L'Art préhistorique*, Dossiers d'Archéologie 209: 18–19.

Lorblanchet, M. and P. G. Bahn (eds.). 1993. *Rock art studies: the post-stylistic era, or, Where do we go from here?* Oxford, Oxbow.

Lorblanchet, M., M. Labeau, J.-L. Vernet, R. Fitte, H. Valladas, C. H. Cachier and M. Arnold. 1990. Etudes des pigments des grottes ornées paléolithiques du Quercy, *Bulletin de la Société des Etudes Littéraires, Scientifiques et Historiques du Lot* 111(2): 93–143.

Martinho Baptista, A. and M. Varela Gomes. 1995. Arte rupestre do Vale do Côa. A. Canada do Inferno. Primeiras impressoes, in V. Oliveira Jorge (ed.), *Dossier Côa*, pp. 45–118. Oporto, Sociedad Portuguesa de Antropologia e Etnologia.

Oliveira Jorge, V. (ed.). 1995. *Dossier Côa.* Oporto, Sociedad Portuguesa de Antropologia e Etnologia.

Riek, G. 1934. *Die Eiszeitjägerstation am Vogelherd im Lonetal.* 1: *Die Kulturen.* Tübingen.

Ripoll Lopez, S. and L.-J. Muncio Gonzalez. 1994. A large open air grouping of Paleolithic rock art in the Spanish Meseta, *INORA* 7: 2–5.

Sahly, A. 1966. *Les Mains mutilées dans l'art préhistorique.* Toulouse, Privat.

Ucko, P. J. 1987. Débuts illusoires dans l'étude de la tradition artistique, *Bulletin de la Société Préhistorique Ariège-Pyrénées* 42: 15–81.

Ucko, P. J. and A. Rosenfeld. 1967. *L'Art paléolithique.* Paris, Hachette.

Valladas, H., H. Cachier, P. Maurice, F. Bernaldo de Quiros, J. Clottes, V. Cabrera Valdés, P. Uzquiano and M. Arnold. 1992. Direct radiocarbon dates for prehistoric paintings at the Altamira, El Castillo and Niaux caves, *Nature* 357: 68–70.

Watchman, A. 1995. Recent petroglyphs, Foz Côa, Portugal, *Rock Art Research* 12(2): 104–8.

Watchman, A. and D. Lessard. 1992. Dating prehistoric rock art by laser: a new method for extracting trace organic matter, *INORA* 2: 14–15.

Zilhão, J. 1995a. L'art rupestre paléolithique de plein air.

Vallée du Côa (Portugal), *L'Art préhistorique*, Dossiers d'Archéologie 209: 106–17.

1995b. The age of the Côa valley (Portugal) rock art: validation of archaeological dating to the Palaeolithic and refutation of 'scientific' dating to historic or protohistoric times, *Antiquity* 69: 883–901.

Zuechner, C. 1996. The Chauvet Cave: radiocarbon versus archaeology, *INORA* 13.

Richard Bradley

# 8. Daggers drawn: depictions of Bronze Age weapons in Atlantic Europe

The rock-engravings of far western Europe are dated by a very few direct stratigraphic contexts and by linking their images to objects of known prehistoric date – although many of the figures are 'abstract' and undatable that way. As they are far earlier than any historical record, and set in an ancient frame of values for metal objects to which we have no direct access, formal methods are in order. This chapter considers the carvings of weapons found in the Bronze Age art of Atlantic Europe and the ways in which they can be studied. It discusses the connections between these drawings and deposits of prehistoric metalwork and investigates their siting in the landscape.

## Atlantic Europe and its rock-art

Following conventional usage, 'Atlantic' Europe is defined as the coastal region extending northwards from the Straits of Gibraltar as far as Britain and Ireland (Fig. 8.1). My main concern is with the rock-art of north-west Spain (Galicia), although I compare this with material in the British Isles with which it has much in common. I also refer to a series of decorated stones in the Alentejo region of southern Portugal, and compare the weapon carvings in all these areas with a rather later phenomenon: the Bronze Age stelae found in the south-west of the Iberian Peninsula (Fig. 8.1).

## Rock-art of north-west Spain: chronology and cultural context

The main period covered in this chapter is the Early Bronze Age, which extends between approximately 2300 and 1500 BC in calendar years. This estimate for the age of the carved figures is based on identifiable images in all the regions considered here. They take three distinct forms. There are daggers of kinds

which are also known from dated burials and hoards; there are depictions of halberds (dagger-like blades hafted perpendicular to long handles) with similar associations; and there are less common drawings of axeheads which can be identified with objects whose chronology is well established through hoard finds and metal analysis. Carvings of daggers and halberds are a feature of sites in Spain and Portugal, whilst drawings of axeheads are found in the British Isles.

The objects themselves are distributed far more widely, although occasional details in these drawings suggest quite specific links between different areas. The axeheads appear in a variety of types which are well documented in Britain and Ireland. These seem to span the entire sequence of development from the flat axes, which are found in both copper and bronze, to examples which compare closely with finds belonging to the end of this period (Needham *et al.* 1989). The daggers are of types which are widely distributed in Early Bronze Age Europe, although occasional details suggest more specific links. Thus a few of the drawings in north-west Spain resemble finds from Brittany and Wessex (Peña Santos 1979), whilst the drawings of halberds found in the same region of Iberia have been identified with artefacts in northern Portugal (Peña Santos 1980). In the same way the swords and halberds depicted on grave slabs in Alentejo have been compared with finds in south-east Spain (Almagro 1966; Chenorkian 1988). Their chronology seems to overlap with that of the other motifs, but the tradition perhaps continued after the last weapon carvings in Galicia and the British Isles (Barcelo 1991). In this chapter all three groups are compared with recent

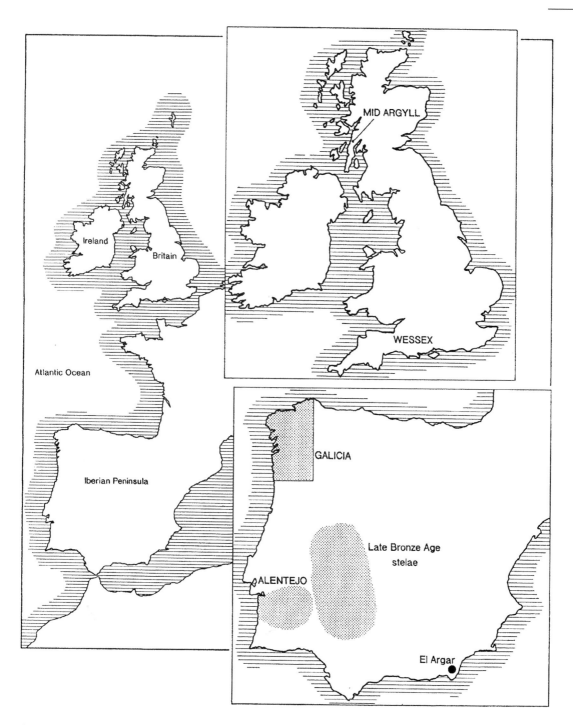

**Fig. 8.1.** The regions of Atlantic Europe discussed in the text.

interpretations of the Late Bronze Age stelae of south-west Iberia (Almagro 1966). Their precise chronology is controversial, but again they depict a wide range of identifiable artefacts. Despite some differences of detail, most schemes concur in assigning these images to the ninth and eighth centuries BC (Galan Domingo 1993).

Such striking links between the drawings of Early Bronze Age weapons and finds of actual artefacts raise the possibility of connections between quite separate parts of Atlantic Europe, and especially between Galicia, north-west France, Britain and Ireland. Such connections are also evidenced by a series of purely abstract motifs which occur in open-air rock-art, in particular the circular devices described as cups and rings. Not only do these elements resemble one another over considerable distances, but the conventions according to which they were deployed were virtually the same in all three regions (Bradley 1995). Such striking links between widely separated areas suggest that access to foreign objects or specialised knowledge may have played an important role in social life. This idea is supported by the evidence of other kinds of artefacts which were not depicted in rock-art, for there are equally close connections between the contents of some burials in each of these areas.

At the same time, there is evidence that the north-western part of Spain shows a different sequence from other parts of the Iberian Peninsula, where a separate style of rock-art (Schematic Art) is quite widely distributed (Gómez Barrera 1992). This shares very few design elements with sites in Galicia and the north Atlantic, and weapons play little part in these paintings and carvings. It suggests the existence of another network of contacts linking sites in northern Portugal with the interior of the Iberian Peninsula and the west Mediterranean.

## The contexts of the weapon carvings

The carvings described in this chapter occur in four different contexts, even when the same kinds of weapon are depicted. The largest group of weapon carvings are those in Galicia (Fig. 8.2a), and these provide the principal focus for this chapter. The main types are drawings of daggers, halberds, and other objects identified as standards or shields; the latter have no counterpart in the archaeological record (Costas Goberna and Novoa Alvarez 1993). In addition, there are occasional drawings of what may be axes or clubs, but it is not clear whether they should be considered as weapons or as tools. All these images are found on natural surfaces in the landscape; at approximately half the sites they are carved on the same rocks as abstract designs. Their overall distribution extends some way beyond the main distribution of cups and rings but again it is confined to a limited area near to the west coast of Galicia. There is some overlap between Galician Art and Schematic Art close to the border with Portugal, but weapon carvings are very rare in the latter style (Bradley and Fábregas Valcarce in press).

Interpretations of Galician rock-art can be compared with weapon carvings belonging to three other groups, two largely contemporary with the evidence from north-west Spain and the third of significantly later date. The first of these comparative samples comes from the British Isles. In this case the repertoire is more restricted and its context is very different. All these images form part of monuments (Fig. 8.2b). One group is in Mid Argyll, western Scotland, where axe carvings are found inside three stone-lined coffins or 'cists' sealed below burial cairns (Simpson and Thawley 1972; Schmidt 1979). Again we cannot tell whether these objects were regarded as weapons, although carvings of daggers are found with depictions of axeheads in southern England (see below). In one of the Scottish examples the drawings of axeheads are superimposed on an existing set of cup-marks, and in this case it seems likely that the decorated stone originally stood in the open air (Bradley 1993: 91–3). A large number of abstract rock-carvings are recorded close to the Scottish sites and these have features in common with petroglyphs in Galicia.

There are two weapon carvings in Wessex. Both

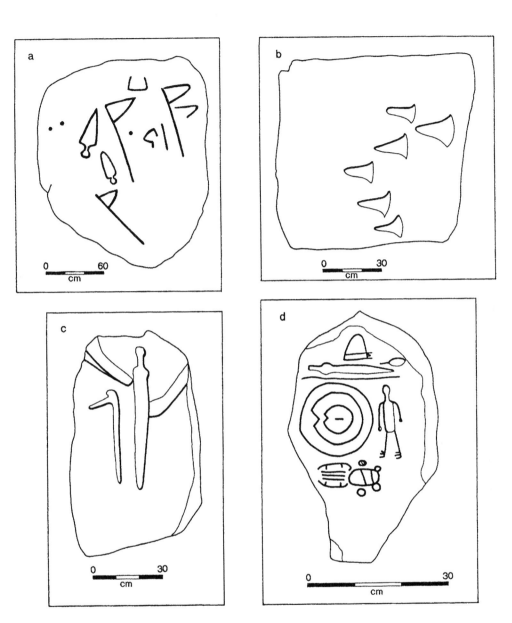

**Fig. 8.2.**

a  Open-air rock-carving at Poza de Lagoa, Galicia.

b  Decorated cist slab at Ri Cruin, Mid Argyll, Scotland.

c  Decorated slab from San Juan de Negrilhos, Alentejo, Portugal.

d  Decorated slab of Late Bronze Age date from Zarza de Montanchez, south-west Spain.

depict Early Bronze Age daggers accompanied by a series of axeheads, although they appear in very different proportions at these sites. The axes are drawn without their hafts, but the daggers are provided with hilts. One group of carvings was on the kerb of a burial mound and was associated with a number of cup-marks (Simpson and Thawley 1972). The second site is Stonehenge, where a dagger and more than forty axeheads were carved on three of the uprights (Cleal *et al.* 1995: 30–3). Rock-carvings are not at all common in Wessex but two cists excavated in the nineteenth century were decorated with cups and rings like those in northern Britain, Ireland and north-west Spain.

Another useful comparison is with the Early Bronze Age weapon carvings of Alentejo (Almagro 1966; Chenorkian 1988). Their contexts are not well documented but, like the finds from Scotland, they seem to have been associated with cist burials. In this case they were employed as covering slabs. It is thought that they had originally stood in the open air, and this would certainly account for the degree of damage that they had sustained before their incorporation in the burial. The main motifs represented in Alentejo are halberds, swords, axes and bows (Fig. 8.2c). There are only two sites with depictions of daggers, but many of the stones also show another kind of artefact described as an 'axe idol', for which there are no parallels among the objects that survive today. Most of the weapons are attached to thongs or belts, as if to illustrate a full set of personal equipment. The axes and halberds are depicted with their hafts, and both the daggers have hilts. The swords seem to be suspended from belts, and this provides one method of working out the orientation of the drawings, and allows us to say that the axes and halberds were shown with their blades uppermost. In some cases, it is possible to interpolate a human figure armed with all these weapons, but although the shapes of the stones sometimes encourage this idea, the body itself is hardly ever portrayed. The only exceptions are found on the edge of the main distribution of carvings and are not associated with graves.

Accounts of the Alentejo cist slabs tell us little about the associated burials, but these do not seem to be found with elaborate grave goods. In fact, similar combinations of artefacts are unusual among the excavated material from this region. Perhaps the carved images provided an alternative for the artefacts themselves. If so, then the links that have been suggested with the El Argar culture of south-east Spain take on a new significance, for in that tradition burials associated with both swords and halberds are thought to be of higher status than the rest (Lull and Estévez 1986).

The last sample of weapon carvings is provided by the Late Bronze Age stelae of south-west Iberia. These are not contemporary with the sites described so far, but are included here because their interpretation raises some of the same issues. Again they contain a wide variety of weapons, including swords, shields, bows, helmets and spears. There are also drawings of personal ornaments and chariots (Fig. 8.2d). The weapon carvings are of two kinds. One group resembles the cist slabs of Alentejo in depicting a set of arms without the person carrying them. In the second group a rather similar range of artefacts is shown, but this time it is accompanied by a diminutive stick figure. That figure is surrounded by a whole series of weapons but these are not attached to the body. Although there have been claims that these carvings marked the positions of burials, there is little evidence for that association.

## Methods of analysing the weapon carvings of Galicia

In the absence of any historical or ethnographic evidence of the roles played by Galician rock-carvings we must study them by formal methods. We can focus on the organisation of the motifs found on individual rocks, and can also investigate the locations of these carvings in the landscape. At the same time, we can learn even more by comparing these different groups with one another and also with the deposits of artefacts found in hoards and graves. In certain cases, this procedure may suggest similarities between the evidence from quite different regions. In other instances, it is the contrasts between these different areas that identify the distinctive characteristics of Galician petroglyphs.

It is unfortunate that so much attention was paid to the chronology of these carvings that until recently little had been said about their interpretation. The same is also true of other drawings of weapons described in this chapter. Consequently, these images were studied in the same manner as the artefacts they portray. As individual weapons were identified among the rock-carvings, rather than investigating the contexts in which these images were created, prehistorians treated them as 'find-spots', of similar status to discoveries of the weapons themselves. As a result, these images have primarily played a part in mapping the distribution of artefact styles. Whilst this information could be used to investigate patterns of production and exchange, all too often its collection seems to have been an end in itself.

It is curious that the study of rock-art should involve such a narrow perspective, since one of its most distinctive features is that these images are fixed at a particular place in the landscape. Their siting ought to provide the stimulus for a more ambitious analysis. In the case of weapon carvings, it is particularly surprising that so little interest has been shown in their placement in the terrain, as this has become an important theme in the study of Bronze Age metalwork. It seems unlikely that the most elaborate artefacts were simply lost; it is far more probable that they were deposited intentionally. Many studies have established that there is a significant relationship between the character of such artefacts and the contexts in which they occur (for a general review of this research see Bradley 1990). Certain types may be found in hoards but not in burials, others are limited to graves, whilst some kinds of object are discovered in isolation. The process of deposition depended on two distinct factors. One was the choice of artefacts for special treatment, and the other was the kind of location in which that treatment would be appropriate. Bronze Age specialists often seize on the first of

these processes because the associations between different artefact types allow them to build a chronology. All too often they overlook the other characteristics of these deposits.

*The character of individual rock-carvings*

If the creation of weapon deposits was attended by strict conventions, might the depiction of these artefacts have been controlled in similar ways? One reason for taking this approach is a recent discovery in Galicia.

When García Alén and Peña Santos (1980) published their definitive account of Galician petroglyphs, it was difficult to relate the weapon carvings to discoveries of the artefacts themselves. This was particularly true of the halberds. It was only in an addendum to his discussion of these artefacts (Peña Santos 1980) that Peña Santos was able to note the discovery of a new series of petroglyphs at Leiro, on the same hill as the only halberd hoard in Galicia (Fig. 8.3). Although the details of this deposit are by no means satisfactory, the coincidence is quite remarkable. On the rock there are drawings of two halberds and two daggers, whilst the near-by hoard contained a halberd and five daggers (Meijide Cameselle 1989). In the absence of complete documentation it is impossible to prove that the two finds are related to one another, but this certainly raises the possibility that the weapon carvings might have played some of the same roles as deposits of artefacts. Alternatively, they could have been created to mark, or even to commemorate, the creation of similar hoards.

In this respect, it is worth contrasting the weapon carvings in Galicia with those in Alentejo. In the latter case the carved stones are associated with individual burials (Almagro 1966). Almost every example seems to depict a single set of weapons (Fig. 8.4b and c), in which no items are duplicated in the same composition (the one exception is a fragment which includes two axes of the same form, but these are of quite different sizes). By contrast, only eight of the Galician daggers (11 per cent) and two of the

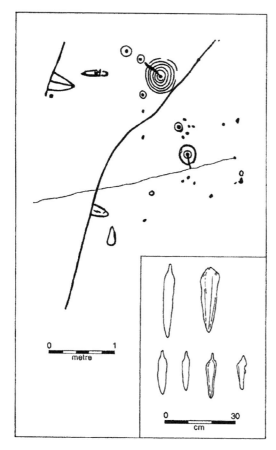

**Fig. 8.3.** Open-air rock-carving at Leiro, Galicia, and the metal hoard from the same location.

weapons on a single rock surface (this figure includes the putative shields but excludes any 'axes' or 'clubs'). The mean is 4.6 weapons. The same averaging method provides figures of 1.4 halberds per carved surface, 2.5 daggers and 0.8 shields. When the individual rocks are grouped according to the 'sites' at which they are found, the mean rises to 7.7 weapons. The figures for individual artefact types are 2.3 halberds per site, 4.2 daggers and 1.2 'shields'.

These weapons share a striking feature, for almost without exception the same kinds of artefact appear in a wide range of sizes. At any one site the shortest dagger may be between 20 per cent and 65 per cent of the length of the largest example; the mean for all the dagger carvings in Galicia works out at 60 per cent. The same approach can be taken with the length of the halberd blades. The shortest example is only a third of the length of the largest example and the mean for all the carvings of halberds is 71 per cent. At any one site the shields are approximately the same size.

There are few patterns of this kind among the Early Bronze Age burials of Iberia (the largest samples are published by Schubart 1975 and Schubart and Ulreich 1991). As in Alentejo, each type of weapon normally appears singly in the graves. There are some exceptions in the El Argar culture, although in certain cases this seems to happen because particular graves contained more than one body. In other cases, daggers of quite different sizes might be deposited together, but this does not apply to the finds of halberds, which are hardly ever duplicated. Daggers also appear in a variety of sizes in hoards, as they do at Leiro where the longest example is twice the size of the smallest. There are too few groups of halberds in Iberia for us to take a similar approach to these weapons, but in Ireland, where 40 per cent of the examples in Bronze Age Europe have been found, there are certainly hoards in which these artefacts appear together in a variety of different sizes (Harbison 1969).

In the weapon carvings of Alentejo the artefacts were arranged as if they accompanied a body. How

halberds (5 per cent) occur singly in the rock-carvings (Fig. 8.4a; Costas Goberna and Novoa Alvarez 1993: 157–81). Even then, one of those halberds is accompanied by two daggers. In the same way, only two of the 'shields' (10 per cent) occur singly, and one of these is associated with five daggers and five halberds and the other with four daggers and two halberds. This suggests a complete contrast with the carvings associated with those burials.

Rather than forming 'sets' of weapons, the Galician carvings exhibit a remarkable range of artefacts (Costas Goberna and Novoa Alvarez 1993: 157–81). There can be as many as 25 separate

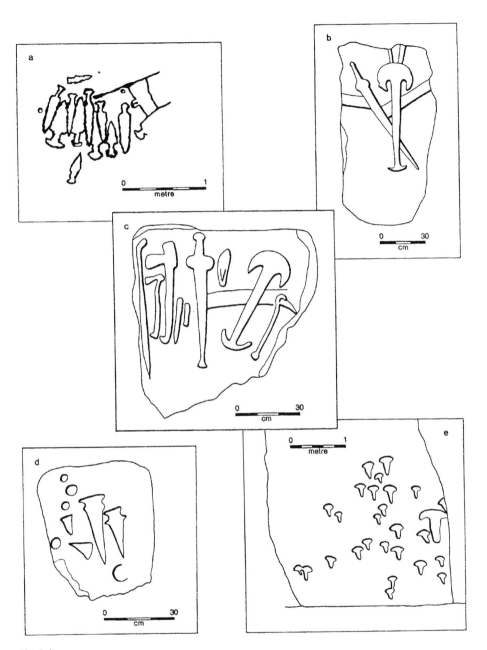

**Fig. 8.4.**

a  Open-air carving at O Ramallal, Galicia.

b  Decorated slab from Santiago de Cacem, Portugal.

c  Decorated slab from Assento, Portugal.

d  The surviving part of a decorated kerb-stone from Badbury Barrow, Wessex.

e  A group of axe carvings at Stonehenge, Wessex.

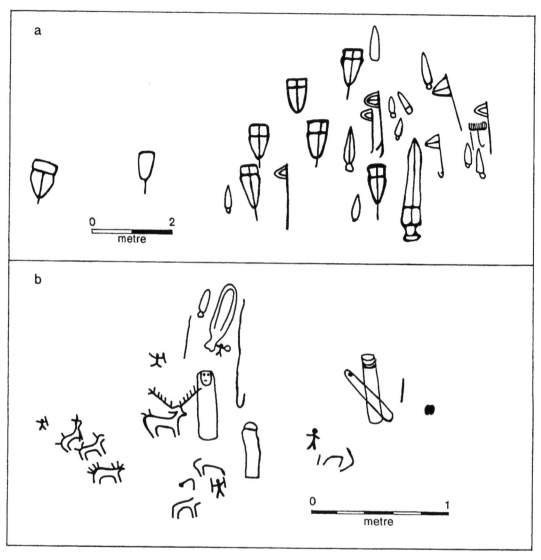

**Fig. 8.5.**
a  Weapon carvings at Auga da Laxe, Galicia.
b  Carvings of weapons, animals, human figure and cylinder idols at Pedra das Ferraduras, Galicia.

were their Galician counterparts organised? There are no absolute rules, but a number of recurrent features do stand out. For the most part Galician weapon carvings are distinct from the other motifs because they are found on quite steeply sloping surfaces. The most impressive group of all, at Auga de Laxe, is found on a massive outcrop (Fig. 8.5a). As a result, the weapons can generally be viewed from below. Although there are certain exceptions, most of these weapons appear to be upright. The blades of the halberds are generally towards the upper end of the carved surface and so are the points of the daggers. The shields or standards adopt the prevailing alignment of these weapons, and in most cases the positions of their shafts follow those of the daggers and halberds. Individual weapons are often related directly to one another, so that unusually large and small examples of the same types may be juxtaposed on the carved surface.

These weapons are organised in quite distinctive ways. Again at Auga de Laxe, where the carvings are exceptionally large, the images are arranged against the rock face in a roughly triangular array which rises 5 m above the modern ground surface. In this case, all the weapons are depicted with their blades towards the top. The apex of this composition is marked by the one dagger which has no hilt. The most conspicuous carving depicts a massive dagger, 2.4 m high; this is surrounded by another nine much smaller examples. One flank of this triangular display of weapons is dominated by a series of 'shields'. The central portion contains most of the daggers, whilst halberds are rather more common on the opposite edge of this composition. The entire group of images resembles a display of trophies piled up against the rock face (Fig. 8.5a).

An alternative is for groups of weapons to be clustered together on the surface of the stone (Fig. 8.4a). In such cases, they lack a single prevailing alignment and instead form a concentrated group of different artefact types. Interestingly, these do not include any shields or standards but one group contains a hafted axe or club. Again these weapons come in a wide variety of sizes. The smallest dagger at O Ramallal is only 38 per cent of the length of the largest example and in the two main groups at Poza de Lagoa the equivalent proportions are 48 per cent and 54 per cent. On the other hand, the halberds at Poza de Lagoa are all of much the same size. It is more difficult to characterise this group of motifs, but the closest comparison might be with the contents of Early Bronze Age hoards where a whole series of different artefacts may be packed into a small space and arranged according to a formal pattern.

*Interpretations and comparisons*

Two features seem to characterise the Galician weapon carvings. The first is the marked variation in the sizes of daggers and halberds. This is also found among the surviving artefacts. It may be that these differences reflect the significance of the individual weapons or even the importance of the people associated with them. In this respect, the carvings resemble hoard finds rather than graves.

Secondly, there is a certain formality in their organisation on the rock face. There seems to have been a particular emphasis on displaying these images, and that may be one reason why they were carved on sloping or near-vertical surfaces. We do not have any evidence for the activities that may have taken place in front of these carvings. Apart from the Leiro hoard, there is only one instance in which an item of metalwork is known to have been deposited at one of these locations. This was a copper flat axe found among a series of abstract motifs and drawings of animals (Monteagudo 1977: 57), but there are no depictions of weapons on that particular site.

I have already suggested that the organisation of some of the weapon carvings has features in common with Early Bronze Age hoards, and this connection is certainly strengthened by the evidence from Leiro. I also argue that one characteristic of metalwork deposits is that their contents may be integrally related to their placing in the landscape. Again the Galician evidence is consistent with this idea, for not only were a number of artefact types displayed in a highly conventional manner but also these carvings were normally made in similar sorts of locations.

Again we need to look at what happened in other areas. Having emphasised how the Galician weapon carvings contrast with those in Alentejo, it is worth comparing them with the evidence from the British Isles.

At first sight we might not expect to find close links between these areas. Although the same style of rock-art is recorded in both countries, the carvings of metal artefacts in Britain appear in very different contexts from those in Galicia. Four of the five examples come from burial monuments and, like those in Alentejo, most of the designs are on cists (Simpson and Thawley 1972). But there is a striking difference between the British material and the evidence from Portugal. In Alentejo it seems likely that the weapon carvings were the equivalent of grave goods, even emphasising links with a style of artefacts found in another region. In Scotland, however, the artefacts depicted inside the burial cists are of types which were only occasionally deposited with the dead (Fig. 8.2b). Even in southern England, where daggers are carved together with axeheads, such associations are uncommon in the funerary record. In fact the role of these dagger carvings has been overemphasised in the literature. There has been considerable discussion of the importance of the example at Stonehenge, but this is outnumbered by no fewer than forty-three drawings of axes. One of these is nearly twice as large as the dagger on Stone 4 (Fig. 8.4d).

If axes are uncommon in Early Bronze Age burials in Britain, they are frequently found in hoards, where they seem to have been deposited according to quite strict conventions. These finds often occur at specific locations in the landscape, including hilltops, springs and bogs. Others had been placed on the sites of existing burial mounds. The contents of these deposits could be arranged with some formality, and it seems most unlikely that these artefacts were meant to be recovered (Schmidt 1979; Needham 1988).

The earlier hoards of axes are especially common in northern Britain, so that the carvings found on Scottish cist slabs might well portray deposits that would be familiar in the region. Moreover, there is considerable evidence that the artefacts placed in these hoards had only rarely been hafted. There are surviving finds of bronze axeheads contained in special bags or pouches and there are many examples whose blades had been decorated. Sometimes that decoration covered the entire surface, and would have been obscured if the axe had been provided with a handle. This is particularly revealing since all five of the British sites show axeheads rather than axes (Fig. 8.4d and e). In contrast to the evidence from Alentejo and to a lesser extent that from Galicia, none of these artefacts was shown as a functioning tool. That only strengthens the connection between the carvings found on British monuments and the composition of the hoards.

If the contents of those hoards were closely connected with their placing in the landscape, why should such deposits be illustrated by carvings located inside monuments? In fact, the decorated cists of western Scotland form part of a much wider tradition in northern Britain. There are far more examples in which the decoration is entirely abstract, and yet it seems most unlikely that these images were created for use in the graves. The decorated slabs appear to be fragments taken from decorated surfaces in the open air. There is even some evidence of the outcrops from which they may have been removed. This apparently bizarre behaviour makes sense if we suppose that in such cases relics of particular places in the landscape were incorporated in the burials of the dead. The decorated cist slab at Nether Largie may very well have been introduced from another site, but there is no evidence that this was true of the other examples. The effect of depicting deposits of metalwork in the fabric of the tomb was to create an association between the funeral rite and other activities which had taken place at specialised locations in the landscape (Bradley 1997: 136–50).

Lastly, it is worth commenting on the evidence from the two sites in Wessex, where the carvings of axes may be later in date than the others. In both cases the carvings were not associated directly with the dead but were displayed on the structure of the monument. At Badbury the axeheads, daggers and cup-marks were carved on the original kerb of a burial mound (Fig. 8.4d), whilst at Stonehenge the drawings of the axes and the dagger are placed in accessible positions towards the base of the stones. The carvings would have been within reach and none would be difficult to see. This recalls the evidence from Galicia where a number of the weapons were depicted on steeply sloping rocks so that these carvings looked like a display of trophies (Fig. 8.5a). The British carvings may have had a rather similar effect, and nowhere more so than at Stonehenge, where the axeheads appear in a wide range of sizes. One of these drawings is approximately twice as large as any of the others. Much the same principle seems to have influenced the carvings of weapons in north-west Spain.

### The local setting of the weapon carvings

The carvings of weapons in Galicia are unusual because so many of them are located on sloping surfaces (Fig. 8.5). That is very different from the position of the other motifs.

In fact the contrasts go much further. The great majority of images in Galician rock-art can be divided into two groups: abstract motifs based on cups and rings; and depictions of animals, mainly red deer. These are widely distributed about the landscape, although abstract motifs tend to be more common towards the coast and animal carvings were found mainly on the higher ground to the east. They share the common feature that both are usually associated with the pattern of everyday activities.

Galician petroglyphs are most abundant in those parts of the country which experience the greatest bioclimatic variation in the course of the year. These are areas that can suffer from drought at the height of summer, with the result that animals must move from the coast to the higher ground. The rock-carvings are generally found near to the settlement areas and along the principal routes leading from the lowlands into the hills. The major concentrations of rock-carvings are found around the edges of shallow basins which still retain some moisture at the hottest time of year. They are also located in areas which afford more protection from the sun (Bradley, Criado and Fábregas Valcarce 1995).

That is not to suggest that these locations were entirely determined by ecological factors. In practice the rocks selected for carving seem to have been carefully chosen from a series of potential sites. They tend to be relatively inconspicuous and rarely command extensive views over the lower ground. Instead, they are located in relation to quite limited parts of the landscape: the damper basins where animals congregate in the summer; the sheltered valleys that allow access between those areas; and places where those separate routes converge. Although these carvings are in positions from which it would have been possible to observe the movement of animals, the rocks that were selected for embellishment offered less cover than others in the vicinity, suggesting they were rarely used as hunting stands. Rather, they overlook parts of the landscape in which artefact scatters are found. Field survey even suggests that the main groups of rock-carvings were located in between settlement areas. Pollen analysis has shown that some of the favoured sites were used over a considerable period, although not necessarily continuously, and that the herding of livestock may have taken place alongside small-scale cultivation. Whilst red deer figure prominently in the petroglyphs, it is unlikely that these provide a rounded picture of daily life. Like the drawings of weapons, the carvings of wild animals provide a partial vision of the world, structured around what Ian Hodder (1990) has termed the *agrios*, (Fig. 8.5b). This is a world in which activities like hunting and fighting predominate. Among the Galician rock-carvings one of the most conspicuous motifs is the stag (Bradley 1997: chapter 13).

Most of the carvings, then, are placed in relatively inconspicuous locations with limited but precisely focused views. However, that is not so true of the images of the stags, especially those with the most prominent antlers. These tend to occupy higher ground than the other rock-carvings and often over-look entire valleys or basins. Here, the stags may be drawn at a much larger scale than the other animals; in a few instances they seem to be portrayed in the act of bellowing. This is especially revealing, for it suggests the showing of these animals in the annual rut when mature stags occupy higher ground and issue a challenge to their rivals. It may be no coincidence that very similar locations were adopted for carvings of weapons (Bradley 1997; Bradley, Criado and Fábregas Valcarce 1995).

It is not particularly common for those weapon carvings to be associated with other motifs. Roughly half the examples are found together with cup-marks or cups and rings, and there are a few cases in which they occur on the same rocks as drawings of stags. They can also be associated with 'idols' of a type known in Portugal and the west Mediterranean (Fig. 8.5b). Other weapon carvings appear in complete isolation. They seem to share several distinctive features. On those sites where they are found together with drawings of stags, there seems to be an emphasis on masculine aggression, as if the halberds and daggers offered the same kind of challenge as the antlers of the rutting stag. Where they are found with drawings of cylinder idols, the emphasis is rather different, for both kinds of object seem to refer to areas some distance away. The halberds express a link with Bronze Age societies in areas as distant as Ireland and the Mediterranean, whilst the occasional cylinder idol forms a connection with more complex societies in central Portugal and south-east Spain.

The siting of the Galician weapon carvings is relevant to both of these issues. These images were located on sloping surfaces where they could be seen from a distance, but they were also located at viewpoints which commanded more of the landscape than the other rock-carvings. In some cases they

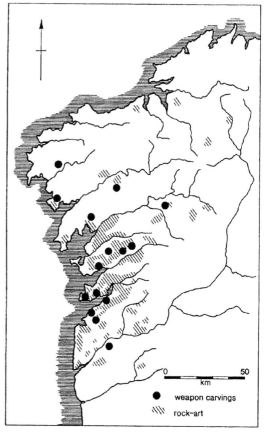

**Fig. 8.6.** The distribution of weapon carvings in Galicia. After Costas Goberna and Novoa Alvarez 1993.

faced away from the shallow valleys and basins where the remaining images were found, as if they looked beyond the settlement system altogether. In other areas they dominated the whole distribution of petroglyphs and were the only carved rocks to over-look the settled area in its entirety.

At the same time, the distribution of weapon carvings extends beyond the range of the other images created in Galician art (Fig. 8.6). Some of these carvings were located outside the local concentrations of rock-art. They overlooked larger tracts of lower ground or even commanded views extending out to sea. Others were located in comparative isolation around the outer edges of the distribution of petroglyphs in north-west Spain. They occupied the same kinds of natural setting as the other weapon carvings in Galicia, but they seemed to bound the region in which they were created (Fig. 8.6). The largest depictions of weapons were created near the limits of their distribution. To the south, the most impressive array of daggers, halberds and shields is close to the Portuguese border. Otherwise, the largest weapons are at the northernmost extent of Galician rock-art.

To sum up, it seems as if the weapon carvings played a special role in the Galician landscape. For the most part they were rendered at a different kind of location from other motifs, a location they sometimes share with depictions of rutting stags. These were places that commanded a more extensive vista than the remaining petroglyphs, often a view that extended outwards from the edges of the settled landscape. Similar images were also created around the outer limits of the distribution of rock-art as a whole. These weapon carvings were often located on sloping surfaces so that they confronted the onlooker, and at the same time they evoked connections with a wider world in which similar artefacts played a specialised role.

## Object, subject, context and the Galician petroglyphs

This account of the Galician petroglyphs has operated at two different scales. It has concerned itself with the organisation of the images on the individual rock face, comparing this evidence with what is known of Early Bronze Age weapon carvings in two other areas, Britain and Alentejo. In each case there seemed to be a close affinity between such groups of drawings and particular kinds of metalwork deposits, hoards in the British Isles and grave goods in southern Portugal. Comparison with these two examples lends weight to the suggestion that the Galician weapon carvings might have been related to hoard finds. The remarkable convergence between these two traditions at Leiro supports that interpretation.

It has become clear that different combinations of Bronze Age artefacts would normally be deposited in different contexts from one another. The same idea seems to apply to the subject-matter of Galician rock-art, for the drawings of weapons were distributed quite differently from most of the other motifs. They adopted quite specific positions in the landscape and their broader distribution extended some way beyond that of the remaining designs. It may be that they helped to establish the importance of particular places in the terrain and also protected them against strangers. In this respect it may be significant that those images could have been understood by people from virtually any part of Early Bronze Age Europe. The same would not have been true of the abstract motifs.

But there are problems in equating these carvings with actual deposits of weaponry, for the role of metal hoards in Galicia remains poorly understood. On the other hand, Iberian archaeology provides an analogy which may be particularly revealing. Perhaps it offers certain clues as to how these images were used.

The Late Bronze Age stelae found in south-west Iberia have received considerable attention in recent years, and the same is true of the metalwork deposits of the same period. Both had been analysed according to a purely functional interpretation. The stelae, regarded as grave-markers, were attributed to a whole series of immigrants, even though there was no real evidence that they were funerary monuments at all (Galan Domingo 1993). The main aim of research was to identify the kinds of artefact depicted on these sculptures and to trace them back to their sources. That was also the approach taken to Late Bronze Age metal finds, which were regarded almost entirely as chance losses. In neither case was the location of these discoveries considered important.

A recent study by Galan Domingo (1993) allows us to consider the stelae in new ways. They fall into six tightly defined regional groups, each of which may be associated with a specific area of land. The most elaborate of these sculptures depict the artefacts

143

that are furthest from their home area, as if knowledge of the exotic provided a source of prestige. The stelae are located in a region with a long history of mobile pastoralism and there seems no reason to suppose that the situation was any different at this time. This emphasis on mobility is important in view of the siting of the stelae. Eighty of these are recorded, but some of their original locations are lost. Among those with positions that can be described with any accuracy, 38 per cent are found in mountain passes, another 21 per cent are on high ground which commands an extensive view, and 32 per cent are located close to fords or the routes leading to them. Another 9 per cent are located by roads which have been in use since the Roman period. They are also found at the intersections of different paths. Galan Domingo (1993) concludes that they provide evidence for a simple territorial system.

The artefacts depicted on the stelae consist mainly of weapons and ornaments. These classes of material are commonly found in hoards and rivers during the Late Bronze Age but until recently the reasons for their deposition had not been studied. This has been remedied in a review by Rúiz-Gálvez (1995), who concludes that they were intentional deposits. The locations of some of this metalwork have a familiar ring. It is found in mountain passes, at fords, at the mouths of rivers – or where routes through the landscape meet. These are the same kinds of locations as those associated with stelae, but in this case Rúiz-Gálvez suggests they perhaps were neutral locations where strangers could meet and where specialised transactions could take place. These might include rites of passage conducted at strategic points on the borders of a territory. Whatever the nature of those rituals, they involved the deposition of a particular range of artefacts.

Once again we discover that a particular group of metal artefacts might be deposited in a strictly determined location, and that both those objects and the copies of them cut in stone might be used to indicate where that transaction had taken place. At one level this procedure played a practical role in establishing territorial divisions, whilst at another it helped to define the relations between different groups of people and sanctioned those relationships through ritual.

Many of those elements are also present in the archaeology of Galicia, even though the weapon carvings there are significantly earlier in date. It is unsatisfactory to claim this as a precise analogy but, like the other comparisons between weapon carvings considered in this chapter, it may help to define the issues more precisely. Rock-art is studied to most effect when it can be related to more general themes in modern archaeology. The Galician weapon carvings fulfil this requirement admirably, for their analysis must also involve a new approach to hoarding and to the interpretation of the prehistoric landscape. This is a volatile combination and needs to be handled with care, but the potential of such work is considerable.

## Acknowledgements
I am most grateful to Rámon Fábregas Valcarce for his comments on an earlier version of this article and to Margaret Mathews for preparing the figure drawings.

## REFERENCES

Almagro, M. 1966. *Las estelas decoradas del suroeste peninsular.* Madrid, Bibliotheca Praehistorica Hispana VIII.
Barcelo, J. 1991. El bronce del sudoeste y la cronologia de las estelas alentejanas, *Arqueologia* 21: 15–24.
Bradley, R. 1990. *The passage of arms: an archaeological analysis of prehistoric hoards and votive deposits.* Cambridge, Cambridge University Press.
1993. *Altering the earth: the origins of monuments in Britain and continental Europe.* Edinburgh, Society of Antiquaries of Scotland.
1995. After MacWhite: Irish rock art in its international context, in J. Waddell and E. Shee Twohig (eds.), *Ireland in the Bronze Age*, pp. 90–6. Dublin, Stationery Office.
1997. *Rock art and the prehistory of Atlantic Europe: signing the land.* London, Routledge.

Bradley, R., F. Criado and R. Fábregas Valcarce. 1995. Rock art and the prehistoric landscape of Galicia, *Proceedings of the Prehistoric Society* 61: 347–70.

Bradley, R. and R. Fábregas Valcarce. In press. Petroglifos gallegos y arte esquemático: una propuesta de Trabajo, in T. Chapa and A. Querol (eds.), *Homenaje al prof. Manuel Fernández Miranda*. Madrid, Editorial Complutense.

Chenorkian, R. 1988. *Les armes métalliques dans l'art protohistorique de l'occident méditerranéen*. Paris, Editions du CNRS.

Cleal, R., K. Walker and R. Montague. 1995. *Stonehenge in its landscape: twentieth century excavations*. London, English Heritage.

Costas Goberna, F. J. and P. Novoa Alvarez. 1993. *Los grabados rupestres de Galicia*. Coruña, Museu Arqueolóxico e Historico.

Galan Domingo, E. 1993. *Estelas, paisaje e territorio del suroeste de la península ibérica*. Madrid, Editorial Complutense.

García Alén, A. and A. Peña Santos. 1980. *Grabados rupestres de la provincia de Pontevedra*. Pontevedra, Museo de Pontevedra.

Gómez Barrera, J. 1992. Manifestaciones de la fascies esquemática el el centro y norte de la península ibérica, *Espacio, Tiempo y Forma* 5: 231–64.

Harbison, P. 1969. *The daggers and halberds of the Early Bronze Age in Ireland*. Munich, C. H. Beck.

Hodder, I. 1990. *The domestication of Europe: structure and contingency in Neolithic societies*. Oxford, Blackwell.

Lull, V. and Estévez, J. 1986. Propuesta metodológia para el estudio de las necrópolis agáricas, in *Homenaje a Luis Siret 1934–1984*, pp. 441–52. Seville, Consejeria de Cultura de la Junta de Andalucia.

Meijide Cameselle, G. 1989. Un importante conjunto del Bronce Inicial en Galicia: el depósito de Leiro (Rianxo, A Coruña), *Gallaecia* 11: 151–64.

Monteagudo, L. 1977. *Die Beile auf der Iberischen Halbinsel*. Munich, C. H. Beck.

Needham, S. 1988. Selective deposition in the British Early Bronze Age, *World Archaeology* 20: 229–48.

Needham, S., M. Leese, D. Hook and M. Hughes. 1989. Developments in the Early Bronze Age metallurgy of southern Britain, *World Archaeology* 20: 383–402.

Peña Santos, A. 1979. Notas para una revisión de los grabados rupestres de 'O Castriño en Conxo', *El Museo de Pontevadra* 33: 3–32.

1980. Las representaciones de alabardas en los grabados rupestres gallegos, *Zephyrus* 31: 115–29.

Rúiz-Gálvez, M. 1995. *Ritos de pazo y puntos de pazo*. Madrid, Seruccio de Publicaciones Universidad Complutense.

Schmidt, P. 1979. Beile als Ritualobjekte in der Altbronzezeit der Britischen Inseln, *Jahresbericht der Instituts für Vorgeschichte der Universität Frankfurt a. M.* (1979): 311–20.

Schubart, H. 1975. *Die Kultur der Bronzezeit im Südwesten der iberischen Halbinsel*. Berlin, De Gruyter.

Schubart, H. and H. Ulreich. 1991. *Die Funde der südostspanischen Bronzezeit der Sammlung Siret*. Mainz, Von Zabern.

Simpson, D. and J. Thawley. 1972. Single grave art in Britain, *Scottish Archaeological Forum* 4: 81–104.

Kalle Sognnes

# 9. Symbols in a changing world: rock-art and the transition from hunting to farming in mid Norway

Dating of the Scandinavian petroglyph sites, with their pecked images on smoothed open-air rock surfaces is exceptionally hard. Most are far too early for any insight from the historical record. In mid Norway, two distinctive traditions overlap – those of Northern hunters and Southern agriculturists. How much is this a chronological sequence, how much the artistic traditions of communities with different concerns which may have been contemporary? Patient formal analysis of the images and inference from their placing in the landscape allow us to see a society in long and slow transition.

## Mid Norway and its archaeology

Mid Norway, located in the western part of the Scandinavian peninsula between c. 62° 30′ and 65° Northern latitude, is one of the major rock-art areas in northern Europe. Most sites are found on the eastern side of central and inner Trondheim Fjord, the main geographical feature in this area, which reaches around 130 km inland. This area is divided into two provinces, Sør-Trøndelag and Nord-Trøndelag; here, I also include some sites in the adjacent province of Møre and Romsdal.

Rock-art has been studied in this area since 1870; after some important discoveries in the 1890s, studies became more systematic (Lossius 1897; Rygh 1908). These discoveries led to an understanding that two different rock-art traditions exist in Scandinavia (Hansen 1904): one has been dated to the Stone Age, the other to the Bronze Age (Brøgger 1906). Both traditions are well represented in mid Norway, the only district in Scandinavia that can be claimed to be a major area for both traditions. Because of their geographical distribution I refer to them as the Northern (NT) and Southern (ST) Traditions, respectively.[1]

The main way to distinguish the two traditions is by subject-matter and motifs: mostly game animals in the Northern Tradition; boats, cup-marks (cupules), and human footprints in the Southern Tradition. There are also differences in terms of sites preferred between the two traditions. In this chapter I concentrate on the chronology and geographic distributions of the rock-art traditions and note important differences.

Informed methods and analogies are less relevant to the mid Norwegian record. For historical times – the last millennium – local peasant societies are fairly well known; ethnological and historical sources may be of relevance for later parts of the Iron Age, that is, for the first millennium AD. For earlier periods, however, these sources give no apparently relevant information.

The Bronze Age of Scandinavia is geographically, spatially and formally separated from any culture or society known from later ethnographic sources. Using ethnographic analogies, therefore, is extremely difficult (Sørensen 1987: 90–1). To a large extent this holds true also for the Neolithic of mid Norway, to which most of the NT rock-art has been allocated.

[1] Several different terms have been proposed for these two rock-art traditions, the oldest being 'South Scandinavian' and 'Arctic'. These terms were, especially in Norwegian literature, replaced by farmers' (sometimes also called agrarian) and hunters' rock-art, respectively. I have found neither of these terms satisfactory. I have a preference for the geographic terms but I would prefer to replace South Scandinavian with 'Nordic', which has become a term frequently used in current Scandinavian languages. Here I have chosen a set of more 'neutral' geographic terms. However, there surely is a need for Scandinavian archaeologists and rock-art scholars to develop a common modern and adequate terminology.

While the Mesolithic pioneer settlements were located at the coast, an expansion towards inland areas, especially along the Trondheim Fjord, apparently took place at the transition to the Neolithic. At this time also a major shift in the use of raw materials for artefact production took place – from flint to slates, schists and other local rocks. Thus, the Neolithic of mid Norway, which was still predominantly settled by hunters – like most of central and northern Scandinavia – differs from contemporary cultures in southern Scandinavia and areas further south. Perhaps, rather than being studied from a European perspective, these northern late hunters should be viewed from a circumpolar perspective (see Møllenhus 1975).

The rock-art of mid Norway is dominated by petroglyphs. However, some NT pictographs are found, mostly at the Fosen peninsula to the west of the Trondheim Fjord and at the Tingvoll Fjord about 150 km south-west of the city of Trondheim. Rock-art appears to have been made in this area for around 5000 years, from Late Mesolithic *c.* 4500 BC through to Early Iron Age *c.* AD 400. Later engravings and paintings exist, especially from post-medieval times, but there seems to be no connection between these 'graffiti' and the prehistoric rock-art.

## Rock-art in mid Norway

The recognition of two separate rock-art traditions in Scandinavia gained prominence during the first half of the twentieth century, influencing virtually all later research. Scholars studied one or other of the traditions; hardly any studied the relationship between them. The relevance of this dichotomy has, however, been questioned (Helskog 1993: 72; Nordbladh 1995: 28).

Traditionally, the transition from hunting to farming in Norway has been studied through glimpses of fairly stable societies, either hunters or farmers. The transforming *processes* involved have hardly been discussed, although these processes were slow; a long transition phase existed, when both hunting and farming were of great importance. Emphasis is put

on documenting and dating the spread of husbandry and agriculture, not on discussing *why* and *how* this transition took place at a particular time. This is also the case for rock-art. The two traditions, not only associated with different cultures and methods of subsistence, have also been claimed to belong to different periods. However, A. Hagen (1969: 127–33) emphasised that there must have been contacts between them in west and mid Norway during the Bronze Age.

Although the Neolithic of mid Norway was dominated by hunters – in archaeological terms by the 'Slate Complex' – evidence of farming is also found; at the Trondheim Fjord we find Europe's northernmost Bronze Age communities, as evidenced by artefacts – bronzes and stone ceremonial axes (Sognnes 1990: 114–16), grave monuments (Rygh 1906) and petroglyphs. Bronzes, cairns and ST rock-art are also found further north, but there are no large agglomerations north of the Trondheim Fjord.

Thus mid Norway constitutes a unique laboratory for studying the transition from hunting to farming in central and northern Scandinavia. Around 200 rock-art localities are known, of which around 50 are of the Northern Tradition (Fig. 9.1). Our knowledge of this record depends on several factors (Sognnes 1989: 82), among which the strategies used for discovering rock-art are of great importance. In mid Norway, hardly any systematic search has ever been conducted, except for some small-scale surveys around already known localities. Natural and social taphonomic processes which strongly affect the preservation of rock-art are also important. The number of localities increases steadily, with an average of between ten and twenty new discoveries per decade. The number of new discoveries is strongly related to research activities, with peaks around 1880, in the 1890s, 1920s, 1950s and, as a result of the present author's work, during the last fifteen years.

Although both traditions are present within the same area, sometimes at the same farms and occasionally on the same panels, the dichotomy in motifs is evident. The Northern Tradition is dominated by

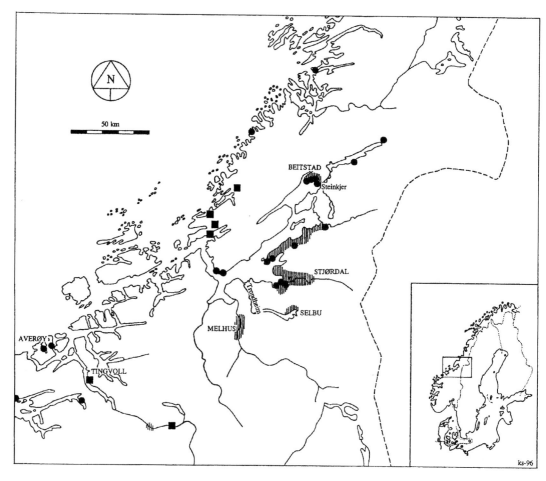

**Fig. 9.1.** Rock-art distribution in mid Norway.
Point symbols show sites (farms) where the Northern Tradition is represented; dots = petroglyphs, squares = pictographs. Major areas with Southern Tradition rock-art are hatched.

representational images. Animals, especially cervids, are most common. Elks dominate but reindeer and red deer are depicted too. Other animals represented are bear and beaver, birds, fish and whales. Boat images are numerous but found at a limited number of sites – often together with whales. Geometric images occur together with the animals.

The NT rock-art of mid Norway has been studied most thoroughly by Gutorm Gjessing (1936). Since this study, the number of localities and of images has

tripled. However, the motifs as well as the geographical and topographical locations of sites are similar, so some of Gjessing's conclusions may still be valid.

Most of the sites allocated to the Northern Tradition are on the eastern side of the Trondheim Fjord (Gjessing 1936; Hallström 1938; Møllenhus 1968b) between the cities of Trondheim and Steinkjer; some sites are found at the coast and at other fjords (Gjessing 1936; Hallström 1938; Møllenhus 1968a).

The majority of the ST sites are found in the same area (Petersen 1926; Rygh 1908; Sognnes 1993). So far, this tradition is represented by petroglyphs only. Around two-thirds of the known localities are found in Stjørdal municipality, Nord-Trøndelag, 30–40 km east of Trondheim. Other concentrations are found in Steinkjer, Nord-Trøndelag, and in Selbu and Melhus, both Sør-Trøndelag, to the south-east and south of Trondheim. Although this tradition has the most abundant rock-art it was until recently the least known. The main reason for this was the focus on the more spectacular and 'exotic' NT sites, especially in the 1890s and 1920s. During the last few decades the ST has been studied more intensively (for example Marstrander 1970; Sognnes 1993); most of the record remains unpublished.

### Rock-art in time: approaches to dating

For more than a century there has been a consensus among Scandinavian archaeologists that the ST rock-art should be dated to the Bronze Age. The 'internal' chronology of this tradition, however, is a rather frail construction. Most chronological systems which have been proposed are based on formal morphological studies of images, especially boats; that is, on the absence/presence of attributes (Malmer 1981) and styles (Almgren 1987; Marstrander 1963). The boat images are the most frequent motif (except for cup-marks) and they have attributes which show great variation, of which some apparently have chronological significance.

The unique panel at Bardal in Steinkjer was used by Gjessing (1935) to create a sequence based on superimpositions. While, in general, very few superimpositions exist, for either NT or ST rock-art, at Bardal between 300 and 400 ST engravings are superimposed on an older 'stratum' consisting of around 50 NT images (Gjessing 1936; Hallström 1938; Lossius 1897). Interestingly, superimpositions are also found on images within each tradition. For the Southern Tradition Gjessing (1935: 133) was able to identify three phases – characterised by certain types of boat images – of which one has two subtypes.

### Pictures of boats and their attributes: a chronology for the Southern Tradition

Gjessing (1935: 132), like most scholars before and after him (such as Coll 1902; Ekholm 1916; Fett and Fett 1941; Larsen 1972; Marstrander 1963), emphasised the difference between images where the hull is drawn with a single line and those with two-lined hulls. The simplest single-line images have been compared with passage-grave art in Brittany, which has been used as an argument in favour of an early date for these images (Gjessing 1935: 133). Malmer (1981: 23; see also Althin 1945), however, claims that the initial boat images had two-lined hulls with two protruding curved lines at one end, one inside the other, identical to Gjessing's type IIa.

I have also studied this problem by means of formal methods, but in a different way. Realising that we are not studying boats but pictures of boats, my starting-point was not the design of the hull, albeit this is frequently the most striking attribute. Rather, I tried to identify the attributes which might represent different kinds of boats. In doing so, I started with a realistically drawn boat image found at Brandskog in the province of Uppland, Sweden, where six people are depicted, paddling the boat (Fig. 9.2a). This 'real' situation – six people paddling a boat showing specific construction characteristics – can be drawn in many different ways, of which I here present eight, all of which have real counterparts (Fig. 9.2b). They look different, but depict the same boat; they differ in style, not in construction. These images all show curved prows at both ends protruding from the gunwale as well as a skid, protruding from the keel, or rather, the bottom plank. These are the attributes which characterise this boat type (Sognnes 1987: 24–5).

Before starting to analyse the Stjørdal record, I conducted a test classification of the boat images using the record from Lower Stjørdal – the parishes of Skatval, Stjørdal and Lånke – based on previous classification systems (Burenhult 1980; Fett and Fett 1941; Malmer 1981; Marstrander 1963). None of these classifications gave satisfactory results. Out of

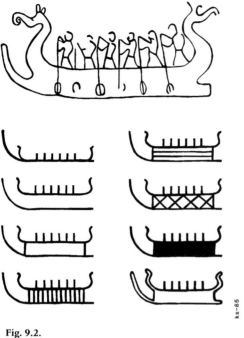

**Fig. 9.2.**
a  The Brandskog ship from Uppland, Sweden.
b  Eight different ways of drawing this boat type.

about 150 images which should have been classifiable, a maximum of 95 (Malmer's system) was actually classified (Sognnes 1987: 22).

The unclassified images showed me the weaknesses and strengths of these systems; I was able to create a new classification system which takes these results into consideration. This system was based primarily on the design of the boats' ends – whether they have protruding lines ('prows'), the number of such protrusions, whether the images were symmetric or non-symmetric and so forth. This resulted in twelve types, of which some do not have 'real' counterparts. Some types, occurring in low numbers, may represent unfinished or weathered examples of some of the other types. The design of the hull was used at a secondary level, creating a set of eight subtypes. The system thus consists of a total of 96 types/subtypes, of which not all have yet been found in the present record. Some of the subtypes not

found in Lower Stjørdal, however, are represented in Upper Stjørdal (Hegre parish).

Four major types of boat designs were found: E, G, H and K/L (which are likely to represent two varieties of the same boat type). Two are identical with types found by Gjessing at Bardal; G is Gjessing's type II, and H is Gjessing's type III. Gjessing's type I, the single-lined images, I have defined as a subtype. Low correlations were found between these four major types (Sognnes 1990: 80–1), which appear to represent four diachronic phases (1–4; see Fig. 9.3). Phase 2, characterised by type G, has been tentatively dated to the Bronze Age (about 1800–500 BC). Stylistic differences indicate that this type may be divided into two sub-phases (see Marstrander 1963: 76–9), which may represent Early and Late Bronze Age; the majority, however, date from the Late Bronze Age (about 1000–500 BC). Phase 3, characterised by type H, has tentatively been dated to the pre-Roman Iron Age (about 500–1 BC). These dates are in accordance with Gjessing's (1935: 135) sequence.

The two other types are not represented at Bardal. However, type K/L is known from west Norway, where it is supposed to be late, as exemplified by an image found at a standing stone erected over a grave from around AD 400 (Skjelsvik and Straume 1957). Hardly any superimpositions exist, but detailed studies reveal that some type G and H images have been redesigned into type K/L. Phase 4, characterised by these types, has been tentatively dated to the Roman Iron Age (about AD 1–400). Type E, which characterises phase 1, has been compared with boat images found at NT sites. Fett and Fett (1979: 67) claim that these images, in fact, represent the same boat type, known from west and mid Norway, as well as Nämforsen in the province of Västernorrland, Sweden. Based on this, phase 1 has been tentatively dated to the Late Neolithic/Early Bronze Age (2000–1500 BC).

These tentative phases provide opportunities for formulating hypotheses concerning temporal developments. We find that phase 1 is represented at four (possibly five) sites in Stjørdal and at one site in

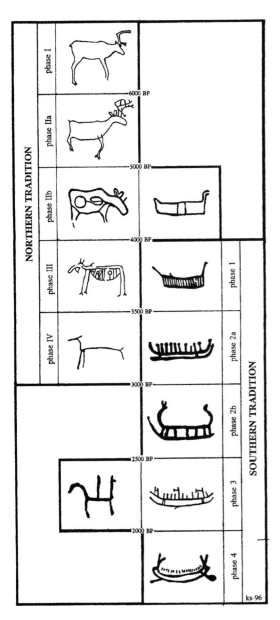

**Fig. 9.3.** Proposed phase sequences for both Northern and Southern rock-art in mid Norway.
  The dates are tentative.

Levanger, between Stjørdal and Steinkjer. The number of sites with boat images increases during phases 2 and 3, and they also show a wider geographical distribution. In phase 4 the number of sites decreases and most images are again found in Stjørdal. Thus, not only was the beginning of rock-art making not simultaneous throughout the district but also the end of it. Interestingly, some of the initial sites are also among the longest-lasting. At the minor concentrations of ST rock-art, phase 1 is not found. In Steinkjer phases 2 and 3 dominate, while in Melhus only phases 3 and 4 are found; Selbu is limited to phases 2 and 4.

The four Stjørdal sites where phase 1 images are found are among the largest in mid Norway; here also boat images are found together with a number of other motifs. This means that – according to the chronology proposed here – petroglyphs were made at these sites for around 2000 years; at Røkke for perhaps as much as 2500 years. This does not necessarily mean that the making of petroglyphs at these sites was continuous. Based on the currently known number of images at each site, the average time between the making of single new images would be between five and eight years (Sognnes 1993: 168). If two or more images were made at the same event, the average time between events would increase considerably.

The other motifs are more difficult to place within this sequence. They occur relatively infrequently with boat images, as evidenced by low correlation values (Sognnes 1990: 14–17), and some motifs, for instance footprints and geometrical designs, were made over a considerable time-period (Sognnes 1990: 104–6). The horse images appear to be late; most likely they are contemporary with phase 3 boat images. Cup-marks, too, may have been made during several phases – but their low occurrence in Hegre parish on panels with late boat images indicates that the majority of the cup-marks are early, but later than phase 1 (Sognnes 1990: 96).

Rock-art production apparently came to an end during the Roman period; but at Stuberg a boat image equipped with mast and beam has recently been found, a sailing vessel which did not come into use in Scandinavia until shortly before the Viking period (Christensen 1985: 201). The design of the boat, without mast and beam, would clearly belong in phase 4.

The number of Bronze Age artefacts (mostly bronzes) found in mid Norway shows a similar pattern. Only a few finds are known from the Early Bronze Age. They are located, like most of the rock-art, in the Steinkjer and Stjørdal areas; at Røkke even at the same farm. Most bronzes are dated to the Late Bronze Age and these artefacts are found over a wider area, much wider than for the contemporary rock-art.

## Stylistic dating and sea-level: a chronology for the Northern Tradition

For the Northern Tradition Gjessing (1936) created a chronological sequence primarily based on stylistic criteria; major parts of this sequence were found to be in concordance with data obtained from studies of the Holocene land uplift. During the Pleistocene, Norway was covered with ice, which pressed down the crust of the earth. After deglaciation this pressure disappeared and the crust readjusted. The readjustment was most rapid shortly after the deglaciation, when sea-levels were much higher than today. In the central and inner Trondheim Fjord area the land still rises 3–4 mm annually. Thus, any traces of human activities which took place along shorelines during the early Holocene are today found high above sea-level.

This phenomenon also affects rock-art studies. As we have no reason to believe than any rock-art was made under water, the altitude of a rock-art panel *might* provide information about the age of the images on it. Fig. 9.4 is a diagram where all known localities at the mouth of the Stjørdal valley are plotted by 5 m intervals. The NT localities lie between around 20 and 50 m above the present sea-level. Compared with results from shoreline displacement studies (Kjemperud 1981; Sveian and Olsen 1984), we find that the relevant shores emerged

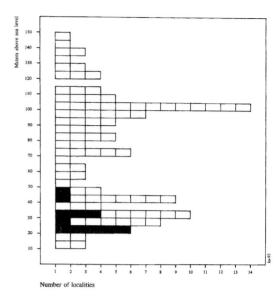

**Fig. 9.4.** Heights above sea-level for rock-art localities in the Stjørdal area, plotted by 5 m intervals.

Open rectangles = Southern Tradition; closed rectangles = Northern Tradition rock-art.

from the sea between about 6000 and 3500 b.p. This means that detailed studies of the localities' heights above sea-level will provide maximum dates for the NT images found on these panels (see Fig. 9.5). A similar approach cannot be used for the ST localities; these, as shown on Fig. 9.4, are situated between about 10 and 150 m above shore level, while relevant corresponding sea-level would be between about 12 and 20 m. Thus, for only a few ST localities can we obtain maximum dates by means of the land uplift.

Shetelig (1922: 150) proposed that a stylistic development took place within the NT rock-art – from large naturalistic to small stylised animals. This was supported by Gjessing (1936: 168), who defined three stylistic phases for mid and north Norway. Gjessing's phase I consists of large, often full-scale outlined animals drawn in a naturalistic way. Gjessing dated this phase to the Middle Neolithic, according to the present chronology, about 3400–2400 BC (see Fig. 9.5). In phase II the animals – still relatively naturalistic – are smaller, and they frequently have

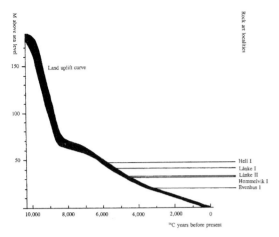

**Fig. 9.5.** Heights above sea-level for NT rock-art localities in the Stjørdal area plotted on to the land uplift curve for Verdal, Nord-Trøndelag.
Curve redrawn from Sveian and Olsen 1984.

some internal body pattern. The appearance of an interior pattern has been considered an important stylistic and chronological marker (Bakka 1975: 28; Hagen 1976: 165). Gjessing dated this phase to the Late Neolithic, about 2400–1800 BC. Phase III animals are small and strongly stylised, their bodies filled with internal lines. This phase was dated to the Early Bronze Age, 1800–1200 BC.

This stylistically based sequence was supported by data obtained from studies of land uplift; phase I localities are situated at higher levels than phase II localities. This indicates that the localities in question were engraved with petroglyphs shortly after they had emerged from the sea. In a study of localities at Hammer, Bakka (1975, 1988) convincingly argued that this actually was the case. At least one of these localities was, when it was discovered, covered by a beach bar, most likely to have been deposited during a storm combined with exceptionally high tide (see Hafsten 1987).

In a recent study of all coastal NT rock-art in northern Fennoscandia and Russia, Lindquist (1994: 77) claims that all sites were shorebound. He divides the record into three major traditions, the most relevant the 'Nordland-Trøndelag' tradition. This tra-

dition he also divides into five phases, of which four are represented in mid Norway (Lindquist 1994: 167–8). Phases I (not represented in mid Norway) and II correspond with the two sub-phases in Gjessing's phase I. Phase II dates to the Early Neolithic. Phases III–V correspond with Gjessing's phase III. Phases III–IV are dated to the Middle Neolithic and phase V to the Late Neolithic. Gjessing's phase III, he claims, belongs to phase I of the South Norwegian tradition. This phase Lindquist dates to the Mesolithic (Lindquist 1994: 161). In general Gjessing, Bakka and Lindquist agree with each other; however, Lindquist arranges Gjessing's sequence in a different order: phase III ( = South Norwegian I) then phase I ( = Nordland-Trøndelag II) then phase II ( = Nordland-Trøndelag III–V).

While discussing this question, one must take into consideration that *any* exposed rock panel can be used for image-making, whether or not it is located near the shore; any panel may also have been used on a number of occasions. Images found on one panel are not necessarily contemporary. Unless proved otherwise, as at Hammer, the land uplift can provide only maximum dates. The location of the NT sites within a narrow range of altitudes surely indicates that this rock-art was made at locations near the sea some millennia ago. As the idea that they were *always* located at the shore is too simplistic, Lindquist's chronological sequence is no better founded than Gjessing's. At Hammer – where a number of small localities are found at an old beach – and perhaps also in Alta in the province of Finnmark (see Helskog 1984), his view does seem correct – but other locational factors should also be taken into consideration. Not all petroglyph panels are located on raised beaches; detailed studies of local topography are necessary before the rock-art-at-the-seashore hypothesis can be deemed probable for each individual locality.

Gjessing's sequence also has been criticised in some studies from north Norway, for instance at Alta, where Helskog (1984: 55–6) could find no relationship between style and heights above sea-level. Nor could Hesjedal (1994) accept this sequence for localities in the provinces of Troms and Nordland. However, like Lindquist, Hesjedal did not study the local topography. Gjessing's sequence was based on a detailed study of localities found in Beitstad parish in Steinkjer – at Hammer, Bardal and Homnes, which are less than 10 km apart. So far, this sequence seems acceptable for the Trondheim Fjord area, and I follow it here.

At Bardal, superimpositions clearly demonstrate this was a multi-phase locality (Gjessing 1936). The first images may have been made shortly after this large panel had emerged from the sea; the superimposed images most likely represent a later phase. Also, at some recently discovered sites, superimpositions are found where images belonging to the older strata are hardly visible, for instance at Lånke in Stjørdal and Rødsand in Averøy, Møre and Romsdal.

Further studies might also lead to a revision of the chronological sequence for mid Norway where Gjessing and Bakka were apparently right; a temporal development within the NT rock-art *can* be traced in this area. This tradition started during the Late Mesolithic – or at the transition to the Neolithic. Lindquist (1994: 161) and Bakka (1973: 173) claimed that it did not last through the Bronze Age. But I am strongly inclined to follow Gjessing (Sognnes 1994: 46–7). Here, three competing chronologies have been proposed. In Bakka's, the short chronology, the production of NT rock-art ended before the Bronze Age, phase III being the latest. Lindquist's longer sequence ends at approximately the same time. Gjessing and I favour a longer chronology, in which phase III may be dated to the Early Bronze Age. That a fourth phase may exist is evidenced by some single-line zoomorphic images found at Holte. These images have been compared with horse images belonging to the ST tradition (Møllenhus 1968b); if we accept this analogy, this phase dates to the Late Bronze Age (Sognnes 1994: 44).

## Rock-art in place: approaches to location
Both hunters and early farmers have manifested their presence in the landscape around the Trondheim Fjord by making rock-art. This happened for a period of around 5000 years, during which the transition from hunting to farming took place. This image-making apparently started at, or shortly before, the transition from the Mesolithic to the Neolithic, that is, approximately 6000 BP, which in this area is represented primarily by a change in the use of raw materials but also by a shift in habitation. The beginning of rock-art production may be linked to this transition as well. Rock-art was apparently not made at the coast – which at that time had already been settled for millennia – but around the central and inner parts of the Trondheim Fjord, at the mouths of large valleys acting as gates to a new and different world consisting of the large forests and mountain areas of interior central Scandinavia. It is tempting here to paraphrase Hodder (1990), seeing the first rock-art in this area as representing the taming of a wild and hitherto alien landscape (Sognnes 1994: 43).

*Rock-art sites, fjords and migration routes: aspects of the Northern Tradition*
Some preliminary patterns can be seen. The Trondheim Fjord can be subdivided into a series of smaller basins. Rock-art is found in all the major basins; in two basins all three phases are found and at two basins two phases are represented (Sognnes 1994: 30–2). Most sites are found at conspicuous topographic features. The site at Hell (Gjessing 1936; Hallström 1938) was once on a small island (later an isthmus) with steep sides, which was separated from the mainland by a narrow sound. The near-by site at Lånke (Sognnes 1994: 41) is located on a crescent-shaped ridge raised around 100 m above the surrounding land and contemporary sea (Fig. 9.6). These sites are within sight of each other. The site at Evenhus is located on an island in the middle of the fjord within sight of most of the central part of the Trondheim Fjord area.

Rock-art is not found at the top of these prominent locations but near their lower edges, often facing the sea. These conspicuous features are located at the border between sea and land, a

# LÅNKE

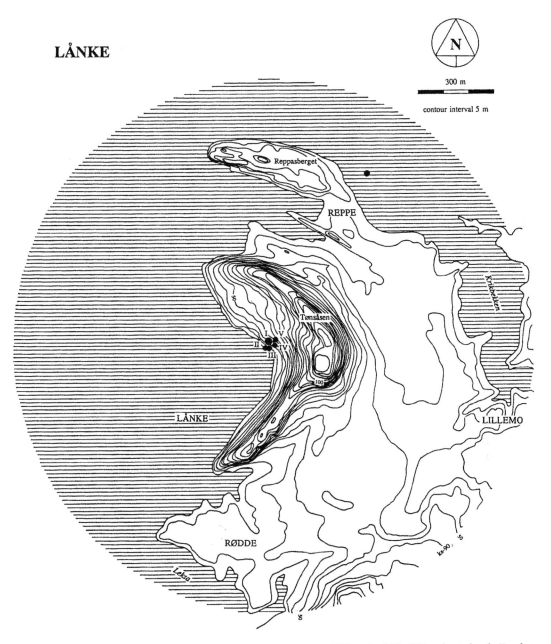

**Fig. 9.6.** NT rock-art is frequently located on conspicuous topographic features. With sea-level 30 m higher than today, the Tønsåsen ridge in Stjørdal, where the Lånke site is found, formed a crescent-shaped promontory at the eastern side of a wide shallow bay. The numbers I–V represent the NT rock-art panels found at Lånke. The dot in the sea to the north of the Tønsåsen ridge represents the ST locality at Reppe.

situation which may have been a primary locational factor. Traditionally, the NT sites have been associated with favourable places for hunting (Gjessing 1936; Hallström 1938) but detailed studies of local topography make this less likely for most sites (see Hagen 1990: 45). Rather, the sites along the Trondheim Fjord may be interpreted as sanctuaries along important hunting trails, for people travelling along the fjord or migrating between the fjord and the large inland forests and mountain areas. In this last case the rock-art might have played an important role in rites associated with territorial passage (Sognnes 1994: 39).

Another concentration of NT rock-art is found 150–200 km inland from the Trondheim Fjord, in the province of Jämtland, Sweden. Morphological similarities between images found in the Jämtland and Trøndelag provinces indicate that close connections may have existed between these two areas; rock-art may signify each end of migration routes between the western and central parts of the Scandinavian peninsula. These migration routes could have been extended to the coast, where the initial Mesolithic settlements were located. However, no rock-art has been found along the outer part of the Trondheim Fjord or on the archipelago outside the mouth of the fjord.

This absence may be due to taphonomic processes, as indicated by remains of earlier images at Lånke and Rødsand. Rødsand is of special interest for this question, since this site, together with the Søbstad site, is located at the coast, on Averøy Island, where numerous Mesolithic dwelling sites have been found. The Rødsand and Søbstad sites most likely would not represent a migration system which also included the Trondheim Fjord area. Rather, these sites should be connected to rock-art at the Tingvoll Fjord and in the Drivdal valley, which leads inland towards mountain areas around Oppdal, Sør-Trøndelag, where some early Mesolithic dwelling sites have been found (Sognnes 1995).

The preference for depictions of large forest animals, especially elk (moose), may represent a focus of interest in these giants of the woods that goes far beyond their importance for subsistence. Later, whales and boats were added to the preferred motifs. This may, as Lindquist (1994: 82) claimed, reflect a change in subsistence, with more emphasis on the marine resources. This seems plausible – but nearness to the sea, and thereby to marine resources, was common for virtually all NT rock-art in mid Norway, including the sites where only land mammals are depicted. The fjord, penetrating far inland with its rich marine life, was within easy reach for most hunters living inland. Numerous boat images are, with very few exceptions, found at two sites only, Hammer and Evenhus, both located at former beaches. These sites are exceptional also because of the great number of images. I find it strange that only these two sites should reflect a change towards maritime adaptation; rather, they may have had functions different from other sites as they are situated at places where relatively large groups could meet – emphasising the importance of the sea for these groups and not necessarily hunting, they may have been important for communications and the maintenance of the group identity. The imagery, then, could represent emblemic symbols signifying the hunting way of life in the Trondheim Fjord area.

*A touching of Southern and Northern Traditions*
During the Late Neolithic and Bronze Age southern and northern Scandinavia went through completely different developments, which show remarkable parallels (Baudou 1989: 41). In south Scandinavia this development is strongly related to the introduction of farming. During these periods farming gradually spread northwards. In mid Norway the transformation process started in the Neolithic, when the local population came into close contact with contemporary farmers living further south. Bronze Age artefacts indicate the existence of two small bridgeheads for the Scandinavian Bronze Age culture at the Trondheim Fjord, in the Steinkjer and Stjørdal areas (Sognnes 1993: 176). Thus a frontier zone apparently existed in mid Norway; it lasted for a long time, perhaps for as long as two millennia.

*Concentrations of rock-art: the key feature of the Southern Tradition distribution*

The distribution of the ST rock-art in mid Norway differs distinctly from that of the NT sites (Sognnes 1983, 1987, 1990). For the vast majority of these sites, nearness to the sea was of no importance; Fig. 9.4 demonstrates that the localities are situated between about 10 and 150 m above the present sea-level, while sea-levels at that time were between about 12 and 20 m. Already the first ST images (phase 1) were being made on inland panels, in the interior of the Skatval promontory and in the Stjørdal valley. Not until much later – in late phase 2 – were ST petroglyphs made on the shores, and then only at a limited number of sites.

In Stjørdal two major concentrations are found, one in Skatval and one in Hegre parish. The localities are clustered, with most sites between 5 and 150 m from their nearest neighbour. At present, fifteen locality clusters are known, which together with five isolated finds constitute twenty sets of sites (Fig. 9.7). Within the two major concentrations, sites are regularly distributed, with distances between neighbouring units (as measured from their centres) between 2000 and 2200 m. Similar patterns are also traced at Steinkjer and Melhus (Sognnes 1993: 158–60).

Although new discoveries are frequently made, and the area where rock-art is known tends to expand, this distribution pattern has been noted since around 1880 in Skatval parish and since around 1920 in Hegre. The earliest sites – Røkke and Auran at the Skatval promontory and Ystines and Leirfall in the Stjørdal valley – are also the largest, and seem to have been known for a longer time. Many panels in the Stjørdal valley are located on the northern side, on small outcrops between alluvial terraces.

This pattern represents the long, continuous use of petroglyphs within a limited area. With possible exceptions for the earliest sites (Røkke and Auran on small hilltops, Ystines and Leirfall at or near valley promontories), these sites cannot be seen until visitors are within just a few metres of them (Fig. 9.8). This rock-art was not meant to be spotted from long distances; on the contrary, it was set back from traffic along the fjord and, in general, also from people migrating along the Stjørdal valley. It must have been meant to be seen only by people familiar with local topography. It is likely this rock-art was made by a sedentary population, by farmers living in and utilising the area near by (Sognnes 1993: 168–70). I think of this pattern as reflecting the rock-art distribution of the Bronze Age and Early Iron Age – and the contemporary settlement pattern. The larger, early sites represent the initial habitations; the surrounding, smaller sites would represent a settlement expansion during the Bronze Age and Early Iron Age.

*Aspects of two traditions in one landscape*

The preferred placing of NT rock-art is at prominent locations, which could be seen from far away – often from the sea; I see the images as used by hunters, as one way of conveying information between distant groups which were constantly on the move (Bouissac 1994: 353). The landscape seems to have played a distinctly different role for the Bronze Age farmers. Although fjords and sounds were of symbolic importance for these farmers too, they created their own landmarks, burying their deceased under cairns located on promontories, hilltops and small islands. Frequently the grave monuments could be seen from the sea. These cairns were one way of signifying that the surrounding land was settled and occupied, symbolising the farmers' possession of the landscape. As symbols mediating messages to people passing by, these human-made features would compete with the natural features used by the hunters, which they soon outnumbered. Their rock-art sanctuaries were located at the dwelling sites, out of sight and reach from travellers and possible aliens. These 'cognitive landmarks' were created places, while the NT sites are at locations which declare themselves to the hunter's view.

The increasing quantity and spread of ST rock-art in mid Norway may reflect a growth in the farming population. Whether there was a continuity from

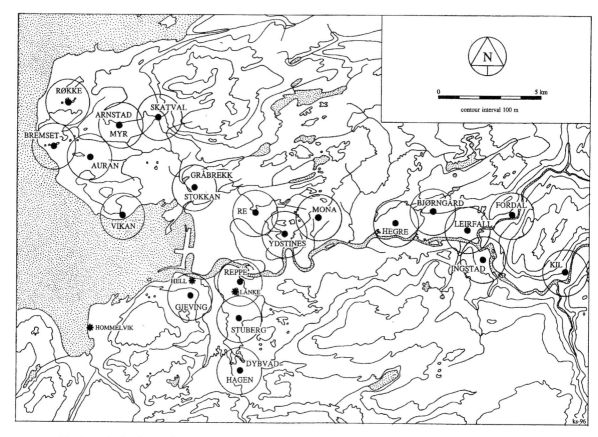

**Fig. 9.7.** The distribution of ST rock-art sites in Stjørdal, Nord-Trøndelag. Circles of 1100 m radius are drawn around the centre of each site.

these Bronze Age settlements to the Iron Age farms – which are known from the Roman period onwards – is unknown.

The growing number of NT petroglyphs during the Neolithic may also have been caused by increased population and internal social stress. To these intra-cultural factors may be added inter-social stress due to the expansion of farming to the area, whether the first farmers were immigrants or some local groups which added husbandry and, later, agriculture to their traditional methods of subsistence. A growing farming population surely must have had some impact on the hunting communities which had lived in this area for millennia, and the supposed social stress must have been increasing for a long

time, most likely reaching its maximum in the Late Bronze Age and pre-Roman Iron Age. If the making of rock-art by hunters was part of a strategy for diminishing and controlling social stress, there would be no reason for stopping this procedure at the end of the Neolithic; rather, one would expect that stress would have *increased* the production of their rock-art during the Bronze Age. On the other hand, acculturation, with a growing farming population as one result, would lead to a reduction in the number of hunters and also to a reduction in the area occupied by them; we would see the number of Bronze Age (phases III and IV) sites decrease.

Little information exists to provide insight into the initial impact of farming on the area. ST

**Fig. 9.8.** Most of the ST localities in Stjørdal can be spotted from a short distance only; here, Hegre VI is today located in the middle of a field.

petroglyphs were probably first made in the Stjørdal area in the Late Neolithic. The first motifs depicted within this tradition were boats, similar, if not identical, to the NT boats, but drawn in a distinctly different style and located in another topographical setting. These petroglyphs also contain a regional emblemic element common for west and mid Norway. Later, new types of boat images were depicted, which seem to represent a pan-Scandinavian symbolic system together with a wider motif repertoire.

The first ST rock-art may have been made when the first farmers settled permanently in Stjørdal and, somewhat later, in the Steinkjer area (Sognnes 1993: 176). The distribution of large and small sites indicates the existence of a hierarchical system. The initial sites were used for more than one millennium, probably as common sanctuaries for people living in a wide area, their potency being renewed and enhanced by the making of new images. At the same time each site, or cluster of localities, may represent social units at a lower level – a family household.

The transition from hunting to farming in mid Norway was slow, lasting perhaps for 2500 years; the period of rock-art production appears to have been somewhat longer. During this transition, both hunters and farmers made their own emblemic rock-art, creating two different rock-art traditions. According to the chronology advocated here, with two long and partly contemporary sequences, there was a period of almost one thousand years, during the Late Neolithic and Early Bronze Age, when images belonging to both traditions were made.

In this perspective the Bardal site is of special interest. At the large locality Bardal I, which measures about $30 \times 10$ m, a major 'iconoclastic' event took place.[2] When it was taken over by nearby farmers, some time during the Early Bronze Age, the potency of the place was altered for the benefit of their own expanding society, which was based on a different form of subsistence. The result was that a new cognitive system, alien to the people who originally created and used this sanctuary, was imposed.

If the two rock-art traditions are to some extent contemporary, this must be taken into account in interpretations. This is especially important for the Southern Tradition, which is believed to have originated in the core area of the Scandinavian Bronze Age culture in Denmark and southernmost Sweden (see Malmer 1981), strongly influenced by several non-Scandinavian cultures, from the Mediterranean, central Europe or the British Isles (Burenhult 1980; Fett and Fett 1979; Malmer 1981; Marstrander 1963). The early occurrence of ST petroglyphs in west and mid Norway, dominated by regional emblemic motifs, may tell a different story. The Southern Tradition may have originated somewhere along the frontier between the early south Scandinavian farming cultures and their contemporary northern neighbours, who still based their subsistence on hunting and had already been making rock-art for millennia.

### Northern and Southern in mid Norway

Scandinavian rock-art often appears to be highly standardised and repetitive, with its cup-marks galore, thousands of boat images, hundreds of elk images and so forth, often drawn in the same manner. Yet research shows a complex story. At least for some motifs, it is possible to provide some provisional dates and to establish tentative chronological sequences. The sites are found within a variety of landscapes, at both macro and micro levels. The rock-art of mid Norway is clearly part of a pan-Scandinavian rock-art tradition, within which numerous regional and local peculiarities can be found. This is the only place in Scandinavia where both the Southern and Northern Traditions are frequent; the number of footprints at the Leirfall site alone almost equals the total number of footprints in the province of Bohuslän, Sweden!

Although the rock-art of mid Norway has been studied for more than a hundred years, much work lies ahead. Important parts of the record are still unpublished. This holds true especially for the Southern Tradition. While virtually all NT sites have been published, except for Gjessing's (1936) monograph, they have mostly been published in local periodicals which are difficult to obtain. It is, therefore, imperative that further investigations are carried out and that the record is published in full.

Both traditions contain unique images, types and motifs, which should make further studies following traditional approaches rewarding. However, the unique position mid Norway holds – as the only major area with both traditions – makes this record especially favourable for studies of the relationship between the two traditions and for questions such as why rock-art was made in Arctic and sub-Arctic Europe. These studies should be conducted in close connection with studies of other contemporary archaeological material which also contains evidence of imagery and symbolism, hitherto hardly recognised or investigated (Sognnes 1996).

Much can be gained by further formal studies of motifs, and also of style, which seems to be of relevance for a limited area like this. These studies surely must include the images themselves; morphological studies as well as studies of frequencies; intra-site as well as inter-site studies. Also the study of the relationship between rock-art and landscape can be developed further, by means of detailed stu-

[2] The term 'iconoclasm' has been used for the breaking and destruction of images for religious worship in later times, for instance for the removal and destruction of specific Catholic symbols (pictures and statues of saints, etc.) during the Reformation in early sixteenth-century Scandinavia. The oldest petroglyph stratas at Bardal were not erased but the superimposition of later ST images defaced the NT images to such an extent that this term here seems appropriate.

dies of panel shape, of the local topography around the panels, and of their wider geographical setting – and by studying the relationship between the rock-art localities and other monuments and landscape features.

Analogies were formerly used both as arguments for the role of hunting magic in the Northern Tradition (Gjessing 1936; Hallström 1938) and for claiming that the ST rock-art was made within the framework of sympathetic magic of a fertility religion (Almgren 1927). For my own studies they have played a minor role. However, if we accept the idea presented here, that the rock-art of mid Norway (and of many other places in Scandinavia) was created in a frontier zone, relevant analogies may be found in other frontiers where rock-art was made. Future research might well benefit from comparative studies, especially those concerned with regionalism, boundary markings and the ways in which different socio-economic groups mark landscapes.

## REFERENCES

Almgren, B. 1987. *Die Datierung bronzezeitlicher Felszeichnungen in Westschweden.* Uppsala, Acta Musei Antiquitatum Septentrionalium Regiæ Universitatis Upsaliensis 6.

Almgren, O. 1927. *Hällristningar och kultbruk.* Stockholm, Almquist and Wicksell. Kungl. Vitterhets Historie och Antikvitets Akademiens Handlingar 35.

Althin, C.-A. 1945. *Studien zu den bronzezeitlichen Felszeichnungen von Skåne.* Lund.

Bakka, E. 1973. Om alderen på veideristningane, *Viking* 37: 151–87.

1975. Geologically dated Arctic rock carvings at Hammer near Steinkjer in Nord Trøndelag, *Arkeologiske skrifter* 2: 7–48. Bergen, Historisk Museum.

1988. *Helleristningane på Hammer i Beitstad, Steinkjer, Nord-Trøndelag. Granskingar i 1977 og 1981.* Trondheim, Vitenskapsmuseet. Rapport arkeologisk serie 7.

Baoudou, E. 1989. Stability and long term changes in north Swedish prehistory: an example of centre-periphery relations, in T. B. Larsson and H. Lundmark (eds.), *Approaches to Swedish prehistory,* pp.

27–53. Oxford, British Archaeological Reports. International Series 500.

Bouissac, P. 1994. Art or script? A falsifiable semiotic hypothesis, *Semiotica* 100–2/4: 349–67.

Brøgger, A. W. 1906. Elg og ren paa helleristninger i det nordlige Norge, *Naturen* 1906: 356–60.

Burenhult, G. 1980. *Götalands hällristningar.* Stockholm, Theses and Papers in North European Archaeology 10.

Christensen, A. E. 1985. *Boat finds from Bryggen.* Bergen, Universitetsforlaget. The Bryggen papers, main series 1.

Coll, A. L. 1902. Fra helleristningernes omraade (andet stykke), *FNFB aarsberetning* 1902: 106–40.

Ekholm, G. 1916. De skandinaviska hällristningarna och deras betydelse, *Ymer* 1916: 275–308.

Fett, E. and P. Fett. 1941. *Sydvestnorske helleristninger. Rogaland og Lista.* Stavanger, Stavanger Museum.

1979. Relations west Norway – western Europe documented in petroglyphs, *Norwegian Archaeological Review* 12: 66–92.

Gjessing, G. 1935. Die Chronologie der Schiffdarstellungen auf den Felsenzeichnungen zu Bardal, *Acta Archaeologica* 6: 125–39.

1936. *Nordenfjelske ristninger og malinger av den arktiske gruppe.* Oslo, Aschehoug. Inst. for sml. kulturforskning serie B 30.

Hafsten, U. 1987. Vegetasjon, klima og landskapsutvikling i Trøndelag etter siste istid, *Norsk Geografisk Tidsskrift* 41: 101–20.

Hagen, A. 1969. *Studier i vestnorsk bergkunst: Ausevik i Flora.* Bergen, Årbok for Universitetet i Bergen. Humanistisk serie 1969: 3.

1976. *Bergkunst: Jegerfolkets helleristninger og malinger i norsk steinalder.* Oslo, Cappelen.

1990. *Helleristningar i Noreg.* Oslo, Det norske samlaget.

Hallström, G. 1938. *Monumental art of northern Europe 1: The Norwegian localities.* Stockholm, Thule.

Hansen, A. M. 1904. *Landnaam i Norge: en udsigt over bosætningens historie.* [Oslo,] Kristiania.

Helskog, K. 1984. Helleristningene i Alta i et tidsperspektiv – en geologisk og multivariabel analyse, in J. Sandnes, A. Kielland and I. Østerlie (eds.), *Folk og ressurser i nord,* pp. 47–60. Trondheim, Tapir.

1993. Fra tvangstrøyer til 90-åras pluralisme i helleristningsforskning, in *Nordic TAG: report from the third Nordic TAG conference 1990,* pp. 70–5. Bergen, Historisk Museum.

Hesjedal, A. 1994. The hunters' rock art in northern Norway: problems of chronology and interpretation, *Norwegian Archaeological Review* 27: 1–28.

Hodder, I. 1990. *The domestication of Europe.* Oxford, Blackwell.

Kjemperud, A. 1981. A shoreline displacement investigation from Frosta in Trondheimsfjorden, Nord-Trøndelag, Norway, *Norsk geologisk tidsskrift* 61: 11–15.

Larsen, G. Mandt. 1972. *Bergbilder i Hordaland: en undersøkelse av bildenes sammensetning, deres naturmiljø og kulturmiljø.* Bergen, Årbok for Universitetet i Bergen. Humanistisk serie 1970: 2.

Lindquist, K. 1994. *Fångstfolkets bilder: en studie av de nordfennoskandiska kunstanknutna jägarhällristningarna.* Stockholm, Arkeologiska institutionen. Theses and Papers in Archaeology, new series A 5.

Lossius, K. 1897. Helleristningen paa Bardal i Beitstaden, *FNFB aarsberetning* 1896: 145–9.

Malmer, M. P. 1981. *A chorological study of north European rock art.* Stockholm, Almquist and Wicksell. Kungl. Vitterhets Historie och Antikvitetsakademiens handlingar, antikvariska serien 31.

Marstrander, S. 1963. *Østfolds jordbruksristninger. Skjeberg.* Oslo, Universitetsforlaget. Inst. for sml. kulturstudier serie B 53.

1970. A newly discovered rock carving of Bronze Age type in central Norway, *Val Camonica symposium 1968*, pp. 261–8. Capo di Ponte (BS), Edizioni del Centro.

Møllenhus, K. R. 1968a. *To nye veideristninger fra Nordmøre og Romsdal.* Trondheim, DKNVS skrifter 1968: 3.

1968b. *Helleristningene på Holtås i Skogn.* Trondheim, DKNVS skrifter 1968: 4.

1975. Use of slate in the circumpolar region, in W. Fitzhugh (ed.), *Prehistoric maritime adaptations*, pp. 57–73. The Hague, Mouton.

Nordbladh, J. 1995. The history of Scandinavian rock art research as a corpus of knowledge and practice, in K. Helskog and B. Olsen (eds.), *Perceiving rock art: social and political perspectives*, pp. 23–34. Oslo, Novus. Inst. for sml. kulturforskning serie B 92.

Petersen, T. 1926. Nye fund fra det nordenfjellske Norges

helleristningsområde, *Finska fornminnesföreningens tidskrift* 36: 23–44.

Rygh, K. 1906. *En gravplads fra broncealderen.* Trondheim, DKNVS skrifter 1906: 1.

1908. *Helleristninger af den sydskandinaviske type i det nordenfjeldske Norge.* Trondheim, DKNVS skrifter 1908: 10.

Shetelig, H. 1922. *Primitive tider.* Bergen, John Grieg.

Skjelsvik, E. and E. Straume 1957. *Austrheimsteinen i Nordfjord. Et nytt bidrag til dateringen.* Bergen, Universitetet i Bergen Årbok historisk-antikvarisk rekke 1957: 1.

Sognnes, K. 1983. *Bergkunsten i Stjørdal: helleristningar og busetjing.* Trondheim, DKNVS Museet. Gunneria 45.

1987. *Bergkunsten i Stjørdal 2: Typologi og kronologi i Nedre Stjørdal.* Trondheim, Vitenskapsmuseet. Gunneria 56.

1989. Rock art at the Arctic circle: Arctic and agrarian rock engravings from Tjøtta and Vevelstad, Nordland, Norway, *Acta Archaeologica* 59: 67–90.

1990. *Bergkunsten i Stjørdal 3: Hegraristningane.* Trondheim, Vitenskapsmuseet. Gunneria 62.

1993. The role of rock art in the Bronze Age and Early Iron Age in Trøndelag, Norway, *Acta Archaeologica* 63: 157–88.

1994. Ritual landscapes: toward a reinterpretation of the Stone Age rock art of Trøndelag, Norway, *Norwegian Archaeological Review* 27: 29–50.

1995. The social context of rock art in Trøndelag, Norway: rock art at a frontier, in K. Helskog and B. Olsen (eds.), *Perceiving rock art: social and political perspectives*, pp. 130–45. Oslo, Novus. Inst. for sml. kulturforskning serie B 92.

1996. Dyresymbolikk i midt-norsk yngre steinalder, *Viking* 59: 25–44.

Sørensen, M. L. S. 1987. Material order and classification: the role of bronze objects in the transition from Bronze Age to Iron Age in Scandinavia, in I. Hodder (ed.), *The archaeology of contextual meanings*, pp. 90–101. Cambridge, Cambridge University Press.

Sveian, H. and L. Olsen. 1984. A shoreline displacement curve from Verdalsøra, Nord-Trøndelag, central Norway, *Norsk geologisk tidsskrift* 64: 27–38.

**Meredith Wilson**

# 10. Pacific rock-art and cultural genesis: a multivariate exploration

Although the European impact on the Pacific islands and islanders was late, awareness of rock-art in the contact period is – as usual – practically nil: we have to depend again on formal methods, although ethnography and ethno-history may offer informed accounts of its social context. A good chronology now for the human settlement of the Pacific islands offers a framework within which we can begin to set a chronology for its rock-art. A mathematical study of similarity between the rock-art motifs found in different regions offers a measure of distance between the images. By these formal means, a pattern of separation and closeness is developed, which can be matched against models developed from other archaeological information.

## Pacific rock-art and its study

Pacific rock-art (Fig. 10.1) is rarely incorporated into broad discussions of Pacific prehistory (Bellwood 1978; Clarke and Terrell 1978; Jennings 1979; Kirch 1984; Terrell 1986; Irwin 1992). Its marginal status derives from two distinct research problems:

- *Difficulty of access.* Rock-art recordings, often unpublished and interspersed throughout various archives and personal field journals, tend to be the by-product of 'broader archaeological, ethnographic or speleological exploration' or 'incidental observations by colonial administrators and other travellers' (Rosenfeld 1988: 119).

- *Incomparability.* Despite an increasing literature describing the rock-art from a number of regions (see, for instance, Roder 1959; Cox and Stasack 1970; Trotter and McCulloch 1971; Frimigacci and Monnin 1980; Millerstrom 1990; Lee 1992), the recordings are not easily compared because little or no attempt has been made to standardise recording methods.

The 'dispersed and disparate' nature of the recorded collection is one of the main reasons why there is an absence of inter-regional comparative rock-art studies. Another likely reason is a prevailing scepticism regarding the informative potential of comparative work, a view that there is no way of determining whether 'related cultural influences' or 'coincidence' accounts for the similarities between rock-art motifs. As Emory (1933: 177) stated: '[p]etroglyphs found to any extensive degree throughout Polynesia . . . are exceedingly simple and appear sporadically throughout the world. Little reliance can be put on them as constituting in themselves a proof of cultural contact. Even in the more elaborate figures possibilities of correspondence through coincidence is too great.'

This chapter presents results from a thesis that explored whether there is a unity in Polynesian rock-art which points to a shared ancestry. In general terms, Pacific rock-art consists of geometric and figurative (particularly anthropomorphic) motifs, many rare and/or localised. Both engravings and paintings are represented, with a majority of one or the other in most regions. There appears to be a greater number of engravings in the Pacific overall.

Because the nature of the information available is variable and limited, the analysis was conducted at the motif level. Multivariate techniques were used to explore the variation of motif types through space. Relative patterns of similarity and difference were observed and tested against models of cultural transformation proposed by Kirch (1984) and by Kirch and Green (1987). The results

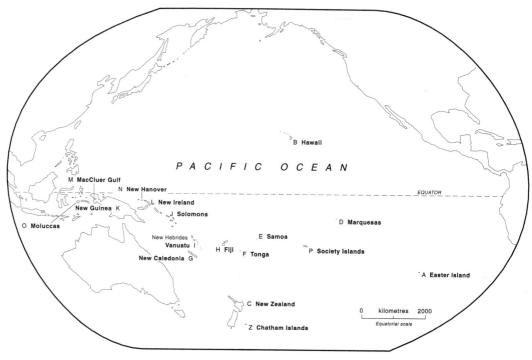

**Fig. 10.1.** The Pacific islands, with the groups used in the study.

force a reconsideration of some explanations for Pacific colonisation proposed by these authors.

This is the first broad-scale analysis of Pacific rock-art using multivariate statistics. Despite small samples and variable records that are hard to compare with one another, this technique has generated patterns which were successfully compared to models for Pacific colonisation.

## Models and issues in the archaeology of Pacific colonisation

The model of colonisation proposed by Kirch and Green (1987), i.e. the 'phylogenetic model of evolution', is founded on a notion of cultural continuity, whereby an underlying cultural substrate in Polynesia, a 'phylogenetic' unit, is traceable to an origin somewhere in South-east Asia. Kirch and Green's procedure for testing this model is as follows: the direction of Pacific colonisation is mapped using lexical reconstructions, and the temporal sequence

understood from dated archaeological deposits. Once branching patterns have been established, they may be explained by evolutionary theory, including the processes of divergence, parallelism and convergence.

Art is one cultural feature that has been examined by this set of procedures. In 1979, Green saw similar decorative elements on prehistoric Lapita pottery and on ethnographic examples of Polynesian barkcloth and tattooing surfaces as sharing inheritance by descendent populations. By the same approach, prototypes of persistent rock-art elements should be identifiable in the Pacific context.

Other models for cultural change in the Pacific during the period of exploration and initial human settlement (for instance Terrell 1988) avoid Kirch and Green's 'evolutionary approach', rejecting its implicit notion of cultural continuity. Because it provides a spatial and, more importantly, temporal framework, the phylogenetic model is the most appropriate for investigating similarities and differences in Pacific rock-art at this stage. It also provides a good point of departure from which to explore rock-art and Pacific prehistory in an integrative way.

Kirch's (1984) 'tripartite' model for Pacific colonisation relies on spatial and temporal regularities for linguistic, archaeological and ethnographic data to identify cultural prototypes. According to its underlying premises, material from the 'colonisation' or 'early' settlement phase of each island should bear closest resemblance to that found in the immediate dispersal region. Fig. 10.2 depicts the lines of variation connecting the series of spatial and temporal units Kirch describes.

Islands and island groups have been classified into five broad regions (indicated by bold rectangular boxes). Divisions reflect the temporal order of colonisation, each region colonised before the one below it in the diagram. Downward-pointing arrows indicate the easterly movement of the initial colonists. Sideways arrows denote inter-island contact and exchange after initial island settlement.

In Kirch and Green's (1987) extension of the tripartite model, an immediate Polynesian origin is proposed in the area of Tonga, Samoa, Futuna and Uvea. A more distant one, believed to exist somewhere in South-east Asia, is regarded as ancestral to the widespread Lapita culture of Island Melanesia.

It is suggested that evolutionary processes lead to patterns of *divergence, convergence* and *parallelism* within historically related groups between 'ancestral' and 'marginal' Polynesia. Key factors described by Kirch and Green (1987: 439–43) to explain divergence (the transmission of homologous traits) include:

- *Isolation*, a quantitative phenomenon, whereby different island groups transform in accordance with the level of isolation experienced. Relatively high isolation is proposed for the uniqueness of Easter Island compared to the archipelagos of Melanesia.
- The *founder effect*, when a small founding population transports an incomplete sample of their parent culture, resulting in rapid differentiation.
- *Colonisation processes*, the experimentation and in-

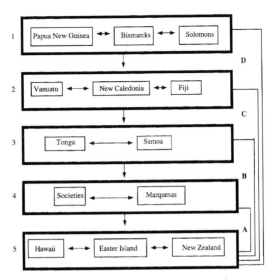

**Fig. 10.2.** The sequence of Pacific island settlement as described by Kirch (1984).

novation in cultural behaviour and technology that arise in adaptation to a new island environment.

- *Long-term environmental selection*, when environmental conditions (for instance, cyclones) and human modifications to the environment (for instance, deforestation) have a significant impact on cultural evolution.
- *External contact*, when people from outside introduce cultural traits.

Convergence occurs as a response to shared conditions (rather than shared origins). Traits which signify a convergent evolution are analogous rather than homologous, arising as a result of similar functional traits.

Parallelism follows from selection pressures on founding populations. If the founding populations of two island regions are small, they may experience parallel evolutionary sequences with regard to reproductive strategies or other mechanisms of population control.

This research aimed to test two features of the phylogenetic model using the results of multivariate analyses: (1) the temporal and spatial sequence of colonisation within and between island groups, and

(2) processes of divergence operating within and between island groups:

1 Kirch (1984) distinguishes two phases of Polynesian history: 'colonisation' and 'expansion and intensification'. The model states that material derived from the colonisation phase should most closely resemble its nearest ancestral form. The colonising rock-art of Easter Island should be most similar to that of a dispersal point locatable in region 4 (Fig. 10.2). In this diagram, where A, B, C and D represent degrees of similarity, A should be greater than B, B greater than C, and so on.

   If locales within region 4 acted as dispersal centres for islands in region 5, the rock-art motifs from the earliest cultural phases of islands within region 5 should resemble each other. As populations adapted to their new island environment and became increasingly different from the homeland, their rock-art should also have changed (albeit at varying rates), retaining fewer homeland traits in favour of localised 'styles'.

2 Since processes of divergence are built into the model, varying degrees of homogeneity between island rock-art should be explicable. In regions 1 and 2, interaction and communication between island groups was purportedly greater than in regions 4 and 5 as a result of inter-island visibility. In Polynesia, the distance between islands impeded interaction so much that certain groups of founding colonists are believed to have been isolated throughout their settlement histories. Where this was the case, degrees of homogeneity in the rock-art should reflect differing degrees of island interchange. Broadly speaking, rock-art from regions 1 and 2 should be more homogeneous than that from regions 4 and 5, where factors of isolation and 'founder-effect' are more acute.

A problem with Kirch and Green's use of the phylogenetic model is its reliance on linguistics to define culture units, for one does not know whether material culture has the same 'coherence' and 'transmissibility' as language (Pawley and Ross 1993: 426). In judging the applicability of the phylogenetic model to rock-art, we need to recognise that linguistic studies focus on form and structure to define linguistic groupings, not on speech (the culturally meaningful use of language). As witnessed by semiotic analyses of 'visual phenomena' using linguistic models (Kechagia 1995: 110), rock-art is more properly compared to speech than language. As Sonesson (1989: 17, in Kechagia 1995) explains: 'It was rather Barthes (notably in 1964) and the French structuralists generally, who conceived of semiotics as a simple transposition of the concepts developed for linguistics by Saussure and Hjelmslev to other domains. Since then the linguistic model seems to have been universally rejected, either explicitly or through the redefining of once linguistic terms.' The rock-art patterns generated for this study conflict with linguistic patterns: the correspondence result for rock-art patterns reveals a greater degree of heterogeneity in Polynesia than in Melanesia, while linguistic patterns suggest the opposite.

## The multivariate analysis

### Choosing the material for study

A degree of temporal control is available for this study by taking the earliest archaeological dates for a human presence on the various island groups as a measure of the maximum age of a regional rock-art body. It remains difficult to establish whether Pacific rock-art is affiliated with non-Austronesian or Austronesian peoples, or situated within the approximate temporal frameworks of pre-Lapita (10,000–3600/3200 BP), Lapita (3600/3200–2500/2000 BP), post-Lapita (2500/2000–750 BP) or 'late prehistory' (750 BP until sustained European contact about 150/100 BP) (Spriggs 1993: 188). If the Melanesian rock-art examined in this study belongs to the post-Lapita period, it is unlikely to manifest prototypes for Polynesian rock-art, which presumably derives from a Lapita cultural base. Both Polynesian and post-Lapita Melanesian rock-art, however, may share a Lapita ancestry.

The notion that Pacific rock-art is an Austronesian phenomenon, initiated during the Lapita period, has found considerable favour. Ballard (1988: 155, 1992) reports that the motifs on Kai Kecil (the westernmost sample included in this study) bear stylistic and other resemblances to rock-art sites elsewhere in Irian Jaya, as well as Melanesia. Ballard (1988: 156) attributes these resemblances to a tradition confined 'culturally to Austronesian speaking enclaves . . . locationally to sea cliffs, with a preference for high visibility and some difficulty of access, and a loose association with local mortuary rituals'.

The existence of a rock-art tradition in the Pacific has been suggested by a number of scholars (Rosenfeld 1988; Roe 1992; Ewins 1995). Ewins (1995: 25) contends that the motifs from a cliff-painting site on Vatulele in Fiji bear signs of this tradition, and also exhibit certain stylistic affinities with rock-art in Polynesia: 'It is suggested here that there are a number of stylistic affinities between various of the Vatulele images and their counterparts in Polynesian art, and Proto-Polynesian and Polynesian presence in Fiji is discussed as providing possible authorship of the paintings.' By this view, a broad analysis should reveal a stylistically affiliated rock-art corpus that extends from Kai Kecil in Indonesia to the marginal islands of east Polynesia.[1]

Prior rock-art analyses, intra- rather than inter-regional, have been conducted with regionally specific research; the rock-art records are therefore not

Table 10.1. *Rock-art regions*

| Code | Region |
| --- | --- |
| A | Easter Island |
| B | Hawaii |
| C | New Zealand |
| D | Hatiheu Valley, Nuku Hiva (Marquesas) |
| E | Leone, Tutuila Island; Fitiuta, Ta'u Island (American Samoa) |
| F | Telekitonga (Tonga) |
| G | New Caledonia |
| H | Fiji |
| I | Vanuatu |
| J | Solomons |
| K | Tabar (New Ireland) |
| L | Goodenough Bay; Sogeri District and Port Moresby hinterland (New Guinea) |
| M | Pulao Ogar, Pulau Arguni, MacCluer Gulf (Irian Jaya) |
| N | New Hanover |
| O | Kai Kecil (Moluccas) |
| P | Society Islands |
| Z | Chatham Islands |

made in the same way. Consistent information about the site context and the arrangement of motifs on a rock surface is lacking. This study is therefore restricted to measuring similarity at the 'motif' level.

The data used derive from recordings of rock-art motifs from a diverse range of Pacific island regions in Near and Remote Oceania, extending from Kai Kecil (Moluccas) in the west to Easter Island in the east (see Fig. 10.1 and Table 10.1). The art includes engravings and paintings, as well as a small number of dendroglyphs (carvings on wood) from the Chatham Islands in New Zealand.

*Methods of analysis: defining motifs, sampling questions, and the focus on anthropomorphs and geometrics*

Initially a formal typology was constructed on the basis of published field illustrations for 2730[2] motifs. Motif categories were defined by shape criteria deriving from the principles of two-dimensional plane geometry (see Clegg 1995; Hagen 1986).

---

[1] There is continuing debate as to whether Austronesian people, claimed as responsible for the rock-art 'tradition' described by Ballard, were also responsible for the initiation of the 'Lapita Culture Complex': was this complex introduced into Near Oceania by Austronesian people or did it evolve out of a pre-existing cultural milieu (Terrell 1986)? Rather than attributing the entire complex to one people, some believe (Spriggs 1996) that the Lapita Cultural Complex is a hybrid of pre-existing and introduced features. The tradition Ballard identifies belongs to the 'late' Austronesian period. This may explain the existence of two different types of rock-art media in the Pacific – the paintings and the engravings. If the 'late' tradition involved painting, perhaps an earlier group of Austronesian-speaking people is responsible for the engravings found across the Pacific – which would account for their profusion in the remote islands of Polynesia.

[2] This figure excludes cup-marks (cupules), the most frequently observed petroglyphs in the Pacific, and motifs which are not illustrated in published records.

Only two categories were sufficiently frequent for multivariate analysis – anthropomorphs and geometrics. The remaining shape categories were found to be numerically dominant in localised areas – itself a telling trend which is discussed below in conjunction with the multivariate results.

The combined total of the two types (anthropomorphs and geometrics) represented over 50 per cent of each regional sample.

Sampling problems arose from the relatively disproportionate representation of anthropomorphs and geometrics between regions; there is just one anthropomorph from Tonga, and 158 from the Marquesas. Nevertheless, small samples were included because there was no means of determining how representative of a region's entire motif range they might be. If the geology of Tonga is unsuitable for creating rock-art, the single anthropomorph recorded for this region could well be the only one that exists. These numerical variations affect a multivariate distribution as the analytical contribution of smaller samples is inevitably limited.

In the study, as many attributes were used as could reasonably be discerned, so that a data-set sufficiently large for further manipulation was achieved, and there would be some protection from bias arising from too few attributes (Tratebas 1993; Taçon, Wilson and Chippindale 1996). The correspondence patterns generated from the 'selected set' of attributes were tested with statistical significance procedures (see Wilson 1994).

Attribute lists, devised with specific 'selection criteria' in mind (see Maynard 1977), were revised as the varied nature and quality of the published sources required. Separate lists for anthropomorphs and geometrics describe the content and structure of each: *content* refers to the individual elements which combine as motifs; and *structure* to the manner in which elements are combined in two-dimensional space.

Attributes of anthropomorphs include shapes named in accordance with the anatomical feature they are identified with, for instance 'nose'. These

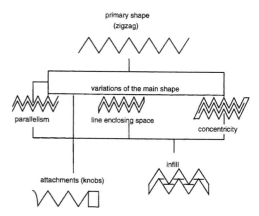

Fig. 10.3. Structural systems used to explore variation in geometrics.

anatomical features were further described according to their form, for instance 'infilled'. Attributes describing geometrics were based on a structural system devised to reveal variations within and between sets of primary shapes (see Fig. 10.3), and to differentiate between:

1 primary shapes
2 characteristics peculiar to certain primary shapes
3 characteristics shared by all primary shapes (see Fig. 10.4).

Each geometric and anthropomorph is described in binary terms (ones and zeros): a one indicates the presence of an attribute, and a zero, the absence. Data in this format are analogous to 'multiple-choice' in the standard form (see Table 10.2) (Nishisato 1994: 24). There are a set of questions: Q1, Q2, Q3, etc., but only one positive (1) answer is possible for any one object. When a set of questions relates to the 'head' of an anthropomorph, the set of possible answers includes 'round', 'square' and 'triangular': a '1' is recorded for the appropriate option, and '0' for the remainder.

The multivariate statistical technique of 'correspondence analysis' (CA) was selected as the most suitable to explore similarities and differences within the data (Wright 1992; Benzecri 1992; Nishisato 1994). The correspondence algorithm measures the chi-squared relationship between variables (at-

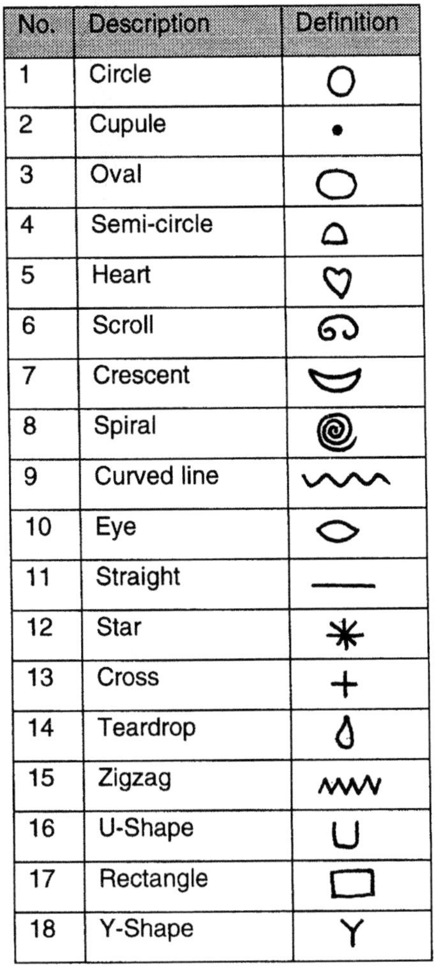

| No. | Description | Definition |
|---|---|---|
| 1 | Circle | O |
| 2 | Cupule | • |
| 3 | Oval | O |
| 4 | Semi-circle | △ |
| 5 | Heart | ♡ |
| 6 | Scroll | ᧓ |
| 7 | Crescent | ‿ |
| 8 | Spiral | ◎ |
| 9 | Curved line | ∿∿ |
| 10 | Eye | ◇ |
| 11 | Straight | — |
| 12 | Star | ✳ |
| 13 | Cross | + |
| 14 | Teardrop | ◊ |
| 15 | Zigzag | ∧∧∧ |
| 16 | U-Shape | U |
| 17 | Rectangle | ▭ |
| 18 | Y-Shape | Y |

**Fig. 10.4.** Geometric primary shapes.

Table 10.2. *Multiple-choice data*

| Question | | 1 | | | 2 | | 3 | | |
|---|---|---|---|---|---|---|---|---|---|
| Option | | 1 | 2 | 3 | 1 | 2 | 1 | 2 | 3 |
| Subject | 1 | 1 | 0 | 0 | 1 | 0 | 0 | 0 | 1 |
| | 2 | 0 | 1 | 0 | 1 | 0 | 1 | 0 | 0 |
| | 3 | 1 | 0 | 0 | 0 | 1 | 0 | 1 | 0 |
| | . | . | . | . | . | . | . | . | . |
| | . | . | . | . | . | . | . | . | . |
| | $n$ | 0 | 0 | 1 | 0 | 1 | 1 | 0 | 0 |

After Nishisato (1994: table 3.3: 2.6).

Table 10.3. *Distribution of anthropomorphs*

| Code | Region | Total |
|---|---|---|
| A | Easter Island | 14 |
| B | Hawaii | 40 |
| C | New Zealand | 38 |
| D | Marquesas | 70 |
| E | Samoa | 1 |
| F | Tonga | 1 |
| G | New Caledonia | 13 |
| H | Fiji | 3 |
| I | Vanuatu | 1 |
| J | Solomons | 3 |
| K | New Ireland | 8 |
| L | East New Guinea | 5 |
| M | MacCluer Gulf | 14 |
| O | Moluccas | 4 |
| P | Society Islands | 4 |
| Z | Chatham Islands | 5 |

tributes) and objects (anthropomorphs and geometrics). The generated scores are represented as scattergrams, one for objects and another for variables, with the relative distances between points making a measure of similarity.

**Correspondence analysis for anthropomorphs**
The analysis of anthropomorphs measured correspondence between 224 anthropomorphs and 169 variables. Table 10.3 lists the number of anthropomorphs from each island region included in the

analysis. Figs. 10.5 and 10.6 present the scatterplots of correspondence scores for objects and variables in the space of the first two correspondence axes. The phenetic correspondence between anthropomorphs in Graph 1 reveals many anthropomorphs aggregating according to their region of origin.

Eastern and central Polynesian anthropomorphs dominate the graph plane and demarcate the boundaries of the scatter. New Zealand anthropomorphs,

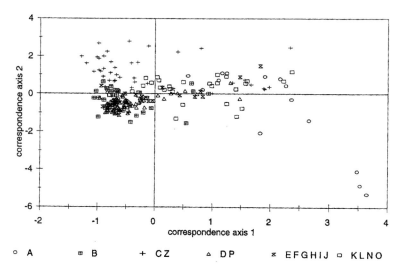

**Fig. 10.5.** Correspondence between 224 anthropomorphs.

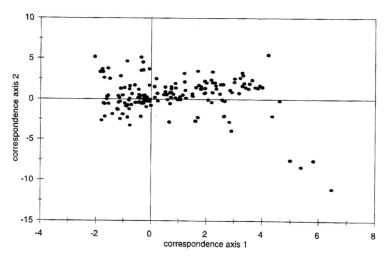

**Fig. 10.6.** Anthropomorphs: correspondence between 169 variables.

predominantly located in the top left quadrat, are the most isolated and homogeneous group. A few Chatham Island dendroglyphs are situated between > 1 (CA axis 1) and < 1, > − 1 (CA axis 2). A single New Zealand outlier (Fig. 10.7), in the top right-hand corner of the distribution, is distinguished by two unique factors: it is the only anthropomorphic specimen included in this analysis that

derives from the North Island, and the only engraved specimen in the entire New Zealand sample.

Easter Island anthropomorphs are represented by an attribute range which – relative to all other specimens – is most unlike New Zealand. Two approximate groups can be identified: the first of three samples located near the periphery of the lower right quadrat are depictions of the distinctive and monu-

**Fig. 10.8.** Easter Island: engraved depiction of *moai* statues. After Lee (1992: fig. 4.15.1:55)

**Fig. 10.7.** New Zealand outlier: engraving from the North Island.
After Furey (1989: fig. 3, 187).

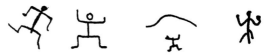

**Fig. 10.10.** Stick figures.
(*left*) Hawaii. After Cox and Stasack (1970: fig. 38, 30)
(*centre left*) Marquesas. After Millerstrom (1990): fig. 8, 35).
(*centre right*) Society Islands. After Navarro (1987).
(*right*) New Caledonia. After Monnin (1986: fig. 4.18, 22).

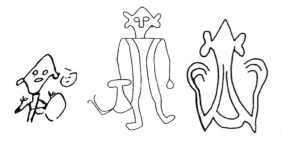

**Fig. 10.9.** Easter Island and Tabar, New Ireland: corresponding engravings.
(*left*) Tabar. After Gunn (1986: fig. 5, 458).
(*centre, right*) Easter Island. After Lee (1992: fig. 4.12, 52; fig. 4.14a, 54).

mental *moai* statues (Lee 1992) (Fig. 10.8); the second includes the remaining Easter Island specimens which share attributes with certain Melanesian specimens, such as 'pointed heads' and 'facial features' (Fig. 10.9).

Anthropomorphs from Hawaii, the Marquesas, the Society Islands and New Caledonia form an interspersed but highly aggregated group in the lower left-hand area of the graph. These inter-regional correlations appear to result from the regular reproduction of 'stick figures', with similar attributes (Fig. 10.10). A statistical significance test confirmed the integrity of this aggregation.

Encircled in Figure 10.11[3] are a number of Hawaiian specimens which do not quite conform to the pattern of invariance characterising 'stick figures'. These figures, converging slightly on the lower scoring New Zealand specimens, are principally located just above or below '0' on the second CA axis. Statistical correlation with this variable group is contingent on a specimen possessing outlined or solidly infilled 'torsos', usually triangular in shape (Fig. 10.12).

Specimens closest to the intersection of the two correspondence axes share the trait of a solid or double outlined 'torso' (Fig. 10.13). In detail, the coherent group of Marquesan, Hawaiian, Society Island and New Caledonian specimens can be inter-

[3] This graph differs slightly from Fig. 10.5 because it is the result of an earlier analysis which excluded samples from the Society Islands, the MacCluer Gulf, the Chatham Islands and the Moluccas. There was no difference in the overall results when these samples were added.

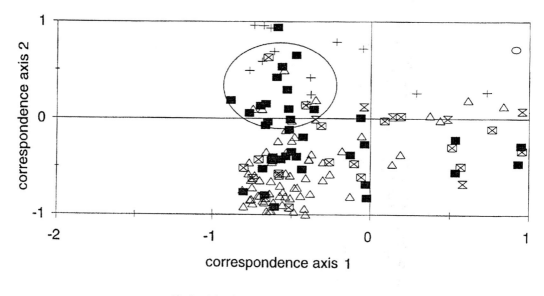

○ Easter Island
■ Hawaii
+ New Zealand
△ Marquesas
⊠ Tonga, Samoa, New Caledonia, Fiji, Vanuatu
⊠ New Ireland, East New Guinea

**Fig. 10.11.** Location of Hawaiian anthropomorphs with inverted triangular torsos.

nally divided on the basis of how 'stick-like' a specimen is. In the lower left quadrant, increased distance from the central origin reveals specimens with an increased number of stick-like features.

An important marker of these 'stick figures' is their high degree of clustering; the relatively close proximity between points is a measure of the stereotyped way images of this group repeat a standard formula of attributes.

The point of convergence on this graph is the central origin, where a suite of variables characterises a number of regionally diverse specimens. Two central, or 'pivotal', traits – the solid 'torso' and outlined 'torso' – appear to direct how inter-regional similarities are revealed by the correspondence algorithm. The single Tongan and Samoan samples have low scores, as do the three Fijian

specimens. Each, marked by a solid or double outlined torso, is situated close to an array of regionally diverse samples (see Fig. 10.10). Low-scoring New Zealand specimens, not bearing traits distinctive of their place of origin, interact with similarly low-scoring Hawaiian and Melanesian specimens (Fig. 10.13).

The relatively dispersed nature of points on the right-hand side of the graph indicates a high degree of variation. This regionally diverse group derives mainly from Kai Kecil, the MacCluer Gulf, Goodenough Bay (New Guinea) and New Ireland in the west, and from Easter Island and Chatham Islands in the east. Similarities are evident between, for instance, the MacCluer Gulf and the Chatham Islands. These figures also have solid or outlined torsos, but are separated from this group by how they display

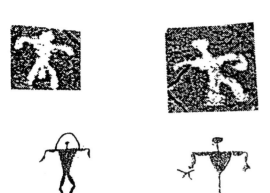

**Fig. 10.14.** Anthropomorphs with facial features.
(*left*) MacCluer Gulf. After Roder (1959).
(*centre*) Kai Kecil. After Ballard (1988: fig. 7.3i).
(*right*) Chatham Islands. After Jefferson (1956: front cover).

**Fig. 10.12.** Hawaiian anthropomorphs with inverted triangular torsos.
From Cox and Stasack (1970: upper left, fig. 5, 9; upper right, fig. 5, 9; lower left, fig. 23, 18; lower right, fig. 7, 38).

facial features (Fig. 10.14). Regionalism is not apparent.

## Correspondence analysis for geometrics

Three primary shapes, the circle, oval and straight line, were selected for independent analysis as they are represented in most regional areas in sufficient numbers.

Another analysis tested the correspondence between the entire geometric sample, comprising 436 motifs (Table 10.4).

**Fig. 10.13.** Anthropomorphs with solid or outlined torsos.
(*top left*) Fiji. After Ewins (1995: fig. 2, 43).
(*top centre*) Marquesas. After Millerstrom (1990: fig. 16, 53).
(*top right*) Solomon Islands. After Roe (1992: fig. 16, 127).
(*centre left*) New Zealand. After Ambrose (1970: fig. 5c, 397).
(*centre right*) Hawaii. After Cox and Stasack (1970: fig. 25, 18).
(*lower left*) Tonga. After Palmer (1965: fig. 1, 36).
(*lower right*) Samoa. After Kikucki (1967: fig. 1, 372).

Table 10.4. *Frequency distribution of geometrics*

| Code | Region | Total[1] | % |
|---|---|---|---|
| A | Easter Island | 71 | 12 |
| B | Hawaii | 31 | 5 |
| C | New Zealand | 25 | 4 |
| D | Marquesas | 12 | 2 |
| E | Samoa | 18 | 3 |
| F | Tonga | 7 | 1 |
| G | New Caledonia | 122 | 21 |
| H | Fiji | 21 | 4 |
| I | Vanuatu | 35 | 6 |
| J | Solomons | 112 | 20 |
| K | Tabar, New Ireland | 14 | 2 |
| L | East New Guinea | 36 | 6 |
| M | MacCluer Gulf | 24 | 4 |
| O | Moluccas | 15 | 3 |
| P | Society Islands | 15 | 3 |

[1]Total reduced to 436 after identical motifs were omitted.

Identical motifs (those consisting of the same number and types of variables) within regions are omitted from the sample. For this study, the *frequencies* of identical motifs are important as they provide an independent measure of variation which was tested against the multivariate results.[4]

### Circles

The correspondence result for the circle motif is generated from a sample of 122 objects and 53 variables. The correspondence algorithm produces very low scores for most of the sample – seen as a highly aggregated and overlapping cluster at 0.1 on the first correspondence axis (see Figure 10.15).

An 'outlier' response of this kind – where the algorithm emphasises 'rare attributes that occur with objects that are otherwise bare of attributes' (Wright 1992: 31) – is common for multiple-choice data (Nishisato 1994: 293). One response is to omit the rare attributes that might mask variation within the main cluster. When correspondence was tested for a data-set reduced that way, to 101 objects and 46 variables, the 'disproportionate' effect of the first result was reduced (see Figure 10.16).

An important observation is made when 'rare' attributes and their corresponding objects are omitted prior to the second analysis. Most of the rare objects are found to derive from Polynesia (areas A, B, C, D, E, F, P), suggesting that Polynesian geometric circle motifs are regionally distinct (see, for example, Fig. 10.17). Omitting eastern Pacific attributes and objects alters the relative patterns of similarity and difference between Polynesian and Melanesian geometric motifs. The first result indicates a high degree of similarity between Melanesian specimens compared to locally distinct and unique Polynesian specimens. The second result shows increase in variation occurring because much of the Polynesian sample is discarded, and there is a concomitant shift in the scale at which spatial variation is observed.

[4] Because identical motifs share the same score they appear overlapping on a multivariate plot.

Despite increased variation in patterns generated from the second analysis, there is still *an absence of correlation between the correspondence axes and region*. Instead, the patterns reflect similarities according to structural affiliations between the infill and appendages of circle motifs.

The result for circles is repeated by the analysis for ovals and for straight lines (graphs not shown): rare attributes are emphasised; they derive principally from Polynesian rock-art assemblages; and regionalism is not apparent.

### All geometrics

The final test on the entire geometric sample calculates the correspondence between 436 objects and 164 variables. The result (Figure 10.18) shows five main groups separated from a dense cluster around the axes' centroid (0,0). Each separate group, represented as a lineal point scatter away from the central origin, is defined by a single primary shape. Objects furthest from the central origin manifest variables unique to their primary shapes; objects close to the central origin embody variables shared by more than one primary shape. Once again, there is an absence of correlation between the correspondence axes and region. Instead, these patterns indicate differences between primary shapes.

## Patterns in Pacific rock-art

### Phenetics

One type of similarity relation used by numerical taxonomists (Sokal 1968; Sokal and Sneath 1963) to describe correlations between living creatures is phenetics, defined by the overall similarity among specimens to be classified (Fig. 10.19). Since no strategy is known for fairly weighting characters according to their evolutionary importance, similarity is defined here by the phenetic relations between many correlating attributes, without differential weighting of certain attributes over others. Clinal variations in motif construction were investigated once the phenetic similarities had been established from multivariate patterns.

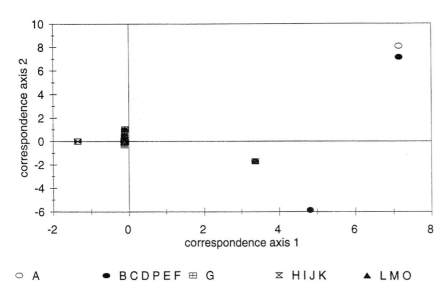

**Fig. 10.15.** Correspondence between 122 circles.

A Easter Island.
B Hawaii, C New Zealand, D Marquesas, P Society Islands, E Samoa, F Tonga.
G New Caledonia.
H Fiji, I Vanuatu, J Solomon Islands, K New Ireland.
L East New Guinea, M MacCluer Gulf, O Moluccas.

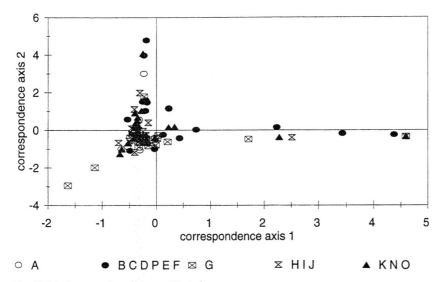

**Fig. 10.16.** Correspondence between 101 circles.

A Easter Island.
B Hawaii, C New Zealand, D Marquesas, P Society Islands, E Samoa, F Tonga.
G New Caledonia.
H Fiji, I Vanuatu, J Solomon Islands.
K New Ireland, N New Hanover, O Kai Kecil (Moluccas).

**Fig. 10.17.** Rare circle motifs from Polynesia.
(*left*) Easter Island. After Lee (1992: fig. 4.63, 81).
(*right*) Marquesas. After Millerstrom (1990: fig. 24, 67).

The *significance* of similarities between geometrics and anthropomorphs is measured according to degrees of 'polytypic aggregation': large numbers of corresponding attributes and objects (Davis 1990: 20). Phenetic and frequency correlations are, therefore, mutually assessed.

Polytypic aggregations are most evident in the results for anthropomorphs, an example being the overall correlation between a large number of both variables and objects from Hawaii and the Marquesas. Figs. 10.20 and 10.21 are the approximate inter-regional correspondence results for anthropomorphs and geometrics according to colonisation time.[5]

Are clinal variations evident in these two figures? The immediate impression is that those islands settled before Easter Island, New Zealand and Hawaii *do* contain prototype rock-art elements for both anthropomorphs and geometrics; an east–west clinal distribution is evident. On the correspondence graphs, similarities tend to decrease further away from the central origin. Samples that occupy the outer areas are generally central or marginal Polynesian; they aggregate with other members of their region of origin.

Discrepancies appear when the phenetic results are examined against the frequency results. Whereas the statistical correlations between anthropomorphic specimens display Easter Island and New Zealand as *polar* groups, the frequency results indicate that both regions share an equally large proportion of anthropomorphs within their respective motif repertoires. In contrast, the high degree of statistical correlation between geometrics in the west is *complemented* by the relative numerical dominance of geometrics in this region. It appears that the similarities between geometric motifs incorporate a much broader geographical unit than the arbitrary zones specified in Fig. 10.2.

This result may be interpreted in two ways. First, the homogeneity of geometric motifs from the western Pacific is a reflection of high degrees of inter-island exchange and communication across this broad region. Second, the result of homogeneity is affected by the small number of variables which describe geometrics. The difference between geometrics may be a matter of one variable, whereas anthropomorphs can be separated by ten or more. Since geometrics are described by fewer variables than anthropomorphs, they are predisposed to producing patterns showing greater homogeneity. I am reluctant to attribute the pattern of geometric invariance in the rock-art of regions to the west of Polynesia to inter-island exchange given that geometrics are inclined to cluster – with this analytical method – according to primary shape rather than their region of origin.

The results of the frequency analysis for both anthropomorphs and geometrics suggest three main regional groupings:

1 Islands of Remote and Near Oceania as far east as Vanuatu and New Caledonia: correspondingly high proportional frequencies of geometrics and low numbers of anthropomorphs.

2 Fiji, Tonga and Samoa: overall lack of either motif type, but particularly depictions of anthropomorphs.

---

[5] The correspondence graphs show the phenetic relations between *individual motifs*. Figs. 10.20 and 10.21 show the 'approximate' phenetic relations between *regional groups*. Ideally, the mean value for each region is calculated for a more precise representation of inter-regional similarity, but the statistical program used for this study was only capable of calculating mean values for six groups at a time.

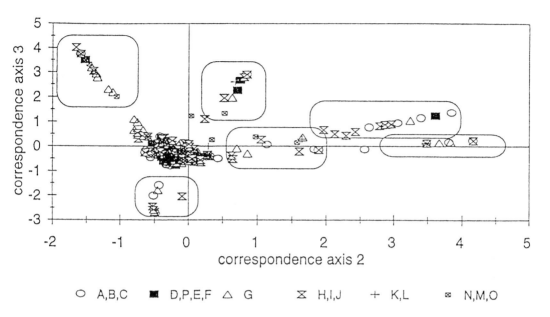

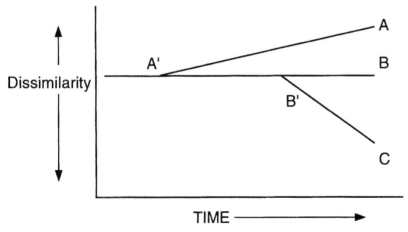

**Fig. 10.18.** Correspondence between all geometrics.
A Easter Island, B Hawaii, C New Zealand.
D Marquesas, P Society Islands, E Samoa, F Tonga.
G New Caledonia.
H Fiji, I Vanuatu, J Solomons.
K New Ireland, L East New Guinea.
N New Hanover, M MacCluer Gulf, O Moluccas.

**Fig. 10.19.** Phenetic relationships.
Phenetically, specimen B is more closely related to specimen A than it is to specimen C, even though C evolved much later than A as a branch of B.
After Sokal (1968: 176).

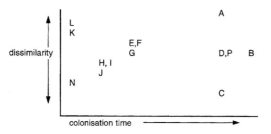

Fig. 10.20. Regional phenetic relationships for anthropo-
morphs.
N New Hanover.
L East New Guinea, K New Ireland.
H Fiji, I Vanuatu, J Solomon Islands.
E Samoa, F Tonga, G New Caledonia.
C New Zealand.
D Marquesas, P Society Islands.
A Easter Island.
B Hawaii.

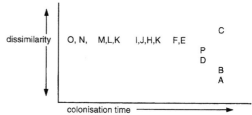

Fig. 10.21. Regional phenetic relationships for geometrics.
O Moluccas, N New Hanover.
M MacCluer Gulf, L East New Guinea, K New Ireland.
I Vanuatu, J Solomon Islands, H Fiji, K New Ireland.
F Tonga, E Samoa.
P Society Islands, D Marquesas.
A Easter Island, B Hawaii.
C New Zealand.

3 Islands of central and east Polynesia: correspondingly large proportion of anthropomorphs.[6]

*Broad-scale patterns*

Some attributes are common to a large portion of the
sample, either because they are real to the subject (for
example, legs are present on anthropomorphs) or
they are markers of the modification which occurs
when a three-dimensional image is transformed into
two dimensions (for example, profile in anthropomorphs). Commonality can cause objects to gravitate
towards the central origin, a trend seen in the correspondence results for circles. Circles constituted by a
common set of attributes form a highly aggregated
cluster close to the central origin. Regionally distinct

objects (mostly from Polynesia), plotting on the
outer edges of the graph, mask difference and/or
regionalism in the main cluster. So regionalism is
most apparent for objects located furthest away from
the central origin.

Regionalism, mainly observed in the patterning
for anthropomorphs, is shown by a set of distinctive
traits repeatedly manifest in objects from remote
island groups. The central origin can be viewed as a
point of departure – the earliest point in the colonisation process. Outwards from this point, modification
over time can be observed.

Read from this temporal perspective, the broad-
scale multivariate patterns – particularly for anthropomorphs – satisfy the predictions of Kirch and
Green's model, supporting the proposition that *Polynesian cultures form a phylogenetic unit deriving from a
common ancestor in South-east Asia.* Meaningful similarities are found close to the central origin, and meaningful differences are found further away. Certain
features common to a group of marginal Polynesian
specimens, such as the New Zealand 'flexed leg' or
'buttressed junction', are located close to the central
origin because they are also found in small numbers
in regions settled much earlier in the colonisation
process (see Fig. 10.22). These traits may have been
successively transmitted in an evolutionary process

[6] This tripartite division of island clusters is based on a count of
observed rock-art motifs rather than distribution figures quoted
in texts. Apparently circle forms constitute at least 60 per cent of
the motif range found in the Hatiheu valley on Nuku Hiva, in
the Marquesas (Millerstrom 1994: pers. comm.), a percentage
ratio quite unlike that tested in this study. However, a brief re-
examination of the frequency distributions described for assemblages recorded in Island Melanesia (see, for example:
McDonalds and Haskovec 1992) reveals that the primary difference between the three broad regions defined here is in terms of
the proportional numbers of anthropomorphs, which are still far
greater in the east.

**Fig. 10.22.** 'Flexed leg' and 'buttressed junction' anthropomorphs from New Zealand and elsewhere.
(*left*) New Zealand. After Ambrose (1970: fig. 5c, 397).
(*centre left*) Solomon Islands. After Roe (1992: fig. 16, 127).
(*centre right*) Kai Kecil. After Ballard (1988: fig. 7.3i).
(*right*) MacCluer Gulf. After Roder (1959).

of Oceanic settlement. Since both the 'flexed leg' and 'buttressed junction' share low correspondence scores (close to 0,0), it is possible that they existed prior to their efflorescence in the New Zealand rock-art context.

Although rock-art from the islands settled earliest in the colonisation sequence (in the west) consists of a diverse range of anthropomorphic designs, each individual depiction is made up of attributes also found in assemblages of central and east Polynesia. An absence of traits distinctive to western rock-art has resulted in a dispersed but interfused group with no evidence of regional clustering.

Is this result affected by the small samples of anthropomorphs from Melanesia and west Polynesia? Probably not. The locations of forms distinctive to Easter Island, New Zealand, Hawaii and the Marquesas – at coordinate points which define the peripheries of the entire distribution – support the notion that east Polynesian rock-art elements are the end product of an evolutionary process of *divergence from a common ancestor*.

Degrees of statistical similarity and difference be-

tween the motifs of different island groups, graphically represented as the relative overall distance between points, may be interpreted according to processes Kirch and Green use to explain divergence. The relatively isolated and diverse set of anthropomorphs from Easter Island might be explained by the effects of remoteness. The impression that the rock-art of Easter Island is the most different of the three marginal Polynesian groups is consistent with isolation as a 'quantitative phenomenon' (Kirch and Green 1987: 440).

Furthermore, relative degrees of statistical similarity across the Pacific are consistent with the proposal that isolation in the east produced difference (isolated intra-regional aggregations), and interactive processes in the west produced similarity (interspersed inter-regional aggregations).

*The attribute: a finer scale of analysis*
An important feature of the correspondence analysis results is the location of the attribute unit. Each attribute is variously configured with others to form motifs. On a correspondence graph, attributes tend

to be peripherally located if they are rare, and more central if they are common. Distance between one attribute and another is generally small if both are commonly depicted together within the same motif, large if they are a rare or unusual addition to a regular motif.

The impact of 'attribute' on the broad patterns is shown by the correspondence between anthropomorphs from Hawaii, the Marquesas and the Society Islands.[7] Close inspection of attributes 'distinctive' to this particular regional group, namely the 'stick figure', elucidates problems with Kirch and Green's 'continuity' argument.

The similarities between anthropomorphic depictions from these three regions can be accounted for cladistically. According to the phenetic relations revealed by the correspondence analyses, there is evidence for a cladistic relationship between the Society Islands, Hawaii and the Marquesas that satisfies the phylogenetic model. In the past, both the Marquesas and the Society Islands have been proposed as dispersal regions for the initial colonists of Hawaii (Cachola-Abad 1993); yet the correspondence between a significant number of attributes and objects from Hawaii and Marquesas suggests the primacy of the Marquesas as the immediate homeland of Hawaiian settlers.[8]

Society Island influence is not excluded, however. Despite the small sample of anthropomorphs from this region, it is quite feasible that the stick figure originated in the Societies. A present lack of absolute dates for the 'stick figure' makes it impossible to determine the direction of influence.

One model for the context of the east Polynesian rock-art is that of 'social interaction'. Founded on a theory of 'information exchange' (Wobst 1977), it views style (encoded in all material culture) in a 'functional as opposed to semiotic way' (McDonald 1994), the idea being that 'part of the formal variability in material culture . . . can be related to the participation of artefacts in the process of information exchange' (Wobst 1977: 321). This model presents, as extremes, 'closed' and 'open' social networks. Certain groups interact and communicate more than others: interaction and communication in an open system leads to similarity, isolation in a closed system leads to divergence.

The high degree of correspondence between Hawaiian and Marquesan anthropomorphs is suggestive of an 'open' cultural network that involved frequent inter-island interaction. The evidence from Easter Island – uniquely remote from other islands – supports this model in that isolation results in increasing cultural divergence.

A recent advance in Hawaiian rock-art research is the use of Accelerator Mass Spectrometry to date 13 of the 423 petroglyphs found on Kaho'olawe (Stasack et al. 1996). This identified two phases of rock-art production. The earliest phase, for which dates of around AD 1000 have been obtained, is characterised by the development of the stick figure (Fig. 10.10). On the correspondence graphs, these figures are found most closely to resemble stick figures from the Marquesas. A later phase, which began around AD 1300, is marked by the emergence of figures with inverted triangular torsos (Fig. 10.11). This group, described earlier as the 'divergent' Hawaiian group, is situated just above the stick figure group on the correspondence graph for anthropomorphs.

If these dates are reliable, and if the chronology identified for Kaho'olawe also applies to other Hawaiian island assemblages, then the model's prediction that the 'colonising' rock-art should be most similar to region B is affirmed.

But now we are faced with a slight problem. When Kirch and Green's model is founded on a notion of cultural continuity, and when the stick figure is one of the earliest rock-art motifs in Hawaii

---

[7] Even though New Caledonian specimens have clustered within the distribution of Hawaiian, Marquesan and Society Island specimens, the number of anthropomorphs from this region is too small to certify the existence of an evolutionary relationship.

[8] Georgia Lee (1994: pers. comm.), who has worked extensively on the rock-art of Easter Island and Hawaii, has commented on the interchangeable nature of Hawaiian and Marquesan stick figure forms. The statistical evidence presented here supports her field observations.

and possibly also the Marquesas, why are there no prototypes for the stick figure in Polynesia's ancestral regions? Given that Kirch and Green's model requires that alteration should be a progression from the preceding region, the noticeable absence of stick figure forms in Polynesia's immediate and more distant homelands is problematic.

Strangely, there appears to be a spatio-temporal continuum for the 'later' Hawaiian forms. The distinctively Hawaiian 'inverted triangular torso' is found in figures from both Tonga and Fiji (Fig. 10.13). Double-outlined rectangular torsos – found in Easter Island, the Marquesas, Hawaii and New Zealand – are also shared by western Polynesian and Island Melanesian forms (Fig. 10.13). Every figure displaying this trait is found at or near the central origin of the correspondence graph, described above as a point of convergence for figures exhibiting traits that have been successfully transmitted between regions.

Could this mean there was a second colonisation of Hawaii, with the attributes which denote the later triangular-bodied style introduced via this colonisation? If so, what are the origins of the stick figure? If the stick figure form was transported and reproduced by the first people to reach and colonise the Marquesas and Hawaii, it is unlikely that its origin lies in western Polynesia.

A reassessment of archaeological evidence from Hane in the Marquesas suggests that artefacts belonging to the early phase at this site lack west Polynesian prototypes, particularly the fish-hook assemblages. Accordingly, the authors 'prefer the view that Hane was settled by people who had not come directly from West Polynesia' (Anderson et al. 1994: 51).

Recent biological studies in the Pacific also question cultural associations between western Polynesia and the east. Pietrusewsky's (1996: 348) recent multivariate craniometric analyses reveal that, while most 'eastern Polynesian groups cluster in a logical manner . . . [w]hat requires further explanation is the association between Hawai'i and Tonga-Samoa, a group that runs contrary to conventional wisdom'.

An alternative, and perhaps more appropriate, explanation for the lack of stick figure prototypes is a prolonged gap in the colonisation sequence. It has been argued that successors of the Lapita culture remained in western Polynesia for a substantial period before continuing their settlement further east (Spriggs and Anderson 1993). The other model – 'fast train' or 'continuous settlement' with no gap (Irwin 1992; Kirch and Ellison 1994) – has recently been criticised on the basis of both archaeological and linguistic evidence. Extending a methodology of 'chronometric hygiene' on early settlement dates in Polynesia, Spriggs and Anderson (1993) argue for a pause of at least 1300 years between settlement of western Polynesia (3000 b.p.) and the earliest sites further east. Linguistic evidence provides further support for the cessation of settlement (for at least 1000 years) to account for the unification of the Polynesian language subgroup (Pawley 1996). For reasons unknown, the scant and regionally discrete rock-art from Samoa and Tonga suggest that the practice of marking rocks was uncommon in this region. If the central and east Polynesian populations reincorporated this practice after a gap of 1000 years, then a break in the transmission of rock-art traits between Melanesia and Polynesia is feasible (presuming traits were not transported via other art media). A picture of continuous colonisation would bear evidence of continuity in rock-art traits. A long gap would allow for substantial changes to the rock-art sequence. Attributes might be lost and completely replaced. Those that survived might have undergone a process of transformation whereby 'linking' forms – attributes that can be traced back in space and time – were completely lost. Assuming the 'stick figure' is not a local (Marquesan, Hawaiian) innovation, it may be that we are unable to reconstruct the process of transformation that led to the production of the 'stick figure' in Hawaii and the Marquesas.

## Pacific rock-art and Pacific prehistory

This study set out to test whether similarities and differences in rock-art satisfy Kirch and Green's 'phylogenetic model'. Limited by an absence of contextual detail, a lack of absolute dates from different regional assemblages, and small and 'uneven' samples, the results show that attribute correlations associated with the 'stick figure' form do not concur with Kirch and Green's claim for cultural continuity in the Pacific region. The lack of prototypes for this Polynesian motif type is at odds with the central notion of Kirch and Green's phylogenetic argument: *cultural continuity*. Prototypical rock-art traits should have been identifiable in ancestral rock-art complexes regardless of whether evolutionary processes of divergence, such as isolation, promoted the development of localised styles.

It has been through the use of Kirch and Green's phylogenetic model that exceptions and indeterminate phenomena have been revealed. How else might a lack of continuity in the rock-art patterns be explained?

- Attributes *not available* to this study were transmitted across the Pacific during the colonisation process; for instance, the locational and technical attributes Ballard (1988, 1992) and Ewins (1995) identified as part of an Austronesian rock-art 'tradition'.
- Similarities and differences in rock-art indicate specific functions which differ from other material evidence.
- Rock-art traits were transferred to and transmitted via other art media, resulting in complex patterns of change that make it difficult, if not impossible, to identify continuity by examining rock-art alone.

These possibilities could be explored with new work on the following areas:

- increased, systematic documentation of Pacific rock-art following the examples set by Georgia Lee's (1992) Easter Island project, and Sidsel Millerstrom's (1990) French Polynesia;
- the demonstration and comprehension of the diversity and range of imagery in the Pacific, and all associated techniques, production stages, locales, associations and uses (Conkey 1987);
- a systematic comparison of rock-art with other art media.

Pacific rock-art need no longer be accorded a marginal status in the field of Pacific research. An increased comprehension of rock-art affinities can only increase our understanding of cultural communication and colonisation in Oceania.

## Acknowledgements

This chapter is based on research undertaken for my BA honours thesis at the University of Sydney (Wilson 1994). I would like to thank Paul Rainbird, Soren Blau, Paul Taçon, John Clegg, Georgia Lee, Sidsel Millerstrom, Matthew Spriggs, Atholl Anderson, Chris Ballard, Andrée Rosenfeld, Richard Wright, Roger Green and Alistair Paterson for comments that improved this chapter.

## REFERENCES

Ambrose, W. 1970. Archaeology and rock drawings from the Waitaki Gorge, central South Island, *Records of the Canterbury Museum* 8(5): 342–437.

Anderson, A., H. Leach, I. Smith and R. Walter. 1994. Reconsideration of the Marquesan sequence in east Polynesian prehistory, with particular reference to Hane (MUH1), *Archaeology in Oceania* 29: 29–52.

Ballard, C. 1988. Dudumahan: a rock art site on Kai Kecil, southeast Moluccas, *Bulletin of the Indo-Pacific Prehistory Association* 8: 139–59.

1992. Painted rock art sites in western Melanesia: locational evidence for an 'Austronesian' tradition, in J. McDonald and I. Haskovec (eds.), *State of the art: regional rock art studies in Australia and Melanesia: Proceedings of Symposium C and D, Darwin 1988*, pp. 94–106. Melbourne, Australian Rock Art Research Association. Occasional AURA Publication 6.

Bellwood, P. 1978. *The Polynesians: prehistory of an island people*. London, Thames and Hudson.

Benzecri, J. P. 1992. *Correspondence analysis handbook*. New York, Marcel Dekker.

Cachola-Abad, Kehaunani C. 1993. Evaluating the orthodox dual settlement model for the Hawaiian Islands: an analysis of artefact distribution and Hawaiian oral traditions, in M. W. Graves and R. C. Green (eds.), *The evolution and organisation of prehistoric society in Polynesia*, pp. 13–22. Auckland, New Zealand Archaeological Association. Monograph 19.

Clarke, J. T. and J. Terrell. 1978. Archaeology in Oceania, *Annual Review of Anthropology* 7: 293–319.

Clegg, J. 1995. *Mathesis drawing*. Balmain (NSW), Clegg Calendars.

Conkey, M. 1987. New approaches in the search for meaning? A review of research in 'Palaeolithic art', *Journal of Field Archaeology* 14: 413–30.

Cox, J. H. and E. Stasack. 1970. *Hawaiian petroglyphs*. Honolulu, Bishop Museum Press.

Davis, W. 1990. Style and history in art history, in M. Conkey and C. Hastorf (eds.), *The uses of style in archaeology*, pp. 18–31. Cambridge, Cambridge University Press.

Emory, K. P. 1933. *Stone remains in the Society Islands*. Honolulu, Bernice P. Bishop Museum. Bulletin 116.

Ewins, R. 1995. Proto-Polynesian rock art? The cliff paintings of Vatulele, Fiji, *Journal of the Polynesian Society* 104: 23–74.

Frimigacci, D. and J. Monnin. 1980. Un inventaire des petroglyphes de Nouvelle-Caledonie: Grande Terre et Iles, *Journal de la Société des Océanistes* 36: 17–59.

Furey, L. 1989. Petroglyph sites on the Coromandel Peninsula, *Archaeology in New Zealand* 32(4): 182–92.

Green, R. C. 1979. Early Lapita art from Polynesia and Island Melanesia: continuities in ceramic, barkcloth, and tattoo decorations, in S. M. Mead (ed.), *Exploring the visual art of Oceania: Australia, Melanesia, Micronesia and Polynesia*, pp. 13–31. Honolulu, University Press of Hawaii.

1994. Changes over time: recent advances in dating human colonisation of the Pacific Basin area, in D. G. Sutton (ed.), *The origins of the first New Zealanders*, pp. 19–51. Auckland, Auckland University Press.

Gunn, M. 1986. Rock art on Tabar, New Ireland Province, Papua New Guinea, *Anthropos* 81: 455–67.

Hagen, M. 1986. *Varieties of realism: geometries of representational art*. Cambridge, Cambridge University Press.

Irwin, G. 1992. *The prehistoric exploration of the Pacific*. Cambridge, Cambridge University Press.

Jefferson, C. 1959. *Dendroglyphs of the Chatham Islands: Moriori designs on Karak trees*. New Plymouth, Polynesian Society.

Jennings, J. D. 1979. *The prehistory of Polynesia*. Canberra, Australian National University Press.

Kechagia, H. 1995. The row and the circle: semiotic perspective of visual thinking, *Rock Art Research* 12(2): 109–16.

Kirch, P. V. 1984. *The evolution of Polynesian chiefdoms*. Cambridge, Cambridge University Press.

(ed.). 1986. *Island societies: archaeological approaches to evolution and transformation*. Cambridge, Cambridge University Press.

Kirch, P. V. and J. Ellison. 1994. Palaeoenvironmental evidence for human colonization of remote Oceanic islands, *Antiquity* 68: 310–21.

Kirch, P. V. and R. Green. 1987. History, phylogeny, and evolution in Polynesia, *Current Anthropology* 28(4): 431–56.

Lee, G. 1992. *Rock art of Easter Island: symbols of power, prayer to the gods*. Los Angeles, UCLA Institute of Archaeology.

McDonald, J. 1994. *Dreamtime Superhighway: an analysis of Sydney Basin rock art and prehistoric information exchange*. Unpublished Ph.D dissertation, Australian National University, Canberra.

McDonald, J. and I. Haskovec (eds.). 1992. *State of the art: regional rock art studies in Australia and Melanesia: Proceedings of Symposium C and D, Darwin 1988*. Melbourne, Australian Rock Art Research Association. Occasional AURA Publication 6.

Maynard, L. 1977. Classification and terminology in Australian rock art, in P. J. Ucko (ed.), *Form in indigenous art*, pp. 385–402. Canberra, Australian Institute of Aboriginal Studies.

Millerstrom, S. 1990. Rock art of the Marquesas Islands, French Polynesia. A case study in the Hatiheu valley, Nuku Hiva. Unpublished MA thesis, Department of Anthropology, San Francisco State University.

1992. Report on the Marquesas Islands Rock Art Project, *Pacific Arts* 6: 19–25.

Monnin, J. 1986. *Les Petroglyphes de Nouvelle-Caledonie*. Noumea, Office Culturel Scientifique et Technique Canaque.

Navarro, M. 1987. *Petroglyphs: Raiatea, Bora-Bora, Huahine: information techniques*. Département d'Archéologie du Centre Polynesian des Sciences Humaines.

Nishisato, S. 1994. *Elements of dual scaling: an introduction to practical data analysis*. Lawrence Erlbaum Associates.

Palmer, J. B. 1965. Petroglyphs in Tonga, *New Zealand Archaeological Association Newsletter* 8(2): 34–8.

Pawley, A. 1996. On the Polynesian subgroup as a problem for Irwin's continuous settlement hypothesis, in J. Davidson *et al.* (eds.), *Pacific culture history: essays in honour of Roger Green*, pp. 387–410. New Zealand Journal of Archaeology Special Publicaton.

Pawley, A. and M. Ross. 1993. Austronesian historical linguistics and culture history, *Annual Review of Anthropology* 22: 425–59.

Pietrusewsky, M. 1996. The physical anthropology of Polynesia: a review of some cranial and skeletal studies, in J. Davidson *et al.* (eds.), *Oceanic culture history: essays in honour of Roger Green*, pp. 343–53. New Zealand Journal of Archaeology Special Publication.

Roder, J. 1959. *Felsbilder und Vorgeschichte des MacCluer-Golfes, West-Neuguinea: Ergebnisse der Frobenius-Expedition 1937–38* IV. Darmstadt, L. C. Wittich.

Roe, D. 1992. Rock art of north-west Guadalcanal, Solomon Islands, in J. McDonald and I. Haskovec . 13–22. Auckland, New Zealand Archaeological Association. Monograph 19.(eds.), *State of the art. Regional rock art studies in Australia and Melanesia. Proceedings of Symposium C and D, Darwin 1988*, pp. 107–27. Melbourne, Australian Rock Art Research Association. Occasional AURA Publication 6.

Rosenfeld, A. 1988. Rock art in western Oceania, *Bulletin of the Indo-Pacific Prehistory Association* 8: 119–38.

Sokal, R. R. 1968. Numerical taxonomy, in *Readings from Scientific American: mathematical thinking in behavioural sciences*, pp. 174–84. San Francisco, W.H. Freeman.

Sokal, R. R. and P. H. A. Sneath. 1963. *Principles of numerical taxonomy*. San Francisco, W.H. Freeman.

Specht, J. 1979. Rock art in the western Pacific, in S. M. Mead (ed.), *Exploring the visual art of Oceania*, pp. 58–82. Honolulu, University of Hawaii Press.

Spriggs, M. 1993. Island Melanesia: the last 10,000 years, in M. Spriggs *et al.* (eds.), *A community of culture: the people and prehistory of the Pacific*. Canberra, Australian National University. Occasional Papers in Prehistory 21.

1996. From Taiwan to the Tuamotus: absolute dating of Austronesian language spread and major subgroups, in R. Blench and M. Spriggs (eds.), *Archaeology and language*, pp. 115–26. London, Routledge.

Spriggs, M. and A. Anderson. 1993. Late colonization of east Polynesia, *Antiquity* 67: 200–17.

Stasack, E., R. Dorn and G. Lee. 1996. First direct [14]C ages on Hawaiian petroglyphs, *Asian Perspectives* 35(1): 51–72.

Taçon, P. S. C., M. Wilson and C. Chippindale. 1996. Birth of the Rainbow Serpent in Arnhem Land rock-art and oral history, *Archaeology in Oceania* 31: 103–24.

Terrell, J. 1986. *Prehistory in the Pacific islands: a study of variation in language, customs and human biology*. Cambridge, Cambridge University Press.

1988. History as a family tree, history as an entangled bank: constructing images and interpretations of prehistory in the South Pacific, *Antiquity* 62: 642–57.

Tratebas, A. M. 1993. Stylistic chronology versus absolute dates for early hunting style rock art on the northern American Plains, in M. Lorblanchet and P. Bahn (eds.), *Rock art studies: the post-stylistic era or Where do we go from here?*, pp. 163–77. Oxford, Oxbow.

Trotter, M. and B. McCulloch. 1971. *Prehistoric rock art of New Zealand*. Wellington, A. H. Reed.

Wilson, M. 1994. Shaping Pacific rock art. Unpublished BA Honours thesis, Department of Prehistoric and Historical Archaeology, University of Sydney.

Wobst, H. M. 1977. Stylistic behaviour and information exchange, in C. E. Cleland (ed.), *For the Director; research essays in honor of J. B. Griffin*, pp. 317–42. Ann Arbor, Museum of Anthropology, University of Michigan. Anthropological Papers 61.

Wright, R. V. S. 1992. *Doing multivariate archaeology and prehistory: handling large data sets with MV-Arch*. Balmain (NSW).

Ralph Hartley and Anne M. Wolley Vawser

# 11. Spatial behaviour and learning in the prehistoric environment of the Colorado River drainage (south-eastern Utah), western North America

The marking of places on the landscape with rock-art is a communicative medium by which the behaviour of the observer is manipulated. In the landscape of the American west where semi-arid plateaus dissected by steep canyons determined the density and routes of movement of people, enhancing places with rock-art was a vital part of the land-use strategies employed by these groups. With geographic modelling and information-theory considerations, varied placement of rock-art can be associated with residential and storage locales and routes of access to them. By these wholly formal methods, a structure for the placement and nature of this imagery on the landscape is developed, guided by concerns which condition how human beings perceive and define their social environment.

## Symbols, rock-art and location in landscape

Over a decade ago Schaafsma (1985: 261–3), reviewing rock-art study in North America, emphasised the functional implications of the position of prehistoric rock-art on the landscape: 'It is a basic assumption that rock art will be located in a patterned way in relationship to both the landscape and other cultural remains, as it is integrated with a variety of specific activities that are in themselves presumed to be non-random' (p. 261). The communicative dimension of graphic displays often underlay functional explanation for the existence of rock-art. The response of humans to form and colour can be influential in attracting attention and manipulating social behaviour (Coe 1992). Can the act of 'making special' specific places in the natural surroundings with petroglyphs or pictographs be adaptive (Dissanayake 1995)? This chapter argues for the utility of investigating the relationship

between location and communicative potential of prehistoric petroglyphs and pictographs in the Colorado River drainage of south-eastern Utah.[1] We suggest that some rock-art in this area was placed so as to direct and manipulate the behaviour of others.

## The study area

The Colorado River drainage of south-eastern Utah lies within the Canyonlands physiographic subdivision of the northern Colorado Plateau (Hunt 1974; Stokes 1977). Here deep meandering canyons are carved mostly in sandstone in the upper Paleozoic and lower Mesozoic formations. Nearly flat-lying sandstone formations form bare, knobby rock surfaces deeply dissected by narrow, rock-walled gulches and small canyons. Drainages fed by snow-melt from surrounding mountains, and springs exposed by down-cutting of the canyons, create micro-climates with fertile soils and riparian vegetation in the canyon bottoms (Fig. 11.1). Surficial deposits of sand cover the rock in several places and both stabilised and active dunes cover extensive upland areas. The field data for this study come from sites in Glen Canyon National Recreation Area, along the Colorado and San Juan Rivers from east central Utah to just south of the Arizona border (Fig. 11.2).

The prehistory of this area is long and varied:

---

[1] We first presented this argument in 1994 (Hartley and Vawser 1997). This chapter, grounded in the same reasoning and set of assumptions, employs a revised method that we believe better addresses the relationship between demographics, resource structure, economic decision-making and the location of rock-art.

**Fig. 11.1.** Area representative of the topography and mountains, mesas, canyons and riparian vegetation in the canyon bottoms of the study area.

archaeological deposits range from Paleo-Indian remains (dating 11,500–9000 BP) to remains of historical American Indian use during and after European contact.[2] Use of the area peaked during the Archaic (c. 9000–2300 BP) and again during the Formative (c. 1560–630 BP). The Archaic hunter-gatherer life-style slowly gave way to the more sedentary horticultural occupation of Formative groups commonly referred to as Anasazi and Fremont. Pre-historic use of the Colorado River drainage by Preformative groups depended on their knowledge of the resource base as well as the social environment, requiring opportunism and mobility. The extensive ranges (c. 10,000 sq. km) of these groups are believed to have overlapped (Hartley 1992a; cf. Kohler 1993), a residentially mobile adaptation during the warm season alternating with a logistically mobile, more sedentary adaptation during the cold season. Anasazi and Fremont – thought of as 'cultures', 'peoples' or 'populations' – constitute archaeological constructs derived from artefactual remains, architectural remains and human remains in the vast expanse of the northern Colorado Plateau and over the course of the last 2–3 thousand years. Anasazi are believed to represent either a developmental extension from the Archaic or a migration phenomenon

[2]  *The general Native American chronology of the study area*

| | | |
|---|---|---|
| Paleo-Indian | 11,500–9000 BP | (c. 10,300–8050 BC) |
| Archaic | 9000–2300 BP | (c. 8050–400 BC) |
| Preformative | 1300–1560 BP | (c. 400 BC–AD 500) |
| Formative | 1560–630 BP | (AD 500–1300) |
| Late Prehistoric | | (AD 1300–1500) |
| Protohistoric | | (AD 1500–1775) |

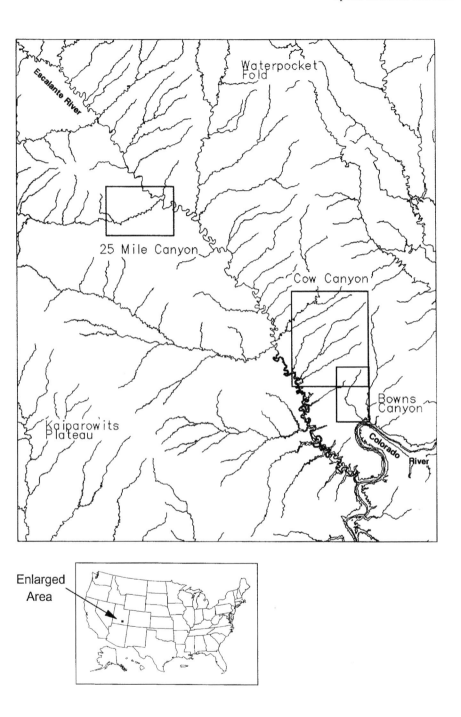

**Fig. 11.2.** The general study area showing the location of the Glen Canyon National Recreation Area in Utah and the Escalante River drainage where it joins the Colorado River.

187

from the south; Fremont development out of the desert Archaic was characterised by extensive variability in 'culture traits'. Regional differentiation in material remains most likely reflected the requirements of adaptation to variation in the resource structure of each area. While residential mobility is characteristic of the Fremont period (*c.* AD 450–1300), settlements indicate a substantial investment in housing and horticulture (see Anderson 1983; Simms 1990; Matson 1991; Janetski 1993).

Intermittent population increase on the northern Colorado Plateau during the Basketmaker and Pueblo periods is inferred from site sizes and density, the size of dwellings and their number, quantities of artefacts and food remains, and skeletal remains. A dramatic decrease in density is indicated archaeologically in the mid to late 1200s (Dean *et al.* 1985: 542–4; 1994: 58–9; Euler 1988). This portion of the Colorado River drainage has been termed a 'no-man's land' in reference to its habitat and position between extensive settlements, at least from the late Basketmaker to middle Pueblo II periods (see Wilcox and Haas 1994: 230–1). The activities of Numic-speaking groups (Ute and Southern Paiute) in this area are documented after AD 1100 (Reed 1994).

Prehistoric rock-art, common in this area, is a mixture of representational and abstract imagery in the form of both petroglyphs and pictographs. The dating of art in the arid west has been argumentative; only recently have radiocarbon and cation-ratio dating been utilised (e.g., Geib and Fairley 1992; Chaffee *et al.* 1994; Dorn 1994). Sites with rock-art in south-east Utah appear to span the range of prehistoric occupation; representational art generally associated with the Anasazi and Fremont is the most common.

Studies of rock-art in south-east Utah have attempted dating, assigned meaning to the images themselves, associated the various styles observed with different cultural groups, and made varied other investigations into the use, construction or meaning of rock-art and its locations. These studies have de-

pended for the most part on formal methods rather than attempted informed methods from a base in ethnography or ethnohistory. While some correlation has been made of images in the rock-art with the customs, mythology and dress observed in historically documented American Indian groups such as the Hopi (Schaafsma 1980; Olsen 1989; Cole 1990, 1992), often considered to be genetic descendants of Anasazi, most research has focused directly on the rock-art itself.

An early study by Turner (1963, 1971) defined five different styles of art, loosely associated with different archaeological manifestations. Other extensive studies since that time (Schaafsma 1971, 1980; Cole 1990) have categorised several somewhat distinct styles and associated them with the Fremont and Anasazi. These cultural assignments are often based on the direct association of buried archaeological deposits or architectural features identified through archaeological methods of documentation such as seriation and absolute dating. Recent studies have dated the rock-art itself. Embodied in this approach are assumptions that rock-art is significant for dating cultural 'commonalities' and that its absolute dating provides a sound basis for tracing the spatial and temporal distributions of cultural groups.

Investigations of the location of rock-art and its relationship to the natural environment have a long history in the arid South-west (Snyder 1966; Weaver and Rosenberg 1978; Ferg 1979; Wallace 1983; Hamann and Hedges 1986; Ives 1986; Martynec 1986; Hartley 1992a; Hyder 1994; Nelson 1995). Bruder (1983), studying northern Hohokam rock-art, suggests that petroglyph sites of two types might explain the non-random distribution of sites in the Deer Valley area: numerous people have visited 'public sites' leaving 'a wide variety of design motifs'; few (or only one person) have visited 'private sites' where rock-art is found to be a 'preponderance of just a few elements'. While these studies have contributed greatly to our knowledge, our interpretations of the utility of rock-art production lean heavily on reconstructing the *social* environment; this chapter claims to be no different. We contend that the positioning of much of the rock-art was the result of decisions that took place at the individual level. A fundamental premiss is that rock-art offered raw 'information' about the presence of past human activities to observers moving about the landscape. In association with material remains and the locale, rock-art was assigned some 'meaning' relative to the social environment and the activities that took place there.

We chose three distinct canyon areas within the Escalante River drainage in Glen Canyon National Recreation Area to explore relationships between the location of rock-art and landscape barriers in this environment and to see what behaviour, if any, could be inferred about the positioning of rock-art and places exhibiting evidence of other activities. Twentyfive Mile Canyon drains the Kaiparowitz Plateau while Cow and Browns drain the southern limb of Waterpocket Fold (Fig. 11.2). Our selection of these areas was determined by highly dissected drainage and by the excellent quality of the archaeological investigations conducted there by Northern Arizona University during the mid to late 1980s (Geib *et al.* 1986, 1987). Accurate record of each site location is important to the analyses. Although thousands of prehistoric sites are recorded in the Glen Canyon area, many were documented before maps of the area were of good quality.

Glen Canyon drainages show evidence of horticultural use in the early Formative. However, Geib *et al.* (1987) believe that residence was confined to the Kaiparowits Plateau during the Basketmaker III period (*c.* AD 600–800). Fremont ceramics are found throughout the Pueblo I period (*c.* AD 800–1000). Geib *et al.* (1987) also suggest that in the Pueblo II period families moved from highland residences into the canyons during the late spring and early summer – but arable land was limited in these canyons. Cow Canyon is believed to exhibit remains of a Pueblo III community (Horsefly Hollow phase AD 1210–1260). Residential sites in upper Cow Canyon are considered to be associated with the many storage facilities observed there (Geib 1993).

Access in and out of Browns Canyon is available through at least five routes as well as through its mouth at the Colorado River; this drainage may have served as an access route to other destinations. Cow Canyon, on the other hand, is a boxed canyon, accessible most easily from its confluence with the Escalante River. At least two trails descend from its rim, requiring the use of hand- and toe-holds (Geib *et al.* 1987: 46).

A recent stylistic analysis (Tokioka 1992) of Glen Canyon (including the Escalante River basin), based on thirty-four morphologically distinct elements, found the rock-art in the Escalante drainage to differ in its associated elements from that of other Glen Canyon areas, prompting Tokioka (1992: 88) to see either 'different cultural identities, or different functional uses of rock-art sites'. Quantitative analysis of the elements showed a strong association of styles that indicate 'warrior-like figures with shields' (1992: 89) in the Escalante drainage. Tokioka (1992) sees the Escalante drainage as a transitional zone between Barrier Canyon style to the north, and Glen Canyon Linear style to the south – both styles assigned to the late Archaic. Also suggested is a cultural association of Fremont with Barrier Canyon style and of Anasazi with Glen Canyon Linear style, seen as reflecting 'different ritual practices based on different cultural traditions' (1992: 96; cf. Manning 1990).

## The placing of rock-art and human use of the landscape

Assessing the behaviour that might underlie the placement of rock-art has been a recent topic of focused investigation in various locales (Sognnes 1994; Taçon 1994; Swartz and Hurlbutt 1994; Bradley 1994). The enhancement of places with markings is rooted in an attempt to communicate information and, in some cases, manipulate behaviour. Places, when marked as a function of symbolling behaviour, often show content that is either explicit or disguised so as to be ambiguous; contemporary urban gang graffiti show how information and the context of a place directs and manipulates spatial behaviour in a highly competitive social environment (Ley and Cibriwski 1974; Brown 1978; Cintron 1991; Gross and Gross 1993; Peteet 1996).

The rock-art of south-east Utah has been observed in a variety of topographical situations – including cliff faces, detached boulders, and on the walls of rock-shelters. The locations are varied in other senses: they may be isolated or they may be associated with other archaeological features – in a cave with buried cultural deposits or on the walls of structures. The images on rock-art panels in different situational contexts vary in content (Ives 1986; Baumann 1989; Hartley 1992a). The present study investigates the relationship between residential behaviour, storage and caching activities, the challenges of prehistoric human mobility, and their relationship to the locations chosen for the application of rock-art imagery. We explore several characteristics of rock-art sites: their topographical situation, the assemblage content of the rock-art itself, and the relationships of these sites to the remains of other activities. With this study we attempt to establish testable hypotheses explaining the positioning and content of rock-art in the canyon country of south-east Utah.

## Assumptions and approach of the study
In a recent analysis of symbolling and material culture in west-central Kenya, Osborn (1996) demonstrated how information regarding rules and expectations in highly complex social settings is reiterated by women in the decorative motifs on calabashes employed as milk containers – a strategy that confers adaptive advantage to offspring. Yet emically generated explanations of the motifs from informants in this social system do not permit the establishment of predictions and hypotheses that can be evaluated and refined to generate predictive nomothetic theory. In a study of prehistoric behaviour the collection of emically generated data is, of course, not possible; the utility of etically derived descriptions increases with our focus on the material remains of prehistoric activities (Harris 1990).

In exploring what role rock-art played in the land-use strategies of prehistoric peoples in this canyon country, we believe two important issues affected human behaviour: *spatial orientation* during human movement, and *spatial 'friction'* impacting decisions about placing facilities for the storage of food and other essential items. We have not approached this research without making assumptions about human behaviour. First and foremost, we assume that the ability to use symbols and icons and to make judgements based on analogical reasoning evolved because it serves some adaptive function in social living. Second, we assume that rock-art functioned as one means of conveying information between individuals and/or groups that enhanced their ability to manipulate social situations and to acquire resources in the environment of south-east Utah. Third, we see communication not simply as an attempt to inform others but also as an energetically inexpensive means by which to manipulate their behaviour; individuals often exaggerate their relative resource-holding power – to the extent that bluffing and deceit are important means of deterrence, especially when the relative difference in strength between competitors is small or when the resource patch cannot be actively defended (Ley and Cibriwsky 1974; Kaplan 1987; Krebs and Davies 1987; Cintron 1991; Cronk 1995).

## Spatial orientation
The concept of orientation includes the ability of an animal to relate the position and movement of its body to spatial cues. Orientation behaviour that leads an individual to a place (a goal) previously determined employs mechanisms whose spatial references are not directly associated with that goal (Schone 1984: 3–16). Variables thought to reflect dimensions of human spatial ability – that is, dimensions concerning the individual's ability to orient the self in a real-world space and to maintain a sense of direction – are:
- landmark memory
- route knowledge
- awareness of geographic direction.

A body of knowledge about large-scale environments is acquired by integrating observations gathered over time. This cognitive spatial description – or 'map' – is consequently used in route-finding and to determine the relative positions of places (Kuipers 1982: 203). The cognitive representations of places, assigned some significance, accumulate to build networks of places; but they do not necessarily provide additional information concerning the intervening terrain (Siegel and White 1975; Kuipers 1983). Growing and repeated experience in that environment makes for highly familiar terrain; new landmarks are identified between old ones; a cognitive spatial description grows of increasing density.

Kaplan and Kaplan (1982: 45) point out that cognitive maps of highly familiar terrain are often packed with salient information. Components of places that are not 'natural' tend to be selected as landmarks; they are distinctive features near places on the landscape where navigation choices need to be made (Kaplan 1976; Allen 1987: 277–9).

The created landmarks are useful in utilising the resource structure of an area efficiently. Localised markers in the environment are usually distinctive stimulus sources which can be used as reference points. To many species visual markers are very important in terrestrial navigation (Hazen 1983; Vander Wall 1990: 164–6). Visual cues, olfaction and spatial memory are a complex set of variables that, especially, help mammals in staying spatially oriented. Visual markers serving as proximal cues – for example, features near food storage sites – facilitate goal-oriented navigation (see Covich 1987: 274–85).

Route-finding is simplified cognitively by representing the environment as a network of places. The accumulation of a chain of sacred places representing the track of an ancestral being of Western Desert Aborigines (Australia) can function in this manner (see Strehlow 1971; Berndt 1976; Lewis 1976). Gould (1990: 153) discusses places with rock-art that, among other functions, serve as 'check-points

during movements across the desert terrain', assisting in orientation to locales of water or other necessary resources.[3]

The role of rock-art as landmarks in the Southwest has been discussed in several studies (see Hayden 1972; Britt 1973; Weaver and Rosenberg 1978; Bruder 1983: 25; Geib and Bungart 1988: 42–7); it is epitomised by the Willowsprings site (Na994) in northern Arizona, where Hopi men, during excursions to procure salt, carved their clan symbols on a landmark boulder along the route to the salt source (Colton and Colton 1931; Titiev 1937; Simmons 1942: 235–6; Michaelis 1981). Informant references to rock-art enhancing a place as a landmark are exemplified for the Hopi by Turner (1963: 71) and for the Zuni by Young (1988: 54–7).

A previous study (Hartley 1992b) of rock-art positioned on detached boulders in south-east Utah saw boulders enhanced with petroglyphs as reference stimuli for storing information about spatial locations and way-finding. Three topographical situations were found among 44 sites:

- on prominent, highly visible places (32);
- along, or in proximity to, documented trails (17);
- at the confluence of creeks, rivers, or unnamed drainages (6).

Some motifs – for example, anthropomorphic images and the depiction of animals – were more commonly produced on these boulders than others. It was suggested that petroglyphs accumulated at these places through time, as they are documented to have done at the Willowsprings site, with significance being assigned to these places by individuals or small groups.

Environmental psychologists know that humans find sight the most efficient medium of cueing their memory of places (Kaplan and Kaplan 1982). Previous research focused only on detached boulders, but

---

[3] A 'trail' is defined by ethologists as a series of markers strung together in a row that convey specific information about the marker (Schone 1984: 31–2, 158). Human use of markers often directs, or is meant to manipulate, the behaviour of others (see Stirling and Waite 1919; Morphy 1977).

other places accentuated with rock-art enhance a landmark. Was rock-art placed so as to serve as spatial reference in this landscape? If it did, we should see that use reflected in similarities and differences observed between rock-art sites in terms of topographical situation and of content.

## Spatial friction and the positioning of storage facilities

Efficient use of space underlies spatial approaches to understanding human activities. Spatial friction – loosely defined as the resistance to movement – generates extra cost and/or inefficiency for every good produced by an individual or group that requires transport. Spatial friction affects choices (decision-making); it is a function of time and a function of cost.

Both primates (Menzel 1978) and human children (Wellman *et al.* 1979) have been shown to use a least-distance strategy when travelling between locations where concealed food or desirable objects are the goal. Although Limp and Carr (1985) emphasise caution in projecting this kind of decision-making to prehistoric human activities, energy efficiency of routes can establish models of human activities on a landscape (see Ericson and Goldstein 1980; Savage 1989; Limp 1991). Access routes to places of food storage, especially for seasonally harvested horticultural products, is likely to have been an important consideration in prehistoric land-use strategies.

The capacity to control the availability of food in space and time offers many animals, including humans, a means by which to minimise the effects of food shortages. For those species which do not store food, intense reductions in short-term nutritious resources can limit population growth. In a competitive environment, those storing food are less likely to suffer scarcity and thereby achieve a better reproductive success (Covich 1987: 253).

The remains of seemingly 'larder hoards' produced by aboriginal groups in south-east Utah are found throughout this canyon country,[4] with storage facilities usually identified as above-ground masonry

structures or semi-subterranean cists (Fig. 11.3). Human 'scatter hoarding' in this area is seen as small caches of one or more ceramic vessels (Fig. 11.4) situated within the home range of logistically organised collectors (see Hunter-Anderson 1986: 36; Wolley and Osborn 1991; Osborn and Vawser 1991). Both hoard types are most often observed in situations where geological or erosional formations provide some protection from the elements. Tools and miscellaneous paraphernalia are also found in cache and storage facilities throughout the study area (see Morss 1931; Lipe 1967: 143–8; 1970: 100–1). These, as well as foodstuffs, require protection from deterioration due to natural processes.

Pilferage of cached or stored food by conspecific competitors is common behaviour across species, and so is the corresponding defence of resource 'patches' such as caches – behaviour that is more adequately studied in animals than in humans (see Covich 1987; Vander Wall 1990). The Raramuri (Tarahumara) of northern Mexico, residentially mobile agriculturists, store corn on the cob in small wooden structures and in natural rock formations enclosed with stone and mortar for protection and concealment (Pennington 1963: 58–61). Graham (1994: 69–70) discusses the conditions surrounding the location of these storage facilities, conditions we believe pertinent to the Utah canyon-lands. When corn is stored at the residence, transport from the fields is required at harvest time. When corn is stored nearer the fields, members of

---

[4] The term 'hoarding' encompasses both storing and caching (Ewer 1968: 50–1), in a spectrum that ranges from 'scatter' hoarding – when a food item or relatively small quantities are stored throughout an organism's range – to 'larder' (centralised or 'nest cache') hoarding – when food is concentrated in one or several discrete sites. The dispersion of scatter or larder hoards is a function of the organism's range of activities and of the need to identify which place offers the best combination of access, concealment and protection. Covich (1987: 274–5) suggests that a large capacity for spatial memory is developed when hoarders specialise in 'nutrient-rich resources that are only seasonally available or clumped in space, and readily transported and stored'. Scatter hoarders rely upon secretive hoarding behaviour; larder hoarders must invest in defensive behaviour, since the relatively larger quantities of food make 'cache pilfering' more attractive to conspecific competitors (Vander Wall 1990: 97; cf. Bettinger 1991: 127).

**Fig. 11.3.** An example of an above-ground masonry storage structure common in the study area.

**Fig. 11.4.** A cached ceramic vessel found in Glen Canyon. Pack rat midden almost completely covered the vessel before excavation.

**Fig. 11.5.** Anthropomorphic figures in a large shelter in Bowns Canyon.

family units must periodically visit the storage facilities and transport the corn to the residence. Graham notes the increased risk of having corn stolen when it is stored away from the residence. Storage structures are also associated with residences. When the residences are not occupied, neighbours and relatives help guard these stores, which are accessible to the owners, even during the cold season. Graham (1994: 69) also notes the caching of 'unused ceramics, tools, and craft items' near the ceiling of the corn storage facilities.

The location of prehistoric storage facilities has rarely been the subject of study. Gilman (1987) and Gross (1992) suggest that storage facilities are found at or near habitation structures under conditions of increased population density and an increased de-

pendence on stored food (cf. Vander Wall 1990: 97; Cordell 1984: 188). The control of access to these stored resources under conditions of population–resource imbalance is a context in which rock-art has been examined previously (Hartley 1991, 1995).

Storage facilities and rock-art believed to be associated with storage were examined at 140 rock-shelters in south-eastern Utah (Hartley 1991). At places where storage facilities are apparent, the rock-art assemblage in most cases had a high redundancy in images depicted (Fig. 11.5). The rock-art assemblage at these sites, it was argued, reflects a competitive social environment where pilferage of stored food stuffs or other resources was a risk. Rock-art assemblages with high redundancy communicated an unambiguous 'message' of ownership or affiliation – making an 'advertisement' of access restriction. Images depicted at these sites were primarily human hands, anthropomorphic images, or mammals. But the majority of the many storage facility sites known in the study area have no rock-art close by.

We contend that some rock-art associated with the storage of horticultural or agricultural products served as a visual marking of restriction. We then ask: Does the topographical position of storage facilities influence the location of rock-art sites in an area that includes arable soil? If so, what are the similarities and differences in assemblage content of the rock-art?

## Methods of analysis

Two procedures are used to address the effects that landscape barriers and social behaviour may have had on the location of rock-art imagery: (1) the quantification of assemblages of rock-art for site comparison, and (2) the use of Geographic Information Systems (GIS) technology in searching a landscape with filters that allow us to see through a noisy bank of information.

## Measuring information in the rock-art assemblage

Alexander (1990: 7) makes clear the interdependence of graphic display, linguistic capabilities and the transfer of information in the evolution of human consciousness: 'We can use signs or symbols to designate places, events, objects, and individuals, and then, through the use of tenses, talk to others about events, objects, or individuals in different times and places. In no other way can detailed information about mental scenarios, which necessarily involve different times and places be transferred between individuals.'

*Information*, in its fundamental sense, is what people seek and exchange to reduce uncertainty about physical and social reality. *Meaning* is the interpretation of the information a message contains. A message is simply the means by which information is

obtained. With these definitions in mind we envisage information, as developed by communication theorists, to be the aspect of messages that increases or reduces uncertainty. Information is measurable, and rock-art – apart from whatever meaning it was assigned in prehistoric socio-cultural systems – is subject to this measure. Subsequently we assign it meaning in our attempts to reconstruct the conditions and dynamics of the socio-economic system. Quantifying assemblages of rock-art with measures of information permits an attempt at objectivity in comparing rock-art panels. The motifs in the rock-art assemblages were categorised into 28 units, 14 each for petroglyphs and for pictographs (Table 11.1).

The Shannon formula (Shannon and Weaver 1949) is used to calculate the initial measures of information for each rock-art assemblage (Table 11.2):

$$\overset{n}{\underset{i}{H}} = - p_i \log_2(1/p_i)$$

where

$H$ = the measure of the amount of information on the panel,

$n$ = the number of rock-art categories in the panel's distribution, and

$p_i$ = the proportion of the $i$th component (i.e. glyph category) of the distribution.

The average amount of information conveyed by a given panel by this formula is, in essence, the statistical uncertainty of the various proportions of the distribution of rock-art categories of each assemblage.

This measure, $H_n$, lies on a scale that ranges from 0 to $\log_n$. Zero, the minimum value, occurs in assemblages where only one category of rock-art image is present: one proportion will equal 1 and the remainder equal zero. The maximum dispersion of a set of proportions occurs when each of the 28 rock-art categories contains the same number of elements (Thomas 1981).

This measure is more useful on a standardised scale. This degree of dispersion exhibited by an

Table 11.1. *Rock-art classification*

| Motif | Description |
|---|---|
| Anthropomorph | Where the human figure is represented in its entirety |
| Fragmentary anthropomorphic | Where only a portion of a human figure is depicted, e.g., torso, headless figure |
| Human hand | Where the figure depicts the human hand, positive or negative image |
| Human foot | Where the figure depicts the human foot, positive or negative image |
| Human head | Where the figure depicts the head of a human |
| Mammalian figure | Where the figure seemingly represents a mammal |
| Mammalian 'tracks' | Where the foot (or feet) of a mammal is represented |
| Bird figure | Where the figure seemingly represents a bird |
| Bird 'tracks' | Where the foot (or feet) of a bird is represented |
| Reptilian figure | Where the depiction suggests a reptile, e.g. snake, lizard |
| Rectilinear | Non-representational figures characterised by straight lines; formed or bounded by straight lines |
| Curvilinear | Non-representational figures consisting of or bounded by curved lines |
| Concentric | Figures having a common centre or common axis, e.g., circles, spirals |
| Abstract geometric | Motifs or outlines that are characterised by both straight and curved lines but that bear no resemblance to natural forms |

Table 11.2. *Rock-art sites in the study area*

| Site | Cultural affiliation | Rock-art Rel. $H_n$ |
|---|---|---|
| **Twentyfive Mile Canyon** | | |
| A | Fremont, early Formative | 0.0 |
| B | Fremont, early Formative | 0.24 |
| C | Fremont/Anasazi, early–middle Formative | 0.0 |
| D | Fremont, early–middle Formative | 0.25 |
| E | Archaic/Fremont | 0.37 |
| F | Fremont, early Formative | 0.59 |
| G | Anasazi, mid-Formative, Archaic rock-art | 0.31 |
| **Cow Canyon** | | |
| H | Kayenta Anasazi, Horsefly Hollow AD 1210–60 | 0 |
| I | Early Fremont | 0 |
| J | Horsefly Hollow, AD 1210–60 | 0.41 |
| **Bowns Canyon** | | |
| K | Mid–late P-II | 0.57 |
| L | Fremont, 675 ± 55 b.p., AD 1250–1400 | 0.32 |
| M | P-III, Kayenta Anasazi | 0.48 |
| N | Archaic/Fremont/Anasazi | 0.39 |
| O | 1200 ± 80 b.p., AD 660–1000 | 0.44 |
| P | Anasazi, late Formative | 1.0 |

observed set of proportions $[p_i]$ on a scale of 0 to 1 is constructed by further calculation:

$$Rel. \ H_n = \frac{-\sum_{i}^{n} p_i \log_2(1/p_i)}{\log_n n}$$

This standardised, or relative, measure of information *Rel. $H_n$* provides what our study needs – an index of uniformity (Krippendorf 1986): the higher the value of *Rel. $H_n$*, the greater the 'information content' of the rock-art assemblage. The value of *Rel. $H_n$* is unaffected by the value of n, permitting fair comparison between rock-art assemblages that differ widely in the number of glyph elements present.

A measure of redundancy gauges the amount of unutilised possibilities for carrying information. Redundancy is the complement of *Rel. $H_n$*,

$$Redundancy = 1 - Rel. \ H_n$$

In communication, as redundancy increases, mistakes in reception are minimised. An assemblage of rock-art that is highly redundant in the images displayed communicates a 'message' that is relatively unambiguous.

Contemporary concepts of information theory, discussed at length by Krippendorf (1975, 1986), do not need to be reiterated; by that theory, the amount of information conveyed by a message is the difference between the uncertainty *before* a message is received and the uncertainty *after* it is received.

## GIS measures of human mobility, accessibility and visibility in the landscape

To evaluate human spatial orientation and spatial friction as factors in the placement of rock-art and storage facilities, site locations in relation to terrain were analysed in several ways using a Geographic Information System (GIS). GIS is essentially a computer technology that allows researchers to account for multiple factors when analysing spatial relationships. Layers of data can be combined to account for topographic position as well as accessibility and visibility, factors important in the placement of rock-art and storage facilities.

A computer model measuring spatial orientation and friction requires data that define the terrain in three-dimensional space. These, providing a record of elevation, slope and aspect (direction of slope), are modelled in DEMs (Digital Elevation Models) created for the United States Geological Survey (USGS). Various analyses were applied using the DEM of the study area to evaluate (1) the efficient routes of travel between arable canyon-bottom land and storage locations, and (2) the visibility of rock-art from those pathways.

We begin with the location of rock-art sites and of storage and residential sites within the canyon area. Using GRASS GIS software on a SUN Workstation, we digitised site locations from 1 : 24,000 scale topographic maps produced by the USGS. The modelling of travel routes begins with the calculation of a friction surface, applying mathematical equations to values of slope (Douglas 1994). With the friction surface created, the cumulative cost of moving across that surface can be determined, and the paths of least resistance – least-cost paths (LCPs) – are identified (see Kanter 1996).

Two different equations were applied to the DEM for this research. The first equation simply squared the slope value stored as percent slope (rise over distance) for each 30 m square grid over the terrain (Fig. 11.6a). This generated a friction surface representing the steepness of the terrain (Fig. 11.6b). The cumulative cost of moving across this surface was then calculated, beginning at the lowest point (arable bottom land) and ending at the edge of the study area (Fig. 11.6c). Paths of least resistance were then identified by using the cost surface and applying a drainage model that linked a start-point at a storage structure with the end-point at the arable bottom land. The model finds the adjacent cell with the lowest value and proceeds step-wise across the landscape in this manner, much the way water drains from a mountain peak. This process using the slope-squared cost surface resulted in paths of least resistance that tended to follow natural channels similar to hydrologic drainage patterns.

The second method of evaluating spatial movement and friction that was used directly reflects potential human movement, representing values of time required to move across a distance. Calculating a friction surface in this manner again required the use of the slope value but in a more complex equation commonly called the 'hiking function' (Imhof 1968; Tobler 1993):

$$H = 6 \exp\left(-3.5 \times \text{abs}\,(S + 0.05)\right)$$

where
$H$ = hiking velocity (kilometres per hour)
$S$ = slope (rise over distance).

This equation results in a friction surface where each 30 m cell is assigned a value which represents the speed at which an individual can traverse that cell (Fig. 11.7a). The results can be generalised: the less

197

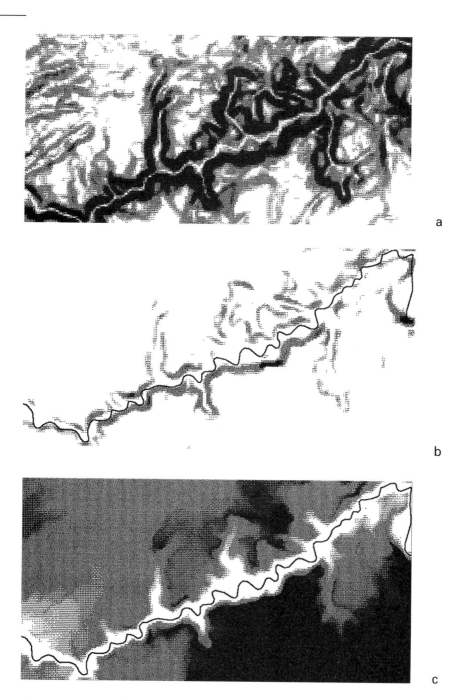

**Fig. 11.6.** Twentyfive Mile Canyon.
a Slope.
b Friction surface created using the slope-squared method.
c Final cumulative cost surface.

steep the terrain, the faster the rate of travel, allowing for a quantification of the obvious and intuitive. Using this friction surface to create a cumulative cost surface (Fig. 11.7b) results in a somewhat different representation of the same area from that of the slope-squared method. Calculating least-cost paths across this cost surface also resulted in paths that were less likely to follow natural drainage patterns.

For each group of calculated pathways it was possible to determine the visibility of rock-art sites using 'viewshed' analysis: a 'viewshed' is that area of ground from which some defined point is visible. In this analysis the computer starts with the location of the rock-art site. It then looks at each surrounding cell in the 30 m grid for a defined distance and determines whether that cell can be 'seen' from that point, as calculated by the elevation of that cell and of those between it and the start-point. In this way a viewshed is defined for the area around the rock-art site, and whether paths pass through this viewshed is determined (see Fig. 11.8). Viewsheds were calculated for each rock-art site for an individual of 1.75 m (5 ft 7 in.) in height and a distance of 500 metres. The viewsheds generated by this process were then plotted along with the locations of storage and the least-cost paths from them. Viewsheds were also calculated for several residential sites in Twentyfive Mile canyon. The process was the same, with the start-point being the location of the residence instead of the location of the rock-art. These viewsheds were plotted along with the location of storage structures and the paths to them. Table 11.2 lists the rock-art sites and map designations used in this study.

### Site location and site association

In asking 'What accounts for the pattern of the distribution of A?', research associates A's variance spatially or areally with the variance of some pattern (B) that is believed to be functionally related. (But sometimes it proves to be only *casually* related.) When two functionally related events occur to-gether, hypotheses link them – 'When B then A', or 'Where a certain proportion of B then a certain proportion of A' – generating answers that are usually covariant in nature. Analysis by area association tends to a static approach; it deals with decision-making, rather than explicitly with the processes generating patterns of spatial distributions.

In this study we look for spatial relationships between sites with rock-art and the remains of other activities, and from those infer group-level behavioural relationships.[5]

Our observed spatial relationships lean heavily on proximity. This approach has pitfalls, especially as chronological controls that establish contemporaneity of activities between places are lacking. In the following discussion we compare the results of our analyses using both the 'slope' and 'hiking function' cost surface. We believe this is one way to establish working hypotheses about behaviour from what we observe about static spatial arrangements.

*Rock-art assemblages measuring a high redundancy are to be expected where the least-cost path (LCP) leading to/from a storage facility intersects the viewshed from the location of the rock-art.*

Use of the 'slope' cost surface suggests this pattern in Twentyfive Mile Canyon at site 42GA3285 (A), at 42GA3272 (C), and in Cow Canyon at site 42KA2722 (I) (Fig. 11.9). The sites in Twentyfive Mile Canyon are both assigned to the early or middle Formative period. Site 42GA3285 (A) is an excellent example of rock-art positioned in a prominent place so as to be seen when storage facilities are being accessed from the canyon. Site 42KA2722 (I), assigned to the early Fremont, is clearly visible from the storage structure and surrounding area.

---

[5] We have categorised sites in this excercise by function. In acknowledging, as did the original surveyors, that distortions can arise with this perspective, we suggest in most cases that artefacts and features indicate that locations were used primarily for specific purposes, such as storage or habitation. Use of these functional terms – not a claim these sites were used for just one purpose – follows from the physical remains of one activity dominating the remains at the site.

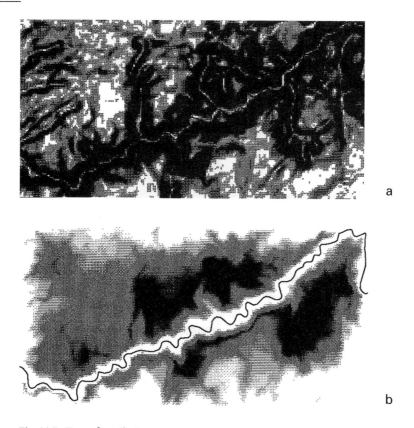

a

b

**Fig. 11.7.** Twentyfive Mile Canyon.
a Friction surface created using the hiking function.
b Final cumulative cost surface.

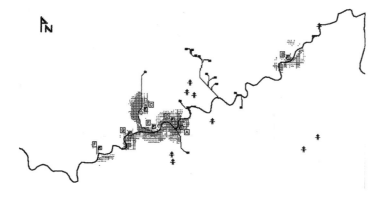

**Fig. 11.8.** Twentyfive Mile Canyon. Locations of rock-art sites (coil icon), storage structures (black rectangle) and residential sites (anthropomorph icon) in relation to the stream. The lines indicates the LCPs from the storage structures. The hatched areas are the viewsheds calculated from the rock-art sites.

Under the 'hiking function' cost surface, this assessment is not substantiated. This model indicates access to storage facilities above 42GA3285 (A) and 42GA3272 (C) in Twentyfive Mile Canyon would have been made without passing within the viewshed of the rock-art (Fig. 11.10). The LCP in the Cow Canyon example (Site I) retains its position in the viewshed with the storage structure.

Where the resource base of two or more groups is the same, or vulnerable to the same fluctuations, then social relationships that permit access rights to the resources of either group are of little benefit to anyone (according to Kelly 1991: 143). To minimise risk to subsistence resources, kin-related groups (for example, families) store food in situations where it can be tended (see Testart 1982: 527; Graham 1994: 69–70; Hegmon 1991).

Recent cross-cultural analyses have challenged reliance upon density-dependent models of resource competition to rationalise the need for proprietary markings related to storage facilities. Witteck (1990) suggests plunder is conducted by low-density societies with food shortages – contradicting that demographical explanation. Small raiding parties or pilfering are considered among the least costly types of aggressive behaviour which low-density societies may exhibit to secure food or other resources. These assertions may support the recent contention of Kohler and Van West (1996: 188) that sharing on the northern Colorado Plateau was more attractive when population was high and less attractive when population was low.

We suggest that rock-art assemblages with an information measure of high redundancy often conveyed a 'message' of ownership and/or access restriction. In these canyons, we believe rock-art with a high redundancy measure was positioned where it was visible to potential thieves. This is appropriate for groups whose population density and dependence on horticultural foods is increasing, but which continue to be residentially mobile for at least portions of the year – making stored or cached goods difficult to tend actively.[6]

*Rock-art is not within the viewshed of many storage facilities or routes, as measured by the LCP leading to them.*

We envisage two kinds of behaviour as accounting for this. In the first, storage or caching by residentially mobile groups in a low-density population environment will be manifested by sites geographically isolated from the remains of other activities; the resource–population balance is relatively stable throughout the year; site defence by rock-art 'advertisement' is not common, due to low risk of pilferage by competitors. Several instances in Cow Canyon (Fig. 11.9), Twentyfive Mile Canyon (Fig. 11.10), and Browns Canyon (Fig. 11.11) appear to fit this context.

Multiple storage facilities are, in some cases, either in close proximity to each other or easily accessible from each other via the LCP as measured to/from the canyon bottom; we see residential sites with substantial habitation structures near by; the storage facilities and the LCP leading to/from them are situated so as to be within the viewshed of these residences. Excellent examples of this spatial layout occur in Twentyfive Mile, Browns and Cow canyons. The storage facilities, positioned across the drainage from the rock-shelter residence, are always within the computed viewshed as here (Fig. 11.12).

In many cases we see storage rooms and/or other kinds of storage features also at these residences. Notable are those residential sites in rock-shelters with rock-art where the remains of substantial storage facilities are observed – good examples are sites 42GA3311 (G) in Twentyfive Mile, 42KA2692 (H)

---

[6] For example, the Khushmaan clan, a nomadic Bedouin group of the Maʿaza tribe in Egypt which uses a range of about 35,000 sq. km, mark places with clan symbols associated with particular valuable resources to communicate to members of other clans their proprietary rights (Hobbs 1989). The cost of actively defending against the use of these resource patches by others far outweighs the benefits, to the extent that 'permission' for use of a resource to non-Khushmaan tribal members is available. This tolerated access is likely a function of the high cost of resource defence (Blurton-Jones 1987; Hawkes 1992), a condition that must be considered when discussing proprietary behaviour in an arid environment.

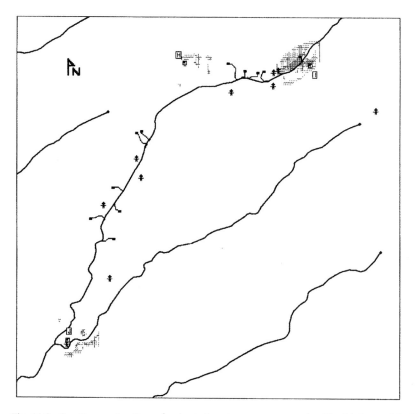

**Fig. 11.9.** Cow Canyon. Locations of rock-art sites, storage structures and residential sites; and the LCPs and viewsheds calculated using the slope-squared method.

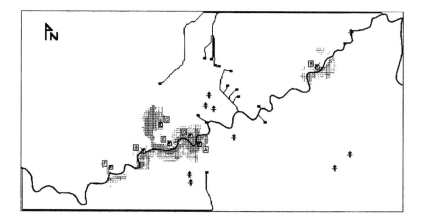

**Fig. 11.10.** Twentyfive Mile Canyon. The different LCPs that result from using the hiking function calculation.

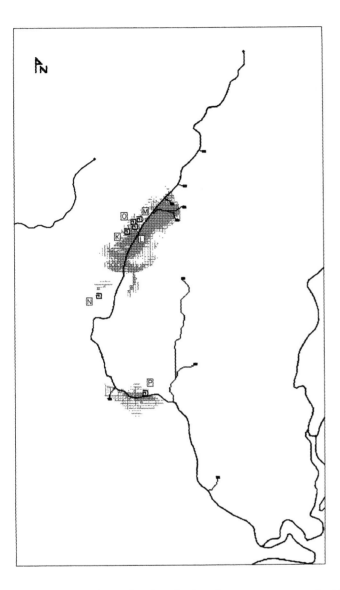

**Fig. 11.11.** Bowns Canyon. Locations of rock-art sites, storage structures and residential sites; and the LCPs and viewsheds calculated using the hiking function. Residential sites are in the same location as the rock-art sites represented by the coil icon.

in Cow, and 42KA2738 (K) and 42KA2754 (N) in Bowns.

When using the 'hiking function' cost surface several storage facilities in Twentyfive Mile Canyon do not appear to be accessed (via LCP) from the canyon bottom (Fig. 11.10). These storage facilities

exhibiting traits consistent with early Formative structures suggest use by mobile groups caching stores of food or seed where the risk of theft was low and the use of rock-art as a proprietary marking less necessary.

Arable land is easily accessible to those residing at

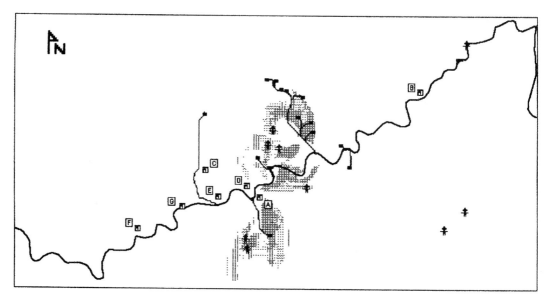

**Fig. 11.12.** Twentyfive Mile Canyon. Storage facilities within the viewshed of residential sites.

sites 42KA2738 (K) and 42KA2739 (L), and access to Waterpocket Fold has been noted by the original surveyors (Geib 1993). At these sites we see Formative and late Formative occupations where the potential for raiding of stores made it more efficient to transport foodstuffs to residences where risk of theft was minimised. Site 42KA2836 (O) in Bowns Canyon is accessible from the residential sites below only by hand- and toe-holds. This kind of spatial structure is considered a response to a highly competitive social environment in which groups are residentially sedentary for at least the cold-weather months and where dependence on stored food grown near by was vital for survival.

Not far from Seven Step Kiva (42KA2692) is the Watchtower site (42KA2690) (H) (Geib 1993), assigned to the Horsefly Hollow phase, where the remains of a small oval masonry room stand atop a pedestal rising above the Kayenta Formation bench. The site is considered by the surveyors as having an excellent view up and down the canyon. Our viewshed computed for a 500 metre distance shows that our ability to simulate an extensive line-of-site up or down a canyon is limited (Fig. 11.13a); when the viewshed was expanded to 700 metres visibility, this site validates its name (Fig. 11.13b).

*Locations of rock-art assemblages measuring a higher information content*

These are found in two situations: (1) at rock-shelters used for extended habitation and (2) within canyons positioned so as to be visible from canyon bottoms, those of the highest information measure being at an entrance to a more densely used portion of the canyon. This rock-art positioning is seen at Five Shield (42KA2807) (Fig. 11.14) (J) in Cow Canyon, at 42KA2734 (P) in Bowns, and 42GA3290 (F) in Twentyfive Mile Canyon. An excellent example is the Five Shield site (42KA2807) (J), considered late Formative (Horsefly Hollow phase). The rock-art is positioned below a prominent, isolated monolith of sandstone between the confluence of Shield and Cow canyons (Geib 1993) (Fig. 11.14).

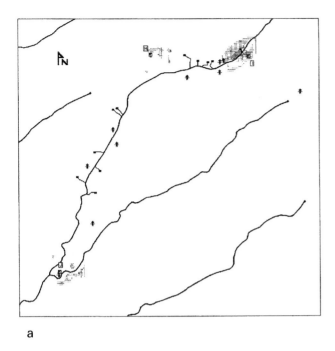

a

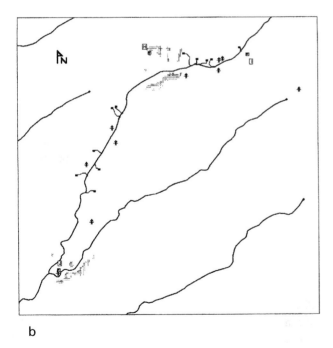

b

**Fig. 11.13.** Area at the head of Cow Canyon showing the (a) 500 m and (b) 700 m viewsheds for the Watchtower site. Note the extent of the canyon viewshed when expanded to 700 metres.

**Fig. 11.14.** Detail of rock-art at the Five Shield site.

We see residential use of the shelters through time as accounting for the accumulation of pecked and painted images at many of these places; we also suggest that rock-art, situated in prominent places on the landscape, helped travellers identify spatial locations. Notable is 42GA3285 (A) in Twentyfive Mile Canyon, a single anthropomorphic petroglyph positioned prominently in the canyon where it can be seen easily by anyone moving up or down the drainage.

### Rock-art, resources and signals in the landscape

Like many drainages and upland areas in the northern American South-west, the Escalante River basin appears to have been used and/or occupied at least intermittently for several centuries. We have looked at three canyons, inventoried as well as, or better than, any other land-parcels in this region; inferences about social and individual behaviour must be speculative, yet are grounded in contemporary discussion of the social environment of the prehistoric northern Colorado Plateau.

Knowledge of the physical geography of the region was necessary for successful access to available resources. The range used by aboriginal groups in the Desert West was extensive, especially as regards the total area used throughout the lifetime of individual members. Memorisation of familiar landmarks was probably essential for route-based navigation, and various kinds of mnemonic cues necessary to a good working knowledge of a territory in difficult and broken canyon country that encompassed thousands of square kilometres. We suggest that rock-art in prominent topographical situations functioned as one medium of information available for coping with the mobility demands of this environment.

Changes in land-use patterns were conditioned by changes in environmental processes and population density. Low-intensity conflicts associated with these changes are acknowledged to be difficult to observe in the archaeological record; sometimes they are manifested archaeologically at sites with a 'defensive' architecture or topographic situation or, as documented more recently, by remains of cannibalism (Turner and Turner 1995; Haas and Creamer 1996; Minnis 1996: 65). Rock-art in this area is not itself a function of a competitive environment, but we do believe that the location of some rock-art was determined by threats to resource patches and by a need to assert proprietary rights.

With these ideas in mind we have developed hypotheses that can be evaluated by focused and analytic research. A field assessment of the LCP as computed here to search for actual evidence of movement routes and a visual assessment of the viewshed from known sites will refine this kind of modelling. A neglected use of GIS studies in archaeology is the potential for well-defined options for behaviour that can be assessed only with concomitant fieldwork; these are not unlike challenges to contemporary urban planners, utility designers, and others who attempt to predict the most useful or sometimes efficient means by which people or some energy source can move. In prehistoric archaeology we are faced with retrodictive tasks – often with opinions being assigned a deictic conclusion. The interpretations we have made here are simply our constructions of a melding of others' opinions. As geographer Peter Gould (1979: 121) once wrote: 'opinions supporting opinions should not be taken too seriously'.

# REFERENCES

Alexander, R. D. 1990. *How did humans evolve? Reflections on the uniquely unique species.* Ann Arbor, Museum of Zoology, University of Michigan. Special Publications No. 1.

Allen, G. L. 1987. Cognitive influences on the acquisition of route knowledge in children and adults, in P. Ellen and C. Thinus-Blanc (eds.), *Cognitive processes and spatial orientation in animals and man,* pp. 271–83. Dordrecht, Martinus Nijhoff.

Anderson, D. C. 1983. Models of Fremont culture history: an evaluation, *Journal of Intermountain Archaeology* 2: 1–27.

Baumann, S. M. 1989. Measuring archaeological assemblage variability: a diversity–redundancy model for rock-art and artifact-feature assemblages from south-eastern Utah. MA thesis, Department of Anthropology, University of Nebraska, Lincoln.

Berndt, R. M. 1976. Territoriality and the problem of demarcating sociocultural space, in N. Peterson (ed.), *Tribes and boundaries in Australia,* pp. 133–61. Atlantic Highlands (NJ), Humanities Press.

Bettinger, R. L. 1991. *Hunter-gatherers – archaeological and evolutionary theory.* New York, Plenum.

Blurton-Jones, N. G. 1987. Tolerated theft: suggestions about the ecology and evolution of sharing, hoarding, and scrounging, *Social Science Information* 26: 31–54.

Bradley, R. 1994. Symbols and signposts: understanding the prehistoric petroglyphs of the British Isles, in C. Renfrew and E. B. W. Zubrow (eds.), *The ancient mind: elements of cognitive archaeology,* pp. 95–106. Cambridge, Cambridge University Press.

Britt, C. Jr. 1973. An old Navajo trail with associated petroglyph trail markers, Canyon de Chelly, Arizona, *Plateau* 46(1): 6–11.

Brown, W. K. 1978. Graffiti, identity, and the delinquent gang, *International Journal of Offender Therapy and Comparative Criminology* 22: 46–8.

Bruder, J. S. 1983. *Archaeological investigations at the Hedgepeth Hills petroglyph site.* Flagstaff, Museum of Northern Arizona. Research Paper No. 28.

Chaffee, S. D., M. Hyman, M. W. Rome, N. J. Coulam, A. Schroedl and K. Hogue. 1994. Radiocarbon dates on the All American Man pictograph, *American Antiquity* 59(4): 769–81.

Cintron, R. 1991. Reading and writing graffiti: a reading,

*The Quarterly Newsletter of the Laboratory of Comparative Human Cognition* 13: 21–4.

Coe, K. 1992. Art: the replicable unit – an inquiry into the possible origin of art as a social behaviour, *Journal of Social and Evolutionary Systems* 15: 217–34.

Cole, S. J. 1990. *Legacy on stone.* Boulder, Johnson Books.
1992. Katsina iconography in Homol'ovi rock-art – central Little Colorado River valley, Arizona, *Arizona Archaeologist* 25: 1–168.

Colton, M. and H. Colton. 1931. Petroglyphs, the record of a great adventure, *American Anthropologist* 33: 32–7.

Cordell, L. S. 1984. *Prehistory of the South-west.* San Diego (CA), Academic Press.

Covich, A. P. 1987. Optimal use of space by neighboring central place foragers: when and where to store surplus resources, *Advances in Behavioural Economics* 1: 249–94.

Cronk, L. 1995. Is there a role for culture in human behavioural ecology? *Ethology and Sociobiology* 16: 181–205.

Dean, J. S., W. H. Doelle, and J. D. Orcutt 1994. Adaptive stress, environment, and demography, in G. J. Gumerman (ed.), *Themes in Southwest prehistory,* pp. 53–86. Santa Fe, School of American Research Press.

Dean, J. S., R. C. Euler, G. J. Gumerman, F. Plog, R. H. Hevly and T. N. V. Karlstrom. 1985. Human behaviour, demography, and paleoenvironment on the Colorado Plateau, *American Antiquity* 50: 537–54.

Dissanayake, E. 1995. Chimera, spandrel, or adaptation – conceptualizing art in human evolution, *Human Nature* 6: 99–117.

Dorn, R. I. 1994. Surface exposure dating with rock varnish, in C. Beck (ed.), *Dating in exposed and surface contexts,* pp. 77–113. Albuquerque (NM), University of New Mexico Press.

Douglas, D. H. 1994. Least-cost path in GIS using an accumulated cost surface and slopelines, *Cartographica* 31: 37–51.

Ericson, J. and E. R. Goldstein. 1980. Work space: a new approach to the analysis of energy expenditure within site catchments, *Anthropology UCLA* 10: 21–30.

Euler, R. C. 1988. Demography and cultural dynamics on the Colorado Plateau, in G. J. Gumerman (ed.), *The Anasazi in a changing environment,* pp. 192–229. Cambridge, Cambridge University Press.

Ewer, R. F. 1968. *Ethology of mammals.* New York, Plenum Press.

Ferg, A. 1979. The petroglyphs of Tumamoc Hill, *The Kiva* 45: 95–118.

Geib, P. R. 1993. *Glen Canyon revisited: summary and conclusions of recent archaeological investigations in the Glen Canyon National Recreation Area.* Flagstaff, Northern Arizona University. Archaeological Report.

Geib, P. R. and P. W. Bungart. 1988. *San Juan archaeological survey: Glen Canyon Year 3 Report, 1987–1988.* Flagstaff, Northern Arizona University. Archaeological Report No. 1010.

Geib, P. R., P. W. Bungart and H. C. Fairley. 1987. *Archaeological investigations along the lower Escalante drainage: Glen Canyon Year 2 Report, 1985–1986.* Flagstaff, Northern Arizona University. Archaeological Report No. 1000.

Geib, P. R. and H. C. Fairley. 1992. Radiocarbon dating of Fremont anthropomorphic rock-art in Glen Canyon, south-central Utah, *Journal of Field Archaeology* 19(2): 155–68.

Geib, P. R., H. C. Fairley and P. W. Bungart. 1986. *Archaeological survey in the Glen Canyon National Recreation Area: Year 1 Descriptive Report, 1984–1985.* Flagstaff, Northern Arizona University. Archaeological Report No. 999.

Gilman, P. A. 1987. Architecture as artifact: pit structures and pueblos in the American South-west, *American Antiquity* 52: 538–64.

Gould, P. 1979. Signals in the noise, in S. Gale and G. Olsson (eds.), *Philosophy in geography*, pp. 121–54. London, D. Reidel.

Gould, R. A. 1990. *Recovering the past.* Albuquerque (NM), University of New Mexico Press.

Graham, M. 1994. *Mobile farmers: an ethnoarchaeological approach to settlement organization among the Raramuri of northwestern Mexico.* Ann Arbor (MI), International Monographs in Prehistory. Ethnoarchaeological Series No. 3.

Gross, D. D. and T. D. Gross. 1993. Tagging: changing visual patterns and the rhetorical implications of a new form of graffiti, *Etc. – a Review of General Semantics* 50: 251–64.

Gross, G. T. 1992. Subsistence change and architecture: Anasazi storerooms in the Dolores region, Colorado, *Research in Economic Anthropology*, Supplement 6, pp. 241–65.

Haas, J. and W. Creamer. 1996. The role of warfare in the Pueblo III period, in M. A. Adler (ed.), *The prehistoric Pueblo world, AD 1150–1350*, pp. 205–13. Tucson (AZ), University of Arizona Press.

Hamann, N. R. and K. Hedges. 1986. Topographical distribution of Hohokam petroglyph sites, *Rock Art Papers* 4: 77–86. San Diego Museum Papers 21.

Harris, M. 1990. Emics and etics revisited, in T. N. Headland, K. L. Pike and M. Harris (eds.), *Emics and etics – the insider/outsider debate*, pp. 48–61. Newbury Park (NJ), Sage Publications.

Hartley, R. J. 1991. Rockshelters and rock-art: an assessment of site use, *Proceedings of the Anasazi Symposium 1991*, compiled by A. Hutchinson and J. E. Smith, pp. 165–90. Mesa Verde (CO), Mesa Verde National Park.

1992a. *Rock art on the northern Colorado Plateau.* Aldershot, Avebury.

1992b. The role of rock art in spatial orientation on the northern Colorado Plateau: some observations and speculation. Paper presented at the Valcamonica symposium, 16–21 October, Capo di Ponte, Italy.

1995. Human hand representations: an assessment, *Bollettino del Centro Camuno di Studi Preistorici* 28: 141–8.

Hartley, R. J. and A. M. Wolley Vawser. 1996. Wayfinding in the desert: evaluating the role of rock-art through GIS, in Paul Faulstich (ed.), *Ecology of rock art*, pp. 55–76. Proceedings of the International Rock Art Congress, Flagstaff (AZ), 1994.

Hawkes, K. 1992. Sharing and collective action, in E. A. Smith and B. Winterhalder (eds.), *Evolutionary ecology and human behavior*, pp. 269–300. New York, Aldine de Gruyter.

Hayden, J. D. 1972. Hohokam petroglyphs of the Sierra Pinacate, Sonora and the Hohokam shell expeditions, *The Kiva* 37: 74–83.

Hazen, N. L. 1983. Spatial orientation: a comparative approach, in H. L. Pick and L. P. Acredolo (eds.), *Spatial orientation – theory, research, and application*, pp. 3–37. New York, Plenum Press.

Hegmon, M. 1991. The risks of sharing and sharing as risk reduction: interhousehold food sharing in egalitarian societies, in S. A. Gregg (ed.), *Between bands and states*, pp. 309–29. Carbondale (IL), Southern Illinois Press, Center for Archaeological Investigations. Occasional Paper No. 9.

Hobbs, J. J. 1989. *Bedouin life in the Egyptian wilderness.* Austin (TX), University of Texas Press.

Hunt, C. B. 1974. *Natural regions of the United States and Canada*. San Francisco (CA), W. H. Freeman.

Hunter-Anderson, R. L. 1986. *Prehistoric adaptation in the American South-west*. Cambridge, Cambridge University Press.

Hyder, W. D. 1994. Basketmaker spatial identity: rock-art as culture and praxis. Paper presented at International Rock Art Congress, 30 May–4 June, Flagstaff (AZ).

Imhof, E. 1968. *Gelunde und Kartz*. Zurich, Bujen Rentsch Verlag.

Ives, G. A. 1986. Rock art of the Dolores River valley, in *Dolores archaeological program: research designs and initial survey results*, compiled by A. E. Kane *et al.*, pp. 235–52. Denver (CO), US Bureau of Reclamation.

Janetski, J. C. 1993. The Archaic to Formative transition north of the Anasazi: a Basketmaker perspective, in V. M. Atkins (ed.), *Anasazi Basketmaker – papers from the 1990 Wetherill–Grand Gulch symposium*, pp. 223–41. Salt Lake City (UT), USDI Bureau of Land Management.

Kanter, J. 1996. Reconstructing the Chaco Anasazi road network using geographic information systems. Paper presented at the 61st annual meeting of the Society for American Archaeology, 10–14 April, New Orleans (LO).

Kaplan, H. 1987. Human communication and contemporary evolutionary theory, *Research on Language and Social Interaction* 20: 79–139.

Kaplan, R. 1976. Way-finding in the natural environment, in G. T. Moore and R. G. Golledge (eds.), *Environmental knowing*, pp. 46–57. Stroudsburg (PA), Dowden, Hutchinson and Ross.

Kaplan, S. and R. Kaplan. 1982. *Cognition and environment*. New York, Praeger.

Kelly, R. L. 1991. Sedentism, sociopolitical inequality, and resource fluctuations, in S. A. Gregg (ed.), *Between bands and states*, pp. 135–58. Carbondale (IL), Southern Illinois Press, Center for Archaeological Investigations. Occasional Paper No. 9.

Kohler, T. A. 1993. News from the northern American South-west: prehistory on the edge of chaos, *Journal of Archaeological Research* 1: 267–321.

Kohler, T. A. and C. R. Van West. 1996. The calculus of self interest in the development of cooperation: sociopolitical development and risk among the northern Anasazi, in J. A. Tainter and B. B. Tainter (eds.), *Evolving complexity and environmental risk in the prehistoric Southwest*, pp. 169–96. Reading (MA), Addison-Wesley.

Krebs, J. R. and N. B. Davies. 1987. *An introduction to behavioural ecology*. Sunderland (MA), Sinaurer.

Krippendorf, K. 1975. Information theory, in G. J. Hanneman and W. J. McEwen (eds.), *Communication and behavior*, pp. 351–89. Reading (MA), Addison-Wesley.

1986. *Information theory–structural models for qualitative data*. Beverly Hills (CA), Sage.

Kuipers, B. 1982. The 'map in the head' metaphor, *Environment and Behaviour* 14: 202–20.

1983. The cognitive map: could it have been any other way?, in H. L. Pick and L. P. Acredolo (eds.), *Spatial orientation: theory, research, and application*, pp. 345–59. New York, Plenum Press.

Lewis, D. 1976. Observations on route finding and spatial orientation among the Aboriginal peoples of the Western Desert of Central Australia, *Oceania* 46: 249–82.

Ley, D. and R. Cybriwski. 1974. Urban graffiti as territorial markers, *Annals of the Association of American Geographers* 64: 491–505.

Limp, W. F. 1991. Continuous cost movement models, in C. Behrens and T. Sever (eds.), *Applications of space-age technology in anthropology*, pp. 237–50. Science and Technology Laboratory, John C. Stennis Space Center.

Limp, W. F. and C. Carr. 1985. The analysis of decision-making: alternative applications in archaeology, in C. Carr (ed.), *For concordance in archaeological analysis*, pp. 128–72. Kansas City (MO), Westport Press.

Lipe, W. D. 1967. Anasazi culture and its relationship to the environment in the Red Rock Plateau region, south-eastern Utah. Ph.D dissertation, Department of Anthropology, Yale University.

1970. Anasazi communities in the Red Rock Plateau, south-eastern Utah, in W. A. Longacre (ed.), *Reconstructing prehistoric Pueblo societies*, pp. 84–139. Albuquerque (NM), University of New Mexico Press.

Manning, S. J. 1990. Barrier Canyon style pictographs of the Colorado Plateau – Part One: Hypothesis and evidence for the existence of post *circa* AD 1300 panels, *Utah Archaeology* 1990 3: 43–84.

Martynec, R. 1986. A comparative analysis of rock art at trincheras sites in the Tucson Basin, *Rock Art Papers* 3: 103–16. San Diego, San Diego Museum Papers No. 0.

Matson, R. G. 1991. *The origins of Southwestern agriculture*. Tucson (AZ), University of Arizona Press.

Menzel, E. W. 1978. Cognitive mapping in chimpanzees, in S. H. Hulse, H. Fowler and W. H. Honig (eds.), *Cognitive processes in animal behavior*, pp. 375–422. Hillsdale (NJ), Erlbaum.

Michaelis, H. 1981. Willowsprings: a Hopi petroglyph site, *Journal of New World Archaeology* 4(2): 3–23.

Minnis, P. E. 1996. Notes on economic uncertainty and human behavior in the prehistoric North American Southwest, in J. A. Tainter and B. B. Tainter (eds.), *Evolving complexity and environmental risk in the prehistoric Southwest*, pp. 57–78. Reading (MA), Addison-Wesley.

Morphy, H. 1977. Schematisation, meaning, and communication in toas, in P. J. Ucko (ed.), *Form in indigenous art*, pp. 77–89. Canberra, Australian Institute of Aboriginal Studies.

Morss, N. 1931. *The ancient culture of the Fremont River in Utah: report on the explorations under the Claflin-Emerson fund, 1928–29*. Cambridge (MA), Papers of the Peabody Museum of American Archaeology and Ethnology 49(1).

Nelson, L. M. 1995. How are these sites different? Investigating petroglyph and site variation in south central Arizona. Paper presented at the 60th annual meeting of the Society for American Archaeology, 3–7 May, Minneapolis (MN).

Olsen, N. H. 1989. Social roles of animal iconography: implications for archaeology from Hopi and Suni ethnographic sources, in H. Morphy (ed.), *Animals into art*, pp. 417–39. London, Unwin Hyman.

Osborn, A. J. 1996. Cattle, co-wives, children, and calabashes: material context for symbol use among the Il Chamus of west-central Kenya, *Journal of Anthropological Archaeology* 15: 107–36.

Osborn, A. J. and A. M. Wolley Vawser. 1991. Adaptive food storage and caching behaviour in the prehistoric South-west, *Proceedings of the Anasazi Symposium 1991*, compiled by A. Hutchinson and J. E. Smith, pp. 215–38. Mesa Verde (CO), Mesa Verde National Park.

Pennington, C. W. 1963. *The Tarahumar of Mexico: their environment and material culture*. Salt Lake City (NT), University of Utah Press.

Peteet, J. 1996. The writing on the walls: the graffiti of the Intifada, *Cultural Anthropology* 11: 139–59.

Reed, A. D. 1994. The Numic occupation of western Colorado and eastern Utah during the prehistoric and protohistoric periods, in D. B. Madsen and D. Rhode (eds.), *Across the west: human population movement and the expansion of the Numa*, pp. 188–9. Salt Lake City (NT), University of Utah Press.

Savage, S. H. 1989. *Late Archaic landscapes: a Geographic Information Systems approach to the late Archaic landscape of the Savannah River valley, Georgia and South Carolina*. University of South Carolina. Occasional Papers of the South Carolina Institute of Archaeology and Anthropology, Anthropological Studies No. 8.

Schaafsma, P. 1971. *The rock art of Utah*. Cambridge (MA), Papers of the Peabody Museum of Archaeology and Ethnology 65.

1980. *Indian rock art of the South-west*. Santa Fe (NT), School of American Research.

1985. Form, content, and function: theory and method in North American rock-art studies, *Advances in Archaeological Method and Theory* 8: 237–77.

Schone, H. 1984. *Spatial orientation: the spatial control of behaviour in animals and man*. Princeton (NJ), Princeton University Press.

Shannon, C. E. and W. Weaver. 1949. *The mathematical theory of communication*. Urbana (IL), University of Illinois Press.

Siegel, A. W. and S. H. White. 1975. The development of spatial representations of large-scale environments, in H. W. Reese (ed.), *Advances in child development and behavior* 10, pp. 9–55. New York (NY), Academic Press.

Simmons, L. W. (ed.). 1942. *Sun Chief: the autobiography of a Hopi Indian*. New Haven (CT), Yale University Press.

Simms, S. R. 1990. Fremont transitions, *Utah Archaeology 1990* 1: 1–18.

Snyder, E. E. 1966. Petroglyphs of the South Mountains of Arizona, *American Antiquity* 31: 705–9.

Sognnes, K. 1994. Ritual landscape: toward a reinterpretation of Stone Age rock art in Trondelag, Norway, *Norwegian Archaeological Review* 27: 29–50.

Stirling, E. C. and E. R. Waite. 1919. Description of toas: or Australian Aboriginal direction signs, *Records of the South Australian Museum* 1(2): 105–55.

Stokes, W. L. 1977. Subdivisions of the major physiographic provinces in Utah, *Utah Geology* 4: 1–17.

Strehlow, T. G. H. 1971. Geography and the totemic landscape in central Australia, in R. Berndt (ed.), *Australian Aboriginal anthropology*, pp. 92–140. Nedlands, University of Western Australia Press.

Swartz, B. K. and T. S. Hurlbutt. 1994. Space, place and territory in rock-art interpretation, *Rock Art Research*

11(1): 13–22.

Taçon, P. S. C. 1994. Socialising landscapes: the long-term implications of signs, symbols and marks on the the land, *Archaeology in Oceania* 29: 117–29.

Testart, A. 1982. The significance of food storage among hunter-gatherers: residence patterns, population densities, and social inequalities, *Current Anthropology* 23: 523–37.

Thomas, R. W. 1981. *Information statistics in geography.* Concepts and Techniques in Modern Geography. Norwich, Geo Abstracts 31.

Titiev, M. 1937. A Hopi salt expedition, *American Anthropologist* 39: 244–58.

Tobler, W. 1993. Non-isotropic geographic modelling, in *Three presentations on geographical analysis and modeling.* Santa Barbara (CA), National Center for Geographic Information and Analysis, University of California. Technical Report 93–1.

Tokioka, K. 1992. Rock art of Escalante Canyon: quantitative analysis of rock art elements of Glen Canyon. MA thesis, Department of Anthropology, Northern Arizona University, Flagstaff.

Turner, C. G. 1963. *Petroglyphs of the Glen Canyon region.* Flagstaff (AZ), Museum of Northern Arizona. 1971. Revised dating for early rock art of the Glen Canyon region, *American Antiquity* 36: 469–71.

Turner, C. G. and J. M. Turner. 1995. Cannibalism in the prehistoric American Southwest: occurrence, taphonomy, explanation, and suggestions for standardized

world definition, *Anthropological Science* 103: 1–22.

Vander Wall, S. B. 1990. *Food hoarding in animals.* Chicago (IL), University of Chicago Press.

Wallace, H. 1983. The mortars, petroglyphs, and trincheras on Rillito Peak, *The Kiva* 48: 137–246.

Weaver, D. E., Jr, and B. H. Rosenberg. 1978. Petroglyphs of the southern Sierra Estrella: a locational interpretation, in E. Snyder, A. J. Bock and F. Bock (eds.), *American Indian rock art*, pp. 108–23. El Toro (CA), American Rock Art Research Association.

Wellman, H. M., S. C. Somerville and R. J. Haake. 1979. Development of search procedures in real-life spatial environments, *Developmental Psychology* 15: 530–42.

Wilcox, D. R. and J. Haas. 1994. The scream of the butterfly: competition and conflict in the prehistoric Southwest, in G. J. Gumerman (ed.), *Themes in Southwest prehistory*, pp. 211–38. Santa Fe (NM), School of American Research.

Wittek, R. 1990. Resource competition and violent conflict: cross-cultural evidence for a socio-ecological approach, *Zeitschrift für Ethnologie* 115: 23–44.

Wolley, A. M. and A. J. Osborn. 1991. *An isolated storage vessel at Site 42SA20779 in Glen Canyon National Recreation Area: adaptive storage and caching behavior in the prehistoric South-west.* Lincoln (NE), Midwest Archeological Center. Occasional Studies in Anthropology No. 25.

Young, M. J. 1988. *Signs from the ancestors: Zuni cultural symbolism and perceptions of rock-art.* Albuquerque (NM), University of New Mexico Press.

# 12. The tale of the chameleon and the platypus: limited and likely choices in making pictures

If a picture is 'naturalistic', then the form of the image follows the form of the subject it represents. We know that this is true for the very many images, from many traditions of image-making, of which we have good informed knowledge. One formal approach to pictures of which we do not have inside knowledge is to suppose that the naturalistic rule also holds there: by observing the traits of the picture, we should be able to figure out the traits of the subject it represents. How secure is this reasoning? What general rules of picture-making may there be which will be instructive?

This chapter has come about because of a number of experiences which have challenged me. At a rock-shelter on Mphunzi Hill in central Malaŵi I was contemplating the beauty of a depiction of a chameleon and marvelling at the powerful mixture of symbolic images that were juxtaposed at the site. Near the chameleon was a python and next to this a monitor lizard, all complex symbols in Chewa cosmology relating to the unified themes of rain, fertility and creation. My thoughts were interrupted by John (a locally born Malaŵian who was working with me) who asked: 'Why do you say that thing is a chameleon? How do you know?' I was devastated. Drawing on knowledge of Chewa cosmology I was starting to see a link between the images and particular symbolic themes. This link demonstrated a connection between the art and Chewa female coming-of-age rituals. However, what was the use of this realisation if even John, a local, was not convinced that the shapes depicted the suggested subjects? The answer in my own mind was to show that the depiction had many of the attributes of a chameleon: the shape of its head, four legs, lizard-like tail, and no other possible subject has all these characteristics.

A year or so later, I was assisting the editors of this volume with their study of rock-art in Arnhem Land, northern Australia. While working through the many wonderful sites at Ubirr in Kakadu National Park we came across a depiction of a duck-billed platypus. It was my first visit to Australia and I had been looking forward to my first sight of a red kangaroo, a koala, a wombat. To my shock, when I got there, I discovered that none of these animals were to be found in Kakadu. The painting of the duck-billed platypus thus excited me and I enquired as to where we could see one of these strange creatures. The answer was 'a few thousand kilometres further east and south' since the platypus lives in eastern Australia. Platypuses do not live and have never lived near Ubirr. This painting, while having many attributes that showed me it was a platypus, the duck-like bill, four legs, wide body, was therefore not a depiction of a platypus. No other possible subject came to my mind but it was my mind that was at fault.

Where did this leave the chameleon? Somewhat up a gum tree it seemed! This brought to mind Clegg and his cautionary words about pictures of '!fish' and 'fish' (Clegg 1977; 1987a). A '!fish' merely reminds one of a fish whereas a 'fish' *is* a depicted fish. However, in the cases of the chameleon and the platypus the problem was not in acknowledging the degree of uncertainty. In both I had been certain; yet in one I was asked to prove my convictions, and in the other it was proved that my convictions could be wrong. Like other researchers who think they grasp what they are looking at, I needed to take a step backwards: to consider the processes by which subjects can be transformed into pictures and the approaches by which they can be recognised. This is the theme of the following.

Macintosh (1977) has suggested that all subject recognition is inherently flawed without informed knowledge. At two rock-shelters in Northern Territory, Australia, using experts from the local Djauan experts from the local Djauan community to judge his observations, he found a '90 per cent failure . . . to diagnose correctly the individual painted items' (Macintosh 1977: 197). This example is a valuable reminder of the need for caution but it is overly pessimistic about the potential of study in that great majority of cases where informed knowledge is absent. In this chapter it will be argued that analysis of the choices taken during the picture-making process provides a formal means of interpretation. Much is obvious, but I have found consideration of the process of picture-creation valuable; indeed, it has altered the way I approach the interpretation of rock-art.

## The making of a picture

Making a picture involves many decisions, each followed by one or a series of actions. The number of choices in each decision and follow-up action is always limited. Some decisions force particular actions: if it is chosen to create a stencil, then pigment must be collected, prepared and blown over the subject onto the chosen surface. What is significant for interpretation is *which* decisions and subsequent actions were chosen rather than forced, and *why* these choices were made. Choices are determined by the wishes of the artist along with the intended purpose of the picture. One wish or purpose may determine many choices in the picturing process. If I want to boast of the size of my latest fishing triumph I would paint an eye-catching picture of a fish, exceptional in size. I would construct a form, using my experience of other fish drawings, and would ensure that this was immediately recognisable as a large fish. The final touch would be to add a figure or mark to show

people that it was I who had caught the monster. The picture would then need to be placed in a position where other people would see it, ideally all other fishermen. A later analysis of what options were available and which were chosen would provide a researcher with indications as to why these choices were made. A formal analysis along these lines can only be carried out from the basis of a good understanding of the picture-making process.

*Preparing to create a picture*

Various decisions have to be taken before a picture can be made. Each decision will affect the appearance of the final picture. All of the choices are limited and limiting.

1 Which place in the landscape are we going to choose for the execution of our picture?

2 On what are we going to draw? At any site there will be many things on which we could make a picture. In this chapter we are concerned solely with rock.

3 Are we going to mark the surface itself or place a mark on it? In the case of rock-art this means choosing whether to make a petroglyph or a pictograph.

4 What method are we going to use to apply the mark? With a petroglyph the mark can be pecked (hammered into the surface) or incised (scraped into the surface). A pictograph can be drawn, painted, daubed, stencilled or printed.

5 What implement are we going to use to make the mark? This is largely conditioned by the choice of method. A petroglyph has to be made with a sharp tool. For pictographs a drawing must be made using some form of crayon; a painting using some form of brush or pointed object such as a stick or a finger; a daubing using the hand or some other large flat object; a stencil by blowing pigment over and around the subject; a print by covering the subject in pigment and then pressing or throwing it against the chosen surface.

6 What pigment, if any, are we going to use? If we wish to make a pictograph we must use pigment;

for a petroglyph, pigment is an optional extra. Charcoal, suitable for drawing, might be found lying near the rock surface; all other forms of pigment must be collected and prepared in advance. This necessitates the collection of a coloured substance which is then ground to powder and mixed with a liquid to create a paste.

Only after these choices have been made and the relevant tools and materials collected can we begin the process of picture-making. The next decision is what image we want to peck, incise, draw, paint, and so forth. Do we intend this image to have a subject?

### Deciding on picture type and subject-matter

Stencils and prints must have subjects since the subject is used in their creation. In other methods the choice of subject is open. If we decide to give our picture a subject then we can create a form that mimics elements of the subject: this is a depiction. We can create a non-depictional mark which represents or stands for the subject: this is a symbol. If we decide to create a picture with no subject, then we create an abstract design. There are thus essentially three picture types: depictions, symbols and abstract designs. The first two have an immediate subject-matter; they may also carry symbolism (meaning deeper than the immediate subject-matter).

The potential choice of immediate subject-matter for any picture is extensive. This will always have been the case. Anything the artist has seen, experienced, heard about or sensed could be depicted or represented. Subject-matter can be non-material as well as material. I am careful not to use the word 'real', as the conception of reality is culturally determined. For any group of artists, in any time-period, the range of possible subjects will be unique and limited. A choice can be made only from the repertoire of known subjects. This repertoire changes through time, with some subjects forgotten and others arriving because of invention or environmental change. Without informed knowledge, the whole range of possible subjects in another place and/or time cannot be known to us.

### Deciding on form

Once the subject-matter (or none) has been chosen, the next decision is to choose a form. For none of the three picture types can there be an unlimited number of forms available to the artist. All are restricted by the nature of two-dimensional drawing and by various choices made during the preparation stage. The form given to an abstract design will be influenced by the artist's experience of other abstract and non-abstract designs: an abstract design must take a form that avoids resemblance to known symbols and depictions. Similarly, the form given to a symbol will be influenced by the artist's experience of existing symbols and other designs. Symbols *must* avoid resemblance to known depictions and existing symbols. Symbols will normally be of simple form since it is usually necessary for them to be repeated.

The form given to a depiction is severely constrained by the necessity for the form to mimic some aspect of its subject. All artists creating a depiction face essentially the same problem: how to transform a three-dimensional subject (material or of the mind) into a two-dimensional picture, a transformation that involves many losses. Even the loss of one dimension is not a simple process. The way an artist tackles this transformation process will be defined by his or her experience of how others have tackled the same problem. This creates, in space and time, complexes of locally interacting artistic traditions where artists belonging to the same tradition use common conventions to overcome common picturing problems and to comply with common picturing wishes. Widely separated traditions sometimes utilise the same convention in dealing with a particular picturing problem. In side-on pictures of large mammals, horns and ears are often drawn as seen from the front (for example, Zimbabwe in Garlake 1995: figs. 9, 153, 182; Algeria in Muzzolini 1995: figs. 86, 196, 214; Australia in Walsh 1988: figs. 147, 154, 156; USA in Whitley 1994: figs. 2, 3). This need not suggest any influence or mixing between these traditions. There can only be a limited number of ways of dealing with any particular picturing problem and it is therefore statistically probable that two groups of people will arrive independently at the same chosen solution. To take this a step further, I would suggest that some answers are more *natural* than others because they overcome the problem more successfully. The best way to depict the distinctive characteristics of horns and ears in a side-on depiction of a large mammal is to shift the perspective to a frontal view for these features. Since this is the best solution available, it is often chosen. This begs the question as to whether there might be a natural and therefore *normal* way of solving some picturing problems irrespective of cultural experience.

## Normalisms

In a recent paper, Deregowski (1995) notes a tendency for animals and humans to be drawn from a lateral (side-on) viewpoint. He suggests that the human eye perceives this as the most 'typical' view which 'represents better' the subject in question and explains this in terms of Attneave's notion of points of concentration of information. According to this, in line drawings, information is most concentrated at the points of rapid change; an outline which shows many corners and pointed bits is, according to this notion, easier to recognise than one which shows few. By this reasoning, the optimum view (in terms of being easy to recognise) for humans and most animals is side-on (ideally walking posture) and for reptiles from above. These are, indeed, common viewpoints, but to suggest that this proves the proposed explanation would be circular reasoning.

Drawing an object from a particular viewpoint makes it impossible to portray all features. I suspect that artists normally choose viewpoints that allow them to depict as many characteristic features as possible. This is usually a lateral view, but not always. Domestic cats, for example, as Deregowski notes, are commonly depicted in children's drawings with their faces front-on (Deregowski 1995: 19). The choice of viewpoint is not therefore to do with the nature of the shape itself (its corners, etc.) but is rather the choice of a view that includes a collection of features which will allow a correct identification of the subject. Lewis has demonstrated how it is not the general appearance or body shape of a picture that is usually key to subject recognition, but certain species-specific characteristics (Lewis 1986: 40). In the depiction of African antelope it is the horns. To be recognisable, the picture thus needs to be a view which is commonly seen and which contains the distinctive species-specific traits. Where there is no single common viewpoint that is distinctive, the natural solution is to twist the perspective slightly or to move body parts somewhat to positions where they can be portrayed. This can be seen in many separated art traditions (for example, Australian 'X-ray style' art in Chaloupka 1993b; Saharan 'archaic style' art in Muzzolini 1995; southern African Bushman art in Lewis-Williams and Dowson 1989).

But do all artists, as Deregowski's paper assumes, want their pictures to convey the immediate subject-matter? Not always. Immediate subject-matter is sometimes disguised; at times it is unimportant, such as when the subject is chosen for some symbolic or mnemonic purpose. The genet cat is depicted on the trunk of a tree as part of the coming-of-age ceremony for Nsenga girls in eastern Zambia (Apthorpe 1962). The image helps the girls to remember instructions concerning sexual practices and taboos. The immediate subject is not important, and it would not matter if the genet cat was wrongly interpreted as a monitor lizard or crocodile. The secondary subject-matter is key: the sexual instruction which is recalled by the phallic nature of the tail hanging between the creature's legs. There is thus no need to add those features that would make the depiction an unambiguous genet cat. The genet cat painting is unusual; in most cases Deregowski is correct that artists wish to convey the immediate subject-matter. This is why a distinctive side view is a common choice for depiction because it most successfully achieves this normal wish. When it is not used one needs to consider why not. Was the artist unaccustomed to lateral depiction and/or using another method to convey the immediate subject-matter or did he/she have a different wish? The realisation that the artist had a more important concern than conveying the immediate subject-matter would be a highly significant finding.

Considering normal behaviour returns us to the question of choices. Why is a particular choice made from the limited number available? Answer: because it most successfully achieves the wishes of the artist. Tradition may play a part in the choice but this does not negate the truth of the above. Traditions will only be continued while they complement the wishes of the artist. The purpose and the product are inherently linked; one defines the other. A formal study of the product (the picture) can therefore assist us to understand the purpose. Consideration of which wishes lead to which choices and which are usual and expected should play an important part in this. Where a picturing choice is made that is rare and unexpected this is an indication that the painter has an unusual wish/purpose in mind. Normal wishes can be known because they are repeated and lead to the same choice being made often and in many places. The choice of the lateral view is a case in point: the product of the normal wish to convey immediate subject-matter. Individual unusual wishes will not occur often but this does not mean they must remain unknown. A picture is the end product of a few wishes and many choices; any one choice may not give away the wish but taking the whole range of choices together should provide strong indications as to the wish. This can be seen in my hypothetical example of the fish painting where I wished to boast of the size of my latest catch. The choice of lateral profile for the fish would not have given away the wish to boast about the catch, only consideration of the many choices that were made.

Clegg is one of the few people to have given norms due consideration. Norms can be applied to all stages of the picture-making process, not merely the choice of manner of depiction. Clegg notes that most of us use unstated norms even though we do this partly subconsciously (Clegg 1987b: 32). An example from my work comes to mind. The hunter-gatherer art of south-central Africa is executed al-most entirely in red ochre. Like many researchers in other areas, I asked why this is the case when yellow ochre, white clay and other pigments were also available. This assumed a norm. Although unstated, I had assumed that if artists assigned no importance to pigment colour they would normally choose pig-ments in accordance with their availability. I was working on the expectation that because red was particularly chosen this implied that the choice of red was significant. This may be a valid expectation but without my having stated and discussed the norm, the value of this research was reduced. Many hun-dreds of specific norms such as this could be drawn up; another example would be that if the final pic-ture, rather than the method of making the picture, was important, then one would expect to find picto-graphs rather than petroglyphs on protected surfa-ces. Petroglyphs take more time and effort to execute and end up being less easy to see; if the image rather than process is key, the petroglyph is therefore less satisfactory. If survival was important then a petro-glyph would be normal as its enduring nature would make it the more satisfactory.

Many specific norms derive from a smaller number of more general normal expectations. The example concerning colour of pigment derives from the ex-pectation that: if thing $X$ is not significant in itself to the artist then thing $X$ will be chosen in accordance with its availability. $X$ could be colour of pigment, subject-matter, nature of surface, orientation of site, etc. The choice of petroglyph or pictograph example derives from another general norm, the laziness norm by which: if action $Y$ is not significant in itself to the artist then the easiest option will be chosen. Clegg has published a depictional norm which is another form of this: 'subjects are depicted as easily as possible: pictures contain only the minimum infor-mation necessary to recognise the subject' (Clegg 1987b: 33). The laziness norm should mean that we find a predominance of very small and very simple pictures. This is not the case. The reason is because achievement of purpose is also important and the simplest picture will not always allow this. There is thus another norm, the satisfaction norm, acting as a counterbalance: the finished product must be satisfying to the artist. A picture will only satisfy if it successfully achieves its purpose. There is thus a balance to be decided by the artist between the amount of effort expended and the extent to which the product satisfies the wishes of the artist; where this balance is struck will be determined by the purpose. Analysis of this choice thus provides another tool for the investigation of picture purpose.

The Clegg norms concerning composition (Clegg 1987b, 1995a) proved particularly valuable to my research. Study of art by primates, children and students caused Clegg to note that when an artist paints on a surface: 'the centre of the space is preferred and tends to be the location of the earliest, as well as the largest, and the most important marks in an agglomeration picture. Edges are avoided, but corners preferred over other margins; pre-existing marks both attract and repel marks, so that marks cluster together, but are not purposely superimposed' (Clegg 1987b: 33, 1995a). The recognition of these normal trends is of value itself, but we should also consider *why* these trends occur. Given that purpose and product are inherently linked, these trends must be the result of normal wishes. Why is the central space the preferred and earliest choice? On a rock face, I suspect this is because of a normal wish for an easily accessible space and one where the limits of the picture will be least restricted. The fact that this first central picture tends to be large suggests a common wish to utilise a reasonable portion of the space that is available; by implication, therefore, use of only a small portion of the available space would be perceived as looking silly. Later pictures are then normally arranged around, following the same wish to utilise that space where the limits of the picture will be least restricted. The reduction in size of picture through time would therefore be a product of the reduction in the size of the space available. Following the least restriction norm should bring about overpainting not avoidance. The fact that avoidance is more common means that there is an avoidance norm, superior to the least restriction norm, which stems from a wish to use clean space or a wish not to disturb existing pictures.

Kampika, in central Malaŵi, provides an example of a site that follows the compositional norms (see Fig. 12.1). Here the central figure is the largest and the oldest. It is slightly overlaid by the smaller figure to its left and by the meandering line above, it is also relatively more faded. Other figures arranged around use up the remaining protected space. Newer figures can be seen to become increasingly small as the remaining space is used up. A few very small recent designs have been squeezed into tiny spaces. At this site the Clegg composition norms allow one to suggest a model of how the site developed, picture by picture. One is given confidence that this model is valid because it is supported by those overlays which exist and by the relative states of preservation. It is also logical that figures squeezed between others will be later. Without the expectation of the normal composition one could easily have missed all sequencing at this site.

Norms are only normal, they are not rules and will not occur always. Many sites exist where the normal composition does not occur. This is also significant. If we were to examine another site and decide that the normal composition had not occurred, this would indicate that the normal wishes outlined above (easy accessibility, lack of restriction, non-overlay of other figures) no longer applied. One could then consider what wishes applied to this non-normal composition. Again this would take us a step closer to understanding why a particular picture was created.

## Conventionalities

In recognising the value of norms it is important not to lose sight of the value of local conventions and regional differences in picturing choices. Some choices made during the picturing process are predetermined in that, having been made at some point in the past, they have then been copied by subsequent artists. Repeated copying turns a choice into a con-

**Fig. 12.1.** Daubings at Kampika, Dedza District, Malaŵi.

vention. Over time, a convention thus becomes the accepted way of doing something. Conventions can grow up relating to any of the choices in the picture-making process described above but are particularly notable when associated with the choice of manner of depiction. Despite being habitual, conventions should still tell us something about the wishes of the artist because they will originally have been chosen for their suitability and success at fulfilling some particular artistic purpose.

Recognition of sets of conventions which seem to belong to particular times and places has led to the grouping of rock-art into 'styles', each a body of pictures that use common conventions. These 'styles' have then been placed in sequences. In recent years the value of the concept 'style' has been questioned (e.g. Lorblanchet and Bahn 1993). Some have called for the abandonment of the term, arguing that it is ill defined and confusing while others have leapt to its

support, arguing that the categorisation of art is essential to meaningful discussion and analysis of rock-art. The problem with the word 'style' would seem to be that it appears to suggest a unified and separated body of art. However a 'style' is actually just a body of pictures that have been collected together by their common use of conventions. The boundaries of such a unit are unlikely to be clear. Both in time and space it should be expected that some conventions will cease and new ones take over, some will be adapted or developed, others will continue as they are. The spatial and temporal boundaries of a 'style' are therefore inherently fuzzy. This does not undermine the concept of the 'style'; it is in its nature. This fact is rarely discussed, perhaps due to the misconception that if you acknowledge the fuzziness of the grouping you undermine its validity. In fact, an examination of the nature of the fuzziness (change/variation) may assist in our understanding of what the grouping represents and why it occurred. Where one grouping merges with another so that at the boundary the conventions are found to be mixed, the implication must be that these groupings occurred for reasons that were mutually compatible. Those elements that merge must be complementary. A clear and sharp divide indicates that the two groupings occurred for reasons that varied and between which there could be no cross-over.

That 'styles' have been identified in almost every place where rock-art occurs demonstrates that there is an inherent tendency for artists to copy picturing conventions. The tendency to copy conventions creates the 'style' but it does not explain it. In south-central Africa I have noted how various 'styles' co-existed within the same geographic/temporal distribution and can be shown to have belonged to a single cultural group (Smith 1995). In this example the coexistence of differing 'styles' may be explained in terms of varying artistic traditions relating to gender and gender concerns. Similar overlap between 'styles' has been noted in other areas (e.g. Arnhem Land: Taçon and Chippindale 1994; central Tanzania: Masao 1979; Anati 1986), no doubt explained by differing reasons. The importance of these examples is that they show that when sets of conventions are copied this is not done mindlessly. The original choice of these conventions was made for a particular reason. The conventions were then copied because this reason remained relevant or at least continued to complement the wishes of the later artists. Conventions from other 'styles', although known, were not copied because they were not relevant. The pictures grouped within a 'style' can thus be expected to be united by a common strand. Judging by those examples of 'styles' about which we have secure knowledge, the common strand seems normally to relate to function. The value of any particular 'style' as an archaeological unit for study will differ according to the reason for its existence: why a particular convention or set of conventions was first used, why it was copied, and why it then ceased to be used. In addition to studying informed

sources, formal examination of the nature of what changed may help to suggest this reason.

Formal study of 'styles' and thus of the decisions taken by artists in choosing particular conventions may be valuable in a number of ways, in addition to helping us explain the reason why those 'styles' came about. Study of the geographical extent of the usage of particular conventions can give a measure of the extent of spread of artistic influence. An understanding of conventions is also one way of getting at subject-matter. In identifying the subject of a particular picture, people who are local contemporaries of the artist should be able to interpret the picture since they will be familiar with the artistic conventions and the possible range of subject-matter. Those of us who study pictures long after they were made, often in parts of the world that are strange to us, are ignorant both of the local artistic conventions and of the possible range of subject-matter. The artistic conventions can usually be learnt by formal methods: essentially by studying the art closely.

A proportion of the potential subject range (animals, plants and natural features) can be known since it will continue into the present, if not in the environs of the site then in other similar areas. Another section can also be learnt from relevant ethnographic, archaeological, palaeontological and palaeobotanical data. Where a picture bears resemblance to known subject-matter then that picture can be unpacked to see what conventions would have been needed to transform the suspected subject into the picture in question. The same conventions can then be used to create expected depictions of other subjects. If such depictions are found to occur in the rock-art, then the identification of the subject-matter of the first picture must have been correct and the conventions were correctly identified. The more detailed analysis of depiction of subject-matter that this then allows will result in a greater depth of understanding in what and how conventions were used. While it seems fair to assume that in a particular time and place the conventions belonging to a particular 'style' will have remained constant for most subject-

219

matter, it should be borne in mind that perceived categories of subject may have been treated somewhat differently. Although the understanding of conventions must initially stem from a recognition of subject-matter, the subsequent deepening knowledge and consideration of the application of these conventions should allow a productive discussion of the subject-matter of many pictographs that would otherwise be considered unrecognisable.

## The normal and the conventional

An awareness of what is universally normal (and why) and what is locally conventional (and why) thus provides scope for the analysis of both subject-matter and picture purpose along formal lines in any area regardless of the existence of informed knowledge. Where does this leave the pictures of the chameleon and the platypus?

*The !chameleon* (see Figs. 12.2 and 12.3)

The chameleon picture belongs to a tradition of art associated with Chewa girls' coming-of-age ceremonies (Smith 1995). This knowledge has come from informed (ethnohistorical) methods. During the ceremonies, pictures were made of a selected group of subjects chosen for their symbolic relevance to the concerns of women. Each picture was used as a mnemonic device to ensure that important teachings were learnt by the girls. The chameleon, a crucial figure in Chewa creation symbolism, thus occurs regularly in the art. Its presence at a site is expected. I am therefore convinced that this is a depiction of a chameleon. This conviction has been allowed because in this instance we enjoy the rare fortune of being able to draw information concerning the picture (which is demonstrably relevant) from modern traditions and practices. For the vast bulk of the world's rock-art we are not in this fortunate position. The point of this chapter is to show that a formal study of the choices that were made in the making of the chameleon picture could have brought us at least some of the way to the understanding that was gained from informed methods.

Without informed knowledge, I think there is sufficient information in the picture to identify it as a chameleon. The form is sufficiently zoomorphic to eliminate the possibility of its being a symbol or abstract design. Exactly why it seems 'sufficiently zoomorphic' is more hard to quantify; even harder would be to quantify the minimum requirements of a zoomorph. I would quantify the zoomorphic elements of this picture as follows:

(A) A central mass mimics the shape of a body seen in lateral profile.

(B) Four protrusions stretching downwards from A mimic in shape and size the four legs found on most creatures.

(C) Two protrusions at opposite ends of A, one long and thin, one short and fat, mimic the usual form for the head and tail of a four-legged creature.

The combination of all of these elements together and alone allows confidence that this is a depiction of a four-legged creature: !body, !legs, !head and !tail have thus become body, legs, head and tail by virtue of the improbability of these features occurring together and alone by chance or in any other object or thing. Next we must try to decide which four-legged creature is depicted.

The relative body part positions identify this as a side view. Using the depictional norms we can thus expect this creature to be taller than it is broad (creatures that are broader than they are tall seem to be more distinctive when viewed from above). Since the creature was daubed, there is no fine detail in the depiction and recognition depends on just a few major features. If it was desired to convey the immediate subject-matter, the artist will thus have formed these few features carefully in order to make the subject recognisable. A wish to convey the subject-matter can be determined from the layout of the legs. This side view should only allow us to see two legs; the two on the far side should be hidden exactly behind those on the near side. In the picture the artist has shifted the legs on the far side so that they can be portrayed. This shift was essential to our recognition

**Fig. 12.2.** A tracing of the !chameleon from Mphunzi Hill, Dedza District, Malaŵi.
Tracing made by Alison Gascoigne from slides; as a disinterested Egyptologist not knowing the rock-art, she traced what she saw.

**Fig. 12.3.** Photograph of the !chameleon from Mphunzi Hill, Dedza District, Malaŵi.
This picture had been outlined in chalk some weeks before this photograph was taken. This was done by someone whose enthusiasm for culture should not be confused with knowledge – the line is inaccurate in a number of places and is best ignored.

221

that this was a four-legged creature. Other clues have also been left. The relative size and proportion of both head and tail mimic only a particular range of subjects. Of modern African creatures only rodents and reptiles have tails of that relative length and width. The relative size and form of the head and neck are unlike any rodent. By a process of elimination this is either a reptile or an unknown subject.

If this is a reptile, then the upward protrusion on the head is strange. The obvious interpretation is that this is an ear; reptiles, however, do not have protruding ears. Going back to the legs, our artist was careful to shift the unseen rear pair to assist subject recognition. If this protrusion was an ear we could thus expect that the artist would, by the same logic and convention, have shifted the second ear so that it too could be seen. The absence of a second protrusion on the head suggests this is not an ear but some single large protruding feature on the head of the subject creature. Among African reptiles such a feature is unique and distinctive to the chameleon. The identification of this picture as a chameleon helps to explain a number of other depicted features: the bobbles on the underside of the head mimic the characteristic wrinkled neck of the creature and the regular bobbles on the top mimic the regular spikes along the creature's back. The chameleon is also one of the few reptiles that is more successfully (distinctively) depicted in side as opposed to top view, which explains the choice of profile. Such subsequent explanation of those features chosen for depiction provides considerable confidence that the proposed subject is correct.

Study of other choices made in the creation of the chameleon could also have informed about the wishes of the artist and the intended purpose of the picture. The picture of the chameleon belongs to a tradition or 'style' of art that is found in central Malaŵi and eastern Zambia. As is typical (conventional) of the 'style', the chameleon was daubed in a large recessed shelter. Despite there being a great number of varied shelters in the area, this 'style' of art is crammed into just a few that are particularly large.

Analysis of the choice of site showed not only a preference for large protected rock faces but also for sites with a large sheltered floor area (a factor not necessarily linked to the size of the protected rock face) and an orientation that is most comfortable for overnighting in the shelter: towards the setting sun. These are not choices that one would expect if the site itself was of little importance. A normal choice in this circumstance would be a random sample of available protected surfaces distorted in favour of ones that were easily accessible. The choice of site seems so significant that the compositional norms were often superseded by the wish/need to remain at the chosen site. When a rock face became full and the preferred choice of avoidance (a preference seen in Fig. 12.1, Kampika; also see Phillipson 1976: figs. 109, 117, 123) was no longer possible, rather than change site, artists chose to superimpose their work upon earlier images. The nature of the chosen sites best fits a connection to some group activity that involved spending a fair amount of time there. The thin spread of sites within the landscape supports this and the nature of the scatter suggests connection to a village-level activity.

There is a clear choice by artists to make new images in this 'style' rather than reuse older ones; this can be seen in Fig. 12.1 where similar daubings have been made alongside one another. It seems that the process of making a picture was at least as important as the image produced. The chosen method of application, daubing, is relatively unusual in world rock-art. I suspect this is partly because it requires a considerable amount of pigment and thus necessitates much effort in the preparation stage. It must also be said that the final picture appears rather crude. That it was chosen here means the method had some advantage that made it appealing to these artists. The obvious advantage of this method is that it is one of the quickest and easiest to execute. This supports the suggestion that the making of the picture or the message which the picture put across (or both) were particular concerns. The chameleon is placed on a high ceiling. This is not a normal or expected position because it is a place where execution is unnecessarily awkward. The result is a picture that stands out from all other places in the shelter. In order to justify the expenditure of effort (and some risk to personal safety) the artist must have considered the visibility of the picture to be of considerable importance. That it was visibility and not height that was important can be seen from choices made in other pictures of the same style. Being viewed must therefore have been important to the function of these pictures.

Although this is merely a brief formal analysis, it is clear that we are progressing towards an understanding, a real understanding (demonstrated in this case by informed knowledge), of this picture and its purpose.

### The !platypus (see Figs. 12.4 and 12.5)

What about the !platypus that is not a platypus? In this case, like most rock-art researchers, I do not enjoy the privilege of informed knowledge to ensure that those formal deductions which I present in publication are correct. The choice of this picture may prove a mistake as it is an example that one has nightmares about: the picture is unique. I have not seen, either for myself or in publications, anything exactly similar within Arnhem Land. Chaloupka (1984, 1993a, 1993b) has recognised a series of 'styles' in the art of Arnhem Land which he and others (see Chippindale and Taçon this volume) have tied to a calendrical framework. This picture fails to follow closely any of the conventions that define these 'styles'. The mixture of filled and unfilled internal space is a convention peculiar to the 'early/simple X-ray style'; however, none of the other internal features comply with this 'style'. The picture therefore gives away no plain clues as to its age; what is more worrying is that we can derive no clues to the real form of its subject from our knowledge of how particular features are depicted in Arnhem Land art. If the subject is not immediately recognisable, can we therefore hope to know it? Many might say no, but an understanding of norms allows us a means to suggest the probable subject.

The picture is somewhat zoomorphic but may fall to the wayside of a 'sufficiently zoomorphic' dividing-line. The zoomorphic elements are:

(A) a central mass that mimics the shape of a body seen in top view.

(B) four short protrusions extending outwards from A, each with five sub-protrusions (one with six). These mimic the form of four legs, each with five toes, as they are found on most creatures. These features are positioned as would be expected in a top view of most creatures.

(C) a protrusion at one end and the possibility of another, now damaged, at the opposite end. These occur at the expected positions of the head and tail of a creature viewed from above.

It is a demonstrable fact that depictions of animals and humans make up by far the greatest proportion of subjects in rock-art around the world. This is true also of Arnhem Land. These are expected subjects for any picture. In this case, the form and placement of various zoomorphic elements occur in positions compatible with a creature viewed from above. No anomalous features occur to contradict this. This provides me with confidence that there is a high likelihood this is a top view of a creature. To move on from this and to discuss which creature is depicted does not inherently compound uncertainty to a point where the final chosen option will be less likely than it is likely. If a particular subject explains the shape of the depicted features, then this will increase confidence in our initial judgement that this picture depicts a creature.

In retrospect I can pinpoint why I thought this was a platypus. Taking the left end as the head, I had placed weight on the resemblance between the filled area and a platypus bill. The shape of the left end is more typical of a tail than a head; our expectation should therefore be that this is the tail. A number of subject options can now be ruled out: this is not a fish, bird, insect or spider; it is a quadruped. The choice of top view may be very significant as it means that this is most likely to be a creature wider

**Fig. 12.4.** Tracing of the !platypus from Ubirr, Kakadu National Park, Northern Territory, Australia. Tracing again made by Alison Gascoigne from what she saw on slides. The arc outlined to the right is damaged.

**Fig. 12.5.** Photograph of the !platypus from Ubirr, Kakadu National Park, Northern Territory Australia. Reproduced by permission of the Australian Nature and Conservation Agency on behalf of Kakadu National Park traditional owners. Photograph by Christopher Chippindale.

than it is tall. Even though this artist appears to have consciously decided to ignore prevailing conventions, he/she must have been aware of existing art traditions and this is something we can utilise. Some elements of tradition are easier to shake off than others. A certain section of received conventions of depiction is so ingrained that it is difficult for an artist to conceive of it as received; it seems automatic and necessary for depiction. If I had only experienced pictures using actual proportions, then, although I might make certain form changes such as to move or twist features, or perhaps use decoration in a different manner, I doubt that I would consider choosing to depict using proportions different from real. To do so would not seem 'innovative', 'challenging' or 'clever'; it would simply create a 'bad' picture. It is thus my belief that there are some conventions that are so basic they become rules which underpin local depiction for long periods of time regardless of change in the choice of manner. In Arnhem Land such rules include:

1 Features of a subject are depicted using a form that mimics their actual shape.

2 Although the size of some 'important' features may be exaggerated for emphasis, the proportions of most depicted features mimic the actual proportions of those features in the subject.

3 All sizeable visual features of a subject are depicted.

The reasonable expectation that such rules will apply to our picture provides a good basis for analysis. While it is possible that this is a 'bad' picture, it is reasonable to expect that these rules will apply.

Working from these rules, which subjects are made likely and which unlikely? It has already been established that this is (in all likelihood) a quadruped pictured as from above. We should start with the most likely option: that the left end depicts the tail and that the head is missing. It would be dangerous to read too much into the shortness of the legs. Although it is a common convention in top-view depictions to splay the legs out, in a precise aerial view one would only see the feet (perhaps not even

the feet) whatever the height of the creature. The length of the tail in relation to the body is roughly correct for most Australian marsupials, rodents, lizards or crocodiles. Bats, marine mammals and other creatures without prominent tails can be ruled out. The shape of the tail is odd. It is relatively even in width, getting slightly wider and rounded at its tip. This is utterly wrong for most Australian creatures. The tip is too rounded and the base too narrow for any lizard or crocodile; it is too wide for any rodent, most dasyurids, bandicoots and bilbies. This leaves only wide-tailed marsupials. The regular arrangement and number of toes on each foot rules out the macropods, narrowing the possible range of known subjects to possums. The missing front, the presumed head, now becomes a problem. This missing section is too small to have fitted any large features. Possums and most of the smaller marsupials have prominent and protruding ears, which would have been depicted were a possum the subject. The ears are larger than the feet and should therefore be seen extending beyond the missing area. Since they are not, this cannot be a possum. Taking the left end as the tail thus leads to the elimination of all known subjects because of the shape of one or more features or the omission of another.

Having eliminated what seemed the most likely option (that the left end was the tail), we must now consider the remaining possibilities:

(A) The left end may be the head.

(B) The subject may be unknown.

(C) This may be a bad picture.

(D) This may not be a quadruped.

It has already been established that options C and D are unlikely; A and B must therefore be considered in preference. Any picture might depict an unknown subject, in this case an unknown creature (either material or of the mind). The existence of an unknown material quadruped is unlikely since we have a good knowledge of the faunal changes in Arnhem Land during both Holocene and Pleistocene periods. It is unlikely the artist would have invented a unique creature. A non-material creature of the mind, learnt

225

about from others, would be most probable were this an unknown subject. Many such 'mythical' creatures are known and painted by artists in Arnhem Land today; the forms used are based on particular material creatures or an amalgam of features from a number of material creatures. The Rainbow Serpent is a well-known example with a snake body and macropod head. If our picture depicts one of these non-material subjects, then its uniqueness is particularly odd because non-material creatures, like the Rainbow Serpent, show remarkable regularity in their adherence to particular conventions.

Understanding what is unlikely leads us to what remains likely: that the front end of this picture is the head of a quadruped animal. In this case the shape of the head is unique to three subjects: the echidna, the long-necked turtle[1] and the platypus. The echidna and long-necked turtle appear quite frequently in Arnhem Land art, the platypus seemingly never. The platypus has never inhabited this part of Australia. The echidna and the long-necked turtle are therefore much the more likely subjects.

The body shape and position of the feet are roughly correct for an aerial view of either an echidna or a long-necked turtle. The left end is too long for the beak of an echidna, but, as one of the

creature's species-specific distinctive features, this might have been exaggerated. In the late Pleistocene a species of long-beaked echidna used to inhabit Arnhem Land which is now found only in the highlands of New Guinea (Augee 1983). The beak of this animal is almost exactly the relative length of the form depicted. The neck/head of a long-necked turtle is likewise almost exactly the relative length of the form depicted. The feature that most clearly decides between the two possible subjects is the bulbous point at the far left end of the depiction. Viewed from above a turtle does indeed have such a bulge: the head at the end of the neck. The beak of an echidna, by contrast, gets progressively narrower towards its tip. The right end would fit with the rear end of either creature. There is little room for any significant feature in the missing section and it seems most likely that the form was just rounded off.

The form given to the feet is somewhat problematic for the turtle interpretation. The turtle has webbed toes with four claws on each foot. The echidna has five clawed feet, with an additional poisoned spur on the rear feet. The depicted feet are thus more suggestive of an echidna since five separated toes are visible on the front feet and six can be seen on the back foot at the top. The zigzagging lines within the body could be explained either as the spines of an echidna or as the shell markings of a turtle. The lines are rather more like the honeycomb shell markings of the turtle. The boxed divisions at the top and bottom edge of the body could be explained as the segmented edge of a turtle shell or the spines of an echidna. Long-beaked echidnas have much shorter spines than the short-beaked echidnas currently living in Arnhem Land. These short spines are largely covered by fur and their appearance in section would bear close resemblance to the boxed divisions on either side of the body in our picture. The number of depicted divisions is too great for the segmented edge of a turtle shell. The box divisions therefore seem to me more suggestive of an echidna.

There are thus some elements of the form that are like a turtle and some that more closely resemble an

---

[1] In an earlier draft of this chapter I overlooked the possibility of the long-necked turtle. This fact was pointed out by Paul S. C. Taçon (a man with informed knowledge who was no doubt much amused by the outcome of my formal approach). This oversight led me to conclude with some conviction that the picture depicted an echidna. In this revised version I have included the possibility of the long-necked turtle and have updated the conclusions accordingly.

Taçon expresses certainty that this is a long-necked turtle; this certainty stems from his long experience of Arnhem Land art. It was important to the chapter that I had no idea at the start as to what the painting depicted and had no particular informed knowledge of Arnhem Land art. That this was so is proved by my error. Taçon's expression of certainty as to the subject is an unexpected bonus. It allows my discussion to be assessed. Most of the deductions were correct: this is a material creature viewed from above; the left end is indeed the head; the subject creature is wider than it is tall; the relative proportions of those features depicted mimic the proportions of the actual creature; all major features are indeed depicted. In the light of this, it is disappointing that the long-necked turtle was overlooked since the procedure would have led to the correct subject.

echidna. How, therefore, do we decide between these two subjects? Our observations concerning the normal choice of profile provide some assistance. The normal viewpoint for the depiction of a turtle should be from above since the creature is wider than it is tall and more of its distinctive characteristics can be depicted in a top view. All depictions of turtles in Arnhem Land that I have seen are shown from above, as expected. The echidna is equally as tall as it is wide and therefore the expected choice of profile would be mixed. Its distinctive spines are most easy to depict in a lateral profile, which would suggest that this profile is likely to be preferred. The actual choice of profile for echidnas follows this expected pattern (Taçon pers. comm.; Clegg 1995b). In Arnhem Land the lateral view is used in almost all echidna depictions (Taçon pers. comm.). Therefore, while the choice of profile does not rule out the echidna, it makes the turtle much the more likely subject.

In choosing the long-necked turtle interpretation we need to accept that this artist has been somewhat inexact in the depiction of detail. The honeycomb pattern of the shell is represented in a stylised manner by zigzags and the number of segments along the edge is exaggerated. In the light of this it is easier to accept the inaccuracies in the form of the feet, since a lack of attention to detail seems to be a consistent feature throughout the depiction: it is a part of the manner employed by this artist. Despite my initial worries about certain features, I think we can have a fair degree of confidence in the long-necked turtle interpretation. It is the only one that explains the bulbous point at the left end as well as fitting with and helping to explain all other features depicted. Thus, in spite of this being 'the nightmare example', we have been able to make a firm stab at the subject by considering what, in this case, was likely.

So ends this tale of the chameleon and the platypus but it need not be the end of their story. Only some of the many choices made during the making of these two pictures have been examined here. Given space, there is scope to take this approach

further. The value of the chameleon and the platypus (that wasn't) is that they challenged my approach to the interpretation of rock-art. Considering these two pictures led me to a collection of ideas that I have found useful in many areas of rock-art analysis. I hope that others will derive similar value from them.

## Acknowledgements

Much inspiration for writing this chapter was gained in remote parts of Arnhem Land while discussing and contemplating matters with Christopher Chippindale (while I was field assistant to him). I thank him for everything (except submerging me near the centre of a crocodile-infested river). The considerable influence that reading John Clegg has had on my thoughts will, I trust, have been obvious. I would like to thank Alison Gascoigne, who made the two tracings.

## REFERENCES

Anati, E. 1986. Rock art of Tanzania and the East African sequence, *Bollettino del Centro Camuno di Studi Preistorici* 23: 15–68.

Apthorpe, R. 1962. A note on Nsenga girl's puberty designs, *South African Archaeological Bulletin* 17: 12–13.

Augee, M. L. 1983. The short-beaked echidna, in R. Straham (ed.), *The complete book of Australian mammals*, pp. 7–9. Sydney, Australian Museum.

Chaloupka, G. 1984. *From palaeoart to casual paintings: the chronological sequence of Arnhem Land plateau rock art.* Darwin, Northern Territory Museum of Arts and Sciences. Monograph Series 1.

1993a. You gotta have style, in M. Lorblanchet and P. Bahn (eds.), *Rock art studies: the post-stylistic era or, Where do we go from here?*, pp. 77–98. Oxford, Oxbow.

1993b. *Journey in time.* Chatswood, Reed.

Clegg, J. 1977. A Saussurian model of prehistoric art, *The Artefact* 2: 151–60.

1987a. Style and tradition at Sturt's Meadows, *World Archaeology* 19(2): 236–55.

1987b. Human picturing behaviour and the study of prehistoric pictures, *Rock Art Research* 4(1): 29–35.

1995a. *Notes towards mathesis art.* 3rd edition. Balmain, Clegg Calendars.

1995b. About pictures of echidnas and cats. Comment on Deregowski (1995), *Rock Art Research* 12(1): 11–13.

Deregowski, J. B. 1995. Perception – depiction – perception, and communication: a skeleton key to rock art and its significance, *Rock Art Research* 12(1): 3–22.

Garlake, P. 1995. *The hunter's vision: the prehistoric art of Zimbabwe.* London, British Museum Press.

Lewis, D. 1986. The Dreamtime animals: a reply, *Archaeology in Oceania* 21(2): 140–5.

Lewis-Williams, J. D. and T. A. Dowson. 1989. *Images of power.* Johannesburg, Southern Book Publishers.

Lorblanchet, M. and P. Bahn (eds.). 1993. *Rock art studies: the post-stylistic era or, Where do we go from here?* Oxford, Oxbow. Oxbow Monograph 35.

Macintosh, N. W. G. 1977. Beswick Creek cave two decades later: a reappraisal, in P. J. Ucko (ed.), *Form in indigenous art: schematisation in the art of Aboriginal Australia and prehistoric Europe*, pp. 191–7. Canberra, Australian Institute of Aboriginal Studies.

Masao, F. T. 1979. *The later Stone Age and the rock paintings of central Tanzania.* Wiesbaden, Franz Steiner Verlag.

Muzzolini, A. 1995. *Les Images rupestres du Sahara.* Toulouse, Préhistoire du Sahara 1.

Phillipson, D. W. 1976. *The prehistory of eastern Zambia.* Nairobi, British Institute in East Africa.

Smith, B. W. 1995. The rock art of south-central Africa. Ph.D thesis, Department of Archaeology, Cambridge University.

Taçon, P. S. C. and C. Chippindale. 1994. Australia's ancient warriors: changing depictions of fighting in the rock art of Arnhem Land, NT, *Cambridge Archaeological Journal* 4(2): 211–48.

Walsh, G. L. 1988. *Australia's greatest rock art.* Bathurst (NSW), E. J. Brill – Robert Brown.

Whitley, D. S. 1994. Shamanism, natural modelling and the rock art of far western North American hunter-gatherers, in S. A. Turpin (ed.), *Shamanism and rock art in North America*, pp. 1–43. San Antonio (TX), Rock Art Foundation. Special Publication 1.

Carolyn E. Boyd

# 13. Pictographic evidence of peyotism in the Lower Pecos, Texas Archaic

The grand rock-paintings of Texas, in the arid country of the Rio Grande, are known for their great anthropomorphic images. They preserve sufficient organic residues for radiocarbon dating of their paints; this, with stratigraphic sequences of styles, places them into an Archaic era beyond any direct ethnographic informed knowledge. An earlier paper (Boyd and Dering 1996), bridging from the plants depicted in the paintings to the plants known from desiccated deposits in the shelters, has demonstrated the iconography of plants is one of hallucinogens. This chapter, using striking congruences between the traits of the paintings and recent associations of hallucinogens, extends that insight by analogy to the animal iconography of the paintings.

## The Lower Pecos region and its rock-art

The Lower Pecos River region is located at the north-eastern reaches of the Chihuahuan Desert within south-western Texas and northern Mexico (Fig. 13.1). The arid landscape of this region is dissected by three major rivers: the Pecos, the Devils and the Rio Grande. The deep canyons and arroyos formed by these rivers and their tributaries contain hundreds of rock-shelters which provided shelter for prehistoric inhabitants. Housed within these dry rock-shelters are some of the most impressive rock-art panels in the world.

These rock-paintings have been categorised into four distinctive and successive styles; the Pecos River, Red Linear, Red Monochrome and Historic (Kirkland and Newcomb 1967; Shafer 1986, 1988; Turpin 1982, 1995). This chapter is concerned with the Pecos River Style, the best represented and oldest of the recognised styles. Ancient DNA was extracted from the Pecos River Style rock-art and subjected to polymerase chain reaction (PCR) and phylogenetic DNA analysis. The results of the analyses indicate that the organic binder utilised in the paint was from a mammal, probably an ungulate (Reese *et al.* 1996). The colour-producing agents identified in the paint are iron oxide minerals. These minerals can be used to produce the earth colour pigments characteristic of the Pecos River Style rock-art; including reds, oranges, yellows and black (Hyman *et al.* 1996; Zolensky 1982).

The presence of an organic binder in the paint has allowed researchers to obtain radiocarbon ages through Accelerator Mass Spectrometry: AMS dates for Pecos River Style art range from > 2950 to 4200 years ago (Chaffee *et al.* 1993; Hyman and Rowe 1996; Ilger *et al.* 1995, in press; Russ *et al.* 1990). These dates place the Pecos River rock-art style to the latter part of the middle Archaic, 4100–3200 years b.p. Only one date each has been obtained for the two more recent prehistoric styles: 1125 ± 85 b.p. for Red Monochrome and 1280 ± 150 b.p. for the Red Linear (Ilger *et al.* 1995).

The central motif of the Pecos River Style is polychrome and monochrome anthropomorphic figures accompanied by an assortment of enigmatic designs (Fig. 13.2). Anthropomorphs range in size from approximately 13 cm to 8 m in height. There is a high degree of variability in the manner in which the anthropomorphs are depicted. Head and body shape, ornamentation, size and colour vary between sites as well as within each rock-art panel.

The bodies of the anthropomorphs are usually depicted facing forward with arms extending

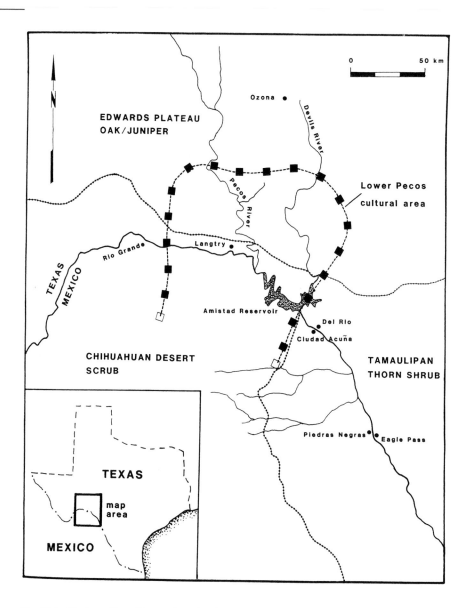

**Fig. 13.1.** The Lower Pecos River region of south-west Texas and northern Mexico. The southern limits of the Lower Pecos cultural area are undefined.

After Turpin (1995: 542).

**Fig. 13.2.** Panther Cave (41VV83), Seminole Canyon. Pecos River Style anthropomorphic figures. This illustration represents 8.5 m of the 40-m panel depicted on the shelter walls of Panther Cave.
Redrawn from Kirkland and Newcomb (1967: 63).

outward or with their bodies in profile. Heads are either absent or depicted in a rectangular, square, oval or other geometric form, or in a manner resembling a particular animal, such as a bird or feline. Frequently the anthropomorphs are depicted with some type of head ornamentation, such as a feather or antler head-dress and with paraphernalia hanging from their arms or at the waist. Commonly found in association with these anthropomorphic figures are design elements such as atlatls, dart points, depictions of animals, serpentine lines and geometric forms.

## Approaches to the rock-art

### Informed methods

Because of the considerable antiquity of the Pecos River Style art, researchers are unable to utilise informed methods, such as historical records or living informants, to gain insight into the meaning of the

rock-art. Early historic Native Americans who inhabited the Lower Pecos region abandoned the area before ethnographic data could be collected.

### Formal methods

Through formal methods, researchers approach the Pecos River Style rock-art as prehistorians. Meaning is inferred from the location of the art in the landscape or the geometry of a pictographic element's shape (Boyd 1992, 1996, in press; Boyd and Dering 1996; Campbell 1958; Turpin 1994a, 1994b). Additional insight has been gained through a formal analysis of the rock-art, leading to the identification of patterns in motif association and variability in motif distribution (Boyd 1992, 1996, in press; Boyd and Dering 1996).

### Ethnographic analogy

Although ethnographic or ethnohistoric information on indigenous groups of this region is absent, re-

231

searchers have effectively utilised ethnographies of groups spatially removed from the study area (Boyd 1992, in press; Boyd and Dering 1996; Campbell 1958). Studying the prehistoric art of the Lower Pecos through analogy has allowed for interpretation of a period in remote prehistory for which we have no modern knowledge or direct ethnohistorical accounts. The patterns and variability identified through formal methods can be understood in the light of similar patterns identified in ethnographies.

## Pictographs and peyotism

In this chapter, I explore how the pictographs in the Lower Pecos River region of Texas provide insight into the antiquity of one of the strongest pan-Indian movements in the United States and Mexico, the peyote religion. Analogies drawn between contemporary Huichol peyotism and the results of a formal analysis of the art, show that the 4000-year-old Pecos River Style rock-art panels contain pictographic representations of a peyote ritual. Environmental explanations and archaeological evidence within the region support this interpretation.

The primary subject of this analysis is a pictographic panel located in a rock-shelter along the Pecos River near its confluence with the Rio Grande. This 'White Shaman' site (41VV124) has no archaeological deposits preserved within the overhang of the shelter. However, numerous mortar holes, slick surfaces and sharpening grooves are present. Scattered cultural debris has been observed in the colluvium below the mouth of the shelter.

The patterns revealed during a formal analysis of the art can be interpreted through ethnographic analogy by identifying the analogous relationships between the elements within the 'White Shaman' site, rock-art panel and elements of Huichol peyotism. Additional Pecos River Style rock-art sites and ethnographies can be used to illustrate the regional distribution of this motif. The resulting interpretation can then be assessed within the context of environmental and archaeological evidence, and this is the approach I detail below.

## A formal analysis of Pecos River Style art

In the autumn of 1990, I began formal analysis of the Pecos River Style rock-art contained within the canyons of the Lower Pecos region of south-west Texas and northern Mexico (Boyd 1992). In this analysis, examinations and analyses of the pictographs were conducted to determine spatial variability and patterns in motif association. I began by producing a colour rendering of each rock-art panel included in the analysis. This approach has allowed me to become acquainted with each pictographic element and its relationship to other elements within the panel. This method has also aided in the identification of variations and consistencies in artistic styles both within a single panel and with others included in the study. Most importantly, it has allowed me to study the rock-art at each site as a single unit or composition.

### The 'White Shaman' rock-art panel (41VV124)

I have spent approximately seventy field hours sketching and photographing the pictographs at 41VV124. From these, I have produced a colour rendering of the 3.66 m × 7.32 m panel (Fig. 13.3). The panel consists of the following:

1 Five black and red anthropomorphic figures across the length of the panel, each approximately the same size.

2 Long, slender black objects with red tips associated with each of these main anthropomorphic figures, one in each hand.

3 Other anthropomorphs depicted in an X-ray or skeletonised fashion, as well as zoomorphic and other enigmatic figures, associated with each of these main anthropomorphic figures.

4 Numerous black dots, both free-floating and decorating the figures in the panel. Over 100 have been counted.

5 An element resembling a deer that is covered with black dots. The deer appears to have been impaled by a dart point.

6 An antlered anthropomorph with tines decorated with black dots, at the far left end of the panel, near the impaled deer.

**Fig. 13.3.** Rendering of the 'White Shaman' (41VV124) rock-art panel located along the Pecos River near its confluence with the Rio Grande. The entire panel extends 3.66 m × 7.32 m.
Rendering drawn by author.

7 A large undulating arch, under the antlered anthropomorph. This anthropomorph is the only one depicted with a weapon, distinctly painted and in this case clearly an atlatl (spear-thrower).

8 Red dots that appear to have been impaled by dart points, close to the antlered anthropomorph and the impaled deer.

9 An object located just above the impaled dots that consists of a straight line with numerous branching lines projecting from one end.

10 A white line extending the entire length of the panel, uniting the five anthropomorphic figures. At the far left end of the panel the line changes to black.

**Ethnographic analogy and Pecos River Style art**

The formal analysis of the Pecos River Style art revealed distinct patterns in motif association (Boyd 1992, 1996, in press). One of the patterns identified at several sites in the region is the association of impaled deer, impaled dots and antlered anthropomorphs with black dots on the ends of their antler tines (Boyd and Dering 1996). The 41VV124 rock-art panel described above contains this motif association.

While conducting an extensive review of the ethnographic literature on cultures within northern Mexico, I identified a similar motif association in Huichol peyotism. Further study identified numerous analogies that could be drawn between the elements contained in the panel and elements of a Huichol pilgrimage taken annually to collect the hallucinogenic peyote cactus. Each rock-art element described above has its analogue in contemporary Huichol peyotism.

## Botany of peyote

Peyote (*Lophophora williamsii*) is a spherical, spineless, chalky blue-green coloured cactus with a height of less than 5 cm and a diameter of seldom more than 6–8 cm (Fig. 13.4). It is most frequently found growing in shallow, rocky upland soils under the thorny shrub canopy provided by plants such as mesquite and acacia. Peyote grows in clusters from a tuberous taproot associated with a much larger nurse plant. During drought conditions, peyote crowns descend below the ground into the taproot to reduce exposure to transpiration losses. When the rains return, the cactus swells and rises slightly above the surface of the soil (Benitez 1975; Boke and Anderson 1970; Bruhn and Holmstedt 1974; Morgan 1983).

The plant's geographic range is primarily in north-eastern and central Mexico and along the Texas borderlands (Fig. 13.5) (Boke and Anderson 1970; Morgan 1983). In the Lower Pecos River region, modern peyote populations are located on south-facing slopes overlooking the western side of the Pecos River canyon, on the uplands above Seminole Canyon just east of the Pecos River, as well as in the area of Langtry, Texas. There are probably many more populations within a few miles of the rock-shelters in this study, but locating them is difficult because of restricted access to private land.

The cactus is harvested by slicing off the small exposed crown. When dried, the sliced segments of the cactus resemble hard, brownish discs that are referred to as peyote buttons (Fig. 13.6). Among more than thirty alkaloids chemically identified in peyote, the major active alkaloid, mescaline, is capable of producing psychic effects and hallucinations in humans (Aberle 1966; Anderson 1980; Bruhn and Holmstedt 1974; Litovitz 1983).

Taken in small quantities, less than 5 mg/kg, peyote produces wakefulness, mild analgesia, loss of appetite, and allaying of thirst (Aberle 1966; La Barre 1975). As each button contains on average 45 mg of mescaline, four to twelve buttons must be consumed to produce vivid visual hallucinations, including reports of shimmering intensification of colour and texture, frequent geometric imagery, and distortions in body image and depth perception. Although peyote intoxication is most commonly associated with visual hallucinations, both auditory and tactile hallucinations, and a variety of synesthesias, are also reported (Anderson 1980; Bye 1979; Klüver 1966; Litovitz 1983; Schultes 1969; Siegel 1984).

## Origins of peyotism

Because of the plant's powerful hallucinogenic properties, pre-Columbian groups in south Texas and throughout northern Mexico utilised peyote in religious ceremonies (La Barre 1975; Morgan 1983; Safford 1916; Schultes 1972; Shonle 1925; Slotkin 1951; Stewart 1987). In the nineteenth century, peyote use spread northward to Oklahoma, where the modern peyote religion of the Native American Church became formalised during the 1880s. There is considerable controversy regarding the origins of peyotism and the content of the earlier cult from which it emerged (Campbell 1958; Howard 1957, 1960; La Barre 1957; Opler 1937, 1938, 1945; Shonle 1925; Slotkin 1955; Stewart 1974, 1987; Troike 1962).

Peyotism in the United States is recognised as having its origins in northern Mexico and southern Texas along the Rio Grande (La Barre 1975; Ruecking 1954; Stewart 1974, 1980, 1987), the northernmost reaches of the natural growth-range of peyote. During historical times, various Indian groups such as the Comanches and the Kiowas and tribes from Oklahoma journeyed to the Lower Pecos region to harvest peyote for ceremonial use. The Comanches and the Kiowas reportedly collected peyote along the Rio Grande and Pecos River (Slotkin 1955;

**Fig. 13.4.** Peyote (*Lophophora williamsii*).
About 3 cm diameter.

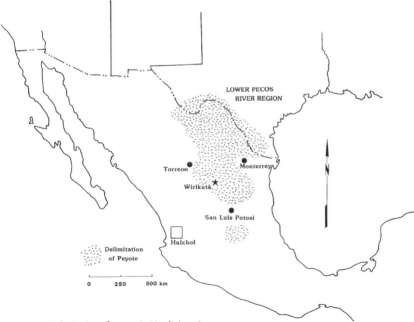

**Fig. 13.5.** Delimitation of peyote in North America.
Modified after Morgan (1983: 74).

**Fig. 13.6.** Peyote buttons recovered from a rock-shelter in the Lower Pecos River region, radiocarbon dated to 7000 b.p. The larger is about 3 cm diameter.

Photograph courtesy of the Witte Museum, San Antonio, Texas.

Stewart 1987). According to Jack R. Skiles, a botanist living in the area of Langtry, Texas, the 'Indians from Oklahoma made trips to Langtry for many years gathering peyote for use in their religious ceremonies' (Stewart 1987: 13).

The earliest historical reference to peyotism was made in the 1560s by Friar Bernardino de Sahagun. In his *General history of the things of New Spain* he credits the primitive nomadic tribes of northern Mexico, the 'Teochichimeca', with the discovery of the hallucinogenic properties of the peyote cactus. The 'Teochichimeca' peyote ceremony, as described by Sahagun, shares many features with the peyote ceremonies conducted by the modern Huichol Indians of northern Mexico (Furst 1972; La Barre 1975; Myerhoff 1974; Stewart 1987). Researchers have suggested that the ancestors of the modern Huichol migrated as nomadic Chichimec hunters into the Sierra Madre Occidentales from a northern homeland, perhaps even the American South-west (Furst 1972).

**Huichol peyotism**

At the core of the Huichol belief system, the peyote hunt unites peyote, deer and maize into one inseparable sacred symbol. Deer, peyote and maize are so intimately interwoven that the Huichol believe that maize is deer, peyote is deer, and maize is peyote; one cannot exist without the others (Furst 1972, 1976, 1978; La Barre 1975; Lemaistre 1996; Lumholtz 1900; Myerhoff 1974; Schaefer and Furst 1996; Zingg 1977 [1938]).

Huichol religion is very complex, the desire for rain its driving force. In Huichol myths both peyote and rain sprang from the forehead of the deer; without the deer there would be no peyote and no rain; consequently there would be no maize. Peyote is therefore sacrificed each year to Grandfather Fire, to ensure rain and a bountiful crop (Lumholtz 1900, 1902).

The only peyote that may be used as a sacrifice in these ceremonies is peyote the Huichol have obtained from their sacred homeland, Wirikuta. In myth, and possibly in history, Wirikuta is the place from which the Ancient Ones came before settling in the Sierra Madre Occidentales in north-central Mexico. Each year, preceding the spring rain-bringing ceremonies, small bands of Huichol unite and set out on a 480 km pilgrimage across the desert, journeying north-east to their land of origin where the peyote grows (Fig. 13.5) (Benitez 1975; Furst and Myerhoff 1966; Furst 1972; Myerhoff 1974; Lumholtz 1900).

In order to be able to enter the sacred homeland, each pilgrim must be transformed into a spirit-being. It is the responsibility of the shaman or *mara'akame* to assist in this transformation, and to assign a new name to each of the pilgrims. The shaman who leads the group on the hunt always becomes Grandfather Fire. He carries the antlers of the Huichol divine ancestor, Kauyumari, Sacred Deer Person. Kauyumari is the intermediary between the shaman and the gods, and the guide and protector of the pilgrims along the journey (Benitez 1975; Furst 1976; Lumholtz 1900; Myerhoff 1974). The Huichol describe him as follows (Myerhoff 1974: 87): 'We call him *Kauyumari*. We call him *Maxa Kwaxi*. It is all one. *Kauyumari* aids Grandfather Fire. He aids Father Sun. He guides the *mara'akame* in what must be done. So that the peyote can be hunted. So that the *mara'akame* can take the peyote from the horns of the deer, there in Wirikuta.' Kauyumari is conceived of both in the form of a deer and as a person wearing antlers. The Huichol believe that when the deer god descended from heaven he brought peyote on his antlers to the sacred homeland, leaving the divine peyote cactus behind in his tracks (Benitez 1975; Lemaistre 1996; Lumholtz 1900; Myerhoff 1974). It is also believed that Kauyumari uses his antlers to open the portal to the Otherworld on the peyote pilgrimage (Furst 1972; Myerhoff 1974).

Another major ritual that must be conducted before the pilgrims can be completely transformed into divine beings is that of purification and confession. The term 'confession', according to Myerhoff, is misleading in that it implies the western religious tradition of confession. Rather, the primary function of this ritual 'is to transform the participants spiritually by making them new' (Myerhoff 1974: 132).

Sexual misdeeds are the only actions confessed during the ceremony. Each participant declares publicly his or her sexual transgressions. The shaman makes a knot in a husk fibre cord for each transgression mentioned. After all of the pilgrims have confessed, the shaman throws the knotted cord in the fire. By this action, the transgressions have been absolved and the pilgrims are no longer considered mortal. To signify a new beginning and unity among the pilgrims, the shaman removes from his pouch a fresh cactus fibre cord which each pilgrim is instructed to grasp. The shaman then takes and scorches the cord over the fire before placing it back in his pouch (Myerhoff 1974; Benitez 1975). When they arrive in the land of Wirikuta, the sacred cord will be knotted by each pilgrim and then unknotted at the end of their journey back home (Furst 1972; Lumholtz 1900; Myerhoff 1974).

Once the confessions and transformations are complete, the group leaves the village, in single file. The shaman-leader goes first, and carries the bow and arrows with which the first peyote will be shot. He also carries deer antlers, which represent Kauyumari (Benitez 1975; Myerhoff 1974).

Strict attention is given to preserving the order of the pilgrims as they proceed in single file. This order

must be maintained no matter how awkward or inconvenient, just as their ancestors did on the First Peyote Hunt (Benitez 1975; Furst 1972; Lumholtz 1900, 1902; Myerhoff 1974).

Candles are an important element within the peyote pilgrimage. At designated points along the journey to Wirikuta, the pilgrims display the offerings they have brought to the peyote. Each stands before his or her offerings while holding candles towards the ascending sun (Benitez 1975; Myerhoff 1974).

About mid-morning, after arriving in the sacred homeland of Wirikuta, the shaman signals for the hunt to begin. The pilgrims fan out across the desert, breaking their single-file order as they search for the peyote/deer. Myerhoff (1974: 153) describes the pilgrims' behaviour to be 'precisely that of stalking an animal'. Once the shaman has found the peyote/deer, he takes aim and shoots it with an arrow. Bursts of colour like a rainbow are said to spurt upward from the slain peyote/deer. The coloured rays, the *kupuri*, represent the soul of the peyote and of the deer. The shaman coaxes the soul back into the peyote/deer with his sacred feather plumes (Benitez 1975; Furst 1972; Myerhoff 1974).

The pilgrims proceed to gather peyote to take back to those who remained at home. After a sufficient amount has been collected, the peyote is sorted, cleaned and packed. The shaman selects five of the finest peyotes, each with five sections. The number five is a sacred number among the Huichol because it signifies the four cardinal points and the sacred centre. It also stands for completion. The five peyotes are strung together and hung on the antlers of Kauyumari. The next day, the pilgrims begin their long journey home (Benitez 1974; Furst 1972, 1978; Myerhoff).

### The 'White Shaman' site: an interpretation by analogy

Specific elements of the Pecos River Style rock-art are analogous to specific elements in the Huichol ritual peyote pilgrimage. Virtually every major aspect of the ritual has its corresponding rock-art representation, and virtually every pictographic element at 41VV124 can be linked to some aspect of the ritual.

*Five black and red anthropomorphic figures extend the length of the panel, each approximately the same size.*
The artist(s) of the 41VV124 rock-art panel utilised the full expanse of canvas provided on the shelter wall. The black and red anthropomorphs are placed evenly across the panel. This is analogous to the Huichol peyote pilgrims observing strict single-file order while on the pilgrimage.

*Long, slender, black objects with red tips are associated with each of the five anthropomorphs.*
The red-tipped black objects associated with the anthropomorphs are analogous to the candles held up by the pilgrims towards the ascending sun when making offerings to peyote at various points along the journey. In this case, these objects would represent torches as opposed to candles.

*Anthropomorphs depicted in a skeletonised fashion, zoomorphic and other enigmatic figures are associated with each of the five black and red anthropomorphs.*
Each of the five black and red anthropomorphs appears to be going through a metamorphosis and is associated with zoomorphic, anthropomorphic or other enigmatic figures. This is analogous to the transformation of the pilgrims into spirit beings prior to their journey to the sacred homeland to hunt peyote.

Guiding the pilgrims in this transformation are the skeletonised depictions of the shaman and his spirit helpers. Modern Huichol artists depict shaman and spirit beings in a skeletonised or X-ray fashion in their yarn paintings. When asked why it is done that way, Ramon Medina, a Huichol shaman and artist responded, 'because that is how it was established in the time of the ancestors' (Furst 1978: 23).

The five black and red anthropomorphs are *not* depicted in a skeletonised fashion. These anthropomorphs, therefore, represent the pilgrims prior to their transformation into spirit beings.

*A white line extends the entire length of the panel, uniting the five anthropomorphic figures. At the left end of the panel, the line changes to black.*
A white line unites each of the five anthropomorphs, just as the cactus fibre cord used by the Huichol shaman unites all the pilgrims following purification and confession. At one end of the white line, the colour changes to black, possibly to symbolise the scorching of the sacred fibre cord by the Huichol shaman.

The number of anthropomorphs is also significant. As stated earlier, among the Huichol, five is a sacred number representing completion. The pilgrims, following their transformation and confession, are considered complete and perfect.

*An antlered anthropomorph is superimposed over the top of a large undulating arch. This is the only anthropomorph in the panel associated with a weapon, in this case an atlatl.*
At the far left end of the panel, passing through a motif identified in an earlier paper as that of the Otherworld (Boyd 1996), is the image of a polychrome antlered anthropomorph (Fig. 13.7). The antler tines of the head-dress are decorated with small black dots, analogous to the peyote buttons brought on the tines of the Huichol divine ancestor, Kauyumari. This figure is also the only anthropomorph in the panel associated with a weapon, in this case an atlatl. This motif is analogous to the shaman-leader who carries the antlers of Kauyumari to open the Otherworld portal and who carries the weapon to shoot the first peyote/deer. This may also be an indication that the panel is to be read from left to right.

*Impaled dots, impaled deer decorated with dots, and elements resembling feather plumes*
There are over 100 dots in the 41VV124 panel. Black dots are depicted on the bodies of the anthropomorphs and free-floating throughout the panel. There are at least five impaled red dots, the clearest

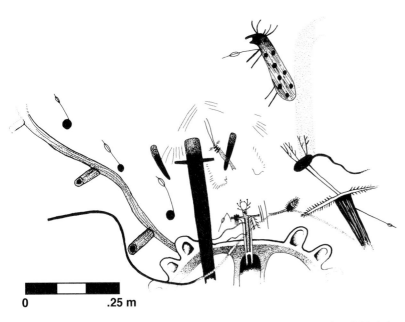

**Fig. 13.7.** 'White Shaman' (41VV124), Pecos River. An antlered anthropomorph with black dots on the ends of each antler tine is found in association with impaled deer and impaled dots. The anthropomorphic figure is passing through an opening in a serpentine arch which has been interpreted in an earlier paper as that of the portal to the Otherworld (Boyd 1996).

on the left end of the panel above the antlered anthropomorph. These impaled dots are analogous to the peyote/deer shot by the Huichol shaman.

There is also an impaled deer covered with large black dots. This image closely resembles depictions of the peyote/deer in Huichol sacred art. The Huichol decorate the body of the deer and antler tines with either dots or flowers to represent the peyote button (Fig. 13.8).

Found in close proximity to the impaled dots and impaled deer illustrated in Figure 13.3 is an element resembling the feather plume used by the shaman to coax the soul back into the peyote/deer after being shot with the arrow.

## Patterns in art and ethnography

The association of peyote with deer in the ethnographic literature is not restricted to Huichol peyotism, nor is the motif association of impaled deer, impaled dots and antlered anthropomorphs restricted to 41VV124.

**Fig. 13.8.** Huichol yarn painting by Chavelo González de la Cruz which illustrates the birth of peyote from the antlers and body of the Great Deer in Wirikúta.

Partial rendering of yarn painting redrawn from Lemaistre 1996: 312.

239

*Patterns in Pecos River Style art*

The association of antlered anthropomorphs with black dots on the ends of their antler tines, impaled deer and impaled dots is found at several sites in the region. At 41VV74 (Fate Bell) in Seminole Canyon the antler tines of a winged antlered anthropomorph are bedecked with black dots (Fig. 13.9). On this panel is an additional element – a winged antlered anthropomorph – which may be understood through analogy. According to the Huichol, deer have the ability to fly (Myerhoff 1974: 201). The sacred deer which brought the First Peyote to the ancestors flew down from the heavens with peyote on his antler tines. Close to the winged, antlered anthropomorph are impaled dots bursting with colour and numerous depictions of antler racks. The impaled dots bursting with colour are analogous to the Huichol description of the soul of the deer escaping as coloured rays from the peyote after being shot by the shaman.

At 41VV83 (Panther Cave), also within Seminole Canyon, impaled dots and impaled deer are repeatedly found in association (Fig. 13.10). The association of black dots on antler tines, impaled deer and dots is also present on a panel located near 41VV76 (Black Cave) in Pressa Canyon, a tributary of Seminole Canyon (Fig. 13.11).

The panel at 41VV76 provides further analogies with Huichol conceptions of the peyote/deer and rain-bringing. Approximately 3.05 m to the right of the antlered anthropomorph is an anthropomorph surrounded by impaled deer (Fig. 13.12); above it is an antler rack with rays resembling a rainbow extending from it. This may be analogous to the Huichol notion of rain springing from the forehead of the deer or of the coloured rays representing the soul of the peyote/deer trying to escape after being shot.

Approximately 25 km to the east of Seminole Canyon is 41VV696, a site located along the Devils River referred to as Cedar Springs (Fig. 13.13). The rock-art panel at 41VV696 contains impaled dots, impaled deer, and black dots on the tines of an antlered anthropomorph.

*Peyote/deer in ethnography*

Other groups, in addition to the Huichol, associate peyote with deer. The antiquity of this association is suggested in Zapotec material culture (Furst 1976). An effigy snuffing pipe from Oaxaca dating to 400–200 BC depicts a reclining deer holding a peyote cactus in its mouth.

The association of deer with peyote, although less direct, is also present among the Papago. Ruth Underhill ([1969]: 264) states that Papago 'shamans owned love magic. A mushroom which corresponds with the Huichol description of peyote, was a strong love charm. A man stalked it like a deer, and shot it with an arrow before it had a chance to disappear into the ground.'

Also according to Underhill, there is a mysterious connection between an unidentified plant used by the Papago as an intoxicant, *pihuri*, and deer. She suggests that the Papago *pihuri* may be analogous to the Huichol *hikuli* (peyote) (Underhill [1969]).

The association of deer and peyote is also present in the ritual racing of various Mexican groups. Use of peyote to increase stamina during ritual racing is known for the Tarahumara, Huichol, Tamaulipecan and Axacee tribes. The association of deer with peyote is demonstrated by the Axacee, who during a race tied strips of deer hide or hoofs to their insteps to help them climb hills while racing (La Barre 1975). The Tarahumara and Huichol carry the peyote/deer during ritual racing (Lumholtz 1902; La Barre 1975).

## Environmental explanations and archaeological evidence

*Peyote/deer and rain*

Today, as in 1900 when Carl Lumholtz conducted his research, the Huichol sacrifice the peyote/deer as an offering to the gods to bring rain and insure against drought. They believe that peyote must be offered to the gods every year 'or they would be unable to catch deer: consequently it would not rain and they would have no corn' (Lumholtz 1900: 23).

The purpose of the ritual for the prehistoric

**Fig. 13.9.** Fate Bell Shelter (41VV74), Seminole Canyon. Winged antlered anthropomorph is associated with impaled dots and antler racks.

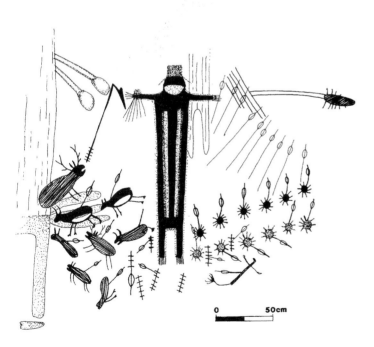

**Fig. 13.10.** Panther Cave (41VV83), Seminole Canyon. Impaled deer and impaled dots are found in association.

241

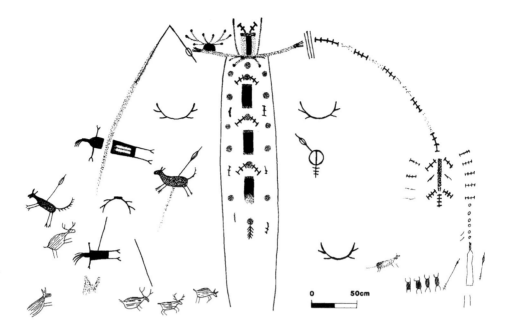

**Fig. 13.11.** Black Cave (41VV76), Pressa Canyon. Pecos River Style rock-art panel located under an overhang approximately 90 m to the left of Black Cave. Black dots on the ends of antler tines, impaled deer and dots are found in association at this site.

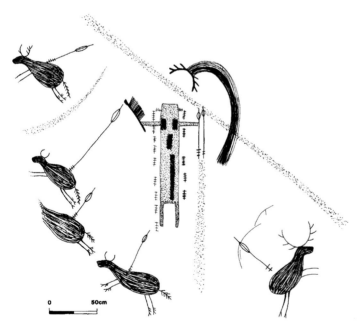

**Fig. 13.12.** Black Cave (41VV76), Pressa Canyon. Pecos River Style rock-art panel located approximately 3.05 m to the right of the panel illustrated in Fig. 13.11.

**Fig. 13.13.** Cedar Springs Shelter (41VV696), Devil's River. Pecos River Style rock-art panel contains an antlered anthropomorph with dots on the end of its antler tines.

hunter-gatherers of the Lower Pecos River region may have been very similar. By studying peyote and deer ecology, I was able to identify a possible explanation for the peyote/deer/rain complex among the hunter-gatherers of the Lower Pecos.

Rain falls primarily in the summer, often as widely spaced torrential rains of short duration. These rains increase the production of desert ephemerals, and they trigger leafing and flowering of important forage and fruit-bearing shrubs. The peyote/deer would have been sacrificed to bring rain to increase the quantity of desert plant foods available for harvest, as opposed to bringing rain for the crops.

Additionally, as deer ecologists have identified in the Chihuahuan Desert, deer travel rapidly to areas where it has just rained in order to eat vegetation that emerges following rainfall (Rautenstrauch and Krausman 1989). When the rain comes the deer come, sometimes from considerable distances. Rainfall not only increases plant food availability but game availability as well.

Rainfall also brings peyote. Peyote has an extensive growing range within the Chihuahuan Desert from central Mexico to southern Texas, including the Lower Pecos River region. The hallucinogenic peyote cactus grows in shrub microenvironments on east- and south-facing slopes to receive moisture from prevailing Gulf winds. During dry periods, peyote descends below the ground surface, becoming difficult to find. But immediately after a rain the peyote swells, becoming visible on the surface of the ground (Benitez 1975; Morgan 1983).

Thus we have the relationship of the deer, the peyote and the rain. When the rains fall, the deer come and peyote appears on the ground where the deer have been feeding on the fresh vegetation. As the Huichol say, wherever the deer has stepped, peyote will grow in his tracks. The addition of maize into the peyote/deer complex by the marginally agricultural Huichol may have been an extension of the already existing relationship identified by the hunter-gatherers between rainfall and the arrival of peyote, deer and wild plant foods.

*Archaeological evidence*
Additional evidence to support the argument for the presence of peyotism in the Lower Pecos comes from the archaeological record. George Martin (1933), an archaeologist working in the Lower Pecos region

during the 1930s, reports having frequently found peyote in the debris of Shumla Caves. The peyote excavated from Shumla Cave no. 5 has been radiocarbon dated to 7000 b.p. (Furst 1989). Peyote was also reported by Woolsey at Fields Shelter and by Sayles in several Texas sites (Campbell 1958; Sayles 1935).

Various items of material culture that were recovered from the Shumla Cave excavations are similar to paraphernalia used in peyote ceremonies by various aboriginal groups. These include rasping sticks made from bone or wood, a rattle made from deer scapulae, a pouch and reed tubes containing cedar incense, and feather plumes (La Barre 1975; Lumholtz 1900, 1902; Schultes 1937; Stewart 1987).

## Interpretation by analogy in relation to archaeological and environmental evidence

Three separate lines of evidence have been presented in this chapter to support my interpretation of the rock-art panel at 41VV124 as a pictographic representation of peyotism:

- Analogies drawn between the patterns in motif association identified through a formal analysis of the rock-art and the ethnographic accounts of Huichol ritual peyote pilgrimages indicate that the rock-art contains elements strikingly similar to those of Huichol peyotism. In addition to 41VV124, the primary subject of this study, the motif association of black dots on deer antler tines, impaled deer and impaled dots was identified at several sites within the region. Furthermore, the peyote/deer association was also identified within ethnographies of other indigenous groups in Mexico.

- The presence of peyote and peyote paraphernalia in the sediments supports the identification of peyotism in the art. The radiocarbon date of 7000 b.p. for the peyote recovered from one of the sites in the region indicates that peyote was being utilised by the peoples of the Lower Pecos during the Archaic period.

- Ecological and environmental factors provide a possible explanation for the relationship of deer, peyote and rain and its presence in the belief system of the peoples of the Lower Pecos Archaic. The hunter-gatherer inhabitants of the Lower Pecos region recognised the existing relationship between the arrival of rain and the arrival of both peyote and deer.

It is only recently that rock-art studies have been given serious consideration by professional archaeologists in North America. The attitude has been, and in many cases still is, that rock-art research geared towards interpretation cannot be accorded a scientific status. This long-standing empiricist approach to rock-art has been concerned solely with documentation and data collection. In an effort to remain scientific, researchers have persisted within this purely descriptive method. If, however, we are to gain an understanding of the art, we must step beyond the confines of data collection and documentation.

All too often, archaeologists have failed to recognise rock-art as a part of the archaeological assemblage and, as a part of that assemblage, a critical part of the context. Interpretation of site activities or land use in areas rich in rock-art must include adequate consideration of the rock-art.

The previous failure to recognise the Lower Pecos rock-art as a part of the archaeological assemblage within the Lower Pecos stems, to a large degree, from the assumption that interpretation of rock-art from remote prehistory is impossible. In this chapter I have demonstrated the explanatory power available to researchers studying rock-art from remote prehistory for which informed methods of study are not available. Insight into prehistoric art can be gained when the results of a formal analysis are combined with ethnographic analogy and assessed within the context of environmental and archaeological evidence. In the Lower Pecos region, previous conclusions regarding site activity, land use, cultural stability or instability, which were reached without adequate consideration of the rock-art, are being revisited.

# REFERENCES

Aberle, D. F. 1966. *The peyote religion among the Navajo.* Chicago, Aldine.

Anderson, E. F. 1980. *Peyote: the divine cactus.* Tuscon (AZ), University of Arizona Press.

Benitez, F. 1975. *In the magic land of peyote.* Austin, University of Texas Press.

Boke, N. H. and E. F. Anderson. 1970. Structure, development, and taxonomy in the genus *Lophophora*, *American Journal of Botany* 57(5): 569–78.

Boyd, C. E. 1992. Archaic codices along the Lower Pecos. Paper presented at the 63rd annual meeting of the Texas Archaeological Society, Corpus Christi, Texas.

1996. Shamanic journeys into the Otherworld of the Archaic Chichimec, *Latin American Antiquity* 7(2): 152–64.

In press. Jimsonweed, peyote, and their animal counterparts in the pictographs of the lower Pecos, Texas Archaic, in D. Whitley (ed.), *Ethnography and western North American rock art.* Albuquerque (NM), University of New Mexico Press.

Boyd, C. E. and J. P. Dering. 1996. Medicinal and hallucinogenic plants identified in the pictographs and sediments of the Lower Pecos, Texas Archaic, *Antiquity* 70(268): 256–75.

Bruhn, J. G. and B. Holmstedt. 1974. Early peyote research: an interdisciplinary study, *Economic Botany* 28: 353–90.

Bye, R. E., Jr. 1979. Hallucinogenic plants of the Tarahumara, *Journal of Ethnopharmacology* 1: 23–48.

Campbell, T. N. 1958. The origins of the mescal bean ceremony, *American Anthropologist* 60(1): 157–60.

Chaffee, S. D., M. Hyman and M. W. Rowe. 1993. AMS [14]C dating of rock paintings, in J. Steinbring, A. Watchman, P. Faulstich and P. S. C. Taçon (eds.), *Time and space*, pp. 67–73. Melbourne, Australian Rock Art Research Association. Occasional AURA Publication No. 8.

Furst, P. T. 1972. *Flesh of the gods.* New York, Praeger Publishers.

1976. *Hallucinogens and culture.* Novato (CA), Chandler and Sharp Publishers.

1978. The art of being Huichol, in K. Berrin (ed.), *Art of the Huichol Indians.* New York, Harry Abrams.

1989. Book review of *Peyote religion: a history, American Ethnologist* 16(2): 386–7.

Furst, P. T. and B. G. Myerhoff. 1966. Myth as history: the jimson weed cycle of the Huichols of Mexico, *Anthropologica* 17: 3–39.

Howard, J. H. 1957. The mescal bean cult of the central and southern Plains: an ancestor of the peyote cult?, *American Anthropologist* 59: 75–87.

1960. Mescalism and peyotism once again, *Plains Anthropologist* 5: 84–5.

Hyman, M. and M. Rowe. 1997. Plasma-chemical extraction and AMS radiocarbon dating of pictographs, *American Indian Rock Art* 23: 1–9.

Hyman, M., S. A. Turpin and M. E. Zolensky. 1996. Pigment analysis from Panther Cave, Texas, *Rock Art Research* 13: 93–103.

Ilger, W. A., M. Hyman, J. Southon and M. W. Rowe. 1995. Dating pictographs with radiocarbon, *Radiocarbon* 37(2): 299–310.

1996. Radiocarbon dating of ancient rock paintings, in M. V. Orna (ed.), *Archaeological Chemistry V* pp. 401–14. Washington (DC), American Chemical Society.

Kirkland, F. and W. W. Newcomb, Jr. 1967. *The rock art of Texas Indians.* Austin, University of Texas Press.

Klüver, H. 1966. *Mescal and mechanisms of hallucinations.* Chicago (IL), University of Chicago Press.

La Barre, W. 1957. Mescalism and peyotism, *American Anthropologist* 59: 708–11.

1975. *The peyote cult.* 4th enlarged edition. New York, Schocken Books.

Lemaistre, D. 1996. The Deer that is peyote and the Deer that is maize, in S. B. Schaefer and P. T. Furst (eds.), *People of the peyote: Huichol Indian history, religion and survival*, pp. 308–29. Albuquerque (NM), University of New Mexico Press.

Litovitz, T. 1983. Hallucinogens, in L. Haddad and J. Winchester (eds.), *Clinical management of poisoning and drug overdose*, pp. 455–61. Philadelphia, W. B. Saunders and Company.

Lumholtz, C. 1900. *Symbolism of the Huichol Indians.* New York, American Museum of Natural History. Memoirs III.

1902. *Unknown Mexico*, vol. II. New York, Scribner.

Martin, G. C. 1933. Archaeological explorations of the Shumla caves, *Witte Memorial Museum Bulletin* 3.

Morgan, G. R. 1983. The biogeography of peyote in south Texas, *Botanical Museum Leaflets* 29(2): 73–86. Cambridge (MA), Harvard University Press.

Myerhoff, B. G. 1974. *Peyote hunt: the sacred journey of the Huichol Indians.* Ithaca, (NY), Cornell University Press.

Opler, M. E. 1937. The influence of aboriginal pattern and white contact on a recently introduced ceremony, the mescalero peyote rite, *Journal of American Folklore* 49: 143–66.

—— 1938. The use of peyote by the Carrizo and Lipan Apache tribes, *American Anthropologist* 40(2): 271–85.

—— 1945. A Mescalero Apache account of the origins of the peyote ceremony, *El Palacio* 52(10): 210–12.

Rautenstrauch, R. K. and P. R. Krausman. 1989. The influence of water availability and rainfall on movements of desert mule deer, *Journal of Mammalogy* 70(1): 197–201.

Reese, R. L., J. N. Derr, M. Hyman, M. Rowe and S. C. Davis. 1996. Ancient DNA from Texas pictographs, *Journal of Archaeological Science* 23(2): 269–77.

Ruecking, F. 1954. Ceremonies of the Coahuiltecan Indians, *Texas Journal of Science* 6(3): 330–9.

Russ, J., M. Hyman, H. J. Shafer and M. W. Rowe. 1990. Radiocarbon dating of prehistoric rock paintings by selective oxidation of organic carbon, *Nature* 348: 710–11.

Safford, W. E. 1916. Narcotic plants and stimulants of the ancient Americas, *Annual Report of the Smithsonian Institution* 387–424.

Sayles, E. B. 1935. An archaeological survey of Texas, Gila Pueblo, *Medallion Papers* XVII. Globe (AZ), Gila Pueblo.

Schaefer, S. B. and P. T. Furst (eds.). 1996. *People of the peyote: Huichol Indian history, religion and survival.* Albuquerque (NM), University of New Mexico Press.

Schultes, R. E. 1937. Peyote and plants used in the peyote ceremony, *Harvard University Museum Leaflets* 4: 129–52.

—— 1969. Hallucinogens of plant origin, *Science* 163(3862): 245–54.

—— 1972. An overview of hallucinogens in the western hemisphere, in P. T. Furst (ed.), *Flesh of the gods.* New York, Praeger.

Shafer, H. J. 1986. *Ancient Texans.* Austin, Texas Monthly Press.

—— 1988. The prehistoric legacy of the Lower Pecos region of Texas, *Bulletin of the Texas Archaeological Society* 59: 23–52.

Shonle, R. 1925. Peyote, the giver of visions, *American Anthropologist* 27: 53–75.

Siegel, R. K. 1984. The natural history of hallucinogens, in B. L. Jacobs (ed.), *Hallucinogens: neurochemical, behavioral, and clinical perspectives*, pp. 1–18. New York, Raven Press.

Slotkin, J. S. 1951. Eighteenth century documentation on peyotism north of the Rio Grande, *American Anthropologist* 53: 420–7.

—— 1955. Peyotism, 1521–1891, *American Anthropologist* 57: 202–30.

Stewart, O. C. 1974. Origins of the peyote religion in the United States, *Plains Anthropologist* 19(65): 211–23.

—— 1980. Peyotism and mescalism, *Plains Anthropologist* 25(90): 297–308.

—— 1987. *Peyote religion.* Norman (OK), University of Oklahoma Press.

—— 1988. Peyotism in Idaho, *Northwest Anthropological Research Notes* 22(1): 1–7.

Troike, R. C. 1962. The origins of plains mescalism, *American Anthropologist* 64: 946–63.

Turpin, S. A. 1982. *Seminole Canyon: the art and archaeology.* Austin, University of Texas. University of Texas Survey Research Report 83.

—— 1994a. On a wing and a prayer: flight metaphors in Pecos River pictographs, in S. A. Turpin (ed.), *Shamanism and rock art in North America*, pp. 73–102. San Antonio, Rock Art Foundation, Inc. Special Publication 1.

—— 1994b. The Were-Cougar theme in Pecos River Style art and its implications for traditional archaeology, in D. S. Whitley and L. L. Loendorf (eds.), *New light on old art: recent advances in hunter-gatherer rock art research*, pp. 75–80. Los Angeles, Institute of Archaeology, University of California. Monograph 36.

—— 1995. The Lower Pecos region of Texas and northern Mexico, *Bulletin of the Texas Archaeological Society* 66: 541–66.

Underhill, R. [1969.] *Papago Indian religion.* Originally published 1946, New York, Columbia University Press. Reprinted, New York, AMS Press.

Zingg, R. M. 1977 [1938]. *The Huichol: primitive artists.* Millwood (NY), Kraus Reprint Company.

Zolensky, M. 1982. Analysis of pigments from prehistoric pictographs, Seminole Canyon State Historical Park, in S. A. Turpin (ed.), *Seminole Canyon: the art and archaeology*, pp. 279–84. Austin (TX), University of Texas. Texas Archaeological Survey Research Report No. 83.

Pieter Jolly

# 14. Modelling change in the contact art of the south-eastern San, southern Africa

That the rock-paintings of southern Africa span a huge time-range is proved by the painted figures, many millennia old, from the Apollo XI Cave, Namibia. These images contrast with the much later contact-period paintings of Nguni, Sotho and European farmers with their characteristic forms of dress and equipment. Informal insight into the art comes from San ethnography, which is used to relate much of the imagery to the religious ideology of the San, including their trance experiences and mythology. But the religious ideologies of many San groups, like other people in culture contact, changed in response to contact with other peoples. We must ask just how these changes were represented in their art.

'Cases show that meanings, themes and motifs associated in an icon at a given time are unstable. They can change independently of each other and have their own histories' (Vansina 1984: 120).

## San painters and black farmers (Fig. 14.1)

The migration of Nguni and Sotho farmers into areas adjacent to the south-eastern mountains of southern Africa brought them into direct contact with the original inhabitants of these areas, San hunter-gatherers. It is these people who are considered to have executed most of the rock-paintings in these mountains and adjacent regions,[1] and it is in these areas that the rock-art of southern Africa attained a peak of beauty and symbolic complexity. While the oldest rock-paintings of southern Africa, those from the Apollo XI Cave, are many millennia old, rock-paintings continued to be made by San or by people of mixed descent until at least the later years of the

nineteenth century. The painting tradition therefore spans a huge time-range.

We can expect changes to have occurred in the art over this time, particularly changes resulting from the influence of competing ideologies and rites introduced by black farmers on San culture. The south-eastern San – like all peoples in culture contact – did not exist in pristine isolation; many San are known to have established close relationships with Nguni and Sotho farmers. What was the effect of these people on the culture and art of the San? How does this contact affect the ways in which we study the art? Some documented and hypothesised changes which the cultures of black farmers introduced in the ritual practices and religious ideologies of the south-eastern San communities, and the possible expression of these changes in their rock-paintings, are discussed here.

## Black farmers in the art

Unambiguous depictions of black farmers in the rock-art of the Drakensberg and adjacent areas can be found in the scenes of battle between San and these people (Fig. 14.2). The differences in weaponry and physical sizes of the groups have made it relatively easy to distinguish black farmers from San here, although we cannot be certain that all figures with bows and arrows in the art are San. As black farmers and Khoi herders are known to have used these weapons, farmer groups may sometimes be represented in the art with these arms.

Relations between many San and black farmer groups were also harmonious, however, and we can expect San to have painted not only their enemies but also their trading partners, friends and relatives

---

[1] These areas and the approximate location c. 1850 of some black farmer groups with whom south-eastern San came into contact are illustrated in Fig. 14.1.

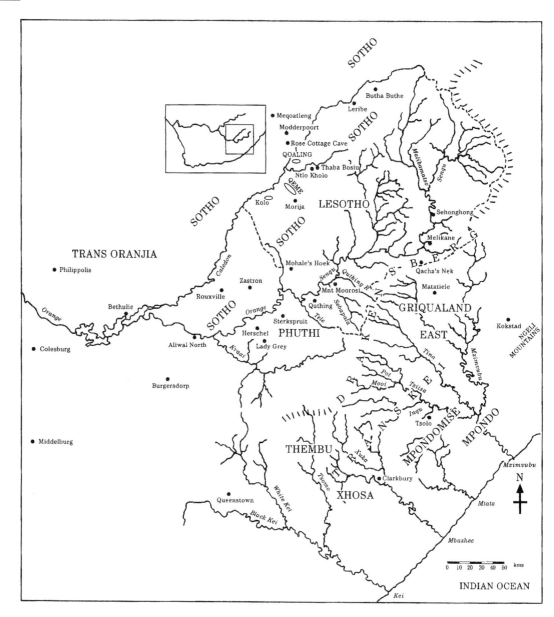

**Fig. 14.1.** The main study area showing the approximate location *c.* 1850 of some black farmer groups with whom the south-eastern San came into contact.
Map compiled from a variety of sources including Vinnicombe (1976) and especially Wright (1971).

**Fig. 14.2.** Conflict between Sotho and San. Lethena River, Lesotho.

**Fig. 14.3.** Ox and herder. Ngcengane Cave, Transkei.

within Nguni and Sotho communities. In the light of the long history of symbiotic interaction between some San groups and Bantu-speakers, we should not assume that the art is almost exclusively concerned with the activities of San people rather than Bantu-speakers (Schofield 1949; Walton 1956: 28). When the context is not that of conflict, identifying black farmers in the art can be difficult, particularly when they are not depicted together with the more gracile

San. It is nevertheless clear that some of the people depicted in the art are black farmers. People depicted herding cattle or sheep outside a cattle-raiding context, for example, are as likely to be Bantu-speakers as San (Fig. 14.3). Where neither livestock nor weaponry are associated with the scene, the dress, associated ritual and other accoutrements of people portrayed in the art may provide clues as to the cultural group to which they belong.

### Domestic ungulates in the art

Paintings of domestic ungulates provide some elements in the art which point to contact between south-eastern San and other groups. Domestic animals introduced by black and by white farmers which appear in the rock-art of southern Africa include sheep (Fig. 14.4), horses (Fig. 14.5) and cattle (Fig. 14.6) – although other paintings executed within the known period of contact may show the influence of interaction. Studies of African rock-paintings of domestic ungulates have been undertaken by Manhire *et al.* (1986) and by Loubser and Laurens (1994), amongst others.

Many paintings of domestic ungulates are painted in a distinctive style. Loubser and Laurens (1994: 89) point out that paintings of domestic animals in the Caledon River valley are seldom shaded; they usually have a blocked, graphic appearance, unlike the shaded polychrome paintings. The pigments used in these paintings also differ from the shaded polychromes, which are less uniform in appearance and bond poorly with the sandstone support. Since the blocked paintings of domestic ungulates and shields are almost always superimposed on shaded polychromes where these paintings occur in the same panel, it can be inferred that the style and technique associated with the former is a later development. These observations accord with those of Vinnicombe (1976: 141), who remarks that the apparently later art in the Natal Drakensberg is characterised by block-like representations which deteriorate relatively rapidly due to lack of a binding medium.

### Dating of the rock-art

A date of between 19,000 and 26,000 years has been obtained for a painted stone from the Apollo XI Cave (Wendt 1976), and a set of paintings on a fallen slab of rock in a shelter in the south-western Cape has recently been dated to about 3500 years (Yates and Jerardino 1996). These paintings were dated by their association with archaeological deposits. Progress has been made in recent years with regard to

**Fig. 14.4.** Sheep. Boskloof, Western Cape.
Reproduced with permission of the Spatial Archaeology Research Unit, Department of Archaeology, University of Cape Town.

radiocarbon dating of paint taken directly from the rock face; the first rock-art dates obtained using the Accelerator Carbon-14 dating method came from a sample of paint taken from a painting from the south-western Cape (van der Merwe *et al.* 1987). Mazel and Watchman have recently begun a programme to date some of the Drakensberg paintings directly (Mazel 1996: 194) which promises to advance our understanding of the painting sequence.

We know that those paintings of the south-eastern mountains which display elements clearly associated with contact cannot be older than the date at which agropastoralists established themselves in the south-eastern areas of South Africa. This had occurred on the Natal coast by about AD 300, and black farmers had spread into Transkei and the upper areas of Natal by AD 700 (Cronin 1982; Maggs 1984). On the other hand, the southern Highveld was only occupied by agriculturists about AD 1400 (Maggs 1980: 12), and we can reasonably expect this to be the earliest possible date for contact elements in the art of this and the adjacent more westerly areas of the south-eastern mountains. Loubser and Laurens (1994) estimate that depictions of domestic ungulates in the southern Orange Free State are not much older than 300 years. While the influence of contact elements may have been felt at a distance, so that

**Fig. 14.5.** Horse. Villa Maria, Lesotho.

**Fig. 14.6.** Ox. Lethena River, Lesotho.

contact motifs were depicted in the art without direct contact between farmers and hunter-gatherers there (Loubser and Laurens 1994), the consensus is that much of the art of the south-eastern mountains was executed during the contact period.[2]

[2] See Thackeray (1983) and Solomon (1995) for a fuller discussion of the dating of southern African rock-art.

## Methods in southern African rock-art research

*Informed methods*

Unlike those in areas of the world where the tradition of rock-painting continues, the San artists are long since dead, and we must depend on a very few first-hand accounts and some second-hand accounts for direct information on the art. Some early travellers and others managed to obtain limited information concerning the composition of paints and the manner in which the paintings were executed (Rudner 1983), but we know little directly about the meaning of the paintings for the artists themselves. An old woman of San descent from Transkei, who claimed that her father had been a painter, provided information concerning this aspect of the art, although we cannot use it with complete confidence (Jolly 1986; Lewis-Williams 1986; Prins 1990; Jolly and Prins 1994). The only known detailed commentary on rock-paintings by a San person directly acquainted with the art is that provided to Joseph Orpen in the nineteenth century by a San man, Qing, from the south-eastern mountains (Orpen 1874). A key text in southern African rock-art studies, it has been frequently used, often in conjunction with the ethnography of San groups from other areas, to throw light on the meaning of rock-paintings in southern Africa.

*Formal methods*

The distribution pattern of paintings of domestic animals in the rock-art may provide insights into this theme. Paintings of cattle and horses on the one hand, and of sheep on the other, differ markedly in the way they are distributed, both within the south-eastern mountains and over southern Africa (Willcox 1971; Vinnicombe 1976; Mazel 1982; Manhire *et al.* 1986; Loubser and Laurens 1994; van Rijssen 1994). Paintings of cattle are situated almost exclusively in the southern, rather than the northern, Drakensberg; and they are entirely absent from the south-western Cape. As Manhire *et al.* (1986) remark, very few paintings of cattle have been recorded anywhere in South Africa other than in the Drakensberg and adjacent areas. Paintings of snakes are similarly distributed: many in the Drakensberg, practically none in the south-western Cape. Possible reasons for these distribution patterns will be discussed towards the end of this chapter within the context of symbiotic interaction between south-eastern hunter-gatherers and black farmers.

*Ethnographic analogy*

The almost complete lack of first-hand explanations of the symbolism of the rock-art in the south-eastern mountains has encouraged researchers to look to the ethnography of San groups in other areas to interpret these paintings. Interpretation is by analogy with the beliefs and customs of San who had or have no tradition of painting and who were or are far removed from the south-eastern mountains. It has been proposed that sufficient similarities can be demonstrated in the ritual practices and belief systems of

San groups widely separated in space and time for us to be able to assume the existence of a structurally unchanged pan-San ideological complex, with some regional variants, for at least the last 2000 years, and possibly the last 27,000 years, amongst all San-speaking hunter-gatherers and their forebears in southern Africa (Lewis-Williams 1980, 1981, 1984, 1995). It is further suggested that continuity in the ideological systems of the San through space and time allows us to interpret paintings in the south-eastern mountains through recourse to the ethnography of twentieth-century Kalahari-San or the nineteenth-century /Xam San of the northern Cape.

This approach has been shown to be valid in certain cases as some San rites and beliefs *were* shared in greater or lesser detail in different areas of southern Africa. We nevertheless need to be careful not to generalise too widely from the ethnography of Kalahari and other San groups to the south-eastern San who executed much of the art. As Hannerz (1987: 550) remarks: ' "A culture" need not be homogeneous, or even particularly coherent. Instead of assuming far-reaching cultural sharing, a "replication of uniformity", we should take a distributive view of cultures as systems of meaning.' Kent (1996) and Guenther (1996) point out, for example, that many significant differences exist or existed in the religious beliefs and rites of San groups, not only between groups separated in space and time but also within the same group at any one time. This variation has implications for studies of south-eastern San rock-art, and specifically for the ways in which ethnographic analogy is used in these studies.

## Change in San religious ideology and ritual practice

The experience of other societies indicates that change lies at the heart of all religious systems (Van der Leeuw 1964: 609–17). Ogot has remarked of African religions: 'traditional religions have histories which are closely interwoven with the social and political organisations of the different African societies' and 'as the latter changed, new religious ideas were either produced from within or borrowed from without to deal with the new situation' (cited in Ranger and Kimambo 1972: 9). This is particularly true for San people, who, as Guenther (1996: 73) aptly puts it, 'forage as much for ideas as for *veldkos*'.

South-eastern San were drawn into the economic and cultural networks of those farming communities with whom they established good relationships, and San communities had been in contact with iron-using farmers long before their eventual incorporation into these groups. Trading, marital and other ties bound some San communities closely to their farmer neighbours over considerable periods of time (Jolly 1994). This close contact brought about changes in the religious ideologies and rites of many San groups, and probably also certain changes in Nguni and Sotho cosmologies and rites. Since it is widely accepted that much, although not all, of the rock-art of the south-eastern San is concerned with their religious beliefs and ritual practices, a corollary is that the overt and symbolic content of some of their art would have changed to reflect, and perhaps even to promote and disseminate[3] the new beliefs and rites to which south-eastern San were exposed. These new rites and beliefs would have included syncretic forms and *bricolages* created from the cultures both of black farmers and of San people.

Although it is not assumed that the kinds of changes that occurred in the religious beliefs and rites of other peoples in culture contact *necessarily* occurred also in San religious ideologies and rites, these changes can help in modelling possible shifts in south-eastern San cosmologies after contact with agriculturists. In the following sections some ways will be explored in which the beliefs and rites of San and other groups may have changed as a result of the influence of other cultures. Examples of ideological and ritual change will be related to hypothesised

changes in the overt content and underlying symbolism of San paintings. Where possible, these changes are discussed with reference to specific paintings. As research into the possible expression of Nguni and Sotho symbolism in San art has only just begun, systematic studies of this form of cultural influence on the art have yet to be undertaken.

*New rites and symbols, as they are adopted from the donor culture, are stripped of their original meanings and given the meanings of existing symbols within the host culture.*
In this form of ideological and ritual change, there is a conscious adoption into the native culture and religion of foreign elements – but they are fitted into an indigenous frame of reference. Core signs may be appropriated, revalued and resituated within a different 'holistic landscape' (Comaroff 1985: 197). This process Campbell (1987), Hall (1990, 1994), and Loubser and Laurens (1994) see as characterising the influence of black farmers on San culture. These scholars have detailed possible ways in which particular elements – but not ideas – associated with the cultures of black farmers and others were absorbed and integrated into existing San religious and symbolic systems and expressed in the art.

It has been convincingly argued, for example, that cattle came, in some cases, to supplement the eland in the power-symbolism of San shamans: eland and cattle became so closely related – possibly equivalent – symbols in San thought that paintings of cattle symbolise beliefs similar to or identical with those in the paintings of elands (Campbell 1987). Similarly, it has been suggested, cattle came to be substituted for both elands and mythical rain-animals in the symbolic system of the San; Hall remarks, 'new economic elements to the San had to be grafted on to existing ritual metaphors underpinning productive relations, thereby rationalising these relations and providing the basis for social and economic reform in the contact period . . . Cattle paintings are one clear expression of this' (Hall 1990: 267).

Symbol substitution of this kind is illustrated in a painting of 'trance cattle' from Lesotho, in which

---

[3] As Vansina (1984: 157–8) remarks, art is not necessarily a passive epiphenomenon. It can crystallise unfocused ideas and mobilise people. Lewis-Williams (1982), Campbell (1987), Hall (1994) and Dowson (1994, 1995) point out that San rock-art, not just a reflection of religious beliefs, was actively implicated in the reproduction of social relations.

**Fig. 14.7.** Trance bull/ox, bleeding from the nose. Sebapala River, Lesotho.

cattle are depicted bleeding from the nose (Fig. 14.7), a feature of the art sometimes associated with dying elands. As Lewis-Williams (1981) has argued, it links these elands to depictions of human figures bleeding from the nose while dancing in trance. Cattle bleeding from the nose can therefore be similarly linked to the trance imagery and symbolism of San shamans.

*New, and sometimes incongruous, rites, beliefs and symbols are added to old to form mixed forms and religious bricolages.*

Studies of culture contact and change indicate that, while symbols may be appropriated and given new meanings unrelated to the culture from which they derive, aspects of the meaning – or even the entire meaning – originally attached to these symbols are often adopted by the culture into which they have been incorporated. Although revalued, the symbol still carries with it pre-existing meanings. As Comaroff (1985: 198) points out, 'purposive reconstructions invariably work with images which already bear meaning . . . *bricolages* always perpetuate as they change. These *bricolages* represent "texts" which both press new associations and reproduce conventional meanings' (Comaroff 1985: 253).

With increasing symbiotic interaction and intermarriage between south-eastern San and black

farmers, some of these hunter-gatherer groups are likely to have been influenced by the rites and beliefs of their black neighbours, as occurred with other San groups. In some cases this would have resulted in the adoption of Nguni and Sotho rites and symbols, which were given meanings derived partly from the cultures from which they originated and partly from San cultures. These syncretic forms or *bricolages* appear to be represented in the art. A rite depicted in a painting from a cave at 'Upper Mangolong' in Lesotho (Fig. 14.8), which was commented upon by the San man, Qing, referred to above, is a case in point. The meaning of this rite appears to have derived from both San and Sotho/Phuthi culture.

Phuthi influence on Qing's religious beliefs is partly suggested by the fact that Qing could speak the Phuthi language and was staying with Nqasha, son of the Phuthi chief, Moorosi, and a San woman, when interviewed by Orpen. The very close association between Qing and the Phuthi, a group known to have intermarried and fraternised extensively with some San communities – as well as analysis of the comments which Qing made on this painting to Joseph Orpen – suggests that the Upper Mangolong painting depicts a Phuthi rite or a San rite strongly influenced by Phuthi culture. When commenting upon this painting, Qing probably drew both on his knowledge of Phuthi religious ideology and rites, in which San are likely to have participated, and on his knowledge of San rites and beliefs (Jolly 1995, 1996a).

Aside from Qing's comments on this painting, the dress, body decoration, ritual accoutrements and weaponry of the people depicted can all be related to initiation rites of south-eastern black farming communities. The spots painted on the body of one of the tailed figures are similar to those painted on the bodies of *abakwetha*, male Nguni initiates. Three of the people depicted are holding knobkerries, weapons associated much more with Bantu-speakers than with San. The long tails are possibly the long woven grass tails worn by the companions of some Sotho initiates at the initiation lodge. The round

**Fig. 14.8.** Tracing of a copy of a painting from Upper Mangolong Cave.
After Orpen (1874).

objects attached to their heads are probably the inflated gall bladders of sacrificial animals associated with the ancestral spirits which are attached to the hair of certain Nguni and Sotho ritual functionaries, particularly diviners. Or they may represent the *kola* worn by some Sotho people attached to the top of their heads (see Arbousset and Daumas 1968 (1846): 83).

The mythologies, as well as the rites, of San and other societies have also been affected by contact. Ellis (1954: 680) demonstrates the complete integration of Indian and European culture elements in Pueblo mythology. Hybridisation of religious beliefs commonly occurs in the mythology of San societies (Barnard 1988); even the biblical story of the Tower of Babel has been adopted and interwoven within the narrative tradition of particular San groups (Barnard 1988: 228).[4] Ideological *bricolage* characterises

the beliefs of !Kung San concerning their mythological trickster, ‡Gao!na, who is represented in two very different ways by the !Kung. The all-powerful sky god image of ‡Gao!na appears to have been adopted from another culture by the !Kung; introduced into their cosmology, it supplements the older trickster image evident in their mythology (Marshall 1962: 228). Similar processes were at work amongst the south-eastern San: Schmidt (1979: 216) points to the possible 'blending of different Bushmen and Bantu tales' by Qing. If San mythology can throw light on the meaning of the art, as Solomon (1994, 1995) and others have suggested, we may find culturally hybrid narratives of this sort expressed in their paintings.

In societies that are culturally liminal, the meaning of a symbol or rite may be drawn from more than one cultural context: the rite or symbol may

---

[4] The missionary Schmelen (1815) recorded similarly hybridised mythologies and religious beliefs amongst San he encountered in Namaqualand. He was told of a great flood that had occurred in the past. One man, his wife and their children survived this flood in a large dish. Once the waters had subsided they disembarked on a high mountain, from where they moved into the surrounding country. In this story we can hear a retelling of Noah's survival of the biblical flood.

The religious beliefs of other Namaqualand San who had had contact with missionaries and had seen European sailing ships were greatly changed. Schmelen (1815) asked San he met in

this area what they believed happened to them after death. They replied that they went 'over the water at that side where the devil is'. They continued: 'He is not good. All the people run to him.' Asked how the devil treated the dead they said: 'he does good to them. You shall see all our people who have died over there in the ships. Those people in the ships are Master over them.'

At least one rock-painting of a ship exists (Fig. 14.9), although we do not know that any religious significance was attached to it, either by the San who painted it or by later generations.

**Fig. 14.9.** Galleon. Heilbron, Western Cape.
After Townley Johnson (1960: fig. 8).

simultaneously have different associations (Pye 1969). It is almost always wrong, Vansina (1984: 114) points out, to attribute only one meaning to an icon. In some cases, we can hypothesise that certain symbols in San rock-art acquired multivocality through association both with a particular San culture and with the culture of a black farming community. At a particular stage in the history of interaction, we can expect paintings of cattle to have had associations both with the symbolism of elands in earlier hunter-gatherer society and with the structurally different symbolism of cattle within Nguni and Sotho society. There are paintings which depict cattle 'massed' in a similar manner to 'massed' eland in the art (Fig. 14.10). Furthermore, different San groups, living at the same time but influenced by the culture of black farmers in varying degrees, may have interpreted a painting of the same image, say a bull or cow, in ways that reflected the varying impact which the cultures of farmers had made on their religious ideologies and ritual practices. This potential for semantic complexity and variety needs to be taken into account.

*New beliefs, rites and their associated symbols are adopted, but they exist separately and in parallel with old beliefs, rites and symbols.*

Two separate religious systems, indigenous and new, may operate in tandem, each brought into play in different circumstances. Frequently the new religious system copes with the circumstances associated with culture contact and rapid social change, a role for which the indigenous religion is ill equipped. People often stand on both sides of cultural boundaries, adopting new forms of worship as useful supplements (Fisher 1978). This response to the introduction of new religious systems as a result of culture contact is evident among a wide variety of peoples. It is particularly marked amongst the Mbuti pygmies, of whom Turnbull (1983: 31) remarks, they 'see themselves in the forest as one thing and in the village as something else. Their manner of speech and behaviour are correspondingly different; they follow different customs, even (apparently) in such

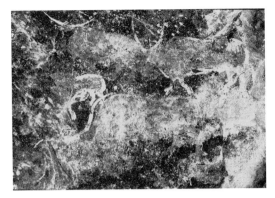

**Fig. 14.10.** Cattle. Ha Khoanyane, Lesotho.

vital areas as marriage and mortuary ceremonies, and initiation into adulthood.'[5]

Those San who were moving between two different cultures, 'living in two worlds',[6] could well have executed paintings that reflected this cultural split: we might find rock-paintings of two different rites, one essentially San in form and meaning, such as a trance dance, and the other essentially Nguni or Sotho, such as a circumcision rite, depicted by the same San group. For example, it is common for Mbuti pygmy youths to be initiated with villager youths according to the custom of the villagers (Turnbull 1965, 1983), and Kratz (1980: 363) remarks that Okiek Dorobo sometimes send their children to neighbouring Maasai or Kipsigis settlements to take part in initiation ceremonies.

A particular set of San beliefs and rites relatively unchanged by contact may have operated in one context, while beliefs and rites borrowed from black farmers operated in another. San are known to have participated in the male initiation rites of black farmers, and where San groups with close ties to black farmers had been greatly influenced by their

---

[5] Woodburn (1982: 194–5) provides examples of Baka pygmies' religious beliefs influenced by those of neighbouring Bantu-speakers and missionaries.
[6] This phrase is borrowed from Bürhmann (1984), who uses it in a different context.

initiation practices, or were initiated together with Sotho or Nguni youths according to their custom, we can expect these rites to have been expressed in their art, alongside paintings of essentially San rites. Schoonraad (1968: 28) and Battiss (1948: fig. 1, opp. p. 226) have drawn attention to rock-paintings which may illustrate circumcision rites. The painting traced by Battiss (Fig. 14.11) comes from a cave in an area known to have been occupied *c.* 1822 by Phuthi farmers, including Moorosi; they lived with San in caves at this time (Ellenberger and Macgregor 1912: 159–60). The figure illustrated in the painting, like one of the figures in the painting from upper Mangolong, has dots painted on his body. As mentioned above, this practice is known to have been associated with the puberty rites of some Nguni groups (see also Broster 1981: plates 26 and 27, for similar spots painted on the torso of a Xhosa diviner initiate).

*New beliefs, rites and symbols are adopted in an almost completely unchanged form.*

There are many examples of hunter-gatherers and others adopting the rites and beliefs of neighbouring peoples almost in *toto.* Chenchu hunter-gatherers of India have adopted the religious beliefs and rites of Hindus, rather than vice versa (von Fürer-Haimendorf 1945); Punan hunter-gatherers of Borneo are closer in customs to affiliated sedentary peoples than to other Punan groups (Hoffman 1984); and Dorobo have taken on the customs of pastoralists to whom they are attached (Blackburn 1974, 1982; Kratz 1980). A central rite adopted by San people from Bantu-speakers is the initiation rite of Lake Chrissie San 'medicine men'/diviners (Potgieter 1955: 30). This rite – almost identical to that undergone by initiate Swazi diviners – involves the capturing of a water-serpent and the use of its skin in an initiation dance. The Lake Chrissie San have been heavily influenced by the Swazi, having lived amongst these people for many years and intermarried with them; this important rite reflects that influence.

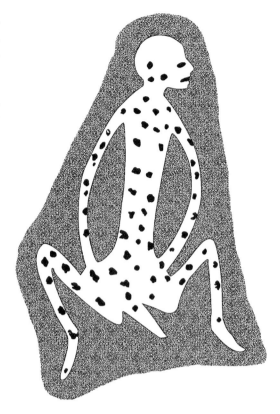

**Fig. 14.11.** Possible initiation scene. Moorosi's Cave, Barkly East.
After Battiss (1948: fig. 1, opp. p. 226).

In general, the more closely San were acquainted both with the economic base of farmer society, and with its rites and beliefs, the greater the likelihood that these rites and beliefs were depicted and symbolised in their rock-art in a relatively unchanged form. The imagery of a painting from Sand Spruit, Lesotho, copied by George William Stow in the nineteenth century (Stow and Bleek 1930), fits well with concepts associated with the initiation of certain Nguni and Sotho diviners as well as concepts generally characteristic of agriculturist cultures in many areas of Africa.

The painting (Fig. 14.12) illustrates an underwater scene. A highly decorated bull is surrounded by fish and accompanied by a water-serpent, as well

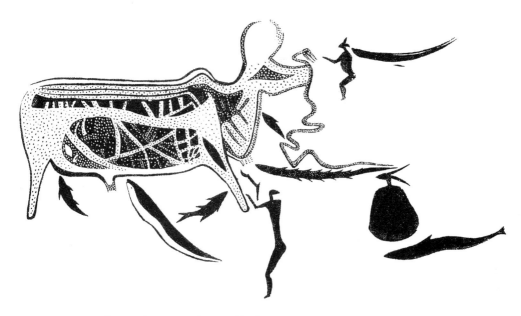

**Fig. 14.12.** Painting from Sand Spruit, Lesotho, copied by Stow. From Stow and Bleek 1930: plate 67a.

as by three buck-headed figures;[7] it appears to express experiences related to altered states of consciousness, possibly the experiences of initiate diviners. During the period of their initiation, diviners from many Nguni groups travel in dreams and trance to underwater realms in rivers, where they encounter a large underwater serpent, the *ixanti*, surrounded by snakes which are directly associated with the ancestral spirits (Kohler 1941; Berglund 1976; Broster 1981). Initiates are required to capture one or more of these snakes, the vertebrae of which are made into necklaces for ritual accoutrement. Other ancestral beings known as the River People, *abantubomlambo*, are also encountered in this realm, as are cattle (Moqotsi 1957).

While experiences related to altered states of consciousness and associated with the initiation of agriculturist diviners may well be depicted, the motifs in

this painting also appear closely related to a complex of religious beliefs, widely spread through Africa, which links snakes, cattle, rivers and ancestors in various ways. These beliefs, not restricted to areas occupied by San people, are connected to complexes of belief peculiar to agriculturist rather than San hunter-gatherer cultures.

Hambly (1931) remarks that snakes are widely held by black agriculturists, including many South African groups, to be manifestations of the spirits of ancestors; they are very often associated with rivers and deep pools by these people. He also tells of the offering of sacrificial cattle by a 'medicine-man' to sacred snakes living in a river near Lake Victoria. African 'medicine men'/diviners, including Nguni diviners, are commonly associated with snakes; they are believed to be able to control snakes, and in some cases to turn into these creatures (Hambly 1931). The association in this painting of a watersnake with a bull, an animal closely associated with the economy and culture of agriculturists rather than with San people, is of particular interest as

---

[7] A painting from Ventershoek in the Orange Free State displays a similar association of a serpent, fish and cattle (Loubser and Laurens 1994: fig. 8), which suggests that Stow's copy is reasonably accurate.

cattle-breeders from a variety of areas in Africa associate these two creatures (Schmidt 1979). A further link between cattle and snakes in the cultures of African agriculturists is evident in the belief that sacred snakes should be given milk; sacred cows are sometimes kept to provide this drink (Hambly 1931).

Cattle, like snakes, are strongly associated by many southern African and other African agriculturists with the tribal ancestors; they are consequently very important symbolically. The realm of the dead is believed by certain agriculturists, including Nguni groups, to be inhabited by the spirits or shades of cattle. Sheddick's (1953: 79) account of the sacrificing of an ox by the Sotho–Nguni group, the Vundle, to their tribal ancestors demonstrates links between cattle, ancestors and rivers. This rite involved the cutting up of the sacrificed beast and the throwing of pieces of its flesh into a river associated with these ancestors. African chiefs were sometimes buried in rivers; in this way rivers, in some cases, became associated with these particular ancestors. For example, during times of drought, cattle were thrown into a deep river pool in which the body of an Mpondomise chief was interred (Cape of Good Hope 1883: 407), thereby supplicating to this important ancestor for rain. Schmidt (1979: 215) cites an account of the sacrificing of cattle by Sotho to the 'Chief of the Water', who lived in a river pool and took the form of a huge snake. This was done during a time of drought. It is also of interest that cattle are known to have been sacrificed by Bantu-speakers to the River People (Young 1834).

These rites and beliefs are all relevant to how we interpret the Sand Spruit painting. They suggest that particular beliefs of cattle-breeders were adopted by the San who executed this painting, and that it symbolises widely held and related beliefs and customs of African agriculturists concerning snakes, rivers, cattle and ancestors. It is well explained through recourse to Nguni and Sotho religious concepts, many of which appear to have been shared in broad detail by other African cattle-breeders.

*Old beliefs, rites and symbols are retained but are given new meanings derived in whole or part from the donor culture.*

Van der Leeuw (1964) terms this process *transposition*, 'the variation in the significance of any phenomenon, occurring in the dynamic of religions, while its form remains quite unaltered' (1964: 611–12). The concept is very similar to an axiom underlying Panofsky's (1972) principle of *disjunction*, which states that a visible form often repeated may acquire different meanings with the passage of time. As Kubler (1970: 143–4) points out: '[W]hen observing disjunction . . . we . . . face the difficult notion of discontinuity in a temporal fabric of which we know the weave to be unbroken. Continuous form does not predicate continuous meaning, nor does continuity of form or meaning necessarily imply continuity of culture.'

A particularly clear transposition is the manner in which the exterior attributes and symbols of the Sun Dance of the Shoshoni Indians have been reinterpreted according to Christian concepts (Hultkrantz 1969). While the form of the dance remains largely unchanged, interpretations now follow Christian lines. It is said that the dance illustrates how Jesus hung on the cross for three days and was taken down (Hultkrantz 1969: 37–8):

The Dance Lodge is the grave of Christ, through which one passes to go out to a new life; or it is Golgotha . . . The roof-poles are 'the Brothers of Jesus', that is the twelve Apostles. It is also said that the western pole represents the 'good influence' whilst the north and south poles symbolise the robbers at Golgotha. Since time immemorial one has placed a stuffed eagle on the roof-poles; because this pole is cleft it is called the path of life or the Judas pole (Judas spoke with a forked tongue).

The centre pole in the Sun Dance now represents the cross of Christ and the buffalo head attached to this pole is sometimes said to represent Christ himself.[8]

---

[8] Hultkrantz (1969: 31) also cites evidence for the adoption of Christian beliefs by the Shoshoni which relate to the origin of the Sun Dance and the seeking of visions at the sites of 'rock-drawings', a traditional Shoshoni rite. According to a recent tradition, believed by the medicine man who related it to be

Were particular rites and symbols retained by San groups, and continued to be depicted in their art – but given new meanings derived in whole or part from other cultures?[9] While the symbolism associated with elands by San may have been transferred to cattle in some cases, with progressive acculturation the symbolic link between ancestors and cattle, as well as other aspects of the complex of religious beliefs surrounding cattle in agriculturist society, could have been transferred to elands depicted in the art (Fig. 14.13), so that they came to be reinterpreted partly within the context of Nguni and Sotho cosmologies. The assignment of new meaning to elands in this manner would have changed the way it was 'read' within transitional San society. As happened with the Shoshoni Sun Dance, the original form and exterior attributes of a peculiarly San rite, such as the trance dance, may have remained unchanged, but with its meaning and symbolism altered by incorporating Nguni and Sotho religious concepts. This may have occurred over a short period in times of very rapid social change. If change occurred slowly, the meaning of a specific painting on a shelter wall may have altered for successive generations occupying the cave as acculturation took its course and the religious beliefs, rites and associated symbolism of farmers were gradually adopted. In this way, the painting would be constantly reinterpreted in terms of new or modified religious beliefs.

The meaning and symbolism associated with the rain-bull, which figured prominently in the mythology and art of some southern San groups (Fig. 14.14), may also have changed while its form remained constant. It is possible that the concept of a rain-animal was not possessed by San people before the arrival of pastoralists and agriculturists in southern Africa. If it was, there can be no doubt that it was altered as a result of contact with these people.

The name given to this animal by the San indicates agriculturist/pastoralist influence. It was usually referred to as a rain-bull or cow, rather than as rain-animal. Moreover, the language which San informants used to describe the rite involving the killing of the rain-bull in order to bring rain is strongly reminiscent of agriculturist or pastoralist, rather than hunter-gatherer, society. Descriptions of San rain-making ceremonies involve the leading or riding of the animal, in the manner of a domesticated animal such as a cow or ox, and the milking of it. Thus a /Xam San man remarked, 'I will cut a she-rain which has milk, I will milk her, then she will rain softly on the ground, so that it is wet deep down in the middle' (Bleek 1933: 309).

Some or all of these elements are present in the rain-making rites of certain cattle-breeding groups in southern Africa. Rain-making ceremonies involving the killing of cows and bulls exist amongst a number of southern African groups that breed cattle (Schmidt 1979). While paintings of rain-animals such as the one illustrated here may depict earlier San concepts unrelated to the rites and beliefs of cattle-breeders, they appear to have been supplemented or supplanted by ideas derived from the cultures of cattle-breeders. Rain-animals in the art were probably

Shoshoni in origin, Christ fasted in the mountains after the crucifixion, praying to God to send the Holy Spirit down the mountains to those who could not read or write. The Spirit then appeared to Shoshoni in dreams at the 'rock-drawings' and gave them the Sun Dance.

9 Stow (1905: 120–4) suggested that the meaning of San rock-paintings might change while their form remained constant; as particular paintings were reinterpreted by later generations, in time the original meaning came to be supplanted. Morris (1988: 117), in considering the rock-engravings of the northern Cape and Karoo, has pointed to studies of ideological and ritual change which suggest that 'particular expressions in art and ritual can undergo considerable change in context and implication and yet retain the same basic "outward and visible" forms and vice versa'.

The meaning of certain rock-paintings in Ngcengane Cave, Transkei, said to have been painted by a San man, Lindiso, may have changed in later years both for this man and for other San who had gone to live with Mpondomise farmers and been influenced by Mpondomise culture (Jolly and Prins 1994; Prins 1994). While some paintings in the shelter appear traditionally San in form, they could later have been interpreted by assimilated San people in religious terms which accommodated concepts drawn from Nguni cosmology, such as ancestor veneration (Prins 1994). We depend on the sometimes inconsistently presented testimony of Lindiso's daughter for information about this man, however, and we cannot be completely sure of the details she provided concerning her father's connection with the paintings at Ngcengane Cave.

**Fig. 14.13.** Elands. Lethena River, Lesotho.

**Fig. 14.14.** Rain-bull. Bamboo Hollow, Natal Drakensberg.

reinterpreted by later generations within this later cultural context, or in terms of syncretic beliefs and rites derived from the cultures of both San hunter-gatherers and farmers. As Schmidt (1979: 211) remarks: 'When studying Bushman rain-making ceremonies and their "rain bull", we have to bear in mind such far-spread beliefs and customs of their Bantu neighbours. Only if we know about the general southern African mental background can we get to a fuller understanding of the Bushman way of life.'

## The distribution patterns of cattle and snake rock-paintings

The hypothesised changes in San art presented here are congruent with the distribution of paintings of cattle and snakes. There have been snakes in the south-western Cape for the entire period that it was occupied by hunter-gatherers, and there have been cattle for more than the one thousand years of joint San–pastoralist occupation of the area. Yet, San of this area did not paint cattle and there are almost no paintings of snakes. On the other hand, there is a considerable number of paintings of these creatures in the south-eastern mountains and adjacent areas where black agriculturists settled (Fig. 14.15).

This unexpected distribution pattern of cattle and snake paintings – something of a mystery in southern African rock-art studies (Willcox 1971; Manhire *et al.* 1986) – can possible be understood as reflecting the various ways in which San of different areas interacted with different peoples (Jolly 1996a). Parkington (1996) has drawn attention to the contrast between the paintings of the Western Cape and those of the Drakensberg, suggesting this contrast may be due to the absence of widespread settled farming in the Cape. He remarks that the presence of settled farmers 'may have caused an evolutionary shift in expressive forms and even performance context', which could explain, at least in part, the marked differences between the Western Cape and Drakensberg art (Parkington 1996: 289).

Cattle and snakes, two key creatures in the symbolic system of black farmers in this area, are also

**Fig. 14.15.** Serpent. Camp Shelter, Natal Drakensberg.

important symbols in the cultures of other African agriculturists further north. While snakes would have had significance in San cultures, these creatures and cattle probably became particularly important symbols for the south-eastern San as a result of the influence of black farming communities on their religious ideology, and were consequently depicted in their art. Where this influence was absent, they were usually not painted. And the fact that cattle paintings are much more common in the southern rather than the northern Drakensberg can be related to the close relationships known to have existed between many San groups and agriculturists such as the Phuthi and Mpondomise, who occupied the southern Drakensberg and adjacent areas. In these San groups, probably heavily influenced by Nguni and Sotho culture, cattle are likely to have become important symbols and subjects for their art (Jolly 1994; for other explanations, see Manhire *et al.* 1986).

Thematic patterning of this sort in the art can be an important indicator of cultural variation amongst San groups. Mitchell (1992, 1996) has proposed that differences in the rock-art of western and eastern Lesotho may reflect differences in social relations and forms of interaction between hunter-gatherers and farmers in these areas. The need to identify regional variations in the art as a clue to differing social processes undergone by hunter-gatherers of different areas is also underlined by Parkington (1996: 289), who remarks, 'some comparisons of the kinds of imagery favoured in the different geographic concentrations of paintings in southern Africa would now seem required, and comparisons that are as alert to the differences as to the supposed similarities'.

## Meaning and form

What evidence we have for the age of the art indicates that most of the rock-paintings in the south-eastern mountains and adjacent areas were executed after the arrival of black farmers about the fifteenth century AD. We need to consider the impact of these farmers on the symbols and rites depicted by the artists. Although many paintings in these areas were probably executed by San largely or wholly unaffected by Nguni and Sotho culture, it is very likely that others reflect, at least in part, the cultural influence of black farmers on south-eastern San society.

This kind of ideological change will not always be easy to detect, or to prove, as disjunction in a rite's or symbol's meaning may be hidden by its continuity of form. Although the south-eastern and other rock-art has almost invariably, and understandably, been interpreted in terms of characteristically San religious concepts and symbols, our wider knowledge of cultural change and hybridity suggest interpretations should take into account the complexities of ideological change as well as the uncertain correspondence between traditional form and traditional meaning in San art.

The influence of the Nguni and Sotho on the San should cause us to reconsider how we use informed methods and ethnographic analogy to interpret the art. We need to draw to an extent on Nguni and Sotho ethnography to interpret the rock-art of the south-eastern mountains (Botha and Thackeray 1987; Thackeray 1988, 1993). In the almost total absence of information from south-eastern San concerning the art of this area, rock-art scholars can profitably utilise the ethnography of Nguni and Sotho groups who occupied the south-eastern mountains and adjacent areas for much of the contact period, and who influenced the religious ideologies and ritual practices of south-eastern San groups.

## Acknowledgements

I am grateful to John Parkington for comments on an earlier version of this chapter. Thanks are also due to Anne Solomon, who assisted with the electronic scanning of slides of rock-paintings used to illustrate my article, and Marg Burton, who helped with the tracing and printing of the map and Orpen's copy of the paintings at Upper Mangolong.

## REFERENCES

Arbousset, T. and F. Daumas. 1968 (1846). *Narrative of an exploratory tour to the north-east of the colony of the Cape of Good Hope.* Cape Town, C. Struik.

Barnard, A. 1988. Structure and fluidity in Khoisan religious ideas, *Journal of Religion in Africa* 18: 216–36.

Battiss, W. 1948. *The artists of the rocks.* Pretoria, Red Fern Press.

Berglund, A. 1976. *Zulu thought-patterns and symbolism.* Cape Town, David Philip.

Blackburn, R. H. 1974. The Okiek and their history, *Azania* 9: 139–57.

   1982. In the land of milk and honey: Okiek adaptations to their forests and neighbours, in E. Leacock and R. Lee (eds.), *Politics and history in band societies*, pp. 283–305. Cambridge, Cambridge University Press.

Bleek, D. F. 1933. Beliefs and customs of the /Xam Bushmen. Part V: The rain, *Bantu Studies* 7: 297–312.

Botha L. J. and J. F. Thackeray. 1987. A note on southern African rock art, medicine-men and Nguni diviners, *South African Archaeological Bulletin* 42: 71–3.

Broster, J. A. 1981. *Amagqirha: religion, magic and medicine in Transkei.* Cape Town, Via Afrika.

Bührmann, M. V. 1984. *Living in two worlds: communications between a white healer and her black counterparts.* Cape Town, Human and Rousseau.

Campbell, C. 1987. Art in crisis: contact period rock art in the south-eastern mountains of southern Africa. Unpublished MSc. thesis, University of the Witwatersrand, Johannesburg.

Cape of Good Hope 1883. *Report and proceedings of the Government Commission on Native Laws and Customs.* Cape Town, W. A. Richards and Sons.

Comaroff, J. 1985. *Body of power, spirit of resistance: the culture and history of a South African people.* Chicago, University of Chicago Press.

Cronin, M. 1982. Radiocarbon dates from the Early Iron Age in Transkei, *South African Journal of Science* 78: 38–9.

Dowson, T. A. 1994. Reading art, writing history: rock art and social change in southern Africa, *World Archaeology* 25(3): 332–45.

1995. Hunter-gatherers, traders and slaves: the 'Mfecane' impact on Bushmen, their ritual and art, in C. Hamilton (ed.), *The Mfecane aftermath: reconstructive debates in southern African history*, pp. 51–70. Johannesburg, Witwatersrand University Press.

Ellenberger, D. F. and S. C. Macgregor. 1912. *History of the Basuto: ancient and modern.* London, Caxton.

Ellis, F. H. 1954. Comment on: *Spanish–Indian acculturation in the Southwest*, by E. H. Spicer, *American Anthropologist* 56: 663–84.

Fisher, H. J. 1978. Conversion reconsidered: some historical aspects of religious conversion in black Africa, *Africa* 43: 27–40.

Guenther, M. 1996. Diversity and flexibility: the case of the Bushmen of southern Africa, in S. Kent (ed.), *Cultural diversity among twentieth-century foragers: an African perspective*, pp. 65–86. Cambridge, Cambridge University Press.

Hall, S. 1990. Hunter-gatherer-fishers of the Fish River Basin: a contribution to the Holocene prehistory of the Eastern Cape. Unpublished Ph.D dissertation, University of Stellenbosch, Stellenbosch.

1994. Images of interaction: rock art and sequence in the eastern Cape, in T. A. Dowson and J. D. Lewis-Williams (eds.), *Contested images: diversity in southern African rock art research*, pp. 61–82. Johannesburg, Witwatersrand University Press.

Hambly, W. D. 1931. *Serpent worship in Africa.* Chicago, Field Museum of Natural History, Publication 289. Anthropological Series 21(1).

Hannerz, U. 1987. The world in creolisation, *Africa* 57: 546–59.

Hoffman, C. L. 1984. Punan foragers in the trading networks of Southeast Asia, in C. Schrire (ed.), *Past and present in hunter-gatherer studies*, pp. 123–49. London, Academic Press.

Hultkrantz, Å. 1969. Pagan and Christian elements in the religious syncretism among the Shoshoni Indians of Wyoming, in S. S. Hartmann (ed.), *Syncretism*, pp. 15–40. Uppsala, Almqvist and Wiksell.

Jolly, P. A. 1986. A first generation descendant of the Transkei San, *South African Archaeological Bulletin* 41: 6–9.

1994. Strangers to brothers: interaction between south-eastern San and southern Nguni/Sotho communities. Unpublished MA thesis, University of Cape Town.

1995. Melikane and Upper Mangolong revisited: the possible effects on San art of symbiotic contact between south-eastern San and southern Sotho and Nguni communities, *South African Archaeological Bulletin* 50: 68–80.

1996a. Symbiotic interaction between black farming communities and the south-eastern San: some implications for southern African rock art studies, the use of ethnographic analogy, and the cultural identity of hunter-gatherers, *Current Anthropology* 37(2): 277–305.

1996b. Interaction between south-eastern San and southern Nguni and Sotho communities *c.* 1400 to *c.* 1880, *South African Historical Journal*, 35: 30–61.

Jolly, P. A. and F. E. Prins. 1994. M. – a further assessment, *South African Archaeological Bulletin* 49: 16–23.

Kent, S. 1996. Cultural diversity among African foragers: causes and implications, in S. Kent (ed.), *Cultural diversity among twentieth-century foragers: an African perspective*, pp. 1–18. Cambridge, Cambridge University Press.

Kohler, M. 1941. *The Izangoma diviners.* Pretoria, Government Printer.

Kratz, C. 1980. Are the Okiek really Maasai? Or Kipsigis? Or Kikuyu?, *Cahiers d'Etudes Africaines* 79: 355–68.

Kubler, G. 1970. Period, style and meaning in ancient American art, *New Literary History* 1–2: 127–44.

Lewis-Williams, J. D. 1980. Ethnography and iconography: aspects of southern San thought and art, *Man* (NS) 15: 467–82.

1981. *Believing and seeing: symbolic meanings in southern San rock paintings.* London, Academic Press.

1982. The economic and social context of southern San rock art, *Current Anthropology* 23(4): 429–49.

1984. Ideological continuities in prehistoric southern Africa, in C. Schrire (ed.), *Past and present in hunter-gatherer studies*, pp. 225–52. London, Academic Press.

1986. The last testament of the southern San, *South African Archaeological Bulletin* 41: 10–11.

1995. Seeing and construing: the making and 'meaning' of a southern African rock art motif, *Cambridge Archaeological Journal* 5(1): 3–23.

Loubser, J. and G. Laurens. 1994. Depictions of domestic ungulates and shields: hunter/gatherers and agro-pastoralists in the Caledon River valley area, in T. A. Dowson and J. D. Lewis-Williams (eds.), *Contested images: diversity in southern African rock art research*, pp. 83–118. Johannesburg, Witwatersrand University Press.

Maggs, T. M. O'C. 1980. The Iron Age sequence south of the Vaal and Pongola Rivers: some historical implications, *Journal of African History* 21(1): 1–15.

1984. The Iron Age south of the Zambezi, in R. G. Klein (ed.), *Southern African prehistory and palaeo-environments*, pp. 329–60. Rotterdam, A. A. Balkema.

Manhire, A. H., J. E. Parkington, A. D. Mazel and T. M. O'C. Maggs. 1986. Cattle, sheep and horses: a review of domestic animals in the rock art of southern Africa, *South African Archaeological Society Goodwin Series* 5: 22–30.

Marshall, L. 1962. !Kung Bushman religious beliefs, *Africa* 32(3): 221–51.

Mazel, A. D. 1982. Distribution of painting themes in the Natal Drakensberg, *Annals of the Natal Museum* 25(1): 67–82.

1996. In pursuit of San pre-colonial history in the Natal Drakensberg: a historical overview, in P. Skotnes (ed.), *Miscast: negotiating the presence of the Bushmen*, pp. 191–5. Cape Town, UCT Press.

Mitchell, P. J. 1992. Archaeological research in Lesotho: a review of 120 years, *African Archaeological Review* 10: 3–34.

1996. Comment on: 'Symbiotic interaction between black farmers and south-eastern San: implications for southern African rock art studies, ethnographic analogy and hunter-gatherer cultural identity', by P. Jolly, *Current Anthropology* 37(2): 277–305.

Moqotsi, L. 1957. A study of ukuthwasa. Unpublished MA thesis, University of the Witwatersrand.

Morris, D. 1988. Engraved in place and time: a review of variability in the rock art of the Northern Cape and Karoo, *South African Archaeological Bulletin* 43: 109–21.

Orpen, J. M. 1874. A glimpse into the mythology of the Maluti Bushmen, *Cape Monthly Magazine* (NS) 9(49): 1–13.

Panofsky, E. 1972. *Renaissances and renascences in western art*. New York, Harper and Row.

Parkington, J. 1996. What is an eland? N!ao and the politics of age and sex in the paintings of the Western Cape, in P. Skotnes (ed.), *Miscast: negotiating the presence of the Bushmen*, pp. 281–9. Cape Town, UCT Press.

Potgieter, E. F. 1955. *The disappearing Bushmen of Lake Chrissie*. Pretoria, J. L. van Schaik.

Prins, F. E. 1990. Southern Bushman descendants in the Transkei – rock art and rainmaking, *South African Journal of Ethnology* 13(3): 110–16.

1994. Living in two worlds: the manipulation of power relations, identity and ideology by the last San rock artist of the Transkei, South Africa, *Natal Museum Journal of Humanities* 6: 179–93.

Pye, E. M. 1969. The transplantation of religions, *Numen* 16: 234–9.

Ranger, T. O. and I. Kimambo. 1972. Introduction, in T. O. Ranger and I. Kimambo (eds.), *The historical study of African religion*, pp. 1–25. London, Heinemann.

Rudner, I. 1983. Paints of the Khoisan artists, *South African Archaeological Society Goodwin Series* 4: 14–20.

Schmelen, Rev. J. H. 1815. Journal of a journey from Pella to explore the mouth of the Orange River and Great Namaqua and Damara countries, January 3rd to December 18th 1815. Unpublished manuscript in the C. W. M. Archives, School of Oriental and African Studies, University of London.

Schmidt, S. 1979. The rain bull of the South African Bushmen, *African Studies* 38: 201–24.

Schofield, J. F. 1949. Four debatable points, *South African Archaeological Bulletin* 4: 98–106.

Schoonraad, M. 1968. Information wanted: Bushmen circumcision, *African Studies* 27: 28.

Sheddick, V. G. J. 1953. *The southern Sotho*. London, International African Institute.

Solomon, A. C. 1994. Mythic women: a study in variability in San rock art and narrative, in T. A. Dowson and J. D. Lewis-Williams (eds.), *Contested images: diversity in southern African rock art research*, pp. 331–71. Johannesburg, Witwatersrand University Press.

1995. Rock art incorporated: an archaeological and interdisciplinary study of certain human figures in San art. Unpublished Ph.D thesis, University of Cape Town.

Spicer, E. H. 1954. Spanish–Indian acculturation in the South-west, *American Anthropologist* 56: 663–84.

Stow, G. W. 1905. *The native races of South Africa*. London, Swan Sonnenschein.

Stow, G. W. and D. F. Bleek. 1930. *Rock paintings in South Africa*. London, Methuen.

Thackeray, A. I. 1983. Dating the rock art of southern Africa, *South African Archaeological Society Goodwin Series* 4: 21–6.

Thackeray, J. F. 1988. Southern African rock art and Xhosa beliefs associated with *abantubomlambo*, *Pictogram* 1: 2–3.

—— 1993. New directions in the study of southern African rock art, *African Arts* 26(1): 74–5.

Townley Johnson, R. 1960. Rock-paintings of ships, *South African Archaeological Bulletin* 15(59): 111–13.

Turnbull, C. M. 1965. *Wayward servants*. London, Eyre and Spittiswoode.

—— 1983. *The Mbuti pygmies: change and adaptation*. New York, Holt, Rhinehart and Winston.

Van der Leeuw, G. 1964. *Religion in essence and manifestation*. London, George Allen and Unwin.

van der Merwe, N. J., J. Sealy and R. Yates. 1987. First accelerator carbon-14 date for pigment from a rock painting, *South African Journal of Science* 83: 56–7.

van Rijssen, W. J. 1994. Rock art: the question of authorship, in T. A. Dowson and J. D. Lewis-Williams (eds.), *Contested images: diversity in southern African rock art research*, pp. 159–75. Johannesburg, Witwatersrand University Press.

Vansina, J. 1984. *Art history in Africa*. London, Longman.

Vinnicombe, P. 1976. *People of the eland*. Pietermaritzburg, University of Natal Press.

von Fürer-Haimendorf, C. 1945. *The Chenchus: jungle folk of the Deccan*. London, Macmillan.

Walton, J. 1956. *African village*. Pretoria, Van Schaik.

Wendt, W. E. 1976. 'Art mobilier' from Apollo 11 Cave, South West Africa: Africa's oldest dated works of art, *South African Archaeological Bulletin* 31: 5–11.

Willcox, A. R. 1971. Domestic cattle and a rock art mystery, in M. Schoonraad (ed.), *Rock paintings of southern Africa*. South African Association of Science, Special Issue 2: 44–8.

Woodburn, J. 1982. Social dimensions of death in four African hunting and gathering societies, in M. Bloch and J. Parry (eds.), *Death and the regeneration of life*, pp. 187–210. Cambridge, Cambridge University Press.

Wright, J. B. 1971. *Bushman raiders of the Drakensberg, 1840–70*. Pietermaritzburg, University of Natal Press.

Yates, R. and A. Jerardino. 1996. A fortuitous fall: an early set of rock wall paintings from the west coast of South Africa, *South African Journal of Science* 92: 110.

Young, S. 1834. Journal of Samuel Young, Unpublished manuscript in the WMMS Archives, School of Oriental and African Studies, University of London.

Anne Solomon

# 15. Ethnography and method in southern African rock-art research

In southern African rock-art studies ethnographic and ethnohistorical materials have underpinned a model which focuses on trance and shamanic visions. Yet the 'ethnographic method' is fraught with difficulties. These include the relationship(s) between verbal and visual texts, and their interpretation; iconographic versus formal methods; and questions regarding presumed consistencies over space and through time.

## San rock-art and its context

San rock-art, found in many thousands of sites in the southern countries of Africa, includes both paintings and engravings. The paintings (on which I shall focus) are relatively well documented in South Africa, Lesotho, Zimbabwe, Namibia and Tanzania (Fig. 15.1). Wars in Angola and Mozambique have meant that our knowledge of San art in those countries is poor. Although we have become accustomed to speaking of 'San art' – implying that it is the work of hunter-gatherers of the same linguistic and cultural group – it is becoming increasingly evident that the reality is probably decidedly more complex. Whilst there is a certain unity amongst the arts of different regions, differences and the reasons for diversity require further attention. Shared features of the southern subcontinental art include the numerical dominance of human figures and large herbivores, executed principally in red, brown and yellow ochreous pigments, with black and white paints also used. Yet there are significant stylistic differences between regions. Recent art, such as nineteenth-century paintings from the KwaZulu-Natal Drakensberg, South Africa, introduces new themes which are not part of the traditional repertoire, such as encounters between in-digenous peoples and colonial settlers. The general rubric 'San art' serves to describe a body of art which, it is generally agreed, is not the work of black Iron Age farmers; yet the term also masks the art's diversity.

The question of the cultural, economic and political identity of the artists is further exacerbated by the poor archaeological contextualisation of the art. We have only two credible direct dates for paintings, neither older than 500 years. Nevertheless, indirect dates derived from excavations suggest that the tradition of painting spans the Holocene (Thackeray 1983; Mazel 1992; Yates and Jerardino 1996); it may be older, if Wendt's (1976) date of approximately 26,000 b.p. from the Namibian cave, Apollo XI, is accepted. Although content (for example, horses, wagons and soldiers) indicates the approximate age of a small number of paintings (Vinnicombe 1976), and it seems likely that many paintings still clearly visible are not of great antiquity, the vast majority remain undated. The dating problem has had profound implications for the kinds of study undertaken on San art. A scarcity of dates but a wealth of ethnographic material has resulted in an inescapable tendency for the focus of San rock-art studies to be synchronic (see Chippindale and Taçon, this volume).

The tradition of San rock-art is now long dead, and we have almost no direct insights into the practice of painting. Exceptions are accounts by a Sotho man and a Xhosa woman, in the 1930s and 1980s respectively (How 1962; Jolly 1986); both claimed familiarity with San artists. However, they could have been familiar only with the most recent art, and

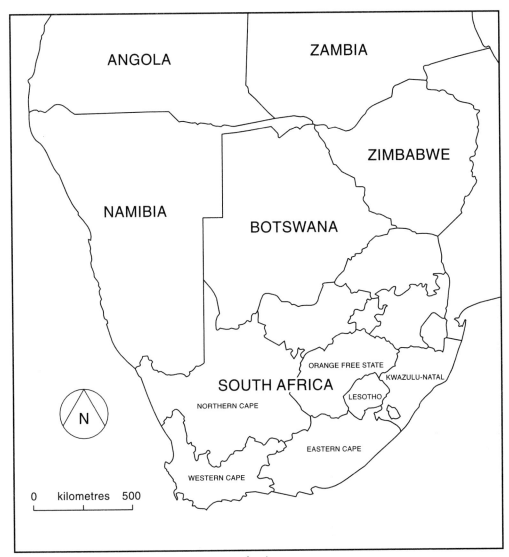

**Fig. 15.1.** Areas where paintings discussed in the text are found.

the extent of continuity between this artistic tradition and the earlier art remains an open question.

Our knowledge of the art via 'informed methods' is minimal, since the practice of painting was not observed. None of the anthropologically documented San groups maintained a tradition of painting. We are, however, extremely fortunate to have an enormous amount of ethnographic and ethnohistorical material which affords insights into aspects of San belief. The Bleek and Lloyd Collection at the University of Cape Town is the largest such source, comprising thousands of pages of stories and lore narrated by /Xam San speakers in the late nineteenth century. This collection and similar material deriving from twentieth-century anthropological studies provide much scope for rock-art research using formal methods and analogy; these two methods are so intertwined that it is difficult to separate them.

Purely formal methods of studying the art have not to date proved particularly illuminating. Commonly, the significance of distributions of images and styles is opaque or inaccessible, until such time as a better framework of dates is available. Although various writers have engaged with formal methods – in the sense of inferring meaning from image form – this has usually been in association with analogical arguments of one kind or another. In these terms, most formal studies arise from a prior process of analogy, or appeal to analogy for their credibility. The important but problematic role of ethnography in San rock-art research, and the interdependence of analogy and formal study in South African rock-art research, are the focus of this chapter.

The dominant model in San rock-art research today is that pioneered by Lewis-Williams (for example 1980, 1981). Ethnographies, especially of the late nineteenth-century /Xam San, alerted Lewis-Williams to shamanic practices in southern San societies; by analogy with shamans in San groups in the Kalahari Desert today, and by comparison of these two ethnographic sources with details of paintings, the model which proposes shamanistic experience as the essence of the art was developed. The process of using ethnographies to interpret San rock-art has become known generally as 'the ethnographic method'. As emphasis has come to be placed on the alleged neurological basis of visual imagery (Lewis-Williams 1984, 1995; Lewis-Williams and Dowson 1988, 1989, 1994), the use of ethnographic analogy has diminished accordingly or changed direction.

Stone and Bahn (1993) have argued that ethnographies and analogies derived from ethnographic studies represent the best – and perhaps the only – way of understanding Palaeolithic art. In the case of San art, the substantial ethnographies offer a multitude of possible templates for modelling the meaning of the visual imagery, and the utility of this wealth of material has by no means been exhausted.

## San rock-art and the creation of the shamanistic model

The existence of large bodies of ethnography on San hunter-gatherers has been a key to South African rock-art studies virtually since their inception in the late nineteenth century. In 1874 the linguist W. H. I. Bleek wrote, 'A collection of faithful copies of Bushman paintings is . . . only second in importance to a collection of folklore in their own language. Both such collections will serve to illustrate each other' (Bleek in Orpen 1874: 13). Recourse to ethnographic material in interpreting San rock-art remains standard practice, but the ways in which ethnographies are used have altered. Early researchers emphasised the relation of the art specifically to mythology (for example, Orpen 1874; Stow and Bleek 1930); but it has become increasingly apparent that incidents, scenes and characters from mythology are not identifiable. Nevertheless, the connection proposed between art and mythology served to underscore the idea that the art was a complex expression of San religious thought.

The earliest studies were focused on iconography, in both senses of the term: the first referring simply to the range of subject-matter; the second to the referents of the images. The notion that the art illustrates the mythology (second sense) has been severely criticised on theoretical and methodological grounds, especially from the perspective of art history. Damisch (1975: 31, cited by Preziosi 1989: 195) has argued that 'iconography as a method is founded on the postulate that the artistic image . . . achieves a signifying articulation only with and because of the textual reference which passes through and eventually imprints itself in it'. Preziosi (1989: 37) criticises such 'mechanical processes of text matching' as mere verbal paraphrasing of the visuality of the image, and relates it to logocentric paradigms.

The prioritisation of word over image highlighted by such critiques was barely addressed in San rock-art until recent inputs from art historians, who have urged archaeologists to conduct formal studies focusing more rigorously on the visuality of San art (see Skotnes 1990, 1994). Nevertheless, given the distance separating contemporary researchers from the art, ethnographies and verbal sources remain crucially important. Of more concern to rock-art researchers through the decades has been the question, 'Which verbal commentary best illuminates the art?' The notion that the art illustrated mythology – and was thus derived from and secondary to it – did not persist. However, recourse to mythology in interpretations of the art did not altogether vanish. Until the 1970s it was customary for enigmatic images – fantastic creatures or strange human-like figures – to be described as 'mythological beings' (Willcox 1956; Lee and Woodhouse 1970; Pager 1971; Vinnicombe 1976); but no direct, linear correlation between the two media was explicitly proposed. Vinnicombe's use of mythology in her landmark work, *People of the eland* (1976), illustrates this. Vinnicombe organised discussion of the paintings by subject-matter (for example, 'eland', 'domestic animals'); each category of images was accompanied by a textual commentary, citing mythological, archaeological, historical and other relevant information. The use of mythology in this context is allusive and non-linear, without the implication of direct links between mythological reference and specific paintings. Rather, references to recorded myths serve primarily to illustrate the culturally specific meanings associated by San-speakers with particular creatures or phenomena, and to underscore the need for understanding San imagery as far as possible in terms of San cosmology. In contrast with earlier theories about the art, the putative linkage with mythology survived in a very general sense. Although the view persisted that the art was linked to 'mythology and other social and religious practices' (Vinnicombe 1972: 195), researchers no longer sought to draw explicit parallels. Theoretical innovations in the 1970s perpetuated this trend.

In the wake of the impact of Leroi-Gourhan's work on Palaeolithic art, Vinnicombe (1972, 1976) and Lewis-Williams (1972, 1974) engaged with structuralism and structural analyses. Vinnicombe explored the possible relation of San art to social structure, while Lewis-Williams began to examine the layout and patterning of images within sites, in terms of syntax and grammar. Both these new directions initiated new ways of thinking about the referents and 'meanings' of the art, as well as an implicit move away from more narrowly iconographic studies. In particular, Lewis-Williams's studies of this time moved in the direction of formal analysis. The importance of ethnography remained; it was indeed consolidated in Lewis-Williams's subsequent work, which initiated dramatic changes in the (sub-)discipline.

The basis of the shamanistic model, which has become the dominant interpretive frame for many researchers, was detailed by Lewis-Williams (1980, 1981). As Vinnicombe had also done, Lewis-Williams explored the utility and problems of using San ethnographies from distant times and places for understanding the rock-paintings of the Drakensberg mountains in the eastern parts of South Africa. He outlined 'various areas of thought where equivalences could be demonstrated' between the beliefs and practices of a range of San groups; these included notions concerning supernatural potency, initiation and trance performance (Lewis-Williams and Dowson 1994: 207). Having established such equivalences, ethnographies – notably the massive Bleek and Lloyd Collection of /Xam San lore – were used to elucidate features of the art.

Fundamental to this endeavour was the identification of trance 'metaphors' (Lewis-Williams 1980). Lewis-Williams's interpretation of southern San texts led him to believe that trance experience and hallucinations were central to understanding aspects of both the ethnographic texts and the art. It was argued that

The metaphors and beliefs which I have so far described suggest that the southern informants' reports of 'death', journeys beneath the water and the capture of a fantastic rain animal should all be seen as accounts of trance experience rather than other events. At least some of the paintings of rain animals therefore probably record hallucinations of medicine men in trance. (Lewis-Williams 1980: 473)

The shamanistic model offered new insights into many paintings: dances with dancers bleeding from the nose are well explained by this model, as are certain other previously enigmatic images. Extension of the model continued apace, and all manner of images have been claimed by proponents of the model as trance-derived. Therianthropes and other figures departing from naturalistic representation came to be seen as hallucinatory forms or metaphors for trance experience (see Lewis-Williams 1984), where previously such figures had commonly been interpreted as 'mythological'. The old dependence on ethnography in general and mythology in particular declined as Lewis-Williams and Dowson developed the model they have called the 'dual ethnographic–neuropsychological approach' (Lewis-Williams and Dowson 1994).

Lewis-Williams and Dowson (1988) considered certain geometric and abstract forms allegedly characteristic of the hallucinatory experience of all anatomically modern humans, who by definition share the same neurological circuitry. Seeing such forms as the building blocks of certain images, Lewis-Williams and Dowson propose that shamanic visions may be implicated in the very origin of the human capacity for image-making. In this vein, Lewis-Williams and Dowson (1988, 1993; Lewis-Williams 1995) have also considered European Palaeolithic and Bronze Age imagery in relation to shamanic practices This model, although rooted in ethnography, represents a certain independence from it. Although Lewis-Williams and Dowson still rely on ethnography to explain the cultural 'construal' of entoptic or hallucinatory forms, the derivation of the imagery from the operations of the nervous system is emphasised. In various respects, the model is diametrically opposite to those which had been in place before, particularly with regard to the emphasis placed on the relation of the art to ritual rather than myth. And, in keeping with an incipient tendency, the neurophysiological approach moves in the direction of formal study, although questions of iconography remain. The innovations wrought by Lewis-Williams

and proponents of the shamanistic model are legion; they have thoroughly reshaped aspects of our understanding of San art. Questions of method nevertheless remain a focus for debate. A topic which has received renewed attention of late concerns the ritual affiliations of the art and, by implication, the use of ethnography more generally.

## The ethnographic method 1: relationships between words and images

Various writers have recently addressed the relationship of the art to mythology or 'folklore'. Barnard (1992: 93) notes that recent researchers have focused on the relationship of the art to ritual, 'whereas previous generations of writers have sought in vain the connections between /Xam myth and prehistoric painting'. That affinities of the art with myth required further attention was recognised by Lewis-Williams and Loubser (1986); recently Guenther (1994) and Deacon (1994) have pursued this question. Deacon (1994: 252) states that 'recent models show a relationship between art and trance, but a correlation has not been established between art and folklore'. Deacon's investigation is a quantificative comparison of themes in the /Xam texts and in the rock-engravings found in the environs of the /Xam home territory in the Northern Cape Province. The absence from the engravings of various subjects and characters featured in the myths and narratives leads Deacon to conclude that there is no direct correlation between folklore and art in that area. Ultimately Deacon endorses the view that the art arises from trance experience, although she concedes that 'Rock-art draws on the same reservoir of experience as folklore, ritual and social relations' (1994: 253).

While Deacon's analysis usefully itemises differences between art and narratives, it is questionable whether these non-correspondences confirm or deny a link between art and folklore. Deacon's method is fundamentally iconographical; it does not aim to problematise the relationship of verbal and visual, nor to theorise the significance of differences of medium or genre. This long-standing problem within the ethnographic method is highlighted by critiques of logocentrism. Guenther (1994), addressing the question in detail, discusses 'textual and symbolic divergences among the three genres of Bushman expressive culture, art, ritual and folklore' and 'some of the methodological implications of this lack of homogeneity within the expressive domain for students of San rock-art' (Guenther 1994: 257). He (1994: 267) also finds that 'art and ritual are part of the same religious enterprise' – but 'relationships between art and myth and myth and ritual are much more tenuous'; with regard to the latter, Guenther adds, 'it is only with respect to the one ritual – the trance dance – that myth seems to be mute'. Indeed, there is good reason to believe that San myth and ritual are closely interwoven; recent models have been underpinned by a dualistic notion of myth and ritual which has obscured such connections (Solomon 1995). Undoubtedly the absence of mythological references to the trance dance has militated against the extensive use of mythology for understanding the rock-art, in the context of a model in which certain mythological images are seen as derived from trance. Examination of a key text suggests that an unjustified separation of myth and ritual has contributed to the prioritisation of ritual in understanding San art.

## The ethnographic method 2: what is a trance metaphor?

In 'Ethnography and iconography: aspects of southern San thought and art', Lewis-Williams (1980) drew on a nineteenth-century commentary published by Orpen (1874). Orpen was a colonial official who travelled to Lesotho in the course of his duties with a guide of San extraction named Qing. According to Orpen,

When happy and at ease smoking over campfires, I got from him the following stories and explanations of paintings, some which he showed and I copied on our route. I commenced by asking what the pictures of men with rhebok's heads meant. He said they were men who had

died and now lived in rivers, and were *spoilt at the same time as the elands* and by the dance of which you have seen paintings. (Orpen 1874: 2; original italics)

In the course of the account, Qing described the 'dance of blood' – 'a circular dance of men and women following each other ... [which was] danced all night' (Orpen 1874: 10). References to nasal bleeding, physical collapse and curing of the sick unequivocally identify this as a reference to the trance dance as ethnographically recorded (for example, from the !Kung; see Katz 1982). It is this segment of Qing's testimony which Lewis-Williams (1980) selects as the foundation of his hypothesis regarding the shamanic basis of the rock-art. The greater part of Qing's narration recounts a number of myths and stories, which bear many resemblances to those recorded contemporaneously by Bleek and Lloyd from the /Xam in north-western South Africa, as well as to those in collections compiled in the twentieth century (for instance Guenther 1989; Biesele 1993). Like those in other collections, they recount the doings of a 'race' of people who were the San predecessors on earth. Bleek and Lloyd (1911) translated the /Xam term as 'the people of the early race', while twentieth-century San-speakers refer to 'the old people' or some such appellation (Guenther 1989; Biesele 1993). All San groups share a belief in a prior time when animals had not yet been differentiated from people (Hewitt 1986; Guenther 1989). These early people were considered to be stupid and uncultured, lacking customs and manners. Guenther (1986, 1989) has discussed the intriguing San belief in a dual creation: only after a second creation did these primordial 'San' become the civilised San of modern times.

Prominent in San narratives is the trickster 'god', variously referred to as Cagn (Orpen 1874), /Kaggen (Bleek and Lloyd 1911) or Kaang (Arbousset and Daumas 1846). This mischievous character is the principal, but not the only, creator. In the Bleek and Lloyd Collection, numerous narratives recount the origin or creation of various creatures and phenomena, such as the eland, locusts, stars, the Milky

Way and so on. Other narratives explain the features of certain animals: the baboon's hairless rump, the shape of the hyena's hindquarters, and the honey badger's long claws. Stories which are apparently ubiquitous among San groups include those which tell of the origin of fire and the origin of death (see below). Although there are certain clear differences among the narrative traditions of different groups, several writers have commented on the extraordinary unity of San oral literature, regardless of linguistic diversity and other differences between groups (Schmidt 1991; Barnard 1992). Khoi (herder) lore is also significantly similar, to the extent that it is possible to speak generally of a Khoisan oral narrative tradition (see Schmidt 1991).

As noted, few simple iconographic correlations can be established between these verbal texts and the rock-art. Nevertheless, links may be discerned between myth and ritual, and, hence, the art. An alternative reading of Qing's comments to Orpen suggests that he considered mythology to be of relevance in relation to both art and ritual.

Commenting on the rhebok-headed men painted in Sehonghong Cave, Qing stated that they were dead men who had been 'spoilt at the same time as the elands and by the dance of which you have seen paintings'. Orpen continued his enquiry: 'I asked when the elands were spoilt and how. He began to explain and mentioned Cagn' (Orpen 1874: 2). The series of narratives which follows begins with Cagn's creation of the eland and proceeds through narratives apparently dealing with the exploits and misadventures of the people of the early race; only at the end of his narration does Qing refer again to the ritual dance. It seems clear that in Qing's view an explanation of the paintings was in some way dependent upon knowledge of the mythological realm.

It is implicit in Orpen's account that Qing's explanation of the spoiling of the eland is directly linked to his mention of Cagn, and, more specifically, to the narrative which follows – the eland creation story. The time at which the eland were 'spoilt' can thus be located in the mythological past. The story of the

eland's creation may itself be understood as the 'spoiling' of the eland.

In Lewis-Williams's (1980) interpretation, 'spoiling' refers to the attainment of an altered state of consciousness in trance. Another interpretation is possible. In the eland creation story, the eland began as Cagn's special and beloved pet, which he devotedly reared in the water-hole, until one day when it was killed without his knowledge. Cagn gathered its remains in a pot, and Cagn's wife, Coti, stirred up the contents. Where the blood and fat of the eland splashed out of the pot, new eland were created, and these then became the great eland herds which were once found in South Africa (Orpen 1874).

In terms of San mythology in general, the creation of the eland herds parallels the process whereby animals become 'real' (ordinary) animals, whereas before they were people. In this context, the spoiling of the eland may be interpreted as the point at which this animal was transformed into a true animal and its former status as a supernatural being was lost. From this perspective, the spoiling of the eland is an event which occurred in the mythical past. According to Qing, the rhebok-headed men of the paintings were also spoilt, or transformed, at this time. In terms of that reading, these paintings must also be seen in relation to the version of the San past as given in myth, rather than being viewed primarily as trance-related or hallucinatory imagery. And the allusion to the rhebok-headed men living in rivers is in Lewis-Williams's view, another reference to the sensations of trance experience.

Water, the water-hole and rain are given symbolic prominence in a wide range of Khoisan myths and stories. Many narratives refer to water-holes, rather than to rivers, understandable when one considers that the majority of Khoisan groups live in arid areas, rather than the well-watered parts with which Qing was familiar. In /Xam narratives, the water-hole is a powerful symbol of life and death. Various stories describe how /Kaggen's eland, /Kaggen's sister-in-law, and a dead ostrich are revived or regrown after parts of them are placed in the water. Other links between the water-hole, birth and regeneration are found in a !Kung story where a python falls into the water-hole, where she subsequently gives birth (Biesele 1993: 124–8). In other contexts, the water-hole is also a symbol of death. In /Xam menarcheal tales, female initiates and menstruating women are required to undergo ritual seclusion. Failure to do so renders them vulnerable to abduction by the violent male rain, who is constituted in the stories as a bull. Disobedient girls who are abducted by the male rain are drowned in the water-hole which is his home, and turned into frogs. The erring initiate's family is similarly abducted and drowned; their skin cloaks revert to being springbok, and their arrows become reeds growing in the water-hole. The water-hole and rain – apart from their links to birth and death – are also associated with initiation, a third important component of the life-cycle. My interpretation of the complex of San beliefs about gender and water or rain, and its relevance to the art, is described in detail elsewhere (Solomon 1989, 1992). References to the water-hole in relation to the origin of the world are also to be found. In the Kalahari, Thomas (1959) was told that in the beginning, the great god emerged from a water-hole. Vedder, working among the Damara, Khoisan foragers in Namibia, recorded a belief that the home of the mythical being, //gaua, was in a hole in the ground (Schapera 1930). Amongst many San groups, //gaua refers to the spirits of the dead, or specifically to a supreme being who is sometimes identified with God and sometimes with the Devil (Barnard 1992: 259). In the /Xam narratives, the water-hole is the place where dead girls (disobedient initiates) dwell (Bleek and Lloyd 1911), and the G/wi believe that the spirits of the dead live in an underworld (Barnard 1992: 114).

The ethnographic evidence suggests that the water-hole represents an interface with the spirit world. It is from the water-hole that life emerges, at the same time as submersion in it means death, regression and reversion. As such, the water-hole separates the realms of the living and the dead. In Lewis-Williams's interpretation death and under-water are metaphors for the sensory distortions experienced in trance (Lewis-Williams 1980), but the symbolism of the water-hole seems to extend beyond trance alone, encoding notions of space and time, and of birth and death. Rather than referring primarily to the 'death' attained in trance, 'underwater' may be seen as a metaphor for actual mortal expiry, and the passage into another realm, occupied by spirits of the dead. The experience of trancers may be understood in these terms, as a journey to the spirit world. It is well documented that shamans in trance enlist the aid of the spirits of the dead, and their shamanic journeys may be seen as a journey to their realm. From this point of view 'underwater' may be seen as the world described in mythology, the world of the people of the early race and of the spirits of the dead. Instead of understanding trance experience and a bodily sensation akin to drowning as the determinants of San notions concerning death and 'underwater', the causality may be inverted: the experiences of death and underwater recounted by trancers in altered states may be seen as determined by their understanding of the other world as enshrined in myth. In other words, it is at least as likely that a knowledge of the mythological world informs the trancer's experience, as vice versa, with trance experience construed as a journey to the mythological world. However, rather than simply inverting the causality, a more appropriate view takes the relationship between trance experience and mythology to be recursive, with neither ultimately determining. This interpretation permits a necessary reintegration of myth and ritual, accounts for the several facets of Qing's commentary, and offers a new way of conceptualising the relation of the mythology to the rock-art.

This view contrasts with the model of Lewis-Williams and Dowson, in which features of the mythology are seen as epiphenomena of trance. The independence of the mythology from trance has also been discussed by Guenther (1994: 268–9), who thinks it 'unwarranted to read the myths as coded tales about shamans' and 'ill-advised to inject into the myths such trance metaphors as have been identified in the art'. If the view that situates trance experience as the origin of the imagery is modified to accommodate Qing's considering mythology a relevant context for understanding the art, then trance experience and mythology may be seen as closely interwoven.

The question remains: if a connection between myth and art is accepted, how might the myths further our understanding of the visual imagery? A reassessment of the relationship of myth and art still does not permit an iconographic approach, in the absence of correlations that permit 'text matching'. Rather than focusing on iconography as subject-matter in a narrow sense, the organisation and textuality of myths may be a key to understanding formal attributes of San art.

## Formal analysis: the motif of the 'mythic woman'

The staunchest supporters of formal studies of rock-art have been art historians, for whom such an approach acknowledges and accounts for 'the visual as a site of meaning' (Skotnes 1994). In Skotnes's approach, the organisation of the panel is at least as important as the identity of the individual component images. A similar approach is also appropriate for analysing the myths and stories. Because such materials have been viewed as epiphenomenal, and principally as secondary tools for understanding the art, rock-art researchers have paid little attention to the textuality and organisation of the narratives; and mythological and other references are commonly decontextualised from their original narrative setting (Solomon 1991, 1995). The formal characteristics of narratives and myth may be considered in relation to formal attributes of the art.

A reading of San narratives reveals a strong emphasis on the themes of death, regeneration and reversal. These preoccupations are exemplified by a story ubiquitous among San groups, as well as widespread among Khoi speakers: The Origin of Death (Bleek and Lloyd 1911; Guenther 1989; Schmidt

1989; Dickens 1991). The basic story, in the many and varied known versions, concerns a young hare, who cries inconsolably while its mother lies dead. The moon reassures the hare that its mother is only sleeping, and will rise again just as the moon itself waxes and wanes. When the hare is unbelieving, the moon retaliates, declaring that from then onwards, people would die outright, and not return as the moon does. This narrative may be seen in relation to the key notion of dual creation, whereby the people of the early race are transformed into real humans; the acquisition of mortality is part of that process. The cyclic regeneration of the moon is a prominent and recurrent symbol in San texts and expression. The themes of death and regeneration symbolised by the moon are found more generally in a number of narratives. Other stories where the dead are regenerated in the water-hole have been mentioned above. The preoccupation in myth with the cycle of life and death, and with death and resurrection, parallels the central concerns of shamanism and its imagery (but is not necessarily derived from them).

The forms used in the narratives echo these prominent themes. The plot device of reversal may be seen in these terms. Many stories lack the dramatic structure familiar to western readers, as two stories in the Bleek and Lloyd Collection which feature /Kaggen illustrate. In the first he learns how to acquire 'Bushman rice' (ant larvae); in the second he gains the power to enter fire unharmed. In both stories, his stupidity causes him to lose his new-found skills; not only does he end up just where he began, but he is none the wiser for it either. Dialogue in some narratives is similarly circular. The story of !Gwa!nuntu and the elephants tells of the abduction of !Gwa!nuntu's grandson by an elephant. Eventually the child is retrieved, and the story ends in a lengthy dialogue between !Gwa!nuntu and the child's mother, she berating !Gwa!nuntu for his carelessness, he defending himself. This continues for about fifty columns of text in the Bleek/Lloyd notebooks, with neither character altering their stance, and with no particular outcome or conclusion emerging. The construction of plot and dialogue is frequently circular, rather than linear. In a related vein, Watson has commented on other aspects of the textual construction of the material: 'One of the most obvious features of the "verbal surface" of /Xam stories is the frequent repetition . . . of syntactic and other elements . . . It is a feature which creates an apparent "circling" rather than linear progression in many of the stories' (Watson 1991: 14). Related to this is what Watson describes as 'the sense of time and logic which the narratives embody . . . [O]nly a brief acquaintance with the material convinced me of the degree to which its sense of time is not our sense, its notion of causation not ours either' (Watson 1991: 15). Rather, these senses of time and causation may be seen as grounded in the notions of cyclicity and causality which the myths themselves propound. Two prominent features of San oral narrative are the emphasis on cyclical regeneration (at the level of 'content') and, similarly, non-linear or circular constructions (at the level of form). These devices are also evident in aspects of the art.

A motif found from northern Zimbabwe to the south-western Cape Province was first described by Frobenius in 1931. It is a human figure, usually clearly female, portrayed in frontal view with an obese torso, splayed legs and raised arms. Many examples wield sticks, crescent-shaped objects or bows; most show an emphasis on the genitalia. Goodall (1949, 1962) made a particular study of the early examples of these figures, which are concentrated in a small area of northern Zimbabwe. Characteristic of these figures is a genital 'emission', in the form of single or double meandering lines. Goodall (1962: 409), dubbing the figures 'mythic women', speculated that they represented a San version of the European mother goddess. Unfortunately for this interpretation, examination of Khoisan mythology does not reveal any such being (Solomon 1994, 1995).

These figures are not well explained solely by reference to trance and shamanism (Solomon 1994, 1995). An alternative interpretation relates their significance to gender, female initiation and the complex of beliefs which centres on links between femaleness, reproduction and rain (Solomon 1992). The 'mythic women' may be seen as representations of the same complex of symbols focusing on death and regeneration as is found in the myths and stories. Reference to a Zimbabwean example illustrates this.

A panel at Murehwa Cave, Zimbabwe (Fig. 15.2), contains two 'mythic women' figures, one of which was discussed by Huffman (1983) in a paper extending the trance hypothesis to the rock-art of that country. The figure under discussion has a distended torso and a lengthy genital 'emission' drawn as a double zigzag line (subsequently partially eroded). Huffman relates the figure's swollen body and the genital 'emission' to ethnographic accounts regarding the supernatural potency attributed by Kalahari San to amniotic fluid and menstrual blood. Ultimately, though, Huffman related the figure to trance, by reference to the falling figures to the right of the 'mythic woman'. It is arguable whether this constitutes sufficient grounds for a trance interpretation. Although in other contexts falling figures which bleed from the nose are plausibly explained as trancers, this figure may be better understood in relation to the wider symbolisation of life and death in San thought. San gender ideologies attribute to women both life-giving and lethal powers (see Solomon 1992). At the same time as the female initiate's attainment of adulthood is celebrated, her accompanying powers to harm men are greatly feared. Hence, strict rules controlling her behaviour are laid down, including the period of seclusion, with accompanying dietary and other restrictions, described in the /Xam menarcheal stories. The Murehwa painting may be interpreted as encapsulating this dualistic view.

With equal plausibility, the falling figures may be understood as men mortally endangered by contact with femaleness, as repeatedly described in San ethnographies (see Solomon 1992). Numerous accounts describe the danger posed by disobedient initiates to their families, and the specific powers of initiates to

**Fig. 15.2.** Groups of figures from panel, Murehwa Cave, Zimbabwe. 'Mythic woman' figure discussed in text, at centre.

kill, to turn men to stone and to endanger the success of the hunt. Women giving birth also represent a potential threat, especially to men, and amniotic fluid is a powerful substance which is closely linked to rain and weather. In the Murehwa painting, the swollen torso of the female figure suggests pregnancy, and the production of life, while the falling figures suggest death. The juxtapositioning of these two concepts in the painting parallels the preoccupation in narratives with themes of life and death.

Other panels containing examples of the 'mythic woman' also contrast swollen-bodied female (or feminine) figures with images of conflict and death. Willcox's Shelter, in the KwaZulu-Natal Drakensberg, contains a similar swollen-bodied figure in nearly the same posture with splayed legs and raised arms (Fig. 15.3). The figure wields a bow and is equipped with quivers. It is depicted with a red shape, rather than a meandering 'emission' between its thighs. The hunting equipment has led researchers (for example, Humphreys, 1996; Solomon 1996) to believe that it cannot be a female figure;

**Fig. 15.3.** 'Mythic woman' figure from Willcox's Shelter, KwaZulu-Natal Drakensberg.

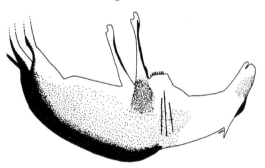

**Fig. 15.4.** Upturned 'dead' eland, Willcox Shelter, Giant's Castle, Natal Drakensberg.
From Lewis-Williams (1983: fig. 19).

ethnographies record taboos on women touching hunting equipment. This objection is not well founded, since gender roles are flexible in initiation ritual; moreover, ethnographic accounts record the use of a bow and arrow by the female initiate among the !xo (Anthony Traill, pers. comm. to Lewis-Williams 1981), and among the !Kung, the initiate is referred to as one who has 'shot an eland' (Lewis-Williams 1981: 51). The figure's body form, frontal portrayal, posture and the genital emphasis relate it to the Zimbabwean 'mythic women'. The figure is directly associated with an upside-down eland (Fig. 15.4), a device which most researchers would agree indicates that the animal is dead. The same contrast, of life potential and death, would seem to underpin this composition. Another example is apparent in a copy of a painting made by Stow in the nineteenth century (Rosenthal and Goodwin 1953). The Knoffelspruit panel (Fig. 15.5) shows a number of human figures engaged in combat. Two of the figures rain arrows upon each other, while others appear to be attacking each other with sticks and clubs. At the bottom left of the scene are two frontal-view figures with splayed legs and swollen torsos, one portrayed with a single genital line, the other with a double line. Although the figures do not show other female characteristics, genital lines appear to be almost exclusively associated with female figures (Solomon 1995). The composition of the panel again suggests that the artists were drawing on a gendered life–death duality in the construction of the panel.

In two further examples, both recorded by Vinnicombe (1976), we see the same contrast. At Hippo Shelter, in the Lesotho Drakensberg mountains (Fig. 15.6), figures with weapons attack each other with vigour. Beneath them is a figure with a moderately thickened torso, splayed legs, a genital emission and a knobbed stick brandished in its right hand. Its head is tilted, giving the impression that it is observing the conflict scene above it. At Magaditseng (Fig. 15.7), a frontal-view figure with splayed legs is associated with a dead or dying human who appears to have some kind of missile piercing his abdomen. The association of the 'mythic woman' motif with scenes of death and conflict suggests that the same concepts which organise the mythology are drawn on in the organisation of the art.

Although direct iconographic correlations be-

**Fig. 15.5.** Figures from panel, Knoffelspruit, Orange Free State. Copy by Stow, in Rosenthal and Goodwin (1953: fig. 20).

**Fig. 15.6.** Figures from panel, Hippo Shelter, Lesotho Drakensberg.
After Vinnicombe (1976: fig. 33a).

tween the myths and the rock-art cannot be drawn, certain thematic, conceptual and formal affinities can be identified. In Deacon's view (1994), commonalities are merely due to the fact that art, ritual and narrative draw on 'the same reservoir of experience'. To some extent, however, there may be structural similarities which go beyond this. Consideration of other formal equivalences between myth and art extends this proposition.

Non-iconographic parallels between art and myth may be identified by comparing aspects of the formal organisation of narratives and the composition of panels. Skotnes (1994) has considered the composition of panels in certain south-western Cape sites. She describes them as 'circular', 'spiralling' and 'centrifugal'; they 'seem to reject the horizontal–vertical axis and are composed in a concentrically dynamic way' (1994: 325). Skotnes relates this circular composition partly to the specific conformation of the sites in which these panels are found, but ultimately attributes it to 'the structure of trance visual experience' (1994: 325). An alternative view does not rely on the determining factor of trance experience. Since circularity and non-linear forms and devices are characteristic also of mythology and its subject-matter, non-linear forms in the art may be related to the ways in which the San experienced and chose to represent their world, independently of trance. Instead of appealing to trance experience, the possibility may be entertained that non-linear compositions were matched to their subject-matter. There are, of course, many paintings which do clearly rely on a horizontal–vertical axis. At one such example, Ikanti 1 in the KwaZulu-Natal Drakensberg, the site is dominated by scores of figures, in several rows, marching towards the viewer's right. In this painting the emphasis on the horizontal axis reinforces the impression of directed movement. Similarly, processions of figures in the south-western Cape also rely on the horizontal axis, reinforcing a sense of directionality, process and narrative (see Parkington 1989).

The 'mythic woman' motif may be considered from a similar point of view. Its portrayal in frontal view sets it aside from most other figures in San art. Pager (1971) analysed 1669 human figures in the Ndedema Gorge, KwaZulu-Natal Drakensberg: 804 faced left, 825 right, and only 40 were in frontal view. No rear-view humans were recorded. This choice effects a disruption of linearity. When a human figure is portrayed in lateral view, the eye is led in the direction in which the figure faces. A running figure encourages the viewer to look to see what the figure is running towards. The lateral view introduces the possibility of narrativity, whereas the

**Fig. 15.7.** Figures from panel, Magaditseng, Eastern Cape Drakensberg. After Vinnicombe (1976: fig. 34).

frontal view which characterises the 'mythic women' does not – at least not to the same extent. Except in Zimbabwe, examples I have seen tend not to be part of more complex panels, and are often directly associated with only a few images. This compositional factor, the frontal view and the figure's circular body form encourage a circular scanning of the image and its associations, rather than a lateral movement. This is especially true with regard to some unique examples of the image at the site of Gxalingenwa Rock 1 (Fig. 15.8). Here the artist(s) painted the figure around pre-existing holes in the site wall which represent the torso. The depth thus created further draws the eye into the centre of the image, rather than laterally. In the 'mythic women' figures, theme, form and compositional factors appear to converge. Although these figures can by no means be said to illustrate the myths, there are parallels in their construction. The 'mythic women' may be understood as embodying the same concerns with life, death, regeneration and cyclicity, conveyed not only by the symbol of the female figure but also by its formal characteristics.

## Ethnography and beyond in San rock-art studies

San rock-art research has been shaped by an abundance of ethnographic material on the one hand, and by a paucity of dates on the other. As a result, research has proceeded in a more anthropological than archaeological vein, with researchers struggling to integrate the art into conventional historical accounts. The use of ethnography remains problematic in this regard, since it accentuates commonalities and minimises differences in the art and its historical contexts over space and through time. For that reason, ethnographic analogies are most appropriate in considering those aspects of San belief which may be less resistant to variation and change – for example, in relation to trance experience or mythology (see also Jolly, this volume).

Iconographical, as opposed to formal, studies are also implicated in the problem of uniformitarian interpretations of the art. In terms of iconography (as subject-matter), the art of different regions is broadly similar, in the predominance of human figures (especially male figures) and large herbivores, the vir-

**Fig. 15.8.** Figure with crescent-shaped object in left hand, painted around a hole on the rock face. Gxalingenwa Rock 1, KwaZulu-Natal Drakensberg.

tual absence of landscape features and the widespread repetition of certain motifs. Differences between the art of different areas (and perhaps different times) lie in form and style, rather than iconography as such. Approaches to the art which focus on understanding its diversity may therefore be expected to rely increasingly on formal studies. However, the reliance of formal approaches on ethnographic analogies of various kinds means that they do not necessarily constitute a much-needed interrogatory or independent approach to the art.

The 'ethnographic method', as it has been called, is something of a misnomer, beyond highlighting its anthropological rather than archaeological affiliations. Nested within the method of using ethnography for rock-art interpretation are other methods; ethnographies may be used in various ways, which require further exploration and evaluation. In this regard, it is important that methods of using ethno-

graphies are recognised as fundamentally interpretive, hermeneutical and open-ended. This was initially acknowledged by Lewis-Williams (1981: 34) when he described the movement between art and ethnography as a 'two-way exegetical process'. The epistemological basis of such an approach is closer to that of art history or literary studies than to that of most archaeology. Questions of epistemology and method are amongst those which require ongoing consideration if integration of strictly archaeological approaches and those which currently characterise San rock-art research is to be achieved.

## Acknowledgements

Thanks to John Parkington and Royden Yates for permission to reproduce the painting in Fig. 15.7; to Yvonne Brink for comments on the manuscript and Martin Hall for comments on the larger body of work from which it is derived. Thanks are also due to Pippa Skotnes and Trevor Sewell for help in preparing the illustrations.

This chapter is an aspect of research conducted for a doctoral dissertation, University of Cape Town, which was made possible by the financial assistance of, *inter alia*, the Centre for Science Development and the University Research Council, University of Cape Town.

## REFERENCES

Arbousset, T. and F. Daumas. 1846. *Narrative of an exploratory tour to the north-east of the colony of the Cape of Good Hope.* Cape Town, Robertson.

Barnard, A. 1992. *Hunters and herders of southern Africa.* Cambridge, Cambridge University Press.

Biesele, M. 1993. *Women like meat: the folklore and foraging ideology of the Kalahari Ju/'hoan.* Johannesburg, Witwatersrand University Press.

Bleek, W. H. I. and L. Lloyd. 1911. *Specimens of Bushman folklore.* London, George Allen.

Damisch, H. 1975. Semiotics and iconography, in T. A. Sebeok (ed.), *The tell-tale sign*, pp. 27–36. Lisse, Peter de Ridder Press.

Deacon, J. 1994. Rock engravings and the folklore of

Bleek and Lloyd's /Xam San informants, in T. A. Dowson and J. D. Lewis-Williams (eds.), *Contested images: diversity in southern African rock art research*, pp. 237–56. Johannesburg, Witwatersrand University Press.

Dickens, P. 1991. The place of Lloyd's !Kun texts in the Ju dialects. Paper presented at the Bleek and Lloyd 1870–1991 Conference, Cape Town.

Goodall, E. 1949. Notes on certain human representations in Rhodesian rock art, *Transactions of the Rhodesian Scientific Association* 42: 1–6.

1962. A distinctive mythical figure appearing in the rock paintings of Southern Rhodesia, in G. Mortelmans and J. Nenquin (eds.), *Actes du IV Congrès Panafricain de Préhistoire*, pp. 399–405. Tervuren, Musée Royale.

Guenther, M. G. 1986. *The Nharo Bushmen of Botswana: tradition and change.* Hamburg, Helmut Buske Verlag. Quellen zur Khoisan-Forschung 3.

1989. *Bushman folktales: oral traditions of the Nharo of Botswana and the /Xam of the Cape.* Stuttgart, Franz Steiner Verlag. Wiesbaden Studien zur Kulturkunde 93.

1994. The relationship of Bushman art to ritual and folklore, in T. A. Dowson and J. D. Lewis-Williams (eds.), *Contested images: diversity in southern African rock art research*, pp. 257–74. Johannesburg, Witwatersrand University Press.

Hewitt, R. L. 1986. *Structure, meaning and ritual in the narratives of the southern San.* Hamburg, Helmut Buske Verlag. Quellen zur Khoisan-Forschung 2.

How, M. W. 1962. *The Mountain Bushmen of Basutoland.* Pretoria, Van Schaik.

Huffman, T. 1983. The trance hypothesis and the rock art of Zimbabwe, *South African Archaeological Society Goodwin Series* 4: 49–53.

Humphreys, A. 1996. 'Mother goddesses' and 'mythic women': an alternative view, *South African Archaeological Bulletin* 51: 32.

Jolly, P. 1986. A first generation descendant of the Transkei San, *South African Archaeological Bulletin* 41: 6–9.

Katz, R. 1982. *Boiling energy: community healing amongst the Kalahari !Kung.* Cambridge (MA), Harvard University Press.

Lee, D. N. and H. C. Woodhouse. 1970. *Art on the rocks of southern Africa.* New York, Scribners.

Lewis-Williams, J. D. 1972. The syntax and function of the Giant's Castle rock paintings, *South African Archae-ological Bulletin* 27: 49–65.

1974. Superpositioning in a sample of rock paintings in the Barkly East district, *South African Archaeological Bulletin* 29: 93–103.

1980. Ethnography and iconography: aspects of southern San thought and art, *Man* (NS) 15: 467–82.

1981. *Believing and seeing: symbolic meanings in southern San rock paintings.* London, Academic Press.

1983. *The rock art of southern Africa.* Cambridge, Cambridge University Press.

1984. Ideological continuities in prehistoric southern Africa: the evidence of rock art, in C. Schrire (ed.), *Past and present in hunter-gatherer studies*, pp. 225–52. New York, Academic Press.

1995. Modelling the production and consumption of rock art, *South African Archaeological Bulletin* 162: 143–54.

Lewis-Williams, J. D. and T. A. Dowson. 1988. Signs of all times: entoptic phenomena in Upper Palaeolithic art, *Current Anthropology* 29: 201–45.

1989. *Images of power: understanding Bushman rock art.* Johannesburg, Southern Book Publishers.

1993. On vision and power in the Neolithic: evidence from the decorated monuments, *Current Anthropology* 34: 55–65.

1994. Aspects of rock art research, in T. A. Dowson and J. D. Lewis-Williams (eds.), *Contested images: diversity in southern African rock art research*, pp. 201–22. Johannesburg, Witwatersrand University Press.

Lewis-Williams, J. D. and J. H. N. Loubser. 1986. Deceptive appearances: a critique of southern African rock art studies, *Advances in World Archaeology* 5: 253–89.

Mazel, A. D. 1992. Collingham Shelter: the excavation of late Holocene deposits, Natal, South Africa, *Natal Museum Journal of Humanities* 4: 1–51.

Orpen, J. 1874. A glimpse into the mythology of the Maluti Bushmen, *Cape Monthly Magazine* 9: 1–13.

Pager, H. 1971. *Ndedema.* Graz, Akademische Druk-u Verlagansalt.

Parkington, J. E. 1989. Interpreting paintings without a commentary: meaning and motive, content and composition in the rock art of the Western Cape, South Africa, *Antiquity* 63: 13–26.

Preziosi, D. 1989. *Rethinking art history: meditations on a coy science.* New Haven, Yale University Press.

Rosenthal, E. and A. J. H. Goodwin. 1953. *Cave artists of South Africa.* Cape Town, A. A. Balkema.

Schapera, I. 1930. *The Khoisan peoples of South Africa:*

*Bushmen and Hottentots.* Reprinted 1965. London, Routledge and Kegan Paul.

Schmidt, S. 1989. *Catalogue of the Khoisan folktales of southern Africa.* Hamburg, Helmut Buske Verlag.

1991. The relationship of the Bleek/Lloyd folktales to the general Khoisan traditions. Paper presented at the Bleek and Lloyd 1870–1991 Conference, Cape Town.

Skotnes, P. 1990. Rock art: is there life after trance? *Proceedings of the Sixth Annual Conference of the South African Association of Art Historians,* pp. 132–7. Cape Town, University of Cape Town.

1994. The visual as a site of meaning: San parietal painting and the experience of modern art, in T. A. Dowson and J. D. Lewis-Williams (eds.), *Contested images: diversity in southern African rock art research,* pp. 315–30. Johannesburg, Witwatersrand University Press.

Solomon, A. 1989. Division of the earth: gender, symbolism, and the archaeology of the southern San. Unpublished MA dissertation, University of Cape Town.

1991. Textuality, historicity and ethnicity: three problems with the use of the Bleek/Lloyd Collection in archaeology. Paper presented at the Bleek and Lloyd 1870–1991 Conference, Cape Town.

1992. Gender, representation and power in San ethnography and rock art, *Journal of Anthropological Archaeology* 11: 291–329.

1994. 'Mythic women': a study in variability in San rock art and narrative, in T. A. Dowson and J. D. Lewis-Williams (eds.), *Contested Images: diversity in Southern African rock art research,* pp. 332–71. Johannesburg, Witwatersrand University Press.

1995. Rock art incorporated: an archaeological and interdisciplinary study of certain human figures in San art. Unpublished Ph.D dissertation, University of Cape Town.

1996. 'Mythic women': a response to Humphreys, *South African Archaeological Bulletin* 51: 33–5.

Stone, A. and P. Bahn. 1993. A comparison of Franco-Cantabrian and Maya art in deep caves: spatial strategies and cultural considerations, in J. Steinbring *et al.* (eds.), *Time and space: dating and spatial considerations in rock art research,* pp. 111–20. Melbourne, Australian Rock Art Research Association. Occasional AURA Publication 8.

Stow, G. W. and D. F. Bleek. 1930. *Rock paintings in South Africa.* London, Methuen.

Thackeray, A. I. 1983. Dating the rock art of southern Africa, *South African Archaeological Society Goodwin Series* 4: 21–6.

Thomas, E. M. 1959. *The harmless people.* New York, Knopf.

Vinnicombe, P. 1972. Myth, motive and selection in southern African rock art, *Africa* 42: 192–204.

1976. *People of the eland.* Pietermaritzburg, University of Natal Press.

Watson, S. 1991. *Return of the moon.* Cape Town, Carrefour.

Wendt, W. E. 1976. 'Art mobilier' from the Apollo 11 Cave, South West Africa: Africa's oldest dated works of art, *South African Archaeological Bulletin* 31: 5–11.

Willcox, A. R. 1956. *Rock paintings of the Drakensberg, Natal and Griqualand East.* London, Max Parrish.

Yates, R. and A. Jerardino. 1996. A fortuitous fall: early rock paintings from the west coast of South Africa, *South African Journal of Science* 92: 110.

Eva M. Walderhaug

# 16. Changing art in a changing society: the hunters' rock-art of western Norway

Like Kalle Sognnes (Chapter 9, above), Eva M. Walderhaug studies open-air petroglyphs that are hard to date and beyond any direct insight. The deriving of a chronology is a necessary goal and a worthwhile achievement. Seriation of specific traits in the distinct and distinctive rules for representing animal bodies gives a dating framework, and permits some knowledge of the sequence in which individual motifs were added to decorated panels. Within this, the developing iconography at the Ausevik rock-art site can be seen in its social context of a region of contact between the world of the hunter-gatherer and the world of the farmer-herder.

## Rock-carvings in western Norway: material and approaches

This chapter deals with questions regarding the content and context of western Norwegian hunters' rock-art, with special reference to a detailed study of the Ausevik rock-art site.

Approaching 400 petroglyph or rock-carving sites are known from the two western Norwegian counties of Hordaland and Sogn og Fjordane.[1] The sites belong to two different Scandinavian rock-art traditions, generally termed *hunters'* and *agrarian* rock-art. Though reflecting an important aspect, the division may be too rigidly applied (see Sognnes, this volume, above; Hagen 1970: 114ff; Helskog 1993: 72; Mandt Larsen 1972: 10f). The majority of agrarian sites contain cup-marks only, but there are also more than eighty picture sites, usually containing between one and one hundred individual figures. In contrast, we find four small hunters' rock-art sites of less than ten individual carvings,

but also two large sites or site-clusters containing several hundred figures.

Hunters' rock-art in Norway is generally dated to the Mesolithic and Neolithic periods; it is also argued – albeit inconclusively – that there is a continuation of the tradition into the Early and Late Bronze Age (Gjessing 1936: 170ff; Hagen 1970: 112; Sognnes 1993: 183). Motifs are predominantly wild game, such as deer, reindeer and elk; other motifs – such as boats, humans and abstract figures – also occur. The agrarian rock-art has a more varied selection of motifs that includes ships, various ring-figures such as concentric circles and spirals, humans and cup-marks; it is associated with the farming population of the Early and Late Bronze Age. There is also evidence of a Late Neolithic origin, as well as a continuation into the Early Iron Age (Mandt 1991; Sognnes 1993, 1995).

Western Norwegian rock-art is entirely prehistoric, leaving us no direct clues as to its meaning, and without the means to study it through any informed method. Different formal approaches have been applied to the study of the hunters' rock-art, though most work has concentrated on documenting and describing the art (Bakka 1966; Bøe 1932; Hagen 1970; Hallström 1938; Fett 1941; Mandt Larsen 1972). Questions concerning chronology have been central (Bakka 1973, 1979; Bøe 1932; Hagen 1970; Walderhaug 1994, 1995). Interpretations have almost exclusively been concerned with hunting-related beliefs and activities (Bakka 1973; Bøe 1932; Hagen 1970). The different views on chronology, on rock-art traditions and on hunting magic have all aimed at understanding the art through its relation to

---

[1] There is also a pictograph site from Årsand in Kvinnherad, Hordaland (Bøe 1940; Mandt Larsen 1972: 27f).

external or abstract factors, through the use of correlation or analogy, and the application of static conceptual schemes. It is time to return to the art, to take an 'inside view', placing it in its rightful context, and taking into consideration the relationship between rock-art and a continuously changing surrounding world. At Ausevik, this has been attempted through identifying and analysing developments and changes in the structure of the site over time; and discussing them in relation to the changing structure of society.

The use of analogy forms the basis for the long-lived 'hunting magic' approach to interpretation, introduced to Norwegian hunters' rock-art research through the work of Gjessing (1936: 138ff). This concept has developed into – until recent years – an almost undisputed truth, the basic analogy long forgotten. In a sense, analogy has also been applied to the chronological debates, possible relationships between similar motifs found within often very different cultural and geographical settings being discussed (Fett and Fett 1979; Hagen 1970; Marstrander 1978). Central to the discussion of chronology, cultural affiliation and meaning content, has been the group of motifs termed *abstract-geometrical* below, that is spirals, ring-figures, cup-marks and so forth. An understanding of these motif forms is also central to this study, which leads us out of Scandinavia, to a discussion of the analogical implications of similar motifs found world-wide (Dowson 1992; Lewis-Williams and Dowson 1988, 1993).

## The rock-art sites of Hordaland and Sogn og Fjordane

Mountains and fjords dominate the natural environment of Hordaland and Sogn og Fjordane; less than 5 per cent of the total land area is cultivable, and more than 25 per cent is found at altitudes of between 900 and 1800 m above sea-level. The hunters' rock-art sites are located near the fjords or coastal zone (see map, Fig. 16.1).

Three small hunters' rock-art sites are known from Hordaland: a deer figure from Rolland outside Bergen (Myhre 1972); and two sites, Rykkje and

Vangdal, from Kvam in the district of Hardanger. The first contains only a single deer figure; and the other five deer and elk figures and two human figures (Bakka 1966; Mandt Larsen 1972: 34f) (see Fig. 16.2). The animal from Rolland was carved on a flat rock surface (now removed) in forest terrain, whereas the two latter sites are both located on steep rock surfaces close to the Hardanger Fjord.

Sogn og Fjordane has a much larger number of carvings, concentrated in two large sites at Ausevik in Flora, in the district of Sunnfjord; and at Vingen, Bremanger, in Nordfjord. The only exceptions are the carvings of four animals, probably deer, on a large sandstone boulder on the island of Brandsøy, also in Flora (Mandt 1980).

The Ausevik rock-art site is located 4 km from the outer coast, on the east side of the Høydal Fjord, one of many smaller fjords opening out towards scattered coastal islands in Sunnfjord. It has a sheltered location, directly below the Skåle mountain, which rises to 800 m. The carvings are spread on sloping panels near the shore. The choice of motifs is both varied and unusual, consisting of animal and human figures of the type associated with hunters' rock-art, but also a considerable number of abstract-geometrical figures. Concentric ring-figures, spirals and cup-marks seldom occur in hunters' rock-art, and nowhere else in such numbers as found here. Instead, they occur within the other, agrarian, rock-art tradition of Scandinavia. These different types of motifs are clearly integrated on the site, in contrast to other *mixed carving sites*, where agrarian rock-art is superimposed on an earlier hunters' rock-art horizon (e.g. Sognnes 1993: 178, 1995: 137).

The large site-cluster at Vingen is found 40 km further north. It is composed of several sites, making up an entire rock-carving area. Documentation of the site-cluster has only in part been published (Bøe 1932; Bakka 1973; Fett 1941; Hallström 1938), though there is a great deal of unpublished material in museum archives. The exact number of carvings is therefore, at present, uncertain but is close to 2000 figures. The main carving area is found in a small

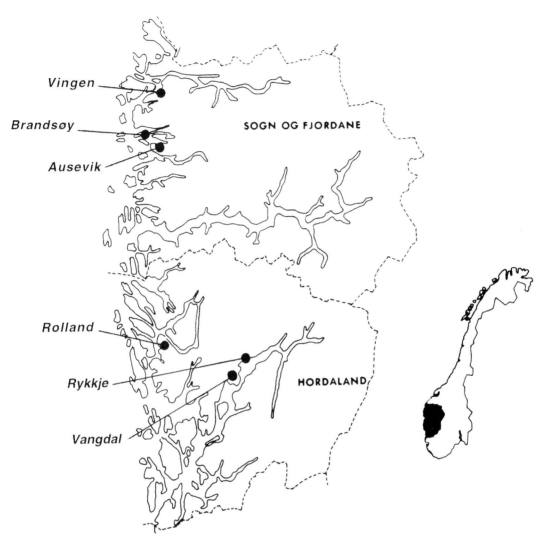

**Fig. 16.1.** Western Norway showing the counties of Hordaland and Sogn og Fjordane, and the hunters' rock-art sites mentioned in the text.

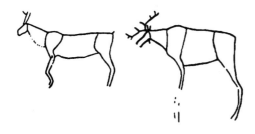

**Fig. 16.2.** Upper and lower parts of a rock-art site from Vangdal in Kvam, Hordaland. The deer figure to the upper left is very similar to one found at Rykkje, also in Kvam.

Tracing by Egil Bakka. Reproduced courtesy of Bergen Museum, University of Bergen.

side-fjord in the Nordfjord district, surrounded by steep mountains. Along the 600 m stretch of the south shore, carvings are found on bare rock, large and small boulders, and even on portable stones. Carvings are also found at several locations within 5 km of this main carving area, both on the north side of the bay and on several locations further out along the main fjord. Motifs are predominantly deer; there are also humans, a considerable number of hook or scythe-like figures, and quite a few abstract figures, mostly different line patterns.

## Chronology of archaeology and of rock-art in western Norway

In this section I refer to the terminology of cultural units, and their calibrated dates BC, following Prescott (1996: 78) and Prescott and Walderhaug (1995: 260):

| | |
|---|---|
| Early Neolithic and | |
| Middle Neolithic A | 3900–2800 BC |
| Middle Neolithic B | 2800–2400 BC |
| Late Neolithic | 2400–1800 BC |

The Hordaland sites, believed to represent the earliest phase of hunters' rock-art in western Norway, can be seen as contemporaneous with – or as the immediate predecessors for – the earliest style of animal depictions found at Vingen (Bakka 1966, 1973). Through the study of similar elements found in carvings and datable archaeological objects, and the study of shoreline displacement, Bakka has attempted to date the Vingen site (1973, 1979). Surfaces which seem suitable for carving and the lower parts of carved panels are often without figures; in addition, many panels, up to 2.5 km apart, show a consistency in their lower levels (Bøe 1932: 39f; Bakka 1979: 116). Four stylistic-chronological phases of animal representation identified by Bakka in the Vingen material (see discussion below) also show consistent variation in the elevation of the lowest carving levels above sea-level. Only figures of the latest stylistic type are found at the lowest levels, at 8.25 m. These variations are linked to decreasing shoreline levels throughout the period of production. Bakka, and also Bøe, argue that the water level must have been *at the very minimum* 5 m higher; in Bakka's view, very likely as much as 6 or 7 m above the present sea-level in the final production phase (Bakka 1973: 176, 1979: 118f; Bøe 1932: 39). Bakka concludes that both archaeological and geological dating methods show that the Vingen carvings cannot have been produced *later* than the end of the Middle Neolithic. He also believes the carving tradition may have its roots in the Late Mesolithic. Current geological knowledge strengthens his suppositions. His arguments for the importance of the sea-levels at Vingen are convincing, but the exact relationship between the placing of carvings and the water's edge, of course, cannot be known. Nor can the starting-point of production be firmly identified by this dating method. Since Bakka views Ausevik as fully or partly contemporaneous with Vingen, the

dating of Ausevik in his opinion also depends on the dating of the last phases at Vingen (1973: 169). Certain similarities between the Vingen rock-art and the rock-art found at Alta in northern Norway have been noted by Helskog (1984: 25). These appear in Helskog's phase 3 at Alta, also dated by way of shoreline displacement to between 2700 and 1700 BC (1987: 19, 1988: 31ff), which falls within the Late Stone Age of northern Norway (Engelstad 1985: 82f). I have previously (1994: 76) argued that there is similarity both in stylistic elements and in selection of motif elements between Vingen and Ausevik and the phase 3 sites Amtmannsnes and Storsteinen in Alta.

Opinions differ on the dating of the Ausevik site, because of the unusual combination of motifs found on the site. Hagen (1970, 1976, 1983) therefore interprets the Ausevik rock-art as an integration of agrarian and hunters' rock-art elements, viewing the abstract-geometrical figures as a loan from agrarian

**Fig. 16.3.** Panel from Ausevik, Flora, Sogn og Fjordane. The panel is damaged through natural weathering processes.

Tracing by Anders Hagen. Reproduced courtesy of Bergen Museum, University of Bergen.

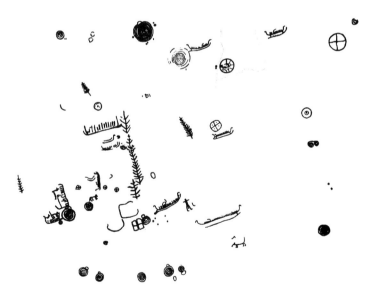

**Fig. 16.4.** Agrarian rock-art. The site, Flote 1, Etne in Hordaland, contains plant motifs and ship figures, also different cup and ring figures and cross-rings, types not found at Ausevik.

Tracing by Gro Mandt. Reproduced courtesy of Bergen Museum, University of Bergen.

rock-art. He argues that the agrarian elements provide the most important chronological link, thereby dating the site to the Early and Late Nordic Bronze Age (more probably the latter), with a continuation into the Early Iron Age (1970: 108ff). He also believes that most of the Ausevik rock-art is younger than the Vingen rock-art (1970: 110). Bakka (1973, 1979), rejecting this point of view, claims that the abstract-geometrical figures should not be interpreted as spirals and so forth, but as *vulva figures*, which he states are also found at Vingen (1973: 169).

Spiral figures and related motifs very clearly *do* occur at Ausevik (see Figs. 16.3, 16.5 and 16.8). However, I cannot agree with Hagen's extremely late dating of the site, or his arguments for a strong influence from the Bronze Age agrarian rock-art milieu. A closer scrutiny of the agrarian rock-art from Sogn og Fjordane (Walderhaug 1994: 69) shows that abstract-geometrical figures of the type found at Ausevik practically do *not* occur within this rock-art tradition; rather the art is dominated by ship figures (Mandt 1991). Agrarian rock-art in Hordaland, on the other hand, contains around 150 different ring motifs, but only 20 of the type found at Ausevik (Mandt Larsen 1972) (see Fig. 16.4). There are, however, certain elements on the site which may in fact be rooted in the agrarian tradition, namely the carvings of two branches or trees, a footprint and a possible ship figure. The latter can be compared to the earliest type of ship figure found at agrarian rock-art sites in Sogn og Fjordane and elsewhere, dating back to the Late Neolithic (Fett and Fett 1941: 137; Mandt 1991; Sognnes 1993: 164).

An alternative explanation for the abstract-geometrical motifs found at Ausevik is proposed by Fett and Fett (1979), who look outside the Scandinavian peninsula. They see a connection from the west Scandinavian agrarian rock-art to passage-grave art, and a lesser connection to Irish and British rock-art. They also argue that impulses from western Europe may have affected the Ausevik rock-art in the Late

Neolithic. Others have also argued for a link between Scandinavian and western European megalithic art and rock-art (Glob 1969; Marstrander 1978; Burenhult 1980). That impulses from megalithic art should have reached western Norway at such a late date seems unlikely in the light of current views on the chronology of the Irish passage-grave art and British megalithic art, which place the tradition within the period *c.* 3200–1500 BC (uncalibrated C-14 years) (Johnston 1993: 267f; Morris 1989: 49; Shee Twohig 1981: 136). One might rather argue for some form of influence from western European megalithic art or rock-art in the Middle Neolithic period. The nature and channels of such possible influences remain to be convincingly described; and with approximate chronologies for the elements in question it is hard to place long-distance events securely in time.

Much of this cultural chronological debate has been concerned with the abstract-geometrical figures; an increasing amount of evidence shows that they appear in very disparate cultural and chronological situations in world-wide rock-art. A strong case, though still debated, for linking these types of motifs to *entoptic imagery*, visions experienced in altered states of consciousness, has been argued by Lewis-Williams and Dowson (1988, 1993; Dowson 1992), starting from the study of southern African rock-art. At this point, one may at least conclude that this group of motifs provides a very weak basis for the dating of the Ausevik site.

As the evidence stands today, Bakkas's dating of the Vingen site to the Late Mesolithic, Early and Middle Neolithic is as good as we can get. The Ausevik and Vingen sites can be seen as partly contemporaneous, I argue below. The Ausevik site must also have been in use in the Middle Neolithic. Certain elements, such as an early boat figure, may reflect some form of contact with the agrarian rock-art milieu in its earliest phase, probably in the early Late Neolithic (Prescott and Walderhaug 1995: 268). Prescott and Walderhaug (1995) have previously suggested that the Ausevik rock-art dates to

Middle Neolithic B, and a transitional phase extends into the early Late Neolithic. This is also in accordance with the Alta dates. The hunters' rock-art found on the boulder from Brandsøy can, on the basis of the carving style, be seen as contemporaneous with both Ausevik and Vingen in early Middle Neolithic B, during which period the tradition of rock-art production at Vingen must have come to an end.

## Archaeological context of the rock-art

*Early and Middle Neolithic A 3900–2800 BC*

Evidence indicating an early agricultural or TRB (Funnel-beaker) phase can be found in the Early Neolithic of eastern Norway, which then seemingly disappears (Hinsch 1955; Østmo 1988: 225f). In western Norway the evidence for agricultural practices prior to the Late Neolithic is scarce or lacking, and, if practised, agriculture has not been intensive (Prescott 1991: 42, 1996; Prescott and Walderhaug 1995: 261), despite certain indications seen through pollen analysis (Bakka and Kaland 1971; Bjerck 1988; Hjelle *et al.* 1992; Indrelid and Moe 1983). A Neolithic hunter-gatherer phase in western Norway, covering the Early Neolithic and Nordic Middle Neolithic A (in cultural terms contemporary with the south Scandinavian TRB), is characterised by technological continuity from the Late Mesolithic (Olsen and Alsaker 1984; Nærøy 1993). With the transition to the Middle Neolithic imported technologies arrive from both north and south Scandinavia, northern slate forms and coarsely tempered cord-stamp pottery are introduced. In addition there are finds of imported flint axes, pottery and amber (Nærøy 1993: 92f; Prescott and Walderhaug 1995: 260f). In spite of these Neolithic elements reflecting contact and interaction with agricultural societies, economy and site character indicate a much stronger traditional element, and a continuing hunter-gatherer adaptation.

*Middle Neolithic B 2800–2400 BC*

Middle Neolithic B – in cultural terms the Nordic Battle Axe phase – is more difficult to assess, because the archaeological record is more limited. A few smaller sites known from western Norway (Nærøy 1993, 1994) seem to indicate a continuing hunter-gatherer economy, alongside indications of possible external pressures influencing production and settlement patterns. The large coastal sites, in use since the Mesolithic, are abandoned at this time. Exploitation of two characteristic greenstone and basalt quarries in Hordaland and Sogn og Fjordane, in use also throughout the Mesolithic, is discontinued at the transition to the Late Neolithic (Olsen and Alsaker 1984); this may also be related to developments in this preceding phase (Prescott and Walderhaug 1995: 261f). There is also evidence of Battle Axe influence – a few graves and stray finds of axes and wedges – concentrated in areas suitable for agriculture in the Oslofjord region of eastern Norway (Hinsch 1956; Nygaard 1989; Prescott and Walderhaug 1995: 261f; Østmo 1988). These different developments may indicate increasing stress within the hunter-gatherer societies of western Norway. This period may also be regarded as a *preparatory phase* for the important changes which took place at the transition to the Late Neolithic (Prescott 1995: 132, 1996: 85; Prescott and Walderhaug 1995: 262).

*Late Neolithic 2400–1800 BC*

The Late Neolithic transition is evidenced all over southern Norway by a significant change in material culture, from domination of local material cultural traits to forms associated with the agrarian cultures of southern Scandinavia (Bakka and Kaland 1971; Nærøy 1993; Prescott 1995). An entirely new set of tools and technology replaces the former (Nærøy 1993: 94). The bifacial flaking technique (Nærøy 1993: 93; Prescott 1986, 1995: 128f), and the introduction of items such as flint daggers, polished shaft-hole axes, and even some metal, are indicators of cultural developments common to southern Norway and to the rest of east and south Scandinavia. For the first time, evidence of cereal cultivation and herding is clearly represented in the archaeological record, as the combined evidence of seeds, bone, faeces, and settlements demonstrates (Bakka and Kaland 1971; Prescott 1996).

The developments in the Neolithic of western Norway have important social and ideological implications. It is within this context of continuity and change that the background for the production of western Norwegian hunters' rock-art should be sought.

## The Ausevik rock-art site

### The material

The Ausevik rock-art is generally known through Hagen's documentation (1970); a thorough examination and documentation of the site was carried out by Bøe as early as the 1930s. His unpublished work proved extremely valuable to me, when in 1991 I returned to re-examine the site. In his field diary, Bøe describes how he found parts of the rock surface at Ausevik in a bad state of decay. The site had decayed further by the time Hagen and his crew arrived to re-document the art in 1963–6. The soft phyllite rock – which originally provided an ideal carving surface – easily weathers under different internal and external influences; the surface crumbles, the outer layers loosen or fall off (Michelsen 1992). Any analysis of the site must take into consideration this destruction, which makes the picture material now available to us incomplete. In piecing together our best picture of the site, Bøe's documentation has become a vital asset.

The carvings are all located within an area of 1500 square metres. Within this limited space, individual panels can be identified, some several metres apart, others quite close to each other, but separated by the natural qualities of the rock. Some panels are found in natural hollows, others are separated by crevices and wide cracks, or in many cases framed by very distinct quartz ores visible in the rock surface. Fourteen different panels have thus been identified, containing from 1 to 108 different figures each (Walderhaug 1994: 27ff).

Through classification of the material, 354 individual figures have been identified (Walderhaug

1994: 32ff), based on on-site observation, and – for 17 figures that have disappeared – on Bøe's documentation. This total number also includes 68 remnants of now unrecognisable, damaged figures, of which 30 remain solely in Bøe's documentation. These damaged figures often consist of only a few remaining lines. Apart from these, five main categories – human, animal, human-animal, plant, object and abstract – have been noted.

The *human* category consists of 22 representations of humans in various forms, their sex either impossible to identify or at best ambiguous. The carving of a bare footprint is also included in this category.

*Animals* consist of 108 four-legged animals, 3 reptiles (snakes), 4 birds and 1 fish. The four-legged animals include 5 depictions of what appear to be dogs or wolves; one-third of the remaining animal figures can be identified as deer by features of their anatomy. For the remaining depictions a positive identification is not possible, although I believe they also predominantly represent deer, the abstract style rather than their species influencing variation in the form of representation. Other members of the larger deer family may, of course, also be present, for example reindeer or elk, but no secure anatomical indications can be found.

The *human-animal* category contains a group of ambiguous figures, with both human- and animal-like (e.g. bird, reptile) features. They were interpreted by Hagen (1970: 53f) as 'dead animals' or 'animal hides'. They cannot be associated with any known animal species. *Plants* include the representations of three branches or trees. Four figures may depict different *objects*: a net (also containing a fish); a scythe-like, perhaps ritual, object; an oval figure, possibly a trap; and a ship figure.

The largest and least homogeneous category is that of the *abstract* figures, which can be divided into the three main groups: geometrical, line-patterns and others. Abstract-geometrical figures consist of cup-marks, spirals, concentric ring-figures or combinations of the two latter; 50 in all. Abstract line-patterns consist of 67 different designs: wavy lines, zigzag

**Fig. 16.5.** Small panel from Ausevik, Flora, Sogn og Fjordane, showing human, animal and different abstract motifs.

Tracing by Johannes Bøe. Reproduced courtesy of Bergen Museum, University of Bergen.

lines, fringe-like figures, complex patterns and so forth, both free-standing and framed. Finally, there is a group of 17 abstract figures of different shapes, such as triangles, labyrinths and double hooks.

*Stylistic-chronological analysis*

The enigma of the Ausevik rock-art lies not so much in the individual motif as in the combination of diverse motif types found on the site (see Fig. 16.5). The site was in use for a considerable period of time, undergoing a variety of influences. As we see the site today, it represents the final picture, which may in fact disguise the differing uses it was put to at various periods in the past. A better understanding of on-site chronology is therefore important, not only for the dating of the site (above), but also as a means to analyse the development and changing structure of the site over time.

In order to identify these structural features an internal chronology of figures must be developed. As this is not possible for the entire body of motifs, a suitable group of figures has been chosen. The analytical approach applied in the following is influenced by the possibilities and limitations inherent in a material both limited in quantity and in part damaged.

The four-legged animals were chosen for a detailed stylistic-chronological analysis, as the group represents one of the largest categories of figures, in which certain similarities and differences can be identified. These may be related to developments in carving style over time. In order to reveal some basic ordering of the material, a simple seriation was performed.

First of all, two independent variables must be identified: 102 deer or probable deer figures have been analysed,[2] and certain recurring elements in what may be termed *body outline* and *body internal marking* were recorded. Thirteen figures were too damaged for either of the two elements to be identified, leaving 89 figures on which the following discussion is based.

*Internal marking* is defined as any form of internal marking (or decoration), but also the intentional lack of it. Three animals are too damaged for marking to be recognised; for the remainder of the animals, five basic forms can be identified. There are also three cases where the internal marking is a *combination* of two of these five forms. It would therefore seem that there have been fairly strict rules governing the way in which the surfaces of the animals' bodies were depicted. The five basic forms are (see Fig. 16.6):

I No, or few and widely spaced lines.

II Horizontal lines from head to tail.

III Vertical lines from back to belly.

IV Weave-pattern. Closely set vertical, horizontal or arched lines combining in different patterns covering the entire body.

V Pecked-all-over.

A fine-grained analysis of details in *body outline* is not possible, as extremities such as ears, hoofs, tails and so forth are in many cases missing because of weathering. The analysis is therefore based on the totality of elements present, which make up the outline or form of each animal's body. Heads are generally very small and not emphasised. Legs are always represented by four single lines, but their positioning varies in an ordered way, influencing the perception of motion.

The representation of body outline shows a much greater degree of individual variation than does interior marking. Fifty-six of the figures can be

---

[2] The dog or wolf figures, and one animal drawn in single line were withheld from the analysis.

**Fig. 16.6.** Animal figures from Ausevik, Flora, Sogn og Fjordane, showing different forms of body outline and internal marking.

From left to right:

*Top row*: Two animals with triangular body outline (type E), internal marking of type IV. Two animals with rectangular body outline (type A), internal marking of types IV and III.

*Second row from top*: Four animals with arched body outline: two animals (type C) with internal marking type III, one animal (type D) with internal marking of type V. One S-shaped animal (type H) with internal marking of type V.

*Third row from top*: Semicircular body outlines. Two animals (type F) with internal marking of type I. Two animals (type G) with internal marking of type V.

*Bottom row*: Individual forms of body outline, one animal with internal marking which is a combination of types II and V, two with internal marking of type II.

**Table 16.1.** *Total number of, and relationship between, different types of body outline and internal marking*

|       | I  | II | III | IV | V  | Comb | Dam | Total |
|-------|----|----|-----|----|----|------|-----|-------|
| A     |    |    | 2   | 8  |    |      | 1   | 11    |
| B     |    |    | 6   | 1  |    |      |     | 7     |
| C     |    |    | 4   | 1  |    |      |     | 5     |
| D     |    |    | 2   |    | 2  |      |     | 4     |
| E     |    |    |     | 4  |    |      |     | 4     |
| F     | 7  |    | 2   |    | 1  |      |     | 10    |
| G     |    |    |     |    | 8  |      |     | 8     |
| H     |    |    | 1   |    | 6  |      |     | 7     |
| Ind   | 4  | 5  | 4   | 4  | 2  | 3    | 2   | 24    |
| Dam   |    |    | 3   | 4  | 2  |      | 13  | 22    |
| Total | 11 | 5  | 24  | 22 | 21 | 3    | 16  | 102   |

Internal marking is shown horizontally, including the five basic forms I–V, combinations of these (Comb) and unidentified marking due to damage (Dam). The different types of body outline A–H are shown vertically, also individual types (Ind), and unidentified body outline due to damage (Dam).

grouped by similarity into various categories, whereas 24 of the figures, although in many cases bearing similarity to figures in defined categories, cannot be placed firmly in any of these. Instead, they are termed *individual* forms. There are 9 instances of figures being too damaged for the body outline to be recognised. The main categories can also be divided into subgroups on the basis of elements such as the relationship between length and breadth of body, angles of the body, degree of arch, position of the legs and so forth (for further details see Walderhaug 1994: 45ff). The main categories and subgroups are (see Fig. 16.6) *rectangular* (A and B), *arched* (C and D), *triangular* (E), *semicircular* (F and G) and *S-shaped* (H) body outlines.

The analysis shows that different animals may have both body outline and internal marking in common; or they may have either outline or internal marking in common (see Table 16.1), which means that these two elements may have varied independently over time, internal marking being the more stable element. I propose a simple seriation, to show how the two elements may vary and develop in relation to each other over time (see Table 16.2). However, this is only possible for defined outline forms (A–H); individual and damaged forms must necessarily be left out. In addition, type II and combination-type internal marking cannot be related to any defined body outline forms.

Table 16.2. *A simple type seriation of undamaged animals*

|   | IV | III | V | I |
|---|---|---|---|---|
| F |   |   | ** | * ******* |
| G |   |   | ******** |   |
| H |   | * | ****** |   |
| D |   |   | ** | ** |
| B | * | ****** |   |   |
| C | * | **** |   |   |
| A | ******* | ** |   |   |
| E |   | **** |   |   |

The seriation includes types A–H body outline (shown horizontally) and internal marking of types I, III, IV and V (shown vertically), excluding individual-type body outline and internal marking of type II or combination forms. The remaining total number (55) of figures is shown by asterisks.

Assuming that the different types of internal marking and body outline each represent phases in time, it is possible to visualise how different forms may be connected in time, through the sharing of one of these elements. Internal marking is seen as the more stable element, thus outline forms may hypothetically be seen as belonging to different 'phases' of internal marking. The start or end-point of the sequence is not at this stage yet defined.

Such a 'static' seriation does not define the start or end-point of the chronological sequence; rather it functions as a hypothetical basis and starting-point for a more detailed chronological discussion and analysis. This has included the entire body of deer figures, in which the individual forms of body outline have also been placed chronologically, in relation to defined forms. Stylistic features of the individual figures, on-site features such as stratigraphy and possible contemporaneous complex scenes have been discussed (further detail in Walderhaug 1994: 50ff). One element of importance for defining the sequence's starting-point in time is the drawing of the front and hind leg-line all the way up to the animal's back. This is found in animals with square, straight-angled hind parts; at Ausevik it is found only in its most characteristic form, in certain animals of outline types E and A

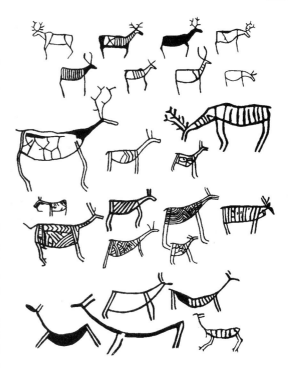

**Fig. 16.7.** Stylistic development of deer figures from Vingen, Bremanger, Sogn og Fjordane, as defined by Egil Bakka (1973).
Oldest phase upper line, youngest phase bottom line.
*Top from left*: Figures 1–8 of Hammaren type, figures 9–12 of Hardbakken type, figures 13–19 of Brattbakken type and figures 20–24 of Elva type.
Reproduced courtesy of Bergen Museum, University of Bergen.

(e.g. animal no. 3 from left, upper line, Fig. 16.6). It has been suggested that this predominant characteristic of the early western Norwegian tradition (see Fig. 16.7) developed from the depiction of the animal's thigh within the body, in the earlier and more naturalistic phases of hunters' rock-art in western Norway (Bakka 1973: 161) (see Fig. 16.2).

Finally, on that basis, a development can be suggested in which the use of internal body marking may have proceeded in the following way:

| | |
|---|---|
| IV–III | (IV dominates) |
| IV–III–V | (III dominates) |
| V–I–II | (V dominates) |

Body outline is seen to develop from triangular and rectangular shapes towards increasingly arched and

S-shaped animals, and eventually towards more semicircularly shaped animals. Motion is increasingly emphasised over time, and also a focusing on large bellies. The most naturalistic representations are seen in the quite unique, S-shaped animals, although they are quite different from the naturalistic types of the early western Norwegian tradition.

The above analysis has not aimed at pinpointing a fixed sequence of events, but rather revealing a tendency which may serve as a basis for further discussion. The approach is highly qualitative, and it is developed through the study of limited material. As a corrective, a comparison can therefore be made to the stylistic-chronological scheme proposed by Bakka for the more abundant Vingen material, developed through 'detailed analysis of a few hundred figures, with the support of stratigraphy' (1973: 162, my translation). Bakka never published the basis for his stylistic analysis in detail. Still, his conclusions concerning the Vingen material are highly interesting. He identifies four phases in the Vingen material (1973: 162ff), and likens the Ausevik carvings to the two youngest phases (see Fig. 16.7). The 'Brattbakken' type is represented by animals with triangular and rectangular body outlines and the characteristic leg-line. Complex internal marking or decoration of a type similar to type IV at Ausevik dominates, and a type similar to type III also occurs. The 'Elva' type, the latest-phase animal, is dominated by type III internal marking; type V is also found. The outline is characterised by arched bodies. Bakka's stylistic scheme is also supported by the systematic variation found in the lowest placing above sea-level of figures from the four stylistic phases. Figures of the Elva type are never found below 8.25–8.40 m above sea-level; the Brattbakken and the older Hardbakken type is not found lower than 9.30 m above sea-level; the early Hammaren type is always found higher than 10 m above sea-level (Bakka 1973: 176).

In my opinion, these two independently developed chronological schemes support each other. They also support the notion of a partial overlap in time between the Ausevik and Vingen sites, although the evidence shows that the final phase at Ausevik represents a younger phase than the Vingen carvings.

*Structure-chronological analysis and interpretation*
The chronological relationship between deer figures and other motifs on the site can be difficult to identify. As figures are seldom superimposed on each other, little is gained from the study of stratigraphy. Stylistic similarity is seen in internal marking of some animals (above) and internal marking found in other animal, human and human-animal figures, and sometimes also in abstract line-patterns. Viewing certain combinations of motifs as contemporaneously carved, *complex scenes* also gives an indication of chronological relationships.

Several of the fourteen individual panels seem to have been in use at the same time. The larger localities have accumulated a large number of figures over time, whereas the smaller panels often represent more limited phases. It is on the latter that the complex scenes are often found, suggesting that meaning and content were linked to the specific combination of motifs, and were not meant to be disturbed by later additions.

An interesting relationship concerns the abstract-geometrical figures, which have been so strongly focused upon in previous discussions. Many of these motifs are – to all appearances – randomly placed, without clear connections to other figures (see Fig. 16.3). However, there is some evidence of intentional combinations of early-type deer figures and abstract-geometrical motifs. An early phase deer figure, calf and bird figure seen in the lower left part of the panel in Fig. 16.8 (nos. 20–23) have been carved so as partly to cover or cross over into one another, without breaking any lines, and have thus been interpreted as a complex scene. The shaman-like human figure (no. 19) and dog or wolf (no. 27) to the right of the group can also be seen as part of this original motif composition. A very similar combination of motifs is found on the smaller panel in Fig. 16.5, also showing an early phase deer figure, closely

**Fig. 16.8.** Panel from Ausevik, Flora, Sogn og Fjordane, showing human, animal and abstract figures from different phases. Tracing by Johannes Bøe. Reproduced courtesy of Bergen Muesum, University of Bergen.

associated with different abstract motifs, such as spirals and cup-marks, and a headless human figure. A net containing a fish with cup-mark eye is placed between the deer's legs, as part of the same figure. I also view this group of figures as a complex scene. Another interesting combination is seen in a now damaged, early rectangular-type deer figure in the upper centre of Fig. 16.3. The hind leg-line is drawn downwards from the animal's back, in characteristic fashion, ending in an abstract-geometrical figure that is also damaged.

Structural build-up is interestingly illustrated by the panel in Fig. 16.8. I have already suggested that the group of figures on the lower left part of this panel were carved at the same time. An important feature is the connecting line drawn between the hind part of the deer figure (no. 23, at the left) and the small pecked-all-over dog or wolf figure behind it (no. 26). This shallowly pecked and rather indistinct figure is in marked contrast to the finely shaped dog/wolf figure straight above it. Directly below is a small, also shallowly pecked animal (no. 25), almost replicating the distinctly carved little calf figure be-

side it. Its legs are terminated by the arched deer figure below (no. 24) but the lines do not cross. A sense of replication is also felt in viewing the human and bird figures in the upper left part of the panel (nos. 45–46). They bear similarity to the shaman and bird figure at the centre of the panel (nos. 19 and 31), although not depicted in such detail.

Another early-type deer figure (no. 32) is found at the centre of the panel. Looking closer, one finds in close connection to this animal's neck a head of the common, unemphasised type. This original head has been prolonged in a strange manner: a new head was added, on which a large set of antlers has been placed. To the left of this figure we find what is interpreted as a late deer figure. A set of lines has been pecked, connecting these two animals.

Several more animal figures of type II internal marking, interpreted as late additions, are found on this panel. Three small and simple, very abstract figures in the lower centre part of the panel (nos. 16–18) are in marked contrast to the detailed weave-patterned deer figures also found here. Typical of late individual body outline figures in general is the mixing of old and new elements, in a somewhat haphazard fashion, in marked contrast to the strict rules of expression of earlier phases. An isolated figure from this same panel is seen extreme left, bottom line of Fig. 16.6. Elements of internal marking of types V and II are here mixed together: the belly bears resemblance to the semicircular-type body outline figures, yet the style is quite different. A similar, but slimmer, type of abstract deer figure (no. 39) is seen in the right corner of the panel in Fig. 16.8, with strange markings between its legs; the combination bears a resemblance to the deer figure with the net between its legs in Fig. 16.5, though of a very different style.

I venture to interpret what is expressed on this panel as resulting from the final use of the site. Older and stricter rules of representation were dissolving, allowing newer and older elements to be jumbled together. Earlier motifs and stylistic elements were being copied, but also integrated in the newer and very abstract styles of representation; or they were being 'reused' through the addition of new lines and elements to older figures; or by new figures being added to complex scenes. Links were made between old and new figures, through the drawing of lines between them. There is an important element which adds to this impression. In the midst of these late figures (Fig. 16.8), in close association with animal no. 16, we find the carving of a bare footprint (no. 15). This may be seen as the introduction of an agrarian rock-art element.

### The place of Ausevik rock-art in society

Not one of the different views and points of discussion outlined can alone firmly substantiate a chronology and interpretation of western Norwegian hunters' rock-art. However, these different strands can be brought together in a meaningful and complementary manner in order to create a more complete picture.

We are able to come quite far in identifying a sequence in the development of the art. Defining its true age, as an absolute calendar date, is more complex, due to the nature of the material. The suggestions concerning chronology may be further substantiated through their relationship to context.

Rock-art has had a function in society, and will therefore relate in some form to social structure; still, we cannot expect to read it as a mirror of society. Rather, we might hope to find what may be termed 'historical relations construed in terms of an ideological production' (Moore 1986: 87). Analysing the art as a solution, we may venture to understand the ideological conflict which necessitates it (Moore 1986: 90).

The hunters' rock-art sites in Hordaland are few, and probably date to the Late Mesolithic. Rock-art is also introduced at Vingen at this time, developing into a strong and stable tradition. The introduction of previously unseen elements, such as abstract line-patterns and hooks, may be related to changes occurring in the Early and Middle Neolithic A, as discussed above. Continuing tradition is also expressed through the vast numbers of deer figures produced at the site, giving much the same image of the society as is seen in other archaeological material. With the advent of the Ausevik rock-art, the picture changes, new elements being forcefully introduced into the older rock-art tradition. The developments inherent in the structure of the site may also be given meaning in relation to the larger social context, and can be related to stressful events within society in Middle Neolithic B. We have seen suggestions that the abstract-geometrical elements found in the art are the result of direct influence from agrarian cultures, southern Scandinavian or western European. Be this as it may, I have argued that these new motifs are integrated into the older local tradition from the start. But this image of harmony conceals the latent conflict and threat to society which these new images represent. The art, therefore, may have been used to *mediate* in a society which was inevitably drawing closer to encompassing dramatic change, occurring at the transition to the Late Neolithic. This capacity to mediate is not so clearly evidenced in the Vingen rock-art, perhaps explaining why rock-art production is discontinued here, at this time of internal struggle. At Ausevik the struggle continues until the end, the final carving stages showing attempts to maintain and reach back into the traditions of the past, the associated knowledge already passing from memory. There is also a brief, but futile, attempt at introducing the symbols of a new cosmology and ideology. With the final carving of a footprint, a new era symbolically places its mark on the site. The hunters' rock-art tradition of western Norway comes to an end; the symbolic expressions of a new economy and ideology takes its place.

In conclusion, what are we to make of the much-discussed abstract-geometrical motifs found at Ausevik? Are they in fact evidence of agrarian influences, or simply the reflections of entoptic imagery? Trance and shamanism are likely to have been components of the hunter-gatherer societies of western Norway; trance-related imagery might well have been symbolically expressed. But why only in this place and at this time? It has recently been suggested that the meagre pre-Late Neolithic occurrences of pottery and grain in Norway are related to the ritual use of intoxicating substances, derived through the exchange of gifts between agricultural and hunter-gatherer societies (Prescott 1996: 84). Evolving social competition may eventually have been expressed through competitive feasting and the accumulation of resources in what were once egalitarian hunter-gatherer societies. This, in turn, led to a Middle Neolithic B/Late Neolithic 'profanisation of grain', preparing the way for the introduction of an agro-pastoral economy at the transition to the Late Neolithic (Prescott 1996: 85; with reference to Sherratt 1991). Such developments may have altered the access to and enactment of rituals, and led to a shifting focus in symbolic expression. Lewis-Williams and Dowson (1993: 55) have stated that 'Altered states of consciousness can become a site of struggle'; they argue that in situations where hallucinatory experience is a common element, an emerging elite may attempt to seize control of it 'as an adjunct to its ideological ar-

moury' (Lewis-Williams and Dowson 1993: 59). In seeking to balance the different lines of argument outlined above, I offer the opinion that both internal and external developments led to altered forms of ritual and symbolic expression in the late Middle Neolithic of western Norway. Rock-art has functioned as an important agent in legitimising and mediating status and inequality in a period of stressful social transition.

## Acknowledgements

The basis for this chapter is an in-depth study of the Ausevik rock art site, carried out in 1991–3, and presented in fulfilment of the Cand. philol. degree at the University of Bergen in February 1994. An abbreviated version was presented at the TAG conference 1994, Bradford University.

My thanks to all the people who assisted in various ways during my work with the study and thesis on which this chapter is based. Special thanks to Christopher Prescott for inspirational discussions, helpful in the development of some of the ideas presented here.

## REFERENCES

Bakka, E. 1966. To hellersitningar frå steinalderen i Hardanger, *Viking* 30: 77–95.

1973. Om alderen på veideristningane, *Viking* 37: 151–87.

1979. On shoreline dating of Arctic rock carvings in Vingen, western Norway, *Norwegian Archaeological Review* 12(2): 115–22.

Bakka, E. and P. E. Kaland. 1971. Early farming in Hordaland, *Norwegian Archaeological Review* 4(2): 1–35.

Bjerck, L. G. B. 1988. Remodelling the Neolithic in southern Norway: another attack on a traditional problem, *Norwegian Archaeological Review* 21(1): 21–33.

Bøe, J. 1932. *Felszeichnungen im westlichen Norwegen I. Vingen und Henøya*. Bergen, Bergen Museums skrifter 15.

1940. En helligdom med malte bergbilder i Hardanger, *Viking* 4: 145–53.

Burenhult, G. 1980. *Götalands Hällristingar. Del 1.* Stockholm, Theses and Papers in North-European Archaeology 10.

Dowson, T. A. 1992. *Rock engravings of southern Africa.* Johannesburg, Witwatersrand University Press.

Engelstad, E. 1985. The Late Stone Age of Arctic Norway: a review, *Arctic Anthropology* 22(1): 79–96.

Fett, E. N. and P. Fett 1941. *Sydvestnorske helleristninger. Rogaland og Lista.* Stavanger, Stavanger Museum.

1979. Relations west Norway–western Europe documented in petroglyphs, *Norwegian Archaeological Review* 12(2): 65–92.

Fett, P. 1941. *Nye ristningar i Nordfjord: Vingelva og Fura.* Bergen, Bergens Museums årbok 1941. Historisk-antikvarisk rekke 6.

Gjessing, G. 1936. *Nordenfjelske ristninger og malinger av den arktiske gruppe.* Oslo, Instituttet for sammenlignende kulturforskning. Serie B: Skrifter XXX.

Glob, P. V. 1969. *Helleristninger i Danmark.* Odense, Jysk Arkeologisk Selskabs Skrifter VII.

Hagen, A. 1970. *Studier i vestnorsk bergkunst. Ausevik i Flora.* Bergen, Universitetsforlaget.

1976. *Bergkunst. Jegerfolkets helleristninger og malinger i norsk steinalder.* Oslo, Cappelen.

1983. *Norges Oldtid.* 3rd edition. Oslo, Cappelen.

Hallström, G. 1938. *Monumental art of northern Europe from the Stone Age* 1: *The Norwegian localities.* Stockholm, Almqvist and Wiksell.

Helskog, K. 1984. Helleristningene i Alta: en presentasjon og en analyse av menneskefigurene, *Viking* 47 (1983): 5–41.

1987. Selective depictions; a study of 3,500 years of rock carvings from Arctic Norway and their relationship to the Sami drums, in I. Hodder (ed.), *Archaeology as long term history*, pp. 17–30. Cambridge, Cambridge University Press.

1988. *Helleristningene i Alta.* Alta, Alta Museum.

1993. Fra tvangstrøyer til 90-åras pluralisme i helleristningsforskning, in C. Prescott and B. Solberg (eds.), *Nordic TAG: report from the third Nordic TAG conference 1990*, pp. 70–5. Bergen, University of Bergen.

Hinsch, E. 1955. *Tragtbægerkultur-Megalittkultur.* Oslo, Universitetets Oldsakssamlings Årbok 1951–53: 10–177.

1956. *Yngre steinalders stridsøkskulturer i Norge.* Bergen, Universitetet i Bergen Årbok 1954. Historisk-Antikvarisk rekke.

Hjelle, K. L., A. K. Hufthammer, P. E. Kaland, A. B. Olsen and E. C. Soltvedt. 1992. *Kotedalen – en boplass gjennom 5000 år 2: Naturvitenskapelige undersøkelser.* Bergen, University of Bergen.

Indrelid, S. and D. Moe. 1983. Februk på Hardangervidda i yngre steinalder, *Viking* 46 (1982): 36–71.

Johnston, S. A. 1993. The relationship between prehistoric Irish rock art and Irish passage tomb art, *Oxford Journal of Archaeology* 12(3): 257–93.

Lewis-Williams, J. D. and T. A. Dowson. 1988. The signs of all times: entoptic phenomena in Upper Palaeolithic art, *Current Anthropology* 29(2): 201–45.

1993. On vision and power in the Neolithic: evidence from the decorated monuments, *Current Anthropology* 34(1): 55–65.

Mandt, G. 1980. Variasjon i vestnorsk bergkunst, *ARKEO* 1980: 12–15.

1991. Vestnorske ristninger i tid og rom. Unpublished manuscript. Bergen, University Library.

Mandt Larsen, G. 1972. *Bergbilder i Hordaland.* Bergen, Årbok for Universitetet i Bergen. Humanistisk serie 1970: 2.

Marstrander, S. 1978. The problem of European impulses in the Nordic area of agrarian rock art, in S. Marstrander (ed.), *Acts of the International Symposium on Rock Art*, pp. 45–67. Oslo, Instituttet for sammenlignende kulturforskning. Serie A: Forelesninger, XXIX.

Michelsen, K. 1992. Conservation of rock art in Norway, in G. Mandt, K. Michelsen and K. H. Riisøen (eds.), *Conservation, preservation and presentation of rock art*, pp. 17–52. Bergen, Arkeologiske Skrifter No. 6.

Moore, H. 1986. *Space, text and gender.* Cambridge, Cambridge University Press.

Morris, R. W. B. 1989. The prehistoric rock art of Great Britain: a survey of all sites bearing motifs more complex than simple cup-marks, *Proceedings of the Prehistoric Society* 55: 45–88.

Myhre, B. 1972. Nyoppdaget helleristning i Hordaland, *ARKEO* 1 (1972): 11–12.

Nærøy, A. J. 1993. Chronological and technological changes in western Norway 6000–3800 BP, *Acta Archaeologica* 63 (1992): 77–95.

1994. *Troll-prosjektet: arkeologiske undersøkelser på Kollsnes, Øygarden K. Hordaland, 1989–1992.* Bergen, Arkeologiske Rapporter 19.

Nygaard, S. 1989. The Stone Age of northern Scandinavia: a review, *Journal of World Prehistory* 3(1): 71–116.

Olsen, A. B. and S. Alsaker. 1984. Greenstone and diabase utilization in the Stone Age of western Norway: technological and socio-cultural aspects of axe and adze production and distribution, *Norwegian Archaeological Review* 17(2): 71–103.

Østmo, E. 1988. *Etableringen av jordbrukskultur i Østfold i steinalderen.* Oslo, Universitetets Oldsaksamlings Skrifter.

Prescott, C. 1986 Chronological, typological and contextual aspects of the late lithic period: a study based on sites excavated in the Nyset and Steggje mountain valleys, Ardal, Sogn, Norway. Manuscript. Bergen, University Library

— 1991. Late Neolithic and Bronze Age developments on the periphery of southern Scandinavia, *Norwegian Archaeological Review* 4(1): 35–48.

— 1995. *From Stone Age to Iron Age: a study from Sogn, western Norway.* Oxford, British Archaeological Report. International Series 603.

— 1996. Was there *really* a Neolithic in Norway?, *Antiquity* 70(267): 77–87.

Prescott, C. and E. M. Walderhaug. 1995. The last frontier? Processes of Indo-Europeanization in northern Europe: the Norwegian case, *The Journal of Indo-European Studies* 23(3–4): 257–78.

Shee Twohig, E. 1981. *The megalithic art of western Europe.* Oxford, Clarendon Press.

Sherratt, A. 1991. Sacred and profane substances: the ritual use of narcotics in later Neolithic Europe, in P. Garwood, D. Jennings, R. Skeates and J. Toms (eds.), *Sacred and profane*, pp. 50–64. Oxford, Oxford University Committee for Archaeology. Monograph 32.

Sognnes, K. 1993. The role of rock art in the Bronze Age and Early Iron Age in Trøndelag, Norway, *Acta Archaeologica* 63: 157–88.

— 1995. The social context of rock art in Trøndelag, Norway: rock art at a frontier, in K. Helskog and B. Olsen (eds.), *Perceiving rock art: social and political perspectives*, pp. 130–45. Oslo, Instituttet for sammenlignende kulturforskning. Serie B: Skrifter XCII.

Walderhaug, E. M. 1994. 'Ansiktet er av stein': Ausevik i Flora – en analyse av bergkunst og kontekst. Manuscript. Bergen, University Library.

— 1995. Rock art and society in Neolithic Sogn og Fjordane, in K. Helskog and B. Olsen (eds.), *Perceiving rock art: social and political perspectives*, pp. 169–80. Oslo, Instituttet for sammenlignende kulturforskning. Serie B: Skrifter XCII.

# 17. Central Asian petroglyphs: between Indo-Iranian and shamanistic interpretations

The petroglyphs of Central Asia form a long sequence from the Neolithic onwards. Within a dating framework provided by the internal petroglyph sequence and by bridging from it to the archaeological cultural sequence, the question arises as to where relevant informed knowledge is to be found. One 'Indo-Iranian' tradition of scholarship looks to the ancient Vedas and the old Iranian Avesta for insight, religious texts from around the fourth century AD that incorporate older literature. The other approach turns to the traditions of shamanism known in recent centuries across Central Asia and north into Siberia, and regarded as having ancient roots. How closely does each match what we see in the formal evidence of patterns in the ancient images?

## The petroglyphs and their cultural contexts

Petroglyphs are extremely numerous on the territory of Central Asia (Fig. 17.1). This territory – at least the parts relevant to the study of petroglyphs – presently extends to Tadjikistan, Uzbekistan, the Russian Federation (including the Republics of Altai, Tuva and Khakassia), Kazakhstan, north-west China and Kirghizstan. The environment is mostly mountain or steppe. Three main river basins organise the fluvial systems. The Aral system with the Amu Darya and Syr Darya and their tributaries is a land of early (third millennium) urbanisation oases and civilisation in contact with the steppe world. The Tarim–Lopnur system was apparently later in developing sedentary agricultural life. In the Northern system, the great Kazakh and Siberian rivers cross steppes and taigas: Irtysh, Ienissei, Ob, Lena and so forth. The main mountains, where the majority of the petroglyphs are found, are, from west to east and north to south: Pamir-Alai, Tianshan, Altai-Saian, Kunlun and Himalaya-Karakorum, plus secondary ranges. These

river basins and mountains were connected in the past, as shown by the discoveries of archaeological remains and the study of rock-art (in English see: Jacobson 1993; Martynov 1991).

Leaving aside the urban oases, the early sequence in this part of the world can be divided into six main periods:

- Palaeolithic: Upper Palaeolithic with art objects in Siberia (Buret', Mal'ta) but no unquestionably dated petroglyphs;
- Neolithic: cultures of hunters, fishers, gatherers: rock-art seemingly in the *taiga* zone;
- Chalcolithic (Aeneolithic in the Soviet literature) and Early Bronze Age (fourth–third millennia): herders of the Afanasevo and Okunevo cultures, beginning of copper metallurgy: rock-art and engraved stelae;
- Bronze Age (second millennium): agriculturists and shepherds of the Andronovo group (Alakul' and Fedorovo variants), metal used: petroglyphs;
- Late Bronze Age with the Karasuk culture in the east and the Jaz-I/Tillja/Ferghana group in the west, beginning of mounted pastoralism and of the Scytho-Siberian Animal Style of the steppes: petroglyphs and engraved stelae;
- Iron Age (first millennium): mounted pastoralists of the Scythian group (often called Saka in the east) with subcultures of different names (Tasmola, Tagar, Tashtyk, Early Xiongnu and so forth) according to the various areas, flourishing of Scytho-Siberian art: petroglyphs and engraved stelae.

These cultures are followed by the later Xiongnu (Hunnic) and Turkic cultures and expansion, which are beyond the scope of the present chapter.

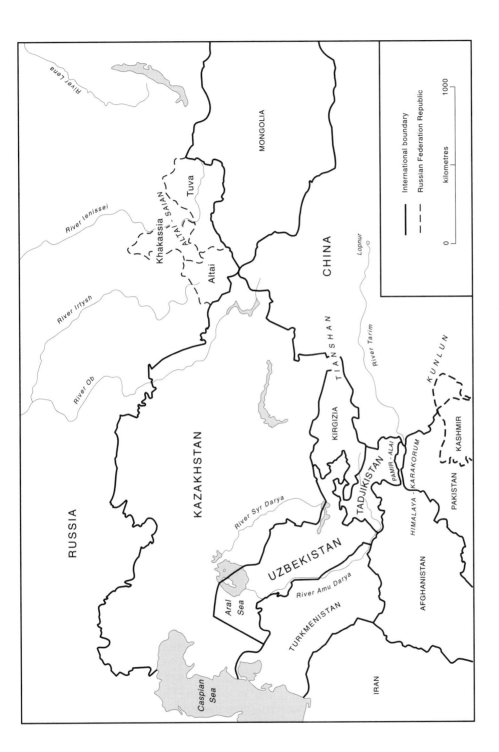

**Fig. 17.1.** The Central Asian region.

This simplified overview suffices for the present purpose. All these cultural phases have developed their own art and used the rock surfaces for the expression of certain feelings and ideas. Central Asian mountains are filled with hundreds of petroglyph sites. Sher (1980) marks 44 on his schematic map, but this figure can be multiplied by 10 at least; see, for example: Kubarev and Matochkin's (1992) map, with 170 locations in the Russian Altai only, and Samashev's (1992, 1993), with 70 in only the Upper Irtysh in Eastern Kazakhstan.

## Studying the petroglyphs

The study of rock-art – begun in Central Asia in the seventeenth century – has been continuous (Sher 1980: 16–20). The most important studies date to this century, an age of regular archaeological and anthropological enquiries, especially during the Soviet period. Slowly a sequence has been constructed, combining the results from excavating thousands of burials in the Kazakh and Siberian steppes with the recording and documentation of thousands of rock-pictures.

The sequence is remarkable, since the great number of pictures from all these numerous sites clearly show a broad continuity (some syntheses: Devlet 1990; Mariyashev and Rogozhinskij 1987; Martynov 1991; Novgorodova 1984; Samashev 1993; Sher 1980, 1994, 1995). To establish the sequence, the relationship between the petroglyphs and the images in the burial sites is basic. In some instances, stratigraphic relations can be made between a rock surface and an archaeological layer burying petroglyphs (in Altai, work by V. Kubarev, D. Cheremisin and V. Molodin, not yet published), but that is insignificant compared with the information derived from the tombs.

Close correspondence can be seen between the rock-art and the representations on stone slabs (Bronze Age), on stone pillars (Bronze and Iron Age), on ornamental bronze artefacts like buckles or daggers (Iron Age), on textile ornaments on dresses and horse harnesses (Iron Age frozen tombs of Altai), on tattooed body ornaments (Iron Age Scythian frozen tombs of the Pazyryk group in Altai), and on engravings on wood artefacts (Iron Age). Once the tombs are dated by the usual archaeological methods and given a safe broad chronology, the relations with rock-art are based upon styles held in common.

A developmental sequence is also built by combining this approach from style analysis with the representation of actual objects – types of knives, daggers, axes, clubs which can be recognised in rock-art and compared with actual finds – and by reference to the culture–ecology–economy sequence. So images of horse-riding and Scytho-Siberian Animal Style cannot appear before a certain date, around or after 1000 BC; pictures of chariots with spoked wheels drawn by horses can hardly be earlier than the mid second millennium, but carts with plain solid wheels drawn by oxen begin much earlier (see below).

The study of composition is also fundamental. Many rock-art surfaces carry a succession of pictures, sometimes intersecting or superimposed on each other (a 'palimpsest' in the Soviet literature). This 'stratigraphy' has to be understood in order to avoid that trap of a generalised synchronism which is the main drawback of the structuralist approach to Palaeolithic art.

In the earliest representations, only large animals are depicted, with no narrative composition. In the Chalcolithic and Bronze Age some narrative structure appears: hunting on foot, with dogs and bow, animals such as *Bos primigenius* or deer; or hunting with chariots. Dances, sexual intercourse, duels and other elementary (mostly binary) narrative compositions are also there, among them the attack of a predatory beast on a herbivore, a subject widely developed later in Scytho-Siberian art. In the Iron Age, besides the change in style, we see the appearance of hunting on horseback with bow and arrow, and the disappearance of *Bos primigenius* as game; now there are more complex compositions – large battles or hunts (Francfort 1995a). Some narrative compositions have been related to ancient epics, but no earlier than the Iron Age (Jacobson 1990a). For the later periods – Turkic notably – the question of narration is made easier by the oral traditions and the echoes of such traditions in the literary sources.

## A choice in research approaches to the petroglyphs: Indo-European or shamanistic?

As far as informed methods are concerned, if we focus upon the Bronze and Iron Age periods, they can be divided into two main groups that are almost mutually exclusive, even when applied to the same body of rock-pictures. A choice has to be made between two bodies of information, the Indo-Iranian or the shamanistic, according to which is thought to be 'informed' in respect of the pictures. Of course, a chapter of the present size cannot give full justice to all the nuances of thinking expressed by the various scholars who have written about the subject; the two ways of interpreting sketched here are really the two main relevant theories.

The first approach uses the ancient Indian Vedas and the old Iranian Avesta as the main sources, adding information from archaeological, ethnographic and linguistic sources (for some syntheses see: Kozhin 1990; Kuz'mina 1986, 1994a, 1994b; Mallory 1987: 56–62, 222–9): in short, the Chalcolithic and Bronze Age petroglyphs were made by the Indo-Iranian and Indo-Aryan tribes moving to the south and especially towards India, while the Iron Age rock-images are the traces of the Iranised Saka tribes, related to the Scythians, peopling the steppe zone from Europe to Mongolia. The Indo-Iranian approach is complicated by reference being sometimes made to the Mycenaean if not Homeric body of knowledge, and sometimes to ethnolinguistic questions – the identifying of the ancient waves of migrant invaders or the determining of linguistic groups like the Tokharians (for a synthesis see: Mallory 1989: 56–62). Within the corpus of rock-images, supporters of the Indo-Iranian theory select images of horse, cattle, deer, chariot, various anthropomorphic figures – those with weapons, with radiating 'solar' heads and so forth. The use of ethnographic data from the Turkic, Mongolian, Finno-Ugrian or in general non-Indo-European-speaking populations is undertaken with the idea that all the relevant elements are there only because they originate in an old Indo-Iranian background coming from protohistory. In this perspective, Europe and Asia are linked culturally, religiously and ethnolinguistically by the congruences between the steppe cultures of Jamnaja and Afanasevo in the third millennium, and of the Srubnaja and Andronovo in the second.

The second, shamanistic approach relies upon abundant ethnographic knowledge from Siberia, Mongolia and even Kazakhstan (some syntheses: Devlet 1976, 1980, 1990; Leont'ev 1978; Martynov 1991: 14–43; Novgorodova 1984, 1989). Reference is sometimes made to the Palaeolithic art of Europe. The main idea is of a local continuous tradition of shamanism from a remote past. The supporters of this theory utilise exactly the same vocabulary of images as do the Indo-European proponents – with some differences: they do not insist on the chariot; they add moose and mask pictures; the anthropomorphic 'radiating' heads are described as 'feathered' heads. In this school, more weight is given to the artistic representations than to the composition of archaeological assemblages of the same period or links with linguistic approaches.

This shamanistic theory admits that some languages can belong to the Indo-European family. Conversely, proponents of the Indo-Iranian theory allow, to a certain extent, a dose of shamanism in the steppe world.

One must observe that the two explanatory theories utilise the petroglyphs in different ways. The Indo-Iranian theory takes the petroglyphs mainly as illustrations of ancient texts while the shamanistic – more concretely – considers them more as the expression of ancient beliefs and rituals.

### The Indo-Iranian theory

We shall not distinguish here Indo-Iranian from Indo-Aryan or even Proto-Indo-Aryan, since those discriminations are not made in the literature about petroglyphs.

From this perspective the rock-art exhibits that picture of deities or sequences of narrative epics and more rarely of rituals which is described in the Vedas or Avesta. The petroglyph sites are open-air sanctuaries, often on mountains, as described for instance by Herodotus writing about the religion of the Scythians.

### Horse

*Pro.* Horse representations are important. The horse was domesticated early in the steppes, in the fourth millennium, where it originated as a wild animal. In the standard theory, the steppe is also the homeland of the Indo-Iranians or Indo-Aryans. That the horse and the Indo-Aryan-speakers are in relation is shown by the Hittite horsemanship treaty of Kikkuli and in various Mittannian texts. Horses were sacrificed both in Vedic India (*ashvamedha*) and in early Persia (king's horse sacrifice of the Achaemenids); as such, the horse is the symbol of the ruling caste. The horse is one of the attributes, possibly the most important, of the warrior aristocracy in Iran and India, pulling chariots and – later – being ridden. Burials of horses, parts of horses or horses with chariots, considered as a sign of 'Indo-Iranity', are known in the steppe from the Andronovo period and in the Swat valley of northern Pakistan (see Bökönyi 1994; Genning 1977; Kuz'mina 1994a, 1994c).

*Contra.* It can be argued that the horse was important in the whole steppe area of Eurasia at any period from the late Palaeolithic – and also later among the Turkic and Mongol tribes (Hamayon 1990; Roux 1966, 1984). It is therefore impossible to assert that petroglyphs of horses were made *only* by peoples speaking Indo-Iranian languages; moreover, pre-Afanasevo horses of the Minusinsk style in Siberia are certainly not related to Indo-Iranians or to Indo-Europeans (Sher 1994: vi–viii, fig. 6).

### Cattle (Fig. 17.2)

*Pro.* Cattle are also important in respect to the Vedic and Avestic literature, with mention of sacrifices (in India) or their prohibition (in Zoroastrian Iran).

Some petroglyphs with human beings and bulls have also been compared with the Minoan-Mycenaean mother goddess (Sher 1994: xxxi–xxxiii).

*Contra.* The same argument as with the horse applies: cattle are important in non-Indo-Iranian contexts as well. Sacrifices and rituals are universal in the steppe zone. An ideology linked with the domesticated bull must have developed after a long period of hunting myths and rituals related to wild *Bos* (Devlet 1990: 85–102; Hamayon 1990; Roux 1966, 1984).

### Deer

*Pro.* Deer are also interpreted as a marker of Iranism, especially as far as the perspective of the Scythians is concerned. In this case, a dose of shamanistic influence is admitted (Martynov 1991: 52–73).

*Contra.* The solar and cyclical symbolism of the deer cannot just be reduced to the Indo-Iranian interpretation, for it is important in many contexts in Eurasia from at least the Neolithic (Hamayon 1990; Jacobson 1993; Roux 1966, 1984). Here, as in the case of *Bos* and of *Equus caballus* (Sacchi 1995), the chronology of pictures shows that rock-engravings of deer largely precede any possible Indo-Iranian or Indo-European intrusion in the Minusinsk or Angara styles of Siberia.

### Carnivores

*Pro.* Beasts of prey may be seen as images of the monsters fought by the Vedic or Avestic heroes – Indra or Verethragna for example (Samashev and Rogozhinskij 1995).

*Contra.* Predatory monsters are simply not a monopoly of the Indo-Iranian mythologies or systems of representations in Eurasia: they appear at early dates from China to Mesopotamia.

### Weapons

*Pro.* Among the weapons, the anthropomorphic beings holding clubs (Fig. 17.3) can be considered as

**Fig. 17.2.** Ustí-Tuba-III, nos. 46.4 to 46.13 (Khakassia, Russia): bovids and 'birth-giving'. Bronze Age. Photograph courtesy of Ja. A. Sher.

images of Indra, the Vedic warrior, or his Avestic counterpart (Mariyashev 1994: 52; Samashev and Rogozhinskij 1995).

*Contra.* The club is a common weapon within Central Asian societies during the Bronze Age, found in excavations and represented in petroglyphs (Kubarev 1987).

*Solar-headed anthropomorphic figures*

*Pro.* Solar-headed anthropomorphic figures (Figs. 17.4 and 17.5), which appear in petroglyphs in isolation, in groups or in relation to chariots, are interpreted as the god Mitra (or Mithra), the solar deity. Comparisons are made between Altaic and Caucasian pictures from the Bronze Age, in support

**Fig. 17.3.** Tamgaly-III, no. 38 (Kazakhstan): complex surface with three 'horned horses' (identified by their non-bovid penises) with riders. An anthropomorphic bird-headed personage hits one of them with a typical Bronze Age axe.
　Photograph Mission Archéologique Française en Asie Centrale.

of the old idea of a Pontic migration eastwards (Kuz'mina 1986: 119–22, 126, 1994b: 456, fig. 17.56; Mariyashev 1979, 1994: 35–6; Novozhenov 1994: 211–13).

*Contra.* The iconographic convention of the radiating head or nimbus, so familiar to us, appears later in the arts of the Middle East; we suspect here an anachronism. And there is no instance in Central Asia where one *cannot* interpret projections as feathers rather than sun rays. Moreover, the Medes (Iranians of the early first millennium) represented on the Assyrian reliefs wear feathered head-dresses. Finally, radiating heads appear not only in the supposed non-Indo-European/Aryan culture of Okunevo in the Minusinsk Basin, but also in the Asiatic cultures of Lower Amur or Ningxia.

*Chariots*

*Pro.* The chariot (Figs. 17.6 and 17.7), along with the horse, is certainly at the core of the Indo-Iranian theory (Novozhenov 1994 offers an extensive survey of the question). The literature is very abundant (some relevant studies include: Cherednichenko and Pustovalov 1991; Genning 1977; Jettmar 1982; Kozhin 1987, 1990; Kuz'mina 1986: 125ff, 1994a, 1994b; Mariyashev 1994: 35–6; Mariyashev and Rogozhinskij 1987; Novgorodova 1978, 1984: 60–1, 74–8, 1989: 140–65; Sher 1978, 1980: 277–85, 1994: x–xiv; Sorokin 1990; Varenov 1990; Zhukov and Ranov 1974). The chariot is the vehicle of the warrior aristocracy, the *rataeshtar* of the Vedic and Avestic texts; it is also the vehicle of the sun god Surya and of Mitra (Mithra). The

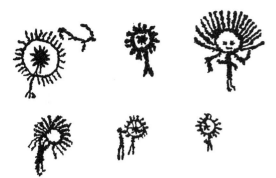

**Fig. 17.4.** Selection of radiating 'solar'-headed anthropomorphs of Sajmaly-Tash (Kirghizstan). Bronze Age.
After Martynov, Mariashev and Abékétov (1992).

**Fig. 17.6.** Sajmaly-Tash (Kirghizstan): chariots with pairs of various animals and drivers plus other animals and signs, Bronze Age.
After Martynov, Mariashev and Abékétov (1992: fig. 17.77).

**Fig. 17.5.** Tamgaly-IV (Kazakhstan): surface with 'solar'-headed and dancing personages.
After Mariyashev (1994: fig. 17.2).

**Fig. 17.7.** Elangash-III (Altai, Russia): chariot with head-radiating driver. Bronze Age.
Photograph Mission Archéologique Française en Asie Centrale.

chariot with spoked wheels originated in the Andronovo (or Srubnaja) cultures of the steppes and spread in Eurasia (Piggott 1978, 1983: 87, 91–3). The presence of chariot burials in the Andronovo group of cultures evidences a warriors' caste, sometimes compared to the Homeric aristocracy; moreover, some horse-bit cheek pieces are similar in the steppes and in the Mycenaean world (Kuz'mina

1994b: 436, fig. 37). Graffiti of chariots depicted in the same manner as the petroglyphs are known on Andronovo ceramics (Kuz'mina 1994b: 433, fig. 34). Some petroglyphs of chariots depict fantastic and, therefore, non-terrestrial pairs of animals, in relation with 'sun'-headed personages, supposed to represent Mitra (Sher 1978: at Sajmaly-Tash in

309

Kirghizstan). The map of chariot terminology in Indo-European languages coincides with the expansion of the chariot from the steppes (Anthony 1995).

*Contra.* It is not certain that the spoked wheel originated in the steppes; the most ancient spoked wheels may be from the Middle East (Littauer and Crouwel 1979: 68–71), and they seem to have existed in Bactria (north Afghanistan) before 1800 BC (Amiet 1986: figs. 8, 9; Francfort 1992a: fig. 10.1) on bullock carts or chariots. A warrior aristocracy mounted on bull or donkey carts existed in all the agricultural societies from at least the third millennium in Mesopotamia but also in Central Asia – Bactria (Francfort 1992a; Jarrige 1995: 22) – and in the steppes of Minusinsk (Sher 1994: x–xiv: Afanasevo date for the Znamenka stele of the Minusinsk Basin, reused in Okunevo grave). Such an aristocracy existed also in non-Indo-Iranian/Aryan societies, with chariot burials, in Shang China after the fourteenth century (Francfort 1992b; Von Dewall 1983; Watson 1978). The graffiti of chariots on Andronovo pots (Kuz'mina 1994b: fig. 34) prove nothing more about Indo-Aryans than does the similarity of the Shang ideogram for 'chariot' (Li 1977: 115) with some petroglyphs. The 'Mitras' shown with paired bulls or mountain goats drawing chariots are not identified with any certainty. The map of Indo-European terminology (Anthony 1995) shows only that the chariot and its parts were described by terms meaning 'chariot' (and its parts) in Indo-European languages; similarly, in China, the chariot was designated by a term meaning 'chariot' in Chinese: so this is not an argument in favour of Indo-Iranity. A balanced view of the introduction of chariots and chariot representations in Central Asia in relation to the earlier presence of carts (Znamenka) and the supposed military Indo-European expansion and ideology has been recently developed (by Jacobson 1990c, 1993: 125–40). In sum, it is impossible to argue that any Bronze Age chariot pictured in the petroglyphs is a mark left by the Indo-Iranians/

Aryans in Central Asia, unless we have other and external data to prove it.

Finally, the Indo-Iranian theory relies upon information from texts, Indian and Iranian, written in India and Iran around the fourth century AD but including parts of ancient religious poems (dated around 1800–1500 BC). There is a big gap in space (the distance between the steppes and India, notably) and in time between the old poems and the archaeological evidence. To fill the gap, a migration of tribes is proposed. This migration from Central Asia is suggested because, among nine archaeological cultures proposed as candidates, not a single one has left material evidence of a crossing through the Hindu Kush range, and there are doubts about a large invasion (Francfort *et al.* 1989: 422–56). On the other hand, in a local evolutionary context, horse-riding, the working of horse bones and some artefacts of Central Asian types are present in Baluchistan (at Pirak) as early as around 1750 BC (Jarrige and Santoni 1979: 32, 171, fig. 90, plates XXVIII, XXXIX, XL; Jarrige 1995: 21–7, fig. 22). This – the requested date and region – does not fit with the expectation of the traditional Vedas analysis; the local tradition is very strong, and the changes occurring at that point were not coming just from the steppes, as is shown by the beginning of rice cultivation. The horse is the only Central Asian creature that we see definitely crossing the Hindu Kush in the first half of the second millennium (Fussman 1989). A comparative study of the petroglyphs of Central Asia and North India shows that the relations have been intense and continuous from the third millennium to the second half of the first millennium BC: there is no longer any reason to advocate a single episode of expansion, even though ancient poems speak of one (Francfort 1992b; Francfort, Klodzinski and Mascle 1990).

In the same vein, we can underline the inconsistency of the Indo-Iranian theory when it ignores or leaves aside the steppic origins of the Western

**Fig. 17.8.** Ustí-Tuba-III, no. 47 (Khakassia, Russia): moose in the Angara style known in the *taiga* since Neolithic, pre-Afanasevo. Photograph courtesy of Ja. A. Sher.

Scythian Iranian epics or ethnographic Caucasian legends (Schiltz 1994).

In conclusion, we must recognise that the variability among the archaeological culture assemblages and among the mythological beliefs – in addition to the possibility of disappeared languages – is greater than falls within the explanatory power of the Indo-Iranian theory as derived only from the Vedic and Avestic texts. But we can also admit that the building of the Indo-Iranian language (Vedic and Avestic) took place in this broad milieu – the steppes and southern Central Asia – and penetrated into northern India, along with horsemanship, in spite of different cultural contexts (Jarrige 1995: 26–7). Because texts give no completely consistent explanations of petroglyphs, the rock-art cannot simply be depictions of the Indo-Iranian deities, myths and epics.

## The shamanistic theory

What about the shamanistic theory?

This theory, which has fewer supporters than the Indo-European or Indo-Iranian, does not exclude the contention that Indo-European – or Indo-Iranian-speaking groups *were* in the area during the Chalcolithic and Bronze Age, but there is no stress on the chariot; it can have been just a means of transport to the other world, as simple animals can be (Mariyashev 1994: 50–1). The sites are interpreted as open-air sanctuaries located in sacred and important places: tops of mountains, passes, fords. Ethnography – fundamental for this theory – draws on the present use of petroglyph sites as places of worship by local Turkic- or Mongol-speaking populations.

*Cervid representations* (deer, moose) (Fig. 17.8) and in general all horned herbivore images can be seen frequently in the frame of shamanism, either as riding animals or in the context of hunting (Devlet 1990: 110–12, 1994; Mariyashev 1979; Martynov 1991; Novgorodova 1984).

Hunting, abundantly represented in Central Asian petroglyphs, is central to the theory of shamanism (Hamayon 1990), including magic or cosmic hunting, in a close relationship between humankind and animals, between earth and the other world (Francfort *et al.* 1993; Jacobson 1993; Kubarev 1987; Novgorodova 1989).

*Representations of masks* (Fig. 17.9), considered as attributes of shamans, are related to a remote past. A particular case is the horned mask or horned anthropomorphic being, frequently compared with Palaeolithic images (Devlet 1976, 1980, 1990: 30–80; Francfort, Klodzinski and Mascle 1990; Jettmar 1982, 1985, 1994; Kubarev 1988; Leont'ev 1978; Martynov 1991: 44–51; Sher 1980: 216–32, 1995: iii–v).

*Radiating head-dresses* are seen as made of feathers or similar ornaments, a part of the ancient eastern Eurasian shaman's or hunter's dress (Leont'ev 1978; Vadeckaja, Leont'ev and Maksimenkov 1980).

*Hybrids of animals or human-cum-animal beings* also correspond to a shamanic view of the world. Composite animals reflect the metamorphosis and constant transformation of nature. Composite anthropomorphic beings express the interpenetrating worlds of the natural and supernatural. In this respect the horned persons and the bird-headed persons frequently pictured on the rocks fit well with shamanistic images (Kubarev 1988: 94ff; Leont'ev 1978; Martynov 1991: 39–41).

*Axis mundi* or any image of a cosmic pillar or vertical view of the world, for example in the shape of the Okunevo stelae with a three-storey universe, reflect again the intercommunication of the upper (heaven), middle (earth) and under worlds (Kubarev 1988: 85–93; Novgorodova 1984, 1989; Sher 1994: viii-xiv; Vadeckaja, Leont'ev and Maksimenkov 1980).

**Fig. 17.9.** Mugur-Sargol (Ienissei Canyon, Mount Saian): masks, 'maskoids', masked anthropomorph. Bronze Age. After Devlet (1980: pl. 20).

There is actually no petroglyph representation that fully contradicts shamanistic theory, but only if one considers a broad Eurasian spectrum of shamanism, not the exact illustration of present-day shamanism (also depicted on rock with recent drums and *ongon* images) (Eliade 1968; Hamayon 1990; Perrin 1995). Moreover, the presence of shamanism in the steppe zone of Eurasia is so ubiquitous that one cannot avoid explaining the Scythian burial material, composite head-dresses and ornaments of Pazyryk, Ukok or Issyk without reference to it (Brentjes and Vasilievsky 1989; Polos'mak 1991).

The shamanistic theory is both in a worse and in a better position than the Indo-Iranian theory for interpreting the rock-images. For the Chalcolithic and Bronze Age, the theoretical situation is not excellent, since we are formally in the same situation as the students of the Palaeolithic art; the shamanistic interpretation of Palaeolithic rock-art has been definitely and incisively rejected by both Leroi-Gourhan (1987) and Lévi-Strauss (1973: 389) as beyond the reach of any kind of demonstration.

In spite of this methodological impossibility (which is formally also a blow to the Indo-Iranian theory), the proponents of the shamanistic theory insist upon a local continuity (Devlet 1976, 1980, 1990; Martynov 1991). First of all, some Siberian peoples maintain a very ancient life-style with aspects of a shamanistic religion. Second, contemporary shamanism is the heir of earlier Turkic and Mongol religion documented by sources. Third, early Turkic and Mongol shamanism cannot be understood without reference to the Scythian data (Roux 1966, 1984). Fourth, one has to accept for the Chalcolithic and Bronze Ages a broad Eurasian shamanism, with links from a very ancient date between eastern Eurasia and America (Chang 1989: 162–5). Fifth, even during the Scythian Iron Age, pure canonical shamanism is not reflected in the archaeological record (Jacobson 1990b).

In this sense, the shamanistic theory fits better with the data and gives better insights into the understanding of Central Asian petroglyphs; but it explains less, in being less specific than the Indo-Iranian interpretation.

## Choosing between the theories

Syncretic and composite mixtures of both theories are sometimes proposed, not always without contradictions. However, we know that traces of shamanism have been recognised in orthodox Iranian Zoroastriansm and that the pre-Christian old Russian pagan religion was encompassing shamanistic and Irano-Scythian elements.

An evaluation is necessary. By examining certain rock-images from the point of view of their relevance (or non-relevance) to the two main proposed explanatory theories we can better ascertain which is more useful. However, it is important to discriminate between universal and local semantics in discrete images or elementary groups.

Analysis – whether in structural or in other terms – will have to respect the chronological and spatial ordering of images and compositions, as we know that from a good record of the surfaces and the superpositioning of the images on them.

It has been useful critically to examine the way we utilise the textual sources in the Indo-Iranian theory and the ethnographic and prehistoric data in the shamanistic theory: there is always a selection of discrete information and/or elementary (binary) structured compositions within a huge body of pictures.

A case-study using material from the Kazakh–French and Russian–French fieldwork carried out in southern Kazakhstan and southern Siberia since 1992 will illustrate this point.

A first part of this collaborative work was to elaborate a corpus or repertoire of the Central Asian petroglyphs, both as a collection of volumes (two issues already printed: Francfort and Sher 1995; Sher *et al.* 1994) and as a database (Martin 1995). The largest and most accurate possible documentation was required, adding newly studied sites to the re-examination of previously recorded sites.

The second part of the work was an in-depth study

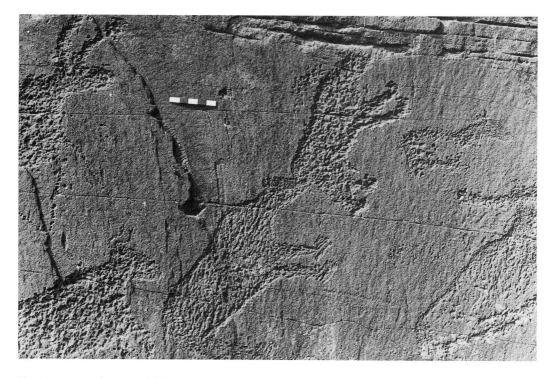

**Fig. 17.10.** Ustí-Tuba-II, no. 6 (Khakassia, Russia): bears, bovid and moose in a large complex surface with thirty-two animals and a horned anthropomorphic figure standing on a boat.
See Francfort and Sher (1995: fig. 17.5, p. xl; pls. 34–9).

of selected parts of sites or surfaces (Francfort *et al.* 1993). The research included the following: geo-microbiological alteration of rock surfaces (Soleil-havoup 1995; Vidal 1995); technological study of engravings and hammering, by stereomacrophotography of superposition of figures and alterations, and by casting of selected parts for microscopic analyses; sampling for physical dating; chemical analyses; search for stratigraphic relations between rock surfaces and archaeological layers (various studies in press).

Amongst the most precise identification of subjects we sought, in particular, those of animal species and artefacts (Fig. 17.10) (Sacchi 1995). An artificial intelligence programme was designed for studying the relation between styles and compositions on a large number of rock-art surfaces (Martin, in preparation).

In one example, the hybrid image of 'horned horse' (Figs. 17.3, 17.11) in petroglyphs and in the archaeological material, our study shows that neither the Indo-Iranian nor the shamanistic theory is relevant to 'explaining' this image (Francfort 1995b). The most remarkable horned horses are the well-known and often-published actual horses, found masked in the frozen Scythian tombs of Pazyryk and bearing artificial horns. Figurines of such horned horses have been found in other tombs of the same culture in Altai too. The horned horse is a widespread (though not too abundant) composite image that can be traced from the Andronovo Bronze Age to the Scythian and later Sarmatian periods in Siberia, Kazakhstan, Gandhara and eastern Europe. The earliest pictures of horned horses are found among the petroglyphs of the Bronze Age

**Fig. 17.11.** Tamgaly-III, no. 23 (Kazakhstan): horned horse. Bronze Age figure renovated later: a personage (not refreshed) is hitting the horse's nose with a Bronze Age type of axe. Stereomacrophotography shows that the horns, here as in other sites, are not later additions. The horned horse in various versions originates in Bronze Age Central Asia.

Photograph Mission Archéologique Française en Asie Centrale.

in Kazakhstan and Altai. The horned horse is not an orthodox image of shamanic or Indo-Iranian mythology. A shamanistic substratum in the broad sense gives, nevertheless, the best possible explanation of this theme: the image of a magic mount for a journey to the other world. Here, again, nothing comes specifically from the Indo-Iranian sources – but also nothing from recorded shamanism except that horns are universally recognised as symbols of power, regrowth and rebirth among shamanistic peoples (there are many examples throughout the Americas, Scandinavia, north Eurasia, Siberia and elsewhere)

(Jacobson 1993: 171–213). But we have to notice that in Central Asia – even for later and far better-documented periods of official Zoroastrianism, like the Achaemenid or the Sassanid-Sogdian – we find great variation in the iconography and burial customs. It is not surprising to observe a great, if not greater, variability in the earlier archaeological data, compared with textual information.

The Central Asian petroglyph pictures include subjects that can be related to the Indo-Iranian sources only because they are parts of the broader Eurasian cultural context of the time. In the same vein, they include shamanistic traits related to a larger substratum. Petroglyphs, as such, are not of any use for the demonstration of the Indo-Iranian identity of their makers. Their variability and potential capacity to be interpreted is richer than the texts that reached us. Consequently, we shall have to encourage local interpretive structural diachronic studies, and to maintain the methodological rigours of the archaeological discipline before we adopt general synthetic theories elaborated in other fields of research. The usefulness of precisely and carefully distinguishing and clearly separating, for methodological reasons, the archaeological (material culture), linguistic, philological, anthropological, artistic, religious, mythological or ideological domains is extremely important at the present stage of research.

## REFERENCES

Amiet, P. 1986. Au-delà d'Elam, *Archäologische Mitteilungen aus Iran* 19: 11–20.

Anthony, D. W. 1995. Horse, wagon and chariot: Indo-European language and archaeology, *Antiquity* 69: 554–65.

Bökönyi, S. 1994. The role of the horse in the exploitation of steppes, in B. Genito (ed.), *The archaeology of the steppes: methods and strategies: papers from the international symposium held in Naples 9–12 November 1992*, pp. 17–27. Naples, Istituto Universitario Orientale, Dipartimento di Studi Asiatici. Series Minor 44.

Brentjes, B. and R. S. Vasilievsky. 1989. *Schamanenkrone und Weltenbaum: Kunst der Nomaden Nordasiens*. Leipzig, E. A. Seemann Verlag.

Chang, K. C. 1989. Ancient China and its anthropological significance, in C. C. Lamberg-Karlovsky (ed.), *Archaeological thought in America*, pp. 155–66. Cambridge, Cambridge University Press.

Cherednichenko, N. N. and S. Zh. Pustovalov. 1991. Boevye kolesnicy i kolesnichie v obshchestve katakombnoj kul'tury (po materialam raskopok v nizhnem podneprov'e), *Sovetskaya Arkheologiya* 1991(4): 206–16.

Devlet, M. A. 1976. *Petroglify Ulug-Khema*. Moscow, Nauka.

1980. *Petroglify Mugur-Sargola*. Moscow, Nauka.

1990. *Listy kamennoj knigi Ulug-Khema*. Kyzyl, Tuvinskoe knizhnoe izdate'stvo.

1994. Pierres à cerfs et images rupestres de cerfs, in *Les Scythes*, pp. 26–9. Paris, Editions Faton. Les dossiers d'archéologie 194.

Eliade, M. 1968. *Le Chamanisme et les techniques archaïques de l'extase*. Paris, Payot.

Francfort, H.-P. 1992a. Dungeons and dragons: reflections on the system of iconography in protohistoric Bactria and Margiana, in G. L. Possehl (ed.), *South Asian archaeology studies*, pp. 179–208. New Delhi, Oxford and IBH Publishing.

1992b. New data illustrating the early contacts between Central Asia and the north-west of the subcontinent, in C. Jarrige (ed.), *South Asian archaeology 1989*, pp. 97–102. Madison (WI), Prehistory Press. Monographs in World Archaeology 14.

1995a. Perspectives de recherches, in H.-P. Francfort and Ja. A. Sher (eds.), *Répertoire des pétroglyphes d'Asie centrale, fascicule 2, Sibérie du Sud 2: Tepsej I–III, Ust'-Tuba I–IV (Russie, Khakassie)*, pp. lxx–lxxvii. Paris, Diffusion de Boccard. Mémoires de la Mission Archéologique Française en Asie Centrale V.2.

1995b. Le cheval cornu, *Bulletin of the Asia Institute 9*: 185–98.

Francfort, H.-P. *et al.* 1989, *Fouilles de Shortughaï: recherches sur l'Asie centrale protohistorique*. Paris, Diffusion de Boccard. Mémoires de la Mission Archéologique Française en Asie Centrale 2.

Francfort, H.-P., D. Klodzinski and G. Mascle. 1990. Pétroglyphes archaïques du Ladakh et du Zanskar, *Arts Asiatiques* 45: 5–27.

Francfort, H.-P., D. Sacchi, Ja. A. Sher, F. Soleilhavoup and P. Vidal. 1993. Art rupestre du bassin de Minusinsk: nouvelles recherches franco-russes, *Arts Asiatiques* 48: 5–52.

Francfort, H.-P. and Ja. A. Sher (eds.). 1995. *Répertoire des pétroglyphes d'Asie centrale, fascicule 2, Sibérie du Sud 2: Tepsej I–III, Ust'-Tuba I–IV (Russie, Khakassie)*. Paris, Diffusion de Boccard. Mémoires de la Mission Archéologique Française en Asie Centrale V.2.

Fussman, G. 1989. Histoire du monde indien, *Annuaire du Collège de France 1988–1989*: 514–30.

Genning, V. F. 1977. Mogil'nik Sintashta i problema rannikh indoiranskikh plemen, *Sovetskaya Arkheologiya* 1977(4): 53–73.

Hamayon, R. 1990. *La Chasse à l'âme: esquisse d'une théorie du chamanisme sibérien*. Nanterre, Société d'Ethnologie.

Jacobson, E. 1990a. The appearance of narrative structures in the petroglyphic art of prehistoric Siberia and Mongolia, in R. S. Vasil'evskij (ed.), *Semantika drevnikh obrazov, (Pervobytnoe iskusstvo)*, pp. 92–106. Novosibirsk, Nauka.

1990b. On the question of shamanism among the early nomads of Eurasia (first millennium BC), in B. Brendemoen (ed.), *Altaica Osloensia; Proceedings from the 32nd Meeting of the Permanent International Altaistic Conference*, pp. 165–79. Oslo, Universitetsforlaget.

1990c. Warriors, chariots, and theories of culture, *Mongolian Studies* 13: 83–116.

1993. *The deer goddess of ancient Siberia: a study in the ecology of belief*. New York, Leyde. Studies in the History of Religions 40.

Jarrige, J.-F. 1995. Du Néolithique à la civilisation de l'Inde ancienne: contribution des recherches archéologiques dans le nord-ouest du sous-continent indo-pakistanais, *Arts Asiatiques* 50: 5–30.

Jarrige, J.-F. and M. Santoni. 1979. *Fouilles de Pirak*. Paris, Klinksieck. Fouilles du Pakistan 2.

Jettmar, K. 1982. Petroglyphs and early history of the upper Indus valley, *Zentralasiatische Studien* 16: 293–308.

1985. Non-Buddhist tradition in the petroglyphs of the Indus valley, in M. Taddei and J. Schotsmans (eds.), *South Asian archaeology 1983*, pp. 751–77. Naples, Istituto Universitario Orientale, Dipartimento di Studi Asiatici. Series Minor 23.

1994. Body-painting and the roots of the Scytho-Siberian Animal Style, in B. Genito (ed.), *The archaeology of the steppes: methods and strategies: papers from the international symposium held in Naples 9–12 November 1992*, pp. 3–15. Naples, Istituto Universitario Orientale, Dipartimento di Studi Asiatici. Series Minor 44.

Kozhin, P. M. 1987, Kolesnichnye sjuzhety v naskal'nom

iskusstve central'noj Azii, in A. P. Derevjanko and Sh. Nacadorzh (eds.), *Arkheologika, etnografija i antropologija Mongolii*, pp. 109–26. Novosibirsk, Nauka.

1990. *Etnokul'turnye kontakty na territorii Evrazii v epokhe eneolita – rannego zheleza (paleokul'turologija i kolesnyj transport)*. Novosibirsk, Avtoreferat.

Kubarev, V. D. 1987. Antropomorfnye khvostatye suchshestva altajskikh gor, in R. S. Vasil'evskij (ed.), *Antropomorfnye izobrazhenija (Pervobytnoe iskusstvo)*, pp. 150–69. Novosibirsk, Nauka.

1988. *Drevnie rospisi Karakola*. Novosibirsk, Nauka.

Kubarev, V. D. and E. P. Matochkin. 1992. *Petroglify Altaja*. Novosibirsk, Institut d'Archéologie de Novosibirsk.

Kuz'mina, E. E. 1986. *Drevnejshie skotovody ot Urala do Tjan'-Shana*. Frunze, Ilim.

1994a. Horses, chariots, and the Indo-Iranians: an archaeological spark in the historical dark, in A. Parpola and P. Koskikallio (eds.), *South Asian archaeology 1993*, pp. 403–11. Helsinki, Suomalainen Tiedeakatemia. Annales Academiae Scientiarum Fennicae series B, 271.

1994b. *Otkuda prishli Indoarii?* Moscow, Vostochnaja literatura.

1994c. Stages of development of stockbreeding husbandry and ecology of the steppes in the light of the archaeological and palaeoecological data (fourth millennium BC – eighth century BC), in B. Genito (ed.), *The archaeology of the steppes: methods and strategies: papers from the international symposium held in Naples 9–12 November 1992*, pp. 31–71. Naples, Istituto Universitario Orientale, Dipartimento di Studi Asiatici. Series Minor 44.

Leont'ev, E. V. 1978. Antropomorfnye izobrazhenija okunevskoj kul'tury (problemy khronologii i semantiki), *Istorija i kul'tura vostoka Azii* 6: 88–118.

Leroi-Gourhan, A. 1987. Le préhistorien et le chamane, *L'Ethnographie* (2): 19–25.

Lévi-Strauss, C. 1973. *Anthropologie structurale* II. Paris, Plon.

Li, Chi. 1977. *Anyang*. Folkestone, Dawson.

Littauer, M. A. and J. H. Crouwel. 1979. *Wheeled vehicles and ridden animals in the ancient Near East*. Leiden, Brill.

Mallory, J. P. 1989 (1991). *In search of the Indo-Europeans: language, archaeology and myth*. London, Thames and Hudson.

Mariyashev, A. N. 1979. Petroglify Semirech'e, in A. P.

Derevjanko (ed.), *Zveri v Kamne (Pervobytnoe iskusstvo)*, Novosibirsk, Nauka.

1994. *Petroglyphs of south Kazakhstan and Semirechye*. Almaty, A. N. Margulan Archaeology Institute.

Mariyashev, A. N. and A. E. Rogozhinskij. 1987. Voprosy periodizacii i khronologii petroglifov Kazakhstana, in A. I. Martynov and V. I. Molodin (eds.), *Skifo-sibirskij mir. Iskusstvo i ideologija*, pp. 55–9. Novosibirsk, Nauka.

Martin, L. 1995. Pétrobase, une base de données consacrées aux gravures rupestres d'Asie centrale, in H.-P. Francfort and Ja. A. Sher (eds.), *Répertoire des pétroglyphes d'Asie centrale, fascicule 2, Sibérie du Sud 2: Tepsej I–III, Ust'-Tuba I–IV (Russie, Khakassie)*, pp. 21–32. Paris, Diffusion de Boccard. Mémoires de la Mission Archéologique Française en Asie Centrale V.2.

Martynov, A. I. 1991. *The ancient art of northern Asia*. Urbana (IL), University of Illinois Press.

Martynov, A. I., A. N. Mariashev and A. K. Abékétov. 1992. *Gravures rupestres de Saimaly-Tach*. Alma-Ata.

Novgorodova, E. A. 1978. Drevnejshie izobrazhenija kolesnic v gorakh Mongolii, *Sovetskaya Arkheologiya* 1978(4): 192–206.

1984. *Mir petroglifov Mongolii*. Moscow, Nauka.

1989. *Drevnjaja Mongolija*. Moscow, Nauka.

Novozhenov, V. A. 1994. *Naskal'nye izobrazhenija povozok Srednej i Central'noj Azii (k probleme migracii naselenija stepnoj Evrazii v epokhu eneolita i bronzy)*. Almaty, Argumenty i Fakty Kazakhstana.

Perrin, M. 1995. *Le Chamanisme*. Paris, Presses Universitaires de France.

Piggott, S. 1978. Chinese chariotry: an outsider's view, in P. Denwood (ed.), *Arts of the Eurasian steppelands*, pp. 32–51. London, Percival David Foundation of Chinese Art, School of Oriental and African Studies. olloquies on Art and Archaeology in Asia 7.

1983. *The earliest wheeled transport: from the Atlantic coast to the Caspian Sea*. London, Thames and Hudson.

Polos'mak, N. 1991. Un nouveau kourgane à 'tombe gelée' de l'Altaï (rapport préliminaire), *Arts Asiatiques* 46: 5–13.

Roux, J.-P. 1966. *Faune et flore sacrées dans les sociétés altaïques*. Paris, Adrien-Maisonneuve.

1984. *La Religion des Turcs et des Mongols*. Paris, Payot.

Sacchi, D. 1995. Quelques aspects du bestiaire, in H.-P. Francfort and Ja. A. Sher (eds.), *Répertoire des pétroglyphes d'Asie centrale, fascicule 2, Sibérie du Sud 2: Tepsej I–III, Ust'-Tuba I–IV (Russie, Khakassie)*, pp. xxxiii–xl.

Paris, Diffusion de Boccard. Mémoires de la Mission Archéologique Française en Asie Centrale V.2.

Samashev, Z. S. 1992. *Naskal'nye izobrazhenija verkhnego priirtysh'ja*. Alma-Ata, Gylym.

— 1993. *Petroglyphs of the East Kazakhstan as a historical sources*. Almaty, Rakurs.

Samashev, Z. and A. Rogozhinskij. 1995. Tentative d'interprétation de pétroglyphes du ravin de Tamgaly, *Bulletin of the Asia Institute* 9: 198–207.

Schiltz, V. 1994. *Les Scythes et les nomades des steppes: 8ᵉ siècle avant J.-C. 1ᵉʳ siècle après J.-C.* Paris, Gallimard. L'univers des formes.

Sher, Ja. A. 1978. K interpretacii sjuzhetov nekotorykh petroglifov Sajmaly-Tasha, in V. G. Lukonin (ed.), *Kul'tura Vostoka. drevnost' i rannee srednevekov'e*, pp. 163–71. St Petersburg, Gosudarstvennyj Ermitazh.

— 1980. *Petroglify srednej i central'noj Azii*. Moscow, Nauka.

— 1994. Commentaire, in Ja. A. Sher (ed.), *Répertoire des pétroglyphes d'Asie centrale, fascicule 1, Sibérie du Sud 1: Oglakhty I–III (Russie, Khakassie)*, pp. i–xxxviii. Paris, Diffusion de Boccard. Mémoires de la Mission Archéologique Française en Asie Centrale V.1.

— 1995. Commentaire, in H.-P. Francfort and Ja. A. Sher (eds.), *Répertoire des pétroglyphes d'Asie centrale, fascicule 2, Sibérie du Sud 2: Tepsej I–III, Ust'-Tuba I–IV (Russie, Khakassie)*, pp. i–xx. Paris, Diffusion de Boccard. Mémoires de la Mission Archéologique Française en Asie Centrale V.2.

Sher, Ja. A., with N. Blednova, N. Legchilo and D. Smirnov. 1994. *Répertoire des pétroglyphes d'Asie centrale, fascicule 1, Sibérie du Sud 1: Oglakhty I–III (Russie, Khakassie)*. Paris, Diffusion de Boccard. Mémoires de la Mission Archéologique Française en Asie Centrale, V.1.

Soleilhavoup, F. 1995. Les supports rocheux: altérations et bioconstructions: témoins d'archéoenvironnements, in H.-P. Francfort and Ja. A. Sher (eds.), *Répertoire des pétroglyphes d'Asie centrale, fascicule 2, Sibérie du Sud 2: Tepsej I–III, Ust'-Tuba I–IV (Russie, Khakassie)*, pp. xli–lxviii. Paris, Diffusion de Boccard. Mémoires de la Mission Archéologique Française en Asie Centrale V.2.

Sorokin, S. 1990. Horse-drawn vehicles of the Eurasian forest-steppe in 'pre-centaurian' times, *Iranica Antiqua* 25: 97–147.

Vadeckaja, E. B., N. V. Leont'ev and G. A. Maksimenkov. 1980. *Pamjatniki okunevskoj kul'tury*. Leningrad, Nauka.

Varenov, A. V. 1990, Etnokul'turnaja prinadlezhnost', semantika, datirovka 'gobijskoj kvadrigi', in A. P. Derevjanko and Sh. Nacagdorzh (eds.), *Arkheologicheskie, etnigraficheskie i antropologicheskie issledovanija v Mongolii*, pp. 106–12. Novosibirsk, Nauka.

Vidal, P. 1995. Conservation, in H.-P. Francfort and Ja. A. Sher (eds.), *Répertoire des pétroglyphes d'Asie centrale, fascicule 2, Sibérie du Sud 2: Tepsej I–III, Ust'-Tuba I–IV (Russie, Khakassie)*, pp. lxix–lxxvi. Paris, Diffusion de Boccard. Mémoires de la Mission Archéologique Française en Asie Centrale V.2.

Von Dewall, M. 1983. Chariotry and burial practice in Zhou China, in P. Snoy (ed.), *Ethnologie und Geshichte: Festschrift für Karl Jettmar*, pp. 96–111. Wiesbaden, Franz Steiner Verlag. Beiträge zur Südasienforschung Südasien-Institut Universität Heidelberg 86.

Watson, W. 1978. The Chinese chariot: an insider's view, in P. Denwood (ed.), *Arts of the Eurasian steppelands*, pp. 1–31. London, Percival David Foundation of Chinese Art, School of Oriental and African Studies. Colloquies on Art and Archaeology in Asia 7.

Zhukov, V. and V. A. Ranov. 1974. Drevnie kolesnici na Pamire, *Pamir* 11.

Jo McDonald

# 18. Shelter rock-art in the Sydney Basin – a space–time continuum: exploring different influences on stylistic change

Records from the contact era, after the First Fleet planted Europeans into the Sydney region of Australia in 1788, give glimpses of Aboriginal social organisation at that time – but not of the rock-art in any specific context. Direct and indirect dating, that set the painting and the engraving traditions in Sydney-region rock-art into their archaeological context, provide a frame for studying the change in art over time. The changing rock-art is related to a changing social milieu, in a trajectory of development reaching that moment of impact with European ways.

## Rock-art of the Sydney region

This chapter explores issues relating to synchronic and diachronic variation in a prehistoric regional art style. The region is the Sydney Basin in southeastern Australia (Fig. 18.1), an area of roughly 300,000 sq. km. Two distinctive media were used in the region, engravings (or pictographs) on open sandstone platforms, and a variety of pigmented forms (stencils, drawings, paintings and engravings) within sheltered locations. These two media represent different manifestations of the same regional style (McDonald 1994). This chapter focuses on the sheltered art component where the contextual information provided by the archaeology in these sites provides evidence about how this art body may have changed over time.

## Age of Sydney rock-art

The time-frame for the region is provided by a well-documented archaeological record (for example, Attenbrow 1987; Kohen 1986; McDonald 1994). While initial occupation here dates to the late Pleistocene, evidence for the main occupation period

dates to the last 5000 years, and the vast majority to the last three millennia. Three distinctive technological phases in stone tool production are recognised within this main occupation period (Attenbrow 1987; McCarthy 1964), the last operating within the millennium prior to white contact. A major research issue relates to whether these lithic phases indicate the types of widely ramified social changes which should also be reflected by the region's art.

By testing the contemporaneity of art and deposit in shelters a continuity over time in art production and occupation evidence is posited. From this, changes in occupation indices over time have been explored – as has diachronic stylistic evidence – to see how art may have contributed to, and been affected by, changing social organisation. Ethnohistorical evidence regarding language groupings and social organisation is given temporal relevance by the archaeological record. It is assumed that the details recorded by observers on the First Fleet (which sailed into Sydney Harbour in 1788) can only be projected back into prehistory for about 1000 years.

## Informed methods

This investigation has been based primarily on formal art and archaeology methods. No ethnographic research was undertaken in the region at the time of first white contact, and the ethnohistorical literature is sparse in regard to the production of rock-art. This analysis has relied primarily on established rock-art dating techniques but has experimented with the use of AMS small-sample direct dating.

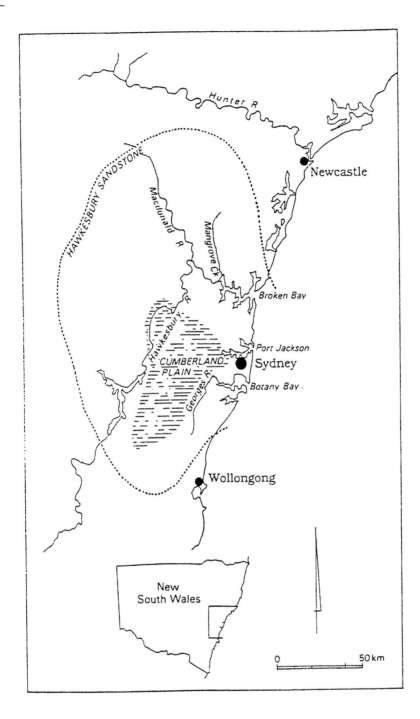

**Fig. 18.1.** The Sydney Basin. The study area showing cities, major rivers and the extent of Hawkesbury sandstone.

## Formal methods

The rock-art from the Sydney Basin is recognised as a distinct and a distinctive regional style (Franklin 1984; McCarthy 1988; McDonald 1991; McMah 1965; Maynard 1976; Officer 1984). What makes it distinctive and what distinguishes it from other regional styles has been addressed previously (Franklin 1984; Officer 1992, 1993; Layton 1992). This art fits the definition (Maynard 1976; Franklin 1984) for the 'Simple Figurative' style, named 'Figurative' because of the high level of recognition (for modern 'etic' observers) between the art and a 'natural' assemblage (human figures, animals, birds, fish and so forth). The 'Simple' part of the label indicates that the schema is not a complicated one, with a minimum amount of detail provided, as required for recognition.

Maynard's (1976: 200–1) definition of this stylistic phase still provides a good general description of the region's art:

the style is dominated by figurative motifs . . . the majority of [these] . . . conform[ing] to a pattern of crude naturalism. Whether the motif is engraved or painted, in outline or solid form, it usually consists of a very simple silhouette of a human or animal model. Most portrayals are strongly standardised. Human beings are depicted frontally, animals and birds in profile, snakes and lizards from above. Normally only the minimum visual requirements for recognition of the motif are fulfilled by the shape of the figure.

Certain variations to this description are necessitated by current research. Human figures are sometime depicted in profile, while some animals (such as the echidna) are not always (Officer 1984; McDonald 1987).

Franklin's (1984) work quantified Maynard's definition for regional Simple Figurative styles. One of her most important results indicated that form, technique and motif contributed fairly equally in the multivariate analysis of style, or at least, in her case, in differentiating between the different regional Simple Figurative styles (Franklin 1984: 89). This result can be interpreted as indicating that each of these aspects of the Sydney Basin assemblage is equally able to provide stylistic information (see also McDonald 1993). This has significance when it comes to evaluating quantitative as opposed to qualitative data (Ashton 1983), and in terms of the analyses undertaken for this research – which have been based largely on motif.

Within Australia, the Sydney Basin is unique in having two extensive synchronous art forms within the region. More than 4000 art sites have been recorded in the region, roughly divided equally between the two art contexts. In no other area of Australia have dual media been simultaneously practised so extensively. In most Australian regions one medium developed to the seeming exclusion of the other (for example Cobar, Laura, Kakadu), or the two forms are diachronically distinct (western New South Wales, central western Queensland). In Sydney, however, the schemata used for the two art components are very similar. This is manifested in the motif range used, in the form of these and – especially – in the general character of the regional motif assemblage (see Maynard 1977). The main difference between the two components is, of course, technique, but also size. Size difference is mostly due to the differences in size of 'canvas' – of the rock surface available.

## Motif

Comparison of the motif range and preferences indicates obvious similarities and differences between the two components in their motif assemblages (McDonald 1994: chapters 5, 9 and 10). The samples used for this research comprised 717 engraving sites (7804 motifs) and 546 shelter art sites (14,424 motifs).

In both components, 'tracks' dominate the identifiable motifs (Fig. 18.2). With the shelter art sites, this is due to the overall predominance of hand stencils; in the engraving component it results from the predominance of human tracks (*mundoes*) and, to a lesser extent, bird and macropod tracks. Given the possible

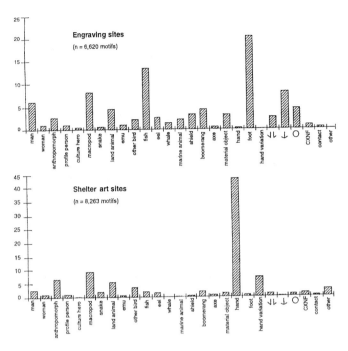

**Fig. 18.2.** Motif preferences for the two art contexts. Motif classification excluding unidentified motifs.

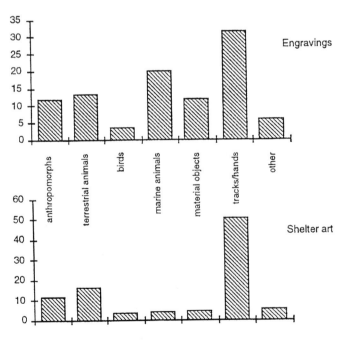

**Fig. 18.3.** Subject preferences for the two art contexts. Clumped motif classes excluding unidentified motifs.

interpretations given to stencils as individual or personalised markers (Moore 1977), and given that this type of art places the artist very firmly within the art, the presence of human tracks in great numbers amongst the engravings is a significant similarity.

Engraved *mundoes* are not in the same representational class as stencilled hands: the former are *conventional* whilst the stencilled hands are *replication*. But the dominance of this motif, and the injection of a human component into both art assemblages, does suggest some semiotic significance.

Other similarities between the two components are the proportions of anthropomorphic depictions, birds and (to a lesser extent) terrestrial animals (Fig. 18.3). The major difference between the two components is in the frequency of marine depictions and material objects – high in engraving sites, low in shelter art sites. The greater number of 'other' motifs in the shelter art assemblage in contrast to the engraved one is a measure (in part) of the more 'stylistically unfettered nature' of this medium (Officer 1984: 72).

Synchronic analyses of the two extensive regional art bodies have shown that they do represent different manifestations of the same art tradition – while demonstrating inherently distinctive stylistic traits because of their techniques. As well as striking similarities in the motif preferences, similar stylistic clines and boundaries are demonstrated by both art bodies, and there is considerable congruence in their locations.

Analysis of the two art assemblages has enabled a much more detailed picture to emerge of how the art may have functioned across the region; and from this a social interactive model based on information exchange theory has been developed (McDonald 1994). In part, congruence between the stylistic clines/boundaries and the ethnohistorically recorded language areas has enabled this interpretation.

## Ethnohistory

Aboriginal society around Port Jackson was not studied systematically, in the ethnographic sense, by those who arrived on the First Fleet. Numerous accounts were made of the more obvious aspects of Aboriginal culture (for example, Collins 1798, 1802, 1804; Phillip 1789, 1791; Tench 1789, 1793). Later, quite detailed references to Aboriginal life in the region were made (such as Barrallier 1802; Threlkeld 1824–59 in Gunson 1974; the Russian expeditions 1814–22 in Barratt 1981), but explicitly anthropological work was not undertaken in the region until the late nineteenth century (Mathews 1896, 1897a, 1897b, 1908; Mathews and Everitt 1900).

Within two years of white contact, an epidemic of (probably) smallpox reduced the local population to less than half (Phillip 1791; Tench 1793; Collins 1798; Butlin 1983; Curson 1985), irreparably changing traditional social organisation across the region. Many of these references then, particularly those made after 1790, need to be viewed with appropriate caution: 'Leaving aside white misunderstanding and prejudice, were whites able, at any stage after 1789, to observe a stable black society? Is the ethnographic evidence not only limited but positively misleading?' (Butlin 1983: 155).

Many of the descriptive accounts, useful in establishing daily activities of the Port Jackson Aborigines in 1788, contain interpretations and conclusions, particularly about the more abstract qualities of Aboriginal life, which require careful treatment.

In 1788, certain differences were observable between groups of people living in the region – according to tribal (family and language) groupings, economic divisions (based on environmental conditions) and social behaviour (gender divisions/prohibitions, ceremonies and so forth). While this information does not suffice for an interpretive model, it does provide material and 'clues' for the interpretation of the stylistic patterning encountered in the art. Of particular importance are the social divisions which were recognised across the region, and the types of social 'boundaries' which might have existed between them. Stylistic behaviour depends not only on social cohesion and the maintenance of social ties, but also on social exclusivity and the maintenance of boundaries between groups of people (Wobst 1977; Wiessner 1983, 1990).

The following ethnohistorical evidence for the region is relevant:

- Four languages are recognised as being spoken across the study area at contact: Darginyung, Guringai, Dharuk and Dharawal.[1] The assumed geographic distribution of the four language groups is based on Capell's (1970) model (Fig. 18.4).

- Residence groups (or 'bands') in the region consisted of named economic units with designated tracts of land. 'Tribes' were perceived as comprising a number of these smaller residence groups, speaking dialects of a common language. Within the range of any one linguistic group or tribe, a number of smaller localised bands (maybe as many as fifteen) would have had kin and/or totemic links with people in other groups and therefore modes of access to resources.

- Considerable social interaction within and across linguistic boundaries occurred. Organised social events (initiation ceremonies, dances and the like), as well as the exploitation of windfall resources (such as whale feasts), resulted in aggregations of large numbers of people of mixed language groups. It would appear that ritual behaviour in the region required the participation, and possibly consent, of neighbouring tribes.

- There is no evidence for a rigid demarcation of territorial boundaries, although many initial observations did occur on the resource-rich coastal strip and possibly within one linguistic group. The evidence suggests that the maintenance of clearly defined territorial boundaries was an unlikely behavioural trait but that social boundaries may still have been significant. It seems that the spatial organisation of art traits would probably not demonstrate characteristics of smaller-scale boundary

maintenance (Wobst 1977), particularly at the band level.

- Linguistic boundaries may be reflected in schematic or other stylistic traits in the art across the region. The presence of distinguishable, localised bands as well as broader language boundaries suggests there may have been a highly complex pattern of artistic behaviour and signatures within and across tribal 'boundaries'.

There is no direct evidence that art played a primary role in ceremonial behaviour, nor that it had any mortuary significance. Unfortunately, the role of art in the society was not investigated by the First Fleet recorders.

- Food resources, economic options and adaptive material culture and personal adornment varied across the region. This could be reflected in the different emphasis on maritime and land animals on the coast and inland, as well as a differential distribution of certain material culture items and the depiction of different modes of personal adornment.

**Archaeological context**

Archaeological evidence suggests that the Aboriginal populations observed in the Sydney region at the time of European settlement had not remained unchanging throughout the Holocene. Changes in stone tool technology (McCarthy 1948, 1964; Bowdler 1970; Lampert 1971a), the apparent late introduction of a specialised coastal economy (Lampert 1971b; Sullivan 1987; Walters 1988), and the possible variations in size and movement of populations in the recent past (Hiscock 1986; Kohen 1986; Attenbrow 1987) all demonstrate a social dynamic (McDonald 1994: chapter 4). One must be wary of a 'timeless ethnographic present' (Meehan and Jones 1988: viii): while the ethnohistory can provide certain behavioural parameters, constraints are placed on this by archaeological 'realities'.

---

[1] This research investigated the question of boundary location in terms of catchments (Peterson 1976) as well as creek-lines (Capell 1970).

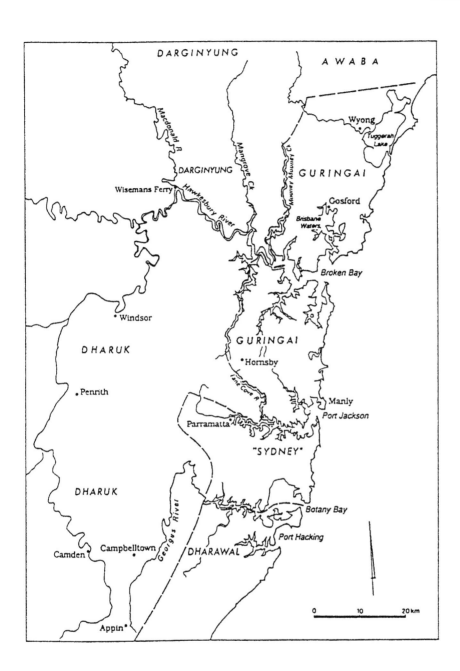

**Fig. 18.4.** The four language areas defined for the region.
After Capell (1970: fig. 1). Drawn by Winifred Mumford.

## How far back into prehistory did the patterns observed in Sydney at contact extend?

The Sydney Basin has been occupied since the late Pleistocene, but only during the mid to late Holocene did occupation increase in most parts of the region, whereupon occupation patterns became much more complex. The lithic Eastern Regional Sequence (ERS), defined initially by McCarthy (1948, 1964), has been refined by more recent research. Attenbrow's (1987) catchment analysis in Mangrove Creek, a comprehensive reanalysis of phases within the ERS, established a local chronology for application at the broader, regional, level. The excavation of four more shelter sites for my research and re-working of Attenbrow's evidence using only her sites with larger assemblages (that is more than 100 excavated artefacts) provides the basis for the following summary (McDonald 1994).

The period of most intensive shelter usage appears to have been between 3000 and 1000 years ago, when enormous numbers of artefacts were deposited within shelters. The beginning of this major increase coincided with the beginning of Phase 3, the Middle Bondaian, when backed blade production was at its peak and the domination of assemblages by bipolar technology using, particularly, quartz began. Its culmination slightly post-dated an increase in the habitation establishment rate, but coincided well with the beginning of a relatively stable period of shelter occupation. In the last millennium, fish-hooks were introduced into the fishing tool-kit. The transition date of *c.* 1000 years ago is proposed for between the Middle and Late Bondaian period – coinciding with the introduction of fish-hooks on the coastal strip and with the declining shelter occupation rates across the region generally.

The following dates have thus been proposed for lithic phases within the Sydney Region Bondaian (McDonald 1994):

Early Bondaian     *c.* 5000 b.p.–*c.* 3000 years b.p.
Middle Bondaian    *c.* 3000 b.p.–*c.* 1000 years b.p.
Late Bondaian      *c.* 1000 b.p.–European
                   contact (AD 1788).

Throughout these phases settlement patterns are expected to have varied. Certain stresses on the population – and artistic mechanisms needed to lessen those stresses – might have been expected.

### Early Bondaian

Population densities were still relatively low at this stage. Use of rock-shelters was increasing, or at least artefact discard increased so as to be archaeologically visible. Early development of the figurative pigment art – and possibly also of open engraved art – could be expected at this time in keeping with developing social interactions and stresses.

### Middle Bondaian

There was an increase in population densities. Following the increased use of rock-shelters for habitation, there was a dramatic increase in these locations for artefact discard. Social pressures amongst the increased population would have necessitated social mechanisms to control interaction and to make it less stressful. There was a proliferation in symbolic behaviour, particularly that allowing the definition of local group social affiliation; symbolic behaviour probably took many forms including – one can suppose – body decoration and scarification. The pigment and engraved art of the region would have developed in this atmosphere and during this period.

### Late Bondaian

There is no real evidence for population decline but a suggestion of changing social organisation during this period. Settlement indices show that rock-shelters continued to be used during this period, but occupation rates – as measured by artefact discard – drop slightly in these locations. Shell fish-hooks are introduced into the coastal tool-kit; backed blade production declines.

## Contemporaneity of art and deposit

The assumption that occupation evidence and art were produced at the same time – and indeed that the two are complementary forms of evidence for the group(s) which produced them – is not new. It has underpinned many analyses both in Australia and overseas. The posited age of European Palaeolithic art has long been based on the dates retrieved from excavated deposits. In various regions of Australia the assumption has often been explicit (or even implicit) in more generalised analyses (such as Chaloupka 1977, 1993; Morwood 1979, 1992; Taçon 1989; Taçon and Chippindale 1993). While a common assumption, the contemporaneity of art and occupation evidence has rarely been extensively investigated on a regional scale.

The contemporaneity of art and occupation deposit was demonstrated at three shelter art sites (Fig. 18.5) during this research.[2] There was a strong suggestion that the main phase of pigment art production in these three sites coincided with the most intensive period of shelter occupation. In multi-phased art sites, it was argued that earlier low-intensity occupation could have had an artistic component, also of low intensity. However, proving this earlier association, with the exception of the Yengo 1 site, is almost impossible.

Prior to this study, more than thirty shelter sites with art had been excavated across the region. While only one was excavated expressly to investigate the context of the art, an analysis of this group of shelters demonstrates broad contemporaneity of art and domestic and/or economic activities across the region (Fig. 18.6). A significant finding was that the patterns of occupation in shelter art sites mirror the indices exhibited by occupation sites generally (Attenbrow 1987: fig. 7.8). This result suggests there are no intrinsic differences in the nature of occupation between shelters used for art production and those without art.

## Diachronic change

A detailed analysis of sixty-five shelter art assemblages in the Mangrove Creek valley was undertaken

[2] Occupation evidence in the fourth shelter was insufficient to test the proposal.

to ascertain whether there was diachronic variability, and to determine the likely effect of diachronic change on stylistic variability across the region. On the basis of superimpositioning, motif preference and multivariate analyses of motif and technical variables, three phases of art production were discerned in this local sample. On the basis of broadly similar patterns identified in a number of sites in different locations (McDonald 1994: chapter 6), this sequence can be extrapolated to the region as a whole:

- *Sydney Basin Art Phase 1* – pecked engravings of tracks and circles.
- *Sydney Basin Art Phase 2* – red paintings, red hand stencils, and possibly white hand stencils (the latter two do not co-occur).
- *Sydney Basin Art Phase 3* – a proliferation of techniques and colour usage, perhaps starting with plain dry black and dry red motifs and then developing into a range of paints, dry bichromes, stencils of varying colours, polychromes and incised motifs. Outline-only motifs end the sequence in many shelters, although European-contact motifs have been recorded in white stencils and in drawn red and white outlined and infill forms.

Across the region, within Phase 3, there may be localised variation in technique proportions, motif preference and timing – identifiable through the synchronic analyses (McDonald 1994: chapter 9) as evidence for stylistic clines. These aspects of localised variation taking place within the most recent phase are significant to interpretations on the basis of the language areas identified at European contact.

A chronology for the Mangrove Creek art sequence was proposed on the basis of associated dates in particular shelter sites (McDonald 1994: chapter 7); it is correlated with the lithic phases identified, and on the basis of association in a number of sites (Table 18.1). These are supported by the small number of AMS dates for the region (Table 18.2) although these dates are not unproblematic

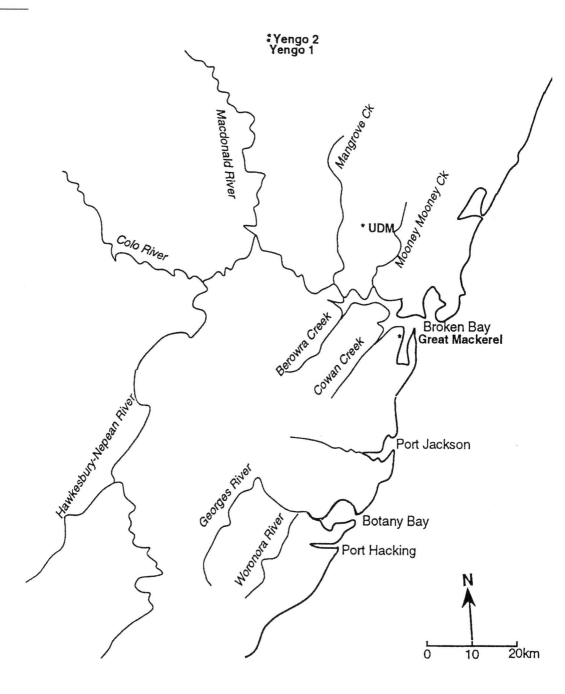

**Fig. 18.5.** The four shelter art sites excavated for this research.

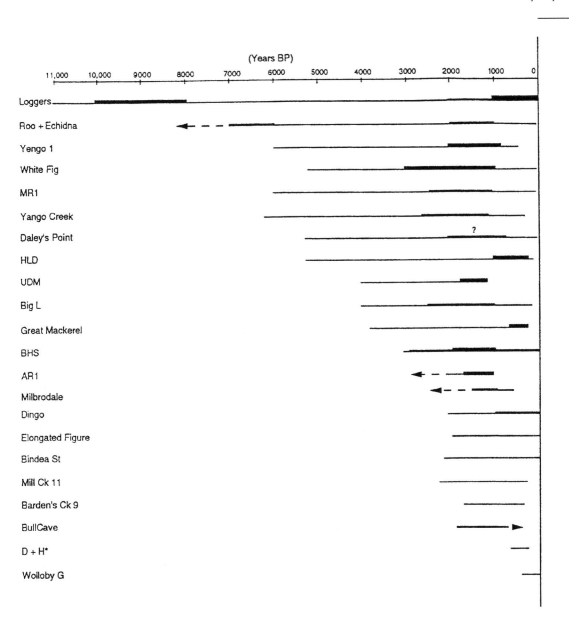

**Fig. 18.6.** Dated shelter art sites showing length of occupation and period of most intensive artefact accumulation.

(McDonald *et al.* 1990; McDonald in prep.). The proposed dates for the art sequence are:

- *Art Phase 1* Pre- or Early Bondaian
  > 5000 years b.p.
- *Art Phase 2* Early Bondaian
  5000–3000 years b.p.
- *Art Phase 3* Middle and Late Bondaian
  3000 years b.p. – European contact

Difficulties encountered in dating followed from the scarcity of sites with art in datable contexts – as motifs covered by deposit and/or evidence of art materials such as pigment – in excavated dated deposits. Furthermore, there are inconsistencies in dating the stone tool phases at a number of sites, and the range of AMS dates returned from direct dating of single motifs also indicates that relying on this technique to date accurately the region's art is premature (McDonald in prep.). A correlation of art phases with broader lithic phases appears the most judicious approach. The main art production period in most sites is contemporaneous with the most intensive period of stone tool production in shelters – the Middle Bondaian. And it is thought that art production continued into the Late Bondaian and, indeed, until contact.

The proposed time-frame for shelter art production indicates that this continued without appreciable stylistic change through the Middle to Late Bondaian stone tool periods, a significant finding in terms of the model for stylistic behaviour in the region.

## Archaeology, art and society in the Sydney region

Archaeological evidence indicates that the period of most intensive shelter usage was between 3000 and 1000 years ago, when enormous numbers of artefacts were deposited in these sites. The beginning of this major increase coincides very well with the beginning of the Middle Bondaian stone tool phase, when backed blade production was at its peak and the assemblages began to be dominated by bipolar technology. This culmination slightly post-dates an increased habitation establishment rate, but co-

Table 18.1. *Excavated art shelters from Mangrove Creek[1]*

| Site | Dates (years b.p.) | Occupation phases[2] | Art phases |
|---|---|---|---|
| Emu Tracks 2[3] | — | 2, 3, 4 | 1 |
| Upside-Down Man[4] | 4030 ± 140 | 1 | 1?, 2 |
| | 1540 ± 60 | 3 | |
| | 1220 ± 120 | 3 | 3 |
| Mt Yengo 1[4] | 6000–4600 | 1 | 1 |
| | 4600–*c.* 2850 | 2 | |
| | < 1950–> 540 | 3 | 3 |
| | < 540 | 4 | 3 |
| Great Mackerel[4] | 3670 ± 150 | 2 | 2 |
| | 560–220 | 4 | 3 |
| Roo and Echidna[3] | 6700 ± 150 | 1 | — |
| | — | 2, 3, 4 | 3 |
| Bird Tracks[3] | — | 4 | 3 |
| Black Hands[3] | 3040 ± 85 | 2 | |
| | — | 3, 4 | 3 |
| Dingo and Horned Anthropo-morph[5] | 581 ± 120 | not analysed | 3 |
| Loggers[3] | 11,050 ± 135 | 1 | |
| | 7950 ± 80 | 2 | |
| | 2840 ± 90 | 3 | 3? |
| | 530 ± 90 | 4 | 3? |

[1]Excavated for this research (Attenbrow 1987).
[2]Occupation phases: 1 = Pre-Bondaian; 2, 3, 4 = Early, Middle and Late Bondaian
[3]Dates from Attenbrow (1987).
[4]Dates from McDonald (1994).
[5]Dates from MacIntosh (1965).

incides well with the beginning of a relatively stable period of shelter occupation.

The combined occupation indices indicate that over the last 3000 years there was continual use of shelters. Artefact accumulation rates suggest that the use of shelters as foci in the landscape, at least for stone tool manufacture, declined in the last millennium. This decline may have resulted from a shift in focus from rock-shelters to open locations. Consistent habitation rates indicate that people continued

Table 18.2. *AMS dates from the four shelters investigated in the Sydney Basin*

| Site | Motif | Art phases | Laboratory number | Date (years b.p.) |
|---|---|---|---|---|
| Gnatalia Creek[1] | 1 | 1? | AA-5850 | 6085 ± 60 |
| | | 1? | AA-5851 | 29,795 ± 420 |
| Waterfall Cave[2] | 1 | 3 | AA-5845 | indistinguishable from modern |
| | | 3 | AA-5846 | 635 ± 50 |
| Native Animals[3] | 2 | 3 | AA-10405 | 1770 ± 205 |
| | | 3 | OZ A 568 | 760 ± 205 |
| | | | AA-10406 | 1080 ± 210 |
| Upside-Down Man[4] | 2 | 3 | OZ B 055 | *c.* 280 ± 90 |
| | | | OZ B 056 | indistinguishable from modern |
| | | | OZ B 057 | indistinguishable from modern |
| | | 3 | OZ B 058 | indistinguishable from modern |

[1] The dating in this site still unresolved (McDonald *et al.* 1990); this motif could be interpreted as a pigmented regional Panaramitee motif.
[2] Same technique in area with a number of faint and/or indistinguishable motifs.
[3] Two motifs in a frieze of apparently related motifs.
[4] Two motifs stylistically and apparently (on the basis of relative weathering) different in age.

using shelters, but they were depositing fewer arte-facts within these locations.

The focus may have shifted at this time to open camp-site locations as a result of changes to the social system (Walters 1988). Ethnohistorical evidence suggests that the focus for habitation in recent prehistory may have been in open 'villages . . . on the sea coast' (Beaglehole 1955; Tench 1793 (1961); Phillip 1789 (1970); Collins 1802 (1975): 460) accommodating upwards of fifty people. A late move to open sites is supported by the establishment dates for open middens generally along the south-east coast (Sullivan 1987), while a similar pattern can be discerned in south-eastern Queensland (Morwood 1986; Walters 1992).

The combined archaeological results and ethnohistorical evidence suggest that, over the last millennium, occupation patterns involved a move away from shelters as a focus for habitation, a trend identified in south-eastern Queensland by Morwood (1986). The ethnohistorical literature for the Sydney region at contact supports the model of bands consisting of large territorial groupings, larger than single residence groups. Studies of camping behaviour (such as Koettig 1976) and spatial relationships indicate that most rock-shelters do not have a large enough floor area to accommodate, on a permanent basis, more than a single residence group.

The move out of rock-shelter sites, then, can be seen not as a shift in perceptions about these locations (see Morwood 1986, 1987) but as a *pragmatic* move to habitation more suitable to the increased spatial requirements of a larger group. An explanation for the increasing size of residence groups over time can be found in the changing social system which accompanied the introduction of fish-hooks at about 1000 years BP (Walters 1988).

Technological changes (particularly the decline of backed blades and the introduction of fish-hooks) would match more socially shared food procurement activities (group hunting pursuits, women fishing). These may have increased the reliability of food supplies, which would be required by larger groups (Bowdler 1981).

The use of shelters on an *ad hoc* basis would have continued. That did, in fact, continue, but lower-intensity occupation of shelters throughout the last millennium can be explained in terms of the patterns of aggregation and dispersal observed at contact (Bowdler 1976; Poiner 1976; Ross 1976). During times of seasonal abundance, groups lived in large, semi-permanent open 'villages'. In times of resource stress, these larger groups dispersed, continuing to exploit their range of already-established rock-shelters, in smaller groups.

During the Middle Bondaian increasing social interaction would have necessitated mechanisms to aid in communicating social identity. With the change to the Late Bondaian, there may have been further need to control interaction and to enforce group identity, but also for mechanisms which required larger-scale group cohesion. Symbolic behaviour would have continued, throughout the last millennium, as an important facilitator of interaction. It is possible that a large number of engraving sites were made during this late period. The increasing social complexity would have produced the conditions required (Wiessner 1989) for demonstrations of group cohesion: fear, real or potential inter-group competition and aggression, and a need for co-operation to achieve certain goals.

Synchronic analyses indicate that the art across this region is relatively homogeneous, revealing broad-scale cohesion. On its periphery, there is evidence of reduced cohesion. The engraved assemblages show a marked decline in numbers and higher levels of heterogeneity to the south of the region. The need for broader-scale group cohesion did not transcend this boundary.

A comparison of differing stylistic homogeneity in the two art components has been used to develop a model of social interaction for the region, founded in information exchange theory, and arguing that these varying levels of heterogeneity reveal different types of social information: the higher levels of homogene-

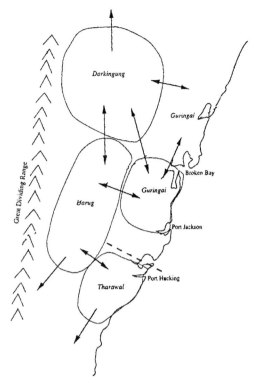

**Fig. 18.7.** Model for territorial organisation and interaction across the Sydney region.

ity in the engraving medium demonstrate larger scale group cohesion; the more heterogeneous medium demonstrates localised group-identifying behaviour. Complex patterns in the levels of variability across the region in both contexts demonstrate the nature of the contacts between language groups, as well as areas where the tensions resulting from these contacts were greatest. The nature of the territorial interaction suggested by these art analyses is depicted in Fig. 18.7.

The varying levels of heterogeneity demonstrated by shelter art sites – across the region but particularly at its periphery – support this model. The high levels of demonstrated homogeneity on the regional margins with this art component indicate that bounding behaviour in these locations was of increased importance.

By using ethnohistorical information – tempered 11 by archaeological data – a time-frame for the social behaviours and languages observed at European contact have been projected back into prehistory. Diachronic analysis of rock-art has identified that there has been no major stylistic change throughout the main period of pigment art production. On the other hand, archaeological evidence indicates a major shift in settlement patterns based on a number of occupation indices during this time of art production. The absence of strong diachronic change in the art indicates that the technological changes shown by the shift from the Middle to Late Bondaian were not indicative of widely ramified social changes, such as would have resulted in changes in the use of art.

Because of this, it is argued that the move out of shelters into open locations did not occur because of changing perceptions about the importance of these locations, but rather that increasing group sizes necessitated this move. The continued production of art was necessary to facilitate continuing negotiation of identity.

The combination of techniques used here – formal and informed – have resulted in an interpretation of this regional prehistoric art body which would not otherwise have been possible. Used in isolation, neither rock-art analysis nor more generalised archaeological investigation would have resulted in this interpretation. Similarly, the ethnohistory alone would not have enabled this interpretation of the region's rock-art. By weaving the threads highlighted as themes in this book, our understanding of the Sydney Basin rock-art is greatly enriched.

## Acknowledgements

This chapter is based on research done for my Ph.D thesis completed at the Australian National University (McDonald 1994). Fieldwork for this was achieved using ANU field funding.

Conventional radiocarbon dates obtained for this research were provided by the ANU Quaternary Research Centre. Some AMS dates have been provided by the Arizona University AMS Facility, and others by ANSTO. An Australian Museum Grant in Aid paid for two of the AMS dates.

## REFERENCES

Ashton, N. M. 1983. Spatial patterning in the Middle–Upper Palaeolithic transition, *World Archaeology* 15(2): 224–34.

Attenbrow, V. J. 1987. The Upper Mangrove Creek catchment: a study of quantitative changes in the archaeological record. Unpublished Ph.D thesis, University of Sydney.

Barrallier, F. 1802. *Journal of the expedition into the interior of New South Wales.* Reprinted 1975, Melbourne, Marsh Walsh Publishing.

Barratt, G. 1981. *The Russians at Port Jackson 1814–1822.* Canberra, AIAS.

Beaglehole, J. C. (ed.) 1955. *The journals of Captain James Cook on his voyage of discovery: the voyage of the* Endeavour *1768–1771.* Cambridge, Hakluyt Society.

Bowdler, S. 1970. Bass Point: the excavation of a southeast Australian shell midden showing cultural and economic change. Unpublished BA (Hons.) thesis, University of Sydney.

1976. Hook, line and dilly bag: an interpretation of an Australian coastal shell midden, *Mankind* 10(4): 248–58.

1981. Hunters in the highlands: Aboriginal adaptations in the eastern Australian uplands, *Archaeology in Oceania* 16(2): 99–111.

Butlin, N. G. 1983. *Our original aggression: Aboriginal populations of south-eastern Australia 1788–1850.* Sydney, George Allen and Unwin.

Capell, A. 1970. Aboriginal languages in the south central coast, NSW: fresh discoveries, *Oceania* 41: 20–7.

Chaloupka, G. 1977. Aspects of the chronology and schematisation of two prehistoric sites on the Arnhem Land Plateau, in P. J. Ucko (ed.), *Form in indigenous art*, pp. 243–59. Canberra, Australian Institute of Aboriginal Studies.

1993. *Journey in time: the world's longest continuing art tradition.* Sydney, Reed.

Collins, D. 1798. *An account of the English colony in New South Wales* I. London, Cadell and Davies. Republished 1975, ed. B. H. Fletcher. Sydney, A. H. and A. W. Reed.

1802. *An account of the English colony in New South Wales* II. London, Cadell and Davies. Republished 1975, ed. B. H. Fletcher. Sydney, A. H. and A. W. Reed.

1804. *An account of the English colony in New South Wales.* Melbourne, Whitcombe and Tombs.

Curson, P. 1985. All dead!, All dead!, in *Times of crisis: epidemics in Sydney 1788–1900*, pp. 41–53. Sydney, University of Sydney Press.

Franklin, N. 1984. Of !macropods and !men: an analysis of the simple figurative styles. Unpublished BA (Hons.) thesis, University of Sydney.

Gunson, N. (ed.) 1974. *Australian reminiscences and papers of L. E. Threlkeld: missionary to the Aborigines 1824–1859.* Canberra, Australian Institute of Aboriginal Studies. Australian Aboriginal Studies 40.

Hiscock, P. 1986. Technological change in the Hunter valley and its implications for the interpretation of late Holocene change in Australia, *Archaeology in Oceania* 21(1): 40–50.

Koettig, M. K. 1976. Rising damp. Unpublished MA thesis, University of Sydney.

Kohen, J. L. 1986. Prehistoric settlement in the western Cumberland Plain: resources, environment and technology. Unpublished Ph.D thesis, School of Earth Sciences, Macquarie University, Sydney.

Lampert, R. J. 1971a. *Burrill Lake and Currarong: coastal sites in southern New South Wales.* Canberra, Department of Prehistory, RSPac.S, Australian National University. *Terra Australis* 1.

1971b. Coastal Aborigines of southeastern Australia, in D. J. Mulvaney and J. Golson (eds.), *Aboriginal man and environment in Australia*, pp. 114–32. Canberra, Australian National University Press.

Layton, R. 1992. *Australian rock art: a new synthesis.* Cambridge, Cambridge University Press.

McCarthy, F. D. 1948. The Lapstone Creek excavation: two culture periods revealed in eastern NSW, *Records Australian Museum* 22: 1–34.

1964. The archaeology of the Capertee valley, NSW, *Records Australian Museum* 26(6): 197–264.

1979. *Australian Aboriginal rock art.* 4th edition (3rd edition 1967). Sydney, Australian Museum.

1988. Rock-art sequences: a matter of clarification (with comments by Clegg, David, Franklin, McDonald, Maynard, Moore, Morwood, Rosenfeld and Bednarik: with author's reply), *Rock Art Research* 5(1): 16–42.

McDonald, J. J. 1987. Sydney Basin Aboriginal Heritage Study: shelter art sites. Stage II. Unpublished Report to NSW NPWS. Report held at NSW NPWS.

1991. Archaeology and art in the Sydney region: context and theory in the analysis of a dual medium style, in P. Bahn and A. Rosenfeld (eds.), *Rock art and prehistory: papers presented to Symposium G of the AURA Congress, Darwin 1988*, pp. 78–85. Oxford, Oxbow Monograph 10.

1993. The depiction of species in macropod track engravings at an Aboriginal art site in western New South Wales, *Records of the Australian Museum, Supplement* 17: 105–16.

1994. Dreamtime Superhighway: an analysis of Sydney Basin rock art and prehistoric information exchange. Unpublished Ph.D thesis, Australian National University, Canberra.

In preparation. AMS dating charcoal drawings in the Sydney region: results and issues, in C. Tunis and G. Ward (eds.), Rock-art dating volume AITSIS and ANSTO.

McDonald, J. J., K. L. C. Officer, D. Donahue, T. Jull, J. Head and B. Ford. 1990. Investigating AMS: dating prehistoric rock-art in the Sydney Sandstone Basin, NSW, *Rock Art Research* 7(2): 83–92.

MacIntosh, N. W. G. 1965. Dingo and Horned Anthropomorph in an Aboriginal rock shelter, *Oceania* 36(2): 85–101.

McMah, L. 1965. A quantitative analysis of the Aboriginal rock carvings in the district of Sydney and the Hawkesbury River. Unpublished BA (Hons.) thesis, University of Sydney.

Mathews, R. H. 1896. The Keeparra ceremony of initiation, *Journal of the Anthropological Institute of Great Britain and Ireland* 26: 320–40.

1897a. The Burbung of the Darkinung tribe, *Proceedings of the Royal Society of Victoria* 10: 1–12.

1897b. Totemic divisions of some Australian tribes, *Journal of the Royal Society of NSW* 31: 154–76.

1908. Some mythology of the Gundungarra tribe, New South Wales, *Zeitschrift für Ethnologia* 40: 291–310.

Mathews, R. H. and M. M. Everitt. 1900. The organisation, language and initiation ceremonies of the Aborigines of the south-east coast of NSW, *Journal and Proceedings of the Royal Society of NSW* 34: 262–81.

Maynard, L. 1976. An archaeological approach to the study of Australian rock art. Unpublished MA thesis, University of Sydney.

1977. Classification and terminology in Australian rock art, in P. J. Ucko (ed.), *Form in indigenous art*, pp. 385–402. Canberra, Australian Institute of Aboriginal Studies.

Meehan, B. and R. Jones (eds.). 1988. *Archaeology with ethnography: an Australian perspective.* Canberra, Department of Prehistory, RSPac.S, Australian National University.

Moore, D. 1977. The hand stencil as a symbol, in P. J. Ucko (ed.), *Form in indigenous art*, pp. 318–24. Canberra, Australian Institute of Aboriginal Studies.

Morwood, M. J. 1979. Art and stone: towards a prehistory of central western Queensland. Unpublished Ph.D thesis, Australian National University, Canberra.

— 1986. The archaeology of art: excavations at Maidenwell and Gatton shelters, SE Queensland, *Queensland Archaeological Research* 3: 88–132.

— 1987. The archaeology of social complexity in southeastern Queensland, *Proceedings of the Prehistoric Society* 53: 337–50.

— 1992. Changing art in a changing landscape: a case study from the upper Flinders region of the north Queensland highlands, in J. J. McDonald and I. B. Haskovec (eds.), *State of the art: regional rock art studies in Australia and Melanesia*, pp. 60–71. Melbourne, Australian Rock Art Research Association. Occasional AURA Publication 6.

Officer, K. L. C. 1984. From Tuggerah to Dharawal: variation and function within a regional art style. Unpublished BA (Hons) thesis, Australian National University, Canberra.

— 1992. The edge of the sandstone: what makes style change, in J. J. McDonald and I. B. Haskovec (eds.), *State of the art: regional rock art studies in Australia and Melanesia*, pp. 6–14. Melbourne, Australian Rock Art Research Association. Occasional AURA Publication 6.

— 1993. Style and graphic: an archaeological model for the analysis of rock art. Unpublished Ph.D thesis, Department of Prehistory and Anthropology, Australian National University, Canberra.

Peterson, N. 1976. The natural and cultural areas of Aboriginal Australia: a preliminary analysis of population groupings with adaptive significance, in N. Peterson (ed.), *Tribes and boundaries in Australia*, pp. 50–71. Canberra, AIAS.Soial Anthropology Series 10.

Phillip, A. 1789. *The voyage of Governor Phillip to Botany Bay: with contributions from other officers of the First Fleet and observations on affairs of the time by Lord Auckland*. London, John Stockdale. Reprinted 1970, Angus and Robertson; in association with RAHS.

— 1791. *Extracts of letters from Arthur Phillip, Esq. Governor of New South Wales to Lord Sydney*. London, Debrett.

Reprinted 1963. Adelaide, Public Library of South Australia. Australiana Facsimile Editions 15.

Poiner, G. 1976. The process of the year among Aborigines of the central and south coast of New South Wales, *Archaeology and Physical Anthropology in Oceania* 11(3): 186–206.

Ross, A. 1976. Inter-tribal contacts: what the First Fleet saw. Unpublished BA (Hons.) thesis, University of Sydney.

Sullivan, M. E. 1987. The recent prehistoric exploitation of edible mussel in Aboriginal shell middens in southern NSW, *Archaeology in Oceania* 22(3): 97–106.

Taçon, P. S. C. 1989. From Rainbow Snakes to X-ray fish: the nature of the recent rock painting tradition in western Arnhem Land, Australia. Unpublished Ph.D thesis, Australian National University, Canberra.

Taçon, P. S. C. and C. Chippindale. 1993. Two old painted panels from Kakadu: variation and sequence in Arnhem Land rock-art, in J. Steinbring, A. Watchman, P. Faulstich and P. S. C. Taçon (eds.), *Time and space: dating and spatial consideration in rock art research*, pp. 32–56. Melbourne, Australian Rock Art Research Association. Occasional AURA Publication 8.

Tench, W. 1789, 1793. *Sydney's first four years: being a reprint of A narrative of the expedition to Botany Bay (1789) and A complete account of the settlement at Port Jackson (1793)*. Reprinted 1961. Sydney, Angus and Robertson in association with RAHS.

Walters, I. 1988. Fish hooks: evidence for dual social systems in southeastern Australia?, *Australian Archaeology* 27: 98–114.

— 1992. Antiquity of marine fishing in south-east Queensland, *Queensland Archaeological Research* 9: 29–34.

Wiessner, P. 1983. Style and information in Kalahari San projectile points, *American Antiquity* 48: 253–76.

— 1989. Style and changing relations between individual and society, in I. Hodder (ed.), *The meanings of things: material culture and symbolic expression*, pp. 56–63, London, Unwin Hyman.

— 1990. Is there a unity to style?, in M. Conkey and C. Hastorf (eds.), *The uses of style in archaeology*, pp. 105–12. Cambridge, Cambridge University Press.

Wobst, H. M. 1977. Stylistic behaviour and information exchange, in C. E. Cleland (ed.), *For the Director: research essays in honor of J. B. Griffin*, pp. 317–42. Ann Arbor, Museum of Anthropology, University of Michigan. Anthropological Papers 61.

John Clegg

# 19. Making sense of obscure pictures from our own history: exotic images from Callan Park, Australia

Other chapters in this book concern the archaeological study of rock-art from other cultures. We close the collection with a chapter about the archaeological study of rock-art from our own culture, placed in the human artificial landscape of a great city and removed in time not far from the present.

In Sydney Harbour, Australia, there is a series of rock engravings on the shores of Iron Cove, Callan Park. A Hospital for the Insane was established there in 1876. The disued 1880–5 buildings are now the Rozelle campus of the University of Sydney. The engravings look like pictures of compass roses, sailing ships, fish or sharks, globes, and strings of capital letters and digits. There are several four-figure number groups which – when interpreted as dates – are for the years from 1855 to 1922. These works of art present a frustrating glimpse of the person who made them, and a subject for archaeological interpretation.

The engravings, on the rocky sea-side cliff-top, are partly covered by soil; they probably continue beneath a lawn. They vary in visibility with time of day, dampness, growth of lichen, obscurity through soil or by overgrowing grass; and – of course – what one sees depends also on one's interests.

As a result, everyone who comments on these engravings finds something different.

## Notice of the Callan Park engravings, and a historical record

My involvement with the engravings began about 1967, when my then brother-in-law told me of the engravings, and I went to look at them and puzzle over them. At that time I was (as I still am) professionally engaged with prehistoric engravings.

Ever since, I have been fond of the engravings at Callan Park, periodically visiting them and exploiting them as teaching material (e.g. Clegg 1977: 121–2). They have never been recorded properly; the recordings used to illustrate this chapter arose from student exercises, and are very varied in quality.

On Thursday, 9 May 1974, the first of a series of paragraphs appeared in 'Column 8' of the *Sydney Morning Herald*, a front-page feature in the city newspaper:

Strolling around the foreshores of Iron Cove, Rozelle, Column 8 was confronted with cryptic inscriptions and nautical drawings carved deeply into rock ledges and boulders on a prominent point. Dozens of sketches – of sharks, windjammers, compass points, globes, profiles of men and women. Probably the work of one man, they are dated from 1855 to 1909. The writing has baffled language experts. Decipher, for instance, WOUHUROPE-FRANHIINSE, or JAMHAMBON?

There follows a photo of a large fish-like figure, then:

We tackled 10 authorities on such carvings and not one had heard of them. Were they gouged into the sandstone by some Indonesian or Dutch sailor trying to write English? Or perhaps an inmate of nearby Callan Park? We may never know.

Then, in Column 8 for Monday 13 May 1974:

Unfortunately, no one has been able to explain definitely the origin of those incredible rock carvings and cryptic inscriptions re-discovered by Column 8 at Iron Cove and reported last Thursday. But scores of readers are convinced the sculptor was trying his illiterate hand at French. Take JAMHAMBON, for example. *Jambon* in French is ham. Ham in English, ham in French – a ham sandwich? The

336

word inscribed on what we thought was a shark — BALENEDLAMR — could also be interpreted as Romanised French for whale of the sea. *Baleine de la mer.* But WOUHUROPEFRAHIINSE? Europe and France, yes, but what of the remainder?

Thursday 16 May 1974:

The rock-carving inscription mystery at Iron Cove thickens. Mr John Clegg, senior tutor in Anthropology at Sydney University, believes the large fish engraved BALENEDLAMR (in illiterate French, 'Whale of the Sea') is an Aboriginal work at least 200 years old, 'tarted up' by our obsessive but still unidentified artist. After examining the site he says the dozens of other carvings conform to the 'outsider art' pattern, gouged by solitary people with no formal training and time on their hands.

The final note in the series appeared on Wednesday 22 May 1974:

Mr R. Black, 89, of Waitara, believes the man who carved and inscribed the rock bluffs at Iron Cove was a crazy old recluse. Everyone was afraid of him and no one knew his name. Mr Black says: 'As a young boy I remember him living on a houseboat below the point at Callan Park. About 60 to 70 years old, he always wore a seaman's cap and shunned the public. Everyone said he was a sea-captain, either French or German. Nobody was allowed aboard his boat, which he seldom left. Schoolchildren said he could draw good pictures. I don't know what happened to him.'

The earliest date (if it is a date) is 1855, the latest 1922. Reading the dates as the year of engraving implies a long, but not impossibly so, working life of sixty-seven years.

Say the artist made the first engravings when he was 20. That makes his date of birth 1835; and his age 87 in 1922. He was known to Mr Black (born 1885), then a young boy (say 10), in about 1895 when the artist was about 60. The span of sixty-seven years, 1855–1922, seems on the long side for any individual artist, and 87 might be uncomfortably old to be occupied with rock-engraving, but the general range is reasonable if we allow some leeway in Mr Black's recollection in creating all the figures. This all fits well enough to be accepted as a working model for the dates when the engravings were made,

and when the artist was active. What can his art add to this portrait of a reclusive European sea-captain who could draw good pictures?

## Common subjects

### Ships

At least 7. The steamer looks like a turn-of-the-century liner (Figs. 19.1 and 19.2: steamer about 1.5 m long), and it flies a tricolour – which could be French, Irish, German, Italian or Belgian (among twelve such flags: Anon. 1990: 660–739). Note the characteristics of the steamship – the forward-projecting bow, the details of screw and rudder, superstructure and rigging – which surely show the artist has studied such ships. All the ships show detail below the water-line, which might indicate that they are models, not real ships sailing. Or it could be an effect of the untrained nature of the drawing to include essential features which may not be always visible.

There are five sailing ships and a skiff (Figs. 19.1, 19.2, 19.3, 19.4). Two have four masts; three are three-masted merchant ships, which were common from say 1880 to 1914. The skiff is an over-canvassed racer with long boom and bowsprit and deep keel, perhaps an 18-footer. One of the ships is labelled JAMHAMBON, another LAVERTE. As we will see, JAMHAMBON is a common message at the site, and its association with the ship may be fortuitous. No sailor would name a deep-sea vessel after Green for deep sea, or Green for trees and Dryads. *La Verte* is therefore an unlikely name for a ship. But the inscription could be a misspelling of *La Vérité*, The Truth, a more suitable name.

I have already mentioned the tricolour on the steamship. The only other flag, clearly Japanese, is attached to one of the common but strange objects called compass roses, which has a thrice iteration of 1883 (Fig. 19.5). Did the Japanese fleet visit then?

### Compass roses

Fourteen counted (three more turned up in late 1996 when some weeds were cleared away). Six have human profiles attached.

John Clegg

**Fig. 19.1.** Incomplete sketch of figures at north end of site. Area shown about 6 by 8 m.

Fig. 19.6 shows more compass roses. The most common motifs at the site were identified on Column 8's first visit as compass points. Some of them point North. They consist of 8- or 16-pointed stars, as in the cardinal points of the compass.[1] Some of the roses are decorated with small discs, which suggests that our artist makes variations for their own sake.

Every one of the fourteen compass roses nestles within a crescent or 'bent banana'. Dr Bernardette

Masters has demonstrated that the dated star–banana figures can be read as records of close astronomical conjunctions between the moon and a planet at the stated date. These vary from big horned things going round 13 of the 16 points (1919) to a bare semicircle (1883 1883 1883 with Japanese flag: Fig. 19.5). Six of the bananas-with-stars (Figs. 19.1, 19.5, 19.6) have a human head, arms and torso appended. The head always appears in left profile, the arms and torso frontal. What looks like the top of a garment appears as a transverse line at about the level of the crescent's end. The faces are equipped with hair, eye, nose, mouth (usually open), an ear (often low to the back) and rather thick necks.

Four of these six left profiles face towards their

[1] I have yet to discover a 32-point one, which must read as nor-nor-east by north, nor-nor-east, nor-nor-east by east, north-east, north-east by east, east-north-east, east-north-east by east, east, east-south-east by east, east-south-east and so on. I enjoyed recollecting all those (though I cannot remember why or how I learnt them), and wonder whether our artist may have experienced some allied pleasure while making the engravings.

338

**Fig. 19.2.** Tracing of engraving of steamboat, about 1.5 m long.

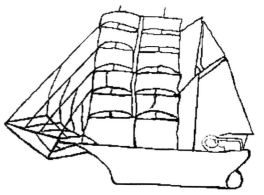

**Fig. 19.4.** Three-master on Mushroom Rock, about 1.3 m long. The area below the sternmost sail – where the wheel should be – is poorly preserved.

**Fig. 19.3.** Partial tracing of figures towards the centre of the site: compass rose and ship with anchor. Area shown about 4 by 4 m.

**Fig. 19.5.** Compass rose with Japanese flag. Maximum length about 2.65 m, star about 1 m.

**Fig. 19.6.** Sketches of two more compass roses. Stars about 1 m. Note the half-moon below the compasses.

compass roses, as though paying attention to them. That is, the faces usually point along the length of their banana. This seems to rule out the figurehead hypothesis: that the bananas represent ships' hulls, and the heads their figureheads. Figureheads simply never look backwards. If the heads are not figureheads, what are they?

Why do the stars always come with bananas? If the stars represent compass roses, it makes sense that people pay attention to them. And compasses are often within half-moons. There are gimbals, a contrivance of rings and bearings for keeping a suspended object, as a ship's compass, horizontal at sea; perhaps that is what is depicted here.

I think the star–banana–person combination represents the activity of steering a ship by compass bearing. Perhaps our artist was a coxswain. The awkwardness of the drawing is consistent with the impossible difficulty of the task undertaken: to show in one view both a person looking and the object of their attention. Among the solutions to this problem two are common. The first is to side-step the task, and require the person to look into the camera, turning their back on the picture they are supposedly admiring. The second is to show the back of the

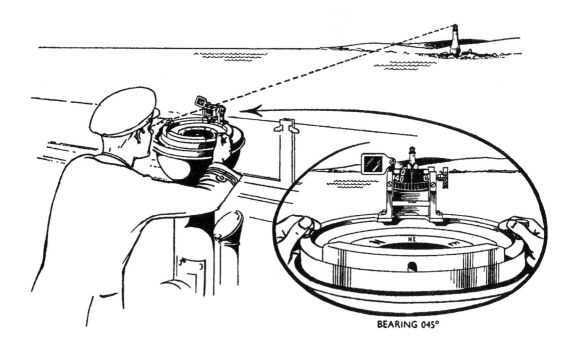

BEARING 045°

**Fig. 19.7.** Taking a bearing.
Illustration from the *Manual of seamanship* (Anon. 1951: fig. 223, p. 215).

person's head. The Callan Park artist chose a third solution, to allow many different viewpoints in one picture. The gimbals are shown in profile, compass in plan, man's shoulders and arms from the front, his head in profile, with a frontal eye. The solution of using multiple viewpoints is employed by the most professional of artists in Fig. 19.7.

A unique incomplete figure consists of a banana with a misshapen circle (partly shown in Fig. 19.3). It looks like the aborted beginning of a new variant of the star–banana theme: banana–circle–star. It may be incomplete because it was abandoned before the rose was added, either because the circle was not good enough, or because the new idea of adding a circle to the banana–rose combination was rejected. A circle would have got in the way of a profile head. This figure provides weak evidence that the sequence of making the motifs went: make banana, then add rose, then add head. The two unappended bananas support the suggestion, by demonstrating that bananas can exist as autonomous motifs.

*Globes*

Two examples (Fig. 19.8).

The artist was not, as the young people reported by Mr R. Black thought at the turn of the century, a ship's captain. Such officers need to know about navigation, and our artist consistently makes a bad mistake about lines of longitude when he is drawing a globe. Lines of longitude are the lines which go north–south, and they converge at the poles. All the mathematics of navigation depend on that simple fact. Our engraver has a general sort of idea about globes being spherical, but he does not make the lines of longitude converge at the poles. He was not a trained navigator.

*People*

Two full-face, 15 left profiles; probably 13 men, 4 women.

I have mentioned the majority of the pictures of people, the six left profiles attending to the compass roses. I assume that they are men, for most nineteenth-

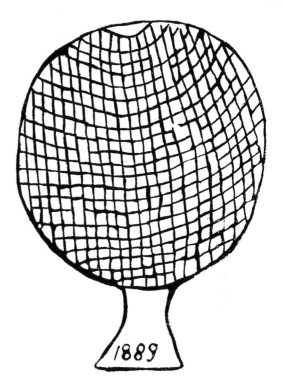

**Fig. 19.8.** Tracing of globe on stand. Diameter about 1.6 m, total height with stand 2.07 m.

century professional sailors were male. There are eleven other people, six probably male heads, and four apparent women. One left profile is like the others, but on its own, deeply cut at the furthest southward extremity of the site, looking towards Rodd Point. Two others look like portraits of individual people: one wears a hat (in 'X-ray' style: Fig. 19.9), the other has his identifying number appended. Having a number does not necessarily make one an inmate of a gaol or asylum; I expect all who have ever been in the armed forces remember their numbers.[2] Then there are four women. Two institutional women with stomping sensible shoes, buckled belts and uniformed wasp waists defining their breasts and hips, with (unfortunately) the standard left profile (Figs. 19.1 and 19.10). Two others are frontal; one appears from

[2] I certainly do, from Portsmouth in 1953: P/M 932351. 351 for short.

**Fig. 19.9.** Head with hat. Total height about 78 cm.

**Fig. 19.10.** Woman. 2.13 m tall in her shoes.

**Fig. 19.11.** 'Queen Victoria'. About half a metre tall.

a banana like the birth of Venus – but sombrely dressed in buttoned top and pleated skirt. The second (Fig. 19.11), dressed the same way, has longish hair. Her arms are akimbo like those of all the other figures. She has ten letters of writing below her, saying DUEMONDROIA.

If Column 8 is correct and the writing is poorly spelt French, DUEMONDROIA makes the royal motto *Dieu et Mon Droit*. That's why I call her Queen Victoria. A stained-glass window with the royal coat of arms and motto was installed in the recreation hall of the Rozelle Hospital, built in 1882.

Extrapolating from these pictures of people, men appear as ordinary people, workers, mates. Women are institutionalised if sensuous. I am sure such an understanding of human nature was all too common last century, especially amongst single-sex workers like sailors.

**Other pictures**
*Fish*
There are at least four assorted fishy creatures (Fig. 19.12), relatively close together. The largest balances a compass on its nose and has the word BALENEDLAMR along its side. It is possible, but not provable, that our artist re-grooved and thus destroyed an Aboriginal rock-engraving of a whale

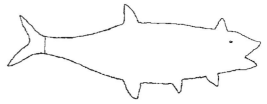

**Fig 19.13.** Illustration of an Aboriginal rock-engraving, published in 1888. This picture in some ways resembles BALENED-LAMR, and could feasibly have inspired it. The original Aboriginal engraving is extant at Bantry Bay, Sydney. The fish-like figure is 5 m long.

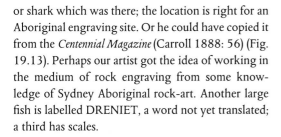

**Fig. 19.12.** Three of the fish. 'Balenedlamr' about 3.5 m, 'Dreniet' 2.5 m, scaled fish about 2 m (with star and crescent adjacent to it).

**Fig. 19.14.** Horse, about 75 cm long.

or shark which was there; the location is right for an Aboriginal engraving site. Or he could have copied it from the *Centennial Magazine* (Carroll 1888: 56) (Fig. 19.13). Perhaps our artist got the idea of working in the medium of rock engraving from some knowledge of Sydney Aboriginal rock-art. Another large fish is labelled DRENIET, a word not yet translated; a third has scales.

*Crescents and horse*
Besides the fish, there are a couple of crescents with no roses or figures, and one horse (Fig. 19.14), clearly derived from the banana motif. The horse is

described by Kerr as an alpaca. Some such creatures occupied a private menagerie near by. When the asylum began to take in patients, the exotic animals were retained for their therapeutic benefit. Unfortunately for this interpretation, the engraving seems to depict a mane, a feature which camelids lack.

*Fouled anchor or ankh*
There is also a fouled anchor (Fig. 19.3), an image which is used by many navies on various insignia. Sometimes the grass grows over and obscures the bottom part of the anchor, and one authority (Powell

**BALENEDLAMR**
*BALEINE DE LA MER*

**LAVERTE**
*LA VÉRITÉ*

**DUEMONDROIA**
*DIEU ET MON DROIT*

**JAMHAMBON**
*GOD THE BUILDER*

**JOSEPHESE JAMHAMBON**
*JOSEPHESE JAMHAMBON*

**JAMARIJAMBON**
*JE MARI JAMBON*

**MSSJAMRIPARJAMBAU**
*MSS JE M'REPIR JAMBON*

**MADAMEWLESINHINGFILETILWDKIKE19109**
*MADAME WLESINHING FILLE ET (ILWDKIKE 19109)*

**f10086 PON**
**MS JAMABIIAMAMBAUWOUTEIO**
**MADAMEWLESINHINGFILETILWDKIKE19109**

**MSS ELHANJANRONWELERE**
**MSS LESAHWELEBEKAHANMAHA**
**HURORANHANSEHAN1912**

**WOUHUROPEFRANHIINSE**
**MSS MARHELINTBAWOUT** ↓ 19109
**DEIOUWOU** ↓ 1908 ⊕
**DRENIET**

**Fig. 19.15.** Transcriptions of some of the engraved letters, with interpretations italicised.

1987: 52) took it for an 'ankh, a cross with a closed semicircular top, [which] was originally an ancient Egyptian symbol which was later taken up by the masons'. This observation led Powell to 'A lexicon of freemasonry compiled by a mason named Mackey in the nineteenth century [which] has a list of "substitute words". Using the book as a dictionary the often repeated phrase JAMHAMBON can be translated to form the appropriate masonic sentiment of GOD THE BUILDER'.

*'Hatched circles and female genitalia'*
Powell (1987: 52) provides the most complete ac-

count of the carvings to date, including the observation that 'the carvings feature symbolic items such as an ankh, hatched circles and female genitalia'. The symbolic female genitalia are associated with writing and have serifs, which is why I reject this interpretation.

*Unfinished carvings*
Near the fouled anchor is a human profile face (Fig. 19.3), as though a face was begun but never completed; and only a couple of metres off is a circle in a crescent, which I interpret as the beginning of a variant on the compass rose theme which was found unsatisfactory.

**Writing: words?** (Fig. 19.15)
The writing always occurs as strings of four or more letters or digits. They look like ordinary English capitals, with serifs. One looks like a Germanic lower-case long S.

Powell gives an analysis of the writing. She notes that JAM occurs in most of the writing, in various combinations, among which are MR JAMHAMBON, JOSEPHESE JAMHAMBON, JAMARIJAMBON. MSS occurs seven times, WILERE three times, MADAME looks a promising beginning, but goes off to MADAMEWLESINHINGFILETILWDKIKE19109

There are currently three theories about the JAM series of letters:

1 Masonic. JAMHAMBON translates as GOD THE BUILDER.

2 Familial. Mr Jamhambon and his daughter Josephese; was our artist attracted to Josephese? JAMARIJAMBON could be about I Husband Ham. *Je mari jambon.*

3 Diet. Mrs Higgs[3] suggested to me that on a long voyage one could get heartily fed up with salt pork in the diet. If there were a French reflexive

[3] The late Marion Higgs was fluent in at least four languages. She contributed to archaeology on (at least) two continents through her husband Eric Higgs and her son-in-law Richard Wright, archaeologists at Cambridge and Sydney.

which indicated dislike, and sounds a bit like JAMRIPAR, *Je m'repir*, then the long string MSSJAMRIPARJAMBAU would transpose as '*Mss Je m'repir jambon,*' and translate into 'Sirs, I dislike salt pork.'

All these versions see the writing as mis-spelt French. The 'letters' towards the bottom of Fig. 19.15 are respectively a broad arrow with serifs on the angled members and a circle enclosing four diameters. Powell (1987: 52) refers to them as 'hatched circles and symbolic female genitalia'. On at least three occasions the artist thought better of broad arrows, and erased them, leaving recessed triangles.

Some of the letter associations feel like words from the Low Countries: WILERE, WOUT and several variants on a boat-sound BAWOUT. Others, HIRI, HANGI, FRAHINSE have a Pacific ring to them. A ghostly character (MA)DAME WLESINH-ING seems to lurk somewhere behind the letters, not quite so visible as the JAMHAMBON family.

## Deducing from the rock-art towards the rock-artist

The mere looking at these engravings, in the light of Mr Black's eyewitness report, produces insights into the personality of the artist, as a shy person with a European seafaring background; he may have spent many hours as a helmsman. He knew a great deal about ships and compass roses, but not the complications of longitude and navigation. To him men were people, women a bit frightening. He may have been fond of a woman by name Josephese Jamhambon, or he may have hated salt pork, and complained to the authorities.

He was an artist of no mean merit, apparently without formal training. It is possible he may have got the idea of exploiting this particular medium from Aboriginal rock-engravings.

Column 8 thought on 16 May 1974 that the artist was obsessive, presumably because of the repetition, and the feeling that he might have been an inmate of the Callan Park asylum. The pictures are not necess-arily evidence of obsession: lots of artists do many variations on the same thing over and over; plenty of archaeologists write the same paper again and again! He may not have been any more obsessive than the rest of us. And if his first carving was made in 1855, 20 years before the first 44 patients were admitted to Callan Park House in 1876 (Anon. n.d.), he was not a patient for the whole of his carving life.

The evidence seems consistent with the four-figure numbers representing dates; in which case he worked at the site between 1855 and 1922. By the last 'date' he must have been into his late eighties. This is as far as I can yet take the study. The turf which covers more engravings could be stripped off for recording and replaced with minimal damage to turf and engravings. The engravings bombard visitors with questions about ships and their names, the writing, the technicalities of drawing. It would be most interesting to hear a psychologist's comments on the whole assemblage. Meanwhile, the engravings are eroding fast under foot-traffic. The site must be preserved and the pictures recorded.

## Acknowledgements

I am greatly indebted to Dr Alison Betts for her comment on the clothing of these women. With a straight neckline, showing their arms and ankles, they are dressed in their underwear: petticoat and chemise or bodice of some sort, drawn in at the waist.

## REFERENCES

Anon. 1951. *Manual of seamanship*. London, Her Majesty's Stationery Office.
 1990. *Guinness encyclopaedia*. Enfield, Guinness.
 N.d. *The Rozelle Hospital*. Pamphlet distributed at the Hospital Fete, 1992.
Carroll, A. 1888. The carved and painted rocks of Australia, *Centennial Magazine* 1(1): 53–6.
Clegg, J. 1977. Sydney rock art, in Peter Stanbury (ed.), *The moving frontier*, pp. 119–24. Sydney, Reed.
Powell, C. 1987. *A river revived: the Parramatta*. Kensington (NSW), New South Wales University Press.

# Index